What is dance, as seen from a philosopher's point of view? Why has dance played little part in traditional philosophies of the arts? And why do these philosophies of the arts take the form they do? The distinguished aesthetician Francis Sparshott subjects these questions to a thorough examination that takes into account all forms and aspects of dance, in art and in life, and brings them within the scope of a single discussion. By showing what is involved in deciding whether something is or is not dance, and by displaying the diversity of ways in which dance can be found meaningful, he provides a new sort of background for dance aesthetics and dance criticism. At the same time, he makes a far-reaching contribution to the methodology of the philosophy of art and practice.

In a witty and personal style that will be familiar to readers of his earlier books, Professor Sparshott makes a distinction between dance and its neighbors (such as work, sports, and games) and points out that it is more profoundly connected to questions of self-knowledge than the other arts. Dance differs from any of the fine arts in that it can be seen, not as the manipulation of a medium, but as self-transformation.

Francis Sparshott is University Professor of Philosophy at the University of Toronto. He is the author of numerous works on aesthetics, including *The Theory of the Arts* (Princeton).

OFF THE GROUND

Francis Sparshott

~~~~~~

OFF THE GROUND

First Steps to a Philosophical

Consideration of

the Dance

PRINCETON
UNIVERSITY PRESS

Copyright © 1988 by Princeton University Press

Published by Princeton University Press, 41 William Street,
Princeton, New Jersey 08540
In the United Kingdom: Princeton University Press, Guildford, Surrey

All Rights Reserved

This book has been composed in Linotron Galliard

Clothbound editions of Princeton University Press books
are printed on acid-free paper, and binding materials are
chosen for strength and durability. Paperbacks, although satisfactory
for personal collections, are not usually suitable for library rebinding

Printed in the United States of America by Princeton University Press,
Princeton, New Jersey

Designed by Laury A. Egan

Library of Congress Cataloging-in-Publication Data

Sparshott, Francis Edward, 1926-
Off the ground : first steps to a philosophical consideration of
the dance / Francis Sparshott.
p.   cm.   Bibliography: p.   Includes index.
ISBN 0-691-07327-9 (alk. paper)
1. Dancing—Philosophy. I. Title.
GV1588.S65 1988
793.3'2'01—dc19   87-34699
CIP

To all who buy it—
and who, having bought it, read it—
and who, having read it all, understand most of it—
this book is dedicated by its author
with gratitude, with respect, and in hope.

CONTENTS

~ ~

CONTENTS

PART II
Theory: On Dance

CONTENTS

CONTENTS

CONTENTS

PREFACE

~ ~ ~ ~ ~ ~ ~ ~ ~ ~ ~ ~ ~ ~ ~ ~ ~ ~

THE AIM of this book is to lay foundations for a philosophical consideration of the art or arts of dance. It begins by asking why dance has historically played little part in the philosophy of the fine arts in general. It goes on to consider what conditions must be fulfilled by the philosophy of any art or practice. It ends by exploring the ways in which the question "What is dance?" can be answered. Other crucial topics in the philosophy of dance are reserved for treatment in a proposed sequel, now in preparation.

My qualifications for this undertaking do not include expert knowledge of any form or aspect of dance, or serious involvement in any form of dance practice. I am not writing as an expert for other experts, though I have tried not to show myself unsuitably ignorant or foolish. I address myself, first of all, to readers who are interested in the philosophy of art in general, and whose interest in dance is not confined to any one form or aspect of dance. What I have to say is not meant to be authoritative or instructive, but to make in my own voice one contribution to cultural conversation.

You will notice that the chapters of this book are elaborately subdivided into numbered sections and subsections. This numbering gives the logical articulation of the work, which is accordingly displayed in the table of contents. Though the book is written informally and without recourse to philosophical technicalities, some of the chapters have a rather tight structure, and attention to the numbering system will help you to keep orientated.

I owe a very special debt to the stimulus and encouragement of Dr. Selma Jeanne Cohen, who first gave me to understand that the aesthetics of dance was a subject that would properly engage my attention.

Special thanks are also due to students from the University of Toronto and York University who came to my seminar on the aesthetics of dance in the spring of 1985, correcting my ideas and providing their own, and to Mary Coros and Professor Selma Odom, who came along and helped.

Preparation of this work was made possible by a Connaught Senior Fellowship in the Humanities for the academic year 1984–1985.

ACKNOWLEDGMENTS

~ ~ ~ ~ ~ ~ ~ ~ ~ ~ ~ ~ ~ ~ ~ ~ ~ ~

CHAPTER 4 of this book was published in substantially its present form, under the title "Some Dimensions of Dance Meaning," in *British Journal of Aesthetics* 25 (1985): 101–114, and appears here by permission of the publisher of the journal, Oxford University Press.

The material in this book dealing with why philosophers have been relatively neglectful of dance aesthetics (*Dance Research Journal* 15 [1982]: 5–30), the reasons why dance was omitted from early systems of the fine arts (*Dance Chronicle* 6 [1983]: 164–183), and the circumstances in which the philosophy of an art or a practice may be expected to be developed (*Grazer philosophische Studien* 19 [1983]: 1–19), appeared in the places named, but in forms different from those in which it now appears.

My thanks are due to the respective editors and publishers for being nice about my recycling of these materials, and to them and others for the stimulus to produce them in the first place.

INTRODUCTION

~ ~ ~ ~ ~ ~ ~ ~ ~ ~ ~ ~ ~ ~ ~ ~ ~ ~ ~ ~

IF ANY ART should attract the attention of philosophers, dance should. Dancing plays an important part in the lives of people everywhere. All human societies dance, just as all have language. But, despite its ubiquity, the activity of dancing confronts the thinker with many puzzles and difficulties. Some of these are conceptual: not all languages have a word for dance, and it is not obvious that we ourselves always mean the same thing when we use our own one word "dance." There are problems about the relation between three ways of thinking about dancing, or three kinds of dance: a spontaneous self-expressive movement of the body, a form of theatrical display, and a set of forms of social interaction. Connected with these problems are further questions, both practical and ideological, about the relation between the sort of dancing that anyone can do and everyone does, and the sort of dancing that can be done only by a dancer who has undertaken a transformation of the body into a performing instrument. These problematic areas combine with other considerations (which will be brought up later) to make the philosophical consideration of the nature and value of dance—of what the word "dance" means—an outstandingly intricate and baffling task, but also an exceptionally intriguing one for anyone who already takes an interest in aesthetics or the philosophy of art.

In most of the major arts, there is a repertory of stock problems and themes, *topoi*, that forms the main substance of what is actually discussed in the philosophy of that art. What one learns in a course on "aesthetics" consists largely of what these topics are and what there is to say about them. Aesthetics thus has a firm operative structure within which the ordinary business of academic debate is carried on and which is not itself to be fruitfully discussed. The structure is frequently called into question and may be denounced as arbitrary, but after a respectfully penitential pause the conversation resumes as though nothing had been said. These centers of perennial debate require perpetual reconsideration as philosophy changes: new styles, new emphases, changing levels of sophistication in different areas may lead to the introduction of new topics and the abandonment of old ones, but are far more likely to produce new handlings of the old themes with only small modifications. It has often been observed that these centers of philosophical concern do not coincide either with the possible scope of the art in question as abstractly conceived or with the problems of artists as concretely encountered, but are centers of an independent theoretical interest. The inference is often drawn that aesthetics is out of touch with reality, a self-contained and self-satisfied logomachy; but that is not entirely justified. Rather, the choice of topics reflects real cruces of cultural concern and philosophical interest. In every field, there are good reasons why the everyday preoccupations of practitioners should fail to coincide with what one would have thought to be the fundamentally important issues, and why theorists encounter a gap between what is fundamentally important and what can be profitably discussed; and it may be conceded that in the philosophy of art, likewise, what we actually do is a fair indication of what can be fruitfully done.

In the case of the art of dance, though certain topics continually recur, no such repertory of stock problems has been established. There is no consensual understanding among aestheticians as to what the problems of dance aesthetics are. The result is that, for practical purposes, the aesthetics of dance might as well not exist. By the reasoning of the preceding paragraph, one might infer that the unspoken wisdom of the community of aestheticians has decided that nothing can be fruitfully done in dance aesthetics. Part of our task here will be to provide grounds for a rational or instructed answer to the question whether that inference is warranted. The rest of our work will go to provide materials for an independent evaluation of its conclusion—a consideration of whether, among all the things that might be said in the aesthetics of dance, any are really worth saying.

We may say at once that the inference from the lack of a repertory of familiar conundrums in dance aesthetics to the conclusion that the art of dance is not worth thinking about should not be drawn too quickly. A vital consideration here is that, in the original formulation of the concept of the fine arts in the sixteenth and seventeenth centuries, dance was not regularly included as one of the fine arts. We will have a lot to say about this matter later. For the moment, it is enough that it was so, and that the repertory of agreed problems in the aesthetics of particular arts has much to do with their status as members of this culturally privileged group. In raising poetry and painting to culturally dignified positions, the scope of what was effectively included in those arts was reduced to intellectually manageable proportions. "Painting" became effectively identified, despite all protests and caveats, with what practitioners of the arts of painting did in the official practice of their art. Deprived of this comfortably validating context, the aesthetics of dance remains amorphous. But what practical or theoretical conclusions can be drawn from this fact is something that can be decided only on the basis of consideration of the complex historical, cultural, and intellectual issues involved.

The present aim is less to establish a structured set of topics for dance aesthetics as part of the main substance of discussion within the philosophy of art than to shed some light on why no such set is current now and to provide a corpus of materials apt to provide a basis for discussion, should people care to discuss them.

The lack of an established structure for our topic makes it unwise to eliminate much that might be judged peripheral. Judgments of relevance and centrality are in place when the scope and shape of the governing discussion have been securely established. Meanwhile, much of this book has to do with the question of how such judgments are to be made and supported. The domain within which it operates is, in fact, that of practical philosophy in general rather than that of aesthetics.

Again, the present aim is not to put forward any particular theory about dance or about dance aesthetics, to favor (by persuasive definition or other such devices of devious rationality) any dance practice or any particular view of such practice. No doubt, prejudices will be revealed and opinions will be expressed; but they are not what the argument of the book is about.

Both because there is no deliberate *parti pris* and because the field we operate in is itself indeterminate, the approach in this book is not linear. Chapters cannot always build on preceding chapters. Retractations of material are not avoided, because that would have called for a definitive assignment of the material to a particular context and its exclusion from others. Little attention is paid to consistency, though it is hoped that there will be no actual contradictions that are not drawn to the reader's attention and accounted for.[1]

The discussion is effectively in four parts. The first part (Chapter 1) seeks to explain why the aesthetics of dance finds itself at a disadvantage. The explanation is partly historical, though history itself explains nothing—or rather, one has to explain why the historical factors were relevant and effective. The second part (Chapters 2 and 3) is devoted to second-order considerations about philosophies and philosophical theories of arts and practices, and about whether dance is indeed best thought of as an art or a practice or in some other way. Something has to be said about how practices and arts are identified and differentiated, in what sense the theory of an art or practice is possible, in what circumstances such a theory may be

---

[1] Consistency, as such, may be an important value only within restricted theoretical contexts. Ian Hacking has argued that, in science, different experimental contexts may call for quite different and mutually incompatible theoretical commitments and that this situation may not be changed by further scientific progress (Hacking 1983, 264 and passim). It seems even likelier that, in the philosophy of practice, the right things to say in one context may contradict the right things to say in a different context (cf. Sparshott 1982, ch. 15). But when this happens, I for one would be unhappy without a higher-order theory about why it should happen.

developed, and what considerations control its development. The third part of the book (Chapter 4) is devoted to the semiotics of dance: that is, to a cataloguing (and in some cases a perfunctory discussion) of the aspects of dance in which meaning may be found. Clearly, such a listing provides the framework within which all issues in dance aesthetics must find their determinate place. The rules by which such a framework must be constructed and judged complete do not at present exist—whether they *could* exist is one of the questions we will have to confront. Meanwhile, we have to proceed as best we can.

The remaining chapters belong to the fourth part of the book, the direct confrontation of topics of straightforward interest: what dance is, what the basic kinds of dance are, what is important about dance, what the characteristic values of dance are, how dance relates to other arts and other forms of activity—stuff like that. Some of these questions have to do with what dance essentially is, and the rest are concerned with the classification, analysis, characterization, and relationships of dance as thus identified. Whether this distinction (made famous by Plato, and often referred to as that between "essence" and "quality") can really be justified and sustained in any particular case has been debated by philosophers. The present work, however, takes it as a practical device and confines itself to questions of the former sort. Questions of the latter sort are left for a later volume, which will inevitably be less systematic than this one, since it cannot have an argumentative core and can be guided only by the author's awareness of matters of actual or possible interest.

One thing this book does not do is run through any or all of the most famous theories in general aesthetics and show how they can be applied to dance. People to whom such application would be interesting and profitable can do that for themselves.[2] Theories and theorists are mentioned and discussed only if and as they help the discussion along, never for their own sakes.

I have already said that my discussion is discontinuous. The chief reason is that the effect of any argument is likely to be that it closes off certain alternatives. But, for a book of merely preliminary and deliberately neutral scope, the alternatives thus closed off might be as well worth examining as the line of argument that eliminated them. One cannot justify one's starting point, if a starting point is what it really is. As an outsider in the world of dance, I am often informed, as a matter of plain fact, that certain doctrines or procedures or definitions or lines of argument are known and agreed on by all competent persons. But, as might have been expected, what one of my informants claims to be the object of such a consensus

---

[2] Some material of this sort is usefully provided by Redfern (1983), but from a rather narrow range.

often contradicts something for which the same status is claimed by an-other. To disagree with such people is out of the question for me: I would be taken to be ignorantly impugning their professional credentials. I can only wait for them to go away.

One may reflect here that learning to be a dancer at a professional level must involve adopting as part of one's very substance a set of values and the language in which those values are articulated, as articulated for singers by Vernon Howard (1982). It may well be that some (or even all) per-formers are personally committed by this self-transformation in such a way that—as a matter of integrity or simply as a psychological impossibility[3]—they cannot afford to take seriously any alternative standpoint. In these cases, the integrity of a particular standpoint and the associated ideology become a necessity within the art, but not, of course, a necessity for all engaged in the art, many of whom will be exponents of rival necessities no less cogent.

The order of treatment in this book is, for obvious reasons, no more logical than it is linear. Logically, one should begin by defining dance and thus delimiting one's subject, then determine the nonaccidental attributes of dance, then proceed to peripheral issues and such second-order matters as the status of one's discourse. Here I follow the opposite order. We start with the meta-issues, and among them consider why dance aesthetics has been neglected—which requires us to consider the relevant doctrines and practices. We do this before we have even mooted the question what sort of theory dance theory could reasonably be. We take it for granted that it is perfectly obvious what theorists would be doing if they did it. Similarly, our historical observations take it for granted that it is perfectly obvious, as indeed it is, what the history of dance is the history of and which theories are dance theories and what they are about when they are about dance. Only later do we raise the question, as if it were still a matter for discovery, of what dance is. Again, the reason is that any definite decision reached in the last area would place constraints on what is now the previous discus-sion, which however deals with issues that arranged themselves without any such determination, and that in many cases no doubt proceeded from starting points that could not be defended. Or one might say: we all know very well what dance is, but we do not know what dance is *strictly speaking*, and we do not even know whether (and, if so, when) we want to speak strictly.

Our topic is, on the face of it, one of alarming complexity. The concept of dance presents us with problems: what forms of behavior are covered by the literal meaning of the word? And how does the word cover them,

---

[3] Thus, Howard (1982) not only identifies skill in singing with the development of the voice but also identifies the *bel canto* style of voice with voice ("natural" voice) in general.

exactly? What favored uses of the word (and its cognates and analogues, of course) are to be considered metaphorical? Or is it the sort of word with which the distinction between literal and metaphorical is better not made? Suppose we get those questions squared away and decide that the word designates a practice, something people do. We may then ask: Is dance an art? Or are there many separate arts of dance? (Are these questions to which it is intelligent to devote one's intelligence?) And is the art (or are any of the arts) a "fine" art (whatever that may usefully mean), and does it matter whether it is or not? If we get that set of issues squared away, we have to enumerate, interrelate, and evaluate the ways in which dance has meanings and values. But there is a more baffling question than any of these, having to do with the mode of existence of dances. Are they visibilia, in the mode of visible bodies in motion? Or do they exist in the first instance for their dancers, kinesthetically, as ways of experiencing one's embodied existence? Or are dances primarily matters of personal interrelation, existing in a social and interpersonal space? Or, finally, is dance a mode of theater, insofar as that can be distinguished from the possibilities already considered? Perhaps these are all possible points of view, or appropriate to different sorts of dance. But, if either of those is the case, how are they mutually related? Do they form any sort of conceptual or practical unity at all? It seems hard to see how they could. And yet we may still feel that the realm of dance is very sharply delineated, a real and very individual and recognizable component in the world we live in. A person who did not know in some way what dancing was would be in some way monstrous. It is by no means obvious that this puzzle can be either solved or dissolved.

Finally, someone might ask: What are the rules by which the proprieties of our discourse submit to be governed? Are we engaged in conceptual clarification, or phenomenology, or empirical description, or experimental research? Not the last, clearly: one does not see what sort of hypotheses should be framed or how they might be tested, since no area of our discourse can be sufficiently safeguarded from the science-precluding qualifier, "it depends what you mean." How can the status of a fact *as a fact about dance* be established? If, on the other hand, it is an empirical study, the domain of experience appealed to must be the history and current practice, world-wide, of dance and dance criticism. And so it is, in the sense that whatever we say must stand or fall by the readers' sense of what that history and practice have been and are. But what makes that history a single history, that practice a single practice, and what do we mean by associating that singleness with the concept of dance? We all know in our nerves what dance is insofar as we all speak a language that articulates a life in which dance is a meaningful part. So, finally, insofar as our investigation is conceptual, it involves not lexicography but the exploration of a domain of practical reason, a common understanding in a social world in which some *among us* are dancers and lovers of dancing. We speak out of a common understanding, as that understanding is formed in a social world in which we participate as different individuals.

PART I

~ ~

Metatheory:
On the Philosophy
of Dance

CHAPTER 1

~ ~ ~ ~ ~ ~ ~ ~ ~ ~ ~ ~ ~ ~ ~ ~ ~ ~

Why the Aesthetics of Dance Has Been Neglected

THE DECADE of the 1960s saw an immense and rapid increase of interest in dance, especially in the United States. It was the most recent of a series of waves of enthusiasm for dance of one or another sort. "As long as the ballet mania prevails," said the London *Morning Post* of March 13, 1843, at the height of the ballerina craze set off by Taglioni, "vain are our protests in favour of the superior rights of the lyrical drama" (quoted in Guest 1984, 113). In the 1920s, in the wake of Diaghilev, both artistic and popular dance spread around the world and established the dance world as we still know it. And so on. What makes the latest epidemic different, if anything does, is that it is accompanied by a great deal of scholarly and scientific activity, giving rise to a mass of historical, sociological, and anthropological studies that are now issuing in publication.

A strange state of affairs in aesthetics has now become apparent. A venerable tradition regards dance as one of the most basic of arts, and this tradition was reinforced in the early years of the present century by evolutionary notions that remarked the ubiquity of dance in primitive cultures and singled out dancelike behavior among primates as one of the principal animal antecedents of human art. Moreover, this evolutionary speculation simply revives in a more up-to-date form a theme popular in the eighteenth-century theorizing about the origins of culture that lies behind so much of our thinking about language and civilization: the idea that dance or dancelike behavior is the first distinctively human trait, the original symbolic activity from which speech and song were derived. To take a mild but influential example, Condillac's essay on the origins of human knowledge assigns dance a key position among the arts. Music and poetry, he writes, "were associated with the art of gesture, an art older than they, which was called 'dance.' From that we may guess that, at all times and among all peoples, some kind of dance, of music, and of poetry, might have been observed" (Condillac 1746, 228). He adopts from William Warburton's

Essay on the Hieroglyphics the theory that ancient peoples, including the Old Testament prophets and Greeks like Heracleitus (according to whom "[t]he king, whose oracle is at Delphi, neither speaks nor is silent, but expresses himself through signs"), as well as the Egyptians, had at their disposal a well-developed language of action and gesture, which they reserved for the most important utterances and which in a refined form became what we know as the dance (pp. 198–199).

Views like those of Condillac were widespread among his contemporaries at the time when the ideas were taking shape that have dominated the philosophy of art and aesthetics ever since. One would therefore expect that theories of dance would continue to occupy a central place in the philosophy of art. But this seems not to be the case. Philosophers of art have contented themselves with this lipservice and have done little work on the aesthetics of the art they have thus determined to be fundamental. Examples of general points in aesthetics are seldom drawn from dance, and separate articles and monographs on dance aesthetics are few. It is possible to sit through an entire conference on aesthetics without once hearing dance referred to. There is an extensive early literature on dance, as well as a great deal of technical and biographical writing; but neither the early literature nor the theoretically significant part of the more recent work is well known to the learned and literary worlds at large. One wonders why this should be so.

It is at once obvious that there are three quite different questions here. The first is why there is so little work done specifically on the philosophy of dance. This question perhaps needs no answer, for philosophers have plenty of work to be getting on with and inactivity needs no excuse. The question is rather: Why should there be any such philosophy? The second question is why, given that there is a philosophy of the fine arts, dance should be excluded from it or given a minor place within it. And the third question is why, given that there is a philosophy of the fine arts in which dance does have a place, dance should receive relatively little emphasis. Part of the answer to that third question could be that the lack of a separate and autonomous philosophy of dance means that there is little distinctive material to draw on.

It might be thought that the question why there should be a separate and autonomous philosophy of dance has already been answered in our statement of the initial problem: since dance is widely held to be the basic and original form of art, anyone who thinks about the theory of art should think about dance first of all. But there are two answers to that, one bad and one good. The bad answer is that speculations about the origins of art and language in the eighteenth-century manner and conjectures about the evolution of art in the early Darwinian manner have long been regarded as irresponsible and unsupported guesswork: far from placing a premium on thought about dance, the supposed original priority of dance contaminates the whole topic with an air of sleaziness. That is a bad answer because usually, once a topic is firmly established, it does not go away merely because it has been disreputably handled: people return to it again and again to see whether it can be reclaimed.

The good answer is, however, very closely related to the bad one. It is, that the alleged primitive priority of dance is based on its actually perceived pervasiveness, a pervasiveness so polymorphous and extensive that there can be nothing distinctive to say about dance as such. Unless one is working in a cash economy, any celebration or ceremony insofar as it is not an exchange of words is bound to have the character of dance, because it can only consist of people making distinctive movements, and what is that if not dancing? Similarly, if anyone deliberately or spontaneously moves his or her body without necessary occasion, nothing prevents us from designating that as dance. And again, if there is to be free intermarriage among families, young people must meet each other freely in intimate but controlled circumstances. Whenever that happens, the result can be called a dance, even if it has only the character of a Friday-night promenade. If it takes place only as a complex of stylized personal exchanges spread out over space and time, we may say that it is a sort of occult dance. In short, the reasons for saying that dance is the origin of all art are reasons for thinking of dance not as one art among others but as a sort of matrix from which arts emerge by specialization. Those arts no doubt include a specific art or arts of dance; but such an art would have no privilege over other specific arts and, because of its close relation to the more pervasive practice, might prove hard to pin down.

Similarly, the fact that (as we shall see in Chapter 2) the literature of speculative cosmology has habitually given the name of "dance" to the movements of the planets around earth or sun, or to the supposedly analogous relation of angels to God, though it certainly assigns enormous importance to the concept of dance, does not suffice to establish a dance aesthetics or any other form of philosophy of the *art* of dance; for what human dancers do can scarcely be made out to be the sort of things that planets and angels are supposed to do.

In considering why the aesthetics of dance has been neglected, we must distinguish between what factors actually made people neglect it and what reasons there were, and still are, why they should have neglected it. As philosophers rather than historians, we are concerned directly with only the latter, though we would be foolish not to take account of as much history as we can master: if accidents without necessities are unilluminating, necessities without accidents are empty. What concerns us is the deliberative question: How are we to think about dancing in the most general terms? We are to build for ourselves an intelligible construction. Events, as such, can be forgotten: they are relevant only as *our* past, only as what is to be contrasted with, overcome by, sustained in, and in other ways related to our present and our future. The present shape we are to give to our thinking is part of the process whereby we make ourselves in our culture.

Our question, then, is: What is there about dancing, about how we have to come to terms with it (as we confront and do it, in order to make the best and most of it) in the context of our philosophy of art and practice (as we confront and do that, to make the best and most sense of it), that resists our bringing it into the center of our aesthetics, either as separate topic or as preferred illustration? And, whatever the resistance is, is it something that could be overcome or that should be overcome; or should we resign ourselves to accepting it as inevitable and even as proper? For the mere fact that dance and dance research are booming, in prestige as well as in popularity, does not entail anything in particular about how the philosophy of dance should be approached and practiced.

1.1 *The Fact of Neglect*

It is useless to try to explain why philosophers neglect the theory of dance unless they really do neglect it. Perhaps they don't. Perhaps what has to be explained is a mere ritual of saying they do. Such a ritual (to which there are well-known parallels in philosophical writing, such as that of deploring the low intellectual standards prevailing in aesthetics) may register an unease about the proper place of dance theory within the philosophy of art. This unease, we shall see, is well grounded. In any case, such rituals as the lament over the neglect of dance theory themselves stand in need of explanation. Rituals must once have served some social purpose and, since not all rituals survive, rituals that continue to be performed must continue to fulfil some function, if not necessarily the function for which they were instituted.

It may well be true that the aesthetics of dance has not been neglected in the sense that little has been written on the subject; it may rather be that what has been written has had a comparatively low intellectual profile within philosophy or in the cultured world at large. My own reflections on this topic started with the supposition that among the data to be reckoned with was a dearth of certain sorts of writing that were in fact abundant; it was only that they did not figure largely in general works. More disconcertingly, my own abstracts and excerpts from works of bygone times turned out to have omitted the materials on dance that they did in fact contain. It may well be, then, that the philosophical neglect of dance is perfectly real, but is not so much a tendency of writers to ignore that art as a tendency of philosophical readers and talkers to ignore what has been written. One must not confuse a lack of available theory with a habit of ignoring what theory there is. But, of course, this second-order neglect would be as strange a phenomenon, as much in need of explanation, as the lack of material would have been.

1.11 PHILOSOPHICAL INERTIA

If contemporary philosophers do neglect dance, at least part of the explanation must be sought in history. Philosophical problems take a long time to shape, and as long a time for their significance to be evaluated. It is largely lost labor to examine contemporary discussions to see why they should have taken this form or that: they are formed by the air they breathe, by the climate of opinion. What formed that climate, today's philosophers are unlikely to know.

The justifiable and inevitable conservatism of philosophy is exaggerated by two tendencies in today's philosophical institutions that are less praiseworthy. In the first place, much recent aesthetics, like other philosophical writing, has in the English-speaking world taken the form of journal articles. Because of this brevity, it has had to be puzzle-oriented, preoccupied with topics that can easily be debated within an unexamined frame of reference. It has therefore had to be parasitic on systems already worked out and on larger concerns articulated elsewhere. The authors have no space to give even such reasons as they have for their starting points.[1] In the second place, what philosophers do has in part to be explained away by a discrepancy (already remarked on by Plato) between the demands of philosophy as ideally conceived and the actual requirements of philosophy as a job.

Philosophy is supposed to be the pursuit of wisdom. Some philosophers glory in that supposition, some accept it humbly, some resent it as a mere etymological imputation for which they should not be held responsible. None the less, they are stuck with it. Other descriptions of philosophy are derived from it or are results of its erosion by history and the rise of the exact sciences. A philosopher cannot evade the exemplary implications of his practice: whatever he does in the name of philosophy reflects, whether he likes it or not, an evaluation of aspects of knowledge and reality.

Philosophy in practice is, however, a school subject. As such, it can be little more than the transmission of received doctrines and methods, and

---

[1] For a more extended and rather different treatment of this difference between journal philosophy and book philosophy, see Sparshott 1985a.

the teaching of it is a highly skilled and exacting but fundamentally mind-less occupation, not much different in its intellectual quality from teaching children the conventions of English spelling. Those who do this teaching are called "professional philosophers"—what else?—and their practice is accordingly taken to have implications about what really matters in the life of the mind, although nothing in what they do requires them to be either competent to assess the importance of intellectual issues or interested in doing so. In fact, such a capacity and such an interest would hinder them in their work, which is to teach "Philosophy 100," the content of which has been settled on political or traditional grounds by a departmental com-mittee.

Teachers of philosophy need to be clever (it is a difficult subject to learn) and dedicated (it is a very hard subject to teach), but nothing in their train-ing calls on them to be wise, or encourages them to become so or to wish to be so, or tends to make them so. Neither wisdom nor the longing for wisdom is either necessary or sufficient to pass one's courses or one's com-prehensives or to satisfy one's Ph.D. committee—it may even be a hin-drance. Nothing in philosophers' training or their daily occupation re-quires them to be intelligent or to use what intelligence they have—that is, to think about the implications of what they are doing. Philosophers can be, and sometimes are, foolish and rather stupid people. Fashions in learn-ing and teaching philosophy can therefore be merely modish, arbitrary, or blinkered. And yet, like it or not, the title of philosopher makes its claim. We are like children who must wear the clothes of our elder siblings whether we are big enough or not.

It follows from what was said in the last paragraph that if aesthetics is almost the least reputable branch of philosophy (and perhaps only the phi-losophy of education crouches lower on the totem pole), that is a result of the way philosophy curricula have come to be organized and does not nec-essarily reflect anyone's considered and reasoned assessment of how the map of the intellectual world ought to be drawn. And if the theory of dance is inconspicuous within aesthetics, that too need not reflect any considered judgment of the place dance should occupy among the arts or among the objects of philosophical reflection. At the same time, philosophy being what it is and supposed to be what it is supposed to be, people interested in dance take the absence of a corpus of familiar materials to reflect a judg-ment on the insignificance or disreputability of dance. And so, at some level, it may; but it need not. None the less, the perceived neglect of the aesthetics of dance is a public fact that has the effect of a public denigration or depreciation of dance. Perhaps more philosophers ought to write on the subject, just for the look of the thing—although, in doing so, they would not be manifesting any very high grade of wisdom, or any singleminded devotion to wisdom, or much intelligence.

1.2 *Alleged Difficulties*

Even if it is true that the neglect of dance aesthetics is to be explained by the dynamics of philosophical discussion and the history of the theory of the arts, that explanation cannot be complete. Past events do not cause present decisions. What we now call the past is our past because we now make it ours. If past patterns of thought can be made out to have determined present practice, it must be because it has not seemed necessary to challenge or change those patterns. Present conditions reflect present pressures, and specific explanations for the neglect have often been attempted. Significantly, these seldom justify it: either they excuse it, of they condemn the forces that produce it.

1.21 LACK OF OCCASION

The first explanation is one we have mentioned already and to which we will return: that the occasion for theorizing about dance has never arisen until very recently. People do not answer a question that no one is urgently asking, even if they can see that it would be a good question. This, of course, is not true: people do answer such questions; but it may be true that their answers languish in obscurity.[2]

1.22 LACK OF AUTHORITY

A more positive reason for the neglect stems from the lack of a familiar and effective dance notation. The original theory of the fine arts, it is argued, relied for propaganda purposes on the records of classical antiquity. Ancient dance, not having been recorded, did not survive.[3] But this argu-

---

[2] Compare, from a different field, Keller's study of how Barbara McClintock's work on the genetics of corn was ignored even while she herself was being honored, because she was answering unfashionable questions and it was not worth anyone's time to master so difficult a field as a parergon (Keller 1983).

[3] John Weaver says this in the course of introducing his presentation of Feuillet's dance notation: "Tho' *Dancing* and *Musick* seem to be of near an equal Antiquity, and even of an equal Extent, yet *Musick* has long receiv'd an Advantage, which *Dancing* wanted. *Musick* has employ'd the Pens of many of the Learned, both Ancient and Modern, and has had the Benefit of an universal character, which convey'd the harmonious Compositions to all Lovers of the *Art* in all Nations. *Dancing*, on the contrary, tho' celebrated by Ancient Authors in an extraordinary manner, and with uncommon Praises, (as I shall shew in a Treatise, which I

ment cannot be sustained. Ancient music was no less effectively lost, and painting hardly less. What survived into the Renaissance was the descriptions, the rhetoric surrounding the works and their alleged effects; Renaissance debates could hinge on the reported features of works that no one had seen or heard for a millennium. Comparable descriptions of ancient dances survived, too. The trouble was, as we shall see, that they were the wrong sort of description.

1.23 LACK OF FAMILIAR REPERTORY

Presumably, if a notation had been desired and practicable, one would have been developed. Notations have been continually developed and widely used since the seventeenth century. The trouble has been that either they fail to capture enough of the complexity of the dance they notate, or they are too unwieldy to be used as musical scores are used, as a means of direct access to the work notated. Perhaps our modern notations will finally do this, as devisers of earlier notations so often promised to do. In any case, the deficiency in question is significant as part of a wider difficulty: writers on dance do not have, as writers on other arts do, a varied and extensive repertory of works with which they could feel entitled to suppose their readers to be familiar. People outside a very few metropolitan centers have had few opportunities to acquaint themselves with dance as understood by the masters and critics of the art.

It is hard to estimate the force of these considerations. For one thing, the repertory of classical ballet, with its standardized technique, is no more inaccessible than any other cultural material. If not everyone knows it well at first hand, that is true of any art. Surely we know it well enough to sustain a conversation. Ballet, however, despite its received status, is held in some quarters to be artistically dubious; and what those who hold this opinion tend to regard as the more artistically sound practice of modern and post-modern dance is accused of being hopelessly fragmented (cf. §1.342 below). It has been virtually impossible for anyone who is neither independently wealthy nor professionally connected with dancing to get any real idea of the scope of contemporary dance. If a grasp of what that dance is depends on acquaintance with the specific works of a large sample of dancers, troupes, and choreographers, few writers are in a position to

shall suddenly publish on that Subject) yet among the Moderns, it has been wholly unknown to the Learned, and destitute of all Pens, in either the speculative or practick part of the *Art*, which for want of an universal Character, was confin'd to the immediate Master and Scholar, or at farthest, to a narrow traditional Instruction, which none could participate of without a Teacher, who had been taught by some other, either Composer, or Scholar of such Composer" (Weaver 1706, the Dedication).

attain that grasp, and none can rely on their readers sharing it. Moreover, no specific branch of today's dance has an adequate hold over our major cultural institutions, in the way that New York painting has had a stranglehold over the major galleries and organs of publicity, so as to form an adequate context of discourse. I cannot *expect as of right* that my readers will know any kind of new dance in the way that I can expect as of right that they will know the work of Barnett Newman or Brice Marden (or whoever it will be next week)—the nationally advertised brands.

One should not be too hasty in correlating insight into aesthetic principles with wide exposure to examples—there is really no reason to think that Kant would have changed his mind about the nature of music if Königsberg had had a better town band. What is missed, rather, is the sense of a sustaining body of shared experience, a context within which mutual understanding makes discussion possible.

To some extent, television has already supplied the sort of common reference we have desiderated, and it is likely that home video will change it further. It is not that video makes the dance *experience* available in the living room, any more than photography takes the student of architecture to Chandigarh, but it does make choreography and dance available for reference and study. The sense in which it enables us to feel that we know what we are talking about is precisely the right sense. And the selective policies of television networks, together with the expensive and highly centralized nature of the video medium, are already beginning to provide Americans with a slate of choreographers *known to be good*, to whom we can all refer as familiar. Specifically, the extensive series of programs produced under the title *Dance in America*, if it continues to be regularly repeated, will saturate us with approved choreography and approved attitudes to artistic dance. When this process has gone a little further, we will all feel comfortable talking about the dance.

1.24 DANCE AS A FEMALE ART

A reason often alleged for the neglect of dance aesthetics is that philosophers have been spokesmen for the official culture of a patriarchal, life-denying, formal, cerebral civilization, whereas dance is essentially orientated toward the body and its life-involvement, inseparable from the suppressed matriarchal values that Jung and others have discerned as dominant in the pre-Hellenic dawn of our civilization (cf. Levin 1977). It is hard to know what to make of this suggestion. One is tempted to dismiss it as a mindless manifestation of doctrinaire feminism, fortified by bad history and worse psychology. To begin with, and decisively, when one looks at dance at all known places and times, dances for women are no more common than dances for men and dances for both sexes together, as a survey of the materials compiled by Sachs (1937) and Hanna (1979) shows.[4] There may be cultures in which institutionalized dance is reserved for women, but none come readily to mind.

In the second place, the association between femininity and the body is implausible. Is there any society in which the ideology represents women as corporeal and men as incorporeal? In most societies, one would have thought, it is the males who are hunters and fighters, and hence physically active in that mode; and in societies that have got beyond hunting and fighting as modes of cultural expression, the niche is filled by athletes, sportsmen, and jocks. English-language popular literature, the surest guide to cultural stereotypes, represents the unathletic and intellectually oriented young male as being at a disadvantage in his culture.

In Aristotle's analysis of sex differences in the animal kingdom (in effect, among mammals, including humans), which presumably embodies the stereotypes of his own place and time, males do not figure as more cerebral than females but as more active, so that in human economies the males tend to acquire and the females to preserve (cf. Sparshott 1985b). That hardly accommodates a stereotype in which it is the females who dance while the males remain immobile, and no society known to Aristotle could have suggested such a stereotype. What it suggests is a differentiation that we find in some later writers, such as Adam Smith (1795): there are two sorts of dance and two sets of dance values, one displaying strength and athleticism, the other manifesting gracefulness. Similarly, in Indian classical dance, both the expressive and the formal kinds of dance (nrtya and nrtta) "are of two varieties, tandava or vigorous, and lasya or gentle. The latter evokes or augments the erotic sentiment while the former represents awe or awe-inspiring emotions" (Sathyanarayana 1969, 9). These types are unmistakably represented in the classical texts as male and female dancing, respectively, the dances of Shiva and of Parvati (cf. §8.211231 below). Neither of these, obviously, is any more dancelike than the other. Perhaps those who associate dance with femaleness are somehow identifying dance as a whole with the sort of dance that women are thus thought of as doing.[5] But I have never seen such an identification stated and defended, and it is hard to see how it could be.

---

[4] Note the emphasis on the materials compiled, as opposed to the opinions expressed; the doctrines and theories of these authorities are not at issue here.

[5] Obviously and notoriously, the kind of dance that expresses a passive stereotype of femininity—balancing on points and jumping into men's arms—is in fact extremely demanding physically and requires that its practitioner be a strong and highly trained athlete. What it symbolizes, and even what it expresses, are at odds with what it represents in terms of human involvement; but that is often true in artistic work.

It is quite true that, when one thinks of the arts of dance, there are contexts in which one thinks of a female dancer in a short white skirt. That is, one identifies artistic dance with nineteenth-century ballet and with dance forms derived from that, and then personifies that form as a "ballerina." One might then think of dance as being at once feminine and fleshly in a derogatory way (because the short tutu functions at least in part to satisfy the voyeurs in the audience) and, hence, as artistically trivial, because that stereotyped image of the girl under a spotlight at the focus of the opera glasses is kitsch (cf. §1.3323 below). But surely this stereotype does not dominate the thinking of anyone seriously interested in aesthetics. Even in the heyday of the ballerina, not only the impresarios but also the choreographers were almost all male—in fact, this continuing male preponderance in ballet choreography is another of those sexual imbalances that feminists have identified and condemned.[6]

What, though, of modern dance? That is, what of the sort of dance that sought to occupy in the artistic pantheon (especially in its United States branch) the niche claimed by ballet as the prevailing art of theater dance? It is quite true that Isadora Duncan, who first revealed to the cultured world at large that dance might be an autonomous art, was a woman and thought of her art as, among other things, a manifestation of womanhood. And it is true that consequently, in a sense, the autonomous art of dance was at first revealed as a woman's art. But that will hardly serve as an explanation of the belittlement of dance, because the significance of the revelation as perceived at the time was precisely that dance could be an art of equal stature with the others. Besides, that was Duncan's own emphasis. She related the significance of her dance not to sexism but to the leading spiritual movements of the day as she from time to time conceived them. It sometimes seems otherwise, so far as the published materials show, only because she as a woman took it for granted that women would be dancers and dancers would be women: the contrast is not between dancing women and undancing men but between dances that defamed and frustrated womanhood and dances that liberated—between her own dance and ballet. "The ballet condemns itself by enforcing the deformation of the beautiful

---

[6] Ninette de Valois remarks in her Preface to Guest (1966) that, even in the romantic ballet in Paris, male dancers and choreographers retained artistic control, though performance and publicity were focused on the female dancers. Suzanne Gordon observes that *Swan Lake* may be interpreted as symbolizing the sex and power relations that still prevail in ballet: "A dominant male—in this case, the evil sorcerer Von Rothbart—controls a flock of women," destroying their humanity (Gordon 1983, 110–111). Isadora Duncan's woman-centered dance can be construed as an attempt to recapture the spirit of the romantic ballet in a less artificial and more democratic form, rather than (as she thought of it) as a rediscovery of the original nature of dance. She supposed, as Levin does, that femininity was part of the original nature of dance as such, rather than one aspect of some recent manifestations of dance.

woman's body!" she wrote; "No historical, no choreographical reasons can prevail against that" (Duncan 1928, 56). And again: "It is not only a question of true art, it is a question of race, of the development of the female sex to beauty and health, of the return to the original strength and to natural movements of women's body. . . . The dancing school of the future is to develop and show the ideal of woman" (Duncan 1928, 61).[7]

It is also true that modern dance, and art-related dance generally in modern America, took root as largely a women's movement, functioning (as Elizabeth Kendall [1979] has so brilliantly reminded us) as both means and symbol of emancipation. Duncan and St. Denis, like Pavlova, could be role models for girls as Nijinsky and Shawn never were for boys. Above all, Martha Graham became the bellwether of "modern dance" as a movement, and the dissemination of her teaching to physical training instructors at Bennington summer schools between 1934 and 1938 firmly established dance as a way in which girls, but not usually boys, could fulfill the physical training requirements usually imposed by colleges.[8] The association of dance with womanhood, once established, is institutionally perpetuated. It is obvious to any observer that American dance education is dominated by women both as teachers and as students (shortage of men is a perennial problem in college dance troupes) and that dance scholarship attracts more women than men. Even in modern dance, however, one has only to think of Rudolf von Laban to realize that the roots of ideology and practice are not exclusively female. Nor is it true that professional-level practitioners of modern dance are predominantly female. Here, where artistic choice plays a bigger part than the exigencies of curriculum, one finds groups that are all male, or all female, or made up of both sexes in all imaginable proportions—though, notoriously, the women usually dance better than the men, because they are drawn from a more extensive pool of potential talent.[9]

---

[7] The reference to race is not casual or accidental. Duncan writes elsewhere of the American dance of the future: "This dance will have nothing in it either of the servile coquetry of ballet or the sensual convulsion of the South African negro. It will be clean. . . . The real American type can never be a ballet dancer. The legs are too long, the body too supple and the spirit too free for this school of affected grace and toe-walking. It is noteworthy that all great ballet dancers have been very short women with small frames. A tall finely made woman could never dance the ballet" (Duncan 1928, 49). There is something in that. The Paris Opera recruited its dancers from undernourished slum children, and Gordon (1983) claims that certain American ballet schools, attempting to make women conform to the unnatural shape preferred by Balanchine and his imitators, drive their students to anorexia. But ballet does not in itself require such excesses, and Isadora may be betraying a personal bias: photographs reveal an earth-motherly aspect to her famous beauty. However, the same emphasis on the essential Americanism of a corn-fed frame appears in Margaret H'Doubler's predilection for the great galumphing girls of Wisconsin (see the opening chapters of H'Doubler 1940).

[8] For the significance of Bennington, see McDonagh 1973, 110ff.

[9] Balanchine once said (I heard him on television) that women dance better than men any-

It is true, again, that among career choices in modern Europe and America, dancing is not a conventional male option: sons are likely to be dissuaded by conventional parents from such a career more vigorously than daughters are from becoming lawyers. This, though, seems to be a local and temporary phenomenon: partly a reaction to the predominant stereotype of the dancer as ballerina, partly a recognition of the plain fact that dancing, like the other arts, is not a reliable way to make a good living. Neither reason represents any particular attitude toward corporeality as such: at most, the objection involves the associations of a particular sort of movement. In the United States, the association of dance with femininity seems to belong to the frontier myth that assigns to the male the sole duty of killing Indians and grizzlies (or, them failing, fish, deer, and pedestrians). As such, it has little to do with the patriarchal organization of official civilization and less to do with the supposed Platonist contempt for the body on the part of philosophy.

Insofar as there is disparagement of theater dance (or, more usually, unspoken and inarticulate distaste for it) as both feminine and body-centered, it may be because the kind of display of the moving body that is associated with theater dance seems to go socially with the self-attitudes that were encouraged in young women and deplored in young men ($3.21 below). If that is so, it belongs to a particular phase in fashion: at other times, women were not supposed to flaunt themselves for the marriage market and young men were supposed to preen and display their knightly valor. But the more one accumulates generalizations of this sort, the more obvious it becomes that the attitudes one is speaking of are not only highly specific to particular social classes and groups but also deeply embedded in specific practices and contexts of behavior. Global attitudes toward the body or toward sexual propriety resist isolation as an independent factor even at a very deep level.— Or rather, perhaps, one has first to isolate a very specific pattern of behavior in a specific context and then inquire how sex bias and attitudes toward the body function in this instance.

If in a patriarchal society dance were indeed thought to be an exclusively feminine matter, that would be a reason for the male establishment to ignore it as necessarily trivial. But no one has ever thought that: at most, what was thought was that the *act* of dancing, of executing a choreogra-

---

way: they are more agile and more precise. But Balanchine was preoccupied with a particular type of dancing and with the peculiar type of body best adapted to it. His genius may have been inseparable from his hang-ups—that is often the way—but that does not entitle his hang-ups to independent respect. Even those who think that Balanchine was the greatest choreographic genius of this or any other age may concede that there may be other ways of dancing well—other styles, and other values, not related to Balanchine's practice, the possibilities of which remain to be exploited by some other star of comparable magnitude.

pher's design, was something mainly for women. Presenters, critics, creators, and connoisseurs of dance, at the height of the ballerina cult, were predominantly male and incurred no stigma from their engagement with dancing. One would expect the emphases of aesthetics to follow those of connoisseurship and criticism rather than those of practice. And, as for the supposed Platonizing devaluation of the body, what that implies is, notoriously, the depreciation of all objects of sensory experience, including music and painting. But what has to be accounted for is a situation in which music and painting are esteemed but dancing is disparaged. Of course, the dancer whose movements are being appreciated is more intensively engaged in bodily movement than the painter is. But so is a sculptor; and, though Leonardo da Vinci made that a reason for disparaging the sculptor's career choice, neither he nor anyone else thought it was a reason for regarding the resulting sculptures less highly than paintings.[10]

In any case, the association of dance with womanhood, however widespread in the age of the ballerina, cannot explain the history of the neglect of dance aesthetics, which (as we shall see) began much earlier. But in fact—and this should really be decisive—the supposed association with womanhood has never at any time formed part of the rhetoric of disparagement of dance as an art. We would have to suppose, then, that the alleged association is either a secret, preserved by some conspiracy among male aestheticians, or else an unconscious bias. But the former supposition is ludicrous, and the latter is implausible: the forces that preserve male domination are usually thought of as conscious assumptions of superiority affording a spurious justification, not as unconscious influences that would as such be abandoned as soon as one was aware of their presence.

We return to this topic in §3.21 from a more positive standpoint, according to which the current disappearance of sexual stereotypes is thought to give dance a new significance.

1.25 PURITANISM

The neglect of dance aesthetics is often attributed to the aftermath of puritanism, which was notoriously hostile to dancing. The word "puritanism" covers a variety of social and religious movements widely scattered in space and time and differing greatly among themselves in their content and their rhetoric. It is therefore as hard to assess the influence of this factor as it is to assess the allegations about sex bias. But two general observations may be made before we consider particulars. First, if puritanical objections

---

[10] Leonardo 1939, 94–97. It is to be observed that dance is not included in the comparisons that Leonardo makes among poetry, music, painting, and sculpture.

did not lastingly inhibit the practice of dance, as they clearly did not, one does not see why they should inhibit dance aesthetics. To explain that, one would have to say that, in general, aestheticians are more susceptible to puritanical influences than other folk. It is of course possible that that is true, but I know of no reason for believing it, and people who go in for this line of argument do not allege it—apparently they have failed to notice the implication. The other thing to say is that puritanical objections to theater are as common as puritanical objections to dance, and no one has suggested that the aesthetics of theater have suffered from any such inhibition. One needs to explain why puritanism should have been more lastingly efficacious in relation to dance than elsewhere. None the less, puritanism must be taken into account.

1.251 *Religion*

The term "puritanism," which in the first instance refers to a theological and moral complex of thought with a specific sectarian context within Protestant Christianity, is usually employed to denote a practice of systematic abstention from and denunciation of "worldly" pleasures on religious rather than genuinely moral grounds. As such, it may mask a more basic sort of religious objection to dancing. Dances almost everywhere are predominantly sacred, components of ceremonies at least part of whose meaning has to do with relationships with supernatural forces. Judaism and Christianity are jealous religions, reluctant to tolerate any truck with deities other than their own. There has been a longstanding tendency in these religions to be suspicious of all dance, as pagan in association if not in intent. Maypole dances look suspiciously like phallus-worship; the Abbots Bromley Horn Dance is obviously up to no good. Alfred Sendrey in his survey of dance in ancient Israel notes a suspicious likeness between the dances current there and the ritual dances practiced in Egypt when the Israelites sojourned there (Sendrey 1974, 221–244). The spokesmen for the official religions could either adopt such dance (as the Abbots Bromley dance was moved to a Christian festival and its equipment stored in the church tower) or try to beat it. When people of the latter persuasion speak of "dance," they are usually thinking of a particular set of suspect dances without considering whether other, unobjectionable dances might not exist.

Fashions in attitudes changed in these matters. At some times and places, "[r]espected rabbis did not consider it beneath their dignity to dance before the bridal couple, and several were so famous for their artful dancing that the rabbinical writers gave them special praise," including "the most distinguished rabbi of his time, Rabban Simeon ben Gamaliel," who "performed a torch dance with eight burning torches, throwing them alternately in the air and catching them, and none of them touched the ground when he prostrated himself, touched the floor with his fingers, kissed the ground, and leaped up again" (Sendrey 1974, 234). Other rabbinical authorities say that "the 'arkestes [= orchestes, a word for "dancer"] is the emptiest of the empty," and so forth (Sendrey 1974, 238).

The religious objections just mentioned are, of course, objections to dancing and not to dance theory. But their effect is both to make dancing taboo and to imply that the main significance of dance is ritual rather than aesthetic, so that a theory of fine art would be inappropriate to it.

1.252 *The Body*

One of the supposed puritanical objections to dancing, which would also be an objection to dance aesthetics, is the way dancing involves the body. We have just now considered this objection as it appears when entangled with sexist considerations; but its real home in its most persuasive form is here. It is not that the dance emphasizes the incarnation of humanity (supposedly congenial to a woman's engagement with tangible reality) as opposed to abstract masculine intellectualism, but that in dance the body is typically revealed, displayed, even stripped for show: not the embodied person, but the body as sensible and sensuous object is the instrument of dance. And the body as thus considered certainly stands for the world, the flesh, and the devil; it is a perfect symbol for what Manichaeans and Gnostics renounce. Such attitudes could inhibit reflection on dance and, as habits of high-minded thought, could persist in a culture in which their religious foundation had been formally renounced. But this fear of nudity and mistrust of physicality (together with the sects in which they prevail) are usually thought of as characteristic of peasants rather than of aesthetes.

1.2521 *Triviality*

The puritanic mistrust of or aversion to the body as body (by contrast with the embodied person) needs to be distinguished from a belief that has certainly done much to discourage dance aesthetics, a belief that has to be taken very seriously indeed. This is the view that, among human beings, concern with the mere fleshly integument trivializes human relationships. An art of which the subject was confined to the motions of the human body, conceived merely as a physical apparatus, would have to be trivial. This view is as old as Western civilization, and has been shared even by dancers writing about dance: dance in and by itself is merely muscular. In the eighteenth century, a dance that merely displayed the vigor, grace, and dexterity of the dancer was compared with the art of fireworks, with derogatory intent.[11] The only dance that could be taken seriously would be one that expressed human qualities through mime. But mime is not pure dance; its means and values are shared with drama. So dance must be either trivial or impure and false to its own nature. In either case, it would not merit the attention of the serious philosopher. To get out of this dilemma, one must either adopt a different attitude toward art (perhaps one that makes all arts equally trivial by reducing them to exploitations of the variability of a medium) or else find a distinctive significance for dance as opposed to mime. But it was a long time before any serious thinker was prepared to take either of those steps.

This whole cluster of topics will occupy us again and again in the course of this book.

1.253 *Theater*

Dance as a fine art is an art of the theater and is regularly associated through its institutions with other theater arts. Often it exists in symbiosis with them, as an element in complex performances; when it does not, it still shares their physical settings and methods of organization. And dance shares with theater its lack of theoretical esteem. This is disguised because theater gets into aesthetics as an adjunct of literary drama, which the players speak, and as an aspect of opera, which the players sing. In these capacities, theater borrows the venerable respectability of poetry and music. But the theater as such has no traditional position of its own: the "legitimate theater," the licenced abode of dramatic art, used to be distinguished from an anarchic mass of miscellaneous showmanship at which official aesthetics has always been reluctant to look. And the dancer as dancer embodies the condition of pure theatricality. Drama and opera offstage are still poetry and music, the dancer offstage is nothing.

Not only can dancers not escape the theoretical nullity of theater; they cannot escape its stigma. That stigma is social and moral in nature. Asso-

---

[11] Noverre 1760, 11. This comparison between dance and fireworks comes from a time when fireworks received more conscious attention than they do now. Originating in Florence, according to D'Israeli, the art spread to Rome in the fourteenth and fifteenth centuries and then took off: "Pyrotechnics from that time have become an art, which, in the degree the inventors have displayed ability in combining the powers of architecture, sculpture, and painting, have produced a number of beautiful effects, which even give pleasure to those who read the descriptions without having beheld them" (D'Israeli 1859a, 17–18). Note the giveaway phrase: with all those talents using the resources of three major arts, the upshot is merely a matter of "beautiful effects"—in other words, superficial, not to be taken seriously. The same imputation of triviality is conveyed by Giovanni-Andrea Gallini with a different comparison: "The dance in action has the same superiority over sheer unmeaning dancing, that a fine history-piece has over cutting flowers in paper" (Gallini 1762, 239).

ciation with the theater as such has traditionally been taken as a sign of immorality and disreputability. This association is often attributed to puritanism, which is why it is mentioned here, but it is much older. Plato's association of the stage with superficiality and moral instability (*Republic* 394E–398B) is notorious and has often seemed plausible: a stage performer must assume an alien persona for the duration of the performance, and it is easy to assume that by doing so one has abandoned one's own character and taken on a different character, so that one's moral personality loses its stable core. (In a dance without mimetic elements this would apply only to the extent that to be a pure dancer is to enact the part of a characterless person; but it was a long time before it occurred to anyone that such dancing was a serious activity at all.) But Plato was only rationalizing an existing prejudice. The bad name of strolling players and vagabonds is at least as old as Demosthenes' *De Corona*, which exploits the presumption that no one who has ever been a professional actor can ever be taken seriously—a presumption that in the early days of Ronald Reagan's presidency journalists unselfconsciously shared. Lucian's *Peri Orcheseos* presupposes that theater dance needs to be defended against the charges of superficiality and hysteria, with effeminacy thrown in.

Even among theater folk, dancers have seldom enjoyed parity of esteem or of reward. A writer in *Der Tanzlehrer* is quoted in 1892 as observing that "[n]ot even the very best solo dancer to-day would dare to take his or her social position by the side of first-class opera singers or actors and actresses. These would all resent it as an unpardonable insult, and let the unlucky votary of Terpsichore feel a full share of their wrath, and still the days are not so very long gone when Fanny Elssler's triumphs put all other artists into the shade." The author adds that (as Gordon [1983] would report of American dancers nearly a century later, but contrasting them now with their European colleagues) dancers do not enjoy salaries, pension rights, and security of employment comparable to those of other theater employees and ends by saying that, though dancers are no more and no less respectable than other people, "everywhere else the utmost is done to hush up shady things, where with dancers on the contrary, trifles are blown out like balloons to a monstrous size, because there is always a large contingent of society who find nothing so *piquant* as scandal about dancers, perhaps because it can be enjoyed without a prick of the conscience, for— of course, who could expect anything else from a dancer" (Crompton 1892, 163).

When Adam Smith's posthumous paper on imitation in the arts segregates the definition of dance in a note that his editors separate from the main text and for which they half apologize because of its trivial theme, one is tempted to discern the influence of the notorious puritanism of the

WHY DANCE HAS BEEN NEGLECTED

Scots; but the puritans were continuing in this matter a tradition they did not originate.[12] Of course, as C. J. Ducasse once remarked, the fact that something always happens does not explain why it ever happens; but a prevailing social stigma, even if itself unexplained, would explain a bias in the general run of cultural writing to which most aesthetics has belonged. The development of aesthetic theory, as of art itself, has a lot to do with prestige.

1.254 *Social Dance and Sex*

As well as objecting to theater, and hence by implication to theater dance, puritans objected to social dance on two grounds: first, it promoted lasciviousness between the sexes; and second, it distracted attention from work and worship.[13] There was no explicit objection to dance simply as dance or as movement of the despised body, nor could there have been: in an age of swordsmanship, it would have been preposterous to decry the cultivation of bodily strength and agility. Rather, an attack on social dancing is presented as an attack on dance as such, or at least on the present state of the practice of dancing. Thus, Christopher Fetherston (1582) does not argue that dancing is necessarily lascivious or that all dancing is in fact so. Rather, he contrasts today's lascivious dance with the decorous dances of ancient Israel.[14] But when he is not attending to this distinction, he simply refers to "lascivious dancing" as though there were no other kind

[12] One must not make too much of this. Both the segregation and the apology are perhaps sufficiently accounted for by the fact that, by the time this essay was published, dance was not considered in the most sophisticated circles to be one of the fine arts, though of course its status as one of the arts of imitation could not reasonably be denied.

[13] Fetherston (1582, B2v–B3r) interprets the fourth commandment as meaning that people ought to work all day for six days and rest on the seventh, leaving no time for trivial amusements like dancing. The objection is partly that dancing is frivolous ("All vanitie doeth dishallow the Sabboath day, but dauncing is vanitie, therefore dauncing doth dishallow the Sabboath day"—Fetherston peppers his text with little syllogisms) and partly that it makes people too tired to work next morning.

[14] He says of the dancers mentioned in the Old Testament that "[t]hey made no mixture of feres in their daunces, but the men daunced by themselues, and the women by themselues; but you in your daunces must haue women, or else the market is marred" (Fetherston 1582, D4v). A later authority partly endorses Fetherston's historical observation: "As in other ritualistic acts, men and women were generally separated at religious dances. Only one Biblical report indicates that both sexes danced together in the dance around the golden calf (Exod. 32: 6, 19). This, however, is not an Israelitish dance in the proper sense, since it occurs at an idolatrous feast" (Sendrey 1974, 229). (Why a dance at an idolatrous feast cannot be Israelitish in the proper sense, Sendrey does not say; perhaps he only means that it was naughty of them.)

21

and at one place (c2v) uses the phrase "dauncing and lasciuiousnes" with a singular verb.

Writing at about the same time as Fetherston, a Catholic priest, Father Jehan Tabourot (under the pseudonym "Thoinot Arbeau"), discerns and extols the social function of that mixing of the sexes that Fetherston deplores:

> Dancing is practiced to make manifest whether lovers are in good health and sound in all their limbs, after which it is permitted to them to kiss their mistresses, whereby they may perceive if either has an unpleasant breath or exhales a disagreeable odour as of bad meat; so that, in addition to divers other merits attendant on dancing, it has become essential for the wellbeing of society.[15]

Now, it is clear that dance as attacked by Fetherston and defended by Arbeau is not so much an art that one might cultivate and appreciate as a pastime one can take part in and enjoy. Fetherston, in fact, has no objection to such an expressive dance as we might expect to find in a fine-arts or ritual context. Dancing as such might be "a moderate motion of the bodie, which serued to set fourth and expresse the ioyes of the minde," and might be well motivated: King David and others "daunced because they had receiued great blessings at the handes of the Lorde, and because they would set forth his prayse; but you daunce because you have obteyned your wicked purposes, and because you will entise others to naughtines" (Fetherston 1582, D4v and D6r). One might therefore dismiss such puritanical strictures as irrelevant to dance aesthetics, since the controversial practices are not those with which aesthetics is concerned. But that is not quite the case. For in Fetherston's day and long after, there was no sharp distinction between social dance and display dance; and what was danced on stage was often, if not always, identical with or a variant on such recreational dances

---

[15] Arbeau 1588, 18. Before we return Sendrey to the shelf (see previous note), we observe that Rabban Simeon Gamaliel seems to agree with Arbeau, for he says that on the 15th of Ab and the Day of Atonement, "[t]he daughters of Israel went forth to dance in the vineyards. And what did they say? 'Young man, lift up thine eyes and see what thou would'st choose for thyself; set not thine eyes on beauty, but set thine eyes on family' " (Tal. Bab. *Ta'anit* 31a, quoted from Sendrey 1974, 230).

Even more striking clerical testimony to the moral salubriousness of social dancing may be found in an editorial in *Dancing*, April 1892: "Terpsichore numbers among its votaries a large number of clergymen of different denominations, including many high dignitaries of the Church of England. . . . A well-known Berkshire rector, some years ago, transformed in his own parish what had formerly been a scene of drunkenness and debauchery into an annual gathering where his friends and respectable parishioners of all classes danced and thoroughly enjoyed themselves. In bringing about this change he was heartily assisted by a celebrated and estimable trainer, whose jockeys and stable-boys formed the majority of the church choir" (Crompton 1892, 123). The stableboys would have known what to do about the camels that troubled Chrysostom (note 24 below).

as the puritans frowned on. Thus, even if the guilt of theater dance is only guilt by association, the association is a very powerful one. And that fact in itself is connected with another factor in the doubtful status of dance aesthetics: the artistic dance with which such aesthetics would be principally concerned is only a specialized form of dance in general, which is a world-wide mode of behavior with complex social connections and ramifications. It is not obvious that artistic dance is from a social and cultural point of view the most important sort of dance or that it can be sharply differentiated from other sorts. Analogous truths hold of the other fine arts, but it may well be that in no other art are the nonartistic connections so wide and deep, so that students of aesthetics could easily find the study of dance dragging them in directions they have no interest in going.

1.3 *The Anomaly of Dance*

The factors we have mentioned as perhaps leading to the neglect of the aesthetics of dance, ranging from the conservatism and ineptitude of academic philosophers to the prejudices of jealous males and indignant puritans, may all be real and even important. But they do not quite convince one that they would have prevailed against the universally recognized ubiquity and centrality of dance in the domain of art. The weightiest part of the explanation must be found elsewhere. My contention will be that the effective context for dance aesthetics must be the theory of the fine arts and that dance does not fit easily into that context. The discussion will, of necessity, be somewhat meandering, since we are dealing with a complicated ideological issue that has a long and tangled history. But it has three strands. First, there is the fact that the classical system of the fine arts has a definite structure into which dance does not easily fit. Second, there is the difficulty of establishing the symbolic and aesthetic character of artistic dance and of vindicating its autonomy. And third, there is the fact that the cultural significance of the dominant form of artistic dance in our society—in fact, the only form that has become securely established—is, as we shall see, equivocal. In later chapters I will go on to adduce a different sort of aspect of the incongruity of dance among the fine arts: that insofar as a single significance can be assigned to dance, it is very different from any that can be attributed to any of the (other) fine arts.

1.31 THE ARTS OF IMITATION

The idea that there is a group of arts, called the "fine arts," of which the function is the imaginative manipulation of symbols and which have an important part to play in civilized life, is a product of the early modern age, taking its definitive form in the middle of the eighteenth century. The system as thus developed had a simple structure. At its center were the "sister arts" of poetry and painting, representing to eye and ear respectively "beautiful nature," the ideal reality of which the perceptible world is a blurred copy. Painting is institutionally as well as theoretically inseparable from drawing, as drawing is from sculpture and architecture, and invokes an underlying geometric order. Poetry is institutionally inseparable from music and from drama, and invokes an underlying algebraic order. That is the developed system of the fine arts, and there is no place in it for dance. Drama loses touch with the system when it loses speech and becomes mime; pure dance is even further removed from the original pairing. Even so, the absence of dance strikes us as strange, and did so at the time. As we shall see later, it was easy to include dance among the arts of imitation; what proved difficult was to explain the distinctive importance of the sort of symbolization that dance employed and to fit it firmly into the interlocked set of practices we have named. Apologists for dance have tried to remedy the defect from the earliest times—long before the concept of "the fine arts" was formulated.

The obvious remedy was to make dance a third "sister" art, a third basic mode of representation: if I want to communicate a situation to you, I can tell you about it, or I can show you in a drawing, or I can act it out, and which way is easiest and best will depend on what it is I want to convey. It is hard to see why the use of bodily movement should be less basic or less capable of artistic development than the other two. The fine art of dancing—mimetic/expressive or abstract—would be related to such informative acting-out in the same way that the arts of painting and poetry (and music) are to graphic and linguistic communication.

Claims for sibling status on behalf of dancing take several forms. Plutarch, in the second century C.E., proposes (at the end of *Symposium Questions* IX) that dance be substituted for painting in Simonides' (c. 500 B.C.E.) famous apophthegm to the effect that painting was silent poetry and poetry was painting that talked.[16] Colletet appeals to the same saying of Simonides, but he would make dance an addition to the pair rather than a substitute for one of its terms:

> If the Ancients called poetry a speaking painting and painting a silent poetry, we may follow their example and call dance—especially that which is performed in our ballets—a mobile picture or an animated poetry. For, just as poetry is a true picture of our passions and painting a discourse, dumb indeed, but still able to arouse whatever our imag-

[16] Plutarch tells us about this apophthegm in his *Glory of Athens*, 3. He adds that the point of it lies in the difference between showing and telling.

ination may hold, so dance is a lively image of our actions and an artistic expression of our secret thoughts. (Colletet 1632, preface; quoted by Prunières 1914, 168; my translation)

Ménéstrier then takes the three sister arts to be music, poetry, and painting and says that dance is their elder brother, though fallen into neglect (Ménéstrier 1682, 1). Gallini quotes the Chevalier de Ramsay to the effect that "[t]o the study of poetry, should be joined that of the three arts of imitation. The antients represented the passions, by gestures, colors, and sounds" (Gallini 1762, 142). Later, Adam Smith (1795) introduces a triad of dance, poetry, and music, and this triad is subsequently taken up by Wagner (§1.341 below). But this last triad, which excludes painting, is based not on a division of the means of expression or representation but on a classification of artistic movement, so that it does not belong to our present topic at all.

Despite the plausibility of these arguments aligning dance with the rest of the arts of imitation, no such triad as they propose ever became current. The difficulty may have been that to think of three modes of representation was easiest when one thought of "imitation" (as our own presentation of the issue suggested) as the production of effective likenesses of one sort or another. But theorists who assigned importance to the arts of "imitation" did so because there was more to imitation than that. For dance to have been accepted as a third sister, it would have been necessary for the "more than that" to have been present as well. And that is where the difficulty lay.

Aristotle, in a work to which all later writers—including the Chevalier de Ramsay—referred, placed dance among the arts of imitation, representing the characters as well as the actions and passions of mankind through dance steps (Aristotle, *Poetics*, ch. 1). But, as we shall see Hegel pointing out, it is hard for such presentation to reach profundity and precision without the use of words, which are after all (as Aristotle himself says in his *Politics*) the means whereby people share their thoughts and values. In fact, the more ambitious mime becomes, the more it becomes a mere display of cleverness, moving to amazed laughter rather than to sympathetic reflection; and this is just because the mime is using immense ingenuity to convey by posture and gesture something that would ordinarily be conveyed quite simply and directly by other means. But if one looks elsewhere in the *Poetics*, it becomes apparent that the only available alternative is for dance to become an ancillary feature of poetic drama—what Aristotle calls "spectacle" and treats, quite rightly, as trivial. The age in which the canon of the fine arts was established was, indeed, familiar with a culturally central and symbolically ambitious form of dance, in the court ballets of France (and to a much lesser degree elsewhere). But in these, as we shall see later, the weight of the meaning was not carried by the means singled out by Aristotle (and all later writers) as specific to dance.

Aristotle's pairing of the sister arts of painting and poetry, which is retained in the fabric of his exposition after the merely schematic enumeration of arts in his opening chapter, goes back to the classification of arts in the quasi-Platonic *Epinomis*, which in turn is a systematization of Plato's epoch-making treatment in *Republic* x.[17] Since Plato's apparent intention there was to denigrate "imitation" (and, hence, to disqualify drama as a source of enlightenment), it seems odd that it should have been his arguments in that passage that became the source of those later relied on to dignify the fine arts. But it is not really so surprising. What was decisive in the long run was the relationships he established; the evaluations were easily reversed.

Plato had merely deplored the absence from "mimetic" arts of one specific sort of value, so that all that was necessary was to find in them a value of a different sort—as Plato himself had in fact pointed out. The *Epinomis* supplied one such value (they are means of entertainment), and Aristotle another (they furnish worthwhile cognitive experiences). But by the third century C.E. Plotinus had hinted at another value, one more congenial to modern readers and more relevant to the present discussion: representation in the fine arts performs a symbolic rather than a straightforwardly descriptive function. On this Neoplatonic view, the idealizing artist produces a "golden world" symbolic of the world's tendency to rationality and order: Pheidias' statue of Zeus is not a likeness of a divine being, but gives force to our sense of justice by enabling us to imagine what the god of justice would look like if he were to make himself visible (Plotinus *Enneads* v, 8.1). A comparable imaginative power was manifested by whoever devised the complex iconography and majestic form of the Indian *Natyaraj*, the Lord of the Dance, Shiva as creator, sustainer, and destroyer of worlds.

1.311 *Plato and the Split in the Fine Arts*

Many writers nowadays say that Plato in the *Republic* condemned what we call the fine arts. The opposite is the case. He recommends for young people an education that is almost entirely aesthetic in its ends as well as its means and in which, though dramatic poetry is excluded, the fine arts play essential parts. Any reader with even a nodding acquaintance with Athe-

---

[17] According to ancient authors, the *Epinomis* was essentially Plato's work, but was edited and published after his death by one of his disciples, Philip of Opus. There is no reason to disbelieve this. The work is little read, partly because of its doubtful authorship and partly because it relates to the parts of Plato's thought that are of least interest to most modern writers and readers. But it is a work of great historical significance.

nian culture can guess that a major component in this curriculum would have been a choric dance in which the young people would have been their own primary audience. The later *Laws* makes this explicit, devoting much space to the principles of dance as the symbolic center of civic activity and carefully distinguishing this sort of dance from dances of professional display.[18]

Plato's *Laws* is little read and less remembered, but its boringness hardly explains why its extensive treatment of dance has been so neglected, not only by the general reader but also by later users of his thought and theorists of dance. People do allude to it, but it seldom occupies an important place in their thinking. So far as the theory of the fine arts is concerned, part of the explanation lies in the way the argument of *Republic* X was made to bear new values and so became the basis of the vindication of those arts and the other arts associated with them. It is because the choric dance does not participate in the original condemnation that it cannot benefit from the later rehabilitation: dance is left in ideological isolation, its justification resting on a different set of principles that could not be brought within the scope of the same theory.

The decisive fact is not that the fine-art side of dance was split off from the side that was regarded as having educational and cultural value, and that the significance of the fine arts depends on the coincidence of the two. The same split is found within music by Aristotle in his *Politics* VIII, a work closely studied and attended to in the formative centuries of our civilization. There, too, the sort of music that a gentlemen learns for his own recreation is contrasted with the sort of thing professionals do for display. But this contrast survives throughout the history of our civilization, in the form of a complex set of contrasts within a single practice of music—erudite versus popular, intellectual versus emotional, musicianship versus technique, and so forth. Music continues to occupy an entrenched position within the fine arts, though its precise status there could be disputed. In dance this does not happen, though it could have. We shall see that none of the reasons why it did not are sufficient.

The fact that dance in Plato is justified by principles differing from those eventually borrowed to afford a rationale for the fine arts could not have been decisive. In Schopenhauer's aesthetics, the same bifurcation of the fine arts into practices requiring contrasting justifications is not only explicit but emphasized. It is in fact Schopenhauer's central notion: the sister

---

[18] In the Athenian tragic festivals that Plato condemned, while the professional actors were up there on the stage, the chorus were amateur singers and dancers privileged to participate on the city's behalf in this ritual worship of Dionysus. Plato would keep the civic chorus and reject the professional display—and, above all, not allow the citizen-students to contaminate themselves with such professionalism.

arts and their cousins are construed as presenting eternal Ideas, whereas music presents the dynamism of the underlying Will itself. And this contrast between Will and Idea can be fairly construed as a revision of the Platonic contrast between the dance which the citizens know by participation and the arts which furnish them with objects for contemplation. But Schopenhauer put music in the place of dance, though dance is in some ways a more direct expression of Will than music is. Why? Partly perhaps because music (essentially involving Time rather than Space) is coupled with Subjectivity as opposed to Objectivity in the Kantian scheme to which Schopenhauer and most of his contemporaries subscribed. But part of the explanation may be that in Schopenhauer's and Hegel's day music was a vital and major art in a way that no form of dance was.

The Greeks had in fact two words for dance: *choreia* and *orchesis*. The relations between these are not simple—we return to them in §2.1 and elsewhere. For now, let it suffice to say that Plato's participatory dance is *choreia* and is essentially a round dance, characterized by the figures that the participants trace out with simple steps in the horizontal dimension. Professional display dance is *orchesis* and is associated rather with athletic virtuosity exploiting the vertical dimension. *Orchesis* is the word used by Lucian, whose work *On Dancing* is the only extended historical and descriptive work on dance surviving from antiquity. So any latter-day aesthetician seeking classical warrant for the dignity of dance finds Lucian readily available, but not Plato. But it was Platonic and Neoplatonic lines of thought that in the crucial decades provided the dignifying ideology for the Arts of Imitation.

1.312 *The Lack of Ancient Exemplars*

The upshot of the foregoing is that ancient ideology was not readily available for the vindication of dance as a fine art. What is equally important is that ancient example was also lacking. One way of claiming dignity for the fine arts was by continual reference to the Hellenistic histories that recorded the cumulative achievements of those arts in the classical age. But this exemplary vindication was scarcely available to dance. No full-scale history of dance successfully ran the gauntlet of the medieval scriptoria, and authors could do no better than cite from Lucian or Athenaeus the isolated examples of the post-Augustan pantomime. True, only verbal descriptions of these were available. But that might not have mattered; as we said before (§1.22), other arts found it sufficient for their purposes to exploit the associated rhetoric—in fact, not knowing just what the ancient masterpieces looked or sounded like gave one room to breathe. What was more important was that, whereas painting, sculpture, and architecture could easily reconcile past authority with present practice, no practice that pantomime could warrant was compatible with contemporary values. As John Weaver said, "The *Actions* and *Gestures* of these *Mimes*, and *Panto-mimes*, tho' adapted to the Pleasure of the Spectator, were never thought a general Qualification fit for Persons of Quality, or Gentlemen, from thence to derive a *graceful Motion, Mien*, or *handsome Assurance* in Conversation" (Weaver 1712, 121). Weaver does not, indeed, accept the thesis that changes in the style of dancing have made classical eulogies of dance inapplicable to modern dance: "As to *Dancing* in its Fundamentals and Expediency," he says, "*Modern Dancing* is of equal Desert," and is closer to the original forms of dance than pantomime was (Weaver 1712, 8). In that, he was no doubt right; but it meant that ancient examples were not available for emulation as ancient rhetoric was for encouragement.

The issue of the incompatibility between dancing, as we understand it, and the pantomime described by Lucian was squarely faced by the Abbé Dubos, in an immensely influential work. He cites from Isidorus of Seville (*Etymologies* 18.50) Varro's opinion that the Latin word for dancing, *saltatio*, was derived not from the word for a jump (*saltus*) but from the name of one Salius, who invented the art of gesture (Dubos 1719, 161).[19] He continues:

> 'Tis easy to conceive that the artificial dances of the ancients, in which they imitated, for example, the leaps and gambols that peasants are accustomed to make after drinking, and the frantic caperings of Bacchanalians, were like to our dances. But the other dances of the ancients, in which they imitated the action of persons who do not leap, or who, to speak after our manner, do not dance, was only an imitation of the steps, attitudes, gestures, and in short of all the external demonstrations with which people are accustomed to accompany their discourse, or which they sometimes use in order to convey their sentiments without speech. 'Tis thus David danced before the ark, testifying by his attitude, as well as by his gestures and prosternations, the profound respect he had for the pledge of the covenant of the Lord and the Jewish people.[20]

[19] The etymology is hardly plausible. The Latin *saltatio* is formed from the verb *saltare*, to dance, which is itself (according to the *Oxford Latin Dictionary*) an iterative form of the verb *salire*, to jump. It is regularly used as an equivalent and translation of the Greek *orchesis*. Anyway, Dubos is lying in his teeth. What Isidore quotes Varro as saying is that Salius (an Arcadian whom Aeneas brought with him to Italy) "was the first to teach the noble Roman teenagers to dance" (*primus docuit Romanos adolescentes nobiles saltare*). Not the same, is it?

[20] Dubos 1719, 161–162. Note how Dubos, like Fetherston and Sendrey (and, in fact, like everybody else), confidently asserts what David's dancing was like and what it meant, though

Dubos's main theme in this part of his book is accordingly that the ancient *saltatio* was invariably mime, usually accompanying a recitative, and not dancing in any contemporary sense. He even goes so far as to advance the thesis that the Greek *emmelia, cordax,* and *sicinnis* were not dance forms at all, but systems of gestures for accompanying tragedy, comedy, and satyr-play, respectively (Dubos 1719, 178).

1.32 D'Alembert's Exclusion of Dance

More important, in the long run, than any of the maneuverings to insert dance among the sister arts or to exclude it was its failure to win a place in certain prominent and influential systems that assigned to the fine arts in general a definite and important position among the exercises of the human intellect. I refer to the systems of D'Alembert and, much more significantly, of Hegel.

In his "Preliminary Discourse" (1751) to Diderot's *Encyclopedia,* D'Alembert presents an overall classification of human knowledge. This, like the work to which it was prefixed, was clearly meant to represent the consensus of the most advanced thought of the day. And it includes a scheme of the fine arts. These are classified as modes of reflective knowledge: "another kind of reflective knowledge . . . consists of the ideas which we create for ourselves by imagining and putting together beings similar to those which are the object of our direct ideas. This is what we call the imitation of Nature, so well known and so highly recommended by the ancients." This imitation, whatever its object, produces pleasure, and that is the purpose it serves (D'Alembert 1751, 37). But it is, in any case, a characteristic employment of the human mind, and an encyclopedia of the human mind and its achievements had to include it.

Among the fine arts, painting and sculpture come first "because it is in those arts above all that imitation best approximates the objects represented and speaks most directly to the senses" (p. 37). Architecture is associated with these, but the scope of its imitation is "confined to imitating the symmetrical arrangement that Nature observes more or less obviously in each individual thing. . . . Poetry, which comes after painting and sculpture, . . . speaks to the imagination rather than to the senses," and music "holds the last place in the order of imitation" because, though it has been developed into a sort of language for expressing the "passions of the soul," its vocabulary and other quasi-linguistic resources remain rudimentary (p. 38). But he adds—and for our present purposes the addition is most sig-

---

none of them had any data and none of them (not even Sendrey; cf. Chapter 2, note 5, below) gave any reason at all for thinking that what they said was true.

nificant—that "[a]ny music that does not portray something is only noise; and without that force of habit which denatures everything, it would hardly create more pleasure than a sequence of harmonious and sensuous words stripped of order and connection" (p. 39). It is these five arts, with their subdivisions, that constitute the fine arts (p. 55), so called because their principal aim is to please. They are distinguished from the other "liberal arts that have been reduced to principle" by their common function of imitating nature and by the fact that they have few if any fixed rules, their practice consisting principally in "an invention which takes its laws almost exclusively from genius" (p. 43) and is guided by the imagination (p. 51). Of these five, D'Alembert says that "[w]e can also include them under the general title of painting, because all the Fine Arts can be reduced to that and differ only by the means which they use" (p. 55).

Nowhere in his classification and discussion does D'Alembert so much as mention the dance. This omission is the more striking because his enumeration of great practitioners of the fine arts centers on seventeenth-century France and specifically on the court of Louis XIV. He mentions by name Lully, but only as a musician, though Lully to us is no better known as a musician than as the eventual organizer of the royal Ballet and the founder of its academy and, hence, of the central tradition of artistic dance in Europe. (Dubos had included Lully, as well as Molière, in a sketch of the development of ballet style.)[21] Since in a work of such general scope D'Alembert not only does not argue for the exclusion of dance but does not even mention it, we are entitled to suppose that he did not think such

---

[21] Remarking that 80 years ago ballet music was slow and sedate and that the accompanying movements "scarce differed from those of common dances," Dubos continues: "Molière had scarce shown by two or three airs that it was possible to improve in this respect, when Lulli appeared, and began to compose what we call quick airs, adapted to the balets. As the dancers who executed these balets were obliged to move with greater celerity and action than had been hitherto practised, a great many people said that the right taste of dancing was corrupted, and that it was degenerating into a low vulgar entertainment. Even the very dancers found it difficult to enter into the spirit of those new airs. . . . The success of these quick airs induced Lulli to compose such as should be both quick and characterised at the same time" (Dubos 1719, 128–129). We note that the contribution made by the dancers in devising the steps they are to execute to Lully's new music is not thought worth mentioning; but Dubos does go on to say that "the dancers improved afterwards to such a degree that they have even outdone the musicians, to whom they have sometimes suggested the idea of airs of a new character, suitable to the balets of which these dancers had first conceived the idea" (p. 130). It may be worth noting that Dubos's work was not uncontroversial: Louis de Cahusac devoted most of the "Avant-propos" of his history of dance to a denunciation of the Abbé's taste and scholarship. His account of ancient dancing was a load of old rubbish, said Cahusac (correctly), and, if Lully's innovations were denounced as corruptions, that is because corruptions is exactly what they were (Cahusac 1754, v–xxxii).

a mention would be expected. We are further entitled to suppose that he was right, that dance was not generally considered one of the fine arts.

Given that D'Alembert does not mention dance, we cannot specify his reasons for not discussing it. But we have observed that the fine arts as such enter into his scheme as branches of knowledge. And of course a branch of knowledge, in the classical understanding, is just what any art is. D'Alembert thinks the fine arts are branches of knowledge because they function through the recognition and manipulation of imitations, and imitation was identified in Aristotle's *Poetics* as basic to human learning: "Imitation is natural to man from childhood, one of his advantages over the lower animals being this, that he is the most imitative creature in the world, and his first studies are through imitation" (*Poetics* 1448b 5–8, Bywater's translation amended). He would thus have returned a dusty answer to a writer in *Blackwood's* in 1844 who asked, "Why not . . . elevate choriography to the rank of one of the fine arts? . . . since all eyes are amenable to the charm of exquisite dancing."[22] The charming of the eye had nothing to do with the matter. "When you have a garden full of pretty flowers," said Balanchine, "you don't demand of them 'What do you mean? What is your significance?' You just enjoy them. So why not just enjoy ballet in the same way ?" This was his way of repudiating pretentious humbug; but it involved presenting himself as an entertainer and artisan, *as opposed to* an artist (Taper 1984, 6).

We may conjecture that D'Alembert's view would be the one later explicitly espoused by Hegel: that dance as an imitative art is an accompaniment or a derivative of the theatrical presentation of poetry—*die aüssere Exekution des dramatischen Kunstwerks*, the execution of the work of dramatic art in an external medium (Hegel 1835, pt. 3, sec. 3, ch. 3, 2c sub fin.). To think of "imitative" dance in that way is, as we saw, to equate it with the "spectacle" in Greek tragedy rather than with the dancers' art as an independent activity.[23] Music gets into D'Alembert's list because it has,

---

[22] Gore 1844, 295. The tone of the article (cited in *OED* as an early occurrence of the word "choreography") is quizzical. Gore's thesis is that Taglioni and Elssler are not only immensely popular everywhere but have been recognized by Royalty as other accomplished women have not; that "[c]lose its eyes as it may, the public cannot but perceive, that the legitimate drama is banished from want of encouragement from the national theatres, and that the ballet is brandishing her cap and bells triumphantly in its room"; and that the least objectionable way of accommodating this state of affairs (especially since very few of the English are gifted dancers) would be to establish a "Royal and National Academy of Dancing of the United Kingdom" (Gore 1844, 298). This is not to make a very strong case for the recognition of dancing as a fine art.

[23] This would not necessarily be a sign of ignorance or insensitivity to the historical realities of dance. Beaujoyeulx's *Ballet comique de la reine* of 1581, which inaugurates the French court ballet and in which the four arts of music, poetry, painting, and dance were meant to be fused,

up to a point, developed a language of expression that is independent of verbal language. Mime, the imitative form or aspect of dance, has no such language but uses clarified forms of "natural" (that is, spontaneous) gestures; and Indian *mudras* and their rudimentary balletic counterparts (such as pointing to one's ring finger to indicate matrimony) are mere translations of words into another form of external symbol. The elevation of dance to the fine arts must await one of two events: the debasement of the idea of the fine arts, as envisaged by the writer in *Blackwood's*, or the broadening of the theory of knowledge to include new modes of cognitive significance such as might be attributed to dance. In our own day, both of these have happened, but (I shall be suggesting) too late. The age of the great encyclopedias is over.

1.33 HEGEL AND THE EMPTINESS OF DANCE

D'Alembert's system of the fine arts has no direct influence nowadays. But Hegel's does. Even those who think Hegel's system preposterous are often effectively under its spell, though this may be so partly because Hegel really did incorporate the consensus of an important segment of enlightened thought in his day. He certainly cannot have been ignorant of D'Alembert's scheme. In any case, unlike D'Alembert, he considers dance with some care and explicitly excludes it from his system of the arts. His reasons require our attention, whether because they affected his successors as they affected him or because his example was influential.

Nothing in Hegel's time suggested any inevitable importance for an art of dance. The *ballet d'action* of J. G. Noverre and his contemporaries had not succeeded in establishing a recognizable alternative to the formalism they had protested against. "The further that modern dancing has advanced in technical skill the more has pantomime sunk in value and disappeared," said Hegel. "The result is that we threaten to see more and more disappearing from modern ballet what alone could lift it into the free realm of art" (Hegel 1975, 1192). A dance of technical virtuosity, however dazzling, could amount to no more than spectacle; and spectacle, in Hegel's terms, is not art. Nor, for that matter, is anything in that mass of acrobatics, pantomime, melodrama, horseplay, juggling, and general showmanship to which the greater part of theater and fairground dancing belonged then as it always has, and which did not even attempt to align itself with what we might dismiss as "official culture" but which people like Hegel and D'A-

---

was intended to realize Jean Antoine de Baïf's ideal of reviving ancient drama through the reduction of dance, music, and verse to a common measure (McGowan 1963, 22). And that measure, I shall be arguing, can hardly be furnished by the dancer (§1.341).

lembert thought of as the accumulated and refined achievements of the self-civilization of humanity.

It can hardly be repeated too often, so remote is the position from any that is nowadays respectable, that Hegel would accept nothing as art that did not contribute to that civilizing endeavor and that, unlike Plato, he did not recognize the mere manufacture of beautiful objects as making any such contribution. When in opera the *music* takes on a value independent of the meaning of the words, it becomes a mere "thing of luxury," and elaborate stage sets and costumes are in order. The subject matter best suited to such decadent splendor is the marvelous, the unintelligible, the fabulous, as in *The Magic Flute*—the kind of thing, in short, that one could not be tempted to be *serious* about. And the same applies to dance.

> The like is the case with our contemporary ballet to which likewise the miraculous and fabulous are agreeable. Here, apart from the pictorial beauty of arrangements and tableaux, what has become above all the chief thing is the changing magnificence and attraction of scenery, costume, and lighting, so that we at last find ourselves transported into a realm where we have left far behind us the logic of prose and the distress and pressure of everyday life. On the other hand, those who know about these things are captivated by the extraordinarily developed bravura and suppleness of the legs, and this always plays a chief part in dancing nowadays. But if some spiritual expression is to glint through this mere dexterity, which nowadays has wandered into an extreme of senselessness and intellectual poverty, what is required is not only a complete conquest of all the technical difficulties but measured movement in harmony with our emotions, and a freedom and grace that are extremely rare. (Hegel 1975, 1192).

The contrast here between dexterous legs and expressive arms, and the complaint about the human irrelevance of academic ballet presentations with their mindlessly decorative exploitation of dead mythologies, are borrowed from the polemics of Noverre and his contemporaries a generation earlier, to which we shall return (§1.3322). Presumably Hegel thought that the promised reform had come to nothing, if he thought at all; but we note his sneer at "those who know about these things," with its suggestion (still fashionable today in some circles) that true lovers of art do not know about ballet, and we infer that he may simply have taken Noverre's word for it. But the dance in Hegel's own day was dominated not by the technically splendid but emotionally arid French ballet, but by the *choreodrammi* of Salvatore Vigano, who had acquired Noverre's ideas from the latter's disciple Dauberval. These productions, though retaining the mythological subjects and the emphasis on production values from the older

34

ballet, had abandoned its formal dance movements, substituting plastic grouping for the chorus and, for the individual dancer, a "rhythmic pantomime halfway between normal imitative gesture and traditional dancing, with a complete subordination of both to the music" (Kirstein 1935, 236).

What Hegel thought, or would have thought, about Vigano's work, we do not know (though it may be that the first part of the quoted passage is meant to apply to such as Vigano and the second part to "classical" academic ballet—granted that it is unlikely that Hegel knew either at first hand). He would hardly have agreed with what Rossini said to Stendhal, that "the trouble with Vigano is, he has too much pantomime and not enough dancing" (Kirstein 1935, 263; Sorell 1971, 412), for he would not have accepted the contrast. In any case, the expressive pantomime version of the art of dance, though it does indeed qualify as true art, never amounts to more than an inferior version of the art of poetry that it displaces: "As soon as mimicry or singing and dancing begin to be developed on their own account and independently, poetry as an art is degraded to being a means and loses its dominion over these other arts which should be merely its accompaniments" (Hegel 1975, 1186)—"speech suffers under music and dancing because it should be the spiritual expression of spirit" (p. 1187).

On reflection, Hegel's judgment on dance seems perverse. Athletic and formal dancing is condemned as inexpressive; expressive dancing is condemned as interfering with poetry. And the double condemnation is supported by the strange judgment that speech should be the "spiritual expression of spirit." But why should it? For what purposes should it? The judgment sounds like a more pretentious version of such familiar nursery injunctions as "God didn't give you feet to kick cats with, but to walk to church on Sundays."[24] But it is time to look at Hegel's system of the arts and see what solid reasons there may be to exclude dance from it.

1.331 *The Hegelian Scheme*

Hegel's system of the arts is roughly as follows. The fine arts are arts that produce beauty. Beauty is the adequation of a form to an idea, so that a

---

[24] James Miller has a real example, from John Chrysostom: "Surely the reason God gave us feet was not to dance like that woman but to process slowly with an orderly and dignified pace; it was not to make a disgraceful spectacle of ourselves or to leap about like camels—for if you find the sight of dancing camels repulsive, think how much more repulsive, how truly disgusting is the sight of women dancing!—but to dance with the angels [*syn angelois choreuô-men*]. For if it is shameful for the body to dance in that other way, it is much more so for the soul. That is the way the demons dance [*toiauta orchountai hoi daimones*]. That is the way their devilish deacons make fools of us" (John Chrysostom, *In Matth. Hom.* xlviii.5, quoted by Miller 1986, 412).

fine art embodies ideas in forms adequate to them. As civilization advances, the arts become more refined. Symbolic arts in which spirit partly informs matter give way to classical arts in which spirit and matter are perfectly fused, and these in turn yield to romantic arts in which spirit dominates its material embodiment. After that, spirit assumes autonomous forms, and art as a whole is superseded—superseded, that is, in the sense that it is no longer the vehicle for the most advanced forms of rational communication, by which civilization defines itself. The paradigm of a symbolic art is architecture; of a classical art, sculpture. The romantic arts are typically painting, music, and poetry. Sculpture is the central art, the most artistic of the arts; among romantic arts, music is central, the most romantic, but poetry is the most spiritual and the most advanced.

These five arts—architecture, sculpture, painting, music, and poetry—"make up the inherently determinate and articulated system of what art is in both essence and reality. It is true that outside them there are other imperfect arts, such as gardening, dancing, etc., which however we can only mention in passing" (Hegel 1975, 626). The reason for considering these other arts as "imperfect" is not really made clear; apparently it is because in them essential distinctions between modes of expression become blurred, but what these are is not specified.[25] Perhaps it comes down to this: as a symbolic art, dance is ineffectual and strained; as a classical art, it is inchoate theater and imperfect poetry; as a romantic art, it is a degenerate form of poetry. Dance can be charming and even beautiful, but it is unstable, because it cannot maintain itself in a form that is both artistically expressive and genuinely dance. No sufficient ground for this judgment is ever adduced, and it may well be that its basis is simply Hegel's hunch that no genuine art of dance has ever established and maintained itself.

Given that dance cannot rival poetry or music as a romantic art, one might still have looked for dance in two places in Hegel's scheme. On the one hand, since the central place allocated to sculpture rests on the ancient thesis that of all natural forms only the human body, being the body of the only theorizing animal, gives natural expression to "the Idea" (ultimately, of an ordered world), one might have expected dance, in which actual human bodies are set in graceful movement, to stand alongside sculpture at the center. That place had been prepared for it by earlier writers, but Hegel

---

[25] The pairing of "gardening" with dancing does not have the belittling tendency one might nowadays suppose. In the later eighteenth century, landscape gardening was assigned great spiritual significance in some quarters. In modifying the landscape, the gardener attunes the indweller to infinity. Hegel is thus conceding, rather than denying, that imperfect arts may be assigned great cultural significance; the suggestion must rather be that they cannot sustain the weight placed on them, cannot really have the significance they are thought to have by confused and sentimental people.

declines to fill it. On the other hand, dance might have been set alongside architecture as the primitive art in which the actual materiality of the body is partly infused with significant properties in the same way that an architect imparts a significant form to actual materials in all their solid strength. But this obvious move is also one Hegel refuses to make. To see why, we must look more closely.

1.3311 *Dance as a "Symbolic" Art*

The analogy between dance and architecture, as it might have seemed to Hegel, is instructive. The dancer's skill and grace imperfectly animate a real corporeal presence, the sweating and straining body, as an architect imparts an illusory lightness to the vault that sustains and is confirmed by the loads imposed on it. And, like architecture, dance has to be recognized as an inevitable and basic art. Human beings will always build and will always dance, just as they always have, and it will always be important to them how they do so. If the origins of dance are prehistoric and even prehuman, that does not mean that dance is superseded. What is at the origin cannot be superseded, in the sense that it can be neither eliminated nor sublated. It can, however, be superseded in the sense that it loses its place at the focus of concern. It was in this sense and not in any other that Hegel held that all art was superseded: science and philosophy are now, and from now on must always be, more central to the concerns of humanity. But art has by no means completed its mission.

Hegel's relegation of architecture to the past corresponds to what several more recent critics have thought to be a historical fact. The architecture of his day was bankrupt, reduced to drawing on a repertory of ornament of which the original significance was lost, in desperate search for any sort of authentic or persuasive style (see Frankl 1968 and Sparshott 1976, and compare Gombrich 1979, ch.8). Similarly, Hegel's remarks on what he took to be contemporary dance that we have already quoted suggest that he saw in it a similarly frenetic and desperate but superficial attempt to resuscitate dead meanings.

Hegel had, in fact, a clear idea of what dance as a "symbolic" art, parallel with architecture, would be and had been. Symbolic arts find, or implant, universal meanings in objects: "Paths in labyrinths are a symbol for the revolution of the planets, just as dances too in their intricacies have the more secret sense of imitating symbolically the movement of the great elemental bodies" (Hegel 1975, 353).[26] Consequently, just as shivarees and

---

[26] What this refers to is the interweaving of earth, air, fire, and water in Aristotelian cosmology. Hegel's interpretation of symbolic dance seems generally to be based on a close but rather fanciful reading of Greek cultural history, in which dance is seen as surviving into

Christmas trees are nowadays enjoyed for their own sakes without regard for the ancient meaning that antiquarians find was formerly attached to them, so was it "in the case of the festal dances of Greek youths and maidens where the interlacings of the dance and their figures imitate the crisscross movements of the planets, as the twists and turns of the labyrinth do also. We do not dance in order to think about what we are doing; interest is restricted to the dance and the tasteful and charming solemnity of its beautiful movement" (Hegel 1975, 495). A merely universal meaning cannot in itself be very interesting; unless that meaning is built very solidly into a current way of life, the only real interest is the charm of the symbol itself. In the case of dance, especially, moving human bodies are themselves too expressive to serve the purposes of a symbolic art: unlike the ponderosities of rock, the meaningful resources of the dancer are necessarily such as cannot be—and could never have been, in no matter how remote a past—exhausted in abstractions.[27]

1.3312 *Dance as a "Classical" Art*

In his dismissal of symbolic dance, Hegel says that the beautiful movements of the dance itself are far more interesting than anything they could convey about the forces of nature they are supposed to stand for—they cannot, after all, convey anything very precise about planetary orbits or plate tectonics. But, in saying that, is Hegel not admitting that dance is a classical art on a par with sculpture? Yet he refuses to admit that, and one wonders why.

One consideration that might have made dance an unlikely partner for sculpture would be that the human body is already perfectly expressive in the only way it can be expressive. This is the thought captured in the notion that "God made man in His own image," which can be taken to mean either (referring to the mind alone) that man is the only animal capable of the intellectual and prudential activity that must be attributed to a demiurge, or that the human body is the only corporeal manifestation of such ratiocinative and purposive capacity. No art of dance, it might be argued, could add anything to that. Dance as the development of gesture, as the epitome of gesture (Lucian), as the idealization of gesture (Fokine), or as the bringing of gesture to consciousness (Adam Smith) could not be, as Lucian argued it was, more expressive of humanity than the undancing body. But if dance expresses something different, what is that? If dance

---

classical times from an archaic past. Perhaps because of Hegel's influence, but perhaps because he was fundamentally right, we still find this approach compelling.

[27] We shall see below (§1.3321) that court ballet, the only form of dance in European history for which cultural centrality could plausibly be claimed, was largely a symbolic art in Hegel's sense.

expresses a new, autonomous realm of artistic reality on the basis of gesture, it reduces to formal fantasy; and for Hegel, as for many others, it could have no more meaning than the fireworks to which, as we observed above, mere abstract dancing was often compared (see §1.2521 above). The appropriate inference from this has indeed been drawn by some recent thinkers: motion itself (or, in less radical minds, *human* motion itself) is already the whole of dance, just as sound itself, in the thinking of John Cage, is all that music could be.[28] No art can be erected on such a basis: if it is taken literally, dance as art evaporates into a kind of yoga.

Unless we can find some definite account of what a dancing body can fitly express, then, we shall have to say that dance cannot take a place among the fine arts. Carpeaux's sculpture of a dance may be art, and one might think that a real dance—as it were, the same thing in animation—could be art too; but it cannot, because the dancer as dancer can express no idea higher than the personality and full humanity his life should already more fully and perfectly show.

The line of argument suggested in the preceding paragraph is specious. The immediate and unreflecting movements of the uninstructed body are only accidentally expressive: adequate embodiment of the idea of humanity for perception requires the transformation of the artist's body into a medium for meaningful gesture. Certainly Hegel never even considers the line we have suggested. What he does say about the possibility of an abstractly beautiful art of dance that would correspond to sculpture is of some subtlety, even if the conclusion he reaches seems ill grounded.

The movements of animals, Hegel argues, unlike their bodies, cannot strike us as beautiful. What we are aware of in animal life is, first of all, capricious movement, the "abstract freedom of changing place from time to time." The reason animal movements cannot strike us as beautiful is that, not being animals ourselves, we do not immediately grasp the principle of unity in those movements: their relation to the animal's life, which is what unifies them, has to be worked out by the intellect, which "struggles to understand the purposefulness in them" (Hegel 1975, 124). The movement of human beings in music and dancing, by contrast, is not capricious but "in itself regular, definite, concrete, and measured—even if we abstract altogether from the meaning of which it is the beautiful expression" (p. 124). But the point is that, just as with animals, there must be a

---

[28] "What was presented in the new dance was the human body as an end in itself, a lucid and sonorous phenomenon in its own right." All that dance can do, if it is not to sink to the level of elitism, is *make the body noticeable* (Sheets-Johnstone 1978, 198). She appears to equate this view with the opinion she attributes on the same page to Merce Cunningham, that all movements are "of equal merit." But that may not be quite what Cunningham had in mind (see §1.342 below).

meaning that is beautifully expressed. And into this meaning we ourselves, since we are also human, should have immediate insight: "If gestures are carried artistically to such a degree of expression that words can be dispensed with, then we have pantomime which, in that case, turns the rhythmic movement of *poetry* into a rhythmic and pictorial movement of *limbs*. In this plastic music of bodily posture and movement the peaceful and cold work of sculpture is ensouled and animated into a dance, and music and plastic art are in this way unified" (p. 1039).

Why, then, is this possibility not taken up? Why is dance refused this place among the fine arts? A dancer's idealized gesture, as envisaged by Fokine, for instance, differs from a natural gesture not by being of a different sort but by being more perceptible: the human meaning it expresses is clarified and isolated for attention as well as being taken up into the musical continuity of the dance movement. And what it expresses is thus, by Hegel's own standards, the individual, the universal in the particular, whereas the natural gesture expresses confused particularity. So the way seems open for an art of dance parallel to the art of sculpture.

Hegel's reason for not admitting dance into the canon of the arts may, in the last resort, be only that it would make his scheme untidy. There is no vacant niche, and the niches were there first. That would explain what may strike one as the incoherence of Hegel's treatment of the topic: he is trying to fit the realities of dance into an ideological pattern established to meet other requirements. In any case, the line he takes is that dance is either abstract, and so does not attain the level of art, or else a degenerate derivative of poetry: pantomime turns the movement of poetry into a movement of the limbs. Adam Smith's conjecture (§1.332, below) that mime in itself is more natural than poetry and might therefore constitute a more basic and independent art is not taken into account. Poetry, according to Hegel, is "the absolute and true art of the spirit," because only speech can present *everything* that is conceivable to the imagination (Hegel 1975, 626). Poetry is the total art because "it repeats in its own field the modes of presentation characteristic of the other arts"; thus, in dramatic art, "poetry also proceeds to speech within a compact action which, when manifested objectively, then gives external shape to the inner side of this objective actual occurrence and so can be closely united with music and gestures, mimicry, dances, etc." (p. 627).

The claim for the priority of poetry has much to recommend it. Human action cannot, in general, be understood without the speech that articulates its intent. We even (it has been suggested) manage to make sense of our own lives only by verbalizing them, telling ourselves more or less explicit stories about what we have done, are doing, and propose to do. Dance, then, is either meaningless or an accompaniment to implied or actual speech, as is made evident in the mimed dances (*natya*) of India, in which the narrative that the dance enacts is chanted (though often unintelligibly or inaudibly) during the dance. In the mimetic dances of nonliterate peoples, we may add, it is typically animals that are mimed, and mimed in the few of their gestures that the human dancer thinks he understands. The miming of a human action is always either a caricature, because the action to be visibly recognizable has to be reduced to its most elementary meanings, or a joke, because its very recognizability is a comment on the transparency of a human action. In drama, as Hegel noted, the visible action is an interpretation of the verbal text that articulates the inner meaning of the action. Without that text, the dance that should interpret the drama becomes a mere fragment, beautiful perhaps, but shorn of the spiritual meaning it should properly have. The stories in Lucian and Athenaeus, according to which a Bathyllus or a Pylades could dance out the meaning of a philosophical text or a diplomatic treaty so that its meaning was perspicuous even to those unacquainted with the original text or even with the language it was written in, would not have convinced Hegel and do not convince me.[29]

And yet, this case for the priority of poetry fails to convince. The claim that poetry can, in some sense, do all that the other arts do is true; but that is perhaps not a very interesting sense. Hegel is merely not interested in meanings that cannot be put into words: this, whatever he may have believed about himself, becomes more and more evident as one reads through the *Aesthetics*. The equations of thought with intellect and of intellect with language effectively prevail in a very crude, not to say fanatical, form. Linguistic behavior is reduced to text: the resources of gesture and inflection are simply brushed aside. We have cited several passages in which Hegel acknowledges the existence of a gesturally significant dance and concurs with his contemporaries in according it artistic supremacy; but as soon as he comes to examine its artistic credentials, he equates it, absurdly, with miming.

1.33121 *Hegel's Original Position.* Before leaving Hegel's treatment of dance as a classical art, I would like to cite H. S. Harris's exposition of the position Hegel had developed in his *Philosophy of Spirit* of 1805–1806. I do not understand much of this, and I do not know how much is uncontrovertibly Hegel's, but the position it represents has affinities with some of those considered in the preceding section, and does much to explain what

---

[29] Marcia Siegel writes of the movements in Doris Humphrey's *Passacaglia* (for instance, the dancers "lift only one arm skyward while using the other oppositionally to create a downward counterforce") that "I can't imagine a clearer statement of agnosticism" (Siegel 1979, 92). But such "statements" are hardly explicit on particular items of doctrine, and she does not say exactly what it is that is clearly stated. Does she mean more than that the dance gives eloquent expression to a mood?

we there called Hegel's fanaticism—the fervor of a disenchanted theologian in search of something to be superstitious about. By way of preface, it needs to be explained that the phrase "Absolute Spirit" invokes one of Hegel's peculiar doctrines. Only a soldier, he argued, could really lose himself in his community, because only he was really prepared to die for it; but the philosopher (as envisaged in Plato's *Republic*, for instance) could achieve a comparable intellectual apotheosis by sacrificing his own personality and ideas and identifying himself with pure thought. The achievement of this universal viewpoint is what fulfills the promise of religion, and it is in the pure beauty of art that we have the first real inkling of it. Now read on.

> Beauty is the *natural* key to entry into the realm of Absolute Spirit because it is only in *beauty* that it can appear at all. But even here it appears sensibly as *love*. The aestheticism that reverences the art *object* as an object belongs to the spirit of scholarship, not to Absolute Spirit. Art is the vehicle of Absolute Spirit only when what it mediates is the awareness of something lovable in and for itself, so that the reverence involved is dedication, i.e. it is as much practical as theoretical. . . .
>
> Because of the absolute importance of the *message*, the linguistic arts are bound to rank higher than the plastic ones. . . . When the fullness of the content is taken as the primary criterion, it is the dance (rather than sculpture) in which the form and content are in perfect harmony. But the dance expresses life in its immediacy, and sinks almost out of consciousness into natural feeling; it is *anschauungslos* [devoid of intentionality]. (Harris 1983, 513–514, citing Hegel 1968, viii 278, 20)

This immediacy of dance is something that Hegel mentioned in his *Aesthetics* lectures as well, but not (as we have seen) as a feature of dance as such: "The peculiar power of music is an elemental one. . . . Dance music even gets into our feet; in short, music gets hold of the individual as *this* man" (Hegel 1975, 906). On this maturer view, what is specific in dance is the figuration, not the musical impulse. But the preference for the verbal arts remains and is thoroughly justified, from Hegel's point of view: the arts are to initiate us into a grasp of and a self-identification with the intellectual community, which is the self-realization of the political community and the only God we know. This viewpoint, however, is not one that people can be expected to take.

1.3313 *Dance as a "Romantic" Art*

A modern art, a living art, in Hegel's time had to be a romantic art, one in which the plasticity of the medium was such that it afforded no resistance to the embodiment of the idea, which, accordingly, could overflow or overpower the medium, as in music, poetry, and painting. As we should say nowadays, these are the arts in which the medium serves for the articulation of a symbol system. A romantic art in this sense is something a corporeal dance could never be, because the human body, however transfigured and manipulated, retains its own articulation. A few days after Hegel died from cholera in 1831, the dance of the nuns in Meyerbeer's *Robert le Diable* (choreographed by F. Taglioni, with his daughter Marie as the Abbess) revealed the possibilities of a romantic art of dance, as the poets of the day understood romanticism. These possibilities transformed ballet into what we still think of it as being. We cannot know what Hegel would have thought of it, but it is certainly not "romantic" in his technical sense. Rather, its "romantic" elements smack of what he described as "symbolic" and would probably have adjudged reactionary on that basis. If so, his judgment would have fallen into line with what we shall be saying about it later (§1.3323).

1.332 *Hegel's Real Reason*

Dance, it now seems, cannot be any of the three kinds of art that Hegel recognizes, because the human body is what it is. It is too expressive for a symbolic art, too saturated in social or linguistic meaning for a classical art, too definitively formed for a romantic art. That does not mean that there cannot be artistic dances—of course there can, and of course there are— but it does mean that no art of dance can be stable and satisfactory as a vehicle of meaning. We said before that Hegel starts with his pigeonholes and rejects what does not fit into them, so that he never looks carefully at dance to see what is actually going on. But that is a little unfair. As a human being he has a human body and knows what it is, and his judgment is based on that intimate knowledge: it is inconceivable that any experience of dance could overrule such knowledge.

Hegel's real reason for excluding dance from the canon of the fine arts, however, is both more obvious and closer to the heart of his thinking. He refuses to acknowledge any split between the rational and the real, and accordingly always bases his schematizations on something very solid and closely observed in history. If dance in his place and time offered no such basis in observation, to have claimed any systematic significance for dance would have been pure ideology.[30]

---

[30] That Hegel knows less history than he thinks he knows is irrelevant in this context. His whole system is, notoriously, based on two suppositions: first, that the human world has a single history, that of the formation of a single intercommunicating world (*Geist*); and second, that Hegel's contemporaries, for the first time, are in a position to grasp that history in

What Hegel is concerned with is the growth of civilization, of human self-knowledge as the inner structure of a social-intellectual world. The arts are important to him as prescientific and subphilosophic modes of such self-knowledge. Consequently, no fine art is important to him, or can even claim reality, unless it has at some crucial place and time been culturally central. For such centrality, it is not enough that it should be widely practiced, enjoyed, and esteemed: it must play a central part in the self-definition of a community in relation to its religion, that is, in relation to the highest spiritual reality it recognizes.

So far as Hegel knew, architecture of the appropriately heavy and symbolizing sort did dominate the early civilizations of Egypt and India. Sculpture was (since Winckelmann) construed as epitomizing Greek civilization, by presenting the ideal image of the gods. But no civilized era had expressed its characteristic orientation in dance. If it could have, surely it would have. Hegel might well have endorsed the opinion common in his day, that dance as an independently important activity belongs to savages and to primitive people whose expression was inarticulate (see Chapter 6, note 5, below, for Jane Austen's presentation of this theme). Adam Smith, for one, had argued that pantomime is more natural than poetic expression and, if accompanied by music, will automatically fall into time with that music. It is therefore reasonable to suppose that mimic dance served to give sense to music before poetry did, so that dance is more primitive than song. And that, he says, is why we hear a lot about dance among the indigenous peoples of Africa and America, but little about their poetry (Smith 1795, 236).

As a means of expression, then, as opposed to a form of recreation or an adjunct to drama, dance is subhuman and pre-artistic. Apes and peacocks dance, and long after Hegel's death such animal behavior would be seen as the ancestry of art. But Hegel is interested in art only as a manifestation of mind—that is, of civilization. Or rather, he confines the fine arts, as D'Alembert had, to practices that contribute to the civilization of civilized peoples, and he is more historically precise than D'Alembert had been about what constitutes a contribution to civilization.

But is it true that dance had, historically, never dominated a civilization? In considering this question for present purposes, we must put aside whatever we may know or conjecture of the dance traditions of Africa, or of India, or of Bali—these form no part of what Hegel means by history. But what about the post-Augustan pantomime of ancient Greece-in-Rome, as

---

its outlines. Even if one or both of these suppositions is false (or even silly), the fact remains that that is what Hegel thought and that it affords such a compelling rationale for the self-esteem of nineteenth-century Europe that its influence, direct and indirect, remains inescapable.

cited by all writers on dance since the Renaissance? Such a dance might indeed have been the preeminent art of the early Roman empire, at a time when Hellenic sculpture had declined and Hellenistic portrait-sculpture represented the most notable successes of statuary. It was not mere aversion to disruption of his system that would have led Hegel to ignore this celebrated phenomenon. One could, and usually does, write a Roman history without ever mentioning mime. Why? Well, the greatest triumph of that art was said to lie in its astonishing success in conveying through gesture alone the content of philosophical and legal texts (cf. §1.3312 above). But, in that case, it would have no significance or value independent of those texts. It is not suggested that there was any domain of meaning accessible only to dance, in the way that only a sculptor (according to Plotinus) could show how Zeus would reveal himself to humanity, should he deign to do so.

A far more serious question could be raised, however, about the modern art of ballet. Degenerate and empty as it might be in Hegel's view, it was the descendant of the French court ballet, which, in the days of Louis XIV, had been the most potent expression of the most striking political phenomenon of its day: the absolutist French monarchy. And the French court ballet was borrowed and developed from the princely courts of the Italian Renaissance, in which it was surely inseparable from one of the significant moments in European civilization: the image of the courtier. Was it anything more than Prussian prejudice that led Hegel (as D'Alembert had also been led) to ignore the *ballet de cour*? The equivocal reputation of ballet is so central to the problem of the neglect of dance aesthetics that it is worth (as the *Guide Michelin* says) a detour.

1.3321 *The Court Ballet*

The idea of the fine arts as such is a product of the sixteenth and later centuries.[31] The occasion of its rise is the acquisitiveness and ostentation of rival monarchs. From this external point of view, the ballet is indeed a culturally central institution. It is a festival in which courtiers and even kings took leading parts, and it is not surprising to find poets, painters, musicians, and architects, no less than choreographers, involved in these evanescent displays. But internally and ideologically the ballet remained marginal. The new order's rejection of feudalism asserted itself through revival of the supposed thought and practice of "classical" Greece and Rome. Poetry, painting, and their related arts, were to be dignified

---

[31] The history of this development is to be found in Kristeller (1951); the relation between autocracy, acquisition, and art is explored by Bazin (1967). I have tried elsewhere to correct the reductively historicizing tendencies of these authors by showing the inherent strength and hence the autonomy of the system arrived at (Sparshott 1982).

through the exaltation of humanity, structurally vindicated by Neopythagorean notions about the mathematical structure of the universe and symbolically justified by Neoplatonic and neo-Stoic figures of reality. We have seen how the arts thus dignified were, in D'Alembert's day, admitted to the rank of modes of cognition. It was thus necessary for dance not only to establish itself at court but to vindicate a position for itself within the aforesaid justificatory framework of the fine arts. And this, for reasons that our discussion of Hegel has already disclosed, it was hard for it to do.

The discrepancy between the external relation to the crass display of economic and political power and the internal relation to esoteric cosmology shows itself already in seventeenth-century discussions of dance. Emphasis is laid on the allegorical meanings of dances, but at the same time it is insisted that a dance is a mere entertainment (see the materials collected in McGowan 1963). Thus Ménéstrier (1682, 146) observes that ballet is a *divertissement*, but deplores the modern habit of abandoning the principles of symbolism in the interests of entertainment value, especially by having the performers lay aside their symbolic trappings before they start to dance. And these two kinds of discourse seem merely to coexist: it is seldom that one finds any attempt to integrate the two functions of ostentation and allegory or to defend their compresence by appealing to Horace's praise (quoted on all sides at this time) for those who "mix the useful with the pleasant."

What tantalizes us is that these court dances did, in a way, have the status of *choreia*, of a society dancing itself at its own center, in the way that Plato in the *Laws* envisaged. Both the social seriousness and the expense of effort and wealth were worthy of a Greek *choregia*. According to M. de Saint-Hubert in 1641, dance was "one of the three principal exercises of the nobility" (Saint-Hubert 1641, quoted by Christout 1967, 27). The nobles danced before the Prince who personifed the State; or the Prince himself might lead the courtiers in dancing.

Court ballets were not, for the most part, cosmologized, except at the allegorical level. If gods were introduced, they were frankly mythological or euhemerized into the excellences of humans. The cosmic center is the Sovereign, the Monarch, the absolute God-on-earth-in-a-small-space that is the great political discovery of the fifteenth century (see McGowan 1963, 174–176, and Christout 1967, passim). And the real meaning of the dance was usually not cosmic at all. As with a Roman triumph (one of its explicit models), the real meaning of the dance was political, and its occasion was probably some political or military or dynastic master-stroke of the monarch.[32]

---

[32] McGowan notes, however, that ballets, unlike plays, tended to be used to promote po-

1.33211 *Court Ballet and the Age of Autocracy.* Insofar as court ballet presents the ideology of autocracy, it is not surprising that it should be involved in its downfall. The fading or overturning of absolutism does not merely make the political associations of dance a liability but undermines its very significance. Yet the other fine arts survived unscathed into other political epochs. Why the difference? Several reasons present themselves. For one thing, ballet was unlike the other arts in having no important symbolic function not connected with the court. Arts that glorify wealth and power can survive revolutions because they can glorify the wealth and power of bourgeois, banks, and bureaucracies; arts that sanctify the hierarchy cannot. In fact, whereas the other arts had long flourished and were merely pressed into service, ballet was developed from insignificant antecedents for purely political ends. And, whereas an allegorical painting of the king as Apollo glorified the king by associating him with divinity, when the king *danced* Apollo things were a bit different. The king was present in person, not merely in effigy, and his emblematic gear was reduced to an enhancement of his political reality.

There is another reason why court ballet cannot survive the demise of monarchy. It was, as *choreia*, an art for participants and not for spectators. The crowds who thronged the palace to see the king dance came to see the king and to see a show, but not to see an artistic performance. The value of such a dance as Plato had envisaged came from the sense of oneself in motion with others and the custom of putting oneself in the way of such sense. When music ceases to be an art of participating amateurs, because professionals raise standards at the same time as social revolution generates a new public whose standards of accomplishment are lower, the audience can still "play the listener's part" and take in the pattern through the ear. But this cannot be done with such a kinesthetic art as *choreia* must at least partly be. The underlying principles of a display dance for spectators must be different, even if they share a common vocabulary. The virtuosi who had served as dancing masters at courts and compiled the technical handbooks had not considered, because they had never needed to consider, the rationale of a dance strictly for looking at.

Ever since Louis XIV stopped dancing and Parisian ballet became the responsibility of an academy rather than of a court, there have been recurrent complaints that ballet keeps relapsing into mere technique and that

---

litico-philosophical ideals rather than to promote specific policies (McGowan 1963, 170). Mark Franko has pointed out (in an address delivered to the Society of Dance History Scholars in February 1986) that many court ballets appear to have been purely erotic in tendency, without any political significance at all. It is quite unclear, he says, whether the traditional emphasis on ideological significance can be maintained for the corpus as a whole. That some ballets had ideological importance is not, however, disputed.

mere technique is not enough.[33] We saw an example of this in Hegel's sneers at afficionados of nimble legs. In no other art is such a complaint so constantly heard. Its recurrence is often explained by saying that dance traditions keep getting lost for want of a notation. But that, even if true, would explain a situation in which specific techniques kept getting lost but the spirit of dance survived, rather than the one actually alleged, in which techniques are stable but the inner vitality of dance keeps fading. A more plausible explanation might be that a dance originally based on participa-

---

[33] Why did Louis XIV stop dancing when he did? Was it just that he got too fat (Haskell 1948, 17)? The question has often been discussed (since the ballet had been an instrument of policy throughout his reign) and has more than anecdotal interest. When Louis withdrew (his last appearance was in *Les Amants magnifiques* in 1670), many other nobles withdrew also. It was this withdrawal that gave Lully his opportunity to take over Perrin's abortive Academy of 1669 and transform the ballet into a fully professional organization. It is this transformation that marks the end of ballet as a socially pivotal institution in Europe. (Thus Christout 1967, 7, 123; but the granting of the privilege to open Perrin's academy in 1669 presumably shows that the King already planned to phase himself out.)

The old tale that Louis's retirement was prompted by Narcisse's speech at the end of Act IV of Racine's *Britannicus* (1669), in which he imagines the senators despising Nero for "se donner luy-même en spectacle aux Romains," though accepted by Erlanger (1970), is rightly rejected by Christout. Narcisse is, as Racine points out in his preface, Nero's evil genius, and the speech in question is one in which he is urging Nero to murder Britannicus. Nor can we imagine Racine being in a position to admonish the King; nor, in view of the long history of ballet at the French court, would such admonition have made any sense.

What calls for explanation is why the court ballet persisted so long. The institution is more suited to the small courts of the petty princes in its Italian homeland. Erlanger (1970, 177) points out that by 1675 the court establishment numbered in the thousands, as opposed to the mere hundred or so of the early sixties. It was obviously impossible to involve such a court *as a whole* in a ballet, so the whole thing lost its point.

In the earlier court ballets, the parts in which the gentry performed consisted mostly of the elementary social and ethnic dances of the time, with the final Grand Ballet not even that but more of a processional walk. However, the increasing participation of professionals kept driving standards up. De Pure (1668, cited by Christout 1967, 139) maintained that the gentry ought to work at learning their steps; but few nobles had the necessary talent and figure, and not all could spare the time. Louis XIV was not only too fat, he was too busy to practice.

The time at which Louis gives up dancing is also the time at which he embarks on military campaigns. It is tempting to think of these as performing in a wider field the function that ballet had performed: that of surrounding the monarchy with visible glory. One has to bear in mind that for Louis XIV, much more than for Louis XIII, the ballets were a deliberate instrument of policy rather than a natural manifestation of princedom. Louis XIV's public career as a dancer began at the age of eight, as part of a desperate publicity campaign by Mazarin to build up the King's personal image against disaffection. (The campaign was renewed after the Fronde; it was then, in 1653, at the age of fifteen, that Louis first appeared as the Sun, in the *Ballet de la nuit*.) Royal participation in the ballet was protracted long after its natural term, as a beloved anachronism. When the King's position was independently strong and secure enough, there was no need to continue it. A king has no need to dance the sun if he *is* the sun.

tion has no intrinsic reason for existing as a spectator art: being inherently arbitrary, it can achieve vitality only accidentally and occasionally, when individual genius happens to coincide with some genuine concern. Since the relation between that concern and what it animates remains extrinsic, the passing of the concern leaves ballet to relapse into barren academicism.

Ballet never loses its connection with autocracy and is still the target of an animus directed against aristocratic privilege and exploitation. The founders of modern dance in America relied on an antipathy to "ballet" of which they seemed to know little other than that they despised it. Already in the day of romantic ballet, Jules Janin wrote a diatribe against male dancers (§1.3323 below) of which the inmost meaning was a bourgeois protest against the symbolism of the old order; the English puritans objected to dance less for the paganism associated with rural dance festivals than for its association with the divine right of kings. If, at the end of the nineteenth century, ballet flourished only in Russia, that may be in part because the czars were the last absolute monarchs. One notes, in this regard, the prevalence in Russian ballet of those scenes to which Janin took special exception, in which the corps de ballet stand around *admiring* the male soloist.

Ballet, then, becomes and remains (like opera) socially and aesthetically suspect in bourgeois and post-bourgeois societies. But until quite recently ballet was the only serious art dance in Europe and America—serious, that is, whatever its connotations of dissipated frivolity, in that it had a well-developed technical and artistic tradition, dedicated professional practitioners, and exacting standards of performance and presentation. There was thus no really existing and available body of art practice in the name of which ballet could be condemned. The effect was that, yet again, dance was excluded from that body of serious practices, the fine arts.

1.33212 *Court Ballet and the Values of Dance.* The court ballet with the king as center can be taken as metaphor for the heliocentric universe. The metaphor or analogy that links human ceremonies and cosmic order is widespread. Plato's *Laws* relied on it; it is central to Confucianism; Louis XIV emphasized it. It is elaborated in Lucian's apologia for dancing, and we shall see (§2.2) Sir John Davies taking the elaboration further in a grandiose vision that seems to provide a splendid vindication for the deep, even cosmic significance of dance in general and court ballets in particular. Our reason for relegating the topic to a section on metaphor, bearing only indirectly on the interpretation and evaluation of dance practice, is that the vindication is too strong. If everything is already dance, nothing in particular seems to follow for what we ordinarily recognize as specifically dance.

The single factor that does most to make the cosmic context unavailable for the theater dance that developed out of the court ballet is the one pointed out by Hegel: conceived as aesthetic spectacle, any dance that models the cosmos is boring. Or at least, the cosmic symbolism and the aesthetic interest are at odds. The underlying truth here was recognized by Plato in his contrast between the true beauty of geometric simplicities and the seductive charm of variegation (*Philebus* 51c and elsewhere). Davies, as we shall see, tries to break this contrast down by insisting that complex patterns represent a repeated application and extension of the principles of simple ones—in the same way, presumably, that snowflakes and "computer art" achieve interest through iterated simplicity. These principles have now been examined and explicated by Sir Ernst Gombrich (1979), but only as the principles of decorative art, and the fine arts must be more than decorative.[34] Davies himself says that the round dance directly modeled on natural change was a crude embodiment of the simplest forms of motion, fit only for primitive man.

Noverre makes precisely this objection to the round dances that symbolize the cosmos, and incorporates it in a more widely ranging polemic against the emblematic, ceremonious dances of the official ballet of his day.[35] These dances took as their usual topic the relationships of supernatural beings. Noverre argues that only a human dance can hold our interest. The movements of human bodies interest us by expressing human emo-

[34] Plato's contrast between beautiful simplicity and seductive variety was picked up by Augustine (*De Ordine* II 32ff.) and became the contrast between rational beauty and perceptible charm employed by Vasari and other theorists of the Renaissance and after.

[35] It is hard to know what to make of Noverre's claim about his historical situation, which seems groundless to us, to the point where it has been fashionable to deny Noverre any originality at all. On the one hand, we have quoted Dubos's description of the preceding century as one of continual, rapid, and revolutionary change, laying (as Levinson says) the foundations of ballet dancing as we know it today. John Weaver's *The Tavern Bilkers* (1702/1703) was already claimed by its author to be "the first Entertainment that appeared on the *English* Stage, where the Representation and Story was carried on by Dancing, Action and Motion only" (Weaver 1728, 45)—a method still said to be a novelty when Jules Perrot introduced it in the guise of a *pas d'action* in the 1830s (Guest 1984, ii and passim). On the other hand, a writer in the London *Morning Post* in 1843 recalls that "[i]n our early days . . . the dancing department presented scarce anything but the most inane and affected mythological absurdities" (quoted in Guest 1984, 113), and the same newspaper in 1846 disparages "the ancient mythological ballets of Noverre, Gardel, and their colleagues, considered the master-minds of the ballet until Perrot and his compeers appeared to adapt dancing to the wonderful improvements of choreography" (ibid., 1984, 176). Perhaps the myth of an ancient, academic, mythological dance remained psychologically necessary as the entrenched enemy of forward-looking dance lovers long after it ceased to prevail, much as today's writers often pretend that we are still boldly rebelling against the High Victorian Age. Or perhaps such polarities as mythological and realistic, formal and mimetic, ceremonious and free, are always with us and always will be, not even dialectically related, while the real dynamics of artistic change depend on quite different factors.

tions and concerns, which is what they naturally do. A human body doing something that has no human meaning not only fails to interest us, it rebuffs our interest. Typically, a dance that embodies reference to cosmic forces will be stiffly ceremonious; perhaps it *cannot but* be so. Such a dance can be made the object only of an educated and austere taste. So the *danse noble*, once the focus of connoisseurship, becomes obsolete. In French ballet it is at least paid lip service until the consummation of the Revolution, but then it vanishes, to be replaced in esteem by the *demi-caractère* dance, whose approximation to mime makes it immediately accessible even if its finest points can be made the object of a refined criticism.[36]

To sum up: the dances for which a cosmic or hierarchic justification was available were essentially dances for participation, and for a variety of reasons they could not maintain parity of esteem among the fine arts. It is in this context that we are to understand a writer in the 1910 edition of *Encyclopedia Britannica*, written before Fokine and Diaghilev changed everything:

> It seems unlikely that we shall see any revival of the best period and styles of dancing until a higher standard of grace and manners becomes fashionable in society. With the constantly increasing abolition of ceremony, courtliness of manner is bound to diminish; and only in an atmosphere of ceremony, courtesy and chivalry can the dance maintain itself in perfection.[37]

That is to say, the flowering of dance depends on a social order that is danced.

The court ballet of Louis XIV, however, did not dance the social order in quite the way we have just envisaged. We have already had a hint of this in the way Ménéstrier complains that the participants, when they begin

[36] In a dance in which distinguished amateurs perform alongside professionals, the parts taken by the former must be technically and athletically modest. The *danse noble* is, fundamentally, a dance that *even a noble* can do. Gallini remarks that "[t]he grave or serious stile of dancing, is the great ground-work of the art. It is also the most difficult" (Gallini 1762, 75). No doubt something of the sort was true, as one might nowadays say that a flashy technique is valueless without purity of line. But there may also be an element of flattery in it, as the gentry consoled themselves for the nimbleness of the professional dancer by reflecting that, however hard the poor fellow worked, he could never attain the all-important quality they themselves already had, of *being a gentleman*. The aristocrat appreciates in his dancing master what he himself is aspiring to do, his own ideal as a dancer. When the amateur disappears from the scene there is no reason to maintain this artificial prestige for the movements of dignity.

[37] *Encyclopedia Britannica*, 11th ed., vol. 3, p. 270. The article is anonymous, a fact that may reflect the low social standing of ballet at the time. (The article was not, like so many in that edition, carried over from the ninth edition.)

dancing, lay aside the emblems that embody their significant identity (Mé-néstrier 1682, 146): a sharp division is implied between dance values as such and the meanings on which the value of the ballet depends. Nor is this a reflection of mere Jesuit prejudice. We find the same emphasis in the libretto of the *Ballet de la délivrance de Reynaud* of 1617: "It was not without choice and reason that the King decided to represent the Demon of fire here." Fire, which purifies and joins like to like, symbolizes his beneficence to his subjects, his power to his enemies, and his magnificence to foreigners (McGowan 1963, 108). Again, much later, the king writes in his memoirs about the *Fête de carrousel* of 1662, the year after he had assumed absolute power:

> I chose to assume the form of the sun, because of the unique quality of the radiance that surrounds it; the light it imparts to the other stars, which compose a kind of court; the fair and equal share of that light that it gives to all the various climates of the world; the good it does in every place, ceaselessly producing joy and activity on every side; the untiring motion in which it yet seems always tranquil; and that constant, invariable course from which it never deviates or diverges—assuredly the most vivid and beautiful image of a great monarch. (Erlanger 1970, 117)

It is obvious that these ideas are to be conveyed by recognition of what the king is representing, not at all by any movements he may be making, on which the significances of his role impose few constraints.

The court ballet, in fact, is not a dance, though it contains dances. It is more of a parade, a spectacle, a masque, as contemporary descriptions make perfectly clear. The dances as units have little significance, the steps have none. The figures danced out on the floor have some geometric and symbolic significance, but not much. No fine art of dance could ever be generated from such practices.

The court ballet's lack of a strictly dance organization and significance is a problem that remains with us. One can give at least a sketchy description of a musical work in musical terms, naming only musical items and relations, and of a painting in painting terms. But descriptions of dances in dance terms do not pass current in any substantial public: such descriptions typically extend only to brief sequences within dances. Thus, in a recent television presentation of her dance *The Catherine Wheel*, Twyla Tharp's verbal commentary said something about the desired quality of movement but was mostly concerned with the motivation of the characters and the symbolism employed. We were *told the story*. No doubt we, the dumb television audience, were being condescended to; but examples of any more dance-oriented mode of discourse are hard to find anywhere. And, significantly, though the video version (directed by Tharp herself) was based on a theater presentation, what we saw was not a dance as it might be seen danced on stage, but a video synthesis of expressive and narrative parts of that. This must have been partly due to the exigencies of the presentation of dance in film space; but that really only accounts for the failure to transcribe forms in an inhospitable medium, not for the evident location of the dance's identity in its expressive and narrative lines.

When the court no longer dances, the emblematic significance of the ballet is lost, and there is nothing to save it from incoherence and vapidity. This necessary loss of meaning, and not a culpable relapse into academic formalism, is what called for the revolutionary efforts of Noverre and later of Vigano. It was necessary to supply a meaning not to the framework of the dance but to the dance itself. To this revolutionary endeavor we now turn. In the end, the effort fails (or succeeds imperfectly) because it never manages to isolate and develop a mode of meaning accessible only through dance, and thus it incurs Hegel's reproach that dance is merely an inferior substitute for or adjunct to literature. Romantic ballet, we shall see, does give us such a distinctive mode of meaning, which no doubt explains why it remains the basis of what is still the standard ballet repertory. Its failure, if it fails, is of a different order.

1.3322 Noverre and the Ballet of Action

The significance of the system of the fine arts, in D'Alembert's version as well as in Hegel's, is that it provides a rationale for taking its members seriously as modes of human activity and manifestations of human intelligence. Noverre professed the intention of vindicating dance as one of the fine arts; Hegel writes as if he were familiar with Noverre's position, but we have seen that he does not accept it. Why should he not have done so?

The potential significance of Noverre lay not only in what he did and what he wrote, but in who he was, in his position in the intellectual world of his time as a personage who could claim membership in the cultivated circles of Geneva, Rome, and London. The court dance masters of sixteenth-century Italy may have had socially dignified positions, but it does not seem that they belonged to the cultural elite. Noverre claimed to do so: "Poets and Painters shall dispute the honour to have you ranked with them," said Voltaire (Haskell 1948, 16).[38] What made it possible for him

---

[38] "I have an additional reason for admiring you, which is peculiar to me; I find that everything you do is full of poetry; the painters and the poets will debate about which of them will possess you [se disputeront à qui vous aura]. . . . Consider me, sir, as one of your most devoted partisans" (Voltaire to Noverre, 26 Apr. 1764; Voltaire 1973, 348–349, letter D11848). Since Noverre argued that dance should be a third sister of equal dignity with

to hold such a position was a general (though temporary) cult of the theater: Diderot placed the actor and his technique at the center of the philosophical interest in nature and culture, and the preromantic cult of sentiment allowed Noverre's friend Garrick a social position in the London
literary set analogous to that which Noverre claimed in Europe at large.[39]

At first sight, Noverre's doctrine looks simple. What he opposes and
condemns as trivial, stilted, and ugly is formal dance; what he proposes
and commends as expressive, natural, and rational is mimetic dance. But
to closer inspection the outlines appear blurred. For one thing, he confuses
formalism with academicism. What he is attacking must be the fossilized
professional transform of the court ballets of the previous century, as nur-
tured and preserved in the Academy—a form of dance strung together
from elements transposed out of an obsolete context and hence without
inner coherence. Such a dance, however, might have been contrasted not
only with mimetic dance but also with a purely formal dance having an
internal logic of its own, graceful and logical though not mimetic.[40] Noverre's presumption to the contrary rests on a facile and hasty equation
between graceful movement and natural gesture.

The dance that Noverre sets up as his contrastive ideal is one aesthetically unified *as human motion*. Such unity he thinks can only be provided
by a unified motivation and hence by a unity in motivated action. The
desiderated dance must therefore be mimetic. The unification is to be carried further by drawing music, costume, and setting into a single vision.

---

poetry and painting, the seeming compliment is a well-calculated insult, whether Voltaire
meant it so or not.

[39] Noverre's *Letters* appear in 1760, the first two volumes of *Tristram Shandy* in 1759,
Sentimental Journey in 1768. Garrick met Diderot and his circle in Paris in 1763 (Diderot's
Paradoxe sur le comédien was inspired by this encounter). The fiasco of the belated Shakespeare
bicentenary extravaganza at Stratford, which should have been Garrick's apotheosis, was in
1769. Noverre's arguments were thus part of a European movement of thought—one of the
earlier manifestations of bourgeois personalism, not an episode confined to dance history.
Their failure to have a wider influence than they did thus calls for explanation. Perhaps, as
our text suggests, they could not be directly related to anything that was happening. In an
earlier letter to Noverre than that cited in the preceding note, Voltaire said that, although his
ideas were very nice, he did not quite see who was to put them into effect: Noverre would
have to become a second Prometheus and create a new race of mankind to perform his works
(Voltaire to Noverre, 11 Oct. 1763; Voltaire 1973, 27, letter D11456).

[40] It should be borne in mind that we have only its enemies' word for the emptiness of the
formal dance that the *ballet d'action* was to replace. Since we have the scores and can stage
revivals, we know that *opera seria* had artistic qualities that its triumphant enemies did not
admit, and we lovers of *La Clemenza di Tito* can read with complacency the words in which
our elders explained that it could not hold the stage. The equally triumphant foes of the
unnotated academic ballet were able to erase its memory and thus substitute their own evaluation for the factual record. Levinson thinks he would have liked it.

And the vision is to be that of the choreographer, not (as previously) that of a scenarist or impresario. What was to be characteristic of *ballet d'action* as such was not merely substituting expression for acrobatics—a perennial topic of polemic—but making unity of action the principle of aesthetic unity and, accordingly, giving choreography primacy among the artistic disciplines that contributed to the ballet.

Noverre's program sounds fine, but something seems to go wrong. Noverre's own description of his favorite composition represents it as a string of highlights, emotional *topoi* from established fables involving the outworn personages of Greek mythology and pastoral. What we are presented with is not the postulated imitation of an action, the third sister art to be set alongside the traditional pair of poetry and painting, but the sort of trifling that still stands for ballet in the minds of its enemies. In fact, it can be argued that the thrust of Noverre's theories is carried through not by his own practice but by Fokine's.[41]

Noverre's polemic, though it purports to offer a single rationale for a unified practice, actually conflates at least five contentious theses, the connections among which are neither logically nor historically very close. First is that perennial polemic, in the name of an expressive dance emphasizing the upper body and arms, against a merely nimble dance of legs and feet.[42] (Fokine and the nineteenth-century analysts of motion would later take the more sophisticated view that expression depends, or should depend, on the whole body as a unit; but if one admits the dichotomy, it is of course true that in conversation it is the top half of one's interlocutor that one looks at for the more subtle manifestations of emotion.)

The second thesis is about the nature and organization of a ballet. Noverre thinks of a ballet as like a wordless drama, unified by its action. The view is concisely expressed by Gallini (1762, 119): "A dance should be a kind of regular dramatic poem to be executed by dancing, in a manner so clear, as to give to the understanding of the spectator no trouble in making out the meaning of the whole, or of any part of it." We have seen that the court ballet, by contrast, had less to do with the ancient drama (with which some academicians liked to associate it) than with such pageants and shows

---

[41] Robert Joffrey's summary of Fokine's choreographic principles in Crabb (1978, 143ff.) reads like a paraphrase from Noverre. See also Fokine (1961). But perhaps we should think rather of a succession of waves of more or less conscious restatements and reinstatements of action ballet, emphasizing different aspects of presentation and technique, among which Fokine's appears decisive mainly because of the art-historical importance of its time.

[42] Gallini (1762, 18) says of the conveniently unobservable Greeks: "Nothing could be more graceful than the motion of their arms. They did not so much regard the nimbleness and capering with the legs and feet, on which we lay so great a stress. Attitude, grace, expression, were their principal object." Gallini's book appeared two years after Noverre's.

as our contemporary float parades, which were as popular then as they are now (§7.6 below). On this view, a ballet would be unified not by its action but by its theme. It would consist of a series of illustrative tableaux strung on that theme like beads on a thread and artistically organized by principles of contrast. And this view of the matter had been explicitly argued by Ménéstrier (1682, 137 and elsewhere). Ménéstrier's position represents the Jesuits' reliance on popular entertainments to reach the people, together with a tacit opposition to elitist and academic theories and practices in the arts. It was important not to allow the proper domain of pageants and processions to be usurped by antiquarian drama:

> Tragedy, comedy, musical representations, and ballet are imitations. That is what they have in common. Tragedy and comedy imitate actions. . . . Ballet imitates the nature of things, and represents men and animals alike. Tragedy and comedy exist for the sake of morals and instruction; ballet exists for the sake of entertainment and pleasure.[43]

The third thesis is the one closest to Noverre's heart: the movement of a dance should be articulated by the motivation it expresses, rather than consisting of a sequence of prefabricated steps. The sort of construction he was attacking is exemplified by Arbeau's *Orchésographie* (1588), which analyzes popular dance forms into a few basic components; and it is still true that it is only such dances that can be quickly taught to miscellaneous groups of amateurs. It is worth remembering, too, how much of secular music as well as dance in the early eighteenth century consists of a few standard dance forms, bourrée, gigue, sarabande, and so forth, each of which was supposed in some versions of the prevailing musicology of the day (the so-called *Affektenlehre*) to be susceptible of analysis into affective elements as well as into component steps. What Noverre is rejecting— anachronistically, as we see from Dubos's account of Lully's reforms (note 21 above)— is presumably reliance on such set forms, not the fundamental ballet vocabulary, which by his day was already standard: without that, there was no basis for the choreographer's work. (We have seen that Vigano, who made that further move away from the stylization of movement, was sometimes felt to have thereby moved out of the domain of dance altogether.) The issue between Noverre and his predecessors had to do rather with the articulation and modulation of these elementary forms.

---

[43] Ménéstrier 1682, 290–291; my translation. Note that Ménéstrier does not contrast dance with drama, but ballet with comedy and tragedy. As the title of his book suggests, he is making distinctions among modes of theatrical presentation, in the manner of Aristotle's *Poetics*; he is not explaining the differences obtaining within an already established set of "imitative" or "fine" arts. Such a "system of the fine arts" does not yet exist to form an authoritative framework for such discussions.

Noverre's fourth thesis is that dance as dance is an independent art form, the works in which are devised by choreographers. That view was not embodied in prevailing practice and is not altogether so even today. Dance was more common by way of interlude in opera or elsewhere, and dance as such had really been no more than that in the court ballet. The creation of a ballet was less likely to be the work of a choreographer, whose concern is with the possibilities of the dancing body, than of a noble patron or a poetic scenario writer or an impresario, to whom the choreographer would be related as stonemason to architect. When we wonder why theorists have neglected the dance, we must not forget that what they neglected was something that more often than not had the status of ancillary amusement or that gave dance form to something the primary significance of which had already been established in other terms. The neglect of dance aesthetics and the exclusion of dance from the dignified circle of the fine arts was not mere ideology but simply reflected the artistic and institutional facts as they were and had almost always been.

Noverre's fifth thesis is that dance and mime are essentially the same. Mime, as we think of it, is a voiceless acting, essentially distinguished from dancing by the absence of musical measure and by the preeminence of the value of representational aptness (see §7.72); in ballet, dancing roles and miming roles are distinct. But Noverre, though himself a dancer thinking and feeling in dance terms, commits himself to the thesis that the values of dance are not independent of the values of mime. He thus lays himself open to Hegel's objection: the values unique to dance are, after all, those of bodily dexterity and hence trivial, and the highest values of dance, those of mime, are but derivative variations of the values proper to poetry.

It was the second and third of these five contentions that were distinctive of the *ballet d'action* as Noverre and his contemporaries conceived and tried to practice it. Perhaps his theoretical positions were too much affected by his wish to vindicate the respectability of ballet as a fine art, with the result that he appears conservative, derivative, and eclectic. Thus André Levinson, in a brilliantly vivid polemic, denounces Noverre for joining the philosophers and confirming "the ancient doctrine of Aristotle, the great misconception that confuses the dance with pantomime and the dance step with gesture," and this at a time when the art of pure dance was achieving great refinement.[44] But joining the philosophers was precisely what Noverre wanted to do, and needed to do if dance was to be culturally respectable. One has only to consider Kant's ranking of the arts in the *Critique of*

[44] Levinson 1927, 50. Aristotle nowhere suggests that all dance is or ought to be mimetic. He only says, in the course of an enumeration of the methods of representing human actions and emotions, that dancers have their own distinctive way of doing so.

Judgment, typical of the cultivated opinion of Europe in his day: however accomplished dance became, it could never rise above the level of "charm" without some mimetic content (Kant 1790, §§51–54).

In claiming dance as one of the three arts that imitate *la belle nature*, Noverre is pressing a prestigious but no longer vital view into the service of a contemporary sensibility that it does not really fit.[45] And when he claims the Roman pantomime as his authority for making expressiveness the primary value of dance, the strategic necessity of finding classical antecedents for practices that are to be deemed respectable blinds him to the unsuitability of his exemplars. Bathyllus and Pylades, as described by ancient authorities, were virtuosi of mimicry (as Garrick was in private life): their skills were an external knack of verisimilitude, not the internally unified and coherently motivated enactment that Noverre (like Gluck in opera) envisaged.[46] But, after all, a decisive fact is that our sources give us simply no *sense* of Bathyllus and Pylades as dancers.

A powerful presence in Noverre's cultural milieu was the sentimentalism derived from Locke and epitomized by Sterne, which celebrates natural humanity as a passionate receiver of impressions unified only by their succession and interrelation—a view that early parodied itself in the phrase that reduced the human mind and personality to "a bundle of sensations." Such a view of humanity can be invoked to explain the inconsequentiality of Noverre's pastoral; but, if it is present at all, it is heavily disguised. It has, in fact, always been hard for a ballet master to admit anything radical into his practice or his theory. A William Blake, a Sterne, a Rousseau can be as daring as they please, since paper costs little. But the choreographer

---

[45] Noverre, like many others, misunderstands the phrase *la belle nature*. He thinks of it as merely ascribing beauty to whatever is natural, as Rousseau might do. But for such writers as Batteux (1746) the phrase has Neoplatonic connotations: "beautiful nature" is nature idealized and irradiated with a reality of a higher order, the "golden world" of Sir Philip Sidney.

[46] This characterization of the ancient pantomimes is based on the extended account in Lucian's *Peri Orcheseos*, sec. 34ff., and especially 62–69. These descriptions are at variance with the claim (sec. 35) that the art of the pantomime requires the "highest standard of culture in all its branches," including rhetoric, the study of proportions, music, and natural and moral philosophy. We have already mentioned the "philosopher-dancer" in the artistic succession of Bathyllus and Pylades, whom Athenaeus describes as expounding the nature of Pythagorean philosophy, "clarifying everything for us more lucidly in his silence than those who claim to give instruction in the verbal skills" (Athenaeus, *Deipnosophistae* I, 20c-d). But the difficulty lies in seeing just what Athenaeus thinks was expounded, and how; what degree of information and sophistication was required of the audience; and, more generally, what actual use the dancer was supposed to make (and did make) of rhetoric and the other arts. Athenaeus is hardly a model of philosophical penetration, and it is impossible to take his claims seriously. Lucian, on the other hand, though intelligent enough, is a professed satirist, and it may be that he is constructing a lampoon. (Lucian's authorship of the *Peri Orcheseos* has been questioned, but on no solid grounds.)

of a municipal or imperial ballet, even if he could retrain his dancers (and persuade them—complaints by innovative playwrights, choreographers, and composers about the recalcitrance of executants are perennial), is subject to external pressures. Ballet is big money. Except in special circumstances when novelty becomes the norm, radical experiments are out.[47]

1.3323 *The Romantic Ballet*

Thus far, nothing in the development of ballet has offered any ground for vindicating the position of dance as one of the fine arts in accordance with the appropriate and available ideologies. No distinctive range of ideas more suitable to articulation by dancing bodies than in any other medium has appeared, except for the cosmological generalities that Hegel stigmatized as inadequate to sustain interesting dance structures. And no European dance outside the context of ballet had aspired to artistic dignity. The romantic ballet, by contrast, centered on the figure of the ballerina dancing on points in a short gauzy skirt, does establish for itself such an identity, and the failure of ballet in this new transformation to establish itself securely among the arts may be thought of as due to sheer snobbery, such as at the same period prevented the recognition of the artistic importance of the novel. But there is more to it than that. In fact, we have already seen that one of the factors in the rise of modern dance, which no one denies to be an art in as full a sense as any other, was a reaction against what was felt to be the human inadequacy of the admittedly autonomous art of ballet dance and choreography: their expression of degrading views of womanhood and dehumanizing political structures.

Romantic ballet, we recall, was born a week after Hegel's death. In a sense, it was born after the death of romanticism itself. Romantic arts, in Hegel's admittedly diffuse and vague exposition, are those that convey a dawning apprehension of the universality of mind; and romanticism had brought in northern mists and infinite vistas to give resonance to classical precisions. Northrop Frye picks the year 1830, which is just before romantic ballet begins, as marking the end of the creative epoch of romanticism in literature and the visual arts (Frye 1963). By 1830, one is often told, the literary posture that was recognized and recognizable as romanticism was a set of escapist mannerisms and gestures, no longer in any vital antithetic relationship to the hardening industrial and urban civilization against which it appeared as an increasingly vain protest. However that may be, "romanticism" is a term with many uses, and in a theatrical context it de-

---

[47] The point is made by Emily Genauer, "Modern Art and the Ballet," in Nadel and Nadel 1970. Don McDonagh (1973, 60) observes that it was because the pioneers of modern dance were too poor to take a theater for more than one night that they learned to do without sets; and because they had no audience anyway, they made no concessions to established taste.

noted an entity with a fairly clear identity. For this phenomenon, as Bournonville saw it, Weber's *Freischutz* cleared the way in 1821. It represented, in his view, "the native, the popular, and the interesting, as opposed to the conventional and the downright boring clad in the guise of aristocratic gentility" (Bournonville 1865, 480).

Ivor Guest's description of the ideology of romantic ballet is convincing and, from the present point of view, damning. "It discovered," he says, "how to fulfil a public need by revealing the unattainable for which people craved as an escape from a world that was grey with their cares and anxieties"; and he remarks how *La Sylphide* (1832), the archetypal romantic ballet, stood for "man's pursuit of the unattainable, the infinite, exemplified in the hopeless love of a mortal for a fairy being"—in effect, for Marie Taglioni, schooled by her father in a new art of "seductive poses and correct and harmonious lines," the first to make systematic use of dancing *sur les pointes* to convey the impression of weightlessness (Guest 1966, 7 and 3).

The ideology of romantic ballet, as Guest conceives it, offers a combination of three important and powerful ideas. The first is the redeeming power of femininity, *das Ewig-weibliche*, as a source of personal value in the competitive, Faustian world of masculine business and politics.[48] The second is embodiment, the individualizing corporeality that sets permanent limits to intellectual abstraction and derealization. And the third is the provision of an otherworldly resonance to counteract the same crippling reductionism of the business world in which people enter only as specimens.

The ballet, as Guest represents it, does not, in reality, so much celebrate and articulate these aspects of reality as subvert them. Humanity's pursuit of the unattainable and infinite is but coarsely symbolized and is certainly not (as Guest suggests) *exemplified* by a mortal's hopeless passion for a sylph. Like its analogue, that curious nineteenth-century phenomenon the fairy play, and like the nineteenth-century cult of faery and "little people" in general, such dances convey a sentimental and impotent nostalgia that its victims are likely to resent even in succumbing to it. Nor is a matriarchal respect for corporeality shown by dancing on tiptoe in an agonizing attempt to appear incorporeal. The ideology, in short, betrays femininity rather than expressing or exalting or even respecting it.

As idealism is reduced to escapism and the human body to a fetish, it is

---

[48] In this vein, Bernard Taper writes: "Balanchine didn't really need to utter his famous statement 'Ballet is woman,' for nearly all his ballets said it, just as they also said that the only way a man can achieve or approach the liberation of his soul is by the homage and devotion he shows woman" (Taper 1984, 253). With respect, I doubt if this is true. Neither the apophthegm nor the ballets reveal to me much more than that the bodies and skills of women inspired Balanchine as a choreographer.

the dominant male's attitude to the female that is superimposed on that fantasizing escapism that Hegel had so damagingly pointed out as appropriate to opera. What lies beneath this compelling beauty is a ghastly vulgarity, the spirit of Biedermeyer: the eternal feminine principle, already somewhat sentimentalized in Goethe's version, has been further degraded into the little woman, the *kept* woman, who must keep smiling through her pain so as not to displease her man. Romantic ballet keeps woman on tiptoe as on a pedestal; and the Jockey Club, who worship at her shrine, are not seriously in search of a metaphor for their impatience with the humdrum grind of their workaday world. The attitude implicit in such a dance is made explicit in Jules Janin's often-quoted diatribe against male dancing:

> Speak to us of a pretty dancing girl who displays the grace of her features and the elegance of her figure. . . . Thank God, I understand that perfectly. . . . But a man, a frightful man, as ugly as you or I, a wretched fellow who leaps up and down without knowing why. . . . That this bewhiskered individual who is a pillar of the community, an elector, a municipal councillor, a man whose business is to make and above all to unmake laws, should come before us in a tunic of sky-blue satin, . . . a frightful danseuse of the male sex, come to pirouette in the best place while the pretty ballet girls stand respectfully at a distance— this was surely impossible and intolerable.[49]

The courtier and the noble who was privileged to dance with the *Roi Soleil*, to whom elegant mastery of his body was as proper as his wit and his courtesy, has been replaced by the whiskery bourgeois as decisively as (in another phrase of Janin's tirade) the agility and dexterity of the fencer had been replaced by the stolidity of the infantryman, "a creature specially made to carry a musket and a sword and to wear a uniform." Historically, Janin's allegation of a discrepancy between the qualities of a dancer and those of a military man represents a remarkable reversal. The 1661 charter of the Académie Royale had emphasized the utility of dancing in teaching the use of weapons. Fencing approximates to dancing of a sort (§7.521;

---

[49] *Journal des débats*, 2 Mar. 1840, quoted in Guest 1966, 21. The language strongly suggests that Janin is not speaking in propria persona but is guying the views of philistines. But Guest speaks elsewhere of "the indifference, if not distaste, which was fast becoming the male dancer's lot" in these years and quotes Théophile Gautier as writing in another journal on the same date: "I do not like male dancing at all. A male dancer performing anything other than *pas de caractère* or pantomime has always seemed to me something of a monstrosity" (Guest 1984, 56–57; the coincidence in dates arises because both Janin and Gautier are reviewing the same performance, and both incidentally say that Jules Perrot's brilliant performance has overcome their objections). Janin's emphasis on "unmaking" laws is presumably a reference to the contrast between post-revolutionary France and the *ancien régime*: male dancers stand for the *douceur de vivre* that we have outgrown.

instruction in an elementary sword dance formed part of my fencing lessons from a former regimental sergeant major). Fokine says that he found it inexplicable that the special subjects at the St. Petersburg Imperial Theater School in 1889 included military gymnastics and fencing, but it really is not at all surprising (Fokine 1961, 17). It is even sometimes alleged that the turned-out positions fundamental to ballet were chosen because they were necessary to stability in the characteristic stances and movements of fencing (the front foot, on the sword-arm side, points at the opponent; the rear foot is at right angles to it, heel directly behind heel). And Lucian's defense of dancing expatiates on the antiquity of military dancing (*Peri Orcheseos* 8–10). In Janin's version of the modern world, all of this is as if it had never been.

A ballet of "pretty dancing girls" idealized by careworn businessmen and drunken jocks is the epitome of a luxury art, a Fabergé art, such as Tolstoy toward the end of Petipa's career would denounce as a perversion of artistic values in the interest of mere titillation. And Guest's descriptions of the methods of recruitment and training at the Paris Opera School bear out the other half of Tolstoy's denunciation, that such luxury arts rest on the oppression and exploitation of the poor by the rich.[50] If that is what romantic ballet is, it cannot be taken seriously as a condign manifestation of the human spirit. The revulsion against what ballet had become by about 1900 is often described as a reaction against the sterile degeneration of what had once been a vital art form. But romantic ballet, for all its charm and despite its occasional triumphs, seems to have been corrupt from the start, at its best demanding from the artistically serious-minded spectator a willing suspension of disapproval.

The picture just presented is no doubt a caricature. Fokine observes that in the Russian ballet of 1890 "[e]verything was directed towards one goal: immediate, personal and loud recognition," and that in consequence ballet was despised not only by public and press but also by artists in other arts (Fokine 1961, 47–53). This stigma (still not altogether removed) and these faults (still not everywhere corrected) have nothing to do with the specific character of romantic ballet but are shared with all performing arts that attract audiences whose enthusiasm and connoisseurship outrun their judgment—in short, all those that attract audiences. It is still possible to hold that Petipa was a great artist betrayed by his patrons and performers, and that romantic ballet was corrupt only in those aspects of it that are captured in Guest's version of its ideology. Bournonville, visiting the Bol-

---

[50] Not all luxury arts are equal in the extent to which they oppress the poor. Tolstoy's observations are religiously motivated rather than sociologically focused. For the exceptional misfortunes of dancers, see §1.253 above.

shoi in 1874 (where already the prevailing manner was reduced to "an unending and monstrous host of feats of bravura, all of which were rewarded with salvos of applause and curtain calls"), found the short skirts in vogue there not only offensive but ridiculous and reports that Johansson and Petipa "confessed that they privately loathed and despised this whole development" but were obliged to follow the taste of the times and "the specific wishes of the high authorities" (Bournonville 1878, 581–582). Twenty years later Alexandre Benois passed the compliment on, remarking that the ballet of the Paris Opéra was

> passing through a period of shameful degeneration particularly evident to us devotees of our wonderful Petersburg ballet. . . . In Paris ballet was regarded as a mere appendage to the opera and there were hardly any male dancers—they had been replaced by hordes of females. This was supposed to be at the insistence of the notorious *abonnés de l'Opéra*, who consisted mostly of very elegant grey-haired old gentlemen . . . who occupied the first rows of seats and who retired whenever they wished, in their top-hats and with their canes, through a special passage to the stage to chat . . . with their ballet beauties. . . . (Benois 1964, ii, 145, cited from Buckle 1979, 29)

A tradition of sound choreography and fine dancing persisted and developed throughout the period when these tendencies dominated, or seemed to dominate, the romantic ballet. When, as in *Les Sylphides*, that tradition is liberated and reborn (the pluralization of the sylphs transfiguring the context from suppressed lust to self-contained ethereality), it is evident that an art of pure dance has been brought to birth.[51] Thus every artistic revolution, once the diatribes are over, can find respectable antecedents in the ancestry it denounced. But before that could happen a new way of thinking about dance and its values had to be developed.

1.34 AFTER THE FINE ARTS

We have quoted an article from the *Encyclopedia Britannica* to the effect that dance cannot flourish in modern industrial societies but only in an

---

[51] The original title of *Les Sylphides* was *Chopiniana*, in which the reference back to romantic ballet is replaced (so to speak) by an invocation of Isadora Duncan's notion that dance expresses the inner meaning of music. In either case, the means of romantic evocation are decontaminated and devoted to the ends of pure dance. When we say, in the text, that an art of pure dance is born, we do not mean that autonomous presentations of "pure unmeaning dancing" had never before appeared in the theater. Of course they had. But even such acclaimed masterpieces as Perrot's *pas de quatre* for Taglioni, Cerrito, Grahn, and Grisi had been offered and accepted as *divertissements* (somewhat as landscape painting advanced from the backgrounds of history painting to become a genre in its own right [Clark 1949]).

atmosphere of ceremony and courtesy. For our purposes, this suggests that the specifically theatrical dance of ballet will be sustained by being made the object of a serious artistic interest only when the inherent values of all dance are esteemed throughout society. It is worth noting in this connection that in his down-to-earth "Thoughts Concerning Education," John Locke is determinedly hostile to poetry but praises dance as an "Accomplishment most necessary for a Gentleman." "Dancing," he says, "being that which gives *graceful Motions* all the Life, and above all things Manliness, and a becoming confidence to young Children, I think it cannot be learn'd too early, after they are once of an Age and Strength capable of it." Indeed, dancing is more steadily a part of general courtly education than either painting or music, let alone poetry. But does Locke's encomium really sustain an art of theater dance, as the *Encyclopedia Britannica* author presumably thought? Apparently not, for Locke continues:

> But you must be sure to have a good Master, that knows, and can teach, what is graceful and becoming, and what gives a Freedom and Easiness to all the Motions of the Body. One that teaches not this, is worse than none at all, Natural Unfashionableness being much better than apish, affected Postures; and I think it much more passable to put off the Hat, and make a Leg, like an honest Country Gentleman, than like an ill-fashion'd Dancing-Master. For, as for the jigging part, and the Figures of Dances, I count that little or nothing, farther than as it tends to perfect *graceful Carriage*. (Locke 1693, §196)

John Weaver followed the same Aristotelian tradition in separating advocacy of social dance from the practice of professional dance:

> To dance too exquisitely is, I must own, too laborious a Vanity; and to be totally ignorant of it, and of that Carriage, Behaviour, Fashion and Address, gain'd by learning it, shews (on the other hand) a Man either stoical, or but meanly bred, or not us'd to Conversation. The best therefore is a kind of Artful Carelessness, as if it were a natural Motion, without a too curious and painful practising. (Weaver 1712, 65).

Part of what this means is that the newly rich take dancing lessons in the hope that they will pass for gentlemen born and bred. And the socially suspect nature of this ambition (which at once recognizes the importance of social stratification and denies its legitimacy) is embodied in the equivocal stereotype of the "dancing master," traditionally placed as an authentic master of conventional elegances which he himself notably fails to embody, a dreaded subverter of the social order that he purports to serve (see note 36 above). The dancing master is caught in a dilemma: if his consciousness of the grace he demonstrates is obvious (as, since he is demonstrating it, it can hardly help being and for pedagogical purposes probably ought to be), he in fact fails to embody the quality he purports to be demonstrating; if he appears to embody it unselfconsciously (and thus really demonstrates what he is supposed to be teaching), he shows himself able to usurp a manner, and hence a position, to which he has no right.[52]

Before the time of Duncan and Fokine, we have suggested, no form of ballet found stable justification by the philosophical systems available at the appropriate time, and no other form of dance afforded any basis for serious consideration as an art form. Corroboration of this view, of a sort, is provided by a work designed to controvert it, a *History of Dancing* produced by a twenty-five-year-old medical doctor in 1906. With the retirement of Elssler and Taglioni in 1845, he says, ballet lost its impetus, though it was revived some years later when ballet dancers began to appear in music-hall programs (St.-Johnston 1906, 110–111; Karsavina was still earning money by dancing for Oswald Stoll at the Coliseum in 1910 [Buckle 1979, 161]).

> But, for all that, the ballet is now a thing of the past, and, with the modern change of ideas, a thing that is never likely to be resuscitated. And in a way it is perhaps as well, for . . . a forced and mechanical

[52] The threat posed by dancing masters might be increased if it was still true, as it had been in the Renaissance, that "an astonishing number" of them were Jewish (Winter 1974, 10). Certainly the stereotype that I recall from an old *Punch* cartoon, which in my youth I took to be generically Latin, could have been meant to be Jewish (see Harry Furniss's drawing "Civilization of the Rough" in *Punch's Almanack for 1882* [*Punch*, 6 Dec. 1881, unpaginated]). The equivocal status of the dancing master is most familiar from Dr. Johnson's statement that Lord Chesterfield taught his son "the morals of a whore, and the manners of a dancing-master" (Boswell 1791, 159), for it was indeed a nobleman who was teaching them! But it is more instructive to compare Jean Jacques Rousseau's exchange with Charles-Hubert Méreau. Rousseau had written in *Émile* that "[w]ere I a dancing master, I would not go in for all the monkeyshines [*singeries*] that Marcel* does, which do very well for the place where he performs them. . . . My model would be an antelope, rather than a dancer from the Opéra," adding the footnote "*A famous dancing master in Paris, who knew his public well, and craftily gave himself airs [*faisoit l'extravagant par ruse*], ascribing to his art an importance which people pretended to find absurd but because of which, fundamentally, they paid him the deepest respect" (*Émile* II, Pléiade edition, IV, 390–391). Méreau retorted in a letter of 14 February 1763 that distinguished people would not have taken lessons from Marcel if he had made monkeys out of them and that in fact he had taught the same principles of balance that Rousseau advocated in *Émile*, the difference being that Marcel made the mechanical implications of those principles explicit. And so on, at some length. Rousseau, plainly left without a leg to stand on, replied on 1 March that the *singeries* in question applied not to what he taught but to his teaching methods: "We could not restrain our laughter at the magisterial gravity with which he enunciated his erudite apophthegms" (Rousseau 1972, nos. 2483 and 2519 [I am indebted to Aubrey Rosenberg for drawing my attention to this correspondence]). That isn't what he said in that footnote, is it?

style cannot contribute to the furtherance of the real art of dancing, and movements such as walking on the extreme points of the toes can only be regarded as unnatural. (St.-Johnston 1906, 113)

What had replaced ballet was skirt dancing, based on ballet movement and continuous with ballet, introduced at the Gaiety Theatre in 1876 by Kate Vaughan in a quartet with Nellie Farren, Edward Terry, and E. W. Royce:

The grace and charm of the new style could not be denied, and the superiority, if only from an artistic point of view, of this form of dancing, built on the old Greek model, over the stiff and conventional movements of the Italian school was so evident that from that time ballet-dancing began to lose a popularity which it has never since regained. (St.-Johnston 1906, 119)

Today's reader notes that grace and charm are the only values the author recognizes in dance. It is just his bad luck, of course, that his requiem for ballet appeared only three years before Diaghilev and his colleagues set Europe on its ear. But we observe that, despite the reference to the old Greek model, he nowhere mentions Isadora Duncan. He does allude to Loie Fuller, but only to disparage her act as irrelevant to dance as such; and this surprises us when we read:

And this skirt dancing, what is it? A vision of laughing eyes and twirling feet, a swift rushing of floating draperies through the air, a twirl, a whirl, now here, now there, yet all with a certainty and precision whose very absence declares its art; then, as the music slows down, a delicate fluttering, like a butterfly, hovering among the flowers, and lastly, as a soft falling snow-flake, silently she sinks to the ground. Is this not something worth living for, to be able to dance it, to be able to see it? (St.-Johnston 1906, 131)

Kate Vaughan, he tells us, was "the creator of all that is best in the dancing of today," "the greatest dancer of her time. And as such her contemporaries justly proclaimed her" (pp. 170–171). And he quotes the wife of the Pre-Raphaelite painter Edward Burne-Jones in evidence: "Another and a different vision also flits across the mind, in the form of the wonderful dancer Kate Vaughan—'Miriam Ariadne Salome Vaughan,' as Edward called her. Never shall I forget seeing him and Ruskin fall into each other's arms in rapture upon accidentally discovering that they both adored her" (Burne-Jones 1904, 121). Now, *that* I should have liked to see.

St.-Johnston may appear to us to value in skirt dancing what has been disparaged in romantic ballet: its reduction to kitsch through the substitution of reverie and association for substance and form. In any case, as we have seen, the justification that romantic ballet and its offshoots might have derived from inclusion in the canon of the recognized fine arts was never available. And the end of romantic ballet comes at a time when the repertory of such justifications is essentially complete. Cultural justifications must be based on the inertia of tradition, and justificatory ideologies could be generated only in a metaphysically sanguine age. Once they get started their impetus may carry them into a skeptical and scientific time, but they can hardly originate in such an age. Purely aesthetic justifications are always available, but they cannot afford ideological support for any specific art or art form, or serve to articulate its discussion, because anything whatever can be aesthetically justified (see §1.342 and note). Justifications in terms of social, physiological, and psychological function are similarly always available, but it is hard to make them both convincing and relevant. The skeptical have to be shown, first, that the need dance is alleged to fulfill is both a real need and, second, that dance is inherently more apt to fulfill that need than other forms of activity. Even if both can be shown, it is likely that what will be thereby vindicated will be not what we esteem as the art of dance but something else: a self-expressive flapping, or gymnastics, or community games, or theosophical therapy.

The effect of the predicament we have just outlined is that artistic dance in our century lacks an authenticating tradition of thought and practice. Modern and postmodern painting and music, for instance, retain their identity and discussibility because, despite the fragmentation of ideology in our pluralistic civilization, there is a commonly accepted heritage of practices and works to which conservatives and radicals alike refer: the children leave home, but they know it is home they have left. It is this security that dance lacks: the justificatory systems of thought themselves stand in need of justification, in many cases more so than the practices they are invoked to defend. In rounding off this chapter, I will not essay a critique of all the alternative ways of thinking about dance that have been mooted without ever becoming respectable among theorists of art, because that failure is due not to their unsuitability or inadequacy so much as to their lack of preemptive cogency; they will fit better into the more positive phases of our discussion. For the present, I will only mention one alternative ideological line that somehow failed to gain credence and some of the features of more recent dance that have been alleged to militate against its playing a featured part in the theory of the arts.

1.341 *Dance as Universal Art: Schopenhauer, Nietzsche, Wagner, Diaghilev*

We saw that romantic ballet developed after romantic thought generally had lost its vital impetus and that it did not participate in the general movement of romantic art. The theory of dance coeval with romantic ballet is not, strictly, a romantic theory and is not related to any form of dance with which it is contemporary or, indeed, with any likely form of theater dance. I refer to the powerful image generated by Nietzsche's *Birth of Tragedy* (1872). Nietzsche reworks Schopenhauer's antithesis between the idea-forming fine arts and the will-embodying art of music and rethinks Hellenic classicism on the basis of a closer scrutiny than Winckelmann's. He sees the civic choral dance, which Plato had extolled and had differentiated from the epistemologically dubious arts of mimesis, as a self-conscious perversion of something more primitive, hinted at in Euripides' *Bacchae*: an ecstatic dance in which a community expressed itself as a chorus of satyrs, a communal half-conscious quasi-mind below the level of individual thought, expressing in its ecstasy the community's will to overcome the agony of universal death. This is the *choros*, the ceremonial ring dance, that is still *orchesis*, the dance of individual rapture. Such a dance is the original and fundamental manifestation of the artistic will. But Nietzsche thinks of the maturer manifestations of that will as taking specific form in song, drama, and the plastic arts; so his theory, far from justifying any actual or even any possible art of dance, confirms the long-established practice of relegating dance to the pre-artistic and subhuman.

Part of Nietzsche's inspiration came from Wagner, who also had come close to providing an artistic rationale for the significance of dance. Wagner advocated a unified art-form in which all arts should find their contributory place, a theatrical art in which a community's dance and dream of itself would be realized. What this calls for is something that actually exists in every civilization, a form of theatrical presentation in which song, dance, mime, and scene are joined. What Wagner contributed was the demand that the whole should be an inseparable artistic unity forged by a single creative intelligence.

It was this comprehensive artistic presentation that Baïf had recognized in Greek drama and sought to reconstitute in ballet but (for want of effective contact with the creative sources of dance in Italy) could not put into effect (cf. note 23 above). Unemphatically by Aristotle in his *Poetics*, emphatically (as we have seen) by Hegel, it had been held that all other components of such a unity must be subservient to that which most explicitly formulates a meaning, that is, the written word, so that all other aspects of theatric art are subsumed in dramatic poetry. Noverre, we have seen, championed the choreographer in a version from which words were excluded. Wagner cut the Gordian knot by being his own dramaturge and poet (a crafty and creative one, however little we may like the results); but the effect of his genius was to dissolve everything in music, and his theory similarly insisted that only the formative power of music could transform the inherently graceless movements of the body and the syntactic necessities of language into art.

Whatever view one takes of the priorities, the difficulty in the notion of a complete and fully unified theatric art is that one cannot very well sing and dance (or, for that matter, act and dance) at the same time, so that the symbiosis of the component arts is uneasy and episodic. Opera, as developed in Europe, with its relaxed canons of unity, included dance as a subsidiary element, but the effect of Wagner's practice was to make music swallow up the dance entirely. Ballet develops into a theater art separate from opera and parallel with it, in which there is dancing but no singing. Ballet and opera share the same social ambience, the same orchestral apparatus, much the same audience, the same sort of decor, and often the same building, the same financial structure, the same management. But they do not share the same music or the same artistic prestige. The triumphs of opera are among the triumphs of music, but outside Russia few great composers have devoted their best energies to ballet. Opera is in some places central, ballet everywhere peripheral, to thought about art.

The Wagnerian *Gesamtkunstwerk* prepares a central place among the arts for dance to occupy. Dance fails to occupy that place; but for one brief period it almost did. The years between 1905 and 1925 could be held, at least as plausibly as any others, to compose the heroic age of modern art. And in those crucial and vital decades the Russian ballet under Diaghilev held a central place in European culture, preoccupying and transforming sensibility, and employing the finest talents (Picasso, Stravinsky) of other arts. But it did not maintain that position, and, astonishingly, it left almost no impression on the theoretical aesthetics of its own day. One wonders why.

Part of the reason for the theoretical invisibility of Diaghilev was yet another inner disharmony between the ideology of ballet and that of the other arts. The ideology of modern art, and the general aesthetic then becoming dominant, was strongly individualistic and expressivistic: the image of the artist was that of the lonely individual achieving and communicating a personal vision. A collaborative art such as ballet does not embody that ideal, whatever its popularity. Aestheticians who speak of dance at all will speak of Isadora Duncan, and then not as embodying the spirit of dance but as representing Art in general—just as the "little tramp" of Charlie Chaplin was idolized at the same time, not as a triumph of the collaborative art of cinema, but as a realization of the essential loneliness of the artist in all of us. Isadora indeed established no tradition, belonged to no school; and within ballet her counterpart is Nijinsky (not least because of his eventual madness), conceived not as a master of dance among dancers but as an isolated and tragic soul.

The revived ballet failed to influence thought because, among other reasons, the Wagnerian notion of the all-embracing and central work of art, despite its long ancestry, was itself without important influence. The idea of centrality was itself peripheral; the shrine at Bayreuth remained an oddity, a backwater. Artists might collaborate wholeheartedly in stage works, but their professional and public positions as artists would depend principally on works conceived autonomously. On the theoretical side, Alain's magnificent conception of a system of fine arts centered on celebrations of public order (1926) was without influence: he had many readers and admirers, but no followers. The idea of a *Gesamtkunstwerk* itself is a sentimental fiction, relating to a way of social life that is not ours and perhaps was never anyone's. The spectacles that unite us in large numbers are (if we leave out the notional unifications effected behind the drapes by popular television programs) sports events, royal weddings, rock or folk festivals, and so on, which evoke in their publics a conscious participation in spectatorship. No work of art conceived in the terms of a modern aesthetic (and that includes Wagnerian music dramas) can do that, because such works call for concentration on what is being performed, not on the shared condition of spectatorship—those who discuss the work they are watching are rightly shushed by their neighbors in the darkened and silenced auditorium.

It follows from what we have just said that the question whether dance might ever take the central and organizing position in such a work of total theater is a question no one was really interested to ask. But suppose that Adam Smith's three "sister arts" of music, poetry, and dance—which Wagner likened to the Three Graces who are never to let go of each other's hands—were indeed to be brought together in a single work of paramount significance: which of the three would call the tune and lead the dance? Surely Hegel and Aristotle and all the rest were right: it could only be the script, the verbal articulation of the meaning. Batteux had indeed argued to the contrary: the three arts of music, poetry, and dance, he said, should be united in a single work, but one of them (any one of them) should predominate: "If it is dance that is throwing the party, music ought not to shine to its disadvantage, but should merely lend a helping hand, to give a more precise point to its movement and character," and the same used to be true of poetry in the old days, when "one danced to the singing voice as one nowadays dances to an instrument" (Batteux 1746, 376, my translation). But he seems not to have thought the matter through: in Tudor's ballet *Dark Elegies*, danced to the accompaniment of Mahler's song cycle *Kindertotenlieder*, it is hard to see how the explicit text can be reduced to an emphasis on a meaning inherent in a sequence of danced movements conceived independently of it.

Wherever there is a script, the script provides the explicit basis of organization, even if it is not in the text that the main interest lies. But suppose that, as in many operas, the poetic value of the script is exhausted in providing that basis: music can then provide the organizing principle, for an essential of musical form is its ability to build and resolve tensions, and music can be or incorporate song. A work that is primarily music can draw poetry into itself, and its flow of impulse can be expressed in the bodily movements of dance. But I, for one, have no idea of what a dance would be like that could from its own resources dominate the forms of poetry and music at once.

Dance in a Wagnerian *Gesamtkunstwerk* seems likely to be structurally trivial, however theatrically important or (like Salome's Dance of the Seven Veils) dramatically focal. If, however, the emphasis on structure and unity is abandoned and the continuity of pure theatricality is left as the dominant value, the importance of dance remains equivocal, for the scope of the theatrical includes comedy routines, acrobatics and juggling, stage effects of all kinds, no less than anything we could reasonably call dance—such things are called "dance" only when and insofar as they appear in a context institutionally identified as that of dance. In short, ballet as an alternative *Gesamtkunstwerk* seems unlikely to provide the rationale for dance theory as such, because the more comprehensive the work, the less likely it seems that dance will form an element within it that is at once autonomous and dominant.

A more specific reason for the evanescence of the artistic influence of the Russian ballet is its dependence on the person of Diaghilev. It was an impresario's art: that is, an art held together by external pressures. Diaghilev's genius for inspiring, persuading, and combining lay in the force of his personality rather than in any artistic vision. His famous and inspired injunction to Cocteau, "Étonne moi," at once reveals his ability to say the right animating word to the right artist at the right time and suggests the failure of his ballet to effect any inner transformation. Buckle's biography makes it quite clear that the enormous impact of the Ballet Russe's first seasons came from dancing of a vigor and precision unknown in Europe, in the service of the extravagant exoticism of Fokine, Bakst, and Stravinsky. But the effect could not be sustained: Fokine's original genius, expressed in "the ballet of local colour, the evocation of past periods and distant lands," exhausted itself (Buckle 1979, 182–184), and there was no center of choreographic conviction by which the enterprise could be held together.

The lack of a choreographic center was not, indeed, accidental, nor can it be reduced to Diaghilev's egoism or his propensity for making choreographers out of his personal favorites. It was the whole point of the *Gesamtkunstwerk* as such that the origin of the ballet could be anything or anyone's and that all talents were simultaneously engaged. The center was not style but the technique of the Russian dancers. Diaghilev did have at his disposal a series of innovative and distinctive dance makers: Fokine, Nijinsky, Massine, Nijinska, Balanchine. But, as in Wagner's Bayreuth, the enterprise depended on a single impresario/genius. It did not arise out of a communal theater, such as Wagner dreamed of, nor did it find one. The Russian Ballet lacked a public meaning, as opposed to a public impact. It may well be, as Buckle suggests, that some of the ballets of Diaghilev's last years are among his finest; but the initial thrill, which enabled him to enlist the most exciting talents in all the arts and stimulate them to work at their best, did not return. No doubt it is true that Balanchine, Diaghilev's last choreographer, was also his best and that Balanchine's best work was done later, in America in collaboration with Stravinsky. But it is obvious to everyone that, after all, it is only ballet, and there is nothing about it to suggest that it might bring to focus the artistic consciousness of its age.

When all is said, though, the failure of Diaghilev's ballet to effect a lasting change in the climate of aesthetics can be overstated. One can argue that Diaghilev made ballet for the first time a European art: hitherto sustained here and there by an itinerant succession of French and Italian masters and dancers, after Diaghilev it became a permanent presence, ubiquitous in Western civilization, with an established possibility of significance—if not at the level of achievement, then at the level of promise.

1.342 *The Elusiveness of Recent Dance*

Classical ballet has a stable technique and is more or less familiar to everyone. It is therefore available for reference in aesthetics: as with other arts, readers may in fact not know what one is talking about, but they will not feel that they have a right to their ignorance. What ballet lacks is rather a recognized position of high seriousness: in the public mind, including that part of the public most in earnest and best informed about the arts, it has long connoted frivolity, reaction, and conspicuous waste, and its institutions and customs of presentation and promotion are still such as to strengthen rather than to cancel this connotation. And it has no anchor to any other source of cultural vitality. It has to be enjoyed and esteemed for its own sake, in pure aestheticism; and, though we may say that that is the condition to which all art aspires, it is a perilous condition. Ballet has nothing to justify it but sheer eloquent beauty. And beauty is not enough. Even if beauty is what art exists for, beauty cannot afford a specific justification for any one art form, since it may be achieved in any medium that admits of the elaboration of differentiations.[53] It will sustain a practice for practitioners and public, until a gust blows the balloon of appreciation elsewhere. But it gives the philosopher nothing specific to justify or explain.

The artistic seriousness that ballet has mostly seemed to lack has been found, for almost a century, in the alternative tradition of artistic dance, a dispersed series of revolutions and counter-revolutions that has rejected or bypassed the vocabulary and discipline of ballet and draws instead on this or that practice of eurhythmics, self-expression, gymnastics, exoticism, or other source or mode of organizing and articulating systems of body movement. The resulting exploration of the artistic possibilities open to dance as such affords the basis for a serious philosophical reflection that it is only beginning to receive. Meanwhile, it may be claimed that at the hands of Balanchine the traditional art of ballet dance has been reborn within this context of earnestness as the art of pure dance that it always potentially was. Just as relief from the burden of representationalism has disentangled from extraneous tasks the pure art that painting always really was, so relief from storytelling has set ballet (to the accompaniment, often, of musical masterpieces independently composed) free to be the art of dance that it never managed to be before. But without the heroic example of modern dance, one doubts whether this could have been achieved: the eyes to perceive it as well as the power to sustain it could not be supplied from within the ballet tradition itself.

The real problem today, then, is why philosophical aesthetics has not met the challenge of this new art, as it has met the challenge of the new art of cinema. The answer most often given is that its practice is uncertainly familiar (§1.23). And one reason alleged for that is that its technique is unstable.

Lincoln Kirstein has contended that no alternative system has managed to work out a "grammar of movement whose end is legible virtuosity," such as could be developed and transmitted to other choreographers and dancers in the way that the resources of ballet have been built up over the centuries. Modern dance studios, he says, depend on the charisma and the body habits of "isolated artists with vivid personalities," whose personal

---

[53] In Sparshott 1982 I insisted repeatedly that "anything can be beautiful" and was well trounced by reviewers who (understandably) did not read to the end. Beauty can be found in anything, but finding it may require a special effort and a disregard of one's normal habits of attention. Similarly here, beauty can be achieved in any medium that can sustain elaborate differentiation, but not all such media can sustain it easily, and to learn such differentiation calls for much experience. An art form can be justified by its beauty in the sense that it may have such a workable medium, and the relevant habits of discrimination may be in place—but in no other sense.

style may be imparted to their immediate students and by them to their own students, but thereafter loses identity (Kirstein 1970, 4).

Let us suppose that Kirstein is right. What, if anything, follows for the artistic identity and seriousness of postballetic dance and for its availability to writers on aesthetics? At worst, it looks as if there is nothing for the aesthetician to take hold of in any such dance, beyond the very fact of the special relation between body and temperament on the one hand and style on the other. But there is that, and it is of great interest as a very special manifestation of a phenomenon universal in art: the way in which artists' personal experiences and endowments are transformed into the material for their art. But then we can go a step further and say that the sort of dance that Kirstein describes is the art in which this very diversity of incommunicable manner is the common ground of the art; for Kirstein does not seem to be denying that such dance is authentically dance.

Kirstein's contrast between the impersonal virtuosity of ballet technique and the subjectivity of studio manners is an example of a sort of critique that has come from various quarters in at least three versions. Caryl Brahms, like other European commentators of the 1930s, contrasted the subjectivity and emotivism of modern dance with the objectivity of ballet:

> The greater part of the dancing literature of the Central European school is of transitory material in the form of a personal record of mood or emotion devised by the interpreter. Most of these mood chronicles, being entirely personal and arbitrary, are evanescent. The choreographical approach is subjective and not—as in Ballet Russe—objective. (Brahms 1936, 62–63)

Similarly, Adrian Stokes said that Wigman "tells her pupils to dance the way they feel" (Stokes 1934, 119). Well, so she may have done, but what she writes for her readers is something very different: "the dance becomes understandable only when it respects and preserves *its meaning relative to* the natural movement-language of man" (Wigman 1963, 10; my emphasis). Wigman writes of developing a dance technique for "the new, free-style dance" and of entering on "the most fascinating expedition existing for a dancer: to discover his own body and its metamorphosis from body into instrument" (Wigman 1975, 52). She does also say (and this may explain Stokes's remark) that, although not everyone can be a dance artist, everyone can "profitably engage in dancing and thereby articulate stifled, half-formed emotions" (Wigman 1975, 53). But this clearly upholds the distinction between artistically controlled dance and mere emoting.

Kirstein's dictum takes account of the point just made. His contrast is between two sorts of technique: those worked out impersonally over the centuries, and those developed ad hoc out of the physical and psychological quirks of their inventors. The latter are unstable because they have no source of unity other than the compresence of their elements in the leader's psyche.[54] But in this form the critique is open to the rejoiner that what is praised in ballet is what is condemned in all other arts as academicism: that what is indispensable to art is personal style, the artists's own integrated way of handling thematicized aspects of the art in question. If that view is accepted, artistic dance becomes once more an object of special interest to the student of aesthetics, because the relation between skill and expression (cf. Sparshott 1982, 48–55) seems to be problematic in it in special ways.

The supposed fact that modern dance techniques are subjective and evanescent has presented a different aspect to dancers subjected to them. What to the originator of the technique, Martha Graham or whomever, was a liberation of artistic potentialities must be oppression to anyone else obliged to dance under them. Submission to the impersonal rigors of ballet technique involves no personal capitulation; forcing oneself into a mold made by Martha Graham to fit herself is crippling. As quoted and represented by Sally Banes (1983), the members of Judson Dance Theater in the early 1960s were united in reacting against what they felt as the domination of the giants of modern dance. Albert Reid, for instance, is quoted as saying (in an interview):

My theory of modern dance was that you had certain strong, central figures like Merce [Cunningham] or Paul Taylor, who had their own way of doing something and everybody formed around them and tried to emulate them as best they could. . . . I thought of modern dance as being personalities and idiosyncracies, with everyone but the leaders trying to fall into those idiosyncracies. Whereas ballet is a tradition that no one person is big enough to overwhelm. (Banes 1983, 203)

A dual reaction against the diverse constraints of ballet (impersonal but highly specialized and perhaps academic) and of modern dance (personal and temperamentally specialized) plainly calls for generalization, the de-

[54] The instability of modern dance techniques seems rather overstated, inferred from their "subjective" character rather than observed. Martha Graham's technique, itself evolved from extant technical resources, became a sort of lingua franca (see for instance Murray 1979, 22)—ubiquitous, if not universal. "What makes her so influential," says John Percival (1980, 54), "is that from her experience over the years she evolved a technique that could be codified and taught by progressive exercises in the same way as classical ballet." Don McDonagh complains that Graham's teaching was disseminated at Bennington summer schools (1934 to 1938 and after) to physical training instructors, who took every little movement and made a dance of it, without artistic purpose (McDonagh 1973, 110ff.) The horrible truth of this was borne in on me at a baton twirlers' competition in British Columbia in 1980, at which one corps' ensemble piece was made up entirely of Graham-style movements: the girls sprawled on the floor in angular poses expressive of loss, anguish, and despair, twirling their batons vigorously in their free hands.

mand for a dance discipline that will be artistically stringent but not restricted to any corporeal or mental configuration or to any specific level of technical skill. On my reading of Banes's account, what emerged from Robert Dunn's choreography class as the basis of Judson Theater practice was the idea of a dance task: to begin from the specification of a thing to be done or a way of doing something and then to do something that complies with the specification and can be *justified as dance*—either by giving a reason in dance terms for each decision that was made or simply by having what was done actually accepted as serious dance. The essential point, which went without saying, was that, although one had no preconceived notion of what was dance or what could become dance, one justified one's practice either as a dancer or (if one was not a dancer) in a way acceptable to dancers. And the working definition of a dancer was that one had invested oneself in dancing, by the energy of one's commitment to the Judson collective if in no other way.

The fact that the artistic dance that arose in opposition to ballet could be described from various points of view as subjective does not mean that "modern dance" is merely a name for a variety of abortive manners. In American practice, the centrality of Denishawn and the American adaptors of Delsarte, notably Genevieve Stebbins, is becoming more familiar through the work of such writers as Shelton. "When Delsarte taught that gesture was the mirror of inner emotional states, he established an axiom of American modern dance," she concludes (Shelton 1981, 128). But what he taught was not the practice of emoting: it was the development of an entire body language. And his endeavors were merely part of a diverse and sustained interest in the principles of human movement, which has a history of its own; ballet is perhaps singular in the extent to which it was immune to the social pressures involved.

I will not attempt to present a history of artistic dance in this century: the partial histories available to me do not form any acceptable synthesis. But my present topic of the ways in which such dance resists or invites the attentions of philosophical aesthetics calls for some differentiation. We may perhaps crudely distinguish, against the continuing background both of ballet and of the styles and routines of commercial theater that do not as such enter into art history, five phases. First come the expressivist individuals, typified by Isadora Duncan. Then come the makers of expressivist systems, typified by Graham and Wigman, who combine the subjectivity we have mentioned with the development of styles and techniques that can be systematically taught. Then, in reaction, comes Merce Cunningham and anyone like him, rejecting style and expression as generating a set of preferred movements and ways of combining movement, and substituting for it a method of making movements into dances. Then, in the fourth phase, come the postmodernists of the 1960s, repudiating such methods in their turn and substituting for them the idea of dance in terms of maximum generality: art conceived as dance relationships, as movement in space, as point of view, or as governing ideology, in such a way that, in principle, art occurs at the boundary where dance is manifested as what could not have been dance before. And, fifth, our present condition, in which, as in the other arts, we seem to be in a steady-state eclecticism, in which versions of past traditions survive amicably side by side and mingle, and "avant-garde" almost becomes an affectionate name for one historical style among the rest.

The fifth of these phases presents the philosopher with no evident challenge or opportunity. But what of the fourth? It is in this phase that the systematic attempt to test the confines of dance is found and with this phase that slogans like "anything can be dance" are associated. And it is of the analogous phase in all arts that Arthur Danto (1981) has said that art in fact becomes philosophy.

An apparent difficulty here is that this fourth phase is one in which the procedures and problems of dance become merged in those of the artistic avant-garde at large, so that specific reference to dance adds nothing. Banes suggests that the significance of the Judson Dance Theater was precisely that it was integral to "pop" art and other evanescent revolutionary modes in their Greenwich Village manifestation—was, in a way, central to them, because the human body in movement with accoutrements in a lit space is universal, common, and neutrally available for art as such (Banes 1983). But this means that dance as such reverts to the "matrix" position assigned to it in some eighteenth-century speculations.

Meanwhile, the fact that the art of dance is calling itself into question is nothing new: it was implicit in the work of the preceding generation, notably Cunningham. What seemed to be new was the testing of limits. Only, limits of what? Only the testing would show. It is not surprising that the moment of this phase was so brief: it was a transitory and tentative movement out of which would have to come this or that self-discovery of dance.

In general, vanguard theories of art cannot sustain aesthetic treatments of particular arts or groups of arts but must relate generically to art as such. Specifically, the aesthetic theory according to which anything can be dance is the same as that whereby anything can be music or anything can be painting. There are only slight differences in the rhetoric, and there need be none in the phenomena. The difference is institutional. If I do something in Judson Church, it is dance; if I do the same thing in a concert hall, it is music; if a photograph of me doing it is displayed in the Museum of Modern Art, it is painting. And if that is the only difference, it is trivial. More importantly, it is parasitic. Assigning such practices to specific arts relies on expectations and significances transferred from traditional forms. If someone stands no particular how on a stage and we are told it is dance, we understand what we are told only by contrasting what we see with what we might have expected to see: the more specific possibilities of dance that the dancer must be taken to be, as it were, undancing. If what the dancer does is to have the meaning of a dance, it must be a meaning that other dances have earned by being more specifically and overtly meaningful *as dances*. To see featureless activity as dance, we must have learned to see things as dances by seeing examples that have a distinctive and recognizable character. In one much-mentioned dance in 1957, about which we will have a lot to say later (§5.4216), it is alleged that Paul Taylor simply stood still from the time the curtain rose to the time it fell. In a performance of John Cage's *4'33"* a musician (David Tudor, or someone) does nothing for an indeterminate time. How could we know that Taylor is dancing and Tudor is performing music? Only because the circumstances of presentation invite us to whet our eyes for Taylor and our ears for Tudor. And we must know how to look, and how to listen.

Within the general context of art, particular performances and works are assigned to this or that art, not because of their inherent qualities, but because of their institutional context. But that context can take effect only if it generates a distinctive way of thinking about and relating to whatever is presented in it. To treat something not inherently dancelike as dance must be to scan it for dance characteristics, dance interest, and dance values; and such scanning must, on the hypothesis, be possible even when there is nothing special in the object to evoke or reward it. Dance must then be a system of meanings such as can sustain or be sustained by patterns of attention and scanning. Music is what is listened to musically, not what has musical quality: Cage's *4'33"* is not great music, but it is music and represents a great discovery about music. Paul Taylor's epoch-making dance, had it taken place as the legend has it, would have exemplified the same capital discovery in the realm of dance. Virtually all actual music is designed to reward musical attention, and virtually all dance is designed to reward dance attention; and the reward in each case is so immediate that one is tempted to think that the attitude has no separate existence. But it has. And the relevance of this to our concerns is this: if there were no more to the arts of dance than the occurrence of a variety of dances, identified as dance behavior by their occurrence in a "dance" context, there might indeed be no real place for a theory of dance aesthetics that goes beyond the general aesthetics applicable to all arts. But a system of meanings that sustains an identifiable dance interest is necessarily not only susceptible to theoretical articulation but in need of such articulation.

"Anything can be dance." That is not the same as saying that everything *is* dance. If everything were dance, the fact that any particular phenomenon was dance could not be very interesting. If anything *can be* dance, the interest would lie in the conditions in which the possibility was realized, the potentiality fulfilled. The realization and fulfillment presumably represent in each case some sort of challenge: in the difficulty of meeting the challenge and being sure that it has been met, in the criteria of success (or of responsibility) in meeting the challenge the interest of dance *as dance* would lie. These are eminently issues of the sort in which philosophers have professionally interested themselves. A dance practice that essentially raises such issues is a practice that specifically challenges philosophy. But, as we said before, the challenge will be sustained only to the extent that the sense in which anything can be dance is interestingly different, raises different issues, from the sense in which "anything can be" painting, or music, or poetry, or any other named art.

The slogan "anything can be dance" is deeply ambiguous because the conditions might be of two kinds. They might be conditions under which any phenomenon could be seen or understood as dance or legitimately claimed to be dance; or they might be conditions under which any material (within a given range) could be fashioned into dance—as if one had said "anything can be danced."

Not all conditions of the former sort are equally interesting. Anything is dance if I say so, or if anyone says so, or if the performer says so—it is hard to make much out of such claims, even if one adds some such rider as "in the name of the dance world" (cf. Dickie 1974). Things get more interesting when the condition is acceptance by a dance group or culturally dominant group or some other collective sufficient to sustain a practical or critical continuity, because presumably the consensus of such a collective must be achieved and not merely conceded, and the grounds of the consensus, even if they cannot be put into words, must be practically effective.

In the student movement of the late 1960s, Murray Louis remarks, "Discipline and training were too difficult, too boring, and besides, they were taught by people over forty. The young looked for and followed any banner that proclaimed this cause, and what better banner in dance than 'Any movement is dance'? Had they looked more carefully or listened more intelligently, they would have realized that slogan should have read 'Any movement *can* be danced' " (Louis 1980, 121). Well, there were some students like that, but there were others who found the training boring only because its difficulties were of the wrong kind: they wanted to work very hard at doing their own thing. Could one make a serious challenge out of *experiencing* whatever one was doing as dance? Perhaps not; but it was the middle ground between facile self-expression and mindless conformism that many of them were as anxious to explore as the earnest boundary-stretchers of the previous generation.

Making a challenge out of the thesis that "anything can be danced" is one way in which Merce Cunningham has represented his own practice:

> I started with the idea that first of all any kind of movement could be dancing. I didn't express it that way at the time, but I thought that any kind of movement could be used as dance movement, that there was no limit in that sense. Then I went on to the idea that each dance should be different. That is, what you find for each dance as movement should be different from what you had used in previous dances. (Cunningham 1985, 39)

But the challenge thus described is, in a way, that of cramming an unwieldy foot into a glass slipper. The repertory of movement chosen for the dance has to be molded into something that can be choreographed and performed by someone who is unmistakably a dancer in a quite classical sense. "You have to get the idea that movement comes from something, not from something expressive but from some momentum or energy, and it has to be clear in order for the next movement to happen" (Cunningham 1985, 68). You have to "make it difficult for yourself," "make the movement awkward for yourself, as though you didn't know how to do it" (Cunningham 1985, 127). But, though a certain sort of personal style is thus avoided—the "idea of somebody whom everyone was supposed to look like or be like" that he saw as dominating the "modern dance" of the 1940s (Cunningham 1985, 65)—it is essentially only the limitation to a restricted repertory of movement that is repudiated; a method of dance making remains that, as we saw, seemed as constraining to some of the Judson Theater group as the regimes of Graham or Holm.

What happens to "anything can be danced," as a challenge for serious dancers, when such canons (of continuity, for example) as Cunningham retains are rejected? As we saw, the criteria become those of acceptability or defensibility in the eyes and mind of some individual or group that succeeds in establishing and retaining its authority. But when is a boundary stretched, and when is it crossed? In its short history, says Banes, the Judson Dance Theater had "enlivened the calcifying dance scene by amplifying the definitions of dance to embrace art, film, music, and movement of every sort"; but when they moved to Gramercy Art Theater "several of them refer to their own works or the works of others as Happenings or theater pieces. It is as if in their fascination with the theater space as a theater they forsook dancing" (Banes 1983, 164). What is the difference? We are offered no explanation. It can't just be that the artists choose a different word to designate their pieces, for "[Philip] Corner thought of his Judson performances as musical compositions, not as dances" (Banes 1983, 151), but Banes describes them as dances and offers no hint that they were perceived in a different way from the other dances. Presumably the difference was this: within the dance series in the church, whatever was presented was thought of within the practical context of dancing by performers, audiences, and critics; comparisons were predominantly with the entirety of artistic dance practice as that was being extended but never abandoned by the Judson group. When they went to the Gramercy Art Theater the spell was broken, the pressure of the operative context of dance practice was compromised.

The present discussion began by considering the contention that current artistic dance other than ballet was ungraspable and hence offered no opportunity for systematic philosophical consideration. We took as our text Lincoln Kirstein's contrast between the impersonal balletic grammar of movement, of which the end was legible virtuosity, and the mere codifications of temperament and mannerisms that deprived the rest of the dance world of any coherence. Nothing we have seen, however, supports this contention. In fact, Kirstein's "legible virtuosity" could be represented as a special case of an end common, in one form or another, to all or most artistic dance, which might be termed the clarification of motion. The testing of the boundaries of dance, which cannot easily be seen in these terms, can be seen as exploring the implications of the ideal itself and proceeds in effect by seeking analogies, and extensions, and antitheses to such practices without losing vital relationship to them.

The elusiveness of current artistic dance, then, is illusory. Practice and principles may be diverse, but dance is not conceptually scattered. Yet, given the practice of neglect and the absence of a strong tradition in dance aesthetics, the question remains open whether and how far there is a place for a special aesthetics of dance that is more than the application of general aesthetic theory to a particular field.

1.4 *Conclusion*

The entirety of this chapter shows that dance, both as one of the traditional fine arts and as an art in today's world, is profoundly problematic. In the days when the honorific canon of the fine arts was being formulated, dance, despite its accepted role in genteel education and its occasional ceremonial and sacerdotal importance, suffered from having no evident teachable content, no iconography that could enter into ideological education.

The problematic character of dance as an art is obviously no reason for philosophers of art to neglect it. On the contrary, it is itself a direct challenge to philosophy. Given that the position of dance as an art on a par with other arts is nowadays accepted without question, the less amenable dance seems to treatment as one of the accepted arts, the more central the very concept of dance becomes to the philosophy of dance, which thus derives both content and urgency from the reasons for its neglect. In fact, this chapter on the reasons for the neglect of dance has necessarily contributed to the philosophy of dance. Each such reason is a thesis in the history of the aesthetics of dance or in substantive aesthetics and makes or implies claims about the kinds and meanings of dance and dances. A synthesis of such claims already amounts to a loose sort of theory of dance. If some of the theses are untrue, then their contradictories must be true and can be combined to form an alternative and perhaps a better theory. And the fact that these mistakes (and not other mistakes) had been made would itself be of some interest.

Philosophy, like all other disciplines, admits a gap between its professions and its practice. Every science has a field, a range of problems for which it admits responsibility and over which it claims jurisdiction. But at any given time the attention of its practitioners will be concentrated on only small areas within that field. These are the areas one learned about at school and so has a good start in, or which it is easy to study with the most readily available techniques, or in which new methods promise rich or easy results, or in which fashion promises respectability. It's like fishing: one fishes where one has already caught fish, or where one's father took one to fish, or where one's tackle enables one to fish, or where one can reach in a short drive from home, or where everyone fishes because everyone knows it's the place to fish—none of which are necessarily the places where there are most fish to be caught. These tendencies of practice are not only inevitable but, in a world in which time and energy are severely limited, entirely proper; and philosophers share them. We write on what we have been taught about, or reply to what was said in the journals, or ape the preoccupations of the big names of the moment. A general practice of ignoring dance can thus be expected to sustain itself, even if there is no good reason for it, until some new factor generates the opposite practice, which will then sustain itself in turn. On this view, what is significant is not so much that philosophers pay little heed to the dance as that we have begun to notice that we do.

CHAPTER 2

~ ~ ~ ~ ~ ~ ~ ~ ~ ~ ~ ~ ~ ~ ~ ~ ~ ~ ~

Dance as Metaphor:
World as Dance

WE SAW in the preceding chapter that the French court ballet, the only dance form that has ever been central to official culture in Europe, relied for much of its meaning on cosmic symbolism, the dancing bodies figuring emblematically as heavenly bodies. And we noted and approved Hegel's contention that no dance could be justified as dance by its being symbolic in this sense, in that the dance movements themselves would be more interesting than the stereotyped meanings they were supposed to convey. But it would be wrong to leave the matter there. Hegel's censure rests on his theory of the fine arts, a theory which, for all its imaginative and synthesizing power, can carry no conviction in an age suspicious of all preemptive maps of the intellectual landscape.

The symbolism of the court ballet was no isolated phenomenon; the analogy between danced order and cosmic order has a long and distinguished history that no account of dance theory can ignore, because it is an important and large part of what has been thought about dance even if it has not been thought critically. Imagery and rhetoric are an important aspect of the nexus of behavior of which dance forms a part. What is not thought critically may none the less be thought seriously and felt deeply. Nor is the analogy between earthly ceremony and heavenly decorum confined to our own cultural tradition. It is widespread if not universal among those cultures and civilizations in which there is any ceremonious behavior at all.

Hegel's objections are not, in any case, decisive. What is at stake is not a method of analyzing or criticizing specific dance movements, a theory of technical criticism. It is rather the assertion of a general analogy between human and natural ordering principles. It starts from the imputation to the heavens and to large-scale or prevalent natural processes of rhythmic, purposeful, intelligent and intelligible (though not necessarily simply describable), beautiful, and repeatable movements such as some dances aspire to.

This imputation gives a sort of resonance to dance, and imparts validity to general dance values—values that Hegel so casually dismisses with such words as "graceful" and "pleasing." This general validation of dance would matter even if it contributed nothing to the differential appreciation of specific dances and choreographical methods. Such considerations are clearly important to our sense of who we are in the world and what world we are in, and the perennial task of philosophy is the clarification and rectification of that sense.

It is to be presumed that everyone's sense of the general meaning of dance and of danced ritual coincides with their sense of the world's order. In fact, this coincidence must hold, at some level. If one really thought of the world's order otherwise, it would be that other order that was embodied in one's dancing. What one means by order provides the profoundest categories of one's understanding. This does not of course mean that any random individual's dancing is a key either to that individual's world view or to that of the culture at large; what it means is that a way of dancing that passes current conveys a sense of order, and that a world view expresses a sense of order, and that one's sense of order must at a deep level be unified. The alternative is alienation. For instance, if we are intellectually convinced that contemporary subatomic physics provides the best clue we have to the way the world is ordered, and that way bears no relation to anything we can express in our dancing, that means that the world as we understand it is not a world in which we can live, that theory and practice have fallen apart; and that is what is meant by alienation.

It must be this feeling that the principles of ballet movement fail to answer to our sense of the way the world is that accounted for the rage that ballet once aroused in artistically high-minded people. The mere association with absolutism would account for its rejection, but not for the anger. People could hardly have felt that ballet threatened them; the feeling must have been that it *violated* them.[1]

---

[1] The ponderously didactic narrator of Hugh Hood's novel *The Scenic Art* (1984) tells us that at a dinner party "I seized the opportunity to remark how much I hated and despised the classical ballet, that it was the flower of that most repellent of societies, late Czarist Russia, . . . that the whole tradition was alien and offensive to our lives. I then stated that the greatest dancer of the century was unquestionably Fred Astaire, and that any honest person who had ever seen him perform would at once acknowledge this.
Gasps and horrified silences" (p. 217).
On the face of it, this is very odd indeed. How could seeing one dancer one time assure one that he was superior to innumerable other dancers one had never seen—to Spessivtseva, for instance, or to Earl Tucker? And why should anyone be horrified by the praise of Astaire and the dispraise of ballet, surely neither novel nor unusual at this date? But the context of the scene and of the novel as a whole show that Astaire is taken as exemplifying an ideal of

The present chapter does three things. First, it relates something about the ways in which the metaphor of cosmic order as a dance was developed. Second, it presents an example of an elaborated ideology of court ballet. Third, it says something of a more recent, somewhat rhapsodic, affirmation of the metaphor.

2.1 *Plato and Lucian on Two Ways of Dancing*

We have already remarked that the Greeks, whose writings formed a common background for modern discussions of dance as of most other topics, had two words for dance. The relations between them are not simple. Plato's word is *choreia* (the abstract noun) or *choros* (the performers, or the activity); Lucian's word is *orchesis*. Homer seems to use both words generically for any kind of dance, and in Greek tragedy the *orchestra* (the *orchesis*-place) is the place where the *choros* performs. This suggests that the words were interchangeable. But in later texts *choreia*, as is suggested by the words we derive from it, tends to mean choral dances such as are associated with public religious festivals. When the aged patriarch Cadmus and the aged seer Tiresias in Euripides' play *The Bacchae* go to dance in honor of Dionysus, the verb they use is *choreuein*: they propose to join the dancing procession, and the movements they envisage are foot-stamping and head-tossing rather than leaping and pirouetting. But Lucian's word, *orchesis*, becomes associated with gymnastic display; its civic associations are with war, not with religion, and the movements it emphasizes are vertical rather than horizontal.

The associations of *orchesis* are with professionalism and display, whereas *choreia* is associated with sacred duty in which, as Euripides makes Tiresias emphasize, all must take part.[2] It is the fact that Lucian's *orchesis* was for show but Plato's *choreia* was not that explains why only the former would really be available to provide warrant for theater dance.

The relation between the two Greek concepts remains elusive. If the indications of Liddell and Scott's Lexicon are to be relied on, *orchesis* is a much rarer word than *choreia* and built less centrally into the language—further, then, from the central concerns of Hellenic civilization. Insofar as there is a clear distinction between the words, it seems to be that *orchesis* stands for the movements of dancing, whatever they may be, and *choreia*

---

comic and nonchalant elegance within a society gracelessly constructed, establishing a vital relationship that the ballet (of which the narrator shows no sort of knowledge) never essays.

[2] Ménéstrier (1682, 17–18), writing twelve years after Louis XIV had ceased to take part in ballets, disagrees: he holds that dance is unsuitable for doctors, magistrates, the old, and councillors, but not for young princes.

for the figures of the dance in which one participates and for the act of participating in them.[3]

Lucian is certainly not aware of any such split between the two concepts of dance. He sets a far-reaching precedent for later writers when he derives metaphysical warrant for dancing from the round dance that the heavens lead at the bidding of Eros, and historical warrant from the war dances and other communal jubilations of ancient races. The former of these would be *choreia* and the latter *orchesis*, if the contrast can be made in that way; but what is to be underwritten by both of them is the specific practice of pantomime, an art form whose origins Lucian himself places at the time of Augustus and which shares nothing with its respectable forebears beyond the name *orchesis* and the grace and agility it exacts from its performers.[4]

Lucian's *Peri Orcheseos* is by no means a profound or penetrating work, and some have suspected that it was intended as a sort of extended lampoon. The claim has, none the less, been made that it is the immediate source of all the sixteenth-century theories relating dance to the music of the spheres—certainly, they all cite it (McGowan 1963, 20). James Miller, however, in his brilliant and exhaustive study of early uses of the trope,

[3] Some such distinction as this seems to be present in Plotinus, *Enneads* IV 4.33, when he says that the dance of the cosmos is a manifold dance figure (*poikile choreia*) but a single dancing (*mia orchesis*). But the sequel in this complex passage suggests that the reference is rather to the intricacy of the movements comprised by a single dance.

The content of the Plotinus passage just mentioned is not directly relevant here, but it would be a shame not to say something about it. Plotinus is arguing that the universe is a single living thing of which all other living things are vital parts, related to it not mechanically but with an immediate sympathy, just as an animal is aware of its fingertips without being aware of the intermediate parts of the body. Then he compares this immediate sympathy with the way a dancer moves. "For in dances among us, too, it goes without saying that what is related externally to the dance, the pipes and the songs and the rest of the adjuncts, changes variously in accordance with each of the movements as they contribute to the purpose of the dance. But one could not speak in the same way of the parts of the one who is contributing the dancing, necessarily corresponding to each figure as the limbs of the body follow along with it, bending, one contracting and one relaxing, one exerting itself and the other receiving some respite as the figuration changes.

"The will of the dancer is looking toward something different; he undergoes certain things conforming with the dance and is subservient to the dance and contributes to the perfection of the whole, so that the dance connoisseur would say how for this sort of figuration he chooses to raise this particular limb of the body and contract that, and a third is concealed, and a fourth assumes a lowered position—whereas the dancer does not specifically decide in advance to do this, but in the dance of the entire body this particular part, as it follows the dance through, assumes the necessary position." This is because, like any animal, "he is not operating on another, but is himself all that takes place."

[4] James Miller (1979, 243 n. 6 and elsewhere) argues, on the basis of Lucian's usage, that the word *orchesis* actually *means* pantomime. Dubos, we saw, argued the same. But the position is quite untenable, as regards the use of the word in general; and Lucian himself uses the word for other sorts of dancing as well.

attributes its homiletic and theoretic force to the fact that the vastly more prestigious Plato applied the word *choreia* to the planetary motions in his *Timaeus*, 40A–D (Miller 1986, ch. 1), even though Plato did not there develop the metaphor. At the same time, Miller emphasizes that the trope was already a commonplace in Greek literature (Sophocles, *Antigone* 1146; Euripides, *Ion* 1074–1089, *Electra* 468–469, etc.).

In dance, as Plato conceives it, the dancers make manifest to themselves and to others an order that is in the first instance psychosomatic, then ethical, then civic, and ultimately cosmic. And the attribution of cosmic significance remains a constant. In the epoch-making *Ballet comique de la reine* of 1581, Beaujoyeulx "constantly reverts to the relationship between the harmony of heaven and that which it is desired to restore on earth: the music of the gilded vault not only represents but attracts 'la vraye harmonie du ciel, de laquelle toutes les choses qui sont en estre sont conservées et maintenues [the true harmony of the heavens, whereby all existing things are preserved and maintained]' (p. 5v)" (McGowan 1963, 46; my translation). In much the same way, in the Confucian *Record of Music*, the order of ceremony duplicates and may sustain the order of empire and the order of heaven (Legge 1885). It seems odd that the Western tradition of the philosophy of art, so long hospitable to analogous ethical interpretations of modes in music (with their metaphysical extension all the way up to the music of the spheres) and to the secular transforms of such interpretation, has never incorporated analogous thinking about the dance.

Why did Platonic authority and long-established custom not outweigh such opposing prejudices in this field as were reviewed in the last chapter? The intellectual's mistrust of the body could not have sufficed, since it did not dissuade Plato, who suffered from the prejudice as much as anyone. The social disrepute of the theater was not enough, since we have seen that the highest developments of Western dance have been associated with the highest social classes, sometimes as patrons and sometimes as participants. Nor can the theological prejudice stemming from associations between traditional dances and pagan religion have been decisive.[5] For one thing, the link is weak: though the symbolism of the maypole seems obvious, the habit of indiscriminately ascribing traditional practices to "fertility rites" (such as are imagined in Stravinsky's *Rite of Spring*) was a passing phase, at its peak about 1900 and really past its prime by about 1920. For another

---

[5] Alfred Sendrey writes that "David's ecstatic dance before the ark of the Covenant is akin to that of the sacrificial dance of the Egyptian Pharaohs," and adds that the Hebrews adopted virtually all Egyptian dance practices except for "the frankly acrobatic abuses" (Sendrey 1974, 222). Sendrey does not explain to the reader how he knows this (and much else of what he says), but I know of no grounds for dissent; and, if he is right, the Hebrews' ostentatious rejection of the religious practices of their neighbors seems not to have extended to dance.

thing, ecclesiastical anathemas have seldom succeeded in suppressing practices that have general support, and have least of all been supported by the intelligentsia, whose attitudes are most directly relevant here.

A more promising explanation might seem to be that the Platonic ideology requires an underlying belief in a unified cosmic order, and that no such belief nowadays prevails. Just as the Hegelian scheme might relegate dance to a prelinguistic and hence prehuman phase of evolution, so a positivistic world view might relegate the Platonic ideology (and hence, by association, dance itself as a meaningful form of activity) to the "barbarism and superstition" of a personalized monotheism. But that explanation will hardly suffice. It may be that in an age of official secularism and nominalism no practice can be given substantial support by appealing to its alleged inner meaning, but such meanings can retain effective life in the form of superstition or as psychological or sociological datum. The world of art is the world of imagination, and justifications in the arts can belong to the world of "as if."

One could certainly argue that the danced ceremonies that figure the cosmos are a nonaesthetic form of dance—what we would classify as ethnic dance and contrast with the theater dance that alone presents an aesthetic spectacle. But the argument is suspect. Plato at least postulates for his *choreia* a nonarbitrary formal beauty that would be of a higher aesthetic order than mere display; and its appeal for participants might be to the visual imagination, the sense for geometry, that animates (though not usually under that name) so much Platonic thought. And we shall see later that the question of where and how we distinguish within dance between what is and is not artistic or aesthetic is not a simple one. But one thing we can say is that the analogy between music and dance is in this respect misleading. Whatever the importance of the supposed relation between musical form and cosmic or ethical order, the artificial status of musical materials guaranteed that there would always be a substantive autonomous body of music theory that would extend to popular as well as to elaborated forms, so that the discrediting of the old myths left music firmly in its intellectual place even if (as often happened) its right to that place was challenged. But no such necessary theoretical substratum guarantees the place of dance, in which the stringencies of the body in its proportions and rhythms preempt the place that basic theory might have held.

It is not always easy to be certain what historical complex of ideas will shed the most useful or reliable light on a given practice or theory. But the way of thinking that associates artistic practices with a mathematically articulated cosmic order seems to fit the rationalism of Descartes and Leibniz, and more especially the a priori encyclopedism of men like Athanasius

Kircher.[6] Wilhelm Dilthey argued that this tradition died out because no common ground could be found between it and the notion of aesthetic experience, which by the late eighteenth century had become the common factor in all the traditions of aesthetic thought that were destined to survive.[7] That sounds right, but it is not the whole story. In music, for instance, the aestheticizing tendency was far from killing off rationalist modes of thought, which survive and flourish to this day alongside their more modish supplanters, partly because (as we said above) there is solid reason for them. What we are trying to discover is why the lineage in dance should have been more decisively broken.

The dance that invokes cosmic order relies on the patterns the dancers trace out on the floor—their orbits, as it were—much as rationalist architecture relies more on the geometrical integration of a building's ground plan than on its façade or even on its vaulting. But that presupposes a large, open dancing space with the spectators, if any, looking down from above. It is the sort of dance one does in a gymnasium or a dining hall, not in a theater. When dance is removed to a stage behind a proscenium arch, this planometric organization becomes virtually imperceptible, if not impossible. *Orchesis* is encouraged to displace *choreia*: dance viewed from its own level will emphasize the vertical, if it wants to be seen.

It can be argued that planometric patterns prevailed in court ballets and in the dances at the Athenian Dionysia that are Plato's exemplars, because the dancers, being amateurs, could not manage elaborate steps and acrobatic feats—in other words, *choreia* would be *orchesis* if it could. Obviously there is a lot of truth in that: a large part of Platonic and Aristotelian thought on these matters, as well as Confucian thought, is simple opposition to professionalism (in part snobbish, in part envious, in part truly humane). But the advocates of amateurism certainly made a virtue of this necessity.

If planometric dance, and hence any dance that figures the cosmos, is ruled out by the introduction of stage and proscenium arch, we are left asking why theater and dance should have retreated behind a proscenium. It cannot be dismissed as a mere matter of technique. Some of the factors are explored by Frances Yates (1969). The change goes with a philosophical transition from classical to baroque forms of thought, from emphasis

---

[6] According to one of Descartes' associates, God is "[t]he supreme master of the ballet danced by all creatures, in steps and movements so well regulated that they enrapture wise and learned men and bring contentment to the angels and to all the saints" (Mersenne 1636, 159).

[7] For the nature of this transformation in underlying attitude, see Gadamer (1960, pt. 1). But one must not forget that the contrast between rational beauty and aesthetic attractiveness had long been a commonplace (see above Chapter 1, note 34).

on reality to emphasis on appearance, and specifically with a vogue for stage illusions that called for machinery that an open hall could not accommodate. And it may not be merely fanciful to suggest that such a transition was inevitable once the Copernican revolution had been inwardly accepted and it had been realized that celestial mechanics was incompatible with the geocentric world in which our gravitating bodies anchor us.[8]

It would be wrong to associate cosmological thinking about dance and about the fine arts generally too closely with seventeenth-century rationalism. Such thinking was rife in the Renaissance, but it did not originate then. It was common in the Middle Ages as well, and its medieval form is a Christianizing adaptation of Neoplatonic or Neopythagorean cosmology. What the Renaissance does is effect a second transformation, humanizing and in a sense de-Christianizing the classical originals. A strong theological (and even a specifically Christian) element may remain; what is banished is the anticlassical aspect. Once more, the better-known analogy of music theory may help. In that field, a mathematizing analogy between the three "musics" of cosmic order, moral order, and audible order, familiar from Boethius, antedates the Christian Middle Ages and survives the Renaissance. But something new appears in the early centuries of Christianity, coexists with the Boethian system, and does not survive into the Renaissance: the thesis that an alternative music, an ecstatic howl (*ululatus*) is most proper to a Deity who is in the first instance not a rationalizing Demiurge but a voluntaristic I AM. One might then wonder why a cosmic theory of dance, analogous to the Boethian theory of music, does not undergo a comparable decontamination, demystification, and rejuvenation in the Renaissance, instead of remaining at the level of a literary trope.

The real reason lies in the history of mathematics. The general theory of proportion in Greek mathematics was actually a generalization of music theory, a way of handling theoretically the methods of tuning stringed instruments. The analogy between musical order and other forms of order is

---

[8] The French court ballet resisted this change, and its theatrical housing remained archaic (see Prunières 1914, 150ff.). The end of any court ballet, according to Prunières, was to provide for the final *grand ballet*, a formal dance in which only the nobility took part; for years after an elevated stage had been introduced, the courtiers would descend a ramp into the body of the hall for this formal finale. But eventually, in the *Ballet de la prospérité des armes de France* of 1641, the court does not descend into the hall but remains on stage where it appears in a sort of apotheosis, celebrating the separateness of the monarchy; and in the new Palais Cardinal the stage, behind a proscenium, had neither stairs nor ramp down to the body of the hall (McGowan 1963, 188–190). But, if the demise of systematically planometric dance in modern times is easy to account for, its origin remains obscure. According to McGowan (1963, 36), the first reference to it is in Colonna's *Hypnerotomachia* of 1499. Beaujoyeulx used it for the *grand ballet* of the *Ballet comique de la reine*, emphasizing in his libretto its geometric character.

thus ineradicable. Nothing of the sort is true of dance. No aspect of dance practice required (or admitted) mathematical treatment, much less generated mathematical methods. Analogy between danced order and other orders had to depend on felt congruence. When the feeling failed, the analogy descended to the level of literary ornament. But that works both ways: at the level of felt congruence, the cosmic analogy with dance has something that music lacks. The harmony of the spheres is merely an analogy, or a postulate, but the heavenly bodies visibly do move.

In music, it is really only the worshipers who ululate. That aspect of the Divine Beauty which is an undifferentiated brightness, the light by which we see light, has no counterpart in music. There is nothing heavenly in white sound. It could be that God as Dancer, unlike God as Musician (who is not so much a performer as a tuner of instruments), acquires in the first Christian centuries a nonclassical significance that resists demystifying. If the cosmic dance signifies not (as in the Aristotelian version) that Love is making the world go round but that Divine Grace is dancing, the dance in question is not likely to be one that can be captured for Art by being secularized.[9] And to make God Himself a dancer rather than a choreographer risks blasphemy—blasphemy of the sort represented by the Avocat Général's speech in the Parlement on the accession of Louis XV: "Sire, your Majesty's seat represents the throne of the living God to us. The orders of the realm render homage and respect to yourself as to a visible divinity" (quoted in Erlanger 1970, 25). Considering the popularity of the comparison between the French king and the sun, the Avocat might be alluding here to a famous passage in which Julian "the Apostate," a fourth-century disciple of the Neoplatonist Iamblichus, represented the planets as dancing round the sun as their king:

> The god came forth from an eternal cause. . . . And then he assigned as his own station the mid-heavens, in order that from all sides he may bestow equal blessings on the gods who came forth by his agency and in company with him; and that he may guide the seven spheres in the heavens and the eighth sphere also, yes and as I believe the ninth creation too, namely our world which revolves for ever in a continuous cycle of birth and death. For it is evident that the planets, as they dance around him [*peri auton choreuontes*], preserve as the measure of their motion a harmony between this god and their own movements such as I shall now describe. (*Hymn to King Sun* 146 B–D, translation adapted from Wright 1913, 399–401)

[9] Georg Lukács (1963) takes it to be the chief mission of art as such to rescue artlike practices from magic and religion and to establish their significance as secular.

The phrase "Divine Grace is dancing," used in the preceding paragraph, is from a second-century text, the *Acts of John*, and has been popularized by Gustav Holst's setting it as *The Hymn of Jesus*. Jesus makes the Apostles form a ring around him and hold hands, and they circle around him answering "Amen" as he sings, "Glory to Thee, Father. . . . Glory to Thee, Word; Glory to Thee, Grace. Grace is dancing. I wish to pipe; dance, all of you."—"Amen!"—. . . ."The twelfth number dances above."—"Amen!"— "Dancing belongs to the sum of things."—"Amen!"—"He who does not dance does not know what is happening."—"Amen!"—. . . ."He who dances knows what I am doing, that his is this human suffering that I am going to suffer."[10]

This "Hymn of Jesus" was denounced at the Second Council of Nicaea as "ludicrous" and "blasphemous" (Miller 1986, 101), and the *Acts of John* was never accepted as canonical. Jesus, we note, is not one of the actual dancers (though he presumably is part of the metaphorical dance of Grace that is necessary to knowledge). He remains at the center, piping and giving the time to his disciples, whom he commands to dance, in reminiscence of the implied rebuke of Matthew 11:17, "We have piped unto you, and ye have not danced." The image of motion imparted from a still center is Neoplatonic; we find it, for instance, in Damascius: "Time is the cause of the dancing [*choreuein*] of the radiance of form around the intelligible One. This radiance passes thence downwards into the world of the senses and keeps the continuity of the dance [*choreias*] in order."[11]

But the image of the divine dancer is not confined to the emanationism of deviant Christian Neoplatonists. It is found in some rabbinical descriptions, as summarized by Alfred Sendrey:

> In the Time to Come, the heavenly hosts will be the dancers, and the people of the righteous the onlookers. The righteous follow rapturously the motions of the divine leader of the dance, point to Him with their fingers, and compare it with the dance of young maidens. In the general rejoicing, they surround the leader of the dance and perform a round-dance around him. (Tal. Yev., *Megillah* ii.3 [73b] etc.; Sendrey 1974, 237)

But is this a metaphor or a vision?

Miller (1979, 440) tells us that the reason the church, when it got its act together, rejected all attempts to justify dancing as a part of its liturgy, or indeed as a fit activity for Christians in any circumstances, was to keep the

---

[10] The word for dance is the *choreia*-word *choreuein* throughout, except when Jesus says "Dance, all of you" (*orchesasthe pantes*), where he uses an *orchesis*-word.

[11] Cited by Simplicius in his commentary on Aristotle's *Physics*, 775.12–16, translated by Miller (1986, 488).

eucharist free from contamination by pagan rituals, such as the Eleusinian mysteries, in which dancing had a prominent place. Dancing, unlike song, had specifically polytheistic connotations. We expressed reservations above as to the reliability of this argument. But, in any case, it proved easy to justify the condemnation of dancing while preserving the imagery of the cosmic dance.[12] For that dance, in Neoplatonic terms, is simply the movement of the order of nature, and what it warrants is not the specific order of literal dance but whatever order is most orderly. And a Christian should identify that order with the moral order of a good life directed toward God. Thus, Ambrose can defuse (and mystify) the rebuke implied in "We piped for you, but ye would not dance" by saying that the word "dance" is not to be taken literally: it must mean the leading of a diligent and active life, and the raising of the soul to spiritual grace (Ambrose, *De Poenitentia* II 42–44, *PL* 16 529a-c; cited in Miller 1979, 477). The "leap of faith," as it were. And the prevailing eschatological viewpoint enforces a sharp contrast between the dance of the living body and the spiritual *choros* after death in which the soul joins the choirs of angels, the "single and harmonious choral dance of divine beings" (*miâi kai homologôi tôn hêrôôn choreiâi*) (Pseudo-Dionysius, *Ecclesiastical Hierarchy* III 3 3, cited in Miller 1986, 515).

To dance in honor of the cosmic dance would, on this view, be pointless. It would substitute a trivial and distracting celebration for real participation; and to dance in emulation of the divine dance leader would be blasphemy. From another point of view, Miller sums up the effect of his researches by saying that the idea of the cosmic dance is essentially visual, so that the interpretation of the order that it represents will vary as the idea of "vision" changes. If that is so, it is clear that an order that can literally be danced and thus related to the sense of one's own and others' movements has no privilege; for such a dance, though it must be visually accessible, does not derive its specific value from the modes of its visibility. Making dance a metaphor for cosmic order no more validates dance than calling Achilles a lion promotes big-game conservation.

The story of what the cosmic affinities of dance were taken to be by different sects at different times and places is an intricate one. But, setting aside the more theological aspects of the Neoplatonic imagery we have been glancing at, the dynamics of Neoplatonism reveal another asymmetry between dance and the "sister arts" that may contribute to the explanation of why Plato's arguments about mimesis fail to provide lasting warrant for

---

[12] We must not forget, though, that no Christian condemnation of dance can surmount 2 Samuel 6, in which a woman who despises King David for dancing before the Lord suffers a magical retribution.

the art of dance as they (so strangely) did for the other arts. On a Neoplatonic view, if the cosmic dance is really a dance, involving change, it must be danced on the level of "nature," the most general manifestation of Plotinus' third hypostasis, "soul"—best understood as a sort of force of generalized vitality, productive of change and variety as such. But this level is one lower than that of the Ideas, which belong to the second (noetic) hypostasis. In imitating nature, the "sister arts" point toward that higher level of being, to which we aspire; but the cosmic dance is nature dancing (as it were) downward, and represents the level of being on which we already are. So dance has nothing of intellectual uplift in it and cannot so readily be dignified by Neoplatonic rhetoric.

That is not the end of the matter, of course. In a Christianizing version of Neoplatonism, the noetic realm can be animated and called "angels." But this is a flight of fancy rather than serious cosmology and cannot survive in the humanistic air of the Renaissance. Again, a very simple and stately sort of dance can be taken to symbolize, not nature, but the unmoving dynamic of the Plotinian world as a whole, whereby the One is at rest in itself but the universe is emanated downward from it and returns to it again—the archetypical dance of the Three Graces was sometimes seen as vaguely symbolizing this dynamic. And Miller (1979, 443; cf. Miller 1986, 513–519) tells us that "Dionysius" associates the movements of the bishop at the eucharist with just such a dance: as he moves away from the altar and returns to it again, trailing censer smoke, his movements parallel the *mone, proodos*, and *epistrophe*—the rest, the progress, and the return—of the Neoplatonic cosmology (*Ecclesiastical Hierarchy* III 3 3).

In Hellenistic times, the analogue of *choreia* has to be the circling and epicycling of the heavenly bodies round their still center and the derivative motions choreographed by the sun in its seasonal movements through the zodiac—the unchanging phenomena that the philosophers optimistically hoped to make the focus of a new religion to replace the shenanigans of the Olympians. It is of the planetary motions that Tuccaro would write:

> If one would consider all these things perfectly, one could perhaps recognize that they are justly imitated and represented in the ball. . . . Those fine and varied retreats, advances, and diagonals, so gracefully performed, are the same conjunctions and triangular, tetragonal, even hexagonal oppositions that daily (as it were) relate the planets in their heavenly spheres. (Tuccaro 1599, 36, quoted by McGowan 1963, 36)

Tuccaro here invokes the relations of judicial astrology rather than of physical astronomy. Lucian's rather casual treatment of the analogy had suggested the latter: the underlying image is that of an endless movement caused and regulated by love—love for an object that causes movement but is not itself moved. The standard presentation of this image, if not its origin, is the twelfth book of Aristotle's *Metaphysics*, a treatise that ends with a good question: Is the ordered movement of the world primarily to be attributed to the moving world itself, or to the cause of its movement? Aristotle answers with a military analogy: strategy is the responsibility of the general who sets the soldiers in motion, not of the soldiers themselves.

The choreographer bears prime responsibility for the dance; the dancers are responsible for the dancing of the dance.

2.2 *Sir John at the Court of Gloriana*

According to Miller, as we saw, the typical Neoplatonic interpretation of the cosmological metaphor for dance is visual: the supposed ground plan of a dance is visualized as isomorphic with the schema of whatever the most striking or basic order of the world is taken to be. From this point of view, the metaphor affords no warrant for any actual dance practice, as Hegel's strictures on "symbolic" dance made plain. But we had previously observed that the *choreia*-type dance to which such metaphors are in the first instance applied are originally and essentially dances for participants, and only secondarily for observers, even if (as Plato himself must surely have supposed) the dance works by appealing primarily to the dancer's visual imagination. This leaves the way open for a kind of theory in which the actual quality of the motion as danced should be the bearer of figurative meaning. And then, instead of Hegel's tension between observed grace and imputed significance, we would have a tension between the excitement of moving rhythmically among fellow dancers (surely the attraction of social dancing in most traditional modes) and the awareness of symbolic meaning. As before, there would be no real reason to suppose this theoretical tension to be experienced as such; rather, each component might reinforce the other.

Much richer possibilities for dance as metaphor for abstract order are opened up once we look at the ways in which dances impose order on one's own movements as dancer. Some of these are realized in a remarkable ideological defense of dance—in effect, of court ballet—by the young lawyer John Davies in his poem *Orchestra* (1596). The poem in its entirety seems to be a "naughty" jeu d'esprit typical of the court circles for whom Elizabeth I was "Gloriana." But that would not necessarily deprive it of an undertone of seriousness, as we realize when we reflect that Spenser's sexually titillating *Faerie Queene* is a sort of apotheosis of the same sensibility. Nor do I know how much of Davies's material is original with him, how much is a commonplace of his day, and how much is derived from specific works

95

(though I shall mention an analogue or two that have come my way). I present it at some length because it is important that such an extended apologia for dance was possible.

Davies plainly takes Lucian as a model for his poem as a whole. In both works, a devotee of dance is converting a contemptuous opponent by reciting its lineage, from the first framing of the cosmic order out of a disordered motion of primary particles, through the heavenly dance of the stars in their courses, through the meteorological dance of the waters through earth and clouds, through the mythical, historical, and literary traditions. But whereas Lucian's champions had been a playgoer and a philosopher, Davies substitutes a more equivocal pair: the chaste grass widow Penelope, from the *Odyssey*, is invited to the dance (which she thinks dissolute) by the leader of her suitors and would-be seducers, Antinous. Antinous' intentions are at best ambiguous, and of course in the *Odyssey* he figures as a villain. Davies, as a lawyer in turbulent times, is no doubt covering his rear, and the overall purport of his poem would remain unclear had he not inserted at the end of it an explicitly incomplete and implicitly interminable encomium of that undeniably respectable patron and devotee of the dance, Queen Elizabeth herself.

Antinous begins by urging:

> *Dauncing* (bright Lady) then began to bee,
> When the first seeds whereof the World did spring,
> The fire, ayre, earth, and water—did agree,
> By Loue's persuasion,—Nature's mighty King,—
> To leaue their first disordred combating;
>   And in a daunce such measure to obserue,
>   As all the world their motion should preserue. . . .
>
> This wondrous myracle did Loue deuise,
> For Dauncing is Loue's proper exercise.
>   [17–18][13]

Everything, he explains, dances to the music of the spheres, including the spheres themselves: "their moouings do a Musick frame, / And they themselues still daunce vnto the same" [19]. Penelope very reasonably asks what analogy these natural processes, however dignified and orderly, bear to the "frantick iollitie" [26] to which Antinous is inviting her. His response, convincing or not, is at least relevant and is what makes the poem important to our argument here. He explains how some of the principal dance forms are successive lessons that Love has taught mankind, to civilize their movements and symbolize their aspirations. The round dance [62–64] integrates the basic movements of the human body and is imparted to dis-

---

[13] The numbers in square brackets are stanza numbers.

orderly men as a simple lesson in orderliness, in imitation of the regular movements of the cosmos. We have already encountered this location of dance at a precivilized level of humanity as a pervasive theme in anthropological speculation about dance. Davies is unusual (an advance on later writers) in accepting this connection but systematically going beyond it: "But after these, as men more ciuell grew, / He did more graue and solemn measures frame" [65], namely, the "swift and wandring" galliard corresponding to musical counterpoint [67–68], the capriol symbolizing the soul's aspiration to escape the body, courantoes (Queen Elizabeth's own favorite measure) in which complexity becomes so intricate as to appear chaotic [69], and lavoltas, "the most delightfull kind,"

> A loftie iumping, or a leaping round;
> Where arme in arme two dauncers are entwind
> And whirle themselues with strict embracements bound.
>
> [70]

—Antinous cites as examples of this binary motion the heavenly twins Castor and Pollux, but we may suspect that he has sexual coupling in mind.[14]—"And euer for the persons and the place / He taught most fit and best according grace" [73].

[14] Davies's language is reminiscent of that used by Thomas Elyot in his own allegorization of dance, in words made familiar by T. S. Eliot: "By the association of a man and a woman in daunsinge may be signified matrimonie. . . . In euery daunse of a moste auncient custome, there daunseth to gether a man and a woman, holding eche other by the hande or the arme: whiche betokeneth concorde" (Elyot 1531, 82r-v). John Weaver quotes the same passage from Elyot (1712, 67ff.). The significance of the hand-holding that betokens concord is said to be the conjunction of male and female virtue, part of the idea being the ancient one that concord is possible only between virtuous people, but the more important part being the notion that male and female excellences are complementary, both necessary to full humanity, which is why men and women dance differently in the same dance: "And the meuing of the man wolde be more vehement, of the woman more delicate, and with lasse aduauncing of the body, signifienge the courage & strenthe that oughte to be in a man, and the pleasant sobrenesse that shulde be in a woman. . . . These qualities, in this wise beinge knitte to gether, and signified in the personages of man and woman daunsinge, do expresse or sette out the figure of very nobilitie" (83r-v). Elyot goes into detail about these moral significations, mindful of ancient days when "in euery of the said daunsis, there was a concinnitie of meuing the foote and body, expressing some pleasaunt or profitable affectes or motions of the mynde" (81v).

"The first meuing in euery daunse is called honour, whiche is a reuerent inclination or curtaisie, with a longe deliberation or pause, and is but one motion comprehendinge the tyme of thre other motions or settyng forth of the foot: by that may be signified, that at the begynning of all our actes, we shulde do due honour to god, whiche is the roote of prudence . . ." (85r).

"By the seconde motion, whiche is two in nombre, may be signified celeritie and slownesse"—this is the branle, which typifies "maturitie" (a word which here makes its debut in the English language) (85r).

"The thyrde motion called singles, is of two vnities seperate in pasinge forwarde: by whom

The doctrine this passage implies, and the underlying feeling it expresses, are those of the somewhat later "theory of affect" in music, which makes precisely these dance movements the basis of a musical rhetoric, taking their movements and the associated musical forms to articulate the range of human emotion (as that was speculatively anatomized in the Cartesian theory of the "passions of the soul"). Tuccaro's analogies (cited above) belong to the same world of thought, and I suppose that Davies is here drawing on some common doctrine of which I am ignorant.

Having thus affirmed, as Lucian had neglected to do, that actual dancing can be systematically related to its metaphorical dignifiers, Davies has Antinous return to his encomium on the general principle of dance: "All ceremonious misteries, / All sacred orgies and religious rites . . . / A liuely shape of dauncing seemes to beare" [77]. All the liberal arts partake of the nature of dance, since they set the parts of discourse in order, and even

> Logick leadeth Reason in a daunce . . .
> For with close following and continuance
> One reason doth another so ensue,
> As in conclusion still the daunce is true.
> [94]

Dancing is thus the art of arts. The argument implied is that all arts depend on the articulation of parts within wholes, this articulation being embodied in principles of movement or change prescribing logical and efficient sequences and progressions; that science consists in discovering just such articulations and principles in nature; and that it is in dancing that this natural order is more directly, more lucidly, and more significantly embodied than in any other art:

> Loe this is Dauncing's true nobilitie,
> Dauncing, the child of Musicke and of Loue;
> Dauncing it selfe, both loue and harmony,
> Where all agree, and all in order moue;
> Dauncing, the Art that all Arts doe approue;

---

may be signified prouidence & industrie: whiche after euerye thinge maturely achieued, as before writen, maketh the first pase forwarde in daunsynge" (86v).

"Comunely nexte after singles in daunsinge is a reprinse, whiche is one mouing only, puttynge backe the ryght fote to his felowe: And that may be well called circumspection . . ." (88v).

"A Double in daunsinge is compacte of the nombre of thre, wherby may be noted these thre braunchs of prudence, election, experience, and modestie . . ." (92r).

"And thus I conclude the last parte of daunsinge, whiche diligently beholden, shall appiere to be as well a necessary studie as a noble & vertuouse pastyme, used & continued in such forme as I hiderto haue declared" (94v).

The faire caracter of the World's consent,
The Heau'n's true figure and th'Earth's ornament.
[96]

Penelope dismisses all this as "the tedious praise of that she did despise" [97]. As she had previously questioned the analogy between the supposed cosmic dance and the actual procedures of dancing, so now she questions the analogy between the cosmic principle of "love" and the human passion of love, which, she says, is the source of all evil, "Wit's monster, Reason's canker, Sence's bane" [99]. And, if Antinous' real reason for wanting her to dance with him is to make her more amenable to seduction, she has a point. Antinous has to protest (indirectly) that his intentions are honorable, invoking the long-traditional contrast between idealistic love and sensual desire and reaffirming that "that true Loue which Dauncing did inuent, / Is he that tun'd the World's whole harmony, / And linkt all men in sweet societie" [102]. The true love is directed to beauty and is expressed in graceful and beautiful motion [104–106].[15] Literal dance is simply one special manifestation of this; and love within a community is manifested in concord, which is imaged and reinforced in the intricate dance figures characteristic of ballet:

Concord's true picture shineth in this art,
Where diuers men and women rankèd be,
And euery one doth daunce a seuerall part,
Yet all as one, in measure doe agree,
Obseruing perfect vniformitie;
    All turne together, all together trace,
    And all together honour and embrace.
[110]

Here, as often, "concord" must be taken as principally signifying what the Romans called *concordia ordinum*, that acceptance of a hierarchical social order which Plato had identified as one of the prime virtues of a city. Davies, as a lawyer, would be familiar with the ideology of Roman law;

[15] The immediate allusion here must be to Plato's *Symposium*, in which all love is said to be aspiration for perpetual possession of beauty, realized in all forms of generation—of children, of literature, of laws, or whatever. But Plato's rhetoric is typically centered on permanent entities, not on changes, however graceful; and the underlying thought in this passage is the one expressed more clearly by Aristotle's claim that early thinkers deified Eros to signify "a principle of things which is at the same time the cause of beauty, and that sort of cause from which things acquire movement" (*Metaphysics* A, 984b20ff.). These two versions of the divinity of love are fused in Plotinus' Neoplatonic scheme, wherein contemplation of higher realities gives rise to the generation of lower realities, including the whole moving world of nature. But in Plotinus the "love of beauty" and Eros himself rather lose their identity.

but the idea of hierarchical agreement was itself, as we saw, the animating principle of the archetypal court ballet of France. The thought had been expressed some years before Davies's poem, in an almost embarrassingly explicit form, in Jean Dorat's "Epithalame" (1570):

JOUVENCEAUX:
>   Le monde est faict par discorde accordance:
>   Le Roy craint Dieu, et les Princes le Roy,
>   Qui vont donnans au peuple bas la Loy.
>   Dansons ainsi pour n'avoir discordance.

PUCELLES:
>   L'un doit porter à l'autre obeissance
>   Du plus petit jusques au grant des grans,
>   Sans rompre l'ordre et sans troubler les rangs,
>   Pour danser tous en bonne convenance. . . .

PUCELLES:
>   Nous ne scaurions aller en decadence,
>   Puisque le Roy Charles mène le bal:
>   Comm' un Soleil qui va d'à mont à val,
>   En conduisant d'astres grand'abondance.[16]
>   (McGowan 1963, 21–22)

Antinous' discourse, however, is not so exclusively focused on the image of social concord, and he proceeds to the general affirmation that the beauty and order of dance show the interaction of love and reason:

>   Much more in Dauncing's Art, in Dauncing's grace,
>   Blindness it selfe may Reason's footstep trace;
>   *For of Loue's maze it is the curious plot,*
>   *And of Man's fellowship the true-love knot.*
>   [116]

And with this italicized linking of reason to planometric choreography he ends his encomium. Whether Penelope was convinced by it, and by his assurance that the Queen herself dances all the time, the poet teasingly invites the reader to guess.

---

[16] "Lads: The world is made by discordant concord: / God is feared by the king, and the king by the princes, / who give the law to the common people. / Let us dance, then, to avoid discord.

"Lasses: One should show submission to the other, / from the lowest people to the highest, / without disrupting order and without disturbing rank, / so that all may dance in proper conformity. . . .

"Lasses: We could not become decadent, / so long as King Charles leads the ball: / like a sun, passing from hill to vale, / leading a great multitude of stars."

2.3 *The Dance of Life*

In this chapter we have been looking at a variety of significant relationships that have been alleged to hold between the forms of dance, or the practices of dancing, and important forms of order or ordered movement that have been supposed to prevail in the world. It is not surprising that such relationships should have been detected. Dance movements are those of our own movements to which we have given pattern and interest for their own sakes, so that the patterns we impart and the interest we find can reflect nothing other than aspects of our own ideas of what is beautifully or interestingly arranged—that is, our own ideas of order. Any order that we find interesting in the world, or even are capable of detecting, must obviously conform to those ideas. If new knowledge enlarges or changes our ideas about what counts as significant form, those expansions and changes immediately become available for dancers. It is thus very easy to think of the world as dancing; though we are likely to add that this is only a metaphor, on the grounds that it is only people who literally dance.

If the world is dancing, does this not impart a unique value to actual dancing as the most direct embodiment of that most vital human endowment, the sense of order, and as affording in its diversified practice a repertory of conceivable forms of ordered movement? That has not usually been thought to be the case. In Davies's poem, we saw, Antinous says things that imply it, but the sober and prudent Penelope questions it. The overall forms of natural change do not explain or validate the very precise forms of fashionable dances; the forces of nature do not validate the whole range of human motivation, including evil intentions. In general, Penelope's view prevails in our society: allegorical readings of dance have passed current only in societies and social strata that were both ceremonious and hierarchical. But clearly this restriction need not obtain, and we might expect corresponding analogies to be drawn whenever a distinctive image of cosmic or social order can be identified.

The expectation is not, however, so clearly justified as we have made it seem. If, as the argument supposes, the forms of order embodied in dance are of general interest because they necessarily show our basic feelings about formal significance, the formal principles involved must be exemplified in all art and, to a lesser extent, in all production and praxis. Dance has no privilege, except to the limited extent that it is a universal and spontaneous mode of behavior like speech, rather than a specialized one like sculpture (I suppose everyone at some time molds or whittles something or other; but it is easier to imagine a life spent without either of these activities than a life spent entirely without dancing). Rather than possessing a significance that is both special and universal, dance will be specially meaningful only insofar as the forms symbolized or exemplified are intrinsically or dynamically related to our impulse to set our own bodies, or the bodies of others, in motion.[17] And that, in fact, as we partly saw, is why the analogy with planetary movements had such force in pre-Galilean times: the view then prevailing centered on Aristotle's answer to his own question, What set the heavens in motion?

The argument of this section has assumed that dance in the literal sense of that word is something that people do. But with a small shift of perspective, that might not be the case; we might use the word "dance," *in the first instance*, simply to designate a certain sort of movement, whether it be of waves or of reflected sunlight or of flowers in wind—just those movements of just those things that we do in fact regularly speak of as dancing. The word "dance" would apply to human movements only when and because they were of this sort. And what ground, we may ask, have we for saying that this is not actually the case—that this is not the best short account we can give of how we do actually use our word "dance"? What authorizes us to say that when we speak of humans as dancing we speak "literally" and when we speak of other things as dancing we speak "metaphorically"? And who, in fact, are the "we" who make this decision?

That rhetorical challenge goes too far. There is indeed a test. When we are speaking of the dancing of the light on the waters or the flowers in the breeze, we can add some such phrase as "to speak poetically," or "as it were," or "so to speak" without much absurdity: it would be pedantic and silly, but not unintelligible. (And, in just the same way, we could qualify our use of the word "dance" with regard to human movements that do not actually form part of dances but are perceived as dancelike: "He sparks the torch, and sets a tiny little blue flame and then, it's hard to describe, actually dances the torch and the rod in separate little rhythms over the thin sheet metal. . . . 'That's beautiful,' I say" [Pirsig 1974, 349]. Pirsig says "actually," of course, just to emphasize that he knows the welder is not actually making his tools dance; he is welding, and that is why his response to the narrator's compliment is "One dollar.") But when we are speaking of humans performing a hornpipe, for instance, we cannot intelligibly say that they are dancing "as it were" or add any such qualification: if we do

---

[17] The argument here is essentially that worked out by Langer in 1953, though with a different emphasis and expressed in different terms. Langer's version has it that dance as such symbolizes psychic power. Despite its considerable suggestive force and the importance it derives from being the most extended treatment of dance by any philosopher up to that time, her theory has usually been rejected as far too narrow. And the ideas developed here in fact show why this is the case, though what I have to say in the next chapter about discussions of the "nerve" of practices will suggest that it is not an insuperable objection. We will return to Langer's theory in other contexts, especially §8.21123.

add one, there has to be something special about what is going on to justify it, and unless that specialness is obvious to whomever we are addressing, we will be called on to explain ourselves. The "literal" sense of the word "dance" and its cognates is simply that range of its uses in which such qualifications as "so to speak" are unacceptable.

It is pretty clear that in our society "dance" in its literal sense applies only to human beings and such conceptually humanoid beings as angels (we will have more to say about this whole topic in Chapter 5). But it is not unthinkable that there should be conceptual schemes, current among peoples no less given than ourselves to institutionalized dance practices, in which this did not hold. To such ways of thinking, the thrust of the concept of dance would not go to the human practices in which dance movements were enshrined but to the quality of the movements themselves, whatever it was that moved—or even to a perceived or imputed quality that might be manifested in forms without movement. Robert F. Thompson, in his studies of West African sculpture and dance, holds that this is true in parts of Africa: the Tiv word for dance, *vine*, is applied to many sorts of thing, for instance to the curve of a cutlass. African arts, he says, are not essentially medium-oriented: in considering them, one has to start from the general criteria of artistic performance (Thompson 1974, xii). And this, if true, is important, since not only does dance play a conspicuous part in traditional West African cultures, but (as Thompson shows) the dance traditions and values in question have retained identity and vitality and continue to be a vitalizing influence wherever they have been brought.[18]

[18] Such evidence needs to be handled with caution. Note that Thompson in fact speaks of what the Tiv word for dance is applied to; he does not say that there is a Tiv word *vine* that applies to many sorts of things, some of which are dances. And Thompson is suppressing what he must be aware of—the wide applicability of the English word "dance" that has formed our point of departure here. The depth and magnitude of his contribution to our understanding of African art should not blind us to the possibility that, like many enthusiasts for exotic cultures, he may be insensitive to the subtleties of the one that should be his own. For instance, he writes: "Each time I return to the West from the complexity of this choreographed universe, I am amused by the old-fashioned definitions of the dance in Europe and North America: social grace or theatrical spectacle. . . . For a Western person to comprehend the moral power of danced art in Africa, he must divest his mind of various prejudicial junk and start from the beginning" (Thompson 1974, 152). Well, there is a lot in that, of course; but it does ignore the sort of material, some of it indubitably Western, discussed in this chapter. Like most people who denounce their own traditions, Thompson is in fact appealing to a point of view solidly established and available within those traditions themselves. If he were more sharply aware of and more deeply sensitive to the values already culturally available to him, he could show his readers just how those values differ from (are, perhaps, inferior to) their counterparts elsewhere and thus reassure us that he is not simply projecting onto the African material an alternative Western stereotype.

The sort of generalization of dance quality that we have been consider-ing can, indeed, be carried to a point of absurdity. As we have seen, if dance exemplifies orderliness in general, and whatever can be grasped must be grasped in virtue of its order, we need some special reason for thinking that dance is a more apt metaphor for cosmic order than anything else; and this special reason cannot be merely some specific aspect of it that makes it apt, since innumerable other phenomena might have special qualifications of equal weight. And if, we may now add, we identify dance as essentially "expressive movement" or something of the sort, then we may be tempted by the facts that every vital movement expresses vitality, and every move-ment whatever is easily shown to be in some way expressive of something or other, to make dance a metaphor for movement in general. This meta-phor that represents all movement as dance is, however, as pointless as the metaphor that represented all order as dance. None the less, the temptation is strong, and its delusive strength no doubt accounts for both the imme-diate fame and the subsequent neglect of the best-known English-language book about dance in this century, Havelock Ellis's *The Dance of Life*.[19]

"To dance," says Ellis, "is to take part in the cosmic control of the world" (Ellis 1923, 40). Well, that's very nice. But just how is this participation effective? The answer is that all vital processes are rhythmical, and in all rhythms small cyclic movements are captured by or subordinated to larger ones.[20] But then, "The diversity of the Many is balanced by the stability of the One. That is why life must always be a dance, for that is what a dance is: perpetual slightly varied movements which are yet always held true to the shape of the whole" (p. viii). And this relation between movements is analogous to one between structures. The periodic table of elements shows that the universe is a dance—that is, the subordination of parts to a whole in a unifying rhythm (p. xi)—and, as all the elements may be seen as dif-ferent arrangements of one stuff (Ellis may be thinking of hydrogen, or perhaps he just means "matter"), so all human life may be seen as different formal arrangements of one stuff, namely, art (pp. 34–35). The signifi-cance of dance is, then, that "it is simply an intimate concrete appeal of a general rhythm" . . . "it need not surprise us at all that rhythm, ever tend-

---

[19] Two things account more immediately for its success: first, the prestige of Ellis himself, at that time a heroic symbol of sexual emancipation and advanced thought; and second, the recent discovery of dance as an authentic art (cf. Ellis 1923, 58). The Library of Congress, by the way, catalogues his book under English belles-lettres, not under dance or history or even anthropology.

[20] We have already had occasion to allude to the importance assigned to these part/whole relations by E. H. Gombrich (1979). The more specific point about minor vital rhythms being adapted to larger rhythms is emphasized by Langer (1970). I do not know whether Ellis's book played any part in making these thoughts accessible.

ing to be moulded into a tune, should mark all the physical and spiritual manifestations of life" (p. 37). And such vital rhythms, being dynamic, take precedence over static formal orders, in reality as well as in our experience. Dance is the archetypal and original "art of the person" (that is, involving what one does with oneself and not what one does with materials extraneous to oneself), and arts of the person are naturally prior to the external arts (among which architecture is as basic as dance is among personal arts) (p. 36). There is indeed, then, solid reason for saying that dancing and no other art establishes the form that all human life should take and that all cosmogonic forces exemplify. The metaphor "the dance of life" is far from empty.

The priority of dynamic over static orders, of quality over form, is no necessary part of the argument. We have already seen that one can, from a Plotinian standpoint, equate "dance" with "nature," in the sense of the realization in movement of an order already in some sense choreographed. From this point of view we can equate the dance of life with the dance of Shiva, Lord of the Dance, as he stands in the Ananda tandava pose at Cidambaram, with his foot on the dead, enacting the replacement of the generations. "Does not the Universe bloom forth from inky void when our Lord Siva dances? Is not all organic or inorganic movement but a manifestation of his Cosmic Dance?" (Sathyanarayana 1969, 307). Shiva dances the world process at all levels, which is one of the reasons he needs so many limbs. Among the Dogon of Mali, we find a cosmogonic dance assigned (if our sources are to be trusted) only to the secondary level of ordering:

> The origin of the ritual dance went back to the first days of the world, when the incest of the earth, changed to an ant, had given the jackal possession of the fibre skirt and made him the enemy of God. . . . Dressed as he was in the fibres taken from his mother, the jackal danced and as he danced, he spoke, for the fibres were full of moisture and words. They had in them the first Word revealed by the Nummo to the earth, and it was this water and this Word which made the animal speak.
>
> God's son spoke his dance. His steps left traces in the dust of the terrace which indicated the meaning of his Word. . . . The son of God . . . acted, spoke, and traced out the world and its future. . . . So the first attested dance had been a dance of divination; it had told in the dust the secrets of the Word contained in the fibres worn by the dancer. (Griaule 1948, 186–187)

What is possible for the Dogon, or for traditional Indian thought, or for Neoplatonists under the Roman Empire may not be readily accessible in today's industrialized societies. I feel that I should be impressed or at least moved by what Ellis says. Although most of his book does not put muscle on the bones I have articulated here but offers a mere assortment of packaged lumps of butcher's meat, I still wonder why the argument has so little bite. Others, it seems, share my jaded indifference, since the book is named more often than its content is exploited. Part of the trouble stems from the general form of a key stage in the argument. Given some phenomenon X, one asserts that all X is Y (Y being some emotive appellation of X), for what is Y but Z (Z being some tendentious description of X)? The game is too easy. Effective invocations of "the dance of life" must do something like what Davies tried to do and what Thompson (1974) does for African dances: relate relevant and illuminating descriptions of specific dance phenomena to independently illuminating principles of natural or vital order. And in a culture as pluralistic as ours, the initial descriptions of dance must isolate in some relevantly enlightening way what we shall in the next chapter be calling the "nerve" of dance practice.

In any case, such metaphors as Ellis's can carry no conviction in an alienated world—in a world, that is, in which we do not really feel that our inner dynamics are in tune with the processes that objectively govern our lives. In such a situation, which may well be ours (I do not know how one would acquire the authority to say that it wasn't; and, if one can't be sure it isn't, I suppose it is), serious dance philosophy must deny itself the use of such resources. Dance must be considered existentially: that is, in ways that presuppose no reinforcement from anything outside the individual. One of the reasons philosophers shy away from the philosophy of dance may after all be that claims for cosmic significance of the sorts we have been discussing are too obvious to be shrugged off, but in their combination of large claims with little substance they irritate rather than reward the critical reader.

CHAPTER 3

❧ ❧ ❧ ❧ ❧ ❧ ❧ ❧ ❧ ❧ ❧ ❧ ❧ ❧ ❧ ❧ ❧

Contexts for Dance Theory

CAN THERE be a theory of dance? Some would say no. Theories not only (as said in the introduction) usually arise out of specific problems, they would say, but can only so arise. Words like "art" and "dance" point to areas of life within which specific problems and practices can call for various sorts of theoretical engagement, but do not in themselves constitute an occasion for theorizing or the subject matter for any specific sort of theory.[1]

People who say that are wrong in what they say, though right in what they may intend.[2] They are wrong about art: the concept of art, as we use it today, is not merely theory-laden, it is entirely theory-engendered. Whenever we say "art," what we utter is the aftermath of some strong theoretical commitment, now so thoroughly taken for granted that it has to be teased out by an alert and historically minded hermeneut.[3] That does not hold for the word "dance," which is indigenous to the vernacular. But, even so, there can be a theory of dance. There can be a theory of anything.

Anything whatever can be *named*—obviously, if one can identify it as something, one can tag whatever it is one identifies and fix the same tag to whatever else shares its criteria of identity. Conversely, the use of a name (that is, of a word that by its syntactic use is established as belonging to that sort of word that refers) implies a claim that the sort of thing the name purports to name exists or might exist. Names may pass current for many reasons—we need not know how many. But there must always be some

---

[1] See Tilghman (1984) for a trenchant statement of this position, in Wittgenstein's version of it.

[2] This applies to my younger and sharper but sillier self: I wrote a long book (Sparshott 1963) to establish the fundamental heterogeneity of aesthetic theories and to systematize their relationships. I was right to say that not all aesthetic theories should be construed as attempts to define the word "art"; I failed, through inexperience, to realize the extent to which the word "art" (like the word "dance") was in itself a vehicle of theorizing.

[3] An earlier book (Sparshott 1982) was devoted to exploring these commitments and their origins. The book was not widely understood. At least, most reviewers assumed that the concept of art was unproblematic and treated the book as a prolix attempt to determine which familiar theory about this well-known object was the correct one.

reason, even if we judge it a bad reason: currency is not a random event but a state that is maintained by constant repetition. Consequently, there can be a theory of anything that can be named: the rationale of the currency of the name. Hence, since anything can be named, there can be a theory of anything. At the very least, there can be an explanation of what the use of the name apparently claims and an account of what (in terms of the culture of its users, if not in absolute terms) fits the word for currency. Given any word, then, there can be a theory about the word's implicit claims, about the conditions of its use, about the justification of those claims, and thus about the sort of warrant its use has. (If one happens to have a theory of naming, one's theory will of course include a consideration of whether the word is really a name.)

A general theory of dance is possible because the word "dance" is current and purports to be a name—in fact, certainly is a name, in the sense that there certainly are dances and we certainly call them dances, even if the word "dance" does not always function in a namelike way.

Dance theory, as thus established, immediately acquires density from the fact that there are other languages in which our word "dance" has no single equivalent (see §8.461). Apparently, people who dance can get by without the thought that they are dancing; and the same people will find it odd that we take ourselves to be doing something we call "dancing" when we are doing whatever it is they say we are doing.

The theory of dance directly generated by the sort of thing we have been talking about is, of course, a second-order theory, a metatheory: a theory about what we mean when we say "dance" and so forth. But wherever dance is done self-consciously, in the sense that dancers generally think of what they are doing as "dancing" (however many other things they may also think of it as), such a second-order theory is also a first-order theory—just as, in the well-known theory of Arthur Danto (1981) and others, what artists do in today's art world is radically affected by the fact that they think of it as *art*, so that a theory of the concept of art is directly a theory about artistic practice.

The foregoing considerations are pretty obvious, and inescapable. They are worth stating because they are often, in effect, denied. Some philosophers have confused the issue by alleging that a philosopher must either accept the facts of the way the word is used as ultimate, not to be thought about (and, presumably, not to be stated in general terms—though that is not openly asserted) and certainly not to be explained, or else stand committed to "Platonism," that is, to postulating the existence of an eternal "essence" that the word in question stands for. But neither alternative makes much sense, and one does not have to choose either of them. What is called for is work of the sort that philosophers have long being doing, sometimes under the heading of "conceptual analysis" or "logical grammar."

There can certainly, then, be a theory of dance, in advance of any specific problem or controversy. But, since there can be a theory of anything, and the reasons we have relied on, except for the ones derived from translatability, are entirely general in scope, the fact that there can be a theory of dance does not entail that such a theory will or should be developed. We do not have or want theories about everything. Theories of dance will presumably not be worked out until they are called for. In what sort of situation would a theory of dance be called for? We shall have to see.

3.1 Dance as an Art

We remarked in Chapter 1 how odd it was that dance used to be excluded from the fine arts. Obviously, dance is an art; and if there are such things as fine arts, it seems equally obvious that dance must be one of the fine arts. But what is it that is obvious? What is it that makes an art a fine art? And what is an art, anyway? What are we saying about dance when we say that it is "an art"?

I have elsewhere dealt at great length with the concept of an art (Sparshott 1982, pt. 1). Very roughly, the general notion of an art is that of an organization of knowledge and skill to bring about some end that (in the context of the art, at least) is agreed to be good. This is the old and broad sense of the word in which we still speak of the "art" of medicine, for instance, which is an art aimed at securing health and longevity in human beings. "The arts" in the sense of the fine arts are the subdivision of these to which dance belongs; and nowadays when we talk about "the arts," it is only the fine arts we mean. But for the time being it is the more general notion we need to think about. In a personal context, an art that a person practices is a specific area within that person's activities on which effort and self-improvement are concentrated. In a social context, an art comprises a stock of skill and knowledge that a society cultivates, perfects, preserves, and transmits, with appropriate institutions of instruction and quality control. In the context of philosophy, "art" in this sense used to be a key term in epistemology and still ought to be. The sort of organization, systematic development, and refinement of methodology that an art represents is a halfway house between mere behavioral adaptation and abstract science: it is the reduction of experience to principles. The really significant thing about arts was thought to be that one could teach them in a way that went beyond just showing people what to do in the situation they were in—although, as our mention of Lincoln Kirstein's comparison between ballet and modern dance (§1.342) reminds us, arts as defined actually differ greatly in the extent to which and the manner in which they can be codified and taught as techniques.

Wherever there is an art, there are practitioners of the art ("artists"); there is a public for the art, people who are interested in the outcome, who may or may not be different individuals from the practitioners; and, if the art is well established, there are institutions, more or less clearly defined, devoted to the maintenance, transmission, practice, and promotion of the art. There are also various sets of standards, more or less well integrated, by which performance in the art is judged. Standards current among practitioners may not coincide with those enshrined in formal institutions (which may, for instance, be more conservative, or in these days more radical, than most practitioners); and standards current among practitioners are quite unlikely to be those prevailing among the public (even if practitioners and public are the same people, notoriously, they will judge their performance differently, depending on which viewpoint they are taking at a given moment). Standards may also differ by being more or less technical as opposed to result-oriented: it is common for great artists to achieve their results by methods that teachers forbid to their students, and the faulty technique is not held to be redeemed by the fact that in this instance it works.

The individuation of arts is necessarily a nebulous matter: there is no way of telling what is an art as opposed to a division of an art or a group of arts, or where the boundaries between arts come. (Denis Diderot, quite rightly, said we should really think of arts as foci around which skills cluster; see Sparshott 1982, 44.) The reason for this is that the forces that unite and separate skills are disparate, because of what we pointed out in the previous paragraph.

One factor is the transferability of skills. If a particular cluster of skills is closely integrated and hard to learn, then the exercise of those skills for whatever purpose will tend to constitute a single art. Alternatively, an integrated demand from a public (however generated) will tend to sustain an art, the art of supplying what is thus perceived as a single need. Or unity may be imposed institutionally, even from the outside, as by a granting agency: if a powerful and wealthy foundation devotes funds to what it calls "the decorative arts" or builds a museum for them, then "the decorative arts" as the foundation defines them will become a significant grouping of activities even if no one had ever thought of them in that way before; if UNESCO organizes its activities around the concept "dance," governments of countries in whose vernacular no such word exists will start to adopt the international vocabulary and habits of thought.[4] Or again, a con-

---

[4] The international language of diplomacy implies standards of conduct and codification of

silience of standards (creativity or originality, for instance) may act as an independent force to bring whatever is suitably judged by those standards into the orbit of a single "art." Since these different pressures tend to group practices and practitioners in different ways, anyone who tries to give a simple and uncontroversial account of what a given art (such as dance) is will almost certainly fail in a way that cannot be remedied by making equally straightforward distinctions among different kinds of dance (or whatever). Things simply are not simple in that sort of way.

Despite the foregoing, it is immediately obvious to anyone that dance is an art. There is an easily recognizable dance world with its own language and its own institutions, with its immensely complicated but quite clear internal articulation. The relations of different forms of dance training, different shapes of dance career, form a structured diversity absolutely typical of arts—typical, too, in the way that the art of dance interacts with the profession of dance and is the active core of the dance "world."

We have, however, a problem. We defined an art as an organization of knowledge and skills, or something like that. In any case, the idea was that of an organization; and we rather took it for granted, perhaps, that one could speak of "organization" only if some sort of functioning unity obtained. But what counts as a functioning unity? The sort of artistic unity we sketched for dance depended on an overlap and interchange of training and technique among practitioners of various sorts of dance who recognize what they share even when they differ. But that applies only within a single cultural community of people who have a standing expectation of interaction at a social level. What about the relation between, say, American dance and Korean dance? Each has a developed tradition with its own organization, and the national structures are analogous; but the dances have no common vocabulary of steps and figures and no common repertory of basic comportments, and Korea and America are different countries with different customs and languages. Should we not say that we have here two separate but closely analogous arts of dance? Only at the highest administrative level is there an interchange, based on the fact that international bureaucracies, like airports and Hilton hotels, are everywhere the same: ministries of culture, dance festivals, mass medium transmission, as well as

---

practice: to explain to each other what they are doing, nations must speak as if they shared a common view of human life and observed common standards of behavior, however widely these may diverge from their indigenous way of looking at things. Similarly, there is an international language of cultural organization and distribution. If an African nation sends some of its performers abroad, it will send them as a "dance group" (and as "performers"), whether that is what they are to themselves or not; and corresponding expectations will be aroused and must be met. That is not to say that these international understandings are in any way superior to indigenous modes of thought and practice; it is only to say that, in the international arena, international modes of speech and thought pass current.

UNESCO, impose a certain portability and exchangeability that make mutual recognition of the analogies between the two art traditions a permanent potentiality that can be realized at any time.[5]

It is just possible to speak of an art of dance that Korea and America share, because the sophisticated practitioners of each recognize the common element in what they are doing, can compare problems and techniques, enroll in each others' classes, exchange videotapes, and so on. When each group learns what the other is doing, it becomes evident to each that both are doing different versions of the same thing, in conditions of practice that impose on each of them structures and pressures that, for all the immense local differences, impinge in a way that is recognizably the same. But what about a tribal African tradition, in which the political-economic superstructure has not imposed the "international style" of organization and conceptualization? Judith Hanna writes:

> Whether a ballet series at Lincoln Center in New York City or a performance for a New Yam Festival among the Ubakala in Nigeria, dance may fulfill the same kinds of function for dancers and observers: it may provide group identity, create self-esteem for the dancer and those identifying with the dancer's reference group, reflect on social concerns, be autotelic, or generate income. There are more similarities than differences to be found in Balanchine's students' devotion to a dance form, intragroup competition, and cooperation and that of an Ubakala's youth group. (Hanna 1979, 201–202)

But she also reminds us of the "basic anthropological axiom" that "significance resides in the whole" (p. 13). In this case, then, the shaping features of dance are closely similar, and the cultural settings are analogous. We shall see later that Hanna feels able to produce a definition of dance without specific cultural content; and we could conjecture that the construction of the human body and the needs of social order will likely generate universals of human culture—"food," "language," "dance"—in terms of which cross-cultural contrasts can be safely drawn. But in this case there is no overlap in terms of practitioners, public, institutions, or technical standards (cf. Thompson 1974). And we have seen that Hanna doubts that a dance tradition can properly be studied in abstraction from the entirety of its culture. How, then, can we say that both societies practice the same art of dance? Their respective practices are joined only by analogy, without any integration at all.

We have, it seems, a choice. Either we allow such structural analogies

---

[5] I rely here on a presentation to the Dance Department of York University by Professor Judy Van Zile of the University of Hawaii, based on her research in Korea. The interpretation of her remarks is my own.

and definitional identities as Hanna speaks of to displace integration of thought and action as sufficient to establish "an art"; or we refuse to divorce arts from unified traditions of thoughtful practice and use some other term for such scattered entities as dance appears to be. It is, of course, a matter of indifference what *words* we use; but the internal dynamic of an art, as we initially conceived it, is so important a factor in human culture that it seems better, when we are speaking strictly, to use some different word for unities based only on perceived likeness. I shall call them "practices," and I will say a little about that notion shortly.

Usually, the sort of problem I have been discussing does not trouble us. When we talk about dance, we are talking about a complex of behavior, with its associated attitudes and ways of talking that we experience from the inside as an aspect of the lives we live. We need no information on such things because, in the first place, the texture of our lives makes us authorities, and, in the second place, our closeness to the phenomena makes it as inappropriate as it is impossible to be *informed* about them. In the analogous case of language, for instance, we do of course need linguistics to explain and structure the phenomena, but it is even more a matter of course that our language is what we are and that we know it as well as anyone possibly could (cf. Cavell 1976). The case of dancing is not so clear as that of language: it is not true that everyone is a dancer in quite the same way that everyone is a native speaker of some language. But the analogy holds to this extent: the notion that dance is something alien to us, about which our knowledge is essentially hearsay, can find no purchase on our minds. Accordingly, just as we all talk about language without regard for the real possibility that we could be refuted by evidence from languages of which we know nothing, so we talk about dance without opening ourselves to the possibility that there could be dances utterly alien to us. There can only be languages and dances that we have not learned; time, effort, and a little aptitude are all we need. We are, as it were, in possession of their domains, though we have not beaten their bounds.

Dance is in every way a typical art (in the general sense we outlined). It is also a typical fine art, despite Hegel. But what that comes to is a question we shall postpone until we have said something about "practices" and about the circumstances in which the "philosophy" of an art or of a practice might come to be given serious attention.

3.2 *Dance as a Practice*

Whatever an art is, it is a sort of practice of which the artists are practitioners. If dance is an art, or if it is many arts, or if some dance pertains to an art and some does not, dance is still a practice in that dancing is something people do, and know they do, and are known to do. The notion of a "practice," as I am using it here, is broad and vague.[6] I will try to explain. Anything that can be habitually done, taken up and engaged in, is a practice. Smoking is a practice, and so is smoking cigars. We ask "Do you smoke?" and "Do you smoke cigars?" and are immediately understood. This immediate understanding is not itself conclusive, though. I understand you equally well if you say "Do you mind if I smoke?" though minding is not a practice—it is not a sort of activity one can take up. At one extreme, jogging, playing the oboe, and shopping on Saturday are practices if they are regularly engaged in by anyone, involving as they do a recognizability of repetition and regularity together with a possibility (but not a necessity) of wide variation. At the other extreme, law and other professions, music and other arts, are practices: one takes them up and engages in them, though the actions they comprise are so various that it may be unidiomatic to refer to them as "things one does."

Shall we say that a practice is, at least, something one engages in under the concept of the practice itself? On this view, I could not be said to engage in the practice of dancing unless I knew what dancing was, knew what it was to dance, and knew I was dancing whenever I danced. After all, we may say, people may have unconscious habits, but they can hardly be said to engage in unconscious practices. Yet to insist in this way that my practices must be elements in or divisions of my doing that correspond to the ways I think of my activity seems too narrow—we will have more to say about that issue shortly. And may not unreflective people be said to engage in practices they never name to themselves at all when they participate unselfconsciously (though consciously and intelligently) in activities institutionalized and conceptually recognized in the society they belong to and to which the practice belongs? Perhaps. But animals, at least, cannot engage in practices, however regularly and habitually they perform a set of actions, insofar as we judge that they are not conceptually equipped to reflect on the structuring of what they do.

Practice in general is the sort of doing that there can be a theory about. One speaks of the "theory and practice" of any activity from smoking to accountancy. Theory and practice are correlative: a practice is the correlate of the theory of just that practice. Belching after a meal, however regularly one does it, is not a practice if one does so every time as a response to a

---

[6] The notion of a "practice" unfolded here is not meant to coincide precisely with any prevailing usage. In particular, it is not meant to coincide with the special sense of the term recently assigned to the word by MacIntyre (1981), which makes it involve his own romanticized version of Aristotelianism. His definition is very rich and fraught; mine is as meager as I can make it.

correspondingly regular stimulus. It becomes a practice when belchers (one or more of them) have some idea of what they are doing when they belch, of when it is that they do so, and of why it is just then that they do it. And the theory of the practice, the thought that delimits and illuminates it, may extend, especially in the more elaborately structured cases, to include one or more explicit theories *about* the practice. It is some or all of these theories about a practice that will amount to the "philosophy" of the practice.

If there can be a practice only where there is at least a rudimentary theory of the practice (namely, a reflective identification of it and a structure of intention sufficiently developed to make it possible to engage in the practice *on purpose*), does it follow that theory precedes practice? In a sense, yes. One cannot be said to engage in the practice of belching after meals until one has a theory of belching. But that does not disqualify the notion that practice usually precedes theory: specifiable practices arise out of an inarticulate mass of activity that the practitioners articulate by discovering what it is that they are doing and only then figuring out the rationale of what they have already begun to do. One responds or a society responds to a stimulus; and, insofar as the response is intelligent and (therefore) intelligible, it may generate rationales that determine practices. Even within developed practices, theory is likely to follow the ways of doing things already initiated by practitioners. For instance, the earliest philosophers did not know they were philosophers; they simply did what they did. It took some time for what they were doing to become recognizable as a specific sort of thing that people could do—that is, as a practice. A given theory may precede the corresponding practice in time, in the sense that someone first gets the idea of doing something and people only then start doing it. It may precede its practice in definition, in that the practice may be such that one could not conceive of engaging in it without knowing just what it was to engage in it (one cannot play backgammon at all without knowing a fair sample of the rules of backgammon). It may precede it "essentially," in the sense that the practice is just the practice of doing whatever the theory prescribes. But in general we may ascribe to practice a sort of priority—a *practical* priority—in that human beings are spontaneous agents first and practitioners only by way of development from that. That is an important point for us, since it enables us to accept that dance is a practice in spite of the fact that people everywhere spontaneously do things that we cannot, without being silly, refuse to call dancing. It is easy to say, however, that there will be a dialectic as theory and practice work on each other; and in a complex practice, involving highly skilled work, we will expect theory and practice to operate in an equilibrium from which any departure—theoretically unwarranted practice, impracticable theory—is pathological.[7]

Unlike an art, a practice as such needs no sustaining institutions (cannot have them, in fact), no public, and no more in the way of standards than is necessary to maintain the distinction between engaging in the practice and not engaging in it. It follows, incidentally, that it is hard to find a good word for someone who does engage in a practice that will not make such engagement sound much more formal and deliberate than it needs to be. Even "practitioner" seems too strong a word; "participant" comes closer to conveying what is meant.

Dance may not be a single art, but surely it is a single practice. (But remember what we said about smoking cigars: a "single" practice may include, or be included in, or overlap with indefinitely many other practices in as good standing as itself—as many others as there are things the participants may equally well be said to be doing.) Dancers know they are dancing, that dancing is one appropriate designation of what they do. What about Korean dance, then? Korean dancers, we may say, engage in the same practice as our dancers. Their language, I am told, has a word (*mu*) that they accept as a proper designation of the dances they perform, a word that in many contexts is intertranslatable with our "dance." But what about our own dance and the African practice that Hanna mentions? Here we have a real problem. Are these people dancing? From our viewpoint, certainly they are: we recognize them without qualms not only as dancing but also as practicing an art that is indubitably an art of dance. But, for all we know, no word like "dance" figures in their vocabulary, any more than it does in that of the Tiv. And let us suppose, for the sake of the present argument, that that is the case. They know what they are doing, and what they do in dancing is done in the light of that knowledge: there is something specific, namable, or describable in their language, which they are conscious of doing more or less normally, more or less correctly, more or less well. (If their language and thought did not incorporate the notions of doing things normally, correctly, and well, I do not see how we could say they engaged in practices; fortunately, Hanna's presentation rules out that possibility in the present case.) But their knowledge of what they are doing does not incorporate any equivalent for our concept of dance. Perhaps the ceremony they are performing is regarded as *sui generis* or is classed with other ceremonies in ways that cut clean across the classifications that seem to us so obviously applicable. We shall say, then, that they are dancing. But

---

[7] This is most strikingly true of the Sanskrit vocabulary for dance-related practices and its use in contemporary English-language discussions by Indians of Indian dance. The question is intricate, but I shall essay some remarks later (§8.461).

can we say that they are engaged in the "practice" of dance? Not according to the definition we gave. But both possible answers have definite attractions. On the one hand, they are engaged consciously in a practice of which they have a concept; they know what they are doing; and the practice is dancelike. Surely, if they happened to know English and were asked whether what they were doing was a dance, they would say "Yes" without even having to think about it, just as we do. So the idea of dance is somehow already implicit in the knowledge they have.[8] On the other hand, if they really have no concept very like that of dance, what they are doing must actually be, as an activity, really very unlike what dancers do, however much it looks like dancing to an outsider. The activity must play a very different part in their lives and in their society.

Another writer with anthropological training, Joann Kealiinohomoku (1970, 541–542), takes a very firm line on the issue we have been mulling over. She makes it a matter of definition that dance "is recognized as dance both by the performer and the observing members of a given group," pointing out that "both Japanese and Mandarin Chinese have time-honored words for dance *and related activities*" (my emphasis) and exclaiming: "Can we really believe that only white Europeans are 'advanced' enough to speak about dance?" But that, of course, was never the issue. What Kealiinohomoku means cannot be quite what she says, because it is only in English that "dance" is a word, and her intentions are cross-culturally egalitarian. What she means is that dance must be recognized in its own practical context as belonging to some practice for which the word "dance" *or some reasonable equivalent* is an acceptable designation. But what would count as a reasonable equivalence is something she says nothing about.

We have a choice. Either we can relax the concept of "practice" in this artificial use, or we can stick to our initial definition. If we do the latter, we will need yet another word to set alongside "art" and "practice" to cover those groups of activities that are unified among us and in our own conceptual schemes but not necessarily in the conceptual schemes of their performers. But, since our purpose in introducing this new sense of "practice" was to escape the unsuitable narrowness of the concept of an art, that seems a bit silly. Perhaps we should do better to introduce a distinction among practices: self-defined practices and observer-defined practices.

There is a vagueness in the concept of a practice that can be brought out by asking some questions of a very abstract sort. What must necessarily be true if a person A is to engage in a practice P? Is it necessary that A should be able to say (if asked) "I do P"—that is, that A should have the concept

---

[8] The relations of theory and practice are further explored in Sparshott 1970a, in which, however, the concept of *a* practice, as set out in the present section, is not introduced.

of P and apply it in this case? Or is it even necessary that A should have the concept of a practice and apply that concept to P—that A should be prepared to say something like "I engage in P," or "P is one of the things I do"? That might not be so silly a restriction, for clearly dancers who know that they are dancers, that they go in for dancing, know something that goes far deeper than the knowledge that "dancing" is what some of their activities are called. Or should we go in the other direction and say that it is enough that the person B, who is ascribing to A the practice P, should have the concept of P (and, for good measure, the concept of a practice as indicated by habitual usage of the sort of locutions we were mentioning)? In that case, we would be saying that A's making a practice of P depends on there being *someone* who recognizes that A does so. (Perhaps that is not quite so silly as it sounds; but perhaps it is.) Or should we, finally, be laxer still, and say that A engages in the practice P providing that it is true that A does make a practice of P and that there is someone in existence at some time who has the concept P? We will have to say something like this last, if we are going to accept the possibility that there is somewhere a tribe that dances although no one in the tribe has the concept of dance and no one who does have that concept knows of the existence of the tribe. And that, after all, is something most of us would probably want to admit. The Ubakala very likely performed their ceremony, just as they do now, before anyone who had a concept like that of dance observed them or even knew of their existence; and, if that is the case, I doubt if anyone would want to say they began to dance at the moment someone who had the concept of dance first saw what they were doing.

It would be absurd to decide, otherwise than for heuristic purposes, to use the term "practice" in one of the above ways rather than in one of the others. But different answers do pick out different ways, all defensible, of thinking about the ways people do things and about what they think about what they are doing. And these matters are so crucial for our subject that we must never quite lose sight of the different possibilities.

We have set up a sort of nest of possibilities. An art is a special case of a practice in the strictest sense we have defined. And each of the senses of "practice" we differentiated is a special case of the less strict senses, since A and B may be the same person. This being so, we need not differentiate sharply between the theory of an art and the theory of a practice, or specify each time what sense of "practice" is relevant.

What people mean when they say they dance depends on the context in which the question "Do you dance?" was posed or arose. Usually they are suggesting that they habitually or occasionally make a practice of engaging in body movement of some rhythmical or patterned or ordered sort to which the appellation "dance" is appropriated by some clear convention:

118

that is, that they engage in one or other recognized form of social dance or folk dance, or in one of the recognized arts of dance—tap, ballet, modern, and such others as may be. These have in common that they are not intrinsically directed to any useful end other than recreation; nor are they in the category of games or sport, being inherently competitive, if they are, only insofar as one competes in excellence of dancing. But it is by no means clear that necessary and sufficient conditions can be laid down for what counts as a dance or as dancing in our society, or that the practices thus singled out would coincide with what one would recognize as dance in a different society.

When we reflect on this apparently haphazard element in what the recognized practice of dance actually consists of, we may be led to propose some such thesis as the following: any body movement that is not strictly utilitarian is likely to be called "dance" by someone or other, and it is hard to find solid grounds either for objecting to such usage or for distinguishing among such usages some that are literal and others that are metaphorical. But, if that is the case, are we not equally short of solid reasons for deciding whether one is speaking literally or metaphorically when one speaks of circling planets or wind-swept treetops as dancing? (Our earlier criterion, the propriety or otherwise of adding such provisos as "so to speak," may be dismissed as having to do only with the accidents of this or that vernacular.) And, if that is the case, what comes of our contention that dance is a practice? Surely we are only entitled to say that there are dance practices, and that *sometimes* people who say they dance have some practice in mind and sometimes they do not? And then, we may say, what comes of the theory of dance? It is open to anyone, of course, to theorize for this or that purpose about some phenomena to which the word "dance" is applied; but there is no reason to suppose that such theorizings derive any internal coherence from the fact that the word "dance" can be applied to their subject matter, or to suppose that any such theorizing could generate a coherent field answering to the uses of that word.

The doubts we have been expressing are, in reality, no more than empty gestures of arbitrary skepticism. We can perfectly well say that one can theorize about dance as a practice (or even about dance practices) and that all the other stuff will come in by way of clarification and contrast. The sorts of hesitations we have been ventilating do not tell against the propriety of theorizing or of calling the process (or its upshot) dance theory; they merely express reservations about what form such theorizing might take. One might, for instance, if one adhered to one or another methodology in the philosophy of science, make stipulations about what formal requirements a piece of discourse must have if it is to count as "a theory."

3.21 THEORIES OF ARTS AND PRACTICES

There can be a theory of anything, we said, because to be "anything" it must be identifiable in speech and it must be possible to give an account of how that identification is done, and that account will be theory. But will it be "a" theory, rather than a diffuse mass of theorizing? And if it is a theory, will it count as philosophy? And if it counts as philosophy, will it constitute "a" philosophy "of" the name-bearer? Not necessarily, one supposes. We do not have any systematic way of making such restrictions, but we could invent some. It would be quite sensible to do so in a context where we are wondering about what a philosophy of dance would look like and in general about the conditions governing the generation, development, currency, and criticism of philosophies of practices. We might stipulate, for instance, that we will not call an activity a practice unless there can be a philosophy of it, and we might allow our restrictions on the scope of philosophies to control what we shall accept (for present purposes, of course) as a "practice." To take an earlier example: can there be a philosophy of belching? One might think not. But there are parts of the world where formal post-prandial eructation is de rigueur (in Kiribati, for instance), and the formalities of the practice must involve notions of etiquette, attitudes to repletion, and who knows what else. Perhaps an account of how these cohere into a world view and a theory of communication would count as a philosophy. We could then say that the possibility of a philosophy of belching was proved by the existence of one and that that possibility entitled us to call belching a "practice." (An observer from Kiribati would note that North Americans do, in a sense, belch, but in a naive and crude way that reflects the crassly cerebrotonic world view and epistemology of the West, clear evidence of an almost subhuman condition that would justify the Kiribatese sending their missionaries and war canoes to bring us their civilization, were it not that they considered proselytism and imperialism vulgar.)

A philosophy of dance is presumably possible if by the philosophy of a practice one means no more than any general theorizing about it that is neither preoccupied with its techniques nor within the purview of a specific science. For the question of how the practice is named cannot be either a technical or a scientific question. And if the philosophy of a practice is possible, there can be a specific philosophy of it, if by that we mean only that the account given is unified; for it is obviously out of the question to stipulate that a philosophy must be true or sensible.

One might object that such a notion of what a philosophy would be is uselessly broad. But there are two reasons for not narrowing it. One is that no such restrictions are in fact recognized by anyone except groups of professional (that is, professorial) philosophers, and that each such restriction expresses a particular philosophical viewpoint. The other is that it is widely agreed that philosophy should always be in question to itself. Otherwise, philosophy is reduced to being one special study among others, and we shall need a new word for the unrestrictedly general questioning that philosophy used to be (cf. Sparshott 1975).

To that catholic view of what would count as the philosophy of a practice, one might still object that, although no limit can be set in advance to the diversity of philosophizing, philosophy is still more than idle chatter. It is serious discourse, and the requirement of seriousness imposes severe limitations. There must be standards of order, system, and care; consistency must be observed, and implications must be carried through far enough to make sure there are no hidden inconsistencies. Even if, suspecting that a demand for consistency and system may ensnare one within a too narrow set of linguistic habits and commitments, one tolerates within philosophy a lot of apparently disorganized and undisciplined speculation, one would not call any body of discourse *a* philosophy of a practice unless it satisfied implicit criteria of relevance, consistency, and organization.[9]

Some people want to say that there can be a philosophy of a practice only if that practice is itself sufficiently articulated to be the proper subject of a well-articulated body of theory. It must have a rational basis: that is, it must be governed by rules, and the philosophy of the practice will be the elucidation of the rules, the explanation of the rationality of the rational basis.[10]

The suggestion seems extravagant. Surely no practice rich enough and complex enough to attract a general theory will be governed or guided, let

---

[9] This methodological maneuvering can get complicated. If a practice, properly so called, must be such that there can be a philosophy of it, and if philosophy is a practice, the tightening of restrictions on the concept of practice goes with a corresponding constraint on the concept of philosophy. And, since limiting the scope of philosophy brings its authority into question, the narrower the view of what a practice is that one reaches by this route, the less compelling that view can be. One gets round this, however, by arguing that very general purposes can be served by very strict methods. Such considerations need not trouble us here.

[10] One must distinguish three possibilities here. First, a practice may be *constituted* by rules: the rules of chess define what chess is, and to play chess is nothing other than to do what those rules define. Second, a practice may be *governed* by rules: the practice exists or existed independently of the rules, but practitioners comply with them just because they are the rules for the practice. Third, a practice may be *guided* by rules but not governed by them: the practitioners all know what the rules are and bear them in mind (accepting the rules is essential to the practice), but they do not necessarily comply with them—much as in North America all drivers are guided by local parking regulations but no one is governed by them. These distinctions, essential as they are, are irrelevant to the discussion in the present passage, for which it suffices that a practice be rule-governed and which applies equally to rule-constituted practices.

alone constituted, by anything much resembling a set of rules.[11] Philoso-phizing is called for only where, though rationality seems to be present, there seem to be no rules. Again, a practice, even if it is rational, is less likely to *have* a rational basis than to be such that a rational basis can be imputed to it on the ground of the rationality it displays. The invocation of "rules" and "bases" is surely fictive: people are behaving *as if* there were rules, *as if* there were an independent rational ground. But behind the lan-guage that seems to make such questionable claims we discern the very reasonable notion that it makes little sense to work at the philosophy of a practice unless one can make some coherent sense of the question what those who engage in the practice are up to and why they are up to it. And that is just to say that, whether or not the practice *has* a rational basis and a set of rules (whatever exactly that may mean), one can ascribe such a basis and rules to it without absurdity or arbitrariness.

There can, we saw, be a theory of dance just because we have the word "dance." And dance is a practice in the sense that it is something people do consciously. And the examination of what it is that they are conscious of is an examination of the basis and rules of the practice, if any. We can hardly use the absence of such a basis and such rules as a reason for saying that there can be no philosophy of dance, since only philosophy can determine whether or not the rules or basis exist. As Aristotle said, to give reasons for not philosophizing is already to philosophize. The only way to avoid the philosophy of a practice (or a supposed practice) is never to have consid-ered its possibility. In the present case, to consider whether dance is a prac-tice in whatever sense one thinks most appropriate is already to have em-barked on philosophy—on a typical philosophical inquiry, in fact. And what would that philosophy be, if not the philosophy of dance? Nor could one set about answering that question without raising further questions of an unmistakably philosophical sort. Once such questions have been raised, self-respect requires that they be dealt with responsibly and systematically; and, in doing that, we would be developing a philosophy of the practice. The very fact that our inquiry stemmed from a specific question would suffice to give it whatever unity might be required.

Whatever theoretical qualms we might have about whether the word "dance" picks out any reality that could engage a theorist's serious atten-tion, the fact is that people do actually write histories, anthropologies, so-ciologies, and encyclopedias of dance, and this activity is not usually

[11] It is characteristic of philosophical discussions of such matters that the distinctions made are ingenious but that the implications of the initial decision to make the specific concept of a "rule" central to the discussion are ignored. Philosophers too seldom ask themselves why they choose that word "rule" to drape their discourse around in the first place. In real life, the concept of a rule has a rather narrow and specialized scope. But never mind that now.

thought of as eccentric. Since the writers of such things do not strike the educated public as insane, they must have been able to identify dance as a single practice or a coherent set of practices in a way that made prima facie sense. And what was thus identified must either be really unified in such a way or not. Insofar as it is, it will be possible to analyze its internal articulation, to explore the standards and values invoked or implied, to catalogue the means used and the ends sought. Insofar as the unity proves illusory, the ground of the illusion would call for inquiry. If there is no practice, what rules guide the much-played game of pretending that there is one? Either a sort of phenomenology or a sort of conceptual analysis will always be in place: the failure of either shows the need for the other. For if analysis fails, the unity of our discourse must rest on some unifying factor that is accessible to insightful thought but eludes explication.

Dance is a practice, but the ground rules for the philosophy of dance are not simply those of a philosophy of practice. Some dance practice, we saw, claims to be art and to count among the fine arts; but not all does, just as not all uses of language are artistic and not all artistic use of language belongs to the fine art of poetry—or, at least, these inclusions would require much special pleading. One can do philosophy of dance within the highly structured theory of the fine arts or within the well-charted domain of general theory about the nature of art, as well as within the wilderness of the theory of practice and the unmapped theory of *Lebensformen* (of which more later). The existence of these alternative perspectives complicates things, because one cannot in good conscience content oneself with mere side-glances over the battlements into wider domains. But it makes things easier, too, by ensuring that there will be much to say, as we have already found. One only has to see what comes from applying prefabricated structures and theories to these special areas. The possession of an articulated framework of methods and perspectives simplifies things, too, by enabling one to eliminate quickly a lot of dubious prancing and showmanship that one would otherwise either have to find one's own reasons for excluding or have to include at the cost of all intelligible order.

Our first chapter asked why the theory of dance had been neglected, since there are theories of other arts and dance is a typical art. We found reasons, but it was the wrong question. Neglect and inaction never require explanation. We should first have asked why one should expect there to be a philosophy of dance, and why and in what circumstances philosophies of arts develop. That there can be a theory of anything is no reason for expecting that there should actually be a theory of any particular thing, and the same applies to the general possibility of theories of practices and arts. The arguments that show a theory of the art of dance to be possible also show that a theory of fireworks is possible; but there is no such theory, nobody wants one, nobody is surprised at its absence.

What makes the possible actual? There must be some sustained pressure that moves a theorist to devote time to the specific practice in question or some public that demands a theory to meet a need of its own. Probably neither of these suffices without the other, for unwanted theories fall on deaf ears and unreceptive desks, and sheepish publics may look up and not be fed. Even if the philosophy of music and the theory of tragedy now sustain themselves through the inertia of academic elaboration and rebuttal, there must have been a specific reason why these themes were chosen for philosophizing about in the first place. The theory of tragedy still attracts students, even though tragedy as an art form is long obsolete, because the problem has established itself as independently intriguing, uncontroversially respectable, and eminently discussable. But when Plato started the tradition of thinking about tragedy, he did so not out of abstract interest but because tragic performances were a dominant institution in the culture he was raised in, so that in order to clear a space for his own theory of culture he had to steal the tragedians' thundersheets. So he wrote a critique of tragedy, and Aristotle replied to it. And so we go on.

What, in general, makes theorists undertake the philosophy of a specific practice? Presumably, that such questions as can always be asked begin to call for answers. That could be when they are practically urgent, socially conspicuous, or intellectually puzzling or challenging. The questions become practically urgent if the practice comes under threat, and socially conspicuous if a change in a community's way of life makes the practice newly anomalous or newly central. They become intellectually puzzling if the energies and resources devoted to a practice become disproportionate to the benefits apparently derived from it, and intellectually challenging if the practice seems integrally and distinctively related to issues of current philosophical concern, as for example because it displays an aspect of behavior that is thought significant to the self-image of humanity. No such listing of possibilities can be exhaustive, because the dynamics of cultural life are often obscure (it is easy to see why there is a vogue for computer models of intelligence among philosophers, especially those who work near the centers of the computer industry; it is less easy to see why frisbee throwing should have caught on and then fizzled out when it did, in relation to the rise and fall of the yo-yo and the diabolo). But such explanation as those mentioned would be acceptable and may stand for the sort of thing one would be looking for.

The continuing vitality of the philosophy of art in general can be explained under three of our four heads. The practice of the fine arts as such has been a conspicuous feature of our civilization since the sixteenth century, and we have said something of how it soon generated its theoretical justification. The attention lavished on those arts is intellectually puzzling (insofar as it outruns and outlasts the urge to revel in monarchical and entrepreneurial loot) as an economically gratuitous activity. It becomes intellectually challenging as the increasing sophistication of artistic procedures and of their ideological defenses vindicates their place as significant manifestations of the cognitive powers by which humanity likes to define itself and as soon as Darwinian biology makes inter-species differentiations problematic and thus focuses attention on artistic activity as a distinctively human development. These explanations, however, go to art in general, to what unites the fine arts, and do nothing to call for a philosophy of dance or any other particular art.

Within the context of the general philosophy of art, the philosophy of dance (or other specific art) would deal with why artistic activity as thus explained should take the form in question. But that context need not be the only one. The art of dance, for instance, might be practiced partly for such reasons and partly for reasons having nothing to do with dance's being a fine art. It could be that an independently explicable and justifiable activity had been taken over, wholly or partly, by the impulse and ideology of art as such. In fact, since the fine arts were practiced before the concept of art was formulated, we would expect that to be the case. Leaving that aside, though, the four sets of circumstances we singled out as making the philosophy of any practice and of art generally worth pursuing can apply to the philosophical treatment of specific arts.

First, then, it could be that an art makes large demands for attention, esteem, and the commitment of public funds—as ballet in fact does. The decline of monarchies, the diversion of civic pride with the rise of the welfare state, and massive taxation of the fortunes of magnates leave expensively ceremonial arts threatened with withdrawal of subvention if ideological vindication is not maintained. Second, an art may impinge unavoidably on public attention: any change in architecture, for instance, is socially conspicuous because it is thrust into the midst of social life and inevitably redirects it. Third, an art may become socially conspicuous, as cinema did between the two world wars, simply by playing a new and large part in cultural life. Fourth, an art may become intellectually puzzling as the nature of the interest or gratification it offers becomes obscure, as with contemporary art forms of which the value seems to be discontinuous with those by which the gratuitous activity of art in general is traditionally vindicated. And fifth, an art may be epistemically significant, as are the arts of literary and pictorial mimesis, which attract philosophical attention even when artists are spending most of their best energy on nonmimetic forms, because mimetic art offers help in the philosopher's perennially baffling task of explaining how human beings represent the world to themselves.

Is there anything to show that the possibilities for a philosophy of dance are ripe for actualization and that the present flurry of interest will establish a self-sustaining trend? Before we take up that question, another more general issue deserves attention.

There are three ways of conceiving the relationship between the possibilities for the philosophy of a given practice and the way those possibilities will be actualized at a given time. One way is as follows. Practices are things people consciously do. That being so, whatever is done as part of the practice is done for a reason, and the reasons are interrelated. Practices develop organically, by historical processes of development, modification, and reaction; it follows that they have a dynamic internal unity, though the unity may not be of a simple kind. And the reasons why things are done must, being reasons, be intelligible. It follows that the philosophy of a practice has a definite, permanent reality. It is the standing possibility of exploring the totality of these intelligible relationships. Not all of these possibilities will ever be explored, but it is in principle open to anyone to take any of them up at any time. What actually gets discussed will need to be explained by the contexts of inquiry that prevail at particular times and places; but, once a set of possibilities has been discussed, the point of that discussion can always be seen. The repertory of possible theoretical modes—that is, the possible ways of organizing the field or part of the field—itself constitutes a standing possibility, a permanent reality of a second order. These realities do not exist in advance of the practice but are generated and established within its context. If dance is a practice, the full content and structure of the philosophy of dance are realities to be explored rather than invented. This way of looking at things seems extravagant, being open to the objection that it downplays the role of historical accident in a way that (because admittedly not all possibilites will ever be realized) can be neither effectively disputed nor interestingly confirmed; but it gains support from the fact that one really can grasp the nature of obsolete art forms, see how what was said about them makes sense, and relate all of that to what is nowadays done in art and said about what is done.

A second way of looking at the matter is as follows. What goes under the name of a given practice at a given time is an indeterminate mess of things done and proposed. At any such time, only a few limited sets of such doings and proposals will be such that a philosopher can give a coherent account of them, making them jointly intelligible as a single practice by whatever criteria are available and acceptable; and available philosophical methods are likely to reduce the options still further. Once a philosopher has isolated such a set, thus implicitly defining a practice, the very indeterminacy that made it necessary for him to do so means that his discovery of a manageable set of intelligible relationships will not only strengthen those relations but also suggest new connections, which he and others can then elaborate and extrapolate. His intervention will thus directly and indirectly generate new organizations of practice. Aristotle's theory of tragedy illustrates this process: initially, the theory applies to aspects of a few rather heterogeneous plays picked out for polemical purposes from among those presented in a specific institutional context; but it then comes to be applied to a particular type of play without regard to its context of presentation and thus in effect creates the type of play it seems to define.

The third way of thinking about how theories of practice work is the following. In advance of theorizing, all organized activities are intrinsically amorphous. The organization, however tight it may be, is extrinsic, imposed by institutions of control, presentation, and transmission. It is the philosopher who creates the intelligibility of the practice after the event and thus, one might say, creates the practice as such. But this assigning of a significance cannot be arbitrary: if it is a significance of the practice, it must be something that, once assigned, can be seen by any competent observer to be signified (and the criteria of competence in observers cannot be arbitrary either). Depending on who sees it, how easily, how willingly, and in what light, theoretical and practical developments of the newly meaningful practice become possible without further creative theorizing, simply by following through the implications of the perceived meanings and the further meanings that are dialectically developed from them.

What these three possibilities come down to, in brief, is that, in advance of theorizing, a practice may be inherently meaningful as a whole, in part, or not at all. It could certainly be the case that each of these possibilities holds for some practices and that none is true of all. Whether that really is the case depends in part on what one allows to count as a single "practice"; the important thing is to grasp what the possibilities are, not which of them actually obtains.

Of the three possibilities mentioned, one might hold at the one extreme that the first always obtains, as a matter of logic. Intelligibilities are, necessarily, timeless (even when they are intelligible sequences), so that all intelligibilities of practice somehow subsist eternally as essences in an intellectual heaven. At the other extreme, one might insist that potential explicability is chimerical in the absence of actual explanations: possibilities are artifacts of the theorizing activity that invokes them, so that the third possibility is the only one to take seriously. To make that plausible, we have to remind ourselves that, if one cannot engage in a practice without somehow knowing what one is doing, practice already involves an element of theory that, in the case of a complex practice, may well require a firm grasp of intelligible articulations that admit of verbally explicit formulation. That being so, the sort of creative philosophizing we suggested would usually be the work of such an intelligent practitioner in the course of developing a personal version of the practice, or the work of someone in contact with such development. The postulated initial amorphousness of the practice cannot fully characterize what a specific individual or working group makes of that practice. This leaves us with a situation in which what some self-conscious individual or group makes of its practice has its own coherence, while the great mass of the practice as generally carried on is such that intelligibilities may be imputed to it almost as freely as one sees "pictures in the fire." But not all pictures are visible in all fires, and all practitioners know they are doing the same thing. So an order of one kind is being imposed on an order of a different kind. No doubt the philosophy of a practice explicates this intersection of orders and compares rival claimants among imposed orders.

Even if every theorist who essays the philosophy of a practice is freely and imaginatively imposing system on a relatively unstructured mass of doings, the theory succeeds only insofar as theorist and public are convinced that the disclosed intelligibilities were always really there, have been discovered and explained rather than constructed and imposed. If it were not so, how could the theorist find confidence to advance the theory, and on what grounds should it be accepted?

However successful and influential a theory for a given practice may be, so that the whole idea of what the practice is is revolutionized, the theory will fail to fit a lot of what one might beforehand have expected it to fit. There will continue to be activities that are merely institutionally, adventitiously, or suppositiously within the confines of the theory and of which the theory simply is not true. People will continue to do what they need to do or feel like doing and will say of it what seems to them to need saying, whether or not that involves paying lip service to some theory whose prestige seems worth borrowing. This unruliness of humanity should not worry anyone: not only are we resigned to it, we share it when it suits us. We cannot then say that the philosopher has described the practice in its entirety. What the philosopher has done is uncover its nerve.

What do we mean—or, rather, since the concept is not in common use, what do we mean to mean—by the nerve of a practice? We mean that part or aspect of a practice that gives the practice its point, makes it worth engaging in and taking seriously in the light of whatever wider and deeper interests may be appropriate, even if (as is often said to be the case in the fine arts) most practitioners do things that can be justified as pertaining to their art only by way of such autonomous technical and institutional criteria as give the art its identifiable unity rather than its human or cosmic justification.[12] People who can properly be said to engage in a practice do many different things, for many different purposes, many of which have little to do with each other and could be achieved by other means. What we shall call the nerve of the practice is that for the sake of which, if the practice did not exist, it would be desirable (if not necessary) to introduce it.

Clearly, the wider interests that justify a practice may shift, and what was originally identified as the nerve of the practice may then become questionable. The philosophy of the practice will perpetuate itself as it becomes necessary to accommodate, to explain, to resist, or to promote such changes.

The notion of the nerve of a practice is not precise, and I do not mean to make it so, since all I am trying to do is make some general points about the shape of inquiry. I will, however, take up two questions. First, what sort of unity is being attributed to the nerve? Here the only answer can be that it must be such an interrelation of meaningful actions as we have already indicated; it may involve a polarity of alternative methods or purposes, or any sort of system. The criterion is pragmatic: that the offered account shall be acceptable as a single account of a single practice, in relation to which activity and criticism can be coordinated. The other question (one I have been asked by someone who was really bothered by it) is whether there can be any method for determining what the nerve of a practice is and, hence, when (for instance) the nerve of a practice has changed. And here it should be clear from the way the concept was introduced that there can be no method, since it is the formulation of the theory that identifies the nerve. To offer a theory of a practice is to propose a way of making sense of it, in such a way as to privilege that part of the practice that really would be made sense of in that way. The notion of making sense of something obviously cannot be made precise or reduced to method, since it is our notion of what does or does not make sense that licenses acceptable methods. In determining what the nerve of a practice is, one is deliberating rather than discovering: one is deciding what to make of it. It seems to me quite obvious that this is how we do go on and that it would be absurd to act otherwise. Deciding how to think of our practices is part of our deciding how to live, what strategies to adopt in shaping our lives individually and together. Any methods we adopted would be heuristic, subject to the control of our critical intelligence.

---

[12] Richard Bernheimer (1961) thus argued that almost all art is irrelevant to what art really exists for: the generation of sacred images. Philosophers have averted their eyes from his book, but that has not made it go away.

To be more precise, there are two reasons why there cannot be a method for determining the nerve of a practice. First, it is a matter of social discernment: one must isolate the phenomena, then describe and weigh them. It is obvious that there cannot be a rule for the first of these, since the presupposition is that the antecedent situation is relatively unstructured (in fact, one must determine what the "situation" is). One does not see how there could be a rule for the other two. One might compare the sentence with which Aristotle ends the first book of his *Posterior Analytics*, pointing to the gift of sharp-sightedness (*anchinoia*), the faculty of rapidly discovering middle terms—scientific intuition, a nose for significance. It's the hallmark of the good scientist, and it is just what there is no method for. It is more like a bodily skill, built up through the experience of responding physically and intellectually to certain sorts of stimuli.

The second reason one cannot have a method for determining the nerve of a practice is that in the act of describing the nerve one gives it definition and thereby facilitates both its adoption and its rejection: one simply changes the nature of the practical situation in which the practice is carried on. Saying what the nerve of a practice is is something like predicting which current tendencies will bear what sort of fruition and something like persuading people to act in the light of such a prediction, whether as promise or as warning. The mother who told her child not to put beans in its ears created the practice by describing it.

This chapter began by wondering in what circumstances a practice might become the target of actual theorizing, and what conditions the theorizing should fulfill before we could call it philosophy. Perhaps the answer to the latter question is: When the field of the theory is so organized that something can be identified as its nerve and we can conceive what it would be for that nerve to change. A reason must be given or suggested for not dealing with the field piecemeal or as a mere means to a simple end. The claim that only a rule-governed practice can be the object of a philosophy was on the right lines after all; only we shall say that what is required is not rules, not even rules for changing rules, but the means of convincingly interpreting differences as intelligible transformations. And we will not admit that the philosophy of a practice has been established until it has shown itself strong and flexible enough to accommodate such transformations without losing its own integrity and force.

3.211 *The Present Prospects for the Philosophy of Dance*

What are the prospects of a philosophy of dance? Our first chapter mentioned obstacles that seem to have been removed. In the last quarter century, audiences for dance in America have vastly increased; my own home town swarms with dance companies, resident and transient. Dance scholarship flourishes; the present book is part of a trend. Enough excellent dance is now available on television for a cultured public to constitute an adequately informed readership for such works. But it is not clear whether all this amounts to cultural centrality. Perhaps it is just a passing fad, such as we have seen before. Nothing in today's revival comes even close to the wild enthusiasm aroused by Marie Taglioni and her successors in the 1840s—until Jenny Lind came along. Edwin Denby conjectured that the sudden rise in the popularity of ballet in the United States during the Second World War (a similar enthusiasm was noted in Britain) was that in ballet nobody speaks, thus offering welcome relief from the oppressive torrent of propaganda—"nobody speaks a foolish word all evening" (Denby 1949, 36). Perhaps the current wave of enthusiasm could be related to the Vietnam war and other phenomena of the preachy sixties. The cultural centrality we had in mind must at least be such as to sustain a lasting and genuine concern. It must at least approximate to what Hegel had in mind: that an art should appear to embody the self-definition of a civilization.

If the new conspicuousness of dance is more than a passing fad, what is its inner meaning? I do not know. But one would expect it to answer to a new attitude toward ourselves or to a new mode of access to the world. What could these be? Stanley Cavell attributed the rise of film between the wars to the pressures of nineteenth-century mass society: the new technical possibilities of cinematography, together with the opportunities for public performance opened by the perceived staleness of vaudeville, were used to satisfy a yearning to have access to the world, or to a world, without exposing oneself to that world (Cavell 1971). And it is in a later phase of the same world that the narrower new public for dance has arisen. Two suggestions that are often made promise to be relevant here.

At one level, the rise of phenomenology as a distinctive mode of philosophizing may have drawn the sting of the overintellectualizing of thought that Plato exemplifies—not that philosophers have thought too much, but that much of their thinking is an ideology of intellectual life masquerading as a view of human life in general. (The theme is a commonplace among philosophers; you can find my version of it in the essay "Speculation and Reflection," in Sparshott 1972.) Especially in France, phenomenologists have begun to show how our experience is that of beings embodied in the world, and this change of attitude gives a new importance to dance as a uniquely exquisite manner of experiencing that way of being. In earlier times, Platonic intellectualism was harmless because it could not be effective. Even the rich lived in hard conditions that made it impossible to forget the vulnerability of the flesh: there was no painless extraction for the teeth of the mighty, and Plato himself (the old story tells) had been a slave.

In an age of climate control and cellophane, affective corporeality begins to appear as something we might lose.

At another level, it is argued that the ideological triumph of the "women's movement" and the advent of "gay liberation" should combine to remove the social stigma from dance in America and other places. As we saw in §1.24, it is supposed that dance is an essentially feminine art and is a sign of effeminacy when practiced by men, and that in either case it symbolizes adoption of a socially subordinate or deviant role. Although I emphasized earlier that in the overall context of world history and anthropology dance has not been the prerogative of either sex and is obviously not so even in the world of Merce Cunningham and Robert Desrosiers, that objection is irrelevant in the present context; the choice of dance as a career has not had the same meaning for the two sexes in our society.

One of the ways in which dance in the Western cultural context has been predominantly feminine, it was argued, and hence might be put in a new perspective by a change in sexual roles is that women, as passive partners in a sexual pairing through which the public meaning of their lives was to be fulfilled, have necessarily been trained to regard their bodies as fit objects for attractive presentation. Dancing before an audience thus fits into the general pattern of their lives. For a man, by contrast, such "showing off" relates only to the personal and not to the public aspect of his life, and even then traditionally takes the form of a display of strength and dexterity rather than a manifestation of beauty and grace.[13] A man who takes up dancing is therefore moving out of the ordinary patterns of his career. But it is precisely these sexually stereotyping patterns of career orientation, these prejudicial divisions between the private and the public, that have recently become so suspect in enlightened circles, so that this overpowering obstacle to a recognition of the possible dignity of dance (as opposed to its attractiveness, which has never been challenged) is rapidly disappearing.[14] Suzanne Gordon observes that the rise to stardom of the glamorous refugees, Nureyev and Baryshnikov, has provided aspiring male dancers

[13] For the equation of dance values with what are here identified as the feminine forms of self-display, compare Théophile Gautier: "Dancing after all has no other object but the revelation of *beautiful* forms in *graceful* attitudes and the development of lines which are agreeable to the eye" (quoted in Sorell 1971, 423; my emphasis).

[14] The point about the place of self-display in traditional feminine culture and its relevance to dance is made by Feinman (198?, 46). A word of caution is in order when we are considering these prognostications of change: the legal and social reforms being produced so rapidly by feminist and other idealists arise from the clear perception of evils but are seldom accompanied by any idea of what sort of social order will replace what we have now. But presumably there will be *some* sort of social order. And it is the totality of that order that will govern the quality of our lives—not the absence of specific evils, however gross.

with an acceptable role model, so that ballet dancing has become an acceptable career choice for men.[15]

More questionable in this context is the thesis we considered and scouted in Chapter 1: women as women are body-oriented and men are mind-oriented, so that the new recognition of women in public life should lead to a renewed esteem for the body and for the body's art of dance. I doubt this. Contempt for the body as opposed to the mind is not noticeably characteristic of most males I know. An equally popular stereotype has it that women emphasize the "spiritual" and despise the lusty physicality of their male assailants. It might be more realistic to say that our social norms prescribe different forms through which men and women respectively can acceptably express whatever degree of body-centeredness or body-aversion they may adopt.

The proposed contrast in general tendencies is many-sided, whether it be considered as a cultural phenomenon (but one common to most widespread cultural configurations, for whatever reason), as broadly anthropological, or even as proper to mythical cosmogony in which sex-pairing is reduced to the union of earth-mother and sky-father, the material and the formal. In any case, the contrast seems to obtain between those shapes and movements that carry through the implications of what is in the material and the shapes and movements imposed on the material by a shaping impulse whose source lies elsewhere. That contrast is operative in all arts, rather than differentiating some arts from others. Within dance, this contrast might indeed take the form of a male choreographer putting a female dancer through the hoops, as it were, as opposed to the female dancer herself expressing the sense of her own corporeal personhood. But there are female choreographers who work with male dancers, and the contrast really amounts to that between dances that conform to a preconceived pattern and dances that evolve from personal impulse. The sexist imputations merely confuse the issue. Similarly, some of my feminist colleagues argue that women typically take a person-centered and context-emphasizing approach to their professional undertakings, whereas men tend to treat them as specialisms isolated alike from related activities and from their contexts in the lives of their practitioners. Men, they say, as part of the same syndrome, turn everything into a competition. Dance, as the art of people moving among people, would typify the more feminine way of doing things, they might say; and it is becoming evident to everyone that it is

---

[15] Gordon 1983, 32–33. The earlier idolization of Nijinsky did not have this effect. His dancing is always described as having a strangely epicene quality—it wasn't the sort of thing one could imagine oneself as doing. Nureyev and Baryshnikov, in their appearance and their relation to the means of publicity, as well as in their dancing styles, are continuous with the rock stars who are already idols for the young.

only this way of approaching things that can save the world. (How, you may ask, is this sexual stereotyping reconciled with the tooth-and-nail tactics popularly ascribed to ballerinas and their ballet mothers? Answer: by special pleading, of course. Women like that are imitating men in a man's world.)

It is hard to sort the sense from the nonsense in sexual polemics. But two things do seem to be true and relevant to the new importance of dance. One is that, in North America at least, there is a dance world that is professionally dominated by women. Dance as art is associated with dance as physical education, and there is this enormous establishment of dance education in which the great majority of teachers and students are women. Whatever the future may bring, a change in the status of women is necessarily a change in the status of this industry: the head of a dance program becomes a more important figure in the hierarchy (though the immediate effect is likely to be that some male, ignorant of dance, will be appointed to the position), the activities of a dance department achieve greater recognition within a school of fine arts.

The other important thing is that dance does emphasize sexuality in a way that no other art does. It almost always matters what sex a dancer is, not only because of typical differences in physical equipment and capacity, but also because the sexuality of the dancer is a normal part of the dance. Men dance and women dance, but they do not always dance in the same dances, and, when they do, they do not typically dance in the same way. Dance certainly does celebrate the physical, corporeal reality of humanity and glorifies and dignifies sexuality as part of that celebration. In our times, sexuality has come out of the closet in a new way, though it is hard to say just where the novelty lies. Sir Thomas Elyot (quoted in Chapter 2, note 14) had argued the importance of dance as expressing and promoting full humanity through the complementarity of the conventional excellences of the sexes, as those had been described by Aristotle in his *Politics* and *Historia Animalium*:

> A man in his naturall perfection is fiers, hardy, stronge in opinion, couaitous of glorie, desirous of knowlege, appetiting by generation to brynge forthe his semblable. The good nature of a woman is to be milde, timerouse, tractable, benigne, of sure remembrance, and shamfast, diuers other qualities of eche of them mought be founde out, but these be moste apparaunt, and for this time sufficient.[16]

[16] Elyot 1531, 82v–83r. C.-H. Méreau remarked in his open letter to Rousseau in 1763 that men and women should have their dancing lessons together; if women learn to dance alone, this will tend to reduce them to sex objects (Rousseau 1972, 180). That, of course, is

In this, Elyot was expressing the ideology of that dance-oriented milieu we have mentioned as centered on the court ballet. So what, apart from the substitution of new stereotypes, is new? Of course nothing need be, since dance would be regaining a significance it had before. But something is. What is new, I think, is what we get from Freud. As before, the alleged sexual differences symbolically displayed in dance are fundamentally different ways of being human. What is new is the recognition that the human being thus differentiated is a fundamentally sexual being and that dance is not merely symbolic of it but also an expression of it, both in its unity and in its differentiation, that is direct and central as no other expression can be.

Not all dance celebrates sexuality. It is rather that such celebration is a permanent possibility of dance as it is of no other art, a possibility central enough that it could be made the nerve of a dance practice. And "celebration" is not the only significantly danceable relation to sex. Eros in dance may be affirmed or denied, may be transfigured or civilized. In each case, the fact that the moving body is a sexual engine makes it possible for this central aspect of human reality to find an unforced and direct expression in dance. It must be admitted, however, that the palmy days of Marcuse are over and that the erotic is less fashionable than it was, perhaps because modes in feminism have turned against the liberation and democratization of eros, or perhaps only because the changing demographics of the baby boom have made it profitable to pander to a slightly older group.

One of the meanings of modern dance, as we said in connection with Duncan and the whole generation celebrated by Kendall (1979), was the emancipation of women within the contexts of their own activities: the release of the female body from constraining costumes, the freeing of the dancing body from the oppressions of ballet. "Not so much freedom to compete with men in the marketplace," as Jowitt says, "but the freedom to put away corsets, take lovers, bear children out of wedlock, and to dance like that kind of woman (powerful, supple, fecund) instead of like some man's vision of the seductive fairy as an antidote to the respectable wife" (Jowitt 1985, 135). Power, suppleness, fecundity—it sounds like a revolution. This meaning goes beyond the literal emancipation of the individual woman, the female form unbound. And, insofar as modern dance was seen as strictly an American movement, it could be represented as a nationalistic vindication of American democracy against the aristocratic European decadence of ballet. Duncan herself at one time equated this liberation with the Jeffersonian dream as expressed by Walt Whitman, the sense

what happened in the romantic ballet, in which such critics as Janin and Gautier so strongly objected to the presence of male dancers.

of expansive hope and ungirdled freedom that may be the best dream the world ever dreamed, the dream from which the wakening has been the saddest. The opening of the frontier let in the plow that broke the plains; and it may be that, with the acceptance that Vietnam and Watergate were not aberrations of Americanism but part of its inner truth, such a dance as Duncan envisaged could still preserve for the imagination the benign illusions by which an earlier generation had aspired to live.

A later version of the "Song of Myself," insofar as public institutions are now sensed as repressing rather than expressing expansive freedom, was the ideology of personal liberation inside an alienating society described by Paul Goodman as "Growing Up Absurd," with the generation gap playing the part the Atlantic Ocean used to play in dividing the rotten old world from the new (Goodman 1960). And, sure enough, one commonly finds dancers' control over their bodies and their creation of an artistic space by their dancing enlisted in the aid of just that set of ideas. Symptomatic of this interpretation of the inner meaning of dance is the way the theme of regimentation and release keeps turning up in the choreographies of college dance groups, a theme in which the contention between constraining ballet-type movement and liberating modern-dance-type (or even jazz-dance-type) movement becomes an allegory of the deeper contention between social constraint and the emancipating self-expression of dance as such. If this is what dancing can mean to people, it has much in common with the filmgoing that, in Cavell's argument, represented the yearning of urbanized humanity for some symbolic combination of power and refuge. This new emphasis on dance as an affirmation of a very personal power and freedom is visible in the "break dancing" in which the spontaneous vigor of dance lately renewed itself. Such dancing involves an explosion of dexterity and energy in relation to a small part of the surface of the ground: the dancer exerts power over a territory in a way comparable to that in which rival street gangs, without resort to metaphor, used to establish their domains in a city. Such gangs fail because they cannot separate their rumbles from the domain of police power. The metaphors of the art of dance create their own spatial world and exercise undisputed dominion over it.

If dancers and publics can really experience in dancing the sorts of meaningfulness I have been sketching, dance could merit a place of central significance among the arts. It would afford symbolic expression for certain personal values that have always been important but that are felt to be more threatened by today's manipulated and mechanized societies than they used to be, so that they have become objects of conscious attention rather than being taken for granted. These values are: first, corporeality, the physical presence of persons in the world, as symbolized in the emphatic movement or stillness of the body; second, the sexuality of humanity, as expressed in the way we dance with and for each other; third, the autonomy of the person as symbolized in mastery of movement; fourth, the liberty of the person as symbolized in freedom of movement; and fifth, perhaps, the humaneness of the person as symbolized in the expressiveness of movement. This is very platitudinous, but that does not matter. The problem for a theory of an art is not how to say something new but how to choose the right set of banalities to vitalize and how to give them life. What this particular set of banalities converges on is what Sartre (1943) called "the body for others," the dimension of corporeality whereby we are aware of others (and thus indirectly of ourselves) as matter suffused with consciousness, not bodies in which minds are captured but corporeal entities vital through and through. Sartre's brilliantly suggestive exploration of the relation between this and other ways of being embodied illuminates what could be the nerve of the art of dance as it can be meaningful nowadays (see Sparshott 1984).

A dance of which the essential point was the realization of the authority and integrity of individuals embodied in a world would be one readable in terms of movements of the body as a human body, not as a soft equivalent of sculpture moving in Euclidean space or as a semaphore for general or universal meanings—that is, not in the terms envisaged by Hegel for any of his three kinds of art. The psychology of perception discovers and explores the fact (which we might have expected) that as human beings we are sensitive to, and capable of making minute discriminations among, visible and audible expressions of our fellow humans in a way that we are not sensitive or capable in other areas. The communicative aspects of these minute discriminations in voice, gesture, and facial expression, which escape measurement, are the material the actor works in.[17] It should not be surprising if there were an art or art forms that exploited the same subtle capacities without relation to explicable content, and perhaps without relation to any communicable content at all. It is that sort of art that the art of dance as here envisaged would be. The relevant values of such an art would be articulated in terms of our mutual presence and visibility as humans. In a mechanized and computerized age, in which social relations are felt no longer to be an arena for the courtesy of a graceful mutuality, an art of dance in which that mutuality is isolated, emphasized, and celebrated, might be felt to be supremely important.

Akin to the dance of human mutuality would be the dance practice de-

---

[17] Some observers are so impressed by this divergence between the measurable and the perceived that they feel that the expressive meanings must be conveyed telepathically (or by some other obscure communicative channel) rather than by audible and visible cues. But that need not be the case. The human sense organs, with their associated cerebral mechanisms, are not calibrated in the same way that our measuring instruments are.

scribed by John Miller Chernoff as pervasively African and spreading throughout the world wherever African music and dance have been influential. It is a practice in which the mutual responsiveness of dancers to each other, to the musicians, and to the spectators has a profoundly ethical meaning in embodying as well as symbolizing self-control and mutual respect: "As the dance gives visible form to the music, so too does the dance give full and visible articulation to the ethical qualities which work through the music, balance in the disciplined expression of power in relativity" (Chernoff 1979, 144). The values realized in this practice are repeatedly invoked, as we have seen, by ideologies of dance in Western society, but not in close relation to the actual art forms of any specific society. One wonders what Hegel would have said (§1.332 above).

The possibilities we have canvassed are easy to see. But what we easily see now may not be what, a few decades hence, people will easily see we should have easily foreseen. The nerve of dance practice on which a viable dance philosophy centers may be quite different from anything in our sketch, which may be based on obsolete or chimerical ideas of what dance is and on notions about art that, though now central in what makes art important for most of those to whom it is important, are about to wither as they lose support among the intelligentsia (or, of course, as the class whose ideology they represent loses its purchase on power).

Even if the nerve of dance practice for our time were as I have suggested, it might well be that the center of a significant art of dance would be found elsewhere at other places and times—in a choric liturgy such as Plato envisaged, perhaps, or a civic processional, or a trance-inducing round dance. It is easy to imagine such a dance as the Catalan Sardana, already a focus for national sentiment and a symbol of national unity, being thought of as the archetypal dance and dominating the imagination of a people of dancers.[18] We might object that such a practice would not be art but social or

[18] I do not know how to dance the Sardana, but at the Aplec at Santa Coloma de Farners in April 1981 what met the tourist's ignorant eye was like this. The dancers form concentric rings *ad lib*, in which men and women alternate. The dance has two alternating phases, one relatively calm, the other excited, accompanying alternating passages of quieter and louder music. The footwork is, properly, intricate, but most participants reduce it to a seemly shuffle and concentrate on going in the right direction and getting the jumps and the arms right. The dancers form a throng; the music starts, but for a while no one dances. Then one or two rings begin to form, and their number grows until dancers in rings are scattered through the throng. But then, as the last cycle of the louder music begins, all of a sudden everyone is dancing, as new rings quickly form and rings within rings; and so they continue to the end. What struck me as the distinctively significant pattern (repeated, at this meeting, every time) was the sudden exuberant participation after the slow spreading of activity—essentially a celebration of the dynamics of mass movements and immensely exhilarating. What one sees in pictures is the people dancing in the rings; what struck me was the way the rings formed. My

"folk" activity; but centrality for such a dance might go with a shift in the significance assigned to art as a whole, which might become more clearly what Tolstoy argued that it always was, the expression of the sentiments that unite us in our societies and in humanity at large. Or again, the central dance, identifying the nerve of the practice and thus prescribing the essential meaning of dance as dance, might be the pairing dance in which sexual union is symbolized and perhaps encouraged. Our social dances have usually been of this sort, and a prevalent form of it is what young people who learned to dance as part of their general education, in my place and time, used to learn. It was not high art, not art at all, for most people hardly even artistic—good dancers were esteemed, and esteemed for their artistry (though that word was not used), but it was not necessary to be a good dancer so long as one was not a bad one (a bad dancer was not inartistic but embarrassing and awkward, bumping into people, treading on toes, losing the time: goodness and badness were not symmetrical!).

More than one philosopher to whom I have presented the argument of this chapter has asked whether I thought disco was art. The question cannot be answered simply: it is as obvious that a disco dancer can dance skillfully and/or artistically as it is that not every disco dancer is expected to be an artist in any ordinarily accepted use of that word. One might say that there may well be an art of disco, but, if there is, not all disco dancers practice it or even know what it is.[19] We think of the art of dance as pertaining essentially to a different sort of practice. But it is obvious that a society could channel such of its artistic passion as is given to dance through a form of social pairing dance such that everyone took part in it but few did so as artists (as, in the days of the tango, most people just sort of tangoed, some people were really good at it, and a few won competitions and gave displays). No form of ballroom dancing, of course, ever won the esteem of high art; but the society we are imagining is one in which the values of dance would be concentrated there. In such a society, again, the meaning of art and artistry would be rather different from what it is among us, something closer to what the arts-and-crafts people envisaged. But such a view of art might come to prevail.[20]

Catalan is too sketchy to be certain, but so far as I can see the handbooks do not say anything about that (cf. Mas i Solench 1981, who says repeatedly that the only really important things are not to break a couple when you join a ring and to follow the leader's instructions).

[19] For a little more on disco as art, see §6.252.

[20] The three sorts of dance here picked out as possibly constituting the nerve of dance practice—the dance conveying the essential meaning of dance, to which other dances merely approximate at best and of which they are at worst perversions—actually answer more or less to three forms of animal activity, which in the palmy days of sentimental Darwinism were often picked out as forerunners of dance. These are the "round dances" observed in some of the higher apes (complete with fluttering rags in the Denishawn manner, Sachs 1937, 10–

Where does this leave us? We have considered three alternative centers for the art (rather than the practice) of dance, three ways of dancing or reasons for dancing with enough substance to sustain a claim that dance is worth doing for their sake. The philosophy of dance, we have suggested, could be organized around such claims. But two possibilities are left open.

First, some one of these might be held to be what dance essentially is and is for, with other forms of dance treated as peripheral or secondary, as applications of dance means to unworthy or inappropriate ends, or in some other way shown to be necessarily inessential. Second, taking a more Olympian view and posing as a philosopher rather than a pamphleteer, one might take all three of these (and any comparable rivals) as together constituting what dance timelessly is, the nerve of dance practice. To argue that, one would have to show how they are necessarily interrelated—the claim to necessity is what makes it philosophy. Dance would be essentially that practice in which these quite different sets of forms and motives achieved some recognizable unity.

Two further reflections are in order. First, we have been switching back and forth between dance as practice and dance as art, with occasional reference to dance as essentially artistic practice. As with other arts that are closely related to things people do all the time, the philosophy of dance would have to come to terms with the relation between highly developed arts of dance, dance as well-formed but not technically organized modes of behavior within a society, and dance as an ubiquitous tendency in human beings to do things with their bodies.

The other thing that remains to be said is that, whatever dance may be said to be essentially, a lot of intellectual energy will be spent on preserving its integrity from mere technicians. In Chapter 1, we remarked how constant in the literature of dance has been the polemic on behalf of significant dance against mere dexterity. Similar polemics arise in all the arts but are most constant and most intense in dance, presumably because the enormous skill needed to master the techniques of the most developed forms of dance competes most directly, as a center of interest, with the human significance for the sake of which the technique might be thought to exist. Or, if one takes the opposite view: attempts to develop a pure art of dance as such are continually running up against resentful amateurs who hate to be disturbed in their vague humanistic muddle. The only other art in which the same battle is nowadays fought with comparable intensity is architecture, which, like dance, impinges directly on the quality of life. As first

---

11); the display dances of some birds; and the mutual courting dances of other birds. I do not know whether the selection of these animal behaviors as paradigmatic reflects a prior sense that three modes of dance are primary. See §§5.51241–2 below.

Ruskin (1849) and then Roger Scruton (1977) argued, architecture has continually to be rescued for humanity from the aesthetes who would reduce it to mere beautiful pattern-making. We live in our bodies and in our houses; an art that concerns them must go beyond aesthetics.

It is useless to speculate about what the future holds for the philosophy of dance or of any other practice, or indeed for philosophy as a whole. The successive transformations of the positive sciences and of technology have necessarily had the result that the philosophy that is to explain ourselves to ourselves is held in suspense while we make up our minds about what most needs explaining, or becomes unmanageably multiform as so many different things call for so many different sorts of explanation. The real world right now is much too interesting for philosophy. All I can do is rehearse the possibilities I see, hoping that less timid and unimaginative souls will see why they are real possibilities and will be able to make something of them—or will be driven by fury to do better.

3.3 *Dance as a Fine Art*

When we talk about "education" or about "sport," we easily understand each other. These are prominent, familiar, and readily identifiable aspects of or areas in our civilization, as well as in the fabric of our individual lives: loose collections of concerns, attitudes, practices, ways of speaking, too vague and pervasive to be characterized in any simple way, but certainly real and recognizable. Religion is another such: there is hardly anything of which one might not assert or deny that it was or had to do with religion; and yet we all know very well what religion is. These amorphous and undefinable but familiarly and intimately known complexes are what Wittgenstein called *Lebensformen*, forms of life. Art is another of them. However much we differ in our attitudes toward art and our theories about it, there is a way in which we all know perfectly well what art is: we know what it is to collect, criticize, produce, subsidize, appreciate art; we are familiar with the sorts of institutions that foster and control art; we know what it is to have a mild interest in art or a passion for it, to have an aversion for it, to be uninterested in or ignorant of it. We know jokes about art, and often we know why they are meant to be funny—we may find some of them funny ourselves. We have stereotypes of artists and the artistic life at various levels of authenticity and success. We are, if we are conventionally educated, aware of the history, psychology, sociology, economics, and philosophy of art and have some idea of what most of these might be like. Even if we have no interest in art, we all have the sort of competence that enables us to place this sort of concern in the context of our lives: if it is not a concern we imagine as even remotely possible for ourselves, we know what it is in us that rejects it and what it thus rejects, and we are aware of its possibility for others.

Dance is not only an art and a practice. Dance is art. That is, as the earlier part of this chapter showed without even meaning to, when we talk about dance, we immediately place it in the context of the form of life that is art and find the appropriate attitudes and habits already in place. For theoretical purposes, we may categorize dance or particular dances and dance forms in other ways and conscientiously abjure the concept of art in doing so. But dance is art all the same, and we know it. Later, in Chapter 6, we shall talk about what in dance has to do with art, and what has not, when we are making that distinction; when we are not making that distinction, dance belongs with art.

What we call "the Fine Arts," or these days more usually just "the arts," are those arts (in the sense sketched in §3.1) that are devoted to making, producing, performing, creating (and so on if necessary) within the domain of art as just described.[21] In fact, the notion of art itself has arisen from the custom of thinking of these arts as intimately related to each other. Their typical product is called works of art (or, in some specialized circles, "artworks"). Among these arts, we saw in Chapter 1 that a handful—poetry, painting, sculpture, music, architecture, perhaps one or two others—tradition-laden and partly institutionalized, have a special status as "the" fine arts. These are as familiar a part of our lives as art itself, and in something of the same way. Just as everyone knows what art is, so everyone knows what music is, even if no two people would define music in the same way or would agree on everything that should be excluded from music or included in it. And though some people, perhaps even most people, might say that not everything that is properly classed as music is included within art in every sense of that term, there is no interesting doubt that a lot of music is art (in a familiar sense that does not cry out for immediate explanation) and that music is art. Even people who think that only a few arts are really fine arts will agree that music is one of them: to deny it is either to show oneself more ignorant than one can plausibly claim to be, or to say something deliberately odd.

That another of the fine arts is the art of dance is nowadays not seriously disputed. As with painting or music, we identify without hesitation the artists, the critics, the patrons, the entrepreneurs of dance. Given any theory of art or of the arts, we see at once how it applies to dance just as easily

[21] The phrase "the fine arts," with or without capitals, is obsolescent and suggests obsolescent attitudes toward art. I occasionally use it nevertheless, despite these associations, because I do not want us to lose sight of the existence of those arts that are not "fine arts" and have nothing to do with art.

as we see how it applies to sculpture or drama. As with poetry or music, we see at once how to apply the distinctions between the academic and the original, between high art and folk art, between the traditional and the modern and the contemporary. The relations among these, and what exponents and opponents and proponents say about them, conform to what corresponding people say in similar contexts about the other arts. Dance, we may say, is absolutely typical as one of "the arts." The doubts we have about applying the categories mentioned (and others like them), the hesitations and objections to saying that dance is really an art, are exactly the same doubts and objections that are familiar from discourse about the other arts.

Most of what needs to be said about dance as one of the arts has been said in Chapter 1, in considering why dance was often excluded from the fine arts as they were originally defined. Only a brief recapitulation is needed here, together with a summary version of what I have written elsewhere (Sparshott 1982) about that in the concept of the fine arts which survives the circumstances of its origin.

3.31 THE FINE ARTS AS A CLOSED SYSTEM

We saw in Chapter 1 that the fine arts in the scheme that got its final and most pretentious form from Hegel consisted of five named arts: painting, poetry, sculpture, music, architecture, and no others. These were dignified activities, parts of civilized life, their appreciation and criticism worthy of a place in the education of cultivated people, affording "the pleasures of the imagination" through their presentation of ideas necessary to a sensitively intelligent grasp of the natural and human worlds. And they were distinguished from each other by the medium through which ideas were presented. What we did not mention before, and what does not appear from the theoretical treatment by Hegel and other philosophers, is that, though the name of each of the fine arts is definable in the abstract terms we have suggested, each of the names actually designated a definite and limited tradition of practice, with a set of preferred subjects and forms as well as media. In theory, music might be the art of expressing feelings through melody and rhythm or simply the art of developing and exploiting tonal systems; in theory, painting might be the art of representing three-dimensional reality on two-dimensional surfaces or simply the arrangement of pigment on a plane. In reality, painting was very definitely the art of painting the sorts of things painters painted in the ways painters painted them. An apprentice painter learned the accepted subjects and symbolisms, as well as the techniques: paintings look like other paintings. Similarly, music as musicians produced it belonged to a fairly small set of familiar genres, played on a limited range of highly developed instruments or sung by voices trained in highly special ways. The history of painting or of music is the history of the gradual transformations in these acceptances.

It is, then, utterly misleading to equate one of the fine arts with the total range of the possibilities available to its medium and its defining aims. If that equation comes closer to holding nowadays, it is partly because many contemporary artists are governed as much by art talk as by art practice, and partly because the idea of the fine arts as a system has lost such clear application and compelling force as it used to have. When the eighteenth-century writers wrote of the fine arts, they were referring to definite and well-structured bodies of practice with a determinate place in what they hoped was the educational system of a developed civilization, as represented by the blessed phrase "polite society." That is why it was futile to argue that dance was really one of the fine arts: in fact, no body of dance practice had reached and maintained just that position. It kept reverting to the position of entertainment.[22] One could not argue that it *ought* to be one of the fine arts without finding an empty niche in the educational system that it might fill. Ballet had, as it still has, the requisite structure and fixed repertory of devices, subjects, and contexts; but, though all dressed up, it had nowhere to go.

The old, closed list of the fine arts, as we sketched it in §1.31, was not developed by working out Hegel's analysis or by any clear decision about cultural importance, but by association. People started with that analogy of poetry and painting: a picture is worth a thousand words, but a picture needs a title—showing and saying are complementary; and, on the old way of thinking, language was the communicative medium that relied on hearing, painting the one that relied on seeing. But then, painting and drawing

---

[22] The presumption that dance is entertainment rather than art may be found entrenched, not to say enshrined, in some odd places. For instance, in the *Oxford English Dictionary*, the entry on "music" (issued by Bradley in 1908) begins by saying that music is one of the fine arts. In the entry on the noun "dance" (issued by Murray in 1894), the word "art" does not figure at all: "1. A rhythmical skipping and stepping, with regular turnings and movements of the limbs and body, usually to the accompaniment of music; either as an expression of joy, exultation, or the like, or as an amusement or entertainment; the action or an act or round of dancing." No other section of the entry comes as close to recognizing the art of dance. In the entry under the verb "dance" the avoidance is even more striking: "To leap, skip, hop, or glide with measured steps and rhythmical movements of the body, usually to the accompaniment of music, either by oneself, or with a partner or in a set." It is not easy to see, from the quotations given in this supposedly historical dictionary, what justifies this differential treatment of music and dance and the effective suppression of the existence of theater dance. Why is it a fact about the English language that music is one of the fine arts or that music is never performed "as an amusement or entertainment," as dance is? Or are these supposed to be facts about the real world, necessary to the understanding of what music is? Perhaps it is only the difference between Murray and Bradley, or between 1894 and 1908.

(and the graphic arts generally) come to the same thing, are parts of one body of practice. And it would be ridiculous to make a sharp line between painting and sculpture (via impasto and low relief), between drawing and sculpture (most sculptors work from drawings), between sculpture and architecture (think of the Parthenon), or between drawing and architecture. If one of them gets into the fine arts, surely they all do. On the other hand, poetry is mostly song (not all languages differentiate them sharply), and so is a lot of music, though not all poetic words go to music and not all music has words. Thus, whatever status poetry and painting have, architecture and sculpture and music are sure to have it too. And that gives you the five fine arts. The list seems absurd to us because it omits the theatrical arts, drama and mime and dance. Why does the chain from poetry through drama to mime and hence to dance not have the same pulling power as the chain from poetry to music? Because staged drama was thought of, by Aristotle as well as by Hegel, simply as the appropriate mode of presentation of a kind of poetry. A performance of *Hamlet* is, first and foremost, a performance of the play that we can read in Shakespeare's written works. So there is no chain to link the established arts with a set of theater arts, of which drama might be one and dance another.

If staged drama is merely written drama with embellishment, we are tempted to go on to say that pantomime, which as we saw was the form of dance that was accepted as most nearly akin to the fine arts, would be identified as drama without words. But an art thus defined is not being assigned any independent communicative power. Instead of filling a vacant niche, it merely finds ingenious ways of doing what dramatic poetry already does, only with reduced means. It is thus essentially a frivolous exercise of ingenuity. Nor is the judgment absurd, once this approach is taken. In the film *Les Enfants du paradis*, in the scene where Baptiste reveals his powers as a mime by showing that it was not Garance who stole the watch, it is obvious that he could have done so just as reliably and more explicitly and precisely by simply *saying* what he had seen. In fact, the whole point of the scene is that Baptiste is succeeding in showing the policeman what he could have told him—and no more.

3.311 *Dance as a Mimetic Art: Aristotle and Batteux*

From any common-sense point of view, dance is uncontroversially one of the arts of imitation as Plato and Aristotle conceived them and one of the fine arts as they were redefined in the eighteenth century. Dance, or one well-known kind of dance, is covered by the formal definition of such an art, and there is no problem if one leaves it at that. Dance has to be deliberately *excluded* from the fine arts by overtly or covertly adding provisos, even if the exclusion comes to be generally accepted.

The texts to which all early modern formulations of a list of fine arts looked back were not the Platonic arguments we think of nowadays but Plutarch's citation of Simonides on the "sister arts" and Aristotle's *Poetics*. The *Poetics* had extraordinary currency and prestige from the middle of the sixteenth century on (especially in connection with the proprieties of dramatic method). What Aristotle says in his opening chapters amounts to the following. Literature is a practice devoted to the representation of human actions, emotions, and characteristics. It is one of a number of practices devoted to doing this in various media: what literature does with words, picturing does with paint, and instrumental music with harmony (that is, a tonal system) and rhythm. And he ends the list by saying: "The imitations of dancers imitate by rhythm itself without harmony; for they, too, through their figured rhythms, imitate both characters and passions and actions as well" (1447a 26–28). The point being made is, first, that the medium of dance is body movement alone (though dancers, then as now, used musical accompaniments) and, second, that a dancer represents human action (*praxis*), not by straightforward mime or dumb-show, but by movements that are formally patterned and rhythmical—in other words, by dance steps and dance figures. Moreover, if we look at the precise wording of the sentence quoted above, we see that Aristotle is not simply characterizing mimetic dance; he is describing the sort of mimesis that dancers actually perform. That is, there is a group of people, dancers, who make a practice of doing this. Dance is a socially established art, including this kind of mimesis in its scope. We keep one eye on the formal scope of the medium and the other on the actual organization of social practice.

As to why imitations of human *praxis* should constitute a family of actual arts, Aristotle simply says that imitation is one of the chief ways of learning things, so that we are naturally interested in it; and it is an exercise of our cognitive faculties, which is inherently enjoyable. Mimesis is a natural and typical manifestation of our humanity. Mimetic dance needs no separate justification and receives none—any more than poetry does. For the *Poetics* contains no specific rationale for poetry as such. What is justified is the generic practice of mimesis and the specific genre of tragedy, with its highly specialized stories and context of presentation. By parity of reasoning, we would expect from an Aristotelian treatise on dance a rationale for particular dance practices (the romantic ballet, for instance, or the electric boogie), but not for dance as such.

Among the moderns, the formulation in which the canon of the fine arts took on its definitive shape and content is usually said to be that of Charles Batteux's *Les Beaux arts reduits à un même principe* (1746), where the "common principle" is the imitation of "beautiful nature" (*la belle nature*). The bulk of his work is concerned with principles of taste, a great preoccupation in that age of collectors and connoisseurs. (He devotes 250 pages to poetry, followed by 3 on painting, then music and dance together get about 20.) In the bits that do have to do with the canon of the arts, at the beginning and end of his book, his general approach is in line with Aristotle's; but there are some basic differences. The general object of mimesis is no longer human affairs but the ideal archetypes on which nature, including human nature in its hierarchical articulation, must be patterned by a Platonic demiurge. Ever since Christianity went up-market, intellectual theologians had followed Philo of Alexandria in supposing that the first thing a Creator did was create the world of Platonic ideas.

Batteux defines an art in general as not merely rule-governed but rule-constituted: it is "a collection or assemblage of rules for doing well something that can be done either well or badly." These rules are merely generalizations drawn from, and consistently verified in, repeated observation (p. 24). There are three kinds of arts: those that serve human needs, those whose object is pleasure, and those that aim at the useful and agreeable together. The third group includes architecture and oratory; the second group is the fine arts strictly so called, namely, music, poetry, painting, sculpture, and "the art of gesture, or dance" (p. 27). And Batteux insists that the fine arts do not use nature, even as a basis of embellishment, but imitate it (p. 28), by which he means that the procedures their principles regulate are not species of fabrication or ornamentation but manipulations of meaning. Consequently, "[t]ous les Arts dans tout ce qu'ils ont de vraiment artificiel, ne sont que des choses imaginaires, des êtres feints, copiés et imités d'après les véritables" ["in all their truly artistic aspects, all the arts are nothing but things of the imagination, feigned realities, copied and imitated from the true"] (p. 38). It follows that, when dance extends to feats of virtuosity ("des secousses et des sauts de fantaisie)," it exceeds its proper bounds; its true task, like that of music (which succumbs to analogous temptations), is to be "the artistic portrait of human emotions" (p. 36).

Batteux' placement of dance among the fine arts is initially straightforward. The fine arts differ only in the media in which they carry out their mimesis: painting, music, dance, and poetry use colors, sounds, gestures, and discourse, respectively (p. 20). But in the sequel things become complex, if not confusing. Dance is lined up with painting and sculpture in its use of visual presentations, and with music and poetry in its function of expressing emotion. It is the only one of the fine arts that is involved in any such duality. The art of gesture, says Batteux, differs from painting and sculpture only "in what it consists of . . . because, in the dance, the subject to which the gestures are attached is natural and living" (p. 59). On the other hand, "Men have three media for expressing their ideas and their feelings (*sentimens*), speech, tone of voice, and gesture," and among these, though speech takes pride of place, the others have several advantages: their use is more natural (we have recourse to them when words fail), more extensive ("it is a universal interpreter which follows us to the ends of the earth, which makes us intelligible to the most barbarous peoples and even to animals"), and immediate (p. 336).

There is another way in which dance differs from painting, to which it was initially said to be analogous. Like speech and tone of voice, gesture can pertain to any one of the three kinds of art initially distinguished: a gesture may simply convey what one feels, or do so with embellishment, or be used for the artistic representation of feeling (p. 338)—in which case it is only by irrelevant coincidence that what it expresses should be what the dancer as a person actually feels (p. 350). But what really messes the discussion up is that Batteux insists that music used to include versification and dance as well as song and that this connection is intrinsic: their separation is due to artists rather than to the arts themselves, which remain intimately related, to the point where Batteux proposes to treat them as one (pp. 333–335).

Even Batteux, then, who begins with a forthright enumeration of the fine arts in which dance figures among the rest on an equal and distinctive footing, ends by making the place of dance equivocal. Dance, as an analogue of painting, presents scenes of persons in action; but as an associate or division of music, it is a matter of gesturing, which is not the same thing at all. It is as though Batteux were thinking sometimes of what it is like to be a person dancing and sometimes of what it is like to be watching a stage performance, and never related the two.

The positions of Aristotle and Batteux are alike, at least initially, in that they plant dance firmly among the arts they are considering. But in the substance of what they say, they are very different—even if much of the difference arises from the fact that Batteux devotes many more pages to the matter than Aristotle does words and that dance belongs to Batteux's proposed topic as it does not to Aristotle's. Aristotle presents dance mimesis as something dancers do, without saying that their art is itself one of mimesis. Batteux presents the art of dance as included within the scope of imitation, any dance that is not mimetic being an abuse of the art. Most important of all, Batteux thinks of the medium of dance as significant movement, feigned and idealized; Aristotle says the medium is movement subjected to figure and rhythm.

We must bear in mind that although Batteux, unlike D'Alembert, makes dance unequivocally one of the fine arts, he does not, as D'Alembert did, assign any cognitive significance to the fine arts as such: they exist only for pleasure (as we should say, for entertainment). As we saw when considering Levinson's strictures on Noverre (§1.3322), people concerned with the prestige of dance were not satisfied with admission to fine-art status on those terms. Aristotle's view of the matter had been different. The eighteenth-century thinkers were much occupied with the idea of "polite society," with the achievement of a level of civilized existence such as savage and superstitious people had never attained, but Aristotle was more relaxed. Humanity had always existed, civilization was natural and would be attained when conditions were right; refined enjoyments were their own justification, a component in the highest form of life attainable by humanity. But there is more to it than that; and Levinson's diatribe, though it is wrong in what it says about Aristotle, may be right in what it implies.

In his *Politics*, Aristotle contrasts genteel music with professional music: the sort gentlemen learn for their own entertainment (singing to the lyre) is different from the virtuoso stuff they get experts to perform for them (tootling the flute). Fair enough, we can grasp the combination of class associations with careerism. But, as we look, we see that the actual contrast of genres is between vocal and instrumental—or, as we might put it but they never would, between music organized verbally and music organized musically. And the same contrast can be made in dance, between dance with a practical or narrative organization, of which the basis in the last analysis is a verbalized or verbalizable text, and dance organized in autonomous dance terms. It is the Indian contrast between *nrtta* and *nrtya* (cf. §8.4611 below). Levinson was right: what Hegel and the rest were really opposed to was *dance organized as dance*. But then, Hegel had no interest in, placed no value on, the arts of dance or music as such. As we suggested in §§1.3312 and 1.33121, he followed the Platonists in valuing only the verbalizable shell of the phenomenon. Music was rescued for such thinkers, in Hellenic and Medieval times, by finding in it a manifestation of mathematical and celestial law. But no analogous backing could be found for dance organization: appeal to the supposed cosmic dance supported, as we saw, the wrong practice. The difficulty appears already in Plato's *Laws*, Books 2 and 7: as we plough through these stupefyingly dull pages, it dawns on us that though Plato may know something about what musicians say about music, he knows absolutely nothing about dancing as dancing. In fact, he cannot conceive how there could be anything to be known about it.

3.32 Ways of Viewing the Fine Arts

Once the fine arts are detached from the historical setting in which they were first identified as a distinctive group of skilled practices, it is seen that they can be described in various ways, each of which picks out something that serves to unite them and give them a common character, and each of which contributes something to the ways we still think about the arts—and will probably continue to do so, because once we have noticed the things that made our forefathers formulate the idea of the fine arts it is hard to see how they could be lost sight of. They remain there to be seen, and it does not occur to us that our forebears may once have found other things better worth looking at. As before, I merely recapitulate material developed at length elsewhere (Sparshott 1982).

3.321 *Arts of Imitative Play*

Within the development of Western philosophy, a set of arts roughly corresponding to the fine arts was first distinguished by Plato and Aristotle as arts of imitation; and these were a subdivision of the arts that contributed to recreation ("play") or simply to the quality of one's life. The important (and surprisingly difficult) thing for us to remember nowadays is that this was not a clumsy attempt to describe a set of practices that had already been grouped together as the fine arts; it was itself the original classification. In the eighteenth-century formulation of the concept of the fine arts, the description of these arts as "arts of imitation" was retained. People nowadays reject the idea, for two reasons. First, they associate it with photographic or journalistic realism, which is no longer a prevailing value in art—if it ever was. Second, the idea is associated with official eighteenth- and nineteenth-century values in general, a bundle of academic attitudes and practices that we still find threatening. And these are indeed good practical reasons for not using this language any more. Taken by itself, however, with regard to its basic intention, and cut loose from all historical associations, the idea still makes a lot of sense. We can bring this out by putting it in the following way.

Humans are distinguished by the extent and elaboration of the part played in their lives by information processing and communication. What we call the (fine) arts are systematic developments of these means of formulation and communication beyond necessity and in the absence of necessity. The means of conveying factual information or formulating necessary communication can be and are developed to formulate and communicate ideas beyond experience, either for the interest of the ideas or for the interest in the potentialities of the means themselves, and, at a further level, simply to see what developments in the methods of development are possible. The arts comprise these fictive and exploratory practices, which remain "imitative play" (or "disengaged communication") even when it is abstract formal possibilities that are being explored. And to say

150

(as is often said) that humans are essentially symbol-using animals is already to make it likely that the arts will be important in human life.

The traditional fine arts, in their avant-garde developments no less than in their most academic manifestations, are arts of the sort just described. But so are the theater arts, including dance. Theater is no longer merely a presentation of poetry in dramatic form: it is the exploration and exploitation of the limits of theatrical resources, whatever they may prove to be. Even in dramatic poetry the drama is no longer supposed to be the presentation of thought and action in dramatic form but is the progressive discovery of what dramatic form is. Theater dance as such immediately becomes a fine art in its own right. Again, the art of mime, in abstraction from a theatrical context, becomes a fine art with its own terms of reference: to see how far meaningful gesture can be developed, what degree of refinement is possible, what can be mimed that cannot be conveyed in any other way, and even *what can exist only as mimed*. And it has usually been taken for granted, even by those who also distinguish mimetic from "pure" or "classical" or "abstract" dance, that either mime is a form of dance or dance is a development of mime.

In terms of the line of thought just sketched, dance figures among theater arts and as an art akin to mime. But dance needs no introduction. Dance is the art of meaningful movement, and its exclusive field, whether in the theater or out of it, is the exploration of the possible meaningfulness of body movement as movement. Saying that such movement must be inherently musical or rhythmical adds little or nothing, for those terms can be construed in such a way as to mean no more than that the movement is perceived as inherently significant without reference to any extraneous criteria or definition of what is meant. (Since rhythms can be jerky and irregular, to call a movement rhythmical may be only to say that it is not random.) In any case, the terms of our present argument require us to say that the development of the resources of the meaningfulness of body movement must be within the domain of the fine arts and that dance plainly fills the bill, even if actual arts of dance as practiced do not explore all the territory open to them.

3.3211 *Noverre Reviewed*

If the phrase "imitative arts" can be (and indeed, if it is to be taken seriously, has to be) understood in the way we have just considered, we can see what went wrong with Noverre's apologia for his new "action ballet." He claimed for dance the status of one of the "sister arts," pursuing the same ends by other means. By basing ballet on sequences of ordinarily motivated action, dance became another way of representing significant *praxis* and thus aspired to the dignity already accorded to painting, epic, and tragedy. But, as we have suggested, there was nothing in that line that dancing could do and its legitimate siblings could not: *praxis* does not lend itself to being danced, in any significant way. In fact, the doings of mythological beings, however uninteresting, offer dance a better opportunity, both because of the affinity between formal dance and the ceremonies in which deities are ritually invoked and because the specialness of dance movement fits the special status of supernatural beings better than it does the transactions of mankind. Nor was the conventional polemic against fancy footwork well judged, from our viewpoint: it would be more promising to ask what significance such footwork might have, or might be given. It is as if Noverre went out of his way to make dance superfluous by emphasizing ways in which it was like its legitimate siblings rather than any unique contribution it might make to the quality of life. In fact, all significant practices and theories in dance in the last hundred years have represented ways of solving this problem: what meaning can dance have that is both unique to the sorts of things that make dance different from all other arts and, by tapping some profound level of human significance, immediately accessible and evidently important to audiences? Noverre saw that danceable meanings must be human meanings but assumed that they must therefore be identical with what gave an accepted human significance to the established fine arts. It was, in fact, only when the status of straightforward mimetic modes in the other arts was called into question that dancers and thinkers began to perceive and exploit the special range of dance meanings. That is why we often say that the art of dance as such is really a development of the last hundred years.

3.322 Arts of Beauty

It is hard to give an account of what is meant by "arts of imitation" that is adequate to all that has been meant by such phrases without becoming so vague as to be empty. Consequently, there is another way of thinking about the fine arts—the way, in fact, that in German and French is conveyed by the very phrases we translate as "fine arts." One simplifies matters as follows. What the arts of imitation do is produce things for looking at or listening to, things in which, in order to understand and appreciate the meaning, we concentrate simply on what that meaning is. And we do so simply out of interest, for enjoyment (in a sufficiently broad sense); insofar as the works are works of art, their value consists of what the public can appreciate in them. That value is what philosophers have always called *beauty*, even though that word (like its equivalents in other languages) is used in the vernacular in rather different ways.[23] This notion of what the fine arts are (or, if you prefer, this way of singling out a group of arts having affinities with each other and with such arts as painting and poetry) comes to much the same thing as the notion of "arts of imitation": how could a work repay looking and listening if not for the special way it stretched the means of expression and communication it used?

Rhetorical questions are tricky. The correct answer to the one in the last paragraph is not "It couldn't" but, at strongest, "We don't see how it could." The difference is important. What were once called "the pleasures of the imagination"—that is, in the usage of the early eighteenth century, the pleasures derived from looking and listening and from visual and auditory imagery—were thought of as pleasures of *taste*, and it was possible to think of a relish for them as not fundamentally different from the enjoyment of nature. Thus the poet Mark Akenside assimilated the difference between Shakespeare and Waller to the difference between two sorts of scenery:

> What then is taste, but these internal powers
> Active and strong, and feelingly alive
> To each fine impulse? A discerning sense
> Of decent and sublime. . . .
>   When lightning fires
> The arch of heaven, and thunders rock the ground,
> When furious whirlwinds rend the howling air,
>   . . . Shakespeare looks abroad
> From some high cliff, superior, and enjoys
> The elemental war. But Waller longs,
> All on the margin of some flowery stream,
> To spread his careless limbs amid the cool
> Of plantane shades. . . .
> Such and so various are the tastes of men.
>   (Akenside 1744, III, 515–567)

In the cases of poetry and painting, in which the place of depiction and narration and hence of meaningfulness in a robust and obvious form was taken for granted, this confusion of nature and art was easy enough. In the case of dance, it was not; and the alternative account of what the fine arts are makes an important difference. Dancers have never tried to be realistic or naturalistic (success would be either boringly complete or farcically impossible); once the notion of mimesis ceases to be built in to the very con-

---

[23] Mary Mothersill has recently made an imposing attempt to reinstate the expression "*x* is beautiful" as "the generic aesthetic predicate" (Mothersill 1984, 3, 253, and passim).

cept of a fine art, it is open for the art of dance to become an abstract arrangement of moving limbs in space. "The concept of a dance as a bodily construction in space and time . . . appears to have been at the basis of most civilized dancing for two hundred years," says Arlene Croce.[24]

To put the matter more generally: dance arts could be defined as arts based on movements of the body that can be appreciated, whatever the grounds of that appreciation may be. Dance movements are movements that can be the object of a developed taste, a distinctive branch of connoisseurship. Such connoisseurship, as Hegel remarked, may be in itself contemptible, not being connected with general cultivation or with any socially and humanly valuable characteristics in the connoisseur. But one may retort that Hegel was a relentlessly pretentious and sanctimonious theory builder, in whom philosophy was a continuation of theology by other means; and that, as Jacques Maritain insisted in a work now too little remembered, the independent values of artistic appreciation may come to roost in the niche, not antisocial but supersocial, formerly assigned to the contemplative lives of saints and scholars (Maritain 1930).

3.323 *Arts of Expression*

In a note to the last section, we found a distinguished critic insisting on the primacy of a dance art based on pure movement and at the same time disparaging a dance of meaningless movement on the ground that dance should not be mindless but should go beyond mind: if dance is pure expression, it should still express *something*. People often say things like this, and in many cases it is their way of voicing their adherence to a view that is in fact widely held as to what the fine arts are. This view picks out roughly but not exactly the same set of practices as the two other such views we have considered, but it characterizes them in a rather different way, so that different arts are given prominence as typical or exemplary of what the fine arts are really all doing.

The view we are now to consider may be approached by considering the case of painting. A painting nowadays need not be a painting *of* anything; but an abstract painting should be as fully meaningful as a representational

---

[24] Croce 1978, 253. Croce also writes that "[t]oo many choreographers are making the same kind of bad ballet. . . . The ideal is absolute expression, dancing for its own sake—what might be called 'dance totalism.' . . . Today it is possible to speak of overtrained audiences who presuppose meaning where there is *only* movement" (1978, 320–321). Some years separate this pronouncement from the one quoted in the text; it is not clear how, if at all, they are to be related to each other, unless by such statements as, "It isn't mindlessness but the state beyond mind that moves us in perfect dancing. It's what moves the dancer, too" (1978, 420).

one and can be experienced as such. If it were not so, abstract painting would not have the status it does among art lovers. Besides, painting is a single art, unified by more than the mere fact that pigment is being spread on surfaces: nonrepresentational and representational painters are obviously in the same line of work, and it is common for one painter to produce works of both sorts. How can this be? One way of conceiving the matter is that artists of both sorts are engaged in "expression." Representational painters present their personal visions of what they paint and do so by expressing their personal feelings about it—if they did not, if they had nothing of their own to say about it, why should they bother to paint it at all? If a less biographical way of putting things is preferred, we can say that representational painters present feelingfully individualized visions of what they paint. But now we can say that abstract artists do exactly the same thing: they present feelingfully individualized visions, which happen not to be visions *of* anything. Since it is the quality of the feelingful vision that matters in both cases, the presence or absence of a representational content is of secondary importance, so far as the fine art of painting is concerned. Painting, we shall now say, like the other fine arts, is first and foremost an art of expression.

The foregoing way of conceiving the fine arts has been very popular for at least four reasons. First, as we saw, it allows us to think of representational and nonrepresentational modes of art together. Second, it allows us to recognize and explain the fact that the most esteemed music for the last two centuries has been "absolute" music, which is not about anything other than itself, and still treat music as the same sort of art as poetry and painting. Third, it differentiates abstract painting from scenery in a relevant way: a painting is something someone has painted and is valued as such. Fourth, and perhaps most important, it takes account of the fact that for many decades artists have not typically worked to please an extant public but to satisfy themselves as harbingers of a public that may not yet exist. In fact, the public for a fine art demands that the work of an artist shall not be aimed at pleasing them. That is part of what we mean by saying that works of art call for appreciation: it is our responsibility to live up to the standards of feeling and understanding that the artist's vision imposes. We may feel that this relation between artist and society is pathological, but we can hardly deny that it is the relation that obtains.

Before the thesis that the fine arts are essentially arts of expression in the above sense took hold, it was often said that music was "the language of feeling," though people who said that at different periods did not always mean the same sort of thing by it. Part of the reason for saying that was that one can make up a song as one goes along, and the time of the song can be real time. A piece of music can come out as a spontaneous effusion, as easy and direct as talking; and since the music neither affirms nor depicts, we can say that it is like language but is not about anything.[25] But we can say the same about dance, with very little change: a dance can be and can be experienced as a spontaneous effusion, a direct manifestation of a feelingful vision that is not a vision of anything. If the arts are arts of expression, dance is not only a full-fledged art but may be thought of as the exemplary fine art, with music as its only possible rival. Expression theories of art in the foregoing sense first appeared in the 1870s, so far as I am aware; it was in the intellectual climate thus prepared that Isadora Duncan's dance was created and perceived.[26]

The only difficulty in accepting dance as an art of expression is that, in a way, the fit is too good. No one can seriously hold that the practice of an art typically consists of giving expression to what the creator or performer happens to be feeling at the time. Theorists who think of art as expression are rather concerned to show how the meaning of a work depends in some close but complex way on its making some aspect of human subjectivity available to appreciation (cf. Sparshott 1982, 85–89). But in dance, even more than in music, things are complicated by the fact that voices and bodies can be artlessly used to show how their owners feel. There is a temptation for writers of general works on dance to begin by mentioning such spontaneous manifestations as the origin and root of dance and thus to suggest that they are archetypally dance. The examples, however, are never of dancers engaged in any actual dance practice: they are always children gamboling, apes stomping, or imaginary "primitive" people leaping and gesticulating. This rightly exasperates people who care about dancing, and writers on dance aesthetics have to spend more energy than others in giving expression its due without committing this infuriating faux pas (e.g., Langer 1953, Sirridge and Armelagos 1977, Carroll 1981).

[25] The logical point is that the feeling expressed in a song may be in line with, or run counter to, or be quite irrelevant to what the person singing the song may be feeling at the time. Since these are logical possibilities, music must at least sometimes express feelings that people can have. People like Stravinsky who say that music *cannot* express feelings are committing themselves to the position that the first sentence in this note is not simply untrue but nonsensical. But is it?

[26] The first theory to become famous as equating art with the expression of feeling seems to be that of Eugène Véron (1878). Theories that talk about expression are a mixed bag, and few are formulated in a way that withstands scrutiny. In general, the kind of theory I am talking about here is to be differentiated sharply from the theory put forward by Benedetto Croce and modified by R. G. Collingwood, according to which art is the expression of an "intuition" or of emotion in a rather special sense. In this latter kind of theory, dance has no special place—in fact, none of the arts has any theoretical standing at all. See Sparshott 1982, ch. 12.

3.324 *Arts of Creation and Imagination*

In the same sort of way that a simplification and generalization of the concept of "arts of imitation" led to the concept of the fine arts simply as arts for the production of objects for appreciation, the notion that the fine arts are to be thought of as in the first instance arts of expression can be simplified and generalized into a less informative but less tricky notion, as follows. What, we ask, was the original point of substituting the concept of expression for that of imitation as the defining characteristic of the fine arts? Simply that what is esteemed in works of art as such is not their relation to some antecedent reality but their issuing from a distinctive sensibility and capacity. That is, they are valued for their originality—not in the sense that each is unlike any previously existing work, but that they depend on and transmit the distinctive point of view of an individual. That is, they represent the active development of trained and refined feeling and perception.

If we follow the train of thought just outlined, we find that the fine arts (or that group of activities that comes closest to what other viewpoints distinguished as the fine arts) are arts of imagination or arts of creation. Both of those words, like all the key words in discussions of these intricate matters, are tricky, usually employed tendentiously in relation to some more or less elaborate and controversial theory about the way we live in the world. That is inevitable, since we are professedly attempting to give a general account of those human activities in which pains are taken to be extraordinary, to probe the limits of what can be made sense of. The use of the words "creation" and "imagination" in such contexts as this has a long and complex history. But for present purposes, which are neither historical nor exploratory but merely those of preliminary orientation, it will be enough to say that by "imagination" we mean simply the ability to form and apprehend sensible and thinkable complexes, and by "creation" we mean bringing into being entities of which the distinctive features cannot be traced to anything in their origins. The important parts played by creation and imagination, in these senses, in human intellectual and practical life is by no means confined to the fine arts. But perhaps it could be claimed that it is in art that creativity and imaginativeness are developed and their products enjoyed for their own sakes.

On the last page of his autobiography, Fred Astaire says that although ballet training is "the finest training a dancer can get," he never cared for it, because "I wanted to do all my dancing my own way, in a sort of outlaw style." He knows nothing, and wants to know nothing, he says, about the history and philosophy of dance. "I have no desire to prove anything by it. I have never used it as an outlet or as a means of expressing myself. I just dance" (Astaire 1959, 325). What does he mean by this? He wants to dance in his own way (since, as he says, he knew he was not going to be a ballet dancer but would continue to be a dance entertainer as he had been since the age of seven), but not to express himself. That is to say, presumably, he wants to develop a distinctive way of dancing that is just dancing. And when he says he just dances, he should not be taken as meaning that his dancing is spontaneous, "doing what comes naturally": the entire book that he is now concluding reveals (or displays) him as a worker and a worrier, a perfectionist, who starts with a danceable idea and transforms it into an idea for a dance number, a number that he then laboriously works up and perfects simply as a dance. The art of dance, as Astaire conceives it, is an art of expression, in that its value lies not in that which the dance relates to but in what Astaire and other artists develop as distinctive danceables. But in Astaire's unforgettable and unmistakable way of dancing, nothing depends on there being a viewpoint or a personality that is being communicated, a state of mind that we share and explore: rather, the Astaire persona expressed is exhausted in the possibilities of the dance style that he has worked up, develops, and exploits. To call what he does a dance of expression is, therefore, a little misleading, even if it is technically correct. It is much nearer the mark to call it a dance of creation and imagination. And that is what justifies so self-conscious and laborious a dance maker in saying "I just dance."[27]

3.33 Cognitive Significance

The fine arts, as conceived in what became the definitive, restricted system, were picked out as having a distinctive importance in general culture, representing a serious use of the mind and earning a place on the map of intellectual undertakings. Within that system, dance had no place because no distinctive contribution to that function could be assigned to it, either on theoretical grounds or in virtue of accepted practices and valuations. We suggested at one point that the later admission of dance to the canon of the fine arts represented not a higher valuation of dance or the discovery of a new range of dance meanings but merely a lowering of standards. It was no longer demanded of a fine art that it be integrated into what was expected of a mature and responsible member of the cultivated classes. Art was trivialized, knowledge devalued: in a democracy, respect for the mind

[27] The same defensive move was made by Balanchine in an interview, in response to a question about why he denied himself certain choreographical adjuncts: "I am not doing anything in particular. I simply dance. Why must everything be defined by words? When you place flowers on a table, are you affirming or denying or disproving anything? . . . I don't have a 'logical' mind, just three-dimensional plasticity" (Balanchine 1984, 31).

and recognition of serious standards for art are rejected as elitist, if they are understood at all. But that way of looking at things is not necessarily the right way. The sorts of people who value art and intellect still exist and occupy the same sort of social position they always did. Art is taken more seriously (or at least solemnly) than ever, if anything, and artists work with as much dedication and intelligence as they ever did.

What has changed is rather that the idea of general culture, of *paideia* or *Bildung*, has gone. The sciences are too complex and change too quickly to fit on a map of knowledge, and a map that excluded them would be silly. In general, the ideal of a general education with a determinate content that would make people free of all the best their culture had to offer is discredited. People who cling to that notion prove thereby that they are either too ill educated to understand the basic tendencies of the world they live in or too scared and resentful to acknowledge them. It is because there is no map of knowledge that the fine arts can no longer be located on such a map, and the exclusion of dance makes no sense.

What has replaced the old idea of an educated and knowledgeable person is the idea of the person of resourceful intellect, able to think and learn, crafty and streetwise as well as quick on the uptake, imaginative, and creative. Insofar as that is our ideal, the fine arts as areas in which imaginativeness and creativity are especially cultivated and celebrated have as important a place as ever—more important, if anything. And from this point of view, dance is no less to be esteemed than any other art. In fact, because at one level dance is accessible to everyone, in that we all have bodies and have learned to use them with some dexterity, dance takes a place beside the literary arts as the art in which creative activity should be immediately possible without having to learn the use of such possibly unfamiliar equipment as brushes, chisels, and saxophones. Of course, serious dance and serious literature are not accessible without arduous training, the remaking of the body and the formation of prose style, but that is another matter.

The idea that our whole notion of what education is about has been transformed in the way I have suggested is not one that has been widely disseminated in any clearly articulated form, much less one that has been generally accepted, even among the educated and educating classes. Consequently, the new significance of the immediate accessibility of dance is not so much affirmed as shown in how people regulate their lives. But that is because almost no one knows how to live in the world as we have made it. Humanity lies undiscovered before us; meanwhile, we do the best we can.

Another thing that has changed the relative significance of dance and the other fine arts is the decline in realist philosophy. The maps of knowledge on which the fine arts held their set place assumed that there is a real world within which we are placed and must place ourselves. That is true even in Hegel's "idealism," in which it turns out that we are ourselves that real world. More recent philosophies have dismissed that position as superficial. Existentialism recognizes that we have access to existence through the act of existing and that the subjective point of view, from which the world is simply that which is present to us, is a viewpoint that cannot be escaped. Phenomenology recognizes that the real world is a selection from what we know, from the totality of objects of intuition, and that the knowable realm of essences must be charted before the frontiers of the domain of science can be drawn within that realm. Linguistic modes of philosophizing, which have dominated academic philosophizing in the English-speaking lands, have diverted attention from facts to meanings, from the objects of knowledge to the workings of the language in which that knowledge is given shape. In the last two of these modes of philosophizing, dance is no less important than any other art. In existentialism it may be of prime importance, in that it celebrates our way of being present to the world. On the older ways of thinking, dance could celebrate social reality; on the new way of thinking, it is more nearly true that in the first instance it celebrates interpersonal reality and that elaborately structured dance forms celebrate the generation of society from interpersonal relations in which the relation between irreducible individuals remains primary.

The foregoing accounts of the drift in philosophy over the last century are no doubt so coarse as to be objectionable. But they should suffice to carry my main point, which is that in any account of the basic structure of today's intellectual life the fine arts can be found a place at least as strategically significant as any they ever held and that, among the fine arts as thus placed, dance seems at least as likely as any to have an important position. And that position will be, as it used not to be, an autonomous one. It was the obsolete epistemology enshrined in the old system of the fine arts that made dance seem parasitic on arts in which the scope of mimesis was more sharply defined or more comprehensive.

3.331 *Non-natural Embellishment*

Something can be said about the possible cognitive significance of Western theater dance as it used to be without invoking any new era in the world of learning. We have observed more than once (e.g., §1.253) that ballet and opera are institutionally intertwined, often sharing management and facilities as well as competing for space and funds. Song and dance in this cultural context have functioned, it seems to me, as non-natural embellishments of drama. They elucidate something that the spoken and acted drama cannot. Notoriously, opera singers take an unnaturally long and noisy time to die; as drama, it is very funny. But what happens is that the *situation* sings. Time stands still while the significance of the situation unfolds in an aria or an ensemble. Perhaps "action ballet" functioned in a similar way. Bournonville certainly thought something of the sort: "The art of *Mime* encompasses all the feelings of the soul. The Dance, on the other hand, is essentially an expression of joy, a desire to follow the rhythms of the music" (Bournonville 1865, 133). (Deborah Jowitt's description of the Bournonville centenary gives an indication of how this works in dance terms; Jowitt 1985, 138–145.) What is celebrated can hardly be, in this context, the sense of the body (that would be analogous to the sense of temporality in music, which is not the primary concern in opera). It must be more like the character of the *Lebenswelt*, the sense of humanity as lived in the enacted experience, that is shown and celebrated (cf. §8.211231).

3.34 AESTHETICS AND CRITICISM

So long as we consider dance within the context of the fine arts, we may be tempted to equate the philosophy of dance with the aesthetics of dance, which in turn might be equated with the theory of dance criticism. The project of basing the philosophy of a fine art on the criticism of that art has much to recommend it. Criticism already exists as an established mode of thinking and writing, and the extant work of critics affords a corpus within which one may expect to find much of the most penetrating and best organized thought about the art. A good critic provides sensitive descriptions of performances, evoking their quality for those who have not seen them and recalling it for those who have. Investigation of how such descriptions are written should reveal much about the nature of the art. The same holds of what critics say in analyzing and explaining the structure and symbolism of performances. Discussing how such analyses and explanations are constructed and defended gives philosophers plenty to think about: How, in general, are symbolisms articulated and understood? What principles determine the relevance or irrelevance of a particular structure imputed to a particular presentation? Again, good critics relate performances to the standards prevailing among those who know the art best—something that few in any audience can know and knowledge of which contributes to the appreciation of further performances. In addition, they may relate those standards to the standards that ought to prevail. How such standards are established, and what their logical standing is, are prime topics of philosophy. Finally, critics may relate performances, as perceived, interpreted, and evaluated, to the large concerns about the beautiful, the useful, the good, and the true by which their readers may be supposed to regulate their lives and thoughts. Criticism thus implies a general theory of values, hierarchically articulated or relatively autonomous; and this, when doggedly pursued, becomes a philosophy of life.

All this being so, the work of any critic has direct philosophical implications. Even the worst criticism has such implications by default, and the work of all but the most superficial critics actively incorporates some philosophizing.[28] Why, then, should not the philosophy of an art simply be the systematic outgrowth of its criticism? No reason, surely, except that the philosophy thus generated would tend to go direct from that in the art which was immediately available in experience to the concerns that the public already recognized as ultimate. If there is a middle ground, it would tend to be left vacant and thus condemn our philosophy to superficiality, if only to the superficiality of premature profundity. It is in this middle ground, in which the unobvious connections between what is obviously true and what is obviously important are worked out, this no man's land, that philosophy has always maneuvered.

The equation of aesthetics with the theory of criticism has been popular among English-language academic philosophers. Its most determined and systematic proponent was Monroe Beardsley (1958). The basic idea is that all philosophy is logic, examining this or that aspect of reasoning in discourse. (The idea behind this is that philosophers are concerned with meanings, not with facts, which are investigated by scientists and historians; and it is supposed that language is the sole domain of meaning.) Philosophy is thus parasitic on discourse, in the sense that the philosopher has nothing to say until someone else has said something. Criticism is equated with argumentative and explanatory discourse about works of fine art as such, considered as objects for appreciation in the way we considered above. Aesthetics, on this account, would consider the arguments critics use to guide appreciation, the canons of relevance implied in what they say, the standards they explicitly or implicitly appeal to, their characteristic ways of describing and explaining works of art, the bases of critical agreement and disagreement, and so forth. A great deal of influential writing on aesthetics has fallen within this domain. And from this point of view, the fact that there have been relatively few careful and sophisticated critics of dance would not only testify to the dubious status of dance as a fine art but

[28] This is not to say that a critic's report on experience should be construed as an inference from philosophical premises; see the interchange between Marcia Siegel and Gerald Myers in Fancher and Myers (1981, 52–68). Nor is it to say that every verdict or evaluation implies a full-blown theory. It is only to say that the professional practice of a critic must imply a philosophical position. (Siegel, in the exchange referred to, relates her own practice to general theses about the nature of perception and language.)

would also help to explain why philosophers have found little to say about it.

The above way of determining the scope of the philosophy of dance is obviously questionable in two ways, whether or not one accepts it in the long run. First, the critics of any fine art operate with a limited perspective. They are directly concerned with the aspects of a work to which the public consciously responds and in terms of which it makes its choices. The deeper implications of those responses, and the attitudes and understandings that are so ingrained as to go without saying, tend not to enter into critical discourse. But it is just those deeper implications that most concern philosophers, whose starting point is thus needlessly far from their destination. Besides, the status of the initial restriction to dance-as-a-fine-art, which is seldom if ever an issue for critics, is one that philosophers cannot pass over. They must also consider dance as a practice, as a form of life, as whatever else it may be—viewpoints that are not embedded in a body of discourse as clearly recognizable and as conveniently accessible as criticism, which is a recognized branch of journalism and of literature. In short, the restriction of aesthetics to the philosophy of criticism closes off too many avenues of inquiry too soon.

The second obviously possible objection to equating the philosophy of art with aesthetics and aesthetics with the philosophy of criticism is a special case of the first. The equations really assume that human intelligence begins to be systematically employed in the fine arts only when the public begins to articulate its appreciation of the work. The work of art is treated as if it were a natural object, not something produced within a thoughtful tradition of intelligent making. This approach to the philosophy of art was robustly and strenuously advocated by Beardsley, but it strikes me as quite monstrously perverse. Its motivation, the will to disentangle criticism from biography and to establish for aesthetics a well-ordered domain, is clear enough. But the price is high.

The present work, though sympathetic to the traditional emphasis on aesthetics as representing the viewpoint of an appreciative and articulate public, with the corresponding downplaying of the professional procedures of specialists, refuses to be limited by it. Apart from the inherent limitations of the approach, which have just been mentioned, there is the fact on which we have insisted: the status of dance as a fine art is not established in the same way that those of poetry and painting are. It is not that the credentials of dance as an art are in doubt and that it is up to me to establish them; it is rather that a looser, more far-ranging, less well-ordered discourse is called for. It is not so much that the philosophy of the other arts is more firmly based and more securely held together by chains of reasoning; it is rather that custom has shown in their case what questions can be begged without anyone complaining.

Because of the lack of secure precedent, the second part of the book begins with a survey of some aspects of dance in which meaning can be found. A comprehensive philosophy of dance would deal with all of them.

PART II

~ ~ ~ ~ ~ ~ ~ ~ ~ ~ ~ ~ ~ ~ ~ ~ ~ ~ ~ ~

Theory: On Dance

CHAPTER 4

∾ ∾ ∾ ∾ ∾ ∾ ∾ ∾ ∾ ∾ ∾ ∾ ∾ ∾ ∾ ∾ ∾ ∾ ∾

Some Dimensions of
Dance Meaning

WHAT SHOULD a general aesthetics of dance and a general theory of the art of dance take into account? Everything for which dance is esteemed and the reasons for esteeming it. But the range of dance values must reflect the totality of the ways in which dance can be found meaningful. One has therefore to begin by trying to ascertain the scope of the meaningfulness of dance.

It is remarkable how much of what is actually written on dance fastens on one set of values answering to only one range of meanings, which is taken as uniquely determining how dances are to be interpreted and evaluated. The starting points of alternative views are either denied or, more often, ignored. The usual justification of this procedure, if any, is that the alternatives neglect or underestimate one's own preferred values. The basis of that preference itself may be affirmed but is never established, and by the nature of the case it cannot be. The basis could only be, in effect, that dance is an art with a set of aims and methods. The existence of such an art cannot, however, undermine the existence of alternative arts with their own aims and methods, nor can it deprive of legitimacy the existing practice of dance that does not pertain to any art. Many writings on dance thus combine an exploration of the values and methods of a way of dancing, which may be sensitive and intelligent, with a claim for the exclusive validity of that way of dancing, which is invariably stupid.

The topic of the present chapter is the scope of the meaningfulness of dance. It is much the most important thing we have to talk about, because everything else depends on it. But it is not clear how the task is to be begun, on what principles it should continue, or how it might be concluded. No applicable framework exists, no way of generating such a framework is recognized. Those writings that extend beyond the articulation of a single practice or a single value (such as "expressiveness" or "quality") seldom go beyond the set of polarities generated by their topic and its converse. I know of no serious attempt even to enumerate the dimensions of dance meaning as here conceived, let alone to order them.

The present chapter confines itself to the preliminary task of enumerating some main dimensions of dance meaning—that is, some mutually irreducible respects in which meanings of dance may be differentiated. The completeness of the enumeration, the proper ordering of the dimensions enumerated, and their relations with each other are problems that remain to be tackled. Merely to present the materials supplied here is a step worth taking, and one that might be compromised by systematic ambitions: reasons for including and arranging must lead to reasons for excluding, and systematic exclusion is just what we have to avoid here.

The treatment will mostly be schematic: most of the ways of being meaningful will merely be enumerated. In any case, it is a chapter about dimensions of meaning, not about qualities. If, for instance, music turns up as an essential dimension of dance meaning, that does not require that every dance must be musical or accompanied by music: it means that the question of how any dance relates to music, if at all, is a question that inevitably arises. Null values are not ruled out. Once a dimension becomes recognized as relevant to dance, whether or not it is explicitly formulated, a null value becomes significant to the observer who recognizes it, even if it has no significance for the participant; and it even has meaning for the participant if the unnoticed possible dimension is one for which the participant's culture makes provision.

Is it in principle possible that the following materials (or others like them) could eventually be arranged in a complete and well-ordered array? I doubt it. What is meaningful has meaning for some persons or in relation to some set of interests, and the relations among these must change in history. (That is why the nerve of a practice changes.) For practical purposes, the meaningfulness of any human action is inexhaustible, as our own changing practice suggests new contexts of acceptable human significance and renders old preoccupations incomprehensible. In fact, there could be a single system only if dance were a single rule-guided practice; but it is not and cannot be, since societies that have no communication with each other have their own ways of doing things that we insist on calling dance. Not only methods and values, but also dimensions of meaningfulness must be supposed relative to culture, if not in the sense that we cannot understand each other's questions, at least in the sense that it may never occur to us to formulate some of them. What follows can only comprise the questions I have thought of or have found raised by others.

Because the different dimensions really are different, no real connection between the parts of the chapter can be guaranteed. What seem to be the most fundamental significances will be presented first. The aspects of dance most discussed by critics and aestheticians figure toward the end of the chapter.

4.1 *Existence*

It is often said and seldom denied that most or all human societies dance, in the sense that they have institutionalized behavior patterns that we unhesitatingly recognize as dance, whether or not the society under consideration thinks of them as dance or possesses the concept of dance. Since the behavior is institutionalized, it must be meaningful to them: they do what they do neither unwittingly nor incidentally, but knowingly and on purpose.

Here, then, is the first dimension: the very fact of dance has meaning. The fact that a society dances tells something about that society. And, since every such society is a human society and virtually all human societies dance, the fact that there is dancing tells something about humanity.

Meaning, then, may be found in the very fact of the existence of dance and, by the same token, in the fact of its prevalence. And this fact may be a fact about a culture or a fact about humanity. But to say that is to make premature assumptions about what dance is: we have not yet established that only human beings dance. The locus of the relevant value might be all-embracing (perhaps a cosmic "dance") or might be found in some wider genus to which humanity belongs: the significant fact might be that all living things, or all animals, or all vertebrates, or all mammals, or all primates, dance—though of course we cannot say of all of them that they *engage in the practice* of dancing. In the opposite direction, the locus of meaning and value might be humanity as a whole, or a society or culture, or an institution, or a group, or an individual, or an occasion, or an activity to which a dance character is assigned. By the same token, it may be the existence or prevalence of a specific style or type of dance that is found significant or, by the same token again, a specific dance. And that being said, it becomes necessary to say that the meaning may lie in the opposition between *some* dance and no dance, between *this* dance and no dance, or between *this* dance and *that* dance.

In all of the cases mentioned in the preceding paragraph, the meaning may be one recognized by those engaged in the practice in question, or it may not. And we should note that the meaning-bearer ("dance as such," "this sort of dance," or "this dance") is in each case an inferred entity: someone has to judge that a dance is being danced. (No further notice of this fact will be taken in the present chapter.) It should be emphasized, too, that because we are concerned in this chapter not with qualities of dance but with dimensions of dance, it is not our business now to affirm that dance is present here or there but rather to say that, when present, its presence is meaningful; and, if its presence is meaningful, so is its absence. Still less is it our business to catalogue the meanings assigned (or properly assigned) along these dimensions or to endorse any specific one or set of such meanings.

4.2 *Self-Defined and Other-Defined*

Most or all human societies dance. But perhaps few such cultures have a word that translates the word "dance." We distinguish, then, between behavior defined by the dancing community as dance and behavior defined as dance only by observers. Within the former, we distinguish at least the following. First, behavior for which "dance" is the preferred designation for general purposes. Second, behavior for which "dance" is one accepted designation (in some circumstances at least) among others. Third, behavior for which the proper answer to "Is it dance?" is affirmative, but for which "dance" is never a spontaneous designation. Fourth, behavior for which the answer to "Is it dance?" is negative, but for which some acceptable argument can evoke the concession that it is dance after all (as often with avant-garde phenomena). And fifth, behavior for which such an argument can be put forward but would not be accepted by whatever judges are deemed authoritative. If we wanted a term for this dimension of dance meaning, we could call it "degree of dance-awareness" or something like that.

In each of the foregoing cases, the link between the behavior and the concept of dance may be of various kinds. The behavior may be of a type that is acknowledged to be dancelike by whatever judges are deemed authoritative. Or it may be perceived as having a generically dance quality. Or it may be classified as dance institutionally (for example, by being presented as dance by accredited dancers on a dance occasion). Or, if dance is a "form of life" in the way that sport and religion are, marking out large regions of language and behavior, behavior might be recognized as pertaining to that form (though I am not sure what it would be for this last possibility to be distinctively realized). We could call all of this not degree of dance-awareness but *mode* of dance-awareness.

In all the foregoing cases, part of the meaning that a dancer's activity has for the dancer is that *it is dance* in the appropriate sense. This cannot be the case when the activity is identified as dance only from a stranger's point of view. In such cases, the identification as dance must rest on some recognized dance features. Among such cases, we must distinguish those where a dancelike quality is detected in the behavior from those in which it is recognized that *a dance* is being danced. The latter is probably more usual; but having a dancelike quality and forming part of a dance are presumably interdependent to some degree.

4.3 *Meanings for Dancers and for Others*

The distinction between people for whom what they do is culturally defined as dancing and those for whom it is not suggests our third dimension. There is a difference between meanings for dancers as such and meanings for others who are relevantly defined as other than dancers. "Dancers" here may mean persons who are categorized as dancers or persons who are now dancing; and the other-than-dancers may simply be nondancers or may be defined by some specific but external relation to dancers. They may, for instance, be the dancers' clients, on behalf of whom they dance in the same way that singers give their people a voice.[1] Or they may be observers, spectators of dance. Or they may be demanders of dance, or meditators on dance. And so on.

Meanings, then, may vary along the dimension of engagement in as opposed to disengagement from the practice of dancing. But we must not think of the relationships involved as simply occupying points on a one-dimensional scale from complete detachment to direct involvement. Relations, as our examples showed, differ significantly in kind. To take a more structured example, if we reflect on the way an art is organized, we see that the nondancers are divided into those who are concerned with the art and those who are not, and that some of the former group are consumers (the public for the art) whereas others are involved as judges, as a reference-group concerned with standards; and among those involved in the production and practice of dance, there are some who actually make dances and others who maintain the institutions of management, teaching, and so forth.

4.4 *Experience and Reflection*

The range of distinctions between meanings for dancers and meanings for others has affinities with the difference between meanings delivered in the experience of dance and meanings delivered in reflection on dance. This

[1] Mark W. Booth remarks that a song comes to its proper audience as a voice without context. The song sings itself in us; we are the song while the song lasts, identified at once with the singer and with the community (Booth 1981, 15–16).

is not quite the same as the difference between meanings taken in the presence of dance and those in its absence, for dancers or spectators may reflect on what they do or perceive while they are doing or perceiving it. Meanings delivered in reflection, as opposed to ways in which dance is actually experienced as meaningful, would pertain to knowledge and beliefs about either the existence or the character of dance as such, or of this or that dance or kind of dance. And the "dance as such" reflected on might be the concept of dance, or the global phenomenon of dancing (the sum of dance activity), or the general character or "essence" of dance.

The close connection between the three different distinctions mentioned in the preceding paragraph suggests that among the ways a dance has meaning for the dancer in the act of dancing, some will be connected with the experience of dancing, but others with the idea of dance and of oneself as dancing. And this suggests a distinction between two ways in which the dancer may experience the dance: kinesthetically, in terms of the way the bodily movement is sensed as a phenomenon within the musculature, however that may take place; and in terms of the sense of the body image, one's learned or imagined sense of the visible form one is taking as a dancer.

4.5 *The Essentials*

There is a nursery song in which a crow lures a suspicious frog onto dry land by promising to make the frog a dancer. The key words in the seduction are: " 'O! there is sweet music on yonder green hill, O! / And you shall be a dancer, a dancer in yellow. . . .' "[2] The crow says nothing of any special dancing skill or aesthetic quality or specific symbolic quality in what is to be danced. The four requisites in the lure are: (1) the music, already playing and ready to be danced to; (2) the place for dancing, the green hill; (3) dressing up in costume or body paint;[3] and (4) not dancing, but *being a dancer*. These four essentials of dance will afford our next dimensions.

The essentials, as I have here called them, seem jointly to be distinctive of dance and give importance to what I think may be a unique phenomenon: that of joining the dance—and, conversely, of leaving the dance. The strikingness of this change of status is obscured in stage performances, where the emergence onstage from the wings (or the emergence from in-

[2] "The Frog and the Crow" (Walter 1919, 156). I am indebted to the staff of the Osborne Collection of Early Children's Books for enabling me to retrace this early child's recollection.

[3] A friendly critic points out that the text here need mean no more than that the frog, dancing on hind legs, shows a yellow belly. But later, on shore and about to be eaten, the frog asks "Where are all the dancers, the dancers in yellow?" So the point is indeed that the dancers should be all dressed up.

visibility as curtains are parted or lights turned on) is almost an automatic part of the theater set-up; but it is a notable feature of dance generally.

4.51 DANCE AND MUSIC

To say that music is one of the essentials of dance is not to say that every dance must have a musical accompaniment. It is rather that some music is expected, even if it be only a drum; and if there is no music, the dance is danced *in the absence* of music. (When I presented a version of this chapter at a seminar, the organizer asked me if I would need music; if my topic had been the semiotics of music, he would not have asked me if I needed a dance floor.) The question of what music a dance is danced to is always legitimate, even though the answer may be "none."

The meaningful relations between dance and music are too complex to be recapitulated here, but I will mention a few distinctions. First, one might illuminate dance qualities by comparing them with music, exploring the relation between being dancelike and being musical; and that would not be the same as exploring the relations between music as an art and dance as an art (whether they be functional interrelations or analogies); and neither of those would be the same as considering relations (of whatever sort) between actual dances and musical pieces. Second, since both dance and music proceed by the articulation of time, one may consider whether they divide time in essentially the same way or in basically different ways. Third, one may consider whether (in general, or on occasions) music tends to generate dance, whether dance generates music, or whether they are independent. And the "generation" considered may itself be a meaningful relation (as when one "expresses" the other or what the other expresses) or simply a causal one. Fourth, an observer may relate a dance practice to the music of the dancers (that is, the sort of music the dancers make and enjoy when they make and enjoy music) or to the observer's own music—or, of course, to some other observed musical practice that is not of either group.

People who discuss music and dance do not usually consider with any sharpness which alternatives in these sets they have chosen, what reasons there might be for doing things otherwise, or the implications of the choices to which they have so unselfconsciously committed themselves. And it is quite generally true that no one has ever even tried to chart the whole domain of the relation between dance and music. But it is usually simply taken for granted that music and dance go together: "It goes without saying that the character of dance is determined by the music that accompanies it" (Gunji 1970, 76).

4.52 THE DANCE PLACE

The green hill where the frog was to be a dancer figures in the song as a special place. The relations of dances to places afford an essential dimension of dance meaning. Every dance is danced somewhere, and it matters where. If it does not matter where a particular dance is danced, that fact is an important aspect of the meaning of that dance. If it does matter, places differ in important ways. Home is one sort of place; and then there are special dance places and places otherwise special. Dance places are not homogeneous: studios are not stages, and both the experience of dancing and the character of the dance itself undergo changes that may be disconcerting when the transition is made from one setting to the other (cf. Humphrey 1962, 72–90).

Among places for dancing that are special otherwise than as specifically dance places, there are many importantly different kinds. Especially, we must distinguish between sacred places and secular places. And, however many kinds there are, we must distinguish dances that are danced in a single place (or a single kind of place) from dances (processional dances, especially) part of whose meaning is the way they move from one kind of place to another. Finally, we must distinguish places that are dance places before they are danced in from those that are made dance places by being danced in. Every dance makes the place where it is danced a special dance place for the nonce, because it necessarily occupies that place in a way that makes it its field.[4]

4.521 *Dance Occasions*

Much that we have just said of place could be said no less of time or occasion. Some dances can be danced at any time, others only at special seasons or festivals. Some occasions for dances are special for private reasons, some for public reasons. And when the relevant distinctions are all charted, we will still have to distinguish dances danced on the right occasion from those danced on the wrong occasion and analyze the ways in which dances can be right and wrong for times.

Some dances are proper only at certain ceremonies, to which they are integral; others are proper only at certain seasons (midsummer, for instance), although they neither constitute nor belong to ceremonies.

---

[4] Paul Weiss argues that the way dancers generate a spatial field that they occupy is characteristic and different from the space of theatrical representations—more like a force field (Weiss 1961, 210–211).

Others, though not linked to a time or a season by such canons of propriety, are felt to be suitable to certain times or seasons—Saturday night rather than Sunday morning, teatime rather than two in the morning—rather than to others. Other dances, not in themselves special in such ways, can acquire occasional significance by being used to celebrate or adorn such ceremonies as weddings or convocations. (In certain segments of our society, wedding dances occupy an ambiguous position: the dances are ordinary dances, but they are part of the ceremony, and they are experienced and sometimes even danced in subtly special ways because they are part of the wedding.)

Some dances generate occasions; others are called for by occasions. Sometimes the occasion that calls for the dance is a dance occasion (such as the Helston Furry Dance, an occasion special only as being the time when that dance is to be performed). Sometimes, like a wedding, it is an occasion otherwise motivated.

It seems quite often to be the case that even in a language that has a generic word for dance, that word may not in fact be applied to dances that are felt very strongly to be integral to certain ceremonies; but that as the general tone of the culture changes, from internal pressures or from exposure to cosmopolitan interchanges, the general word may come to be felt at first permissible and, in the end, perfectly appropriate. In Japanese, the generic word for dance, *buyo*, was coined for the purpose in the Taisho era (1912–1926); before that, "there was no abstract term for dance in the Japanese language" (Gunji 1970; 74, see §8.4611 below).

A dance formerly appropriate to one sort of occasion may be transposed for a quite different sort of occasion, or it may be extracted from its proper occasion and presented in such a way as to suggest that its occasion is not essential to it. In fact, the latter very often happens in these days of international tours and widespread interest in "ethnic dance." But this practice may be thought of not as a transformation of the dance by a realignment of its meanings, but as preserving whatever was of interest in the dance strictly as dance. In this way, the scope of dance meaning is drastically reduced—perhaps to what can be captured by a given system of movement notation.

A matter that will not be taken up here is how far a discussion of dance places should run parallel to a discussion of dance times. Should our term "occasion" be taken as involving both places and times as factors? We should not go that far. The dance place may be a dance place even when no one is dancing there: in the song, the green hill stands as one element in the seduction, and the striking up of the music is another.

4.53 SPECIALNESS

The promise to the frog was that he would be a dancer in yellow;[5] that is, he would be a being other than he now is, special, singled out. Dance behavior is special, set apart from ordinary behavior, not part of our everyday business. This specialness is an important dimension of dance meaning and a very complex one: it is not yet clear what it should cover, how it should be charted, and how it should be related to other dimensions. But I have already drawn attention to the significance of *joining the dance*. That is an aspect of one mode of specialness, which I shall call *standing forth as a dancer*; and, conversely, leaving the dance may be considered as an aspect of abstaining from dance.

4.531 *Not Being a Dancer*

There are many significant ways of not being a dancer. One may be an absentee, or one may be a spectator; one may be excluded from presence, as unsuitable or as forbidden; one may be excluded from participation, as incompetent or by disqualification; or one may be someone to whom *this* dance, or *any* dance, is simply irrelevant. A dance into which I must not enter has a meaning different for me from that of a dance into which I am unable to enter (and within these, simply not having the qualifications is different from being unable to acquire the qualifications), and both of these differ from a dance in which I choose not to enter (that is, exercise my option of not entering), which in turn is not the same as a dance in which I refuse to enter even though I may be expected or even required to do so. Euripides in his *Bacchae* provides a subtle variation on this theme when Pentheus first refuses to enter the compulsory dance of Dionysus and then destroys himself by entering it in violation of what he wrongly takes to be a taboo on his entry. And there is another category of dances that I cannot imagine myself entering because I do not belong to the kind of beings whose dance it is. I am not *excluded* from the courtship dance of the crested grebe or from the dance of the planets round the hearth of heaven; I do not even think of playing in those leagues.

4.532 *Being a Dancer: Role, Presence, Participation*

There is more to say about the meanings of being a dancer than about the meanings of not being one. Standing forth as a dancer is possible at

---

[5] He, not she: the crow calls him "Sir."

three levels (if not more): first, self-characterization in a dancer's role; second, presenting oneself at a dance occasion; and third, taking part as a dancer in a dance. Merely to dance is not, as such, to stand forth as a dancer.

What it means to identify oneself as a dancer depends on, first, how the dancer's society specifies roles—whether by economic division of labor, or by craft-castes, or however it may be. It depends, second, on what alternatives the society offers among the roles it recognizes and to whom and how those options are opened. And third, it depends on what significance is assigned to taking up those options in various circumstances. The second of these can vary without the first, and the third without the second: as many of us have to learn, the public meaning of a career choice does not stay constant throughout a lifetime.

The significance of one's self-characterization as a dancer depends on whether or not one conforms to the standard requirements of the role. Most societies, perhaps all societies, show some form of tolerance for some forms of aberrant self-characterization. Nor is the precise way in which one's self-identification conforms or fails to conform to this or that form of expectation a simple matter: it constitutes an entire dimension or sub-dimension of dance meaning.

A society may offer divergent and contrasting roles for dancers. To take up a career as a dancer is not, among us, the same as to be a dance goer (as opposed to a stay-at-home sobersides); to be an ethnic dance hobbyist, however enthusiastic, is not to be a dedicated dance artist. And these roles do not just exist inertly side by side: the way one is a dancer depends on how one plays these possibilities against each other, in practice or in speech. The way one is a ballet dancer depends partly on one's demonstrated or avowed attitude toward modern or ethnic dance.

In a labor-dividing society, a specific dancing role (such as that of a professional ballet dancer) may bear different social connotations for different sexes and different classes. By exploiting these public significances, individuals can give their own choices of their roles different private or domestic meanings—as rebellion, as means to advancement, and so forth.

The fact that in a certain kind of situation a culture offers a wide or a narrow range of options (or no option at all) is in itself significant, and the meaning of a choice depends on the range of options one has to choose among. Adherents of structuralism like to reduce all such options to systems of binary choices. This can always be done, but one should not give undue weight to the possibility: there need be no single way of effecting such a reduction, and effecting the reduction in any way at all risks concealing, to no good purpose, the actual way the choice was made.

4.533 *Significances of Dance Going*

So much for self-characterization as a dancer. We come now to attendance at dance occasions. In general, attending a dance is a declaration of alignment. In the case of music, which in this respect seems analogous with dance, three ways of aligning oneself have been distinguished (Willis 1974). In the first case, one simply aligns oneself with those who share one's interests at some appropriate level of specificity. In the second case, the chosen dance form or music is perceived as congruent with one's individual or social self. The third case is that in which the dance form or music is integral to the substance of one's choice of life. The second of these cases may be seen and heard exemplified in the foyer at any theater dance performance; the third was a familiar phenomenon among the devotees of pop music in the sixties, and to some extent still is. In this connection, it is noteworthy that, in a multicultural or colonized society, dance can have special significance as a cultural expression: to join an ethnic dance group may be a way of affirming one's ethnic identity; to dance such a national dance as the Sardana may be a political act.[6]

To present oneself at, or absent oneself from, a dance occasion is to identify oneself as one who dances or does not dance, or at least as one who countenances or does not countenance a dance of this sort (or, in some circumstances, any dance). It is a means of self-definition. But it is always possible, though in some cases it may be outlandish, to attend a dance occasion without dancing. Such occasions may offer a variety of well-defined roles for non-dancers as well as for dancers. Thus, at social dances among us, there are dancers, voluntary wallflowers, sitters-out, chaperones and old-timers, among others less easily named. There may even be a curmudgeon or two. The elaborate social dance affairs called "balls" are elaborate dramatizations of what are primarily sexual roles. Presumably in other societies, too, those who are present but not dancing at this or that sort of dance are likely to be nondancing in specific capacities.

In relation to European-style social dancing, it is striking how the significance of "being a dancer" varies because of the high symbolic charge carried by the role of professional dancer. Throughout the eighteenth and nineteenth centuries the status of the dancing master, combining the value

[6] For my naive observation of this Catalonian dance, see Chapter 3, n. 18. In the present context, it is relevant that Mas i Solench (1981) ascribes the revival of the Sardana, with the music and choreography in approximately their present form, to the work of Josep Maria (Pep) Ventura i Casas and Miquel Pardas i Roure in the fifth decade of the nineteenth century and that the *Encyclopedia Britannica* ascribes to the same date the rise of articulate Catalonian nationalism, with the establishing of Catalan as a literary language. Mas himself does not explicitly make the connection.

of social decorum with the disvalue of professionalism, maintains a highly charged ambiguity.

4.534 *Costume*

It was promised that the frog should be a dancer *all in yellow*. What a dancer wears relates to the specialness of the dancer before it relates to the specific meaning of the dance. Dress is among our "essentials" of dance, as an index of specialness. One dresses up to go dancing, separates oneself from the workaday world. Even among us, this is not invariable: there are many dances that one can join without dressing up, many dance institutions (Greek tavern dancing, for instance) that, calling for spontaneity, do not and cannot call for distinctive costume. The case is rather that, in such a society as ours, the question of how a dancer is to dress is one that necessarily arises, even if the answer is "come as you are." "Ordinary clothes" mean one thing if they are mandatory, if it would be wrong to dress up; something else if one could have dressed up but refrained from doing so; and something else again if no one notices how one dresses. No doubt there are societies in which there is no dance that calls for distinctive dress or body-paint and for which the question of costume does not arise at all—and the fact that it did not arise would be something that we, as observers, would find significant about what dance means (and about what costume means) in that society.

The distinctive costume for a dance may be that of a dancer (or of a professional dancer) as such or of a paradigm dancer: dancing pumps (or even, as in the movie of *The Red Shoes*, toe shoes) carry the generic meaning of "dance," and people who wear them to the supermarket are telling us something. Or one may dress in pointed relation to professional dance: for instance, to wear "practice clothes" may be taken to signify professionalism together with a studio orientation rather than a stage orientation, to dance barefoot rather than on point shoes was at one time a declaration of independence from dead tradition, and to dance on stage in "ordinary clothes" may make a statement in favor of "democracy of movement" in an avant-garde context.

There is dressing down as well as dressing up. Near-nakedness is common in dance, and not necessarily in connection with sexual stripping or to free the limbs for movement (or for the perception of movement). Public nakedness is special and is a direct way of marking the specialness of the dancer. And acts of dressing or of undressing may be incorporated into dances with a variety of social, sexual, aesthetic, or other meanings. We resume this topic in §8.213.

Many costumes mark the wearer not generically as a dancer but as dancer of a specific dance: ethnic dancers wear ethnic costumes reserved for such ethnic displays, and morris dancers wear a distinctive uniform. In the case of the morris dancers, the costume has no further symbolic meaning (none, anyway, that the dancers avow), but the ethnic costumes independently declare allegiance to the idea, if not to the reality, of the nationality to which they pertain. In African masked dances, the masks identify the dancers as dancers of the specific ceremony but usually also claim for the dancer identity with a particular kind of being or with a being of a particular quality. Again, the ballet dancer's tutu and point shoes may be taken to symbolize the values of romantic ballet, and Isadora Duncan's bare feet and filmy draperies evoked the sentimental Hellenism of the nineteenth century (cf. Jenkyns 1980, esp. chs. 7–9).

A dance costume may identify the wearer as a specific sort of dancer or danced character, whether by mimetic representation or (as in the French court ballets) with emblematic accoutrements. Or it may identify a specific function within the dance, such as that of the blackface characters in the morris who differ from the other dancers in their appearance and in their movements.

Lastly, dance costumes may have only aesthetic meaning, relating significantly to nothing but the overall appearance of the spectacle. And they may do this either by entering into the décor or by becoming props and instruments of the dance (as in the "serpentine" dances of Loie Fuller). In such cases, by assuming a merely aesthetic or pictorial quality, the costuming may undermine rather than enhance the danced meaning by superimposing on it a sort of separate dance *of costume*. In this capacity, costume clearly belongs not at all to the present subdimension of "specialness" but to the dimension of "meanings in dances." And it is sufficiently obvious that in many or most of the other forms and aspects we have considered the way a dancer dresses performs a double duty, signifying the way the dancer is special and contributing to the meaning of the dance as a whole. This doubleness should not lead us to submerge, as most writers on dance seem to, the distinctive meaning dimension of clothing in the general meaning of the dance.

4.54 DANCERS IN RELATION

Dancers dance in relation to other dancers and to others who are not dancing. Insofar as these relationships form part of the dance itself, they will be taken up in later chapters. But there are many other sorts of significant relationships that seem to call for attention in their own right. There are, for instance, differences in attitude: not in the dancer's private feelings, but in the way the dance is danced in relation to others. Dancers may dance *to*, or *for*, or *at*, or, for that matter, *against* (and we may not have a prepo-sition handy for every such attitude) some or all of their onlookers or fel-low dancers. The onlookers may be related to them in any of many ways: colleagues, friends, teachers, pupils, royalty, gods, the gallery, critics, or whatever; and the meaning of what one does may differ significantly in each case, even if one says one is really dancing to satisfy oneself alone. The onlookers may be actually present or notional. In either case, the relation-ships are central to the meaning of the dance.

Dancers may dance with other dancers, who may be dancing the same or differently. They may dance as soloist with soloist, as soloist with en-semble, as group with group. They may dance in pairs: paired dances, with partners of opposite sex, are a favored genre in our society. As part of the dance, these are considered elsewhere; but again, there are other compo-nents of meaning that call for recognition. In any of these cases, as with onlookers, the dancers may dance with, or at, or to, or for, or against each other; and I may dance *at* someone who is dancing *for* me or is trying to dance *with* me, and so on.

The human articulation of the dancing group, as dancers in relation, may be (in Sartre's terminology) that of a series or of a group: we may be simply joining as separate individuals in a common task, or we may be dancing as an interactive unity. The difference is profound and subtle, a matter of our whole way of being in the world with other people; and insofar as dance is a practice that is typically both communal and intense, this dimension of meaning should take on a special significance in dance. Within this dimen-sion, I think there may be exemplified a special sort of relationship that is neither that of the series nor that of the group, and that is not quite that of the loss of identity in the impersonal "They" (Heidegger's *das Man*)—that in which dancers are merely iterations of each other, each of them being "the dancer of the dance." It seems to me that this happens in certain elab-orate and ritualized dances in which dancers perform the same steps in unison, not as members of a squad as in a corps de ballet, but each as fully enacting the dance.

Mutual relations of dancers as they dance may be related or unrelated to two other sorts of relationships: those outside the context of the present dance but within a wider dance context, and those outside dance but in the context of this or that social grouping. In any case, here also we have an important dimension of dance meaning. And we should not forget the senses in which every dancer, like every artist, dances for and against all fellow artists past, present, and to come.

Within this dimension of relatedness we might find a special place for proprietorship. In §4.532 we mentioned the different significances of put-ting oneself forward as a dancer of dances to which one had different levels and kinds of entitlement. What I now propose is close to that. Dancers of dances have also different rights in them *as against other dancers*. A dancer may be teacher, learner, demonstrator, established in the role within a company, and so on. A dancer may occupy several such places on a single occasion (an advanced student may give a lesson in the teacher's presence, to which the public may be admitted as to a concert)—we are used to such complexities in real life. In addition, one may have a prescriptive right to a dance one has choreographed or made one's own. Martha Graham in old age had trouble in her company because she felt not that no one else could dance her roles but that no one else had a right to (Stodelle 1984). And there has been, I think, some feeling that no one other than José Limon should dance *The Moor's Pavane*, not because no one else could—it "can apparently survive any number of second-rate performances," says Deborah Jowitt (1985, 133)—but because it would be a sort of desecration. In a rather different way, Pavlova established a special right in *The Dying Swan*: it was her party piece, and anyone else dancing it is, as it were, dancing it in her presence to the point where it is almost impossible to do the dance nowadays otherwise than as parody.

The dimension of proprietorship has other manifestations in other dance traditions. Among Australian aboriginals, for instance, it has been observed that within a group "seemingly all dancing in much the same way," it was discovered on notating each dancer individually that "the dance was actually led by one amongst the large group. It was conjectured that he in fact owned it" (McGuinness-Scott 1983, 64). Australian aboriginals do not go in for ownership much; and one supposes that among them, and other peoples whose social structure differs from ours, different variations of property meaning, and interdancer meaning generally, are important in a way that we are in no position to understand.

A dancer may dance in solitude. But that solitude will have many meanings, depending on who is deemed to be absent and on the quality of that absence. Insofar as dance is a strictly visible art, however, and the dancer cannot see the dance as it is being danced, solitude in dancing takes on a depth of meaning of its own.

4.6 *The Meaning of Dance*

The topics dealt with so far have mostly not been among those dimensions of meaning explicitly treated by theorists and critics of dance. Among the latter, we often find general meanings assigned to dancing as such—the sort of thing we considered in Chapter 2. Obviously, given the variety of behavior to which the word "dance" is applied, these meanings must either be trivial or else inapplicable to much dancing; but presumably what is intended is that the assigned meaning explains why people should dance at all—a core significance necessary and sufficient to justify the practice of dancing as such (the sort of thing we discussed in §3.21 as the "nerve" of dance practice). Such general meanings usually take one of two basic forms. First, one treats dance as a proto-language of gesture and assigns it the function of expressing grief, joy, and such other feelings as a public expression may seem appropriate to. Second, one fastens on the specialness of dance behavior and ascribes to dance the function of marking "the sacred" or some such concept (the theory of "powers" in Langer 1953 is a theory of this sort). In general, dance is made out to be, in one way or another, an emphatic celebration of enhanced vitality (cf. §8.211231).[7]

The dimension of dance meaning afforded by the general meanings assigned to dance is perhaps not entirely different from the dimension of "existence" with which we began our catalog. The difference is, of course, that in the former instance what was found significant was the very fact that people do dance; here, the fact is assumed, and the elucidation or interpretation of the fact becomes the object of attention. The objection would be that the distinction is empty: the interpretation has no point unless dance exists, and the existence of dance has no significance unless it admits of an interpretation. True. But discourses often fall clearly enough into one category or the other, so we will let the distinction stand.

In any case, theories assigning a general meaning to dance as such are shadowed by theories assigning similarly general meanings to named dances and dance genres, and even to particular dance performances. Thus Ruth Katz, in "The Egalitarian Waltz," finds in the difference between waltz and minuet an extensive and profound expression of a contrast in social and political attitudes; and Judith L. Hanna, in contrasting what dances mean for dancers with what they mean for audiences, goes into detail about the rise of specific dance forms, dance movements, and dance companies, by contrast with the aestheticism and uninstructed associations of the onlookers (Katz 1973; Hanna 1983).

4.7 Meanings in Dances

Most discussions of dance meaning in the context of aesthetics fasten on specific meanings of specific movements. That this tiny part of the field

---

[7] Thus Paul Valéry says, in a celebrated lecture, that a dancer "encloses herself as it were in a time that she engenders, a time consisting entirely of immediate energy": dance is "quite simply a poetry that encompasses the action of living creatures in its entirety," and "all the arts can be considered as particular examples of this general idea" (Valéry 1936, 203, 210, 208)—a line of talk that, as a Japanese commentator observes, seems not to fit Japanese dance at all (Gunji 1970, 68). I return to Valéry in §8.21122.

should almost monopolize attention is not surprising: these are indeed the meanings to which critics and connoisseurs attend, the ground of appreciation. They are what critics handle best, and this book says little about them.

How does one identify the dance within which meaning is to be found? Some confine dance to the moving bodies of dancers or, more narrowly yet, to the dance movements of those bodies. At the other extreme the dance may be held to include the entire presentation of a dance spectacle in a theater, including the state of the carpeting in the foyer and the times of the last buses. Between such extremes, the focus deemed appropriate may vary. One may fasten on the dance as choreographed; the dance as choreographically realized by the performers; the dance as actually performed by them (which may add something to the realization of the choreography, if any, depending on how inclusive the latter was); the bodies and looks of the performers, as dancers or as people with bodies; the dancers' costumes, as included in the dance or as irrelevant or enhancing or detracting; the space of the dance as the field of the movements-in-relation intrinsic to the dance or in relation to the real space of the stage (a relation that may or may not be conceived as extrinsic); the dance as including the scenery but excluding the lighting, or including that too. How someone criticizes a dance shows what the dance is being taken to consist of, whether or not the critic makes that explicit; and the arguments sometimes produced to show that only one way of delimiting the dance is legitimate are never such as to convince those in possession of arguments for a contrary view.[8]

Meanings in dances may also be distinguished, even when the object for attention has been delimited in the above respect, by the perceptual modality to which the dance is taken to belong. Is dance strictly a visual medium? Or are sounds (the music, and perhaps the thuds and scrapes) part of it? And what about kinesthesia, a mode of access that presumably only those dancing have directly, though other dancers may empathize and nondancers perhaps sympathize and imagine? And, if we say that dance is essentially visual, do we want to mean that its meanings can themselves be

---

[8] Sheets-Johnstone (1966), for instance, deduces a prescription for dance composition from a definition of dance supposed to articulate a phenomenological intuition of the essence of dance. But the definition turns out to be a direct application of an account of the temporal structure of being-in-the-midst-of-the-world as articulated by certain French phenomenologists. Why should we suppose that that and nothing else is what dance is? Even if we suppose that that particular version of phenomenology is a uniquely privileged truth, and even if we suppose that dance can somehow embody an essential intuition of that sort, it still does not at all follow that that is what all dances should do or that dances that do that are better than dances that do other things. Philosophical foundations are not practical prescriptions.

relevantly explicated in visual terms (so that dances become visible patterns), or only that relevant dance meanings of all sorts are only those that can be mediated by what is visible? And, if we take the former of these alternatives and say that dances belong to the visible as such, do we want to mean that literally or, as so many theorists have argued in so many different ways (to which so many other theorists have shown themselves so variously impervious), mean that dances are virtual objects, objects posited as nonreal by the visual imagination? Or do we even want to advance these modes of meaningful variability as somehow mutually exclusive? In any case, we have in this domain of sensory modality an unmistakable and necessary dimension of dance meaning.

Suppose now that we equate a dance with a set of dance movements (or a single differentiated movement sequence) to which dance meanings may be appropriated. How is one to single these out as dance movements in the first place? In accordance with what we said in §4.2, there are at least three ways. They may be singled out as dance movements by the dance context alone, or they may be perceived as having some distinctive quality, or they may be identified as belonging to systems of differentiated movement with which differentiated meanings are associated. In the last case, the systems will usually, if not always, be related to specific ways of dancing developed in specific cultural contexts; but that specificity of origin and association does not prevent us from generalizing about kinds of differentiation as such.

Meanings of movements may be differentiated by what is referred to, by what is expressed, or by how movements relate to other movements. In all three cases, the meanings may be regarded as conventional or as natural— or, less tendentiously, as requiring to be specially learned or as learned in the general processes of maturing and acculturation.

Movements may have meaning by forming parts of movement systems. Dance traditions tend to develop systems of "steps": specialized movements and sequences susceptible of demonstration and repetition. These may be systems of gestures or abstract postures and movements. In the latter case, a particular pose or motion may from time to time be assigned a gestural meaning or an expressive value. In dance systems, the set of recognized steps would normally go with set ways of combining steps, acknowledged ways of selecting, introducing, and organizing movements not recognized as steps, and more or less acceptable ways of modifying the resulting system as a whole.

In addition to the systems of steps developed within dance traditions, a number of general systems of human movement have been worked out and adopted for descriptive purposes or as bases for dance practice, and meanings have been assigned accordingly on a variety of principles. These general systems usually invoke some natural foundation for their classifications, from physiology or psychology or cosmology.

Dance movements are movements in space. But what sort of space? The dancers move in "real" space, in the sense that their positions, accelerations, and velocities can be plotted in a Euclidean three-dimensional space and time. But, since dancers are people and their movements are human movements, they may also be perceived in a topological or hodological space—that is, one constructed from feasible approaches, tracks, passings, and the like, in terms of facilitations and resistances. In addition, because the dancers are necessarily seen as human (or we could make no sense of their movement at all), we may also find their movements meaningful in terms of the sort of social space of interaction that Edward T. Hall (1966) has explored. This intractable topic of alternative "spaces" will require our attention later (§8.44).

The meanings of movements are usually differentiated as mimetic and abstract, by what is represented and by inherent structure. This intricate topic, including that of the dimensions on which mimesis is differentiated—most crudely, by what is represented and by how it is represented—we leave to other occasions and other writers.

Normally, dancers are human, and their dances are movements of their bodies. We remarked that this may affect the "space," the kind of relatedness, within which the movements are perceived as taking place. By the same token, the meanings of the movements themselves vary according to the manner and extent to which the movements are typical of the human body or are body-oriented as opposed to pattern-oriented. And any movement that a dancer makes can be construed simply as an observed movement, or in relation to the dancer as dancer, or in relation to the dancer as human being. Similarly, meanings of dance movements vary according to their relation to movements made in everyday life and according to their relation to such conditions of humanity as sex and age. Again, as human actions the dance movements cannot escape being assigned (at least some of the time) the sort of "expressive" meaningfulness that human actions have (see Carroll 1981, 101–103). And on this dimension an action may be seen as inherently meaningful, or as significant of a state in the agent, or as indicative of an intention to communicate a state to the recipient of the message: possible variations are innumerable, and the literature of general aesthetics discusses them endlessly (cf. Sparshott 1982, 206–233). The whole area broached in this paragraph is one of bewildering complexity; and it is the inextricability of this sort of tangle, as we shall be saying in Chapters 8 and 9, that makes the aesthetics of dance such a formidable and daunting subject.

4.8 *Conclusion*

This chapter has been little more than a roughly ordered catalog of largely empty pigeonholes, but it does seek to make three points. First, unless some such attempt to canvass the possibilities is made, any concrete discussion of dance meanings lacks foundation. Second, there is no a priori reason to suppose that any limited set of the meanings here listed is uniquely privileged in its relevance to dance or that there is any identifiable set of them that it is improper to take into account. Nor is there any reason to think that attending to some precludes attending to others. The literature on dance is cluttered with high-minded denunciations of people who perversely, or vulgarly, or ignorantly, or snobbishly, or in some other easily denounceable way fail to dance in the uniquely right way, or to look at the only right things, or to describe the only relevant aspects of the only right things. I hope to have supplied a corrective: denounce all you want, but remember that you are taking a stand, not stating a fact. And third, extant discussions of dance meanings are heavily crowded in one corner of the terrain. Theorists usually discuss at a deeper or more abstract level the very same topics that practitioners and their critics discuss. They are entirely right to do so: if they did otherwise, they would be little read and would be dismissed as irrelevant and unhelpful, if not as pedantic and ignorant. Practice is what matters: problems that arise in practice are the only ones that need discussing and the only ones whose discussion can have a fruitful outcome. My aim is to provide a background for such discussions, not to replace them or even to influence their direction.

CHAPTER 5

~ ~ ~ ~ ~ ~ ~ ~ ~ ~ ~ ~ ~ ~ ~ ~ ~ ~

On What Is and What
Is Not Dance

5.1 *Definitions*

I HAVE WRITTEN a great deal already without attempting to define dance or otherwise delimiting the topic of our discourse. The omission has not impeded us. It is in fact unusual to begin a philosophical treatise with a definition of its subject matter, and by no means the rule to include one anywhere. Nor is it the task of such a treatise to arrive at a definition or to lay the ground for one. When one finds phrases purporting to be definitions quoted from other authors, they often turn out to be slogans extracted from argumentative passages, misleading when removed from their contexts. When one comes across what looks like a definition of dance, a sentence beginning with the words "Dance is . . ." or even "Dance may be defined as . . . ," it is a mistake to take it at face value. One has to look and see just how the sentence is related to other sentences and what function it performs in the argumentative or other context of which it forms part. That also applies to dictionary definitions (like the one quoted earlier) and to Judith Hanna's definition, which is quoted toward the end of this chapter (see p. 263).

I have already insisted that we all know what music (for instance) is, though we differ about the status of marginal cases and about the propriety of including certain practices. It is time to say a bit more about the provenance and scope of this kind of knowledge that we all have. In part, it comes from the extreme obviousness and familiarity of standard cases. Mozart's "Jupiter" Symphony and the like are music and unlikely to be taken for anything else: they come to mind when we think "music," familiar denizens of our thoughts, as if they had always lived there. But such knowledge also shows itself in the whole way we behave and talk about things; there is no need to suppose it could or should be encapsuled in a summary statement. What we know about music is shown in everything we say about music, about musical compositions and performances, and in what we do about them; the limits of our knowledge appear in all the complexity of the ways in which talk and behavior are understood to be out of line or irrelevant (or contentious, or bizarre, or platitudinous).

How could a definition of dance either replace or enhance our understanding of dance? It would have to be based on that understanding and subject to correction by it. It would be better to let the course of one's discussion be guided from point to point by the understanding of what dance is that one has built up over a lifetime. Of course, my own understanding as philosopher and dance goer will not coincide with that of a dance journalist or a dancer or a promoter. But a definition would do nothing to bring our respective habits of mind closer together. And the gap is not troublesome, for two reasons. First, everyone who reads this book understands that this is what and how a theorist thinks, just as when I read what dancers write I understand that what they say reflects an experience that I can respect and partly enter but do not expect to share. And second, part of my lifelong understanding includes the continuous learning of how my perspective on dance does relate to other perspectives and is continually corrected by them.

A person who generalizes about dance will have in the forefront of the mind some particular kind of dance, or way of dancing, or range of dances, or some specific contrast between things that are being thought of as dancelike and undancelike. This is the effective target of the generalization, and what it is will vary habitually for different people and different classes of context. And for each particular person, this effective target will be different at different times, depending on the context of thought. Something excluded as undancelike will be rejected for some specific reason, the strength and relevance of which will be determined by the point at issue in the current discussion. No possible statement that purports to sum up in a definition what dance is (and hence what is not dance) could possibly sum up the purport of all such generalizations: being made on different context-bound principles, they are inherently unsummable. The most one could manage would be an account of the ways in which such contrasts and emphases typically vary. This whole matter has been explored in depth for over a century by the most acute philosophers and linguists. Any theorist who simply puts forward a general definition of dance in this day and age is showing crass ignorance and insensitivity.

A special futility besets the project of defining an art: a definition simply invites counterexamples, which can only result in endless and pointless caveats, qualifications, and complications (see §5.241 below). A definition in cultural matters is not to be such that no counterexamples can be discovered or imagined, but it carries with it an implicit understanding of how particular sorts of apparent counterexamples are to be dealt with. The understanding is implicit because no definition could spell them out without being uselessly long, if it could be done at all; and, if the principles are understood without being formulated, one's understanding of the art in question must be such that it neither needs nor admits formulation. The definition turns out to be useless after all.

It may be, however, that the case of dance is different from that of some other arts, perhaps from all of the (other) recognized fine arts. It might be held that the practice of the art of music, for instance, is a cultural fact with which we can acquaint ourselves: the reason we need not define it is that there are cultural cues to how we can learn all about it, and these cues are reasonably consistent. But we have seen that the institutionalization of dance is many-centered if not incoherent. Social dancing is not organized as a fine art, though social dancing may be practiced artistically or even as an art. In understanding dance, we can neither organize our thinking around the question what sort of art dance is nor avoid that question. In the case of music, we can get by with an understanding built up through experience, because in fact the consistent institutionalization of music in our society has given our experience a certain shape. If our experience of dance does not embody a similar articulation, perhaps we do need something like a definition to help articulate our discourse. (I do a lot of perhapsing here, because it is by no means clear that what is alleged of music is true.)

There is another peculiarity of dance, by contrast with other arts, that might call for a more explicit statement than usual of just what it is we are talking about. Prima facie, dance is non-utilitarian body movement. But we do that all the time: we are always in motion or in repose, and during much of the time we are neither pursuing a useful end nor quite unaware of what we are doing. It may be said that we are always on the verge of dance. Dance cannot be assigned an institutional identity because it ubiquitously precedes institutionalization in a way that most other arts do not. A child's scribbling, for instance, however spontaneous, is a specific anticipation of graphic art and uses paper and pencils developed for that art. But the skill with which we move our bodies, even if not presocial (since every child grows up within some society in which every possible movement has social meaning), cannot be preemptively caught up into the ambience of any institutional organization, because it is involved in everything we do and therefore in every possible institution.

Shall we say that dance is like song in the above respect, that dance is an outgrowth of the spontaneous use of such skills as are involved in all movement in the same way that singing comes from the spontaneous use of the voice in which we say everything we say? No. Speech is untuneful: the intonation whereby we utter sounds at a definite pitch is special, a way we use the vocal apparatus in singing, in chanting, in calling, and not in other ways. In a Southern Baptist sermon, oratory may spill over into chant, but a boundary is first approached and then decisively crossed as the pitch variation of speech is emphasized and transformed. In dance, on the other hand, in the way it has just been presented, there is no boundary. At least, if one burst into dance as one bursts into song, it is not clear what the sign of that bursting would be. Hence the significance of the formal moves described in the last chapter as "joining the dance."

Rather than song, it is literature that affords an analogy to dance. In all that we say, except insofar as we respond to urgent exigencies, we are on the verge of literature. The skills of speech, used in all our saying, allow for an element of spontaneity in that we can always try to express our meaning better and hence more eloquently and more artistically. The concept of eloquence invokes the institutions of elocution and rhetoric, but what it formalizes is a pervasive skill that does not depend on them but rests only on our ability to mean something by what we say.

If dance differs from other typical fine arts in its many-centeredness and in its closeness to highly generalized aspects of human skill, a reason for essaying a definition of dance might be to minimize a risk that discussions of art and arts notoriously run: that of confining one's attention to one kind of example. (Hanna's definition, and the whole enterprise to which it belongs, is certainly aimed at this error, which she finds fatally pervasive in Sachs [1937].) Section 3.2 sheds light on the forms such failure might take: mistaking the scope of a practice, wrongly combining or separating practices, mistaking the nerve of a practice for the practice itself, misidentifying or misdescribing the nerve, and so on.

It follows from what we have just said that, although to put forward a definition of dance as a context-free formula that would somehow tell everyone for all time what dance really *is* would be a very silly thing to do, a review of what one would have to do if one wished to arrive at such a definition might be instructive. It would amount to a review of the principles and contexts typically involved and invoked in generalizations about dance.

The task of defining dance is one of some delicacy. Today's philosophers seek to define words and concepts, not realities; they think it is too hard to envisage just what a reality would be if there were no theory or verbal classification imposed on it. This is especially true of things like dance that are largely matters of human practice anyway. What makes the task exceptionally delicate is that the last thing we are likely to determine is the extent to which defining dance will be defining a term "dance" as opposed to describing a practice or manifestation of the reality of dance, or the other way round, or both separately, or both together. In fact, the best way to proceed is to say what we want to say and then see what, if anything, it comes to. The risk is, of course, that our discourse will defy summary in just the same way that we said diverse, well-grounded generalizations about dance do. But we can't help that.

What is it that we would like to catch in the net of our definition? We can distinguish at least eight different things, all of which we might want to take into account somehow or other. First, there is the essence of dance, what we mean to pick out in something by calling it "dance." Second, there is the necessity of dance, that in dance which fills a place that only dance can fill in any life-world we can envisage. Third, there is what we think of as dance and what we think of dance as, that which comes to mind when we think "dance." Fourth, there is what we regularly apply the word "dance" to without thinking twice about it, so that we would be non-plussed if we were challenged. Fifth, what we regularly apply the word "dance" to, but in such a way that we are not taken aback when our use of the word is challenged—we recognize that it is not the most danceish sort of dance, but dance is what we always call it none the less. Sixth, what we sometimes call and sometimes decline to call dance, depending on the context of the discourse or on the context of the activity to which we refer: we might want to classify something as dance rather than, or as well as, athletics or figure skating for some purposes and in certain contexts, or to differentiate it from dance, depending on what point we were trying to make. Seventh, what we call dance for want of a better word, knowing that it is not really dance but hoping to be understood; or, conversely, what we are surprised to hear someone else call dance, though we see what is meant and why the word was chosen. And, eighth, there is what we call dance by metaphor, to indicate something dancelike about it, where part of the point of our calling it so is that we all know it is not "really" or "literally" dance.

Concepts do not all have the same shape, as any good dictionary shows. Some have a single center, some many; some branch into thickets, some metamorphose; and so on. Nouns enter into our discourse in different ways, which we master as part of the skill at speaking that takes up so much of the human brain. We have no satisfactory way of reducing these variations to rule and classification. Modern linguistics, when it ventures into such areas, tends to treat them extensionally without much regard to the dynamics of such extension; and the simple distinctions philosophers have introduced by the phrase "family likeness" mislead and disappoint us in much the same way. Some words are used for classifying, some for characterizing, some for qualifying, and so on; and no doubt a given word will do lots of such things in ways that are interwoven. Perhaps concepts differ as much as bones do, of which each is a separate shape that is a function of the special set of pressures and tensions and attachments that determine its contributions to the body's work.

5.2 *Four Strategies*

It looks at first as though we might have a choice. On the one hand, we could look into our hearts and write: I could decide what I myself mean when I call something "dance," and, since you and I speak the same language (for you read this book in the same language I wrote it in), what I mean must be more or less what you mean. This alternative would look at dancing from the inside, subjectively. On the other hand, I could consult the anthropologists and historians and find out what dance everywhere is and has been, objectively. Then we could combine the two somehow and get depth and breadth, the inner and the outer, together. But that is an illusion. On the one hand, what people elsewhere do is irrelevant unless we are already prepared to call it "dance"; on the other hand, I have misdescribed what I found in my heart if it fails to fit exotic examples of what I am prepared to call "dance." So, although both those things are what I have to do, they do not furnish the beginnings of a method.

There are books about how to define things, and I could have got one and used it as a manual. But, after all, I am not actually trying to define anything, and such manuals usually tell us everything except what we actually wanted to know. So I will make do with what has stuck in my head after all these years. What has stuck is probably what I can use.

What strategies are available to show the shape of what we mean by dance? Here are four to be going on with.

5.21 TAXONOMY

First, we could enumerate all the different kinds of dances we can think of and then consider how they should be jointly and severally characterized, how the list might be lengthened or shortened, what principles might be discerned as governing the making and modifying of such a list, what different sorts of classifications offered themselves for what purposes and how these classifications differed among themselves. It is easy to classify dances by context: theater dance and social dance, art dance and recreational dance, and so on. Someone might object that we should first determine what we are classifying before we figure out how to classify it. But perhaps the very first thing we should notice about dance is that, whatever it may be, it is something that is easily classified in these familiar ways.[1]

Given that dances and dance institutions admit of such classification, dance also includes whatever is brought (whatever is customarily brought, whatever could be persuasively brought) into the context of these stable entities in any of several ways. First, by a sufficiently compelling analogy (what is sufficiently compelling? Whatever is found to exercise effective compulsion). Second, institutionally, by being adopted as an officially inseparable part of what was inherently dance. Third, by extension of practice, as practitioners extend their interests and the range and use of their skills to incorporate new territories into what was previously thought of as the domain of dance. And fourth, perhaps, by such an artistic dialectic as theorists of music have postulated for their own art, whereby reflection on the implications of what was already recognized as important and urgent in dance called for a new development that had a preemptive right to be called "dance" because it was in the legitimate line of succession.

What is and what is not dance depends, of course, not on what is taken to be dance by any particular group of people or even by everyone, but on what is correctly so taken. But what is the standard of correctness? In matters like the present, I know of no argument that would establish any standard other than a pragmatic one: what will be agreed on by all competent observers. (What makes observers competent? Experience, intelligence, responsibility, and proficiency in a more developed form of such reflections as are engaging us in this book.) It is unlikely that any such consensus will emerge, or even that we could get agreement on who should do the consenting, especially since dance practice itself will certainly continue to change in place and time—if it did not, that cessation of change would be the greatest change of all. In practice, then, we have to forget about correctness and rely on our own judgment and that of those whose judgment we respect. What is and is not dance is after all, then, what is taken to be dance; and the question "Taken how, and by whom?" is not one that admits of a clear answer (see Sparshott 1982, 149–168).

Subject to the provisos of the last paragraph, what is and is not dance will depend in part on the acceptable limits of such considerations as we raised in the paragraph before that: whether an analogy is generally found (or can be made) to be persuasive, whether an institutional context's hos-

---

[1] The point is emphasized by Ellfeldt (1976, 12), who would define dance by saying that "[d]ance is movement organized and patterned to serve its particular 'dance' purpose." That is, generalizations must remain within the context of specific dance methods and reasons. Dance is definable only as a set of recognizably linked practices; all that we can *say* about what they have in common is that they are not nondance practices. Ellfeldt does not, however, work this out in detail.

pitality can be pushed to a certain distance in a certain direction, whether practitioners meet massive resistance to the extensions or restrictions their professional practice dictates, whether a dialectic is felt to lead into a blind alley.

There is also, however, a quite different sort of factor that partly controls what is and what is not dance: the existence and practical availability of alternative contexts of practices and institutions within which whatever one is doing may be classified and subsumed. At different times and places, theater, mime, athletics, pageants, parades, callisthenics, and so on assume more or less distinct practical identities and greater or less artistic and social importance. To take one illustration: the sort of thing that is done in baton twirling would certainly be called dancing if there were nothing else to call it. But, in fact, it is placed in a class of its own and functions within the institutional context of competitive athletics, not within that of dance. To take another example: we have seen that pantomime was at one time taken to be the paradigm case of dance. Someone who did at that time the sort of thing that Marcel Marceau does now would, so far as we can tell, have been thought of as a dancer. Nowadays we operate with a separate art form of white-face mime, of which Marceau is an exponent; he is a mime *as opposed to* a dancer, and we can explain why. Chapter 7 looks at some of these alternatives. There is a great deal of variability in what contexts and affiliations are practically and theoretically available at any given time for relating a given practice to; and that in itself must prevent one from saying definitively what for all time is or is not dance.

5.22 PROFILING

A second available strategy for deciding what is dance is one for which we laid the groundwork in Chapter 4. We rely on our perceptions and recollections, and on what we have heard and seen and read, to compile and sort the dimensions of dance meaning in a way that no longer strikes us as obviously incomplete and unsystematic. Then we can assume that the resulting profile will be unique to dance. We next have to decide how to use that profile to determine the status of anything that is neither obviously dance nor obviously not dance. We might say, for instance, that in calling something dance we are implying that the relevant dimensions of its mean-ingfulness approximate to our profile. Anything for which the implication is reasonable is dance; anything for which the implication is absurd cannot be dance. And what are the criteria of "reasonableness" and "absurdity" here? There can be none; one has to use one's wits. But why, if we were going to have to use our wits anyway, go through the preliminary rigma-role of compiling semiological profiles? Because it would be stupid not to.

5.23 PARADIGMS

A third strategy available for clarifying what dance is would be to start from certain paradigm cases. What Kevin Pugh does in a ballet, what Isadora Duncan did alone, what Ram Gopal used to demonstrate are indisputably dancing. If they did not dance, nobody dances; if what they did was not dancing, there is nothing else it could be called. Or, more precisely: someone who said that what they did was not dance would be trying to tell us what dance ought to be, not what we know it is, or would be performing some other sort of silly-clever maneuver.[2] Or again: the tango is a dance (or a class of dances); the Navajo Way Dance is a dance; the *pas de deux* from *Nutcracker* is a dance. Our ideas of what dancing and dances are rest on such clear cases as these. If anything is in some way like one of them but is either clearly not dance or not clearly dance, what it is to be dance would be elucidated by the precise differences between clear and doubtful cases.

5.24 THE DIRECT APPROACH: NECESSARY AND SUFFICIENT CONDITIONS

A fourth strategy, which might be an alternative to the above or might be a continuation of them, would be the direct approach. We know what we, as embodiments of our culture and speakers of its language, mean by calling something dance, in the sense that our use of the word in conversation with other members and speakers is a responsible exercise of our informed intelligence. (I was about to say, our *serious* use of the word, but that proviso is wrong: to use the word flippantly or otherwise nonseriously requires the same mastery of language as its serious use.) If we do know that, there is nothing to prevent us from trying to explain what we mean and from summing up that explanation by spelling out what conditions something must fulfill before we can call it dance and what conditions would be sufficient to warrant our doing so. Of course, we cannot be sure, to start with, that any such conditions can be found; but, equally, we can-

---

[2] Rayner Heppenstall (1936) says that what Isadora Duncan did was not dancing but sexual self-expression—a judgment in which he felt all the more secure because he had never seen her perform. But what he meant, as his book as a whole makes clear, is that Duncan had no technique comparable to that of the Russian ballet. For reasons that are not altogether clear, English ballet-fanciers around 1930 seem to have found it necessary to deny the status of alternative forms of dance, of which they had little or no direct knowledge. Remarks in the same vein as Heppenstall's can be found in Haskell (1948, 80–82), who also disparages Wigman ("a very remarkable personality, if not a great dancer," p. 88) and the whole "Central European school of dancing," which he dismisses as "a form of war neurosis" (pp. 77–78). But Haskell does not go so far as to say that these people were not dancing *at all*.

not be sure, to start with, that they cannot. In either case, the attempt should be instructive.

In the particular case of dance, however, the attempt to spell out necessary and sufficient conditions seems not worth making—or at least, the conditions specified must include the unavailability of alternative, overriding practices. Even if we leave out of account anything that might be affected by that, the multiplicity of dance practices leaves one wondering what all dances could have distinctively in common, unless there is some core of skills and concerns that all dancers must have. Even if such a core could be identified, it would still be true that what goes on at a Saturday-night hop is very radically different from what goes on in the dance theater at Harbourfront and has a very different personal and social significance. To specify necessary and sufficient conditions of dance is the wrong thing to do even if it is possible, because it distracts attention from these divergences in substance and significance. It could be that everything of interest and value is outside the common core. (In an apple, the core is the fruit's reason for being; but it is the part we throw away.) In fact, concentrating on conditions conceals the very fact of divergence, because that is not a characteristic of any dance but is a fact about the overall practice of dance throughout the world.

Another objection to looking too singlemindedly for necessary and sufficient conditions of dance is that it presupposes that to call something dance is essentially a way of describing it. But it may not be. It might be, at least in part, a way of saying that certain sorts of standards are relevant to its evaluation. To call something dance is not to say what it is like but to say in what context it has to be appreciated and judged. Dance, in any case, relates to institutions of presentation, to skills, and to specific activities, and to emphasize what dances have in common can only conceal this essential complexity.

5.241 *Reflexivity and Perversity*

Even within the narrow domain where it might be expected to work, that of specifying what counts descriptively as dance within a given context of presentation and evaluation, an enumeration of necessary and sufficient conditions must necessarily fail to include everything that could legitimately be called dance unless we allow ourselves to stipulate what the criteria of legitimacy are to be. The reason for this necessary failure is that creators of dances are conscious beings capable of innovation and include self-conscious persons animated by a zeal for emancipation. Any or all conventions may be perceived as restraints. There is nothing to prevent such a person from reading a definition of dance and, in his or her capacity as qualified dancer or choreographer or promoter, doing *as dance* something that defies the definition. "That is a red flag to us," says Senta Driver. "Anything they say isn't a dance we are going to go and try to disprove" (Fancher and Myers 1981, 93). We note, however, that *disproving* is required; and she has to try, which suggests that she might fail. What would the disproof be? She doesn't say, but I suppose it would be to make or do something that defied the definition and yet was accepted in the relevantly authoritative circle as indubitably dance. The choreographer says NO to this, NO to that, NO to the other (cf. Rainer 1966). But, if the dance is accepted (and repeated), it is probably because of what the choreographer is saying YES to; and the content of this affirmation either turns out to be something that was always essentially or sufficiently dance after all, or becomes part of our modified notion of what dance now is.[3]

The position just derived from Driver is that any definition may be challenged but that such a challenge need not succeed. (That may suggest that at some future time all further challenges will fail—we will finally have discovered what dance was all along—but I will not explore that avenue.) What the criteria of such success might be is a hard question. To bring out the particular issue of principle that is relevant here, let us consider an imaginary case. Any conceivable definition of dance might be confronted by a statement like the following:

> Clayton Clevarass presented a dance called "Absent Fandango" in the window of an empty store around the corner from Judson Church on April 17, 1965. The window was left exactly as it was. Leaflets announcing the performance were prepared but never distributed. Clevarass thought of having tickets printed, but decided not to spend the

---

[3] The nay-saying is given pride of place partly because the idea that art is essentially creative (§3.324) may be taken to mean that art lies in the repudiation of precedent, and partly because modern dance established its status as art primarily by challenging the credentials of ballet. Hence, "We should not try to create a tradition," said Anna Sokolow. "Ballet has done that, and that's fine—for ballet. But not for us. Our strength lies in our lack of tradition" ("The Rebel and the Bourgeois," in Cohen 1966, 29). Without a solid (even though unstated) "Yes," the repetition of "No" becomes a plea, not for endless innovation, but for perpetually renewed artlessness. This would fit in with the claim by Richard Kraus that the growth period of modern dance stems from the activity at Columbia Teachers' College of Gertrude Colby, who around 1913 developed "a physical education program that would be natural and free, and which would permit self-expression" through "a creative dance based on natural movement and on *children's* interests" (Kraus 1969, 132–133; my emphasis). Kraus's view of the matter would relegate modern dance to the enervating and patronizing aesthetics of "child art," which has limited appeal outside pedagogical circles. But his view seems not to be generally shared; he ignores the amount of analytic thought that had gone into the notion of "natural movement" before Colby's day, and the alleged lines of influence are not traced in any detail.

money. It is not known whether anyone attended the performance, since no member of Clevarass's entourage or of the media was present—the media were invited, but the invitations were not sent until Clevarass's return ten days later from Italy, where he had been lecturing on John Cage with prepared piano and unprepared audience.

Anyone prepared to cull the annals of recent art and scour the review pages of appropriate periodicals can amass a body of such "concrete examples" to refute any conceivable definition. The definition is theory, we shall be told; Clevarass's démarche is a fact. It is no use asking whether it is a *relevant* fact, for every smart person knows that judgments of relevance are covert evaluations and hence subjective; and the mention of Judson and Cage (church and priest) is enough to establish Clevarass's credentials. It is therefore thought sufficient to cite the example and leave it at that.

How might someone who wanted to specify necessary and sufficient conditions for dance respond to the citation of such phenomena as the Clevarass "Absent Fandango"—or rather, to the report of such phenomena, since part of the point is that nothing interesting is supposed to have happened? Such a person might concede defeat, on the ground that some dance is art, and art, being essentially creative, cannot be confined. We cannot predict what will be accepted as dance and cannot predict what the criteria of acceptance will be. For Clevarass has indeed been accepted, in some sense: he might have done what he is alleged to have done, and nobody might have paid any attention; or those who did pay attention might have lacked enough influence to get themselves quoted; or their attention might not have taken the form of accepting his alleged claim to have put on a dance performance. There are indeed good reasons for conceding defeat. But one does not have to. One might simply seek to make one's definition immune to such counterexamples by a more cautiously worded reformulation: definitional draftsmanship is, no doubt, a subtle skill. Or one might admit that one's definition only holds for normal cases: some phenomena are not worth covering and are to be discounted.

Some philosophical debates on the defensibility of definition have been bedeviled by too strict attention to the apparent implications of the necessity and sufficiency ascribed to the conditions. An analogy may be drawn with scientific theories. On one view of the latter, a theory is a hypothesis, a guess (perhaps an informed and inspired guess) about what accounts for a phenomenon and hence what the outcome of a certain experiment should be. If the outcome is otherwise, the hypothesis is falsified and the theory should be rejected. But it is generally agreed that that is not what happens, nor should it. Rather, if the theory seems to explain a lot of things, and if one has no better theory to hand, one will explain the unwelcome results away as best one can and hope for better times. The universality and necessity ascribed to the theory are logical features, not practical guides. Similarly, and even more so, in the domain of human action where matters are seldom clear-cut, necessity and sufficiency are part of the logical specification of the sort of definition we are proposing: they do not tell us how we should use our formula, how literally we should take it, what we should let in through the back door.

Another way of responding to citation of "Absent Fandango" is to say that one's definition certainly admits of exceptions, but the point of such exceptions will be precisely that they are exceptional. Clevarass and his reporter certainly did not think that what they were doing was normal dance or would set a new trend in dance. The whole point lay in the aberrancy (and, if they were lucky, the outrageousness) of the claim, which still could not be comfortably denied, that "Absent Fandango" was a dance performance (or, at least, a dance thingy). The definer may then say that whatever counts as dance while failing to fit the definition will be *a talking point*. The definer could be wrong about this, but anyone can make mistakes. What would cast doubt on the definition would not be the possibility of producing cases that are essentially debatable but that of producing cases that are straightforwardly acceptable as dance although not covered by the definition.

A variation of the preceding response would be to say that things like "Absent Fandango" are not examples of dance but foci for anecdotes. Whatever Clevarass has done, he has neither danced nor mounted a dance performance—he was rather exceptionally careful not quite to do any of the things performers and promoters do. (Significant avoidance of this sort requires good theoretical and practical knowledge of what goes on in dance, of course, including knowledge that what one is doing is not that. Without a definition of what dance had to be, Clevarass might not have seen so clearly what he had to avoid doing.) What Clevarass did was provide the occasion for the anecdote we recounted. Part of the history of art is the anecdotes it generates from time to time, such as stories of birds pecking paintings of grapes. In later times, the point of the anecdote we recounted will be that the person who is the source of the anecdote said it was a performance. Who is that person? We have not said, not having bothered to invent him (or her). But *someone* will have to have learned from some source close to Clevarass (Al Terego, perhaps, or Mimi Smiley) or pretend to have learned that Clevarass did all these things; and that same someone must have launched the rumor of them effectively enough for word to have come to me and then been passed on to you. Now, the circulation of a story is not the same as a dance, and a definition of dance is not to be refuted by the currency of tales. There is, in fact, a great cloud of talk that surrounds the practice of dance, as there is around medicine or religion, and this propensity for generating discourse is a very important part of what makes such practices what they are, in the sheer amount of talk no less than in any content it may have. But a definition of dance by necessary and sufficient conditions does not purport to take this vaporous mass into account.

5.2411 *Center and Margin*

What purpose might a definition of dance serve? Many purposes. But one thing it could not do is convey more substantive information than it contains. Dictionary definitions explain unfamiliar symbols by giving their equivalents in symbols supposed already familiar; what philosophers have called "persuasive" definitions tendentiously favor such equivalences that are not quite current, like defining dance as "Graceful movements accompanied by music." In any case, the definition relies on such substantive knowledge about dance as one may have.

Within that limitation, there are two more serious purposes that a definition of dance might serve, and it is unlikely that one definition would serve for both. One function is performed by the old sort of definition by genus and differentiation, answering the question "What sort of a what is a so-and-so?" What that does is summarize a taxonomy, such as the one implicit in D'Alembert's or Philip of Opus's classification of the arts, cited in earlier chapters. Such a definition is suited, in practical matters, only to a unitary practice holding a determinate position in a clearly articulated way of life, such as that which D'Alembert's contemporaries liked to postulate for their own civilization.[4] The other function requires a less tightly organized definition, one that might be approximated by integrating the leading parts of a dictionary entry. That function is to set out those modes or features of a practice that any anthropological or other theorist of the practice will have to take into account, on pain of being found incompetent or partisan. The extent to which such a definition is required to be so comprehensive that valid counterexamples cannot be brought against it will depend on the constraints on the kind of theory one has in mind. And this variability of context gives rise to a third, closely related, function of definition: to indicate what the definer is *prepared* to take into account. Philosophers call such definitions "stipulative." It is customary to preface such declarations of intent with a phrase like "By dance I shall mean. . . ." But definers often delude themselves into thinking that they are laying bare the

---

[4] This is classicism as defined by Michel Foucault (1966), in which entities are classified by their observed likenesses and differences rather than (as has been usual since about 1800) by their functional dynamics, in the way exemplified in our discussion of practices in §§3.2–3.21. In fact, however, taxonomies and the style of thinking they embody are still widely used.

nerve of a practice and indicating what the phenomenon defined *really* is, and the absence of such a warning phrase does not mean that a reader would not be wise to treat a definition as stipulative.

Part of the function of a definition, as of a list of paradigms, is to challenge the citation of deviant and exceptional cases. Far from undermining the original position, as is often supposed, such putative counterexamples may strengthen it by helping us to make clear what is exceptional about exceptions, why marginal cases are on the margin. A definition of music whereby Cage's *4'33"* was decreed not to be music would be defective, but not nearly so seriously defective as one whereby that work figured as normal or standard music.

The point of a practice is to be practiced; it is oriented toward the future. That being so, one does not have to accept all putative counterexamples as real examples. Even without going as far as our imaginary avant-gardist Clayton Clevarass, one does not have to concede even that whatever is presented on stage by a dancer, in performance and as part of that performance, is dance, even though it may be received and reported as such. For it may be something that cannot be taken seriously as dance, something that cannot be related practically to other parts of dance practice, cannot be taken up or meaningfully related to by dancers and others. Such abortive performances and fragments or aspects of performances remain part of the anecdotal history of dance to which we have alluded, along with tales of the childhood of great dancers, of their eccentricities, of the debts of impresarios, of onstage accidents, and of the numbers of curtain calls.

The connections of such dead-end doings as we are now considering are institutional, contextual, associational—all backward rather than forward. They can no more be used as counterexamples to generalizations about dance than monstrous births and freaks are counterexamples to generalizations about the morphology of an animal species. It is understood that such generalizations have to do with what can sustain itself in the life of that species—or that art. The fact that monstrous births do occur is a necessary part of our understanding of how animals in general develop and reproduce, not a necessary or proper part of our understanding of the species. The fact that monstrosities in a particular species occur with a certain frequency and tend to take certain forms is a part of our account of that species, but a separate part that we admit as a footnote and do not allow to affect our general description. The parallel is not exact, of course. In the zoological case we base ourselves on the relative stability of a breeding population with its current genetic repertoire, whereas in the case of the practice we base ourselves on the conscious development of interacting series of imitations and inventions. Moreover, the occurrence of exceptional births reminds us that in changed times different selections of genes may prove viable; in the conscious procedures of practice, on the other hand, whatever is remembered to have been essayed, however abortive, remains a perpetual resource for revival or inspiration in changed times. Until times do change, however, we are right to relegate eccentricities and deviations to the anecdotal penumbra of the practice, not to try to install them within our practical understanding of what the practice has been, is now, and has the potential of becoming.

5.3 *The Fifth Strategy*

We have suggested four strategies for deciding to say what dance is. The first was by induction from all the kinds and qualities of dance one could think of. The second was to construct a profile of the dimensions of dance meaning. A third was to proceed by likeness and difference from a few paradigm cases of what is typically and egregiously dance. And the fourth, which we have discussed at circuitous length, was to find a formula that would sum up one's entire understanding of dance into a list of necessary and sufficient conditions. But there is an alternative to the fourth strategy: instead of drawing on the whole extent of one's experience of dance, one starts from what one takes to be at the center of that experience.[5]

The fifth strategy is the one I take Susanne Langer (1953) to have employed in her discussions of specific arts, including dance. One finds something that seems, subjectively, to offer the key to the whole of one's personal experience of dance. In effect, one treats that as the nerve of dance, without (at least in the first instance) attempting any sort of survey of practice. Rather, one seeks confirmation for one's views from a reinterpretation of what others have written. One takes as much as possible of whatever else has been said about dance and sees how much of it can be understood as the sort of thing a person of different temperament, interests, and intellectual habits might say to express an experience analogous to one's own. One then simply speaks as one finds, explaining how these other findings can be taken as the best sort of corroboration one could expect in the psychologically, linguistically, and culturally diverse world in which our mutual understandings take place. A great deal of writing about dance, perhaps most of the writing that people have actually found it rewarding to read, has had this character—the reason being, obviously enough, that such writing offers a deeply felt and perhaps passionately observed alternative perspective on the very same matters about which one has closely compa-

---

[5] This contrast between extensive and central approaches to philosophical questions is explored in my essay on "The Central Problem of Philosophy" (in Sparshott 1972).

rable feelings and observations. That makes for much better and more heartening reading than any scholarly or analytic review of alternative opinions of which the reviewer, not sharing the concern, has (almost inevitably) missed the point.

The foregoing can best be explained by example, and the only example I can honestly use is my own. The following is what I might do and the sort of thing I might say.

Many years ago I joined a recreational group who did English country dancing. We were not dancers, and few of us got past the stage of getting through the movements without errors. Even so, my experience in some dances was unlike anything else I knew: a transposition into an altered state of being. The state in each dance was different: the "Newcastle" condition, the "Gathering Peascods" condition, and the condition of the "Fandango" were quite distinct. It was easy to recognize that the new state of being, the dance state, incorporated the sense of one's body movements, of the music to which one moved, of one's changing relation to the other dancers, of one's movement within the space of the hall. But the new condition of which one was aware was itself irreducible and distinct: a supervenient grace, one might have said, except that it was neither additional to the specific components of the experience nor a function of them, but, as it were, a new register into which they were transposed and into which I was myself translated. Insofar as I successfully learned any of the dances, in the sense that I came to move within them, a partial transformation of the sort took place; but it was only in a few that the metamorphosis was achieved.

To avoid misunderstanding, I had better add that, of course, in any social gathering (even a cocktail party or a stupefyingly dull committee) or in any team sport, one is directly aware of oneself as partially transposed into a new state of being, a part within a mental whole. The sort of self-transformation I am referring to in dance is not something special or "mystical," discontinuous with everyday experience, but an enhanced version of a quality that, if one troubles to attend to it, pervades experience—at least, if on reflection you do not find that this is a part of your experience, then being a human being is not for you what it is for me. But the experience of becoming part of the dance is something much stronger, with a much more marked savor; one sees why misguided people talk about dance "expressing emotion" even when it doesn't.

A second thing I need to add is that, though the experience of existing as Newcastle was utterly different from that of existing as the Morpeth Rant, they were both recognizably and strikingly ways of existing within dances. That is, self-transformation in dance is a characteristic and unique range of unique self-transformations.

The next thing to say is that in dances where I had imperfectly acquired the dance my experience seems in retrospect to have been that of a partial and unachieved transposition. And now, looking back to childhood experiences of being unsuccessfully taught social dances, in which certainly nothing of the kind took place, I am tempted to say, perhaps sentimentally and fancifully, that the experience was in fact that of being excluded from a state of being into which I had no way of access.

Any phenomenologist will know what to say about the foregoing attempt to put into words my own present sense of the depth of my own dance experience. The phenomenologist will say that everyone's way of being is a way of acting out a life of embodiment within a world that is present to one as well as one's being a part of it. Different phenomenologists will find different ways of putting it. Sartre in his early days would say that each person's way of living his or her life is a personal way of coming to terms with the really impossible task of building a stable self in a world in which one remains, in the last resort, an autonomous and free consciousness; and this, he said, involved symbolically appropriating the world. Whatever nuance the phenomenologist gives it, dancing is going to be a very special sort of activity that is exceptionally heavily charged with symbolism of these basic relationships and not only manifests in an especially poignant way this most universal and basic level in human reality but also symbolizes it in ways that are unique to each dance. The phenomenologist will then say that *of course* I experience dance, insofar as I dance it fully, as a special way of being in ways that are themselves special.[6] As for those who reject phenomenology, even they should concede that the ways of talking it enshrines are widely current, and that currency is all my argument needs.[7]

I am inclined to believe (what I have read somewhere) that people like me who have a heavy personal investment in the literary arts often make bad dancers, because verbal rhythms are inimical to dance rhythms. However that may be, I myself am certainly no dancer, so it seems likely that the experience of dancing that is central for me is quite unlike what would be central for anyone who was by training or temperament a dancer. A dancer must systematically master movements, transforming the body into an instrument tuned the right way, developing methods of mastering and integrating movements by analyzing and reconstructing their components or by marshaling inward energies or by whatever it may be. But then, either dance must become meaningless for such a person by being reduced to

---

[6] The views referred to are those of Sartre 1943, especially in the last part.

[7] One should bear in mind that the alleged experience of self-transformation could itself be the effect of many years of reading phenomenology and thus be an artifact. Philosophers of different schools admit to and cultivate in themselves experiences and ways of perception appropriate to their theories.

technique or it must retain or re-acquire a significance. (It is notorious that sidemen in orchestras may become cynical and bored, merely making a living from their technical facility. But no one has ever suggested that this fatality tells us anything about the human meaning of music and musical experience, however much it may tell us about the sickness of the music business in a labor-dividing society.) And a person like me would simply suppose that that significance would be a sophisticated, subtle, and profound counterpart of what had deep meaning for oneself. How, humanly speaking, could it be otherwise? Or at least, I would look around me for such corroborations and would find them in all sorts of utterances most variously expressed.

Dance, then, is a mode of behavior in which people put themselves rhythmically into motion in a way that transforms their sense of their own existence in a way that is at once characteristic and strongly qualified according to the dance performed. People, at the extreme, dance themselves into ecstasies and trances; and dance conditions, though not involving diminution of consciousness, approximate to trance conditions in the intensity of absorption within the dance. And why would people want to do that? As one of the quickest ways out of Manchester? Perhaps. But it could also be because, at any given time, the specific dances currently in favor induce and symbolize particular "ways of being" or life-attitudes that are currently prized for reasons that (like those considered in §3.21) may be quite obvious. It could be the combination of such an obvious value with the sense of self-transformation that grounded the allure of the dance.

The sort of change I am talking about depends on (and largely consists of) doing specific dance things, and large claims about its significance need more support than they sometimes get. Laban, for instance, makes a swift and unexplained transition from one sort of statement to another:

> A single movement is not dance, no matter how dancelike it might be in its form and rhythm, or however beautiful or expressive it might seem. The lasting, uninterrupted flow of organised movement phrases is true dance. Some single movements can be "dance movements" perhaps, in contrast to "every-day movements," or those of play, sport and so on, but they are not yet a complete dance.
>
> Dance is the transition into a world in which the illusory, static appearances of life are transformed into clear spatial dynamism. (Laban 1974, 93)

People often complain that Laban combines shrewd analysis of movement with fanciful asseverations about reality; but I am not quite sure that that is what is happening here.[8] The transition I am referring to is rather

---

[8] One attempt to wrestle with Laban from this point of view is that of John Foster. He

from the recognition that dance movements are such, not because of their inherent quality, but because they belong to dances, to the assertion that, in belonging to a dance, a movement belongs to a world that is constituted of pure energy. What I find interesting is that Laban seems unaware that he has changed the subject: either a dance as such effects a transposition into the mode of spatial dynamism, or whatever does not take place in that mode is not, properly speaking, dance. It is the former of these interpretations that would bring him close to the sort of thing I am talking about here.

The sort of self-transformation of the dancer that I have been talking about is different from the promise made to the frog in the rhyme, that he should be transformed into "a dancer all in yellow," a transformation that (we saw in Chapter 4) was entirely a matter of his self-image as dancer and had nothing to do with any actual dance he might be doing. Nor has it anything to do with any spectator's image or view of the dancer. If dancing is what we are saying it is, do people watch dancing for the vicarious experience? We said (§4.54) that a dancer may dance *for* people, on their behalf, in a way like that; but that is only one of the possible relationships, and it seems implausible to make it central to the experience of a theater dance audience. What, if I were to continue with this strategy, would I say about that?

One way of dealing with the impasse is to start over and ask myself: What, in my experience as dance goer, has a place of comparable centrality to the experience of self-transformation in dancing? Then I revert to a memory of Robert Helpmann dancing the Master of Trevanion in Ninette de Valois's *The Haunted Ballroom* in, I suppose, 1947. I remember it as a rather scurrying sort of ballet, but Helpmann's first entry I recall as generating by his sheer presence an extraordinary power that in itself made the dance center on him. For me, always, this power of presence has been the core of my experience in watching dance: a power exercised, for me, by very few dancers and almost always by men. It is definitely a dance presence and not a stage presence. And what I mean by that (I can now say) is that it answers to the phenomenological sort of reading of my experience of transformation in dancing: it is an emphatic revelation of human presence to the world.

I seem now to be in trouble with my project of making strategic use of my central experiences to generate a notion of what dance is and is not. On the whole, women dancers on our stages are better than the men dancers, and presence-to-the-world is not an obvious way of picking out the heart

---

links Laban to Gurdjieff, but the links are tenuous: "They both used Movement as a means to spiritual understanding and were both concerned with cosmic structures and knowledge. Both attracted rich patrons . . ." (Foster 1977, 26).

of whatever it is they are doing. But perhaps I am not in such bad trouble as all that. It is not the fact of emphatic presence that is central, but the manner of presence and relatedness—in classical ballet, what many writers have called the "defiance of gravity," for instance, or the rootedness seen in some of Graham's dances. When we *see* the dancer rather than dancing ourselves, the aspect and range of ways of being in the world will be different. And there is this: to each of us, existentially, being is being, we are in the world simply as being there; even if maleness and femaleness should be polar ways of being, they could not be evident *as such* in our being to ourselves. If human being is indeed sexual from the start, it would be in our relation to others and our awareness of the being of others that this would appear. This range of ways of being in the world would become meaningful to us in the dances we saw, not in those we danced. And now I am home free. I can use my sense of the depths of dance meaning, in performance and in observation, to form the basis of an account of what dance fundamentally is, by providing means of translation and mediation between my own ways of talking and thinking and those chosen by others. But will all this help us to say not only what is dance but also what is not dance? Not really. It is a strategy that serves to establish the nerve of dance. What it leaves out is not necessarily other than dance but may well be dance in a way that is peripheral, in one of the ways of being peripheral that are sketched elsewhere in this chapter.

5.4 *Recognizability*

I have said repeatedly that one of the first things to bear in mind when we are considering what is and what is not dance is that we all know perfectly well what it is. One of the things people grow up knowing, if English is their native language, is how the word "dance" is used, including the ranges of cases where such use is normal, exceptional, controversial, sarcastic, and so on. And the reason we know what to say has to be that we know what we are talking about. But, although that is important (we have taken account of it already), what I have in mind here is something more. Suppose we met an anthropologist who went to study a newly discovered tribe whose culture he and we knew nothing about. Suppose he were to tell us that, by extraordinary luck, on the very first day of his visit they performed a dance that took place only every ten years. I do not think that this account would leave us incredulous. And yet it implies that he knew a dance when he saw one, without being told it was a dance or any thing else about it. Just as he would recognize their speech as language, their houses as dwellings, their food gathering as gathering things to eat, he would recognize their dance as a dance.

Mistakes can certainly be made in all these areas. The anthropologist might think they were gathering certain caterpillars to preserve the vegetable crop, but in fact the caterpillars were to eat; he might think that certain huts were dwellings, but they were really shrines. Mistakes about language are not so easy to envisage: one might not recognize that a street merchant's cry consisted of words, or that a "talking drum" encoded language; but, even so, we cannot imagine spending any time among a people and not recognizing that their language was language. It is, I think, almost as hard to envisage spending much time among a people and not recognizing their dance as dance. If our anthropologist told us that he was present at this dance but did not at the time recognize it as dance, we might not be incredulous, but we would certainly feel that an explanation was called for. We would be just as surprised and nonplussed if he told us that what he at first took for a dance turned out not to be one. The circumstances must have been very special. It could not just have been that what he took for a dance was really a ritual. Nothing prevents a dance being a ritual; it is part of our concept of dance that dances are not deprived of their status by a ceremonial context. About the only thing that would explain his remark would be that he at first failed to notice that the movements of the supposed dancers were determined by some such instrumental task as sowing seed or manipulating tools or weapons, slapping insects or avoiding invisible barriers (like the people setting up the exhibition in Jacques Tati's film *Trafic*).[9] At the same time, though we expect a dance to be immediately recognizable as such, wherever on earth it is performed, we are aware that dances differ radically among themselves. On being told we are to see a dance, we do not know at all what sort of thing we shall see, though we can be pretty confident that it will be recognizably a dance.

Dance is dance, we may say, and recognizably so wherever humans are human. In the domain of science fiction, however, we could certainly accept an alien planet on which the space explorers do not recognize the residents' dances until they learn the culture. But then, we could equally accept as part of the same fiction that the explorers did not at first know which of the resident aliens' behavior was language or was most like language. That, though, is the special condition of science fiction: we do not know, until the author tells us, whether the aliens have bodies, or how their bodies are composed of what, or how and whether they communicate with

---

[9] It is not the bare fact of utility that is relevant. Rain dances, initiation dances, and so on are essentially useful. But they are useful *as dances* danced by dance rules; efficacy is not attributed to their component motions.

each other, or how they are individuated. Nothing can usefully be inferred from generalizations about the possibilities of science fiction, for the charm of the genre lies in its exploitation of the licence to ignore constraints on what is really possible or to indulge our fancy where we do not know what such constraints might be.

5.5 *Strategies Applied*

Of the five strategies suggested, the enumeration and grouping of kinds is beyond our present scope, and the construction of a profile of dimensions of meaning awaits a finally satisfactory version of Chapter 4. I have said all I have to say for now on my own materials for a subjective approach. That leaves us with the consideration of paradigm cases and the establishing of necessary and sufficient conditions. We have said enough to show that the latter is in principle impossible, but we also said that the attempt should be instructive. What could teach us more about dance than to weigh the credentials of what may strike us at first as characteristic features of all dance? We will accordingly propose some plausible common characteristics of dance, test them a little, and follow up by looking at a fairly recent attempt to say just what, on the basis of all available knowledge, is common to all the world's dances. But before we do that we will have another look at the remaining strategy by suggesting a few paradigm cases and a few doubtful cases.

5.51 CENTER AND PERIPHERY

What shall be our paradigms of dance? Ballet dance, for one. Movements of the body or bodies, based on types of positioning and movement that the body is, from childhood, exhaustively trained to make, subject to the canons of clarity or beauty or expressiveness and usually all three, the movements linked together in harmonious and rhythmical sequences, the sequences themselves designed and repeated in accordance with the same canons, accompanied (or, by exception, *as if* accompanied) by music against whose rhythms the movements are counterpointed, presented to an audience in an elaborate setting (or devised with such presentations and settings in mind as their guiding norm)—but, above all, examples of a recognized kind of dance, namely, ballet.

Ballet is a paradigm, and was so even when the pioneers of modern dance affected to despise it: it was the unmistakable enemy. But no less paradigmatic is a tribe's rain dance, even for those who would regard it, by comparison with ballet, as a rudimentary or degenerate form. There are dancers who know they are dancing this specific dance and in doing so perform movements of the feet and/or other parts of their bodies that are the specific movements for this dance, arranged in such sequences as properly constitute the dance, accompanied by music, perhaps a chant of the dancers themselves, at least by a regularly or rhythmically beaten drum or drums, the music and the movement fitting together in some prescribed way—if not by synchronizing specific movements with specific sonorous events, at least by co-varying the character of the sound and the character or implication of the movement in some fashion recognized as appropriate. There need be no spectators, actual or implicit. There is likely to be, but need not be, a special occasion for the dance; there is very likely to be a special and elaborate costume, worn for this dance and nothing else. What is essential is that the dancers know that this is their rain dance they are performing. The language they speak need not have the concept of "dance" or that of "rain dance" at its disposal, or even the concept of "performing." What they must know is that they are doing *this*, *now*, and that what they are doing now is a specific manifestation of *this* that they regularly do. Not all of them need even know that: children may be picked up and dragged along, newcomers may be conscripted without explanation to join in and follow along as best they can; but *the group* knows it. That, I would say, is an absolutely typical sort of dance; and when we speak of the ubiquity of dance among human groups that (rather than the highly specialized ballet, so closely tied to a specific history) is just the sort of thing we have in mind.

To make my meaning clear, I provided thumbnail sketches of the particular paradigms I had in mind. But in doing so I was really going against the intent of what I wanted to say here. Descriptions substitute a form of words for what should be at issue, which would be your and my experienced knowledge of such dances, whether by observation or through protracted hearsay—knowledge that would ground such descriptions without becoming exhaustively (or even at all) explicit in them. What I should really do is point to an example of the sort of dance I had in mind and say only, "I mean *that* sort of dance."

The differential availability of paradigms is a complication here. I have seen many ballets in the last forty years, but no rain dances (though I have read narratives, heard recordings, seen films of the sort of thing I have in mind; and I have seen people from a New Mexico pueblo who dressed themselves up and showed us how they did their Basket Dance). Yet I would insist on the rain dance being a dance: though I have no direct knowledge of such dances, they enter into the very basis of my understanding of what dancing is. It seems to follow that that basis is largely an imaginative construction; and your imagination, being based on different access to different paradigms, should lead you in a rather different imaginative direction. What is perhaps remarkable is that this divergence seems not to occur in any very important way. What is good dance and what is legitimate dance are matters of dispute, but the understanding of what the paradigms of dance would be seems less controversial.

5.511 *The Choice of Paradigms*

Whether or not they are supplemented with descriptions of actual dances, our two paradigms will not suffice. Together, they would mislead us. They share something not all dances need: a certain ceremoniality. And they omit things that are important to some equally paradigmatic dances as dances: social pairing, a relation to ecstasy, a relevance to recreation and to physical perfection. Disco and ballroom dancing, balls and hops are no less central to our idea of dance than ballet and ritual dances; and so are dances like the sailor's hornpipe, flings, and reels. We would have to add an item to our list of paradigms whenever we noticed some important trait that some dance has *as dance*, one that is exemplified in something that is indisputably dance but not in any of our admitted paradigms. We have seen that at certain times and places that have been crucial to the development of our civilization the individual and creative dances of Isadora Duncan and her compeers, the choral dances of Greek theater that linked civic sense to dramatic poetry (together with their necessary counterweights, the trance-inducing dances of Dionysus), even the pantomime of which Bathyllus and Pylades were exemplary exponents have been central to what dance meant; and we should no doubt add the courtly dances enumerated by Sir John Davies and described in the instruction manuals of the sixteenth and seventeenth centuries. Whatever made them central to what dancing was at that time must surely be something that no account of what dance is or is not can sanely ignore.

It is evident from the foregoing, however, that the method of paradigm cases is not free from internal problems. We have in fact cited three components in it or three alternative versions of it. We could start from the sorts of dances that immediately strike us as central, here and now, to what we take dance to be; we could start by including dances that have had such a central importance at other places and times whose thinking was exemplary for us ("the Renaissance," "Classical Antiquity"); we could gerrymander our list to take into account our sense of what significant differences there are among dances and why they are significant. And in the last case, at least, one might wonder whether we are in the first instance relying on paradigm cases at all. The question is whether our list of dances is really (but unavowedly) meant to illustrate an antecedent sense of how dances significantly differ from each other, or whether we do honestly start from an unanalyzed sense of how two exemplarily dancelike dances differ. In practice, as in all such cases, there will be an interplay; but we will be entitled to say that we are ultimately basing ourselves on paradigm cases if (and only if) we refuse in principle to affirm at any point that the specifiable differences that make up a sensed difference between actual dances have now been exhausted. In any case, the point of the "paradigm case" method remains that what dance *means* is made to depend on acceptability for such a list, and that the general idea of what dance is depends on the idea of acceptability as *certainly a dance if anything is*.

5.512 *Marginal Cases*

If our account of what is and what is not dance is to be based on a consideration of paradigm cases, it could be usefully supplemented by considering marginal and spurious cases—cases that conspicuously give rise to hesitation as to whether or not they are dance, or that conspicuously provoke debate about whether they clearly are or clearly are not dance. One might also consider reverse paradigms, cases of what is not dance if anything is not; but, since their common feature would be only that there was nothing about them to make anyone want to call them dance, such a discussion would be pointless and interminable. Such cases do in fact play an important part in discussions, but only in a way that is incidental to discussions that derive their focus and structure from something else. "The melted patch of snow on my neighbor's roof this morning is not dance." Well, no, but no one said it is and no one is going to. We will mention it only if there is some way of not being dance that it aptly illustrates (in this instance, it happens to be the first thing that catches my eye as I turn my head to look out of my window in search of a good random example).

I consider ten possible kinds of cases, of which someone might hesitate as to whether they counted as dance or not.

5.5121 *Frisking*

A small child (who has perhaps seen something on television or watched older children?) says, "Look, Mom, I'm dancing." But the child is not dancing, not really: it is jumping up and down, skipping about, like a puppy, gamboling and frisking.[10] Why does the child think it's dancing?

---

[10] Miller (1986, 135) points out that a word Jesus applies to his own dancing in the *Acts of John* (see §2.1) is *skirtan*, the word applied by Plato (*Laws* 653E) to the gamboling of children, and he invites us to compare the Beloved in the *Song of Songs* 2:8, who "cometh leaping on the mountains, skipping upon the hills." Plato is saying that children can't keep still, they suffer from excess energy, their fidgeting and frisking is "as if they were dancing for joy."

Why isn't it? The putative dance is something the child is doing on purpose to be a dance, neither a mere reflex nor a stretch of its activity identified as dancelike by others. The child has grasped the idea that dancing has to do with frisking about and being seen, even frisking about in order to be seen and applauded. The child may even have grasped that it has to do with frisking about rhythmically, though this will be hard to tell, for two reasons: on the one hand, the combined forces of gravitation, the spring action of the muscles, and the pendulum impetus of the limbs suffice to impart a temporally patterned character to any vigorous motion; on the other hand, the concept of rhythm is too elusive to be applied as a criterion. What the child has mainly missed is the importance of imparting to the frisking something worth watching. Dance is something that extorts or merits attention, not primarily something for which attention is *demanded*. The child has not grasped the necessity of governing one's movements by a standard of right and wrong (let alone good and bad, beautiful and ugly, graceful and ungainly) according to which one would be dancing more or less successfully, performing more or less well a specific dance or kind of dance. It is because the child is *just* dancing that it is not really dancing at all. If, however, the child performs motions having a recognizable character and does recognizably repeat them, then we will begin to agree that the child is dancing and invite it to "Show Uncle Mervin how you dance" or "Do your dance for Aunt Edie," just as we would admit it was dancing if we could ourselves discern in its movements some sign of a valued or valuable quality or design.

5.5122 *The Airborne*

We speak of the dance of motes in a sunbeam. Why do we? Is it because most of us lack or cannot be bothered with the concept of Brownian movement? Rather, it is because the particles swirl together in draughts and eddies in movements that remind us of a corps de ballet more strongly than of any other kind of movement, or because, being so light, they move up and down in a way vaguely evocative of the ideal lightness symbolized in that paradigm of dance, the romantic ballet.[11] Dancers in such a ballet should be light and agile; at least they should not thump and stamp.

According to Sendrey (1974, 223), the word used in the *Song of Songs* is one found nowhere else in the Bible: *kafaz*. He says it is a synonym of *dalag*, which means the same as *rakad*, which does mean "to skip about." I don't know how he knows.

[11] Dante in the *Paradiso*, XIV, 112–117, likens the movements whereby the radiant souls form a cross to the movements of dust particles in a sunbeam—but he does not say that they dance. Dorothy Sayers in her translation makes them "dance in the shaft of light." Was it that dancing had become more respectable in Sayers's day, or that the paradigm of romantic ballet was available to her and not to Dante? Milton in "Il Penseroso" does not say that "the gay

The fact that the overall movement of motes is called a dance does not mean that we think of individual motes as dancing. If it is as if they were dancing, it is because of the apparent freedom of their movement, not constrained either by any evident finality or by an imposed force, but free as the wind. In just the same way we speak of the dance of mayflies or midges at evening, although no one insect by itself is doing anything that strikes us as notably dancelike. (I've watched the mayflies to see, and they aren't. They just go straight up and float down again until they bump into another mayfly. Then all hell breaks loose.)

In all these cases, we are (it will be said) speaking metaphorically. But what would that mean? It is not metaphor in the sense of an imaginative transferring of a word from its native heath to a domain where its use represents some poetic or rhetorical insight. We are not finding a new way of looking at a phenomenon for which we have at our disposal other, more humdrum, locutions. We regularly call such movements dance, and there is no other word more regularly used to convey the character of the movement. All that is meant by calling the usage metaphorical is that we are prepared to admit, if pressed, that the motes and insects are not *really* dancing—that they are, in fact, dubious and marginal cases. If this is metaphor, it is only (by the standards here invoked) metaphorically metaphor.

5.5123 *Reflections*

We speak of the dance of sunlight on the water—another metaphor that is no metaphor. This case is like the one before, but it is even clearer here that there is no one thing dancing. Patches of reflection appear and disappear here and there on the rippling surface. What is dancelike in the rippling? It is a light and as if agile motion—twinkletoes—as if a spark were struck out wherever and whenever a lightfooted dancer touched ground. Such intricate lightfootedness is the distinctive and attractive feature in some modes of dance. It is a similar agility in a mechanic's touch that is called "dancing" by Pirsig (1974; cited above, §2.3). We need know nothing of brazing to envision what is meant, and it is about as much like the dance imputed to the sunbeam as it is like any human dance. The movements in question are typically dancelike, then, and "dance" is the word that best catches our meaning. But if I named the dance of light or the danced brazing torch when asked to give an example of a dance or of a kind of dance, I would be out of line. Even if the example were accepted, it would be a tiresome thing for me to have done. And it goes without

---

motes that people the Sun Beams" are dancing, either; but it would not have been relevant for his poem, as in fact it is for Dante's. Actually, none of the quotations in the *OED* article on "motes" makes them dance, even when they are in sunbeams and not in people's eyes (the relevant section, Monopoly to Movement, was issued by Bradley in 1908).

saying that even the mechanic is not engaging in the practice of dancing. As for the dance of sunlight, nothing is doing anything, even in the restricted sense in which the motes in the sunbeam were swirling. There is an appearance that puts us in mind of a quality of certain dance movements, and that is all there is.

The sunlight dances on the waves, but do the waves themselves dance? Not often, I would have thought, and not in open water, where they rather roll. But on the seacoasts of Bohemia they do:

> When you do dance, I wish you
> A waue o' the Sea, that you might euer do
> Nothing but that: moue still, still so:
> And owne no other Function.
> (Shakespeare, *A Winter's Tale*, IV 4)

—I give the First Folio text, for the sake of its splendid punctuation, allowing waves and dancer to move perpetually in place.

The waves, like the dancing lights, are not entities performing a dance; they exist only as dancing. But, unlike the lights, their separate existence is not a function of the appearance of movement. The wave really has a continuous existence, but only as moving water. "You are the music, while the music lasts." When the music of the wind stops playing, the waves stop dancing and stop being waves: they relapse into the prosaic existence of seawater.

To think of a dancer as a wave is a remarkable trope. It is not confined to Bohemia. In Ireland, too, when people hear the Fiddler of Dooney, "they dance like the waves of the sea." I have always imagined that as a specific dance: the dancers link arms and roll down the street until their wave breaks at the door of the pub. But if it is a choppy sea they could be doing a jig, their green caps bobbing at all different angles.

I do not know why we say waves dance, except that they do.

5.5124 *Bestiary*

Many forms of animal behavior are called dances or thought of as dancelike in a much more definite way than the dancing mayflies. In general, these are modes of intraspecific communication or information-bearing interaction. People accordingly have very different views, in each case (though more in some than in others), as to how dancelike the behavior is. The difference hinges on three factors: first, the extent to which the investigator or expositor adopts the category of information exchange as the appropriate framework and as applicable equally to human and other animals; second, the extent to which human dances of the paradigm sort are thought of as primarily exchanges of information; and third, the weight attached to there being a practice that is deliberately engaged in. Since these differences are fundamental, there can be no intellectual victory in the disputes to which they give rise. The best thing to do is to hold the contestants' coats and rifle the pockets.

5.51241 *Grebes.* We speak of the courting dance of the crested grebe and of other animals where the courting behavior includes elaborate mutual posturing.[12] Are they dancing? They certainly do not know they are dancing; but then, humans who do not speak languages close to modern European vernaculars do not know that anything they do is "dancing." The grebes, though, are presumed not to be doing anything of which they can be said to *know* they are doing it. We must suppose that, in whatever sense birds may be said to sort-of-know something, they know they are courting a mateworthy member of the opposite sex; it just so happens that in doing so they produce patterns of movement that sometimes remind us of dancing. But what is it about what they do that reminds us of that? It is not that they look like people performing any particular dance or kind of dance. Perhaps it is rather that they *display* themselves in patterned movement. But in what sense "patterned"? It is an interwoven succession of advances and retreats, rises and falls, nods, turns, and so on, in which the principle of organization strikes us, the observers, as being no other than exactly to be that particular sequence of movements. The dance must be "designed" to attract, in the sense that attraction is its ethological significance; but it attracts not by (for instance) presenting the animals' sexual parts in a way indicating accessibility but by being attractive. The grebes are not really dancing, perhaps; but what else are they doing? It is mating behavior, but what sort of mating behavior? A mating dance, quite obviously. What else would you call it? A ritual, no doubt, which is what Huxley did call it. But what sort of ritual? A dance ritual. A ritual dance.

5.51242 *Apes.* More notorious even than the grebes are the dancing chimpanzees reported by Wolfgang Koehler, because their description was assigned a pivotal place by Curt Sachs in his *World History of the Dance.* His apes enjoyed a "primitive round dance" in which they start by "marching in orderly fashion" around a post, then start trotting and "beat out what approaches a distinct rhythm." In this alleged dance, "the chimpanzee likes to bedeck his body with all sorts of things, especialy strings, vines, and rags that dangle and swing in the air as he moves about." Sachs interprets all this as showing that "on a lower level than that of man, a series of essential

---

[12] The fame of this grebe rests on a long paper by Huxley (1914). He calls what they do a ritual rather than a dance, which begs the same sort of question in the same sort of way.

dance *motifs* has *already* been *developed*" (my emphasis), thus insinuating that the movements described have the status of thematic variables in a cultural form, that the apes developed them in some sort of process of formative elaboration, and that the chimpanzees in Koehler's laboratory on Teneriffe are in some sense among his own ancestors. The historian of dance, says Sachs, is thus "able to distinguish, on the basis of established facts, innate from acquired characteristics" (Sachs 1937, 9–11).

Sachs's reference to chimpanzees, lumped together with birds and "natives," has, not surprisingly, met with fierce repudiation from writers more sophisticated in the behavioral sciences, because it neglects cultural context and systematically associates animal dances with those of nonliterate peoples. Joann Kealiinohomoku (1970) has compiled a disheartening collection of such stupid and vicious equations, from the pages of writers on dance whom one would otherwise have thought reasonably well educated.

As the terms of Koehler's description and Sachs's interpretation show, the interest in the chimpanzee's dances is part of a continuing tendency to seek analogues with human behavior in studies of other primates. If man is a hairless ape, maybe ape is a hairy human. There was an attempt some years ago to make chimpanzees out to be painters, and more recently some investigators persuaded themselves that apes could be taught a rudimentary sort of humanoid language. But these endeavors were less persuasive than the dancing. Human languages do not form part of the apes' intraspecific communication systems, and it is silly to suppose that they could become so. Apes do not practice anything like the art of painting, and their propensity to apply brushstrokes tastefully did not function outside the context of the trainer's provision of materials and knowledge of where to stop: there is no indication that the apes ever learned that there was a task that might be *completed*, a picture to be painted. But the dance as reported by Koehler was part of the spontaneous behavior of the group, and we know that apes (like other mammals that live in groups) do have elaborate social structures with complex hierarchical and communication systems. It is not clear that baboon colonies do not develop something like a culture, forms of structured behavior specific to and learned within the colony. So would it not be perversely doctrinaire to deny that Koehler's apes might have been, in a perfectly straightforward way, dancing? Maybe colonies of some species in some circumstances do develop clearly patterned behavior of that sort, and we call it dancelike not only because some of the behavioral items are much more dancelike than they are like anything else we know but also because what the apes are doing is visibly engaging in what would recognizably be a dance practice if we could concede that it was a practice at all. It is the variable dancelikeness that constitutes the behavior pattern as a structure within the overall pattern of the apes' lives.

It might be so. It is not certain that it is so. Koehler's reports remain exceptional. We have no information about whether and in what conditions and under what forms such behavior occurs in the wild, nor any general account of situations in which such behavior can be regularly observed or induced in captivity.[13] Besides being exceptional, the reports are suspiciously slanted: only German chimpanzees, it has been unkindly said, would march up and down waving flags. The grebes' courtship was too invariable to count as really dance, the chimpanzees' antics are insufficiently regular.

We need to know a lot more about how apes live before we can say what they are up to when they look as if they are dancing. Really, we need more than that. We need to know a lot about social animals in general, how social existence in all orders of animals is patterned. We need to know a lot more about what is common to the behavior patterns of all mammalian species, of all social mammalian species, of all primate species. We need to know what the variabilites are. Only then will we be in a position to pick out groupings of behavior that will be significantly "dancelike." And, when we achieve that, we will no doubt take a new look at what in our own cultures has this character. Such a view of dance would be neither peripheral nor paradigmatic in our thinking. Human behavior that was dancelike in this new sense, but not actually recognized as dance, would be peripheral in one way; animal "dances" would be peripheral in another way (we could actually recognize them as properly to be designated "dance" without extending the accolade to the human behavior in question, on the ground that the animals never do anything more dancelike than that—but humans do!). None of this need change the status of the paradigm dances danced by trained dancers who know what dance they are dancing and know what it is to dance. Everything human beings do acquires its distinctive quality from the way humans construct their lives linguistically, and nothing is going to change that.

Though the material compiled in this bestiary of ours is in one way marginal in the consideration of what dance is, in its totality and its general purport it is by no means trivial. And the stuff about apes is important. It

---

[13] An afternoon spent browsing extensively among recent chimpanzee research (including Mason 1970) unearthed no allusions to any such dancelike practice and no single instance of anything like it, either in the wild or in captivity. Authorities who still cite Koehler omit all mention of the "dance." I infer that the alleged tendency does not exist. What confronts one throughout the literature is that (a) chimpanzees are markedly individual in what they do and (b) component movements (leaping, following) that might enter into such a "dance" are frequently observed, but not in any particular connection with each other. In fact, if one did see a bunch of chimpanzees doing what Koehler said he saw them do, or even if they did it habitually, one would have no reason to infer that chimpanzees as a species had any propensity to do so.

is highly significant that in some influential circles our self-understanding as dancers at one time demanded that we invoke the supposed round dance of the chimpanzees and now no less imperiously demands its oblivion. This willed oblivion involves the repudiation of nature, rather than art, as the dominant context of dance practice; it involves the repudiation of the very idea of "human nature" (as opposed to culture); it implies the rejection of the idea that there are such things as dance movements, in the sense of movements that are intrinsically proper to dance practice. Some would say this change of viewpoint shows a new maturity in our thinking, a turning away from old superstitions and facile ethnocentricities. Others would say it means the obliteration of the world—the replacement of our knowledge of ourselves and of our world by the contents of our undergraduate survey courses.

5.51243 *Bees*. Less anxiety-making than the cavortings of apes around their alleged maypoles are the "dances" of the honeybee as described by von Frisch (1950). Bees returning to the hive from a pollen-gathering expedition perform movements on the face of the comb, or wherever, that indicate by their speed, magnitude, and orientation the direction, distance, and copiousness of the food source. We sometimes refer to these movements as a dance. Why? Like dances, it is patterned behavior isolated from other behavior. There is a specific dance the bees are performing. The movement is patterned in a way that human movements are only when we are dancing or when we are doing things of the sort that make people say "they look as if they are dancing." (Actually, this is a bit of an exaggeration; a skeptic would say that the bees look less like dancers than like a thirsty audience in a crowded bar during a short intermission.) The bees do a sort of serpentine interweaving of some intricacy, a sort of conga line.

We do speak of the dance of the bees. In fact, they and the grebes have got into the dictionary. Number 14 in the article on "dance" in the *Random House Dictionary of the English Language* (1967) reads: "A stylized, instinctive pattern of movements peformed by an animal, as a bird in courtship display, or an insect, as a honeybee in indicating a source of nectar."[14] But, though we call it a dance, we do not ordinarily speak of any one bee as dancing, any more than we do of individual mayflies. The appearance of dance is only the outcome of the summed behavior of the returning and greeting insects. The ethological significance of the way they move is sim-

---

[14] It is interesting—nature notes from all over—that in an article of which the substance is taken verbatim from the *OED* the grebes and bees have been inserted, while dancing bears, to whom we presently turn, have been deleted. The apes, too late for the *OED*, do not make it into the Random House dictionary either, perhaps because they are taken to be straightforwardly dancing in one of the ordinary senses of the word.

ply to transmit information; to say, with the dictionary, that the movements are "stylized" is misleading both as introducing the inappropriate ideas of style and non-naturalism and as suggesting that there is something as special about the bee's posture as there is about the grebe's. We are less inclined than in the case of the grebe to ascribe to the individual critter anything like a dancelike motivation, or indeed anything like motivation at all. A bee is just part of the bee-machine. And yet, because the function of the behavior is to communicate, we can hardly help assimilating it to *gesture*, traditionally a key term in defining dance. The bee is a tiny Pylades. Anyway, if the bee is not dancing, what else would you call what it does?

5.51244 *Elephants*. With grebes, apes, and bees, our readiness to speak of "dance" depends partly on a perceptible patternedness in behavior, partly on the specific appearance and structure discerned in the behavior, and partly on our readiness to attribute to the moving entity some sort of motivation. We might then round out our discussion by mentioning Kipling's story "Toomai of the Elephants" (1894). I know nothing of any folklore or observation that may lie behind the story; my concern is with the fiction. In the story the elephants are dancing not only because their movements are dancelike in a rudimentary way—they shuffle around, "stamping all together" (which artfully implies but does not state that they stamped rhythmically, kept time in their stamping)—but because their only motivation is that they are *going to a dance*. They have themselves a ball, come home in the wee small hours, and are no good for anything all next day, just as the puritan Fetherston complained (Chapter 1, note 13). But this is of no consequence. We speak of the elephants' dance because (in a collection of anthropomorphizing stories) the author and his characters do; and the author has given the dance the character of a ball, partly to nudge the tale along and partly, no doubt, with some satirical intent. (Actually, a close reading shows that at no point is any anthropomorphic motion or motivation actually attributed to the beasts; readers are inveigled into making that attribution themselves.) The way these elephants dance, it seems, tells us more about the resources of fiction than about the boundaries of the concept of dance.

There is, however, more to it than that. These fictitious beasts are not only humanlike in their wisdom, but uncanny in themselves. Their dance is not merely a ball, it is solemnly unmotivated; to have witnessed it is a rare and dangerous privilege. And Kipling's elephants are not the only elephants there are. In India there are places where elephants are included in religious rituals, gesturing appropriately with feet and trunks; and they are introduced into circus acts, where they do the same sorts of things. In European and American circuses, where the animals and acts seem mostly to have come from India originally, elephants do the same sort of minimal dance approximations, but without the ritual significances. Do circus elephants dance or not? They *sort of* dance. And it makes a great difference, in India, that elephants are not ordinary animals but occupy a special place in the economy of human, animal, and divine life. An elephant is associated with the elephant-headed god Ganesh, the eldest son of Shiva, who is Lord of the Dance. It is generally true in the Indian and Sino-Japanese civilizations, as in most cultures, that the significance of what an animal does, and of what people can make it do and pretend that it does, depends on the part it plays in mythology, in the ontology of the imagination. Animals of privilege—monkeys, bears, elephants—may be allowed to dance, where a pig would not be, even if it could. And the same is true of our Euro-American civilization, though in a way that is muddled and muted by our dogmatic humanism and monotheism. One can be sentimental about Swan Lake as one could not about Duck Pond. And my grandmother would have said that Pavlova's Dying Swan looked like a dying duck in a thunderstorm.

5.5125 *Dancing Bears*

In a different category from the bees, apes, birds, and fictive elephants of our bestiary are "dancing bears." We have remarked already that the *OED* gives them a place of their own in the article on the verb "dance" (1 b): "Of animals taught to perform certain regular movements." We call its behavior dance, not because of any dancelike character it is observed to possess, but because the bear is made to simulate a human dancer to the best of the bear leader's endeavor. It is indeed dancing under the concept of dance. The bear is made to stand on its hind legs—and really, this is the point of the show, to see the bear stand up like a man—and to shuffle its feet and perhaps flap its arms a bit while music is played. The bear is exactly in the position of an exceptionally clumsy and stupid dancer displaying the outcome of its training and the choreography it has learned. The bear is dancing, all right. But it is not exactly performing a dance, and it is certainly not a dancer even though it certainly is a dancing bear. Dancers so impossibly dumb as not to grasp the principles on which their dance is organized still know that they are dancing, and that is just what the bear cannot know. Like the stupid dancer, it does what it is told; but, though it presumably recognizes the dance it always does as its invariable response to a certain cue (the music in the trainer's presence), and I would suppose that in some way it recognizes that it is doing *what it has learned*, nothing in its recognitions answers in any way to the fact that what it is doing is a dance. Dancers know that insofar as they understand the dance they can try to dance it better without the choreographer having to dictate every last nuance of every least movement. One supposes that if the bear knows anything of that sort, all it knows is which of its movements have pleased its trainer best. Or should we add, its trainer and its audience? Domestic animals seem in general to grasp the notion of being applauded for what they are trained to do.

The bear, I said, is not *exactly* performing a dance. But, in a way, it is. It is performing *its* dance. Its trainer will have trained it to make certain movements (the traditional ones, or the most dancelike ones he knows how to teach it) and to combine them in some sequences: the most sequential ones possible, and especially, if he can manage it, with a recognizable *end*. Why am I reluctant to say that, whatever the trainer's success in this, the bear will perform a dance? Because it is unlikely that the bear grasps the unity of the sequence it goes through or has any internally programmed determination of the sequence. There is no true synthesis of movements, only an externally imposed and maintained succession sustained by the trainer's command and alien to the bear's ursinity. It is no more dancing than a parrot uttering a sequence of syllables, of which it does not even know that they form words, is speaking a sentence in a language.

Notwithstanding all that, the bear's dancing has another dimension. Bears, like elephants in India, are more than just ordinary animals, as much fiction testifies. They too are uncanny beasts: to make a bear dance to one's tune is a significant humiliation, perhaps akin to bear-baiting. In the fictional Wild West, potent baddies shoot around the feet of feeble goodies in order to impose on them a shuffling sort of dance; the Iroquois hung red-hot axheads round the necks of their captives to make them do something like dancing. If a free dance may express the autonomy of the human spirit, perhaps an imposed dance symbolizes domination.[15]

5.5126 *Orchestral Conductors*

The dancing bear that shuffles to music puts one in mind of the orchestral conductor who waves at his band. What is he doing? Perhaps someone has to beat time, but the conductor does more than that (and may in fact not do it at all). Someone has said that the conductor "performs a dance to interpret the music to the audience." That was a witticism, said just because we all know the conductor is not really dancing. But what else can he be doing? He is moving rhythmically and gesturing expressively to music, and

---

[15] Conversely, Salome and other autonomous dancers may impose their will on others by their dancing. Mata Hari became a legendary figure because she was a dancer who extorted secrets (though not by her dancing). Kipling's repertory of dancing beasts includes a snake luring monkeys to their deaths by its dancing in the dust.

his movements have a purely formal and symbolic meaning.[16] He directs his movements at the orchestra, but surely he cannot be teaching or instigating them now; any real influence he may have on their playing, beyond keeping the time and boosting morale, must have been settled in rehearsal. Perhaps he is dancing at the band for us.

The way a conductor dances for an audience is like the way the bee dances at the hive entrance: the speed, orientation, and amplitude of the movements indicate the direction, the importance, and the relative availability of the nectar. Well, not quite: the conductor shows us rather how the music should affect us, which the bee does not need to dance out because it carries the samples with it. But are we not in the same position? Can we not hear the music? Not necessarily. If music is the language of feeling, the audience may not know the idiom; the conductor can help with a simultaneous translation into the idiom of visible gesture. Again, the structure of the musical forms may escape us on first hearing (in fact, it is bound to do so); the conductor, who has heard the music before, can mime for us some of the architectonics.

All the same, the conductor is not exactly dancing, though some conducting is very dancelike.[17] Conducting is closer to mime than to dance. In a dance, however strictly the logic of the movement may be controlled by the music, that logic belongs to the dance itself. The movements of the conductor, at every point of their articulation and in every nuance of their gestural quality, are referred to the music, which determines them or which they determine. They are assigned no autonomy and they claim none. If one watches the conductor, one does so for reasons connected only with the music, however eccentric and mannered the things he does; insofar as the movements take on a character of independent interest, they become an irritant. Conductors differ widely, not to say wildly, but what they differ in is always their way of conducting the music, reciprocally determined not

---

[16] I saw the young Celibidache conduct Tchaikovsky's Fifth Symphony in a provincial theater in the 1940s. From my seat I could see into the wings, where, at the symphony's end, the maestro staggered off exhausted. He stood nonchalantly waiting until the applause subsided a little, then took out his handkerchief, clapped it to his brow, and bravely staggered onstage again to acknowledge the plaudits of the peasantry. I used to think he was celebrating the intensity of his own efforts on our behalf, but I now incline to the view that he was miming the emotional intensity of the experience we had been through together.

[17] Not all. Sir Adrian Boult, much of the time, simply gave the beat, keeping his left hand in his trouser pocket. True, this was when the BBC Symphony Orchestra was in provincial (bombproof) exile during the war, and the live audience was not paying. Even then, after a concert under a visiting conductor, I heard one of his musicians say "How nice to have a real conductor for a change!" One would get jaded, of course, and a new conductor would have to do more work on the unfamiliar band, but I suspect the meaning was that the temporary conductor was a better dancer.

merely by its gross outline but detail for detail. No criticism based on anything other than the music can be relevant, none based on the music can be irrelevant.

What is the conductor doing, we asked, if he is not dancing? But we have an answer. The conductor is conducting the music and the musicians. And yet we may feel that only in a cultural climate where dancers may be fêted could a virtuoso conductor become a star.

5.5127 *Ice Dancing*

To say that an orchestral conductor is dancing is a sort of witticism, though not a good one: everyone has already noticed that the conductor dances, but everyone knows it is not a dance. But to say that a figure skater or a competitor in the "ice dancing" section of a skating competition is dancing is not even a witticism. The skater performs steps, leaps, figures, in time to the music in just the way that a dancer does. Of course such skaters are dancing and know they are dancing. But no one thinks of them as dancers. Why not? It is not only that we have something else to call them, namely, skaters; we could have gone on calling them skaters and called them dancers as well.

Two things make one hesitate to speak of figure skaters as dancers. First, the prior and dominant skill is that of skating: they are skaters who can dance rather than dancers some of whose dances call for skates. Figure skating does not primarily function as a specialism within dance practice or dance arts. Second, the performance context of figure skating is closer to acrobatics than to any dance practice. What acrobatics requires is the performance of certain movements that demand great strength, skill, precision, coordination, and dexterity in a way that looks effortless and economical and hence graceful. It is a demonstration of prowess in bodily skills and is no more dancing than a dancer's exercises at the barre are. There is no dance context. Movements are carried out not to merit being seen but to witness that they have been mastered. They are done for judges, not for an audience, even if spectators are present. It is true that nowadays acrobatic contests include "free exercises" in which the competitors compose sequences to satisfy their own and (they hope) the judges' sense of form; but the status of these is equivocal. Some find them distasteful because they contaminate the austerely limited values of acrobatics with a simulacrum of dance values that are neither appropriate nor sufficiently understood to impart their own formal organization to what is done. The competitors do not dance; they do acrobatics in a corrupted way.[18]

When we look at a manual on ice dancing, we notice at once how firmly

---

[18] I am indebted to Paul Benacerraf, a gymnastics buff, for telling me about this.

the subject is placed in the context of competition. Although not every rule is taken as an end in itself, we read that "[t]here *must* be a standard; otherwise the professionals do not know what to teach, and the skaters do not know what to skate" (Soanes 1976, 1); and the whole discussion is in terms of the relative gravity of faults at this or that test level. The idea that one might do such things otherwise than in or for competitions is nowhere considered. Even at the "gold" level, where considerations of aesthetics go beyond correctness, we read such things as "[t]he Viennese Waltz should give the feeling of waltzing in a Viennese grand ballroom with massive chandeliers, and the music should also be chosen to give this effect, that is, true Viennese Waltz music. The dance is lilting and graceful" (Soanes 1976, 102). Ice dancing, evidently, does not generate a dance aesthetic of its own but is parasitic on the music and the supposed ethos of ballroom dancing in a way that exactly fulfills the forebodings of those who resent the contamination of acrobatics by alien values.

Should we then say that figure skating is a form of acrobatics that happens to look like some forms of dancing? Just because it obviously does look like dancing, but that is the wrong way to look at it, to call it dancing is not a witticism but a solecism. But matters are complicated by the practice of people like Toller Cranston, a figure skater who has competed as such but whose dominant motivation is aesthetic (he has exhibited as a painter and published as a fabulist, thus firmly establishing the art context as the one in which he has chosen to operate). Judges in competitions have, it seems, found his performances in free-form events excessively dancelike; but he, like John Curry and some others, has evolved a sort of *dance on skates* and has devised, directed, and performed elaborate television fantasies in this genre. What he does is obviously a development from within competitive skating. But how can we deny that it is, quite straightforwardly, a form of dance?

At least three answers seem possible. One is that of course he is dancing: the fact that he dances on skates and in a way suitable to that condition makes no difference. A second is that we would say he is dancing were it not for one thing: the context of figure skating already exists and has a gravitational pull so strong that we cannot honestly see him or think of him otherwise than as a skater. But a third thing we might say is this. Skates are heavy and clumsy. They lend themselves to the effective performance of only a limited range of movements, which are precisely the rapid glides, the leaps and spins of a skater, the pushing of which to their extreme of vigor and grace is what makes up the substance of competitive figure skating. It is not the institutional context but the limitations and the established associations of the actual repertory of movements that keep what

Cranston does within the realm of skating and not that of dance proper. To see it as dance we would have to see an old thing in a new way.

The contrast between typical skating movements and typical dancing movements has been emphasized by Janice Rio. "Basic to the notion of dancing," she says, "is the notion of stepping (generic sense) from one foot to the other. . . . In dancing stepping from one foot to the other is the foundation from which step patterns are built, while in ice skating the foundation lies with the gliding from one foot to the other" (Rio 1981, ch. 6, pp. 8–9). She cites Ashton's ballet *Les Patineurs*, in which the dancers resemble skaters while never ceasing to be dancers, because their skaterly postures and rhythms are belied by the step-founded basis of their movements. And ice dancing of Cranston's or Curry's sort is no more a form of dancing than narrative dance is a form of drama (ibid., p. 10). The point is well taken, and well developed. The fact that, as we have seen, there are occasional dances that lack steps is not relevant, since we are comparing whole practices rather than individual compositions or performances.

If we are to compare practices, though, we must ask: Is it characteristic of all dance practices everywhere that they are built on a foundation of foot-to-foot steps, or is the latter distinctive only of some dance practices, including our own? It does not seem that stepping rather than sliding or shuffling is basic to all African or American vernacular styles, and one ragtime composer is quoted as saying of the Essence that "[i]f a guy could really do it, he sometimes looked as if he was being towed around on ice skates . . . the performer moves forward without appearing to move his feet at all, by manipulating his toes and heels rapidly, so that his body is propelled without changing the position of his legs" (Stearns and Stearns 1968, 50). In fact, if an anthropologist were to tell us that there were cultures in which the characteristic dances were performed sitting down, we might be mildly surprised, but we would not be incredulous, and we certainly would not accuse our informant of misusing language. We may concede that ice dancers are not doing what we should identify as dancing in the most relevant context, that of our own accepted dance practice, but to say without qualification that they are not dancing is a little strong.

Whatever we may think of the status of competition dancing, the restriction to the context of skating may after all be transcended as well as compromised. When figure skaters have won all their championships, they often join such a show as "Ice Capades," a spectacular extravaganza in which skating skill is displayed in the context of showmanship. By the tradition of such shows, what appears may or may not be dance (cf. §§7.6, 1.33212). The figure skaters then become the show's dancers. And, since the whole show is on skates, the fact that they are also skaters sinks into the background.

227

All in all, though we will never accept ice dancing as a paradigm of dance, its status as dance seems variable and complex. When competitors in the "free dancing" section have chosen their dance music, says Soanes, "the next important requirement is that it be adapted to ice skating. It is not enough that the dancers wear figure skates and perform on a sheet of ice; they must *skate*. Excessive use of movements which could be done just as well without skates is to be discouraged and penalized severely." But, he adds, the music "must be *dance* music" (Soanes 1976, 109). Not being a philosopher, he lets his equal and opposing emphases stand in lieu of explanation. And perhaps we can do no better.

5.5128 *Kathakali*

Our last kind of dance that cannot serve as a paradigm is exemplified by the Indian theatrical form of Kathakali. This presents a problem akin to that once posed for the compilers of the Christian scriptures by the Book of Revelation. If it was canonical, they said, it was *certainly* canonical; if it was not canonical, it was *certainly not* canonical. The point was that the decision called on one to make up one's mind about the nature of one's religion, of scripture, of the relation between the human and the divine. The issue could not be treated as that of a borderline case. Kathakali is that sort of test case.

Surely Kathakali is dance if anything is. Starting even earlier and proceeding even more rigorously than in ballet, the dancer is taught to build movements and postures by resynthesizing meticulously analyzed and controlled movements of the body parts. The dance consists of a chain of gestures and steps peculiar to dance and developed in the direction of perspicuousness and visibility. The movement is elegant, graceful, majestic, and eloquent, and it proceeds to a musical accompaniment. What is this if not dance? What is dance if not this? However, what is danced is the story of a text that is being recited. What determines the construction of the dance is not choreographical logic but the narrative. It is somewhat as though a song were to follow, exquisitely, the intonations of a speaking voice. In the latter case we would not speak of song; we would use a different word: "chant." So we might say that Kathakali is not dance but "presentational theater," or some such phrase that would mark its distinctness from any tradition we allow to be dance. It is not quite mime, because many of the movements are constructed from conventional units. A reason for saying it is at least not *essentially* dance appears when one observes other, less exquisitely refined versions of Indian dance theater, which are more clearly hammed and mugged presentations of the story being chanted. They are essentially dumb-show, and the more sophisticated genre differs primarily in the way the detail of the movement has been reconstructed.

Is Kathakali dance, or isn't it? One would need to know much more about it, of course. But, on the present showing, Hegel would have had no problem: certainly it is, it typifies the form in which alone dance can take a place among the fine arts as an embellishment or variant of poetic mimesis. Moreover, the spectators focus their attention neither on the words (which may in fact be unintelligible—inaudible, or in a dead language or an unfamiliar idiom) nor on the music, which functions as accompaniment. They concentrate on the performers and on what they are doing, and what the performers are doing is evidently dancing rather than acting or miming. How could it not be dance? But, if we work with a conceptual space in which dance and drama set up separate and rival fields of force, we may be equally firm in excluding from dance Kathakali and all forms of oriental presentational theater. The linkages and separations of practice here are evidently unstable and not constant between cultures.

When we compare our own impressions with what the Indians themselves have to say, we find the same ambivalence, although they have no one word (in any of their traditional literary languages, that I know of) that makes quite the same contrasts that we use "dance" to make. As we shall have occasion to see later (§8.4611), they have separate words for pure dance, for the "expressive" dance that interprets text, and for such dance-dramas as Kathakali. "Kathakali is purely a dance drama," writes one expert. "The gestural and other expressional modes in it are almost entirely devoted to suggest, elucidate or augment a discursive theme and this leaves a very small percentage for the purely formal meaning" (Sathyanarayana 1969, 238). They are distinctively dance forms, then, but their meanings are not specifically dance meanings.

5.513 A False Center

We devoted a whole chapter to "Dance as Metaphor," to the dominant idea that the universe as a whole is dancelike in the organization of the heavens or in the rhythms of its basic movements or in both. Should we not then think of these as paradigm metaphors, so that the dance of the heavens or of life is acknowledged to stand at the center of our ideas about dance?

No, we should not. It is not true that "the world is a dance, if anything is." We think of it as a dance only if we are forcibly struck by its likeness, in some aspects, to dances that are themselves paradigmatically dancelike in a quite different and more direct way. The world is a dance only when considered under an aspect under which we need not consider it: it is not true that "the world is a dance, if it is anything." The metaphor remains a metaphor. If any culture were to make some modality of movement, not necessarily human, the center of its idea of dance, then either that modality would have to be much more specifically and integrally exemplified in the dances danced in that culture than such cosmic movements can ever be, or else we would conclude that what these people thought of as dance was so fundamentally unlike what we think of as dance that it would be better to use a different word.

None the less, what dance is and has been in our civilization is something it could not have been if the dance of the heavens and the dance of life were less deeply resonant in it.

5.52 NECESSARY AND SUFFICIENT CONDITIONS

In differentiating between central and marginal cases, one explains one's reasons for placing them where one does. Those reasons then provide material for the alternative strategy, whereby one proposes plausibly necessary and sufficient conditions of dance and considers what one should say about proposed exceptions and counterexamples. The main purpose of that consideration, as we said before, is not to get a better list but to make the list meaningful by showing how it works.

Necessary and sufficient for what? The question defeats us at the start. They could not be conditions that have to be fulfilled by anything that anyone could ever honestly, correctly, or usefully call dance—such discourse is too multidimensionally various and too context-bound for that. The conditions would have to pick out some reasonably strict and unified notion of dance that would be relevant to some dominant practical and theoretical concern. But what concern could claim such dominant status? No answer satisfies: we would end with a sense of "dance" defined by the conditions themselves, manifesting without necessarily avowing whatever practical irritations and theoretical discomforts guided its formulation. But we said in an earlier chapter that people do write and read general histories, sociologies, anthropologies, phenomenologies, philosophies of dance. What our conditions should capture would be whatever it is that provides any inherent unity the subject matter of such a book might be expected to have.[19] I consider seven possible candidates for such a position. I consider mostly their necessity and let their sufficiency look after itself: it is tidier to enumerate necessary ingredients, and then see what needs to be added, than to establish a sufficient totality and scrutinize it for superfluities.

---

[19] Remember that by using the words "anthropology" and "history" we have already foreclosed on all possibilities that would extend dance beyond human practice.

5.521 *Conscious Movements*

A dance consists of or is centered on a series of the visible motions of a conscious agent or agents. This is discussible at six points at least.

5.5211 *Movement and Adjunct*

We say "consists of or is centered on." Some would say that, strictly, the dance as such consists of the dancer's danced movements, all else being adjunct. Pure dancers of pure dance dance naked or wear only enough clothing to avoid the distractions of nudity. The *pas de deux* from *Nutcracker* is often performed without scenery or music and in practice costume; it is still the same dance. True. But surely, at a performance of *Nutcracker* with costume and music and scenery, the latter are integral parts of the work presented and legitimate objects of dance criticism. So is the lighting, at least if its complexity is such as to call for craft and care.

In the case of the lighting, if it is just a matter of having enough lights to see by and having them turned on, then the lighting is a proper object for the dance critic in one way, as part of the conditions affecting the way the performance is seen; if the lighting is not part of the conditions with which the dancers have to contend but is the sort of thing that is designed by the team that created the dance, then it is an object of criticism in quite a different way, as part of the production. And then we can say quite generally: the stipulation that a dance be centered on body movements and the fact that some dances are constituted (for their creators, dancers, spectators, critics) essentially by nothing other than those movements do not entail that, in dances similarly conceived, performed, enjoyed, and criticized as involving such other elements as we mentioned, the latter cannot be part of the dance or that the totality is any less properly dance than the stripped-down alternative. If the claims of such minimalism were accepted, in dance as in other arts, it would follow that much of what is done and most of what is prized in the art is not properly speaking an exercise of that art at all. The position is possible and has often been taken, but other positions are defensible.

If we define a dance as consisting of or centered on a set of movements, does it follow that the choreography of a dance is not the dance itself? Is the design for the movements any less "the dance" than the movements of the bodies that execute the design? The question is not worth answering, a sterile conundrum.[20] When Balanchine says (I heard him say it, in a tel-

[20] Students of aesthetics are familiar with this set of maneuvers in the discussion of music. Someone says: the score is not music, only a recipe for making music. Someone else says: a performance is not itself music, only a representation of the music that the composer made.

231

evised film) that "[b]allet belongs to this dancer who is now this moment under your eyes. Choreography doesn't exist," he is not saying something that is either true or untrue. He is eloquently making a point. The design is a design for dancing and, as choreography, has no other interest; but that interest it does have. The possible relations between the danceable and the danced are an important topic in dance theory but have nothing to do here.

5.5212 *Counting Movements*

"A series of the visible motions," we said. That implies that movements can be arranged in series, which implies that we know where one motion stops and the next begins. Does that mean that dance is intrinsically digital, rather than analog? Does it imply that when a person moves we always know the one right way to analyze their movement; or does it mean that, unless we know the one right way, it cannot be a dance? In fact we have no set way of individuating people's movements, either as to their successive parts in time or as to their synchronous parts within a single body or group. Much philosophical ink has been spilled in the last quarter century on the related problem of how one individuates *actions*; and, insofar as what a dancer does in dancing is to move, the movements that are the relevant actions will admit of all the ambiguities and complexities that belong to those discussions, as well as any that belong to what may be this different level of analysis. (Roughly, what a person is *doing* depends on how the person's *movements* are understood; how the person's movements are to be described in the first place is not quite the same question, though bound up with it.) The dancer leaps—at what point do we say the movement starts? A leap requires a preparation—is that a separate movement? A dancer asks a choreographer, "Where is this movement *coming from*?" Presumably, the answer affects the quality of the movement: is that just a matter of the musculature, or does it involve the mental set and a variety of minute adjustments that go along with that? Again, suppose in a dance I turn my head—a single movement? Yes, but several muscles moved to bring it about; and, within the movement, there was a beginning to move and a coming to rest. Besides, if I am performing a *fouetté*, my head turn will be an integral part of that; and, if I am partnering, my turn will be integral to the interaction of our glances, gestures, and holds.

In any case, is a dance really a series of movements? If it is a single dance, will it not be a single complex movement, with beginning and middle and

---

Each has a good point; to try to decide which of them is right, otherwise than in some specific context of discussion, is idiotic.

end?[21] It is a dance because what comes in the middle is not a sequence of separate items but interwoven: it is what comes before the beginning and after the end that is only sequentially connected with the movement(s) within the dance.

The foregoing paragraph sounds precious and captious. After all, if people are dancing, there is a time before which no movement any dancer makes is part of the dance and a time after which none will be; and in between there is a time when all or a significant subset of the movements the dancers visibly make within a given space or in a given context will be identifiable as the dance they are dancing. And who are the dancers? They are the people whose movements are identified as part of the dance. How are you going to get around that?

Suppose we give in. Does it follow that a person is not dancing unless there is some right way of differentiating the movements made, so that it is those movements under that description that constitute the dance? Presumably not. It is part of what we mean by dancing that we should usually be able to recognize steps and positions in a dance, but it is no part of what we mean by dancing that this should *always* be possible. Is it even true that one could not be dancing *a dance* unless one could divide it into some component repeatable movements that one could recognize as constituting *the same dance again*? I doubt it. One could not claim to have created a dance work unless one could specify the conditions of recognizable repetition; but one can improvise dance as a dancer without creating a work. But if, in my improvisation, I do not notice and do not decide how my dancing is divisible into movements, so that I cannot specify at all what I have done and what I shall do next, how shall I know that I am dancing? Well, very easily, just as people could talk with continuous intelligibility before grammatical analysis was invented. I shall simply put my trained dancerly intelligence into play. Anyone who sees me can analyze my dance into component movements, but no such analysis has any authority. We may suspect that some analyses will be more illuminating than others, more vivid descriptions, more closely related to how that dancerly mind of mine was working. But the notion of a sequence of movements is misleadingly definite.

[21] In Japan, "the student of dance is taught a complete dance from beginning to end, then another, then another, until a repertory of complete dances has been learned. In the West a dance student is first taught the basic steps; he drills on these over and over, and only later are the steps put together into a complete dance. . . .

"Psychologically one has learned a dance, total and complete and unchanging, whereas in the West, by learning the basic steps first, psychologically one always tends to view any dance as made up of these separate steps—and hence, as variable" (James R. Brandon in his "Introduction" to Gunji 1970, 65).

I think it is an inseparable part of our notion of artistic action, and even of intelligent action, that what is done must admit of intelligibly analytic and explanatory description: that it must be possible to give a breakdown of what was done that will make sense. And some such descriptions will make better sense, be more enlightening, than others; some will be ruled out by the facts of the case; some will fit like a glove. But it is not part of our notion of art or of intelligence that there should ideally be one and only one correct description, of which all other acceptable descriptions are parts or to which they approximate. In fact, supreme artistry and exceptional intelligence may usually, if not always, have a richness that outruns system: it is as if they had built-in somewhere a capacity for inexhaustibly generating intelligibilities. At least, things like that are customarily said of great art, and there is no reason why they should be any less plausible if applied to comparable exercises of intelligence in other domains. If that is so, the demand that a dance be a definitively describable series of correctly identified motions is misplaced, because it would mean either that the most intelligent and artistic dances are not really dances at all (but, perhaps, matrices of dances), or that artistry and intelligence have no adequate place in dance.

5.5213 *Consciousness*

A dance, on the present showing, must be danced by a conscious agent: dancers must know that they are doing something, namely, that thing to which we (but not necessarily they) give the name of dance. But is this restriction legitimate? We may set aside such phenomena as dancing daffodils and motes in sunbeams, on the ground that they are dances only by courtesy, and we may allow that dancing bears are "dancing" in connivance with the trainer's professional optimism. But what about automata? Marionettes dance. Yes, but they dance vicariously; the puppeteer uses them to dance with. But suppose a roboteer built a dancing robot? Does the robot dance, or does the roboteer dance vicariously in the robot? It is a nice question, and ballets play with it by having real dancers simulate clockwork dolls. Surely the dancers are not pretending not to dance: they are pretending to dance by clockwork. And they conduct the pretense partly by simulating rigidity in articulation and partly by moving their bodies as though they were alienated instruments moved by a limited program. Since I can consciously and deliberately move parts of my body as if they were not parts of myself, it would be doctrinaire to deny that the doll dances, if it is adequately humanoid and if it has been programmed to perform movements that simulate regular dance movements. And it would be impolite not to salute the maker's and programmer's ingenuity by saying that the doll dances, just as it is impolite to computer designers and programmers, who exhaust their ingenuity to make their machines simulate human think-ing, to say that computers don't think.[22] But we are, in any case, ready to attribute actions to lifelike dolls and even to merely functional robots: we will say that they do just those things the doing of which they simulate. They are made to do something, and the maker has not failed, so how can we deny that they do that thing? The doll is made to do something, it is doing something, and what is it doing if it is not dancing? And the better the simulation, the more the doll will look as if it is acting intelligently, knows what it is doing.

In the case of lifelike dolls dancing in a lifelike way, the condition that a dancer must be a conscious agent is not really breached; it is, as it were, observed by courtesy. An animal that happened to perform dancelike movements otherwise than as part of what we would designate as its "dance" in one of the special cases considered would no more be thought of as dancing than a human to whose movements the requirements of some task had given a dancelike quality (cf §7.1). The requirement of conscious agency operates here in a plain way. But what if someone were to build a machine that did not simulate human (or animal) dances but performed elaborate machine movements that the inventor, no doubt in virtue of some kind of intricacy or some aesthetic appeal he had imparted to them, told us were dances? Can we generalize about the difference between cases in which we would let him convince us and cases in which we would tell him not to be silly? Perhaps there would have to be some theriomorphic aspect to the alleged dance, or else some defensible analogy to some kind of movement we were already committed to calling dance. But I think we would have to ask the inventor. Presumably the inventor, in designing the machine to dance, designed it to perform specific sorts of movement that the inventor had himself identified beforehand as appropriately dancelike. So either it would have to be easy for us to see that it was dancing, or else the inventor (or impresario) would have to make a good case. And we cannot predict what case would be made and what would make such a case good enough. This is, in fact, a situation that calls for the judicial reasoning of case law, by precedent and subsumption.

Such a dancing machine as we have imagined would bear close analogy with computer art or with the simpler machine art that is produced by fastening pencils to eccentric cogs. These are all designed to conform to what the designer thinks of as artistic or as aesthetically pleasing. They are

---

[22] The analogy is inexact. In most cases, the reason for building computers that simulate human thought is to help us in the thinking we need to do, to do some of our headwork for us, so it makes more sense here than in the case of dance to say that we do part of our thinking with the machine. Dr. Coppelius does not do part of his dancing through his doll, though one could certainly write a story in which a crippled dancer did so.

machine transformations of accepted art values. Whether we accept the results depends partly on whether we share the designer's views of what those values are, partly on whether we find the transformation affectively acceptable. Our a priori views on the conditions of artistic status have little to do with the matter, because it is often a presupposition of our discourse that these conditions cannot be fulfilled anyway. What would be the point of telling the inventor that the machine was not creative, not original, and so on? The inventor *knows* that.

Another important factor in the way the requirement of conscious intent affects our thinking about the machine designed to perform machinelike quasi-dances lies in the equivocal status of the concept of autonomy. The machine is a machine for dancing; it dances whenever it is switched on or whenever it is programmed to dance. Its dance is "autonomous" in the strict sense that the machine is following the logic of its own design, the law of its own being. Its dance expresses that in it which corresponds to what conscious intent is in intelligently volitional beings. It is not like looking up and noticing that someone (or even some animal) has started dancing—they have taken it into their heads to dance, we say. Machines do not express anything like autonomy by taking things into their heads. Apparent spontaneity in machines is a sign of failure. A machine that started dancing instead of doing whatever it was doing before would almost certainly have broken down. Our washing machine dances across the laundry floor when the tub has come unbalanced; but no one would expect us to reconsider or gerrymander a definition to take account of that.[23] So, in the case of the dancing machine with the mechanical-type movements, the very mechanical quality of the movements, though it made them less like a human or animal dance, might actually be among the things that moved us to say that the machine was, in a sense, dancing.

5.52131 *Nature and Necessity.* We have seen that the privileged status of consciously intended movements gives rise to some problems. Some light is shed on these by considering Aristotle's concept of "nature." (It is worth while looking at this world view, though long obsolete, because Aristotle's intelligent interest in macroscopic vital phenomena was not diverted, as our own interest inevitably is, by information that is inaccessible to unaided observation and therefore irrelevant to the ways we keep ourselves oriented in the minute-by-minute world of practice.) "Natural" entities were defined by Aristotle as those, typically living things, that have within

---

[23] The washing machine dances in that its motions are rhythmical and non-utilitarian, and in that it proceeds across the floor by steps, hops, and leaps. But few washing machines dance really well.

themselves the power to initiate and terminate certain of their own move-ments—those of their movements, in fact, that we call "natural." The point of interest to us here is that, not only are not all the movements of any natural thing themselves natural, but no movement is altogether natural: the overall movement of the physical world includes the movements we call "natural" as parts, not only because they are parts of the whole move-ment-system of the world but also because their energy is causally derived in one way or another from external energy sources. The world thus con-fronts us with a continuity between mechanical and vital movements, be-tween meaningful and enforced motions.

In dancers, as in other living things, the movements of the body are caused partly by impacts and resistances from outside the body, partly by the mechanisms of limbs, muscles and joints and tendons; and partly by the mind, the voluntary innervation that represents the workings of an in-formation system. But the information system itself has to be explained partly in terms of its own dynamics, partly by its structure, however deter-mined, and partly by its inputs. The arts of dance play on this complex interweaving of will and necessity, and one cannot therefore build into a definition of dance any sharp contrast between them.

5.5214 *Humanity*

Is it enough that a dance be centered on movements of a conscious agent? Should we not insist that the agent be human? Dance, insofar as it engages our philosophical interest, is a practice, and only humans engage in practice. Grebes, bees, and robots do not engage in practices. Nor do apes, not really, because they do not have the sort of language they would need to equip themselves with the *concept* of what they were doing. How-ever, the stipulation of humanity would also rule out the angels who make a practice of dancing in Dante's *Paradiso*.

There are arguments on both sides. One argument says that there is no reason for the restriction to humanity as such. If there are nonhuman but intelligent, language-using beings on remote planets, the question whether they engage in the practice of dancing is not to be settled a priori. We would want to know whether they had culture as well as intelligence, whether they were civilized. Above all, we would want to know what their culture (if any) was like, what they did. Only when we were well informed and acquainted would we know whether to say that they danced, or that they did not dance, or that they engaged in dancelike practices that were not quite dance. Come to think of it, we would need the same sort of information before we knew whether to say that they were human, or not human, or humanlike; persons, or not persons, or somewhat personal. I am reasonably sure that it is lack of culture more than lack of personhood, lack of personhood more than failure to be human, that stops the bees dancing. But the concepts of personhood, humanity, linguistic competence, and culture are intimately and intricately connected in ways that cannot be explored here. As for the angels, however, they surely sing; and, if we say they sing, we might as well admit they dance. To say that angels can't dance because they are not human and only humans dance seems extravagant. Being essentially incorporeal, whatever they do cannot express their own corporeality, which is indeed an important consideration—but what's the point of being an angel, if you can't dance?[24]

One reason for restricting dance to humanity would be that, so far as we now are concerned, humanity and personhood and culture are coextensive. We will think about extraterrestrial life forms when we encounter them; meanwhile, the only dance that is meaningful as dance is one that engages much that in our experience is uniquely human. But we could go further and say that dance is inseparable, not from culture in general, but from human culture and from human existence. Dance as we know it is essentially a manner of expressing a specifically human sense of the ways our bodies occupy physical and social spaces. Susanne Langer's celebrated theory of dance (1953) argues for this viewpoint. One may object that, even if this view of dance fits the facts, it fits only where it touches: it applies only to dance as art and hence only to certain selected dances. This objection, however, can be met easily enough. We can tie it in with what I was saying about dance as an alternative mode of being, intimated or vouchsafed. Any kind of dance, we can say, obviously has a specialness of that kind: dance in general is the practice of putting oneself into motions that are experienced as special in ways that are in each case easily identified. To

[24] In fact, angels can sing in a sense in which they can't dance. Angels are interesting. In Christian mythology, they are disembodied minds that figure in human history as bearers of messages from God to humans. To bear such messages, they must be visible and audible, that is, they must have bodies. Since they are disembodied, the bodies they use for communication must be generated for the occasion: they are temporary configurations of local matter. Medieval arguments about angels were attempts to work out the implications of these conditions in ways that would do justice to sacred texts while staying within the bounds of contemporary physics. Angels can talk and sing, because they can intelligently produce the audible phenomena. But can they dance? Not really, because one dances by moving the body in which one exists as being embodied, and an angel exists as disembodied. The body an angel generates is not related to it in that way and is not a spatiotemporal continuant susceptible to change in the physical world. But of course an angel could make its "body" dance in any way it wanted. That old question, "How many angels can dance on the point of a pin?" used to be an object of derision because people supposed that "scholasticism" seriously wanted to know the right answer. But it was a school exercise, and an extremely good one, raising all sorts of questions about the concepts of dance and of embodiment and many other matters, as the sages of the Enlightenment would have realized if they had used their elegant brains for anything other than sneering and drinking chocolate.

be directly aware of one's relationships within the world as meaningful is a large part of what humanity really means for us. Man is the dancing animal because dance is the direct manifestation of the general capacity for culture, for living in a multitude of variously meaningful states.

However far one developed that line of thought, though, it would not evade a second objection: that dance as thus conceived is not specifically human but generically appropriate to any limbed and articulate animal capable of culture—of the reflective elaboration of its own modes of awareness and of itself as an object of self-awareness. The particular dances we dance as humans have a specific character that goes far beyond that, involving the exact number of our limbs, the relative weight and balance of the head, the placing of our sense organs and sex organs, the mass of our planet, and the ways we are sexually differentiated (two alternative sexes, two intergrading sexualities, etc.). If we had different shapes and different bonding arrangements, we would not be human, and we would dance very differently. But surely, if that was the only sort of difference there was, we could still dance. Couldn't we? What would prevent us? And why should we not want to?

5.52141 *Aristotelian Dance.* In considering the requirement of autonomy in dance, I invoked the old Aristotelian idea of natural movement. It may be worth while returning to Aristotle to consider some possible implications of making dance specifically human. The reason for reverting to these archaic and obsolete lucubrations is that Aristotle is the last person in Western philosophy to take an intelligent look at human life as part of the natural world. Here, then, is a version of what Aristotle has to say about animal movement in his *On the Soul*, III 10, with a glance forward at his remarks on the shape of human life in his *Ethics*.

Animals can move themselves because they have joints, on which the moving parts of the animal pivot in relation to unmoving parts. When a dancer moves in space, as a whole, the limbs are moving in relation to what (from the dancer's point of view) remains the still center of the dancer's being.

Why should an animal move? There must be a reason, a stimulus to which it responds. The stimulus is something to which the animal relates in two ways: it recognizes it, and it desires or shuns it as thus recognized. That is to say, the affective aspect of one's relation to the objective of one's action is subordinate to the cognitive aspect. Action is possible only in a world that is found meaningful. But the meanings, to provoke action, must themselves be practical meanings: things desired as perceived must have been perceived as desirable. Aristotle does not say, but phenomenological

239

philosophers have been saying lately, that such meanings must be generated within the context of the world as a field for action.

What we have said of action so far is true not only of humans but of all
animals that can properly be said to "do" anything, even of the sea ane-
mone that merely grips whatever prey comes within its range. What is
characteristic of human actions is that they are based on a sense of time—
that is, on rational imagination. We act in envisaged sequences, taking
means to ends and reflecting on the past as past, comparing alternative
routes to destinations, weighing the near against the far. What enables us
to do this is language, in which the imagined can be fixed and compared:
language use and reasoning are one and the same. Our sense of time, then,
enables us to live lives in which the episodes are related by sequence and
subordination, and by cause and effect. To live such a life, and nothing
else, is what it is to be human (and to live it properly, since it is a linguistically mediated existence, one must live among fellow speakers with
whom one's objectives may be stabilized, refined, and integrated).

If we insist that dance is human, that could mean, in Aristotelian terms,
that a dance is a series of movements meaningful and worthwhile to the
dancer, ordered in time, the parts subordinated to the meaning of the
whole, the series amounting to a sequence in which each episode (each
"step") is related in retrospect and prospect to the others and/or to the
beginning and ending of the whole as a whole, and in which whatever is
done is envisaged as preferable to alternatives that were not done.

Sympathetic readers of the Aristotelian *Ethics* will recognize that a dance
as thus described is a life in miniature. A lifetime is or can be meaningful,
its meaning exhausted in the living of it. A drama is meaningful as the
representation of a life, or a part of a life, in a graspable form. A dance is a
series of body movements so ordered as to have the kind of satisfactory
meaning that a whole life can have. It would be excessive, however, to
make the possession of such an order a necessary condition of something's
being a dance. At most, we could claim that to be a dance must be something that it is appropriate to criticize in such terms.

5.5215 *Visibility*

We specified that the movements of dance must be visible. Should we
have? What did we want to exclude? Certainly we did not mean to insist
that one's movements as a dancer exist for one's vision rather than for one's
kinesthetic sense or simply for one's overall self-awareness as being in the
dance condition. Nor do we want to make it a matter of the definition of
dance that dances exist for spectators, much less that they necessarily exist
for their strictly visual aspects (as opposed to such other aspects of them as
may be accessible by way of visible data). Or at least, I don't; others may.

Roger Copeland, for instance, writes: "[F]or many of the Judsonites, the difference between dance and non-dance has nothing to do with the movement itself, but depends rather on the context in which the movement is perceived. Dance might thus be defined as *any movement designed to be looked at*" (Copeland 1979, 323). But it looks rather as if Copeland or his informants have thought only of the supposed irrelevance of movement quality and have not considered what that is to be contrasted with. Nothing is said about what kind of context is required; as the definition stands, every flasher is a dancer—unless indeed a lot of significance is to be packed into the word "designed." If the word means something like "patterned," we might be able to make a go of it; if it only means "intended," we can't keep the flasher out. In any case, the definition stipulates that one cannot dance for one's own satisfaction and that social dances are not dances at all unless they are performed for the sake of the onlookers. In fact, as with so many avant-garde pronouncements, one cannot tell what is intended because one does not know what alternatives have been considered.

What should a stipulation of "visibility" exclude, if it is to be acceptable at all? We might want to exclude invisible movements, in the sense of internal rearrangements of the body that leave no trace on the surface, or movements of the mind (in case someone wanted to say that any train of thought I entertain is a movement and hence could qualify, if dancelike in some other respects, as a dance). But it is hardly worth while to protect a definition against maneuvers of that sort (cf. §5.512). Suppose, though, that it were stipulated that a certain dance be performed *in the dark*? The "spectators" would hear footfalls and rustlings and breathings and imagine what doings might be producing such effects. But what would they be imagining? What the dance would look like in the light, probably. That something is not seen (like the color of a stalactite in an undiscovered cavern) does not prove that it is not essentially visible.[25] What we principally

[25] There is an instructive and amusing exchange between Paul Ziff and his critics, arising out of a paper on seeing and appreciating dance. Deborah Jowitt commented: "I have seen dances in the dark—you will please take the word 'see' on another level—that is, I have been at dances in which there was no lighting, and I only heard the sound of the dance." "I object strenuously," Ziff replied. "You cannot see a ballet in the dark—I mean pitch dark." Jowitt: "Why?" Ziff: "Because in order to see anything you need radiation. . . . What you can do is to visualize, but to visualize is not to see." Someone from the audience: "I would like to [also] say I think you can see a dance in the dark, if that's what the choreographer intended you to see." Ziff: ". . . You like to speak metaphorically. I do not. I repeat, you cannot see something in the dark; you can visualize it. I don't see any necessity to speak so fancifully. I don't care what the designer of the dance intended; he is not going to get me to see anything in the dark." Senta Driver apparently took this to mean that Ziff wanted to impose restrictions on what choreographers could do: "If I make something I intend you to perceive and experience without movement, without floor, without sound, without living bodies or without any of

want to exclude, I take it, is music and song: the visible dance is to be differentiated from its audible analogs.

Singing and speaking, except as interjection or accompaniment, are excluded from dance by the use of words; language has its own form of syntactical organization. Instrumental music is excluded because (or insofar as) musical instruments are not so much prostheses as tools; the things we do with them are not appropriately thought of as movements of the body as such. But what about wordless song, ululation, vocalization, melisma? We do exclude that; but why do we want to? And should we? Consider the "mouth music" (*puirt-a-beul*) of the Hebrides: when dancing and dance music were proscribed on religious grounds, an elaborate method of simulating instrumental dance tunes by singing nonsense syllables was developed.[26] We think of it as dance music, never as audible dance. But why not? Not so much, I think, because we are using our ears as because we are using our voices.

The animal system of communicating and expressing through audible qualities imparted to the breath—in whistles, calls, squawks, cries, screams, purrs, honks, oratorios, bellows, brays, chirps, groans, chuckles, and such—is very much a system with its own dynamics and its own sort of part to play in life, just as dancing is. Of course they overlap, because animals live lives in which everything runs into everything else; but it is because they are different, not in kind or descriptive features but in dynamic organization, that overlapping is a word for what they do. Music and dance go together, certainly, but whatever is developed from voice is something other than dance. The furthest we would want to go would be to say

---

the other thousands of things dancers have removed, that is what you are given; you cannot wish it to be different. You can wish it to be different, but you cannot make it different. It is not different. The piece does not exist when the lights are turned on if it's intended to be done in the dark. I have seen that piece you're referring to, but unfortunately I have only seen it with the lights on. I wish I had experienced it in performance." But we note that Driver does not say you can *see* it in the dark, and Jowitt picks up her last sentence by pointing out that " 'Experience' is perhaps a more accurate word if we are worried about whether 'see' is objectionable" (Fancher and Myers 1981, 86–93).

[26] Some say the emphasis on the religious embargo is a mistake: mouth music is practiced throughout Gaeldom, a part of the cultural heritage that the Calvinism of the Hebrides merely emphasized. Insofar as mouth music did start from a religious ban, it would bear some analogy with the custom of "patting Juba" among the American blacks of slavery and post-slavery times. The Stearnses, who define patting as "a special routine of slapping the hands, knees, thighs, and body in a rhythmic display," developed from the simple practice of clapping to encourage a dancer, remark that "[i]n Africa, of course, this function would be performed by drums, but in the United States, where drums had frequently been forbidden for fear of slave revolts, the emergence of patting seems to have been inevitable" (Stearns and Stearns 1968, 29). But the analogy is not close: patting is visible as much as audible and becomes incorporated into the dance in the same way that tapping and stamping so often are.

that *puirt-a-beul* follows dance as dance follows music: as we may dance to an imagined tune, to which the dance then gives a sort of ghostly reality, so we may make mouth music to accompany an imagined dance that is thereby almost, but never quite, danced in the mind.

5.5216 Immobility

We spoke of "visible motions." But is motion necessary? Continuous motion is not. Dancers come to rest, stand still. That sounds like a quibble; but fundamental problems often turn on quibbles, and this may be one.

When Eduard Hanslick said that the content of music was forms in tonal movement, it would have been stupid to object that music contains rests during which some or all voices are silent. In fact, no one was that stupid. We might say that the forms at such moments have not really stopped moving but are in a totally dynamic state. We might say that there is indeed movement from the beginning to the end of the rest, from recollection and resonance through hesitance to anticipation. However we put it, a rest is not mere absence of sound; it is part of the sound pattern: as we listen, we maintain our concern with the continuing pattern set up by the musical structure. Musical pieces may even end with a rest, partly as a typographical convention to fill up the bar in a written score, but by no means entirely. So too in dancing. A dancer motionless between movements has not stopped dancing, has not reverted to an everyday habit of body. An analysis of the movement vocabulary of classical Indian dance tells us that held poses in dances have two distinct meanings: "First, they have the same place as silence between the spoken words and the spaces between the written words in language. . . . Second, they often suggest movement by contrast or tendency" (Sathyanarayana 1969, 114–115).

British Army drill distinguishes between standing "at ease" and standing "easy." Standing at ease is a switched-on attitude. Not only is the body position prescribed, but the mental set is one of readiness-to-be-drilled: one is performing the position of standing at ease, not just happening to be in it. Standing easy is switched off: one may fidget and slouch, but what is more important is that one relaxes one's concentration. And standing "at attention" (which is a different position) involves the tensed immobility that comes from being actually engaged in a specific maneuver or state of directed passivity: one is switched on and with the engine running. A similar gradation, though less rigidly articulated, is discernible in stage dancing: one may be in a pose or rest that is keyed in to active dancing; one may be disengaged from the actual dancing that is being done but still poised to dance; one may be out of the dance and blending into the scenery, but still onstage. In none of these cases is one out of the dance altogether, as though one were a civilian who happened to be standing about among the soldiers on parade. There is a difference between standing on-stage as a dancer who is not in this dance and standing on the stage as someone who is not involved in the dancing.

The aforesaid differences in kinds and qualities of abstention and non-participation in a dance that is going on are not, of course, the same as the meaningful ways of not being a dancer that we mentioned in §4.531. But they are also not the same as performing a dance in which there is no movement at all. And there are such dances.

Senta Driver describes a dance choreographed by Douglas Dunn:

> We can talk about a work in which there was no movement. We can tell you why we thought it was a dance. There has been one very note-worthy work . . . that has been very influential, in which the dancer appeared in a completely still form for four hours a day for a month or more, and I still think of that as an act of movement, partly because the performer was not dead. That actually was a very emotionally-resonant situation. (Fancher and Myers 1981, 109)

Well, if the dancer was really *completely* still, it would be. The sustained and repeated effort not to move a muscle would call for immense skill, endur-ance, and devotion. Driver does not say she *saw* the dance. (Suppose she had seen it *all the way through*: would her spectatorship be any less a dance than Dunn's—and would it have been the same dance? Presumably not: she could have shifted and blinked, and anyway she was not *doing* a dance. But I suppose, if one were to witness such a dance, one would treat it as I treat Niagara Falls: once one has got the general picture, one simply goes back every few weeks to make sure the water is still running.) She says nothing, and needs to say nothing, about the quality of the dancing: pre-sumably one does not need to observe it; it is not there to be experienced or enjoyed; it is enough that one knows that it was really done and done as a dance, not just to beat the record for Sustained Motionlessness by an Artist in the *Guinness Book of World Records*.

Much the most famous motionless dance is one peformed by Paul Tay-lor. Popular works on contemporary dance used constantly to refer to it, saying no more than that Taylor stood motionless on stage throughout the dance, and often adding that the dance was reviewed in one periodical by a blank space. These bald statements, when I came across them, used to leave me puzzled. First, what did Taylor actually do? Did he walk on stage, stand there for a while, and then walk off? Did a curtain rise and fall on him standing? It makes a big difference. In the former case, but not in the latter, there was a definite beginning and a definite ending to his stand. And we would need to know just how he effected the entry and exit, if any: Did he do it in such a way as to encourage or to discourage the audience to see the entry and the exit as part of the dance, in which the standstill would then after all be an episode?

Second, how long did he stand there? Two minutes? Ten minutes? Two hours? It makes a difference. Was he *holding* a pose, testing the patience of his audience, or merely conveying the idea that there could be a standing dance? Giving them lots of time to look, or giving them time to get bored?

Third, how did he stand? In a dancer's position? (If so, what kind of dancer? The kind of dancer he was, or a kind of dancer he wasn't?) To attention? Strained or relaxed? Stock still, or making such casual movements (shifting and easing) as one makes when standing? Blinking or unblinking? Some particular how, or no particular noticeable how? How was he dressed? Was there scenery or a backdrop? Stage lighting? A spotlight? There could have been a spotlight directed on some other part of the stage than where he stood. Was there?

One's first reaction to the fact that the episode is referred to *ad nauseam* by people who show no sign that such questions have ever occurred to them may be to classify it with the imaginary Clayton Clevarass. The sole point of the performance would then have been that it derived its status as dance solely from its being institutionally part of a dance program. But then, the point about the power of the institutional context could only have been made by doing something that had no dance quality; and, in that case, the choice of immobility would have tended to show that movement is indeed necessary to dance.

More probably, though, the important thing these writers wish to convey to us is simply that Taylor in a regular dance performance context really did something *of which it could be truly, adequately, and appropriately said* that he "just stood there." Unlike Dunn's dance, on this showing, Taylor's is reduced to the status of peg for an exemplary anecdote and is to be relegated to that penumbra of legend that characteristically surrounds all the arts and functions entirely through the ideas evoked by the verbal content and not through the specifics of any work that may have been performed.

Taylor's actual dance, however, was a real dance, called *Duet* and performed at the New York YM–YWHA on October 20, 1957.[27] Descrip-

[27] The motionless dance, like Taylor, did not stand alone. It was not the whole of a dance performance; it took its point from being one of a series of short, aberrant pieces of the "testing the limits" sort soon to become more popular, presented by someone already established in the professional dance world. And the celebrated "blank review" was not a review of the motionless piece, as is usually said, in which case it might have been construed as implying that without movement there could be no dance. Rather, the nonreview was of the entire program, so that the meaning was quite indeterminate, beyond advertising that the reviewer (Louis Horst, in *Dance Observer*, November 1957) was for some reason unable or unwilling to apply his critical skills to the evening's offerings. There could be many reasons for such a declaration; no doubt the reviewer did not realize how many there could be. This failure to

tions of the dance seem to be hard to come by, but it seems that it was a dance for two people, a man and a woman: Taylor stood, and his partner sat, for three minutes, the duration of the dance (Jowitt 1977, 108–110; cf. Van Camp 1981, 89, n. 106). A recent PBS program on Taylor's career presented what apparently purported to be a photographic still of the celebrated motionless dance.[28] Whatever its credentials, what the photograph seemed to show was a male and a female dancer in a sort of "Spanish" pose (the chair was not clearly visible). It was, in fact, a rudimentary tableau vivant—a familiar form of presentation in its own right, with its own show tradition, but not usually presented as dance.[29] If that is what Taylor did, it is far from what the legend suggests. It is as if there has been a longstanding conspiracy to misrepresent his boutade, no doubt in the interest of a more piquant story. But let us suppose that the picture is authentic. What then?

A tableau vivant is a posed scene that suggests an action by presenting an incident from which the past and future developments of the action can

---

envisage the range of relevant alternative meanings is usual in avant-garde manifestations. The shills fix on one meaning as though it were the only possible one and somehow determined by the piece or ploy in its context, instead of being the only one the PR person or the artist happened to think of. Horst, however, may have relied on his mental habits being familiar to his readers. Being the editor of the journal, he presumably had no one to tell him he was not being as smart as he thought.

[28] I say "apparently purported" because the narration did not say in so many words that it was. In any case, of course, such stills are virtually never photographic records of an actual performance. They may or may not be intended to show what one might have seen, or be going to see, at such a performance. The PR camera always lies, but one cannot be sure what it is lying about.

The dance in the picture may well not be the one to which the rumors relate. In a review of Paul Taylor's *Private Domain*, Lincoln Kirstein recalls: "He was presenting the première of *Epic*, which, compared to today's works of swollen minimalism, was an astronomical black hole. His costume was a nicely pressed business suit. As cleanly shaved as a young broker, he looked like an advertisement for sales at Barney's Men's Store. His accompaniment was the tape of a telephone operator which every ten seconds announced: 'At the tone the time will be. . . .' He remained immobile for about ten, but what seemed like twenty minutes. In about five, the auditorium was less than half-full." In the performance as thus described, the tape's mechanically repeated reference to time would give the dancer's immobility a sharpness of meaning that it would not otherwise have. Kirstein, we note, no less than those who fasten on *Duet*, is sure that the immobility was a feature of a single dance, and he implies that Louis Horst's review referred to that dance only (Kirstein 1987, 30).

[29] At the Windmill Theatre in London during World War II, nude dancing in theaters being forbidden but posing motionless in the nude being permitted, the entertainers were employed simply to strike poses in their nakedness and not dare to sneeze. These were tableaux vivants, but the women were referred to as dancers, presumably because they would have danced had that been permitted. (The theater stayed open throughout the war and its bombardments and thus became a celebrated institution, thereby impressing tableaux vivants on the public consciousness; hence its mention here.)

be read off. The pose in the purported Taylor picture looked like that; even if it was not, the dancers were visibly *striking a pose*. A pose suggests a dance that surrounds it. The Three Graces are supposed to be engaging in a dance, although they are invariably represented in one and the same pose: a pose that can only represent a moment of poise in a dance, of arrested motion transmuted into the "aesthetic moment" of equilibrium.[30] If one were modelling a group of the Graces from life, the models would not be instructed to dance at all but to *stand* so. In much the same way, the image of Shiva's dance of death is that of a *pose*: what is significant is the positions in which all the limbs and extremities are held. We take it that the god is dancing, but we are not aware of his movement. It is not that we catch him in a moment of stopped movement, as in a flashlight photograph (or even as in Carpeaux's sculptured group on the Paris Opéra). The god is striking and holding a pose. It is a dance pose—if the god is doing anything other than having his likeness taken, dancing is certainly what he is doing. But his motion is significantly arrested: "holding" the pose is exactly the right word.

Intervals and moments of motionlessness within dances are not homogeneous. At least five kinds must be distinguished. As will be seen, what is initially distinguished may be the dance implications of paintings and drawings of dancers "in action," where the artist is obliged to decide what quality of the immobile image shall invoke the fact of dance and what relation it shall suggest. In a world where graphic arts are widely practiced—and in which for centuries people have learned to dance and have learned about dancing and dancers from books with pictures—dance practice must become infected with pictorial practice. Bournonville went so far as to speak of his ballets as "a series of pictures bound together by a dramatic thread" (Bournonville 1848, 72).

First, there is the held movement that suggests a before and after in the dance, but without projecting any specific dancing. That seems true of the Three Graces. Such an indeterminate suspension is no doubt more often a pictorial artifact than a dance fact: a real dance has a real context that is inferred by spectators, even if it is not actually projected. But there can be such a coming to a point of determinate position and indeterminate rest.

Second, also something singled out by portrayals of dance but not necessarily created by them, there are the movements of rest or climax built into the dance itself, the moment at which one phase in an articulated motion is replaced by the next or at which the moment of maximum devel-

---

[30] Iconographically, it is not only that the Graces are always shown in this pose: they only exist in that pose. They have no existence separate from each other and no other way of being than posed just so.

opment within such a phase is reached. Pictures of the Sardana always show the dancers with linked hands raised to the highest point or at the lowest, and rightly so, because at every other moment the hands are *being raised* or *being lowered*.

Third, there are dance positions reached and held, separately identified and significant points in the dance, arabesque and attitude. The Graces' posture is posed for the viewer and has its meaning through its own evocativeness and not as part of a dance in which it figures; the arabesque, though also posed for us, should take its dominant meaning from its place in the choreographic structure.

Fourth, there are the motionless gestures of stillness, poses rendered meaningful in themselves in the same way that a movement is meaningful. Indian dance dramas sometimes have the look of being structured around a series of such fraught punctuations.

Fifth, there is the hiatus, the arrested movement as in a flash photograph, inserted so often into video dances these days as the "freeze frame" and adopted into street dancing in the last few years. The technical possibility of arresting any moving picture and taking an arbitrary moment within a movement as if it were a pose or a rest, a possibility long exploited for laughs by comic actors and mimes, becomes a legitimate resource of dance seeing and of dance making.

Since we are making so much here of the interplay between real immobility and the portrayal of movement in an immobile medium, we should add mention of those pictorial representations of movement in which what is shown is a position that does not and perhaps could not form part of the movement it suggests. The stock example is the "flying gallop," the position with all legs extended in which horses used to be painted as galloping, a pure pictorial convention that spread all over the world. No such position ever occurs, as Eadweard Muybridge's photographs finally proved. I suspect that old engravings of dancers in action have the same relation to reality: they do not show what took place, or any part of it, but exemplify the ruling convention of depicting steps and figures of the appropriate kind.

5.52161 *Stillness*. Not all immobilities are rests, pauses, poses, and so forth within the context of action. In the Aristotelian account of natural movement, an animal's power of putting itself in motion is coupled with its power of coming to a stand. An animal does something when it *stops* moving, which is quite different from being checked by an obstacle or simply gliding to a halt. Nor are all stoppings the same. When a cat stalks a bird there is a poised stillness, a withholding of vital movements. Again, a human being who can move meaningfully can meaningfully keep still; and meaningfully keeping still is not quite the same as *refraining* from meaningful movement. In the latter case, what has meaning is the absence of a meaning, which is not the same as a positively meaningful stillness. (Compare the difference between, for instance, not matching a bid at an auction and trying not to move in a game of "grandmother's footsteps.") Or, of course, someone may simply not be engaging in any meaningful movement.

Taylor's *Duet*, if faithfully represented by the "tableau" picture, could have been ambiguous as between a meaningful abstention from movement and several other things: holding a pose, simulating a waxwork, specifically refraining from *dancing*. Different people, no doubt, including Taylor himself, could have taken it in different ways, or in no particular way, depending on their level of information, imagination, and gullibility. But one thing that it might have been, and on this evidence was not, was a stillness. There is a quality of stillness of repose, and dancers might impart that quality of stillness to their presence. It would surprise me if nowhere in the world was this something dancers had to learn. But there is also another stillness, a stillness of movement withheld or denied. It was this quality that Helpmann's initial stillness had in *The Haunted Ballroom*, and that is what the ballet required: as the dancers swirl around him, the Master *rejects* them and repudiates their movement. Neither of these stillnesses seems to be what *Duet* was about.

A quality of positive stillness such as I am referring to was commented on by Isadora Duncan in a performance of *The Second Mrs. Tanqueray*: "I said to myself, when I can come on the stage and stand as still as Eleanora Duse did tonight, and, at the same time, create that tremendous force of dynamic movement, then I shall be the greatest dancer in the world" (Duncan 1928, 121). Duse, though, was not a dancer but a dramatic actress. The stillness of a dancer and of an actor must have different meanings. In all the various possible ways, the one denies such action as a drama may hold, the other abjures such movement as a dancer may make or symbolize. Duncan saw the tremendous force of a denial different from the one she would have had to make.

Even this is not all. A dancer may use stillness to emphasize one of the values of dance we shall discuss later, the quality of bodily presentness. The stage presence of dancers and actors is an important part of their quality as performer and as artist; and, if dance is among other things a celebration of corporeality, bodily presence must play an important part in it. It is when the dancer is not moving that this quality is emphasized and isolated; and in this way, too, *not moving* will be an important phase in dance movement.[31]

[31] The quality of presence may be confused with star quality. When the Queen comes to

5.522 *Pattern*

A necessary condition for dance often proposed is to the effect that the motion of all dances must be patterned. The proposal is plausible. To have a recognizable identity, the dance must have some distinctive order; and if it is to be recognizably dance, the order must be determined by something other than the practical requirements of a task. But it is hard to specify a condition of this sort that is inclusive enough to be persuasive but definite enough not to be trivial.

In a later chapter, we shall say something about the principles of dance order, but these can only be principles characteristically or typically dance-like. To find a principle of order that can be used as a necessary condition of all dances is something else again. It is not at all clear what sort of principle one would want, what sort of false and dubious claimants to the title of dance one would use it to exclude. I enumerate some possibilities, without suggesting that it would be sensible to commit oneself to any of them.

Should one say, first, that all dances must be patterned in the sense that every dance must have an actual pattern, involving symmetry and repetition of distinct design elements? Dances do indeed tend to be patterned in just this way, consisting of repeated figures, steps linked in chains that are repeated until the dance ends, parts built symmetrically into wholes; learning a new dance is typically learning a pattern in just this sense. But not all dances are patterned in this way, and the sorts of dance that qualify most clearly as art seldom are. The most one could say is that the fact that many sorts of dance are thus ordered is an important part of our idea of dance as such, and that all of the sorts of organization of elements discussed by E. H. Gombrich (1979) are characteristic of one or another specific sort of dance.

If the requirement of actual pattern is too strong, should we at least say that dance movement must have a recognizable regularity? Sir John Davies in *Orchestra* invokes as the key to his panegyric on dance Aristotle's definition of time as "the measurement of movement," and the idea that dance is movement "in measure" is a commonplace. To tread a measure was to dance. There is a spectacular celebration of this theme in St Augustine's *Free Decision*. He starts by saying that all inquiry is concerned with forms— that is, with numbers—and that earth, sea, sky, and all that is therein are nothing without forms (or numbers). The thought is a venerable one:

---

town, when the party leader visits the local meeting, when Nureyev makes a rare guest appearance, they attract all eyes and ears. This may be partly because, from the habit of being the center of attention, they gradually acquire an air of expecting-to-be-looked-at that passes for charisma; but it may only be that, knowing they are famous and important and are what we came to see, we ourselves provide the motivation for not taking our eyes off them.

things are what they are because of their formal properties, and these are said to be identified in principle with numerical formulae. The same is true, Augustine continues, of artifacts.

> Then ask what moves the limbs of the artificer himself: it is number, for they also move in accordance with number. And if you take from the hands their work, and from the mind the will to fabricate, and that movement of limbs is referred to pleasure, that will have the name of dance (*saltatio*). Ask, then, what it is that gives pleasure in dance, and number will answer you: "Here I am." Look now at the beauty of the formed body: numbers are fixed in space. Look at the beauty of mobility in the body: numbers are deployed in time. Move inward to the art from which these issue, and look for time and space in that: it will be never, it will be nowhere; but number is alive in them. (Augustine *De Libero Arbitrio* II xvi 42)

The requirement of measure and countability, with or without Augustine's rhetoric, is that there must be something in the movement that is actually such as to lend itself to being counted or measured. Can this be a necessary condition, or is this merely another aspect of typical dancelikeness? It is probably a condition of dancing to music or of dancing with others.[32] How else could one keep together? But is it necessary to all dance? Suppose we were to see someone who was, to all appearance, improvising a solo dance without music, with flowing and graceful movements—would we hesitate to say that such a person was dancing until we were sure there was something inherent to what was going on that we could count or measure? I am, to say the least, not sure that we would, and I do not know what reason we would have for doing so.

A third possible variant of the demand for pattern is that the dancer have in mind a definite (perhaps in principle repeatable) pattern, that some version of patternedness be an internal characteristic of the dance as motion performed. This comes down to saying that dancers must know not only that they are dancing but also what dance they are dancing. Their action in dancing must be rule-guided in a way characteristic of dance. A fourth, weaker version of the same demand, would be that the dancer be guided

---

[32] Yvonne Rainer (1966) operates with a view of dance that systematically explores the ways in which movement can be measurable, whether or not the units are those in which movement is habitually seen. It must be interesting for the dancers, but I do not see how an audience is supposed to know what the system is, unless it is explained and demonstrated beforehand. Is it a guessing game? Or do the dancers contrive to make the measure perspicuous—and, if so, how? But, in any case, descriptions of Rainer's work (e.g., Siegel 1977, 307–308) suggest that it is not this aspect of her work that has most interested her colleagues, critics, and audiences.

by a formal sense, by considerations of the form of what is danced. This requirement could be fulfilled whenever a trained dancer danced as a dancer, but spontaneously, without necessarily thinking about the formal qualities of what was danced. A few pages back, when we were considering the related requirement that a dance be analyzable into discrete movements, we used, as analogy for the way a dancer might dance in such a way without actually performing or thinking of any analysis, the ability of native speakers of a language to speak in a grammatical way whenever they spontaneously exercise their linguistic competence, without thinking either about rules or even about grammaticality. But the analogy is not so close as we made it seem. In the linguistic case, there really is a grammar to which we spontaneously conform (or a set of grammars could be constructed, with any of which our usage is consistent); but we know of no such requirement in the case of dance. The insistence, which we have been considering here, that dance must be formally characterized by a definite inherent dancedness, whether or not a dance was being danced, does not require that it have any further property analogous to grammaticality.

A fifth version of the demand for pattern would be like the fourth, but with the imputation of conscious intent ruled out. To be a dance, we would say, a set of movements must have formal properties capable of engaging a positive interest, but we would not specify what they would have to be. This at least saves us from saying (as the fourth option would) that the only way to find out if it's a dance is to ask the dancer. But not everyone wants to be saved from that.[33] However, if we do make the perceptible possession of a quality of positive patternedness a requirement of dance, we are up against a host of difficulties familiar in aesthetics. Does not the perception of such a vaguely defined and elusive property depend on the formation of an appropriate taste or connoisseurship? And, if patternedness has a sort of interest necessary to dance, do not avant-garde dances that manage to avoid such patternedness have just the same sort of interest?

Rather than wrestle with the difficulties and problems just raised (and a philosopher would certainly advise against making a necessary condition out of something for which one did not have rather solid criteria), one might try a sixth tack and say that a dance must have formal interest in the sense that its formal properties, its pattern if there is one and the mode of

---

[33] To say that dancers are authorities on whether or not they are dancing is not to commit the "intentional fallacy" in criticism. That fallacy consists of substituting what the dancer meant to mean by the dance for what the dance meant; it is a fallacy, if it is, because the dancer may have failed to impart the intended meaning to the materials. That is very different from saying that a dancer is entitled to claim that what is performed has the status of a dance and is open to criticism as such. The point is made by Monroe Beardsley, one of the original discoverers of the intentional fallacy (1977; cf. Sparshott 1982, 573 n. 46).

its unpatternedness if there is none, are something that it is always relevant to attend to when one is attending to a dance. But that is no longer to make pattern a necessary condition that dances must possess in order to be dances. To be a dance is now to be something that, because of the context of its presentation or for whatever other reason, is properly to be received in a certain way. That is another matter entirely.

5.523 *Endotelicity*

Making it a necessary condition of dance that it be in some sense patterned does not work out too well when we try to specify in what sense. We saw that the best bet might be to say that it is a necessary condition of dance that its motions be determined by their being formally the right ones for the dance in question. It is not a matter of what the motions should be, but a matter of why they are as they are. The word "endotelicity" was coined for requirements of this sort: an endotelic activity is one performed for the value actually found in it. It is characteristic of art that it is endotelic: we impose on works of art the serious requirement that they should be made as it is right for them to be and appreciated for their precise rightness without regard to considerations of enjoyment or of utility. Dance, we may say, is endotelic whether it is art or not. But its endotelicity is not general, like that of art: it is a specifically dance endotelicity, to be evaluated by dance criteria. The requirement is that what is done be right as dance or right for this particular dance or dance style.

The requirement of endotelicity being purely formal, no sort of movement can be ruled out. A laborious action, an industrial task can be done as dance. We cannot even specify that the principle of organization of the task must be made dancelike: the dance task could be simply to do the work, and the formal qualities to be attended to as constituting the dance would then be whatever qualities the movements take on when one takes the job seriously. There is a well-known thesis that all labor takes on rhythmical properties, so that the difference between work movement and dance movement is a matter of degree. But that is a thesis about the typical organization of kinds of movements and is irrelevant to the sort of categorial question that engages us here; we return to it later (§7.1).

If a job of work can qualify as dance, provided that its constituent movements are considered endotelically from a formal standpoint, how can we say what is dance and what is not dance? Clearly, its status must be determined by the context in which it is done. But what determines that context? Whatever determines the action's reason for being. But how is that determined? Only God can really decide that. Seriously, though, who is to decide that a dance is a dance? Well, whoever is responsible; we know

253

about responsibility. Sometimes an impresario, often a choreographer or a performer. In a sense, the public could decide; or one could decide for oneself.

A position like the one just enunciated has been worked out by George Dickie (1974) and its difficulties thoroughly canvassed. We return to it later (§6.32). The corresponding definition of dance would go something like this: a set of human movements is a dance if and only if it is singled out as a candidate for (appropriate) formal appreciation by someone representing the dance world. (The point of the last words about the dance world is that this sort of hospitability in classification makes sense only in the context of a prior knowledge of what dance is all about—knowing what we all know, in the sort of sense described at the beginning of this chapter.) Dickie's position gives rise to worries about the responsible exercise of responsibility: can the status of candidacy be conferred arbitrarily, by decree? But that need not worry us here, since we are putting it forward not as a definition of dance but only as a necessary condition: no set of human movements is a dance unless thus singled out, we shall say, but there may be other conditions as well.

The supposed act (or mental act) of singling something out on behalf of the dance world takes on a special significance in the realm of the avant-garde. Dance people know what dance is—they know it in their bones, it is the very shape of their lives. An avant-garde dance that seems undance-like to some (even to most) others is, if authentic, within the compass of this developed and developing dance consciousness of theirs. They have not only a responsibility, but an authority and a right: the same right that, we recall Cavell saying, native and habitual speakers of a language have as to the meaning of their own utterances.

5.5231 *Display*

If dance is to be attended to for its inherent formal properties, should we not say that its movements are to be *displayed*? Adam Smith thought so. The fact that all an opera singer's gestures keep time to the music, he points out, does not suffice to make them dance steps. What is distinctive of dance is that its movements display grace, or agility, or both. This is in contrast with everyday life, where it is good for a movement to be graceful or agile but offensive for it to be deliberately or ostentatiously so. In dance, "The display of one, or other, or both of these qualities, is in reality the proper purpose of the action" (Smith 1795, 250).

Smith is thinking of theater dance, of dance as one of the "imitative arts." But, as we said in §5.5215, it is no part of the concept of dance that it be done for an audience. A dancer may dance alone, for any reason or for no reason, and be dancing no less than when on stage. Ritual dances are not disqualified from being dances because no one (not even God) is watching. As we remarked of the child showing off, what is required is not that the movement be watched or made for watching but that it be made to be worth watching, that it be made such as to pass muster with any qualified watchers.

5.5232 *Getting It Right*

What concerns the dancer of a dance as such is not necessarily that the dance should look right. It is that it should *be* right. The standard is no doubt a cognitive one, and no doubt has to do with visible movement; but the appropriate test may be that it feels right to the dancer or that the dancer knows it is going right. In a choreographed dance, the test may be that the choreographer (or whoever is running things) can see not that it looks right but that it is being *done* right. In any case, dances have to be got right, and they have to be got right by dance standards. More specifically, they have to be got right by the standards for the particular dance that is being danced. The standards are of three sorts. First, the right things have to be done, the proper steps performed. Second, they have to be done in the correct way, without mistakes. Third, they may be judged by how well they are done, in accordance with such values as the "grace" and "agility" that Smith stipulated or other more specific values of all sorts: ballon, aplomb, coolness, and so on.

The standards by which a dance has to be done properly, correctly, and well do not themselves require further justification. That is what we meant by calling dance and dances "endotelic." To perform or participate in a dance involves accepting these standards as absolute and autonomous within the context of the dance itself. The alternative is to substitute a different (and perhaps a better) dance for the dance one had been doing; and then the commitment would be to getting *that* dance right.

Is it a necessary condition of dance that it be subject to specific standards that are standards for dance in general or for the specific dance or form of dance in question? Perhaps. But then, if one wishes to include grebes and motes and other marginal dancers, one has to recognize that the standards are to be invoked by some being other than the dancer. Who is going to say "Those motes are swirling all wrong"? Who is going to listen?

5.524 *Institutions*

If dances are going to be subject to dance standards in any meaningful way, there must be some way of recognizing the appropriate canons of rightness. The practice of dancing must be institutionalized: there must be a socially recognized and structured practice in which the dancers know themselves to be participants and hence know that the appropriate standards really do apply to them. Should we then say that the requirement of the applicability of standards should be either supplemented or replaced by a requirement that every dance should be a recognized instance of such an institutionalized practice? Surely not. But we could hold that it is only by some direct reference to such a practice that anything can be properly considered dance.

What is most clearly a dance, a dancer, etc. is what falls most directly within the scope of dance institutions. What is established as dance is only what is (admitted to be) properly scanned for dance meanings and values, and appropriately challenges such scanning. What can be taken seriously as dance is what is such as to fit effectively into the tissue of meanings that the institutions of dance articulate. Whatever is acknowledged as dance but does not fit appropriately into an institutionalized practice of dance is dance by analogy and extension and courtesy: it is like dance, imitates dance, is derived from dance, as defined by the socially organized institutions of dancing. The young woman who in her spontaneous joy invented the polka, simply by dancing it for the first time, was clearly creating a new dance, one that could be danced in the way other dances were: the practice of dancing already had a place for it and for the standards by which its dancing would be assessed.

David Best suggests that what makes a movement a dance movement is neither its quality as movement nor the intention of the mover, but simply that it is performed within the meaningful context of dance; he concedes, however, that it could be a "movement *normally* made in a dance context" (Best 1978, 80; my emphasis). A mudra, an arabesque, is a dance movement normally made in a dance context, in the sense that it is seldom made otherwise than as part of a dance, or in the course of dancing, or preparing to dance, or illustrating a dance, and so forth. In a different sense, any movement that is actually performed as part of a dance or in the course of dancing is a dance movement, however uncharacteristic it may be of dancing in general or of any particular sort of dance.[34] A dance can be made out of any sort of movement—but not by anyone. Who has the authority to declare that something is a dance or that a context is a dance context depends on the prevailing institutions of art and dance. On the other hand, we will not necessarily refuse to say that a movement is a dance movement if (not the movement itself but) its character or quality is what we should

---

[34] We have to say "performed," not "made," in such a context to cut out slips and tumbles and intrusions—unless we have stipulated that the dance itself, as constituting the context, is to include all such accidents and incidents. Sometimes that would indeed be the right thing to say; the concept of a dance context does not commit us to anything very definite.

expect to find in such a context, whether it is or has ever been in such a context or not. (We can say, if it amuses us to do so, that it constitutes its own context.) The significant point is that the designation of dance is in every case mediated in one way or another through reference to the institution and is not directly a function of quality or intent.

Can the claim that such institutional mediation is a necessary condition of dance be maintained? Perhaps. We will want to say that people danced before any such institutions existed to perform the mediating function. But no doubt only people whose thought has been molded by the presence of such institutions will call such practices and phenomena "dance."

That leaves us with two questions. First, what counts as mediation? We can make the link as tight or as slack as we please; but, before we start stipulating necessary conditions, we will have to make up our minds about the degree of strictness we wish to impose—and how we shall justify it. Second, what counts as an "institution"? We got on quite well with the concept of a practice. What do we add by stipulating that it be "institutionalized"? Philosophers grumble at each other about the vagueness of this word. If an institution has to be something like an academy, with a charter and formal accrediting procedures, the requirement is absurdly too stringent. But what weaker requirement would do the job? One cannot say in general terms, because social organs and instruments of control vary with the whole way a society operates. What is meant is something like this: the practice of dance, as we understand it, depends on there being an acknowledged distinction within the relevant society between the public and the private, and dance has a publicly recognized status in the former domain. If that is indeed what is meant, the claim is a strong one but not absurdly so. The condition has been so long, so amply, and so variously fulfilled in our society that it is hard to say how we should think in its absence.

5.525 *Dancing a Dance*

The crested grebe dances, if it dances at all, only when it dances the mating dance of its species. One could contend that it is a necessary condition of dance that there be *a dance* that is danced; otherwise, one is merely rehearsing, practicing, gamboling, or something. Dances typically have names: the Black Bottom, Swan Lake, the Helston Furry Dance. One dances a dance of a recognized kind or in relation to a recognized kind. When Hippocleides danced away his wife, Herodotus tells us (6. 129), he danced Spartan and Athenian figures (*ourchesato . . . schematia*) before standing on his head on the table and gesturing with his legs. When he was waving his legs, he was deemed to be still dancing—but only, I suspect, because he had begun by dancing those "figures" and establishing the dance context. Again, the woman who danced the first polka was clearly dancing because there was clearly a dance she was dancing, and people saw that, what she was dancing, they could dance too. It had no name, but they gave it one. And again, we said before that a child who claimed to be dancing would more likely be said by others to be doing so if there was a regular or regularly organized sequence that they could recognize as "Little Iodine's dance."

Actually, the expression "a dance" is ambiguous. The Helston Furry Dance is individuated as "a dance" by being a recurrent seasonal event articulated as a dance ceremony. *Swan Lake* is individuated in terms of its internal structure as a dance work repeatable at any time within a tradition of transmitted practice. "The tango" is individuated as a method of freely putting together certain dance components according to certain conventions. These principles of individuation are too diverse to constitute a single "necessary condition": one would have to specify further. But how?

If it sounds too strong to insist that whatever is danced must always be *a dance*, if it is to count as dancing at all, we may reflect that, from the point of view of logic, that is exactly the same as saying that, if people are dancing, whatever they do counts as *a dance*. And then we can dispose of the ambiguity disclosed at the end of the previous paragraph by reflecting that it is what the people in question are doing when they dance that determines the precise sense in which what they dance is a dance. Disco dancing, for instance, is a style in which dancers dance in a certain sort of environment to a certain sort of music, exploiting a partial repertory of movements (Villari and Villari 1978). But "disco" is not the name of a dance. The particular dance that a pair of disco dancers dance is constituted a dance by their beginning and ending it together within the span of a continuity of disco music. But the same considerations that led us to consider an institutional relation as a necessary condition of dance may tempt us to say that there must always be a dance one is dancing in the double sense that there must be a recognized or recognizable style in which one is dancing, as well as a temporal span that bounds the dance.[35] One may not be able to recognize what the dance is, in the sense either of being able to put a name to it or of being able to see how one would dance it (the rules may not be evident); but one must be able to see (an intelligent observer must be able to learn to see) that something danceable is being danced,

---

[35] The halves of the condition can be separated. I can switch styles within a continuous bout of dancing; and I can start a dance here today and take it up in Etobicoke next Tuesday from where I left off. Same dance, or different dance? It's a moot point, surely, so the theorist leaves it moot.

that something is done that could be learned and then done more or less correctly, expertly, and well.

The condition that there be a dance that is danced seems now to have reduced to a crude version of a general principle for individuating actions (which we hardly need to include) and a restatement of one of our other proposed conditions, that dancing of any sort must be something that can be done right or wrong. But the fact that the condition now seems redundant, because it can be inferred from other conditions, does not prove that we should drop it. It might, once inferred, have practical significance. Somewhat similarly, in the field of logic, the fact that the logical relations of conjunction, alternation, affirmation, negation, and implication can all be derived from the relation of mutual incompatibility does not render them otiose or reduce them to the character of mere abbreviations. They retain their own uses in the strategies of argument. Similarly, the question "What is that dance you are dancing?" retains an argumentative point of its own.

What about a "free" dancer like Isadora Duncan? Setting aside her debt to callisthenics, to her brother's interpretation of the iconography of Greek dance, to the complex and entrenched traditions of "free" and "classical" dancing, did there have to be dances that she danced? And were they dances merely because she was a dancer and dancing them in the exercise of her métier? No, she developed a distinctive style of dancing with a repertory of preferred movements and worked up specific dances that were repeatable and structured, the structure typically having as armature a particular piece of music. Given the style, a stretch of her dancing from start to stop would have been a dance; such a stretch with beginning and ending would have been more of a dance; one structured and worked up would have been more of a dance still. And what of Clayton Clevarass and his "Absent Fandango"? Whether it was a dance or not, he was not dancing; that there be a dance is at most a necessary condition, not a sufficient condition.

But what about King David dancing before the ark? Was there a dance he danced? We do not know what he did, how he moved; he was worse reported than Paul Taylor. But, if we believe that he danced, are we thereby committed to the belief that there was some dance he was dancing? This seems to be a real test case. He danced before the Lord with all his might, girded with a linen ephod, and Michal despised him for it. "Leaping and dancing" is the way she saw it, making a spectacle of himself. Can we suppose that he was simply jumping about at random while the trumpets played? And if he was, would it follow that he was not dancing at all? I don't think so. It was a special case, unlikely to be repeated. Can we not conceive that his surprised subjects, like the anthropologist in the unknown culture (§5.4), saw their king just *breaking into dance?* Dancing what? Nothing in particular. Just dancing, that's all.[36]

5.526 *The Sacred*

An anthropologist whose learning and acumen command the profoundest respect once told me that it is not true that, as is so often said, music is necessary to dance; but it is true that dance is everywhere sacred.[37] He was wrong, was he not? Nothing sacred about disco or about the work of Busby Berkeley. Perhaps, like some anthropologists, he felt it unprofessional to acknowledge the existence of any community with more than a thousand members? But, as we saw in our chapter on meanings (Chapter 4), being a dancer is indeed a special and segregated status. Just because it is something we do with the bodies we do everything with, the very existence of dance requires that it be assigned a status that sets it apart. Such demarcation is the mark of the sacred as against the secular or the profane. Dance must occupy a special place, whether we call the place sacred or not. We may profane or desecrate it occasionally, or subjectively ignore its status (as tourists ignorantly trespass on sanctuaries); but we could not make a regular practice of doing so, or dance would cease to exist. It is up to us to look and see, in a society that dances but does not acknowledge the category of the sacred, what the operative analogue of sacredness is. There is sure to be one. Some such conviction as this may lie behind Maurice Béjart's insistence that dance must have a ritual quality (§6.41 below); but unearned sacredness and unoccasioned ritual seem fraudulent, as we remark elsewhere (§7.2 and note 18 to Chapter 6). Unless one is authentically engaged in some real worship, it may be better to let one's dance establish its own special status by the power it generates.

Can we say that sacredness, or a reasonable facsimile thereof, is a necessary condition of dance? No, because any dance can be "profaned" and still be a dance. Clayton Clevarass will find a way of showing us how. But it may well be that the practice of dancing depends on there being some nonordinary domain to which it essentially pertains.

---

[36] Chapter 2, note 5, acquiescently quoted Alfred Sendrey (1974, 222) as saying that David's dance was "akin to that of the sacrificial dance of the Egyptian Pharaoh." But actually he is just *saying* that. As to the words used for what David was doing, "*karar*, 'to whirl about', 'to rotate', occurs in the Bible only once in the sense of dancing (2 Sam. 6:14). As a synonym of *karar*, the same Biblical passage uses the word *pazzaz*, in its strict sense 'leaping', and, applied to dancing, 'to dance hopping' (2 Sam. 6:16)" (Sendrey 1974, 223).

[37] Should we have included (not music, but) "musicality" as a candidate for a possible necessary condition of dance? No, we should not. The criteria of musicality are open to question wherever the criteria of dance are. Music and dance have a common destiny, but not one that can usefully be invoked in the present connection.

5.527 *Specialness*

An inner analog of the specialness that is typified by the sacred, the non-ordinary domain of life to which dance pertains, is that subjective sense of entering into a special mode of being to which I attached such importance in my own experience (§5.3). Could one make that, or rather whatever it is that corresponds to it in the experience of dance generally, a necessary condition of dance, on the ground that whatever does not achieve this transformation is not yet dance? No, one could not. The condition is neither necessary nor sufficient. It is not sufficient, because every activity that engrosses one completely, in bodily activity or in working with materials or in social exchange, transforms one subjectively into the self-engaged-in-this-now.[38] What is distinctive of dance in this regard is rather that the activity engaged in is typically endotelic, exists for the sake of its experienced properties, and consequently is such that the experience of being transformed within it should be sharpened and emphasized as it is nowhere else. All the typical features of dance are such as to make it so. The fact that this whole range of experience is not widely reported on, and hence the significance of its refinement and accentuation in dance has not been emphasized, is not necessarily an important consideration: introspection is unfashionable among intellectuals, the vocabulary available for describing subjective states is impoverished, and people in general are remarkably insensitive to the experienced quality of life as they live it.

Even if we could make the appropriate sense of "self-transformation" sharp enough for us to use it as a sufficient condition for something in dance, it could hardly be a condition of dance itself. What I reported on was that such transformations took place only when I was dancing successfully, in the specific sense that I could be unselfconsciously engrossed in it; and the point at which this stage is reached is not the same as the point at which one has begun actually to dance the dance as opposed to learning it and *trying* to dance it. But, in any case, we certainly could not make anything of that sort a *necessary* condition of any sort of dance. When we rec-

---

[38] The thesis advanced and elaborated here, that one becomes functionally and subjectively a different kind of being in every activity and fellowship in which one is fully engaged, is an aspect of a way of thinking about intelligent behavior that has been made popular in some persuasive writings by Gregory Bateson (1972). Intelligence, he argues, should be thought of not as a property of thinking individuals but as a function of the totality of a conscious being in its environment. In evaluating my remarks about self-transformation, one has to bear in mind that all arguments about identity are tricky. Statements that "this is not the same as that" can only be understood relatively to some stipulated answer to the questions: Same what? Same in what respects? For present purposes, to speak of self-transformation is only to identify certain phenomena and bring out an aspect of their subjective significance: it should imply no metaphysical claims.

ognize people as dancing, we know nothing of their state of mind; nor do people teaching dances require any such self-consciousness before satisfying themselves that the dance in question has been learned.

5.528 *Necessary Conditions: Summary*

The conditions of dance we have now canvassed as perhaps severally necessary (and perhaps jointly sufficient; but perhaps not) amount to this: dancing is patterned conscious movement of one or more agents, not controlled by considerations of mechanical instrumentality but governed by its own standards of rightness and wrongness, in relation to an institutional context that is in the first instance that of dancing, and such that its character as a specific kind of dancing is determinable. But these have turned out to be not specific requirements but classes of kinds of requirements. Nor has the necessity been shown in any one case. Perhaps, borrowing a word from Nelson Goodman (1968), we should call them "symptoms" of dance. If we call something dance, it is likely to be because it is marked by several symptoms or strongly marked by some. But beyond that we cannot go.

5.53 THE INDUCTIVE METHOD

Someone who had reviewed everything recognized as dance throughout the world might try to summarize the results in a defining formula. But how could one be sure that the formula reflected no bias in the collection, interpretation, and evaluation of data, or that the choice of its terms was neither arbitrary nor misleading? As we said earlier, a world of various experience cannot be contained within a phrase. Even if the phrasemaker felt that the phrase was somehow true to the residue deposited on the walls of the mind, this quality would surely be some emblematic subjective rightness rather than any public viability. In the passage that ends his *Posterior Analytics* (much longer and much more famous than the parallel passage at the end of Book I, mentioned above), Aristotle gives an account of how repeated experience leads to the formation of concepts in human and animal minds. Learning the use of a word in a language, with all its syntactic and semantic ramifications, would be a form of that process. But no such process equips us with definitions: defining is an intellectual task, requiring the analysis of causal relations within a determinate discipline. Such disciplines are the product of systematic inquiry. It follows that definitions are relative to bodies of inquiry and are misrepresented when proposed as simple reports on experience.

In her anthropological survey of meaningfulnesses in world dance, Judith Hanna offers what seems to be a definition based on induction. Dance is

> human behavior composed, from the dancer's perspective, of (1) purposeful, (2) intentionally rhythmical, and (3) culturally patterned sequences of (4a) nonverbal body movements (4b) other than ordinary motor activities, (4c) the motion having inherent and aesthetic value. (Aesthetic refers to notions of appropriateness and competency held by the dancer's reference groups which act as a frame of reference for self-evaluation and attitude formation to guide the dancer's actions). (Hanna 1979, 19)

There is no point in discussing this at length; the discussion of proposed necessary conditions, which we have just completed, kept it constantly in mind, and we have already expressed doubts and reservations at many points. But there are six general points I would make, to illustrate the problems that beset such enterprises.

First, the whole is tendentious. The initial selection of the human context defines the anthropological perspective chosen; there is nothing to show it is the right one. Do all the world's dancers think they share their dancing with all humans and only with humans?

Second, almost every clause is deeply ambiguous. For instance, does "intentionally rhythmical" require that all dancers bring the concept of rhythm as such to bear on their dancing? Or does it require, less stringently, that they impart to their dancing a distinctive property of rhythmicality, whether they think of it as rhythm or not? Or does it only require that they attend to the temporal articulation of their dance? Again, does "other than ordinary" mean that there must be special, distinctively dance movements, or that the movements be physically of kinds seldom made when not dancing, or only that they be made otherwise than in the context of workaday activities? We are not told and I cannot guess.

Third, the implications are unclear even where the immediate meaning is not. Consider the mention of "reference groups" and of being "culturally patterned." Does that mean that one is not dancing unless one is dancing a dance that is properly a part of one's culture as a whole and normatively controlled by it? Or is it within the terms of the definition that one can dance for oneself alone and thus be one's own reference group? Or is this possible only in a culture that positively demands that artists work to please themselves alone, so that each one is appointed a first-order reference group by this second-order reference group? In that case, what is culturally patterned will include what one is required by the culture to invent one's own patterns for—unless it is to be part of the definition that the patterns of a dance will inevitably, despite their subjective autonomy, turn out to be typical of the patterns current and approved in one's culture at large. (That is very likely true; but is it true *by definition*)?

The fourth point is more specific. Contrast Hanna's definition with one offered by T. Davidson in the 1901 edition of Chambers's *Twentieth-Century Dictionary*. He defines the verb "dance" as "to move with measured steps to music"—the definition is somewhat Augustinian, and it makes a military march a paradigm case of dance, but never mind that now. My immediate point is that the definition admits of no answer to the question "What are you dancing?" Hanna's dancers, by contrast, necessarily know what they are dancing: they know the cultural pattern and associated standards connected with the other-than-ordinary rhythms and sets of movements they are setting themselves to perform.

My fifth point is a suggestion. Might Hanna's definition as a whole not be taken less as an account of what experience has shown dance to be than as a succinct account of how her own material is organized, listing the questions she has asked herself and the topics she has covered rather than any positive content that has emerged? That would certainly explain the multiple ambiguities.

Sixth and last, Hanna shows no sign of being aware of the difficulties of principle involved in seeking, developing, and offering definitions. For Hanna, as for so many products of advanced education, philosophy has toiled in vain. However, few of her readers will notice anything wrong; and such insouciance is in fact a great help when one wants to say something striking, helpful, and concise—as Hanna does.

The implication of Hanna's definition, and of the research that supports it, is that dance is a practice of a recognizable character in which human beings at all times and in all places engage and have engaged. We may take her word for it. But the question remains: Why do they?

An answer that has been popular for over two thousand years is content to explain all artistic phenomena as aspects of a general tendency in humans as intelligently tool-using and symbol-using animals to explore the possibilities of their bodies and environments for manipulation, development, and elaboration. We explore the capacities of our bodies in expressiveness, in mimetic force, in prowess of strength, speed, and suppleness, and in formal elaboration. To all the outcomes of this exploratory exploitation we give the name of dance, insofar as the quality of the movement itself is directly at issue (for mere contests of who can jump higher, hit harder, and run faster are nowhere dances), until special subsets of such skills acquire some institutional nondance identity of their own.

Dance may thus coincide with a set of variously specifiable movements explicable as connatural to an overbrained body, or with such of them as are singled out for special cultivation as genres within a culture. But that does not mean that restless curiosity is the sole motive, or even a common motive, of practitioners of dance once established. Other compelling and widespread varieties of human motivation may dominate the dances of a given place and time; it could be that in dance everywhere the basic proclivity to generate dance behavior is captured in the interests of some more urgent and specific set of motives, such as self-expression, or the working out of the Oedipus complex, or the inducing of "highs" through superoxidation, or the symbolizing of social taboos—these motives themselves, of course, being manifested in specific cultural forms, in the ways that the substance of Hanna's book demonstrates. Or we may suspect that the experimental development of dance movement furnishes the means of dance but that, wherever dances are danced, those means are at the service of some other end. And we can add that these supervenient ends of dance will themselves be overlaid by the private concerns of individual users of dance in the pursuit of their own life strategies. We will therefore always be suspicious of accounts of dance that purport to isolate the essential significance of dancing in phenomenological or psychological or any other preemptive set of terms, however compelling they may seem and however strikingly they may capture some indubitable and inevitable significance. What a phenomenology or a psychology cannot do is establish its preeminence over possible rivals.

5.6 *Conclusion*

Does this whole chapter enable us to say anything of a conclusive and summary sort about what is and is not dance? Perhaps; though parts of the following have not been solidly prepared, and it ignores and overrides many qualms and objections previously insisted on.

The human intelligence is ratlike in its restless quest for elaboration, the urge to test limitations and boundaries, in the realm of possible thought and action as well as in the physical world (as individuals and communities we may often be lazy; as a species we are explorative under stress and in opportunity). More than ratlike is the logical version of this adventurousness: the drive on to conclusions and back to principles. It is by these drives that all arts and skills develop. The development of dance is to be understood in this light and in these terms.

We find ourselves involved, on a regular or continuing basis, in all sorts of activities that call for our activity as embodied beings, moving and manipulating, as opposed to activities that engage us thinkingly in speech and feelingly in song.[39]

---

[39] Although there is much to be said for speaking of *people* as doing things physically, thinkingly, and feelingly, which is the language used in the text, we could have used nouns: we

Any regularly structured activity tends to have four noticeable characteristics. First, it involves movements patterned (or characteristically disordered and pattern-resistant) in space. Second, the movements are patterned or pattern-resistant in time, are rhythmical or arhythmical. Third, the quality of one's engagement of oneself in the task, as a way of being in the world, is special or humdrum: one becomes axwoman or launderer, and, if one is cooperating with others, one's being becomes that of the specific sort of fellow being one is.[40] And, fourth, the task becomes an engagement of one's prowess (or one's unhandiness), a special manifestation of the glory or ignominy of the body's instrumentality.

The pattern, the rhythm, the special quality of being, and the prowess in any task or engagement in the physical world and the human world can be singled out for attention, dwelt on, and relished; can be emphasized; can be developed and elaborated; can be canceled out and repudiated. These are the ways of making any such action or engagement dancelike.

Once one has experienced what it is to enhance actions by making them dancelike (which need be no more than thinking of them dancelikely), one can devise actions and engagements specially for the purpose of such enhancement. One may then seek out new ways of achieving what may be acted and experienced as analogous enhancements. When actions are done solely for the sake of such enhancement, or when they are special acts designed to be enhanced in such ways, what we have is no longer dancelikeness but dance. But it is to be noted that when we say "before" and "after" here we are referring to logical priority: one must act, action must be capable of enhancement, the enhanced must be capable of isolation, the process itself must be susceptible of development, just because humans are as we said they are at the beginning of this section. It does not follow that there must be priority in time. The reason people used to be fascinated by apes and peacocks was because their cavortings seemed to testify that pure dance behavior could be included in the basic repertory of human activity.

---

dance with our bodies, think with our minds, and sing with heart and soul. But not only has it been thought philosophically bad to reify the mind like that; our words here suggest that we do not have agreement on a third noun: heart and soul, not to mention guts and spirit, have not settled the bounds of their domains in metaphorical anthropology. And now, of course, it occurs to us that mind *and body* are metaphorical in much the same way.

[40] Sartre has confused this phenomenon by seeming to say that, first, such temporary self-transformations, which arise from becoming absorbed in a specific action or cooperation, should always be thought of as role playing, and, second, that such role playing is always a manifestation of bad faith or self-deception, on the ground that one must be kidding oneself that the role relieves one of responsibility for one's choices. Sartre gives us no reason for thinking that either of these assertions is true. The effect of his rhetoric is to make living seem an impossible task before which the only authentic attitude is guilt, despair, anguish, and lots and lots of courage.

In that case, we could say that the basis of the elaboration and ordering and other enhancement was the range of physical movements and resistances specific to human bodies.

Since much actual dance is mimetic, one should add here that a resource for the development of specific dance movements is the movements of other animate and inanimate beings we see or sense around us, movements alien to our lives but possible for us, or suggesting possibilities.

We must not suppose that because pattern, rhythm, self-transformation, and prowess are distinguishable aspects of action they function separately, as if they were separable materials or tools. It would be a long task to explore the ways in which they function as unified or as separate, and this book will not attempt it.

If this is what dance and dancelike behavior are, it will be possible for a human group to develop specific dance practices, recognized and cultivated ways of dancing, and to develop dance arts, systems of teachable dance skills, and all that goes therewith. In fact, as we know, dance characteristically exists in any culture as specific arts superimposed on specific practices, themselves superimposed on the still vital possibilities of dancing in general (not that one can dance in general, of course; but one has a general capacity to do dancelike things and even things that amount to dances, as sketched in this section, without reference to cultural practice).[41]

Once dance as thus envisaged is established, the idea of what dance is can be enriched and refined and extended in various ways. The concept of dance itself and related concepts may be used consciously to formulate *dance methods* and *dance objectives* in relation to recognized practice or to the pure idea of dance itself, however that may be conceived. The institutions that give a determinate social identity to the arts and practices of dance may be used to extend or restrict what counts as dance by bestowing or withholding sanction. And things will be further complicated in our civilization, and any others that may be similarly blessed, by the idea of art: that certain modes of human activity, among which some dance may be counted, have a very special sort of social and spiritual significance of sorts that books about art go on about. If dance not only can be art but has a distinct tendency to be art, that may make a big difference to how we think about dance in general; that tendency might well be the sort of thing one could not possibly leave out when one was considering what was and what was not dance.

---

[41] The point is that one could not be a human being without these capacities, which every human life calls into play. One's culture may of course prevent one from affording them certain kinds of recognition and hence cultivation. Anthropologists, in reaction against what they saw as a romantic ideal of universal human freedom, used to combat it with a no less romantic notion of cultural omnipotence; and maybe they still do.

That's about it, except for one thing. Mimesis actually plays a much bigger role in dance than the foregoing suggests. We made a place for it, but only as a resource. We accepted the modern discovery, or succumbed to the modern pretense, that the arts that have been important in human life through mimesis are essentially not mimetic at all, that mimesis is a perversion. So, in dance, one says that dance is really and truly a way of putting oneself into high-quality motion. But, even if that is a good sort of thing to say about art and about whatever the fine arts have turned into, its merits are irrelevant here, since we have not confined this part of our discussion to a fine-arts framework.

Something is wrong with what we have said, then, if it entails that mimetic dance should be less prominent than it actually is. But the prominence of mimesis can be explained in at least three ways. One way we have mentioned already: observed motions give us lots of examples for free development. A second is by way of theurgy and magic. As uttering the name of a god compels its presence, as a god's likeness captures its sacredness, so making a god's or an animal's proper motions bring it within one's power. This is especially true in dancelike bodily motion insofar as that transports one into a special mode of being: in performing an action organized in a dance way, one's sense of becoming something special is induced, and in mimetic dance it must be as if one became what one danced. And magical action, which is especially emphatic action, would lend itself more than most action to embellishment of the sort that constitutes dancelikeness. Many authors have commented in many ways on how secular art is a transformation of sacred or magical practice; and a lot of sacred and magical practice is bound to be mimetic, for, if you aren't going to sing and dance at a ceremony, what *are* you going to do? But a third explanation of the prominence of mimesis, one that calls for no etiological speculation, is that the mimetic affords possibilities of meaningfulness as extensive and rich as all others together. In Nelson Goodman's phraseology, a symbol system consists of a symbol scheme with a referential domain. Mimesis is not a subdomain of syntax; it is the whole domain of semantics. No more needs to be said.

CHAPTER 6

~ ~ ~ ~ ~ ~ ~ ~ ~ ~ ~ ~ ~ ~ ~ ~ ~ ~ ~

On What Is and What Is Not
The Art of Dance

WE HAVE SEEN that dance is not an art in the classical sense of an organization of knowledge and skill for a specific end. We have seen that dance was not placed unequivocally or unanimously among the arts originally identified as the fine arts, and why not. In the previous chapter and elsewhere, we have slipped from the sort of dance that is nowadays thought of as art, or as artistic, to recreational and other dancing, and back again as occasion required, and have relied on the reader to make any necessary adjustments. And we will continue to do that, without notice.

We do, however, have to confront a general question. The initial and declared focus of this book is on artistic dance, or dance as art, and we are interested in other dancing primarily as the matrix within which artistic dance takes form. We said something in §3.3 about how theories of art apply to dance in general. What we did not do was follow out the implications of our contention that not all dance is art. How is that distinction made? How should it be made? At what point, and on what grounds, do we begin to assign a dance or a dance practice to an art or say that it has become artistic? Is it a matter of degree or of kind? Degree of what, and what kind of kind? Is it that certain standards have become more plainly relevant? or more rigidly applied? or more consistently complied with? Or are there radically different standards, different procedures and practices, different contexts that at different times induce us to draw the distinction between art and not art (and the distinction between the artistic and the inartistic) in different places? What we said in §3.3 provides some materials for an answer: any dance or way of dancing to which what we said there is apposite is, to that extent, art; otherwise, not. But we cannot be sure that there will be no more to it than that.

From the previous chapter, we may surmise that there can be no simple or straightforward answer to the questions we have just raised. Since there is no simple principle on which we differentiate what is dance from what is not, it is most unlikely that we have a single way of differentiating dances and dancing that are art from those that are not. That could not come about unless this latter differentiation were applicable only to a single set of dance practices or to a single mode of dancing, identified as dance by a single set of unequivocal criteria. And that is not likely to be the case.

There are, in fact, at least three distinctions that confront us. The first is between those dance practices that are (fine) arts, in the same league as music and poetry, and those that are not arts in any such sense. The second is between dance or dancing that is art, in the sense of belonging to the domain that pertains to those arts whether or not it belongs to any particular art, and dance or dancing that does not belong to that domain. The third is between dance that is artistic, in the sense of having qualities for which things are praised as art, and dance that is not artistic. The distinctions are mutually independent in application—a dance can be artistic without being art, and so on; but each is only definable in terms of the one before it.

The reason we have to take these questions up is that there is a clear and familiar sense in which not all dance is art or artistic in any way. Leaving out of account the "dancing" of nonhuman agents, which we can brush aside as not eligible, people who roll back the rug at a party, put on a tape, and start dancing do not think of themselves as practicing an art, or of themselves as artists, or of what they jointly produce as a work of art; and they will not spoil their fun by wondering whether what they are doing is artistic. Why should they? Anyone familiar with art theory and aesthetics will be familiar with more than one theory according to which they are doing all those things, and may even hold such a theory; but it is not a point of view people take when they are not theorizing.

Everybody *can* dance somehow or other: point a gun at someone's head and say "dance or die," and they will think of something to do. And practically everybody has at some time wanted to dance and has danced. But not everyone has practiced any art of dance. To do so requires that one transform one's body into an instrument for appropriately controlled movement, though some such transformations are more thoroughgoing than others. Arts of dancing, based on the transferability of a set of dancing skills and mindsets, no doubt call for different instruments: ballet dancers and jazz dancers do different things with their bodies. There are, it would seem, separate and parallel arts of dance. But is there any such thing as being a dancer in general, something that from the artistic point of view all dancers have in common? It could be so, if body-learning is itself a skill: if one could learn, not specific practices or dances or steps, but how to learn dancing. I suspect that this is the case. It seems likely that a dancer trained in any dance tradition can more easily learn any dance, however alien, than someone with no dance training, picking up movements and styles more quickly, reproducing them more precisely, retaining them more readily and surely. What would this facility be based on? A system of kinesthetics, a habit of attending to how one's body feels? A system of body-image use, a habit of knowing and attending to how one's body is disposed in space? Or simply a habit of making fine discriminations in movement and posture? There may be people who know the answers—but there may not; in the related field of academic work, the familiar topic of the transferability of study skills and habits between unrelated disciplines has yet to be reduced to system.

6.1 *Two Methods*

Such distinctions as whether some dance is art, or whether some dance form is an art form, can be made in either of two plausible ways, which may work against each other. One is to make the distinction by criteria already established in relation to other arts or to art in general: art is endotelic activity, or embodies significant form, or expresses emotion, or produces delight through representation, or systematically furnishes symbols meeting certain standards of repletion and density, or whatever slogan or viewpoint one might be using to organize one's thoughts with. There are many such, but they are all open to the same objection from the present point of view. They all assume that we could decide what art is before we started thinking about dance. The objection is that, for all we know, the criteria we are using might never have been adopted in the first place if we had taken dance into account. Accordingly, we might reflect that what all these criteria purport to do is to clarify the principles on which we accept as art whatever we do accept. What we should do, then, is to see what form of dance is accepted as art by the appropriate reference group—the artists, or their society, or theorists, or *their* society, or a sufficient public. If we can clarify any resulting criteria, we may take them as regulative in other areas, just as we would have done with "significant form" and the rest, thus isolating the peculiar contribution that artistic dance makes to the general idea of art. (That, incidentally, is what Havelock Ellis was up to in *The Dance of Life*.)

6.2 *Some Distinctions*

The word "art" is used for many purposes on many occasions, and these are not systematically interrelated. The interested reader should refer to

Sparshott (1982) or to some similarly general work on art theory and make the suitable applications. It would be pointless to summarize the relevant material here: the whole point is that no summary account of the complexities can be given. What is possible is to mention a few distinctions that can be and are made in this area, some contrasts that the word "art" and its cognates are regularly used to draw, bearing in mind that they are not all made on the same principle and cannot be reduced to a single system.

6.21 AFFILIATION

Dance counts as art when, in a culture that has the concept of art in general, or when considered from the viewpoint of a culture that has that concept, it belongs to the art world or to the life-form of art, as opposed to the world of the everyday, or of sport, or of recreation, or of some other rival among the domains into which people sort their lives. Dancing of a certain sort may tend to go with an interest in art, a tendency to associate with artists or their clients, a willingness to accept artistic standards and what goes with them (to tolerate critics and invite reviewers), to prefer praise from people identified by themselves and others as art lovers, to apply and accept the language of art aspiration and art appreciation as relevant to one's own performance. There are unlikely to be clear distinctions in these matters, since what one does may be associated with more than one such domain in ways that may fluctuate and may at any one time be uncertain; but it may well be that the most important reason for sometimes thinking that some dance is art is that its practitioners habitually place it in the context of the art world by their actions and attitudes.

6.22 QUALITY

What makes some dance art may be a matter of the felt quality of experience—what is sometimes summed up as the "aesthetic" quality of experience. If there is a range of feelings and attitudes that are characteristic of our absorbed participation in the practice or appreciation of art, then dance will be art when it regularly evokes those attitudes and feelings, whatever they may be. It does not matter here that theorists deny that there is any distinctive set of such qualities and responses; all that matters is that, in the context of such distinctions, those making the distinction do it on what purport to be such directly experiential grounds. There is no doubt that, when Isadora Duncan was hailed as an artist, it was largely because her dance was felt to have a quality importantly akin to the quality of acknowledged works of art in other media and to demand comparable attentiveness and scrutiny.

There is an important ambiguity in the preceding paragraph. I wrote as if what was in question was a particular, identifiable quality of experience. But what made a particular dance art might rather be the fact that what was important in the dance was the quality of the experience, whatever that quality might be: artistic behavior is behavior in which the quality of experience is what is important. But we must add that it is important not merely as enjoyed but as attended to. That distinguishes artistic dance from merely social or recreational dance, which is enjoyed but in which there is nothing that calls for attention.

One of the reasons one cannot give a straightforward answer to people who ask whether or not disco dancing is art as that any sort of dancing that can be attended to becomes art to the extent that such attention is seriously paid. Insofar as dancing is an endotelic activity, there is nothing for dancers to attend to in their dancing other than the quality of their performance, either as dancing in general or as dancing of this or that determinate kind. The outcome of attention must be the cultivation of pure values of some sort or other; and the possible sorts will be the different recognized kinds of art value, because that is how art values are determined and differentiated.

The requirement of attentiveness would also exclude ecstatic and trance-inducing dances. Such a dance would count as art only if it was the felt quality of the falling into trance that was esteemed for its own sake, as something to cultivated and discriminatingly relished. It is hard to imagine a society in which an art of becoming entranced through dance could be cultivated or could be recognized as art if it were.[1] Part of the difficulty with conceiving of such an art is that we would expect the sort of experience involved not to be differentiated or articulated and to be related only loosely and globally to the movements that occasioned it. Terms like "appreciation" do not fit very well here.

To be appreciated as art, a performance must be discriminatingly attended to. But that has two consequences. First, distinctions between genres become provisional and hypothetical: the presupposition of such attention must be that significant distinctions await discovery. But second, distinctions among arts and genres, though thus provisional, become determinate where they were not before: classes of comparison become established; areas and forms of refinement are cultivated. "Modern bullfighting," says Robert Graves, "did not start until 1907. . . . In this renascence of bullfighting, the many different passes were finally formalized and per-

---

[1] Beryl de Zoete points out that the violent contortions of "kris-dancers" who become possessed in the course of the dance are never called "dancing" by the Balinese (Zoete 1938, 67).

fected, and the sport of bullfighting became an art."[2] As the passes are formalized and standardized, the sport becomes an art in the old "craft" sense; as they become perfected and are made the focus of stylistic refinement, it becomes a fine art. Somewhat similarly in dance, historians connect the transition of ballet from mere show to fine art with the final codification of its formal language in the hands of such masters as Carlo Blasis.

In terms of the contrast we are discussing, then, dance that is art is dance considered as an object of appreciation, apprehended and enjoyed for its cognized properties as dance, as made available through appropriate observation, interpretation, and discrimination. It may prove hard to find quite the right formulation, but that is a question for the general theory of art and need not concern us here. All we need to say is that dance is art when and insofar as it exists for the sake of that in it which lends itself to appreciation—as defined and elaborated in the appropriate general theory of art.

6.23 Art Dance and Ethnic Dance

A bibliographer comments on an article by James K. Feibleman: "An example of how far out of touch the philosopher may be with dance. Fails to distinguish between ethnic dance and dance as an art form" (Kaprelian 1976, 58). What are we to make of this? Why should not ethnic dance be danced for its own sake, for its aesthetic qualities? The argument would have to be that ethnic dance, art or not, is not a form of art, because its primary significance is that it symbolizes cultural identity by contrast with the imperial or metropolitan culture that defines itself not as belonging to this nation or that but as belonging to civilization at large. Dance as an art form, then, is danced as it is because of its dance qualities. If it were no longer esteemed as dance, it would no longer be danced, or would be danced only as a historical reconstruction—and even then, on this argument, it would be reconstructed because it had once been esteemed as art. The ethnic dance, on the other hand, is danced because it is *ours*. Whatever are felt to be its artistic shortcomings, it will not be changed because it would then no longer be our dance; or rather, if it is changed, it will be changed in accordance with ideas of national suitability and not to conform with whatever dance values its proponents may share as members of the wider collective.

The distinction as thus presented applies only within communities

---

[2] Graves 1969, 154. I am aware that some readers may object to this reference to the cruel sport of bullfighting on the ground that, while the bull fights for the love of fighting, the unfortunate matador, drawn almost invariably from the poorest classes of society, is driven to his dreadful trade by sheer economic necessity. But, if I offend, I offend.

where both ethnic dance and art dance exist side by side. If the term "ethnic" is applied in a looser way, to any dancing that is characteristic of a particular culture, then of course all dance is ethnic.[3] And if it is applied, as it often is, to the dances performed by culturally isolated groups whose dancing is neither subject to modification in the light of an abstract idea of dance in general and a worldwide history of dance nor contrasted by the dance community with any other way of dancing, the contrast stated between ethnic dance and dance as an art form needs a lot of explanation. Why should we not say that their dance is ethnic, because it is their cultural property, and also artistic, because it is one of their arts and danced by their aesthetic standards? The contrast might need to be reinterpreted into something like Schiller's famous contrast between naive and sentimental poetry, between dance that is simply danced and dance that is danced self-consciously under the idea of dancing. But even that distinction is doubtfully acceptable, because the conditions stated say nothing about the degree or kind of self-consciousness involved in the dance practice, and there is nothing to say that cultures may not differ widely among themselves in this sort of way.

In any case, it is not only the philosopher Feibleman who is thus out of touch with dance. When Judith L. Hanna says that dance fulfills the same function among the Ubakala and among Lincoln Center dance goers (see §3.1 above), she too fails to make a sharp distinction between ethnic dance and dance as an art form. As she points out, the relevant contrasts may be between rural and urban settings everywhere rather than between the ethnic and the artistic. It may be felt, however, that Hanna is pushing things a bit. Unless the Ubakala have the concept of art, habitually discriminate between art and what is not art, and are conversant with a range of alternative dance values comparable to those available to Balanchine and his public, it is hard to see how the functions and meanings could be the same. The phrase "more similarities than differences" can be deceptive. How does one count? There are more similarities than differences between Mozart and Hitler (both German-speaking males, only one of them a musician), if you count them right.[4]

---

[3] Joann Kealiinohomoku (1970), while protesting against the way some writers treat the dances of most of the world as belonging to a single genre called "primitive" or "ethnic" dance, claims that ballet, as the dance of the Caucasian people of Europe, is itself an ethnic dance. That is a mistake. The ballet is not the dance of any nation but the common property of our civilization, and is what the ethnic dances of Europe are contrasted with. The same is true of any empire: what is common to the empire is contrasted with what is peculiar to specific national groups within the empire. It is the latter that is called ethnic.

[4] For the difficulty of counting similarities, see Nelson Goodman's essay "Seven Strictures on Similarity" (Goodman 1972). But see also the caveat in Sparshott 1982, 532–534.

There are contexts, then, in which the contrast between ethnic dance and dance as an art form seems clear and sharp, and contexts in which it vanishes altogether. Perhaps we should say not only that ethnic dance as such exists only in deliberate contrast to dance as an art form but also that dance as an art form exists only in conscious contrast to other forms of non-art dance from which it is distinguished. A beautifully articulated version of such a contrast may be extracted from the work of Louis Horst (1940). In case after case, he traces a development whereby a simple peasant dance becomes popular at court and is given a suitably polished and elegant form, is then adopted as an episode for formal display in ballets, and finally (usually in our own century) becomes a theme for free variation in the choreography of a modern art dance. At each stage, the dance becomes less ethnic, less associated with the spontaneous fun of a particular local culture, and more artlike, imbued with more consciously cultivated aesthetic characteristics.[5]

6.24 THE PUBLIC

One reason for not thinking of a trance-inducing dance as art ($6.22), even if it were relished for the quality of an experience systematically related to its articulation, is that we think of art as, at least in principle, pub-

---

[5] An interesting light is shed on the transition from country to court by a passage in Jane Austen's *Pride and Prejudice*:

Mary, at the end of a long concerto, was glad to purchase praise and gratitude by Scotch and Irish airs, at the request of her younger sisters, who with some of the Lucases and two or three officers joined eagerly in dancing at one end of the room.

Mr. Darcy stood near them in silent indignation at such a mode of passing the evening, to the exclusion of all conversation, and was too much engrossed by his own thoughts to perceive that Sir William Lucas was his neighbour, till Sir William thus began.

"What a charming amusement for young people this is, Mr. Darcy!—There is nothing like dancing after all.—I consider it as one of the first refinements of polished societies."

"Certainly, Sir;—and it has the advantage also of being in vogue amongst the less polished societies of the world.—Every savage can dance."

Sir William only smiled. (Austen 1813, 25)

Mr. Darcy probably does not really think that the dancing that every savage can do is the same as the dancing that Sir William thinks is a refinement of polished societies; his objection is that all dancing kills conversation. On the other hand, Sir William is a bit silly to think that what the young people are up to is a sign of refinement. We notice that the airs danced to are not English, but Scotch and Irish, and thus not free from the taint of savagery. (In terms of the novel, we have to bear in mind that Sir William is too eager to please everybody, and Mr. Darcy notoriously abrasive. Observe that Mr. Darcy's fury at the death of conversation prevents him at first from noticing that Sir William is trying to engage him in conversation. I am indebted to Eileen Or for drawing my attention to the subtleties of this passage.)

licly accessible, whereas in the entrancement we suppose that each dancer turns aside into his or her private awareness. The dancers may share the incipient ecstasy—the Bacchic dancers are united in their relation to Bromios, it is by no means a private experience of separate individuals but rather a loss of identity—but there is nothing in it for any possible public. Should we then say that the fine arts are arts *for publics* and thus arts of display? Historically, that is certainly how they were conceived: the beauty and significance they achieve are to be comprehended and relished by an audience. We might then say bluntly that dance as fine art is always display dance, involving movement made visible in significant beauty. In fact, dance as art in our civilization is theater dance and exists outside theater only by carrying the implication of its theatrical setting with it.

We have already quoted Adam Smith's account of dance (as an art of imitation) as being concerned with the display of movement, on the elegantly conceived ground that it is precisely the ostentation of grace, which is offensive in ordinary life, that is valued in dance.[6] The same point is made in Selma Jeanne Cohen's definition of dancing as human movement "framed to be seen for its own sake and interest even above its interest of meaning."[7]

Are we then to say that dance as fine art is dance organized around the visibility of movement and its display, whereas ballroom dancing centers on the excitement of moving to music (with contact, or the promise of contact, with a potential sexual partner) and ethnic dance celebrates communal identity? There may be spectators for these latter kinds of dance, and they may have important parts to play, but they do not amount to what we called a "public" for the dance in §3.1. In that case, the mistake in making visibility a necessary condition of dance as such (§5.3215) is that it was misplaced: visibility is a condition of art dance, not of dance in general.

The choreographer Jerome Robbins has told the world (in a PBS telecast devoted to his work) that he preferred the way his dances looked in

6 This is the point of the remarks made about the "manners of a dancing master" in the eighteenth and nineteenth centuries (see Chapter 1 n. 52). Adam Smith's view might be paraphrased by saying that dance movements must be self-consciously well formed, but the self-consciousness must be divorced from ego-consciousness.

7 Cohen adapts the phrase from Gerard Manley Hopkins, who was writing about poetry, in her "Prolegomenon to the Aesthetic of Dance" (Nadel and Nadel 1970, 4–5). Perhaps the phrase meant something rather different in its original application to the reading of texts written in a language, for words as such exist primarily as meaning-bearers within a system, whereas it seems obvious that human movements are in the first instance movements of human bodies and have to dissociate themselves from that primacy to enter into systems of dance movement. Be that as it may, Cohen's borrowing may effect a more radical transformation than she avows.

rehearsal to the way they looked on stage because in the former context the dancers were dancing as opposed to performing. There is evidently a difference between doing something visibly right and doing it to look right, between manifesting something and displaying it. So one sees what is meant: art should not be a matter of showing off. But it is very puzzling. What is it that has to be got right? Apparently, nothing other than getting the motion right for vision. There is no sense in which the motion can be seen to be right, other than that it should be seen to *look* right. And the actual steps rehearsed must be identical with the steps performed. What, then, can the distinction Robbins makes between dancing and performing really be? That a danced movement looks wrong if it looks flaunted? Probably. When the pianist Glenn Gould gave up concert performances and devoted himself to recording, his avowed reason was that in performances one inevitably played for immediate effect, at the expense of fidelity to the inner meaning of the music itself.[8] The stage, as we said in §4.52, is not the studio, and one acts in one's total situation: perhaps all stage performers have to choose between being never perfect in rehearsal and never right on the night. But it is hard to see how one could maintain as a principle either that performance arts are always rehearsal arts that have undergone corruption or that one should always rehearse for the dress rehearsal and never for the first night.

Robbins, like all choreographers, is a (superannuated) dancer and has in mind the feel of a dance as well as its look. His interaction with his dancers in (filmed) rehearsal and in developing a dance is a conversation of movements, with interrogation and response: "Like this?"—"Rather like *that*"—"It goes better for me this way." The words are less important than the movements shown, tried, accepted, modified. In addition, the dancers in rehearsal dance to be seen by a fellow dancer at close range, not to be seen by an audience across the lights and through the arch. Theater dance must be declamatory; there is a corresponding inner difference between opera and *Lied*, between orchestral music and chamber music, corresponding to the rhetorical difference expressed in the old adage that prose is to be heard and poetry to be overheard.[9] And, most important perhaps, since dancer and choreographer are creating together, what each sees in the other is the adumbration of an ideal dance, which the one by gestures and the other by responses show that each inwardly realizes.

In general, such a segregation of performance and audience as we find

---

[8] Gould's somewhat complex position is explored in Payzant 1978. I specify his avowed reason, since those of us who saw Gould in public performance could not help noticing his apparent personal discomfort on the concert stage.

[9] "If we may be excused the antithesis, we should say that eloquence is *heard*, poetry is *over*heard" (Mill 1833, 348).

in dance as a theater art is not a necessary condition of artistic experience, even in the performing arts. Musicians play quartets, sing madrigals, engage in jam sessions, for themselves alone, and it is often said that the deepest experience of any performing art is that of the performer. (Of course, this would only be true in the ideal case, if at all: not every performer's experience would on every occasion be profounder than that of every member of the audience, as countless anecdotes about cynical sidemen and bored comedians insist.) In fact, the contention that theater dance as such is directed to an audience, though obviously true, is only half true and becomes less true the more the dance takes on the character of art as opposed to entertainment.

Though the basic forms of theater dance are developed with public presentation in mind, and the audience is integral to (if not everywhere dominant in) the institution, dancers writing on their art often insist that it demands total dedication, a singlemindedness in which the thought of a spectator plays no part. Certainly none of the choreographers contributing to Selma Jeanne Cohen's *The Modern Dance* (1966) admit to thinking of themselves as producing something primarily to be looked at, much less to give any pleasure in being looked at—though it is equally true that none of them explain why, in that case, their activity presupposes a setting of public performance. And what is one to make of the elaborate curtain calls in which even the most devotedly arty dance companies indulge? Are they, too, conceived without regard to any possible audience? Well, perhaps they are, just as a bow or a courtesy within a dance is performed without regard to the social implications such a greeting might have if it were not in a dance. One would then have to say that a curtain call is a pure dance that just happens to be historically derived from the obsolete custom of acknowledging applause.[10] But I don't think anyone has gone that far—yet. Perhaps what we should really say is that in any case, as we said in Chapter 3, every dance has to be entered and left as one assumes and quits the condition of being a dancer; and all curtain calls, however simple or elaborate, are ways of leaving the dance and may accordingly be in varying degrees and in various ways inside or outside the dance.

Although a dance or a dance form could hardly be theater dance without reference to at least a possible public, it is not so clear that artistic dance as such requires a public. One can certainly imagine a dancer retiring from the stage and developing his or her own art without thought of any public. It seems absurd to suppose that such a dancer would be any the less an artist simply because the art was unseen and unknown, though we have to

---

[10] The last time Pilobolus came to Toronto, the reviewers noted correctly that the curtain calls were the best part of the performance—they were certainly the most loudly applauded.

suppose that, if such a dancer were after all to be observed, the excellence of the dance would be in principle visible (one says "in principle" because such a development might in fact outstrip the appreciative competence of anyone other than the dancer).

Should one then say that the dancer as artist (or as dancer of artistic dance) dances always for an ideal public? In fact one is accustomed to the idea that the pioneers of modern dance in Martha Graham's day danced with a public in mind, but without any reference to whether such a public might ever come to exist. (It is hard for a dancer, unlike a musical composer or a writer, to work for posterity!) Merce Cunningham at one time revealed his compositions to the New York public only in recitals at which no dance was presented in its entirety but various compositions were presented partially and simultaneously. So far as that public was concerned, such dances were never seen, but existed, and were, as it were, glimpsed.[11] We cannot even say that the dancers were themselves their own public, as many artists are, stand-ins for the others who may never show up; for a dance may exist for its dancers not as seen but as danced.

Perhaps what we really ought to be saying here is that the art of dance depends on movement, not as seen but as known or envisaged. Not the way the dancer looks in movement, or kinesthetically feels in movement, or can be seen to be moving, but the way the dancer is actually moving and is moving as a dancer. That is to say, although it is true that dances exist as to be seen, that is misleading; their substance is not visible but is a construction of humanity moving in a special mode. But there is no reason to suppose that that mode is invariably the same, even if we insist that, to be art, there must be some special dance mode or other.

It must be conceded, though, that there is something very questionable in this idea of artistic dance as the realization of an autonomous dance idea to which the presence of a public is at best equivocally necessary. Once again we may invoke the example of Glenn Gould. Gould says that fidelity to the performed music is best achieved through the construction of recordings and that live performance to an audience involves distortions (amounting to spiritual corruptions) as well as imperfections. But others

---

[11] This is the view of the matter taken by Arlene Croce (1978), who complains that if you wanted to see the whole of a Cunningham dance you had to go out of town. John Percival, however, regards these events as self-contained collages, each "being put together with an appearance of informal ease yet with a skill and taste that enables them to build to a climax and gently die away again" (Percival 1980, 64). Not having seen, can't say; however, one might suspect from Cunningham's longstanding involvement with John Cage that a multiple ambiguity was welcomed but not entirely foreseen. Cage likes to compile works from the compresence of independently varying forms, and he believes in sometimes making things difficult to see.

say that even the best recording is not music at all. A truly musical event is the actual performance of a piece in real time on a real occasion. And one important kind of such an occasion is that in which the performer plays to an audience who listen to the performer. So too, it may be said, the art of dance centers on the realization of dance events; and to a very large class of such events, the presence of people who are watching the dancers dance is essential. The phrase "show business" can be misleading here. It is not that the audience are being entertained or being shown things: the dance exists for them, as they exist for the dance.[12] Obviously, there are profound ambiguities here, to which we will have to return. Whatever may turn out to be the right thing to say, it will have to be something that honors both standpoints and somehow reconciles them.[13]

6.25 ART AND ENTERTAINMENT

The converse of the view that dance cannot be art without an implied public, conferring on it a public and social reality as opposed to mere subjective "self-expression" and daydreaming, is the familiar contrast between art and entertainment. This is a contrast that is most at home within the performing arts, where it sets the need to attract and hold an immediate audience against the requirement of constructing an inherently satisfactory work, the fulfillment of which obviously cannot be judged at first sight or by the uninstructed.

The distinction between art and entertainment is sometimes attacked as snobbish, on the ground that the performing arts can have no real reason for existing other than to give satisfaction in performance (and what is that, if not to entertain?), whereas all entertainers have to be artists in the sense that it is not easy to hold an audience. That is very true, but it is not the whole truth, and one cannot argue away the evident polarity between

[12] Beryl de Zoete observes that Balinese audiences do not watch dances closely: "The Balinese, like other orientals, enters into the atmosphere of the dance and remains there as in a familiar landscape" (Zoete 1938, 16).

[13] The issue here is how dance is to be understood, not how individual dancers feel about their relations to the audience. Dancers differ widely in what they say about how they feel. Moira Shearer is reported as saying, "You don't have to work on an audience, it isn't *to* them. You are creating something within the stage" (Newman 1982, 109) (compare Merce Cunningham: "The dance isn't *directed* to them, or done for them. It's presented for them" [Cunningham 1985, 172]); whereas Tanaquil LeClercq tells the same interviewer, "You have to dance for somebody. You don't do it for yourself; that's like contemplating your own navel. You do it for people. That's why I can't understand those modern dancers, dancing away in lofts for just a few people" (Newman 1982, 166). Strictly, these dancers are not contradicting each other: one can dance for somebody without dancing to them, and one can be creating something for them. But Shearer and LeClercq do seem to be taking very different attitudes toward their job—or, possibly, to the interviewer.

the tendency toward concentrating upon immediate effect, devising routines aimed at the amusement of a casual audience, and the development of dances or other performances that are endlessly refined and structurally strengthened and in which the possibilities of a medium are explored and developed. Within the entertainment industry itself, the polarity can be discerned in the contrast in attitude that developed between Fred and Adele Astaire, according to the former's autobiography (1959). Adele is the more talented and precocious dancer, with Fred as her comic assistant; but as they mature, Adele becomes bored with rehearsing, while Fred endlessly worries about developing every detail of every performance and labors to work up new dance ideas, wherever derived, into articulate routines with their own proper endings. Fred clearly thinks and feels like an artist—or conforms to one of our stereotypes of "the artist"—however he may depreciate himself as a "hoofer." A middle position between those into which Adele and Fred are said to have diverged is one exemplified again and again in the Stearnses' book on jazz dance (1968). The dancers pride themselves and congratulate each other on their brilliance and success, but the valued qualities are speed and execution, and the criteria are competitive: the measure is the number of encores, and the highest praise is that this or that world-famous performer refused to follow the hero's act.

6.251 *Art and Craft*

The sort of distinction I have just made between the Astaires is a matter of degree. Presumably all vaudeville hoofers start much the same; some develop into artists, some degenerate into purveyors of tired routines, as more or less of the person comes to be involved and as the performer develops more and more or less and less of the possibilities initially open. But it was argued by R. G. Collingwood (1938) that there is really a difference of kind—or rather, that two entirely different and mutually conflicting principles are involved, although they are usually both operative on any occasion. On the one hand, there is art proper, the working out and clarification of affective mental contents ("expression of emotion" in a rather special sense), the sort of thing that Martha Graham did after she left Denishawn. On the other hand, there is craft and rhetoric, the working out of means to achieve preconceived ends and effects, the sort of thing one thinks of Busby Berkeley as doing. Part of the point here is that Berkeley could be brilliantly inventive, immensely skilled and imaginative in devising novel effects, and still not be an artist, insofar as he remained a showman devising a show, whereas Graham would be an artist insofar as she was concerned only to make clear to herself (and thus, but only incidentally, to others) the idea of a dance that was coming to be created in her.

There is a certain asymmetry in the contrast between Berkeley and Graham. Berkeley (in the work we remember him for) was choreographing for other dancers; Graham was inventing dances for others and for herself.[14] But what about those who dance what choreographers other than themselves have conceived? Is there any sense in which such a dancer can be an artist? The general question of the relation between dance making and dancing belongs to another context. What needs to be said here is that a merely interpretive (as opposed to a creative) dancer is engaged in art in the present sense insofar as the realization of the dance as an artistic unity depends essentially on the dancer's own contribution. Arlene Croce writes: "Gordeyev's dancing . . . is full of those grace notes that weaker technicians leave out. . . . Those little extras of his seem to come from the inside, as tokens of an ardent sincerity toward his ballerina, his public, and the art of dancing" (Croce 1978, 5).

Collingwood would think Croce confused here. "Grace notes" of technique sound like little twiddly bits added on, one more squiggly wire on a Fabergé egg, spoken of here as though they were merely signs of how seriously the artist is taking the job, checking the oil and wiping the windshield. Surely the point ought to be that it is no longer a question of technique, of how well the dancer has solved the mechanical problems: in the best dancers, all one is aware of is the meaningful unity of the dance, in which task and achievement are not separable. Mastery is necessary, not because the rules measure success, but because it is from such mastery that artistry begins. This is what one usually says of technique in other arts;[15] and if technique cannot thus be transcended in creative subsumption in ballet, then ballet excludes art, is not an art medium in the present sense.

The position just presented is open to the objection that it is mere covert evaluation: the distinction between technique and imaginative realization, between craft and art generally, can be made only by imputing to the performer this or that psychological state (perhaps "sincerity" in this case). I think what this popular objection amounts to is that questions about the nature of mental tasks cannot be reduced to measurable distinctions in outcomes, and of course they can't. But the sort of positivist aestheticism implicit in the objection does not seem to me to be a tenable position. Prac-

---

[14] Actually, this statement is misleading. Berkeley was choreographing for himself and not for dancers. "I never cared whether a girl knew her right foot from her left," he said, "so long as she was beautiful. I'd get her to move, or dance, or do something" (Pike and Martin 1973, 51–53). The real dancing was done by Berkeley's camera, as in Judy Garland's minstrel show number in *Babes on Broadway*, which he did in one shot with "about thirty eight" camera moves (ibid., 75) and, as always, in a single take (ibid., 61).

[15] "The necessary rules are craft rules. Beyond that we have the great exemplars that *set* the standards by which we measure our own progress" (Mothersill 1984, 191).

tical questions can be posed only in terms of what it is to set about doing things. Whether it is tenable or not, people who make the distinction between "art" and "craft" do it in the sort of way I have been describing. From our point of view, in any case, the issue is of no consequence, since the point is easily restated in logical terms. Establishing that a rule has been broken or a technique mastered is never directly relevant to artistic evaluation. Insofar as a performance is subject to direct technical evaluation, to that extent it is not art.

6.252 *Genres*

The distinction between art and craft as just made is one that appears, if at all, within any of the arts, or in symbol use, whether it occurs within an art or not. But when Astaire called himself a hoofer he was identifying himself as a dance entertainer in a genre for which it would be pretentious to claim the status of art. And it is not unknown for such distinctions between genres to be given institutional recognition. Friends in the dance world tell me (angrily and contemptuously) that the Canada Council, for instance, in describing its program for dance artists, specifically excludes tap dance and jazz dance from eligibility for support. Such dance is refused the status of art, whatever its creative brilliance, while any third-run epigone of Graham can line up for a hand-out.

Actually the Council's position is defensible in principle. There may well be dance genres in which the accepted institutional structure, the aims and limitations that define the genre, do not encourage art (as opposed to entertainment): persons of artistic leanings will not take it up, there are no possibilities to develop within the genre. Some genres, in fact, are essentially matters of the cultivation and display of prowess; others are essentially matters of development and creation (see §6.42 below).

In a previous chapter, I briefly discussed the question whether disco dancing was art. My dancing days, such as they were, were over before disco came along. The impression I get from the Villaris is that disco is not primarily an art form, that the essence of the disco experience is "total immersion" in the club environment, in which one gets carried away by a strong bass beat as manipulated by a DJ who knows how to control the energy levels of the dancers (Villari and Villari 1978, 101, 19). More like a bacchanal than a ballet. But, they say, there is an art whereby one puts a disco dance together, and they describe what it is to learn it by using the analogy of language learning and use (pp. 41–42). This testimony of a professionally friendly pair of witnesses confirms the more hostile verdict of the Stearnses: "As the dances multiplied," they said, "the quality deteriorated. . . . There were about five thousand discotheques by 1965, but the dancing was erratic. No one could dance with finesse in such crowded darkness, even if he wished, and many patrons were older people who although they liked the darkness emphatically did not wish" (Stearns and Stearns 1968, 5). Put these together and what we get is the following. Disco dancing consists, formally, of a repertory of debased and coarsened movements from Black American vernacular dance, danced to a similarly vulgarized beat in an environment hostile to aesthetic concerns and to any sort of refinement of skill. But, of course, a dancer *can* use these unpromising means in the interests of art; and it would be possible for an authentic dance of disco to arise by the usual means of refinement, imagination, creation, cultivation, and so forth. It would be unlikely, but it could happen.

6.26 HIGH ART

Sometimes, whether or not one makes a distinction between art and entertainment, and even if one concedes that there is a sense in which there can be great artists in the entertainment world, and even if one concedes that tap dancing is an art or an art form in its own right, and that there are many arts of dance, one may wish to make a distinction between what is *really* art and what is art only in a diminished sense. A common way of doing this is to distinguish "high art" from other art and to say that, for purposes of serious discussion, one wishes to confine oneself to "high art." The distinction is akin to, but not the same as, that originally made between the limited set of the fine arts and other arts. The point is that in some societies there are only a few art forms and art practices that are singled out for special attention. Art values of seriousness, integrity, dedication, perfection of accomplishment, depth of meaning, and so on (there is no definitive list) are, if not actually observed, acknowledged to be paramount in these forms and practices as they are not elsewhere. There is a high degree of cultural investment in them. Their supreme practitioners are not so much rewarded as revered, regarded as national treasures.

In dance, in our Western civilization, the historians of ballet have claimed this status for it and for no other art. The leading practitioners of ballet and no other dance form have sometimes claimed and sometimes been conceded a dignified place in national life, comparable to that of leading musicians or painters. Ballet companies, but not other dance companies, can aspire to be National, or Royal, or Imperial, or at least Civic. When modern dance in America sought to achieve a similar position, it could do so only by claiming that ballet was a usurper. The idea plainly is that, in the first place, the art form in question has developed and maintained itself by serious cultivation of its expressive means; in the second place, its seriousness earns it a recognized place in official culture and public life; and, most important, this and no other dance form stands for what dance means for this society as a whole, whether or not it enjoys widespread popularity. And so we come back again to the idea that art can exist only as a public fact, in the public realm, and as in the presence of a public. But now it is by repudiation of any immediate appeal to a public made up of occasional audiences that the art claims the right to speak for the public in its ideal manifestation.

We have seen already that Isadora Duncan and her successors in American dance set themselves up as moral and healthy in opposition to the sick and sinful decadence of ballet. But it was apparently only with Martha Graham that modern dance made a serious claim to the preemptive status of the high art of dance. What, in fact, was Graham's discovery? It is clear that she founded, or helped to establish, a viable tradition of teachable technique in a way that Duncan never did. It is also clear that, unlike the Denishawn group, from which she emerged, she was serious about style, about principles of movement, about discipline, about devotion, about aspirations that were not centered on show business. But what did she do that Wigman did not do? Wigman had the same seriousness, with a much firmer basis in Laban's teaching and training, and established a network of schools throughout Central Europe, which for a while maintained a sort of cultural dominance of its own. Graham, according to myth, simply reorganized and refined her Denishawn material on the basis of a romantic intuition about Amerindian culture. Wigman rethought the body as an expressive instrument—or, at least, thought she was doing that. What happened? Well, Hitler happened. The cult of the body, which gave European dance its popular impetus, was swallowed up in paramilitary *Kraft durch Freud*; Wigman's more talented colleagues emigrated to America, where they endowed Broadway with a new stylishness but where the artistic integrity of the movement evaporated into a collection of mannerisms and an uncontrolled self-expression. What Wigman had done was not enough: she had not integrated a powerful impetus with a technique of movement adequate to articulate and sustain it.[16]

What, then, did Graham do? Perhaps Stodelle (1984) is right in suggesting that Graham was Louis Horst's creation, that he imbued her individual genius and her overpowering sense of her own destiny with the ideas of work and discipline. On this showing, Graham was really sus-

---

[16] The remarks on Wigman and the fate of European dance here are tentative. Accounts of the development of modern dance in the 1920s and 1930s, both in Europe and in America, tend to be distorted by urges to deny and annex influences. The upshot of the "Mary Wigman Centennial Day" held at City College, CUNY, on 17 February 1986 was to leave me at least with the impression that Wigman was more inspiring as a teacher than as a dancer, and more as a talker than as a teacher. For Wigman's own ideas, see Wigman 1975.

tained by the idea of seriousness as such, by an overpowering sense of what it would be for dance to be serious, not only as an aspiration but as an undertaking.[17] The dancer's movement does not reflect experience or convey emotion, but comes from that mysterious entity the solar plexus—which is a metaphorical way, once fashionable, of saying that dance must come from whatever the center of the dancer's individuality is. Since World War I, the unconscious mind has taken the place the solar plexus occupied: we have been passing through an age of "depth psychology," and dance, destined by silence and abstraction to be the domain of ineffable meanings, is the apt art of whatever those depths may be. The perhaps unfortunate character of Graham's own brushes with Jungian notions is beside the point, which is that Jung exemplified the level at which dance, unlike any other art, was fundamentally articulated. And the connection with depth psychology applied especially to modern dance.[18] Ballet, with its beautifully cadenced and disciplined system, operated on formal and social levels that answered less precisely to the age's sense of its deepest motivation.

6.261 *Professional and Amateur*

The distinction between high art and lower art is repeated on a more practical level as that between professional and amateur. This is a multifaceted distinction, but what is essential is the contrast between someone who makes dance a serious business, works at it in a context where he or she expects publicly to be called to account, and someone for whom it is a mere pastime, for whom failure is merely personal disappointment. The distinction is familiar to anyone who works in the arts. It has nothing to do with quality of achievement; it is a matter of whether one claims recognition as having a serious, long-term commitment to the practice of the art, is prepared to stand or fall by one's performance in the art. (Perhaps the best measure of seriousness in any of the fine arts is the extent to which one puts oneself at risk in them.) But, though the distinction is in principle

---

[17] Seriousness is a tricky business. It is one thing to take one's art seriously in the sense that one works at it, another thing to be solemn about it. Of Graham's genius as a dancer and choreographer, and of her seriousness about dancing, there has never been any question. But her seriousness did sometimes verge on a pretentious solemnity that demanded an unearned reverence. This often happens in the arts, when original artists become exasperated with the way the great public refuses to pay attention. The point was accurately made by Richard Watts, reviewing Bill "Bojangles" Robinson's performance in *Blackbirds of 1933* for the *Herald Tribune* (4 December 1933): "This veteran tap dancer is one of the great artists of the modern stage, and is worth in his unostentatious way several dozen of a Mary Wigman, Charles Weidman, Martha Graham,—who are more pompous in their determination to be artistic" (quoted by Stearns and Stearns 1968, 183).

[18] For Graham's encounter with Jungian thought, see Shelton 1983.

a clear one, its application is less clear. Commitment is a matter of degree, of extent and intensity, and of kind. The distinction is further complicated by the fact that, especially in sports, the distinction between amateur and professional is conceived legalistically in terms of compensation: an amateur is someone who receives neither money nor other defined sorts of recompense. That is a goodish measure of professionalism conceived as seriousness, but not a perfect one. In any case, it is the acknowledged professionals who define for themselves and others what the art is. There is not much doubt about who they are, and they are not necessarily the same as those who control the formal institutions of training and presentation.

The contrast between professional and amateur, and consequently between what counts and what does not really count as art in dance, implies a number of contrasts. One is between reliable skill and lack of skill. A professional knows what to do; an amateur need only know what the amateur wants to do. A professional's activity is, in principle (for sickness or unemployment may intervene), regular and continuous; an amateur's is occasional and incidental. A professional has mastered a method; an amateur need not have. Above all, the professional is engaged in an organized undertaking, in which the operations are essentially detached from personal impulses; an amateur is typically engaged in self-expression. Nothing is more indicative of the amateur in the arts than this (especially in poetry, where the medium seems to offer no resistance): the amateur's own feelings of self-satisfaction play the critical role that for the serious artist is fulfilled by the requirements of the piece in hand.

The contrast between artistic work and self-expression comes close to the requirement of public practice that we examined above. And, just as that requirement had to be balanced against the distinction between art and entertainment, so here professionalism is shadowed by commercialism, of which the converse is not self-indulgent amateurism but devotion and consecration. This ambiguity perpetually engenders a lot of mutual suspicion.

6.3 *Significance*

The most basic distinction between dance that is art and dance that is not is that art, as such, has a significance that some dance lacks. As explained at great length in Sparshott (1982), the word "art" is widely used to impute this or that kind of significance that is supposed to be characteristic of the fine arts. Obviously, not all dancers and dance makers need aspire to such a significance, and there may well be dance to which it would be extravagant for anyone else to impute it.

6.31 INTERPRETABILITY

The most fashionable version of the sort of distinction we are now considering is that formulated by Arthur C. Danto (1981). Very roughly, Danto's theory is that to be a work of art is to be subject to a specific interpretation in the light of the sorts of meaning available at the relevant stage of art history. An art work is not, as such, a real thing, but is culturally sustained by its interpretability. Such facts about a dance as that it is nice to look at, or exciting, or fun to do, or that it has other perceptible qualities (however compelling) for participation or observation do not suffice for it to count as art. Since dancing can be done for fun or for exercise (like jogging), this distinction should have a bigger place in dance than it has in (say) painting, which is the sort of thing one does not do otherwise than as art, except in a minimalist mode (like painting a fence).

6.311 *Mere Appearance*

Danto's theory is a more modish version of a way of thinking about art that goes back to Schiller (1795). Art, Schiller's argument goes, is concerned with appearance (*Schein*) as opposed to reality, with objects for the imagination if not with imaginary objects. If a dance is regarded as art, the spectators abstract from their awareness of the person dancing and see only the dance. They do not see Karen Kain, they see only Giselle, even if what they see is Karen Kain's Giselle. Of course, Kain really is dancing Giselle, not just imagining it, and they really do see her really dancing it; they are not imagining anything, not even that she *is* Giselle. They willingly suspend their disbelief; but, as Coleridge meant to indicate by that carefully worded phrase, that is not because they entertain any alternative belief. Equally of course, today's philosophical students of aesthetics have pointed out that whatever one calls "appearance" is usually contrasted with some specific reality, and there is no easy way to specify what set of appearances art contrasts with what realities. But I take it that what is meant is that the art object is considered as though entirely constituted by those attributes that are taken account of in its relevant appreciation. A dance would be art insofar as it was appropriate to subject it to this thoroughly abstractive mode of seeing.[19]

[19] An attempt to define an appropriate sort of aesthetic perception was made by Virgil

Schiller's view seems at first a primitive and nebulous forerunner of Goodman's theory of art, as well as Danto's. If to be a work of art is to be a character in a symbol system, to regard something as a work of art is to attend only to its symbol-related characteristics, and these are all characteristics that it has as signifier and not as any other sort of entity. Why, then, not advance into the twentieth century? Well, in the case of Goodman, there is no way of identifying the alleged system in which the work is a character and no way of specifying what the system would be like if we could identify it. The reality lying behind the "system" is the fact that, when we find something meaningful, we are aware of its having its meaning by excluding alternatives. Similarly, with Danto, there is a wild extravagance in the notion that an interpretive act directed at a work bestows on it the significant characteristics without which it would have had no reason to exist in the first place.

6.32 THE INSTITUTIONAL THEORY

On Danto's theory, a work of art has a sort of significance to which it is entitled by history: a dance that is a work of art is one that is legitimately seen and hence understood in a certain way. But who is to say what is legitimate? Brooding on this question may lead one to entertain a theory of the sort advanced by George Dickie (1974) and touched on in §5.523 (and elsewhere) above. Any dance is a work of art if it is put forward as a candidate for appreciation by someone acting on behalf of the art world, that is, by someone who understands enough about the whole business of art and art appreciation for the proposal to make sense. And one can and should then go on to talk about when such proposals are responsible and when they are irresponsible, why some proposals are taken up and others are not, thus getting away from the supposedly empty question "Is it art?" to a consideration of how in particular cases the standings of specific works are established and contested. The relevant point for us here is the following. Presumably, the practice of distinguishing between dances that are to be treated as art and dances that are not to be so treated arises from the recognition that they respectively have and lack characteristics by virtue of which they really are art, in such terms as are specified elsewhere in this chapter. What the institutional theory affirms is that, once this practice of

---

Aldrich (1963). The attempt is often said to founder on the reef that sinks most theories of this general sort: all seeing and looking concentrates on certain features of what is beheld and neglects others, and attempts to describe the difference between artistic seeing and other seeing always turn out to be either circular or tendentious. However, the mere fact that a theory is untenable is no reason for not holding it—it only shows that you can't, not that you shouldn't (cf. Feyerabend 1978).

discrimination is established, there can be no definitive reasons for saying which dances are to be so treated and which are not. Ultimately, it is a matter of cultural will, the differential investment of energies.

The plausibility of this "institutional" theory of art has a curious consequence. Whereas, on most ways of distinguishing dances that are art from those that are not, the implication is that the former are a select group within the latter, the institutional theory means that the criteria for dance as art are laxer than for other dance. The institutional context can justify anything. Many things are accepted as dance in an art context that would not be accepted as dance in the real world. We must not forget, however, that such acceptance must be motivated, and what motivates is presumably the good will engendered by the more directly appreciable characteristics that sustain the institution in the first place.

6.321 *Derealization*

Sartre presents art as a very special mode of experience, in which (as in other theories we are looking at here) an object is "derealized." That is to say, the object present to the senses is treated as basis for an object cognized in terms of a mode of imaginative construction. (The jargon is explained and defended in *L'Imaginaire* [1940]). But in a later work (1971) he recognizes that this derealization is not something that occurs at random but normally requires an institutionalized setting. Dances that are centers of derealization are art, others are not; and the dancers' status as permanent centers for such derealization demands something like a theater setting in which the audience assemble in order to derealize themselves as spectators. Artistic dance presupposes arts of dance and dancers who are artists, that is, *recognized* centers of derealization. But, of course, once such an institution is established and the appropriate patterns of incitement and surrender are habitual, anyone can issue an invitation to derealization by proclaiming themselves to be dancers, and people can derealize themselves as spectators in relation to anything: imagination knows facilitations, even imperatives, but no limits.

Since Sartre is only describing some of the things that do go on in art, his points can be made in jargons no more and no less objectionable than his own—for instance, by calling a work of art a "character in a symbol system." What is distinctive in Sartre's later approach is that the "appearance" of the work is not so much an abstraction from the marble carved or the person dancing as a transfiguration of them; and the process of derealization in the work is matched by a transfiguration of the person who engages with the work as spectator (Sartre 1971, 785–790). Such a mutual transformation had already been envisaged by Mikel Dufrenne and was common coin among American pragmatists of the 1930s. What Sartre added was a sharpened sense of the symmetry involved and an application of his favorite concept of the "practico-inert," the irreducible material basis and residue of subjectivity. That is, though art and spectator are both fully transformed, the basis of the transformation remains present as what is being transformed.

6.4 *Status and Significance*

Setting aside the variety of ways in which, and the reasons for which, the word "art" and its equivalents and cognates may be applied to dances on this or that occasion, let us continue to concentrate on the status and significance of art as defined by the paradigm of the fine arts tradition and remind ourselves of some ways in which an art of dancing, or an artistic dance form, or even *the* art of dance, might in principle qualify for such status. First, it might be art simply by being institutionally accepted as one of the arts by those whose acceptances amount to appropriate recognition: dictionary makers, granting agencies, journalists and publicists, teachers and school organizers, show promoters, and other people concerned with the categorization and control of cultural life.[20] The layout of a newspaper, for instance, reflects a definite view of how the social world is organized by its division into world news, local news, business, sports, women's pages (nowadays renamed "lifestyle"), and entertainment. (In my home town, everything that artists in any medium do as artists counts as entertainment; their visits and their deaths, but never their works, count as news.)

Second, such an art or art form might be art because those who engage in it think of it as art, enter it or perform it with an avowed art attitude. Once art is established as a "form of life" within a civilization, those who engage in any practice within its ambit will do so, if not in the name of art, then in awareness that what they are doing is art. And this awareness must govern their attitude, their avowed motivation, their apologetics, and the way they set about things.

Third, an art or art form might be an art because of the inner dynamics of the concept of art, by actually having enough or the right assortment of the characteristics by which art is, for the time being, recognized. That is, it might be an art just because it is one; it is the sort of thing that an art is, just as Canada is a constitutional monarchy and the United States a feder-

---

[20] For an example of how a dictionary may decree the status of an art, see Chapter 3, note 22.

ated republic because that, whatever else they may be and however important we may think it, is what they are.

Fourth, an art or an art form might count as art by the dialectic of art, related to such dance as is preeminently art as other practices are related to other high arts as marginal, as anti-art, as deviant, or in such other relationships as there might be.

The four ways suggested are alternative ways in which a practice may be art, and it may be art for one of these reasons and not for others. It is not the case that it must be the same one of these four that in each instance provides the reason why art is art. If someone suggests that only one of these reasons is appropriate, that person is inviting us to exchange our notion of what art is for a different sort of notion.

6.41 ART AND THE ARTISTIC

The preferred locus of art as a kind of significance is not a practice or an art or art form but a particular work or activity: it may be in the practice that the significance is promoted, but it can only be on specific occasions that it is achieved. We may envisage the following sort of model: occasional, sporadic or spontaneous, items of dancelike behavior are found (or believed) to achieve a certain sort of significance; arts and art forms of dance are then developed to foster what is thus found valuable; but, since the value was generated outside any organized practice in the first place, it must be possible for the value still to be realized outside it. The fine arts, in fact, including that or those of dance, exist, in the last analysis, to achieve a certain level of human dignity, or insight, or accomplishment. It is unlikely that that level can often be attained without education, training, or institutional support; but, if it can be, so much the better. We may therefore ask, not what the art of dance is or what is the art of dance, but what dance is art. (Symmetry invites us to add: what art is dance? And it is a good question, because it must often happen in the avant-garde that it is clearer that what is happening is art than that it is or is not dance. But one can answer the question by using the materials compiled in the preceding chapter, if one can answer it at all.)

Given the general human significance of art, what dance achieves that significance, if any does? The question answers itself. The very reasons that lead us to separate art from the arts, so as to distinguish what really has the desired significance from what is only connected with it by ambition and presumption, prevent us from specifying kinds and categories of dance that would be art ex officio. Once one has decided what significance one claims for art, the question of what dance has that significance can only be answered by considering particular dances in the light of one's concrete understanding of dancing and of how dancing can be significant. That really is all.

Well, what is this significance of art? This is no place to recapitulate and defend an account of all the ingredients that severally or in combination go to make up our modern notions of art. I will simply list the ones I can think of, including the ones I have mentioned already, so that you will not think I am trying to make a mystery.

Art may include the notion of a highly wrought skill, virtuosity, and finish, especially when anthropologists are talking, but it may not. It may imply the emphasized or elaborated or enjoyed use of a symbol system or, more generally, the exploration and celebration of meaning. It is likely to imply creation, as opposed to the ritual repetition of practice or the academic repetition of effects. Such creation is often interpreted as the achievement of intuition or unanalyzable and unheralded meaning, and this in turn may be equated with the expression of feeling or of the knowledge of feeling. The implication of this talk about expression is that the work of art must make its effect, as it was achieved, as a unified experience, and not (in the way that discourse does) as a synthesis of denumerable items.

On a different line of thought, whatever is artistic enough to be art may be identified as the proper target of a characteristic aesthetic vocabulary, or as eliciting or meriting aesthetic judgment—as being, in other words, an object of taste. (Many people hate these ideas, but their protests have not succeeded in discrediting them to the general satisfaction.) Being a proper target for all that sort of thing has often been held to require evoking an attitude of "disinterestedness" or "aesthetic distance." Lots of different ways of specifying such an attitude or approach (or even "propositional attitude") have been tried, but lots of people remain unhappy with all of them. Such malcontents sometimes say that all it comes down to is saying that works of art must be produced and appreciated *as* works of art—not in a describable way such as could be tagged with one of the objectionable phrases, but in accordance with the actual complex practices established for the art in question. That is not so emptily circular as it may sound: the point is that, for any actual sort of art, there is a complex way of understanding and appreciating it and dealing with it generally, and we simply have to learn that through relevant experience. (Some of us would agree, but would add that, for anyone who has acquired the relevant skill, such phrases as "psychical distance" may have great value in focusing important aspects of our thought in ways that ought not to mislead anybody.)

Part of the tendency of the preceding paragraph could be, and sometimes is, simplified into saying that, now that we do have the notion of art, together with an idea of what it demands of us, what is art is what is produced and appreciated in the light of the notion of art: all art nowadays is self-consciously art, and whatever is self-consciously art is art, though not necessarily good art.[21]

In addition to the significances we have put forward, which in one way or another belong to favored modern orthodoxies and heresies, there is the view of Bernheimer (1961), unfashionable but passionately embraced by those who do hold it, that what is art is what is in a peculiar way special or sacred or magical, segregated and holy, relating us to the unseen powers of the world. Whatever fails to do that is merely entertainment or kitsch or at best residually art, art by association. Thus we find Maurice Béjart saying: "Dance is a phenomenon of religious origin, and then social, and to the extent that it remains a religious and social phenomenon it fulfils its function. Dance is a rite, sacred and human, and as far as it is a rite it interests me. As a divertissement it is not dance."[22] The people who hold the view we are considering would say that it may well be dance, but such dance cannot really be art. But in fact, all sorts of views are held about the

[21] The idea that what is art is what is done under the notion of art sounds newfangled and is. But in any of the particular arts it must always have been true that much derives its status from its context. Not every brush stroke in a painting can be artistic in its own right and apart from its place in the work; poems are made up of words, none of which is in itself poetic, even if there are some that it is inappropriate to use otherwise than in poetry. And by a short series of steps (there are no inherently poetic thoughts or subjects; a whole line may derive its poetic force entirely from its context) we proceed to the notion that almost any sequence of words becomes a poem, and quite acceptable as such, if it is set out to be read as poetry, with the reader's sense of poetry, scanning for poetic quality.

[22] Quoted in Percival 1971, 57. Actually, Béjart's ballets are not rituals of any specific cult, not even of one the choreographer has invented for the occasion. All he means is that (to dance artistically) one should dance as though one were performing some rite or other. I am not sure what is required, beyond a sense of sanctimonious self-importance and some dramatic lighting. Béjart's detractors would say that rituality without a rite is the apotheosis of kitsch—not religion, but the idea of oneself as religious. Adrian Stokes commented earlier on a "trance-like" quality in the free-style dancing of the 1930s: "A mesmeric kind of movement in Oriental dancing, Indian and Javanese especially, conveys something that is most intense. These movements, often sinuous, are generally of immediate religious significance or are, at any rate, expressive of direct and definite cultural symbols. . . . European 'Yoga,' on the other hand, is just trance-like and expressionist (and bogus) since it is so largely the product of the vaguest of emotions, of a more or less nameless overstretching or discontent often tinged with arrogance" (Stokes 1934, 113). Stokes here combines three different things: the substitution of religiosity and rituality for substantial rite and religious symbolism; the connection between modern dance and the belief systems, such as theosophy and nature-mysticism, allied with "depth psychology"; and the exploitation of a range of dance movement and expression that Stokes disliked.
Marcia Siegel identifies "ritual" with a style of action that has a liturgical air and associates it with the fact that "[m]any people think dancing has its source in man's spiritual being" (Siegel 1979, 49–67). She says in this connection that Graham's *Primitive Mysteries* "seems to be one enormous Hail Mary" (p. 51), but I wonder if it isn't more like a Hail Martha.

relations among art, dance, and the sacred, usually with no solid reason. One scholar held that all dance was originally sacred on no better grounds than that all primitive people dance and that primitive people don't waste time (Oesterley 1923)—but he said nothing about art. Malraux seems to have thought that the concept of art derives from sacred imagery that outlives its context, a fate that may befall dances as well as anything else. Lukács holds that art rescues such imagery for humanity by eliminating its magical contexts. Béjart seems to equate the polarity between the sacred and the secular with that between art and entertainment. I have discussed some of the variants elsewhere (Sparshott 1982, ch. 13); what is especially relevant for us, the relation between dance and ritual, will be dealt with in the next chapter.

The marks of artistic status and significance proposed in this section not only diverge but seem sometimes to be opposed. What William Blake despised in Joshua Reynolds was precisely that on which Reynolds relied for his standing as an artist. And this is not surprising. If artistry in any case is a matter of cultivating depth and range in imagery, cultivation in one direction or aspect is likely to be irrelevant or antithetical to cultivation in some other. All we need say is that a dance is not artistic, or not within the domain of art, if it evinces no concern at all with such deepening or extending. A given dance may not be elaborated or finished, not a vehicle of impassioned expression, not original in vision, and not affiliated with any established practice in which these standards are habitually observed—and so on, for as many immediate or mediated claims to artistic significance or status as have ever been proposed. But, we may say, unless a dance or a dance practice is strongly and distinctly some one of these, it is not art. To say that a dance is not artistic or not art may on occasion be to say that it lacks some particular quality or connection that one happens to have in the forefront of one's mind or that is adopted for the nonce as authoritative for one's discourse. But it may be to make the stronger claim that there is *nothing* artistic about it. The difficulty is that whatever makes it recognizable dancing is likely to make it, on some view or other, recognizably artistic. The solution to the difficulty is that there is no reason why a person's good reasons for calling something dance should also, for the same person and in the same context, be good reasons for calling it art.

6.5 *Conclusion*

Dance is artistic and partakes of art insofar as it has, or aspires to, or submits to be judged in the light of, or can be related to a significance of whichever of the foregoing kinds is adopted or is deemed acceptable by whoever is controlling the conversation. Debates—and, far more frequently, unelaborated and unqualified assertions—abound here, and it would be out of place to express my own preferences. I will simply repeat that, just as the nerve of the practice of dance shifts from time to time, so does the nerve of artistic practice, and they may do so independently of each other. An age of such cultural turbulence as ours is one in which a stable consensus is not to be sought. We look always for the meanings we need.

Whatever they may be, such dignifying considerations as we are discussing, though in principle applicable in the first instance to individuals and not to kinds, may be applied on whatever scale one pleases. One can apply them to particular dances, or to particular performances, or to the style distributed (as a scattered particular) through all or part of a dancer's or choreographer's career.[23] And, since in any performance art one may practice one's art continuously and without any self-contained work being produced, manifesting one's artistry in the continuous quality of one's activity, one may apply these considerations to the dancing and not to any whole that is danced.[24] One can also apply them to particular aspects of or moments in dance that is otherwise not artistic: one can dance, or find others dancing, artistically for a moment or in some respect—the word "epiphany" is sometimes used for such uncovenanted vouchsafings. The Saturday-night hop, we said, is not as such an occasion for art. But one may find oneself swept up into another realm of sudden beauty or significance or mystery, or have inklings or glimpses of such; or one may find oneself thinking of the occasion as art and so transmute it by one's vision.

Such considerations can be applied, in a secondary way, to art forms. Ballet or "modern" dance or "postmodern" dance may tend to be art because those engaged in them tend to impart art to them or to look for art in them: that is to say, because they have been developed as vehicles for art. One of the things that may make people go in for one of them may be the "art impulse" itself, a commitment to one or other of the characteristic

[23] What I mean is that, if a dancer (say, Isadora Duncan) dances in a unique way, the lifelong sum of her dancing in that way constitutes a single, recognizable item in the furniture of the world, no less than one of her dances does, or she herself as a dancing body.

[24] Susan Foster, contrasting the titles of Weaver's *History of Dancing* (1711) and Sachs' *World History of the Dance* (1936), notes a corresponding conceptual shift: "dancing" is a sort of thing people do, on many occasions for many purposes, a practice; "the dance" is a unified practice with a single aim (Foster 1983). Dancing is an ongoing activity; the dance is manifested in the achievement of dances. So there could be two arts: the art of dancing, shown in the manifestation of skilfulness; and the art of the dance, shown in the development and performance of specific dances. It's an important point, though the terminological peg it hangs on may amount to no more than the procedures of noun formation current in different languages at different times.

values of art, or even to the abstract idea of art value as such (these are the people who sometimes get called "arty"); and it would be strange if dance forms and institutions that attract such motives, and may even be founded and sustained by them, did not become saturated with the relevant qualities.[25] All dance, because of what it is and because of the range of interests it is apt to accommodate, trembles constantly on the verge of art; and the forms that are cultivated and criticized in the name of art will naturally be more often and more deeply significant artistically than others. But we need draw no fine lines and should erect no barriers. Histories of dance entertainment are full of performers whose individual skill and style has placed them firmly in the context of art—Astaire as dancer and Chaplin as mime are the examples we immediately think of—and may well bring their genres with them as recognizable vehicles of artistic endeavor.

In any case, in considering other arts, while admitting the contrast between what is art and what is not art, we habitually also admit continuity in principle from the humblest magical practice of utilitarian craft to the highest and most purely significant art. Why not in dance too?

[25] The converse of this point should not be forgotten: the routines of artistic success in the most highly developed genres become so highly specialized that they are readily imitated, and performers devote themselves to producing what has the appearance of familiar works of art. This phenomenon is one of those that go by the name of "academicism," and, as Clement Greenberg pointed out, it coincides with one of the best-known definitions of kitsch, in which artistic endeavor is replaced by work that is given easily recognizable features associated with "art" (Greenberg 1971, 9ff.). Because of their highly developed technique and distinctive mannerisms, respectively, both ballet and modern dance constantly run this risk.

CHAPTER 7

~ ~ ~ ~ ~ ~ ~ ~ ~ ~ ~ ~ ~ ~ ~ ~ ~ ~ ~ ~

Dance and Its Neighbors

WE SAID that what is dance is determined partly by what is nothing else: alternative classifications for practice will mark out certain activities as something other than dance, though in default of the alternative they would probably have been counted as dance. These will be activities that have something dancelike about them, either because they typically have a dancelike quality or because we think of them in ways akin to those in which we think about dance. There cannot, as we said before, be any such thing as a dancelike quality in general, such that all and only dances have it; but there can certainly be dancelike qualities in contrast with undance-like qualities in particular respects and contexts, as well as qualities that serve to differentiate dancing from activities that are felt to be related to dancing but unlike it. It should be illuminating to look at such differentiations.

In what follows, we will not be concerned with definitions. We will be dealing with typical differences, exemplary differences, that hold between our ideas of sorts of activities rather than between observed instances. And here, even more than elsewhere, we will be dealing with dance as organized practice and as art forms more than with dance generally.

7.1 Dance and Labor

I begin, perversely, with what is apparently no neighbor of dance: labor. Dance is characterized in Hanna's definition as "other than ordinary," and one thinks of this phrase as primarily intended to set dance apart from the workaday world.

A professional dancer works very hard, engages in exhausting physical labor. But the dancer is not engaged in a task determined by requirements imposed by some end extraneous to dance. The dance may indeed consist of performing some such task; but, if so, the task becomes dance because its movements either are abstracted from their laborious context and trans-ferred to a performance context or are considered in abstraction from their

practical end and considered for their dance values, their qualities as movements under some mode of movement analysis taken to be relevant to
dance.[1] (In the extreme case, a dance subject may be made of the earnest
endeavor to fulfill a task. But my only example of this is provided by someone who is not a choreographer or interested in dance, and who offers
neither us nor—apparently—himself any explanation of why it was presented as a dance.)[2]

The dancer, if a professional, is working in the sense not only that the
dance is hard work but also that dancing is the dancer's job, in the sense of
the word "job" associated by Hannah Arendt with *homo laborans* (Arendt
1958): it is what the dancer does for a living, for food and shelter. It is
characteristic of human beings that anything can be valued, prized for qualities (such as dance qualities) that are conferred on it by our way of looking
at it. It is equally characteristic that anything can be devalued, reduced to
a mere means of survival.[3] It is such reduction that the word "job" con-
notes.

Dance may also be work in the sense that it is the dancer's proper function in one or more capacity, what justifies the dancer's participation in a

[1] It appears that dances incorporating work-generated actions were a recognizable genre in
the great experimental age of theater dance in the first half of the eighteenth century. An
illustration in Lambranzi (1716, pt. 2, pl. 25) bears the caption: "Two smiths forge a nail,
on the musical beat, until the tune has been completed once; then one lays down his hammer
and dances *chassés, ballonés, pirouettes* and *pas de rigaudon* until the tune has been repeated,
then the first dances, the other forges, and finally they both dance with each other and so
exeunt" (my translation). The plain implication of the caption is that the "smiths" use the
hammers in the ordinary way, except that they do so in time with the music. A quite different
use of work movements in dance is the sailor's hornpipe, in which (in one version at least)
two dancers face each other and alternate sections of a fast jig (immobile from the waist up)
with sections in which some nautical task is mimed.

[2] *Running Out of Breath*, by Tom Johnson (1976). The dancer, who is required simply to
run until out of breath, has to recite a text (which she tells the audience is memorized) while
doing so, ending by saying "I am proving to myself that I can meet the challenge." Note that,
as a person, she is really meeting the challenge but is not really saying that she is doing so,
much less that she is interested in doing so—she is only *reciting* that. I do not know whether
Johnson intended this piquant anomaly.

[3] Ballet dancing as a job has been described by Suzanne Gordon (1983). It is the job aspects
of professional dancing that she describes as the "real world of ballet." The values for the sake
of which ballet exists are dismissed as unreal because they are unrelated to physical survival
and economic welfare. This extraordinarily limited view of what human life is all about is not
justified within her book; but it is part of the argument that in fact the economic exploitation
of dancers is so extreme that ambition, pain, and fear destroy the artistic motivation as well
as the physical and mental health of the dancers. As Tolstoy observed long before, the conditions under which workers in the performing arts live are such as to reduce their work to
the level of a job, however great their talent and devotion. Despite the truth in Tolstoy's and
Gordon's revelations, the emphasis on the job aspect of the arts disguises the fact that even
relatively downtrodden operatives may feel that the job aspects are not central.

wider setting. The dance may justify the dancer as achieving one of those valuable states of being by which humans define their humanity or as fulfilling a role defined as necessary by the society's self-image or supposed to be actually necessary to its continued existence or well-being. The dance may justify the dancer as sustaining in a magical or exemplary manner the processes of the world, as the dancers of the Hopi Snake Dance are said to be doing the most important part of a man's work, sustaining the cosmos in which the Hopi are an essential part. In these cases, there is no contrast between dance and work, between the dance aspects and the work aspects of what is done, because it is through the performance of the dance as such that the function is fulfilled.

It is misleading in such contexts, as in most others, to make "work" the antonym of "play." To do so is usually to imply that some set of human activities and practices is to be set aside as "superfluous" in relation to an idea of seriousness or necessity that is seldom spelled out. It usually turns out that everything is to be considered superfluous except animal survival and the accumulation of material goods (cf. Sparshott 1970b and 1973).

In a more benign opposition to "work" than that just considered, it was once fashionable to speak of "the play element in culture" (Huizinga's subtitle for *Homo Ludens*, [1955]) as imparting a ritualized character to many aspects of human behavior in all human societies, a character that in the end is to be equated with culture itself.[4] Such behavior takes on a partly ritualized character and becomes gamelike (in the analysis proposed by Bernard Suits [1978]) in that one no longer seeks to achieve the purported end of one's activity otherwise than through the particular set of means and operations prescribed for it. Such sequences of actions are gamelike to the extent that the objective is to succeed while complying with the rules, artistic to the extent that the complying actions themselves come to be stabilized and to be relished for being just the actions they are. And, insofar as they are actions embodied in movements, in being artistic they are dancelike.

Labor figures as a neighbor of dance not because of any of the foregoing relationships but because of the rhythmic character of dance. Rhythm, as Havelock Ellis remarked in *The Dance of Life*, is a pervasive feature of vital activity and hence is a quality of all actions that fall under the control of a

---

[4] The idea of culture as play, as the valorization and embellishment of life, has been replaced in fashion (conformably with current information technology) by structuralist interpretations of culture as a system of binary codes that serve as a medium for perceiving (and indeed, creating) the environment. But it is only in intellectual fashionability that the replacement has taken effect. The points made are quite different, indeed complementary: the "play" theory has to do with conscious cultivation; the structuralist theory has to do with supposed unconscious motivations, usually concerned with avoiding incest.

single impulse or a set of coordinated impulses. And that is true of most activities involving physical labor.[5] Karl Bücher pointed out, in a book once famous (*Arbeit und Rhythmus* [1902]), that many jobs involve repeated patterns of movement. Some do so in a very striking way, in that intricate series of physical movements have to be repeated in order to achieve a complex change in material organization. Others have patterns that are less obviously subject to physical constraints, but almost any job involves routines that recur—answering telephones, examining patients, delivering letters, interviewing candidates, auctioning hogs. Any such recurring routine, and any system of such routines, may be developed (and, by an efficient worker, always is developed) so that it is performed with regular economy. When it is so performed, it has a beauty of efficient execution that may be noted and may be deliberately cultivated and enjoyed by the worker (even if it is later transformed into an unconscious routine). Such routines may be developed occasionally or regularly into miniature dance routines or displays.

No job engrosses all one's attention, especially in the repetitious and mechanical parts that lend themselves most easily to such streamlining or embellishment. Nor can the demands such a job makes on physical performance usually be critical. The pace of a job must be set, if it is set at all, in accordance with the capacities of the slowest, and it must normally allow margins for error, weakness, fatigue, and toilet breaks. But, accordingly, the pace must allow for refinement and exuberance when those margins are not used up. Observe the symmetry here: the urge to economy of effort produces a dancelike elegance and neatness; the relief from pressure affords opportunity for a dancelike elaboration. When the pressure of a task is notably intense or notably relaxed, the quality of movement comes to the fore.

Work, then, tends to involve as part of its substance rhythmically patternable elements. It is, in fact, Bücher's thesis that in preliterate societies (*Naturvölker*) physical labor is avoided unless it can be given such a pattern, normally with the aid of the work songs and other musical accompaniments to which most of his book is devoted. The elements thus structured

---

[5] What is intended by "rhythm" here is the sort of strong order suggested as the first version of "pattern" in §5.522. Pending a full-scale inquiry into the concepts of rhythm and rhythmicality, let us say for now that rhythm is a perceptible orderliness in movement such as can actually be experienced as controlling the flow of that movement, in such a way that whoever judges the movement rhythmical feels able to tell whether continuations of the movement observe the same rhythm or not. It seems to follow from this requirement that rhythms be structured as Ellis says, because radical heteronomy would preclude a principle of continuation. But one would have to add that movements are said to be rhythmical in a strong sense when perception of the rhythm incites the perceiver to move in the same rhythm.

may, insofar as they are patterned, be dignified with the name of dance. But the job itself is not a dance, unless one's job is dancing. It is not a requirement of the job that it be susceptible of such patterning, much less that it actually be patterned, whereas such patterning in a dance is essential to its being the dance that it is. On the other hand, the external motivation for the dance (to make money, to placate the gods, to celebrate an anniversary) does not mechanically dictate the dance movements in the way that the task of changing a tire dictates what movements must be made.

It works both ways. In changing a tire, one has great freedom in the timing, sequence, and style of the movements one makes, but it is essential that the movements include those necessary to raise, loosen, remove, replace, tighten, and lower in such a way as to get the wheel changed. In a dance, by contrast, the quality of every movement that counts as part of the dance is restricted by the requirement that it be made in the way specified by the dance and its values. At the same time, however, there is no required product or outcome imposing practical limits on what will be effective. There may indeed be ritual or artistic requirements that the dance must fulfill, so that certain gestures and steps must be included, a certain sequence observed, certain stages gone through; but these are elements in the structure of the movement itself and, if imposed on the dancer, are imposed not by the proposed outcome of the task but by the dancer's knowledge of what the rules of the dance require. Again, there are limits placed on the dance by the size of the dance space, the length of time available, one's own dimensions and abilities and those of one's partner. But these are side constraints on what dances are possible, not objectives determining what has to be brought about. And we have to remember that, if the dance task is to perform some nondance task (as in *Running Out of Breath*, perhaps), that nondance task is dance only as a dance task. (That is a formal, not a material, requirement: it is a matter not of what movements a dance can consist of, but of what it is for any movement to form part of a dance.)

Bücher was not interested in the definition of dance. His concern was with perceptible dancelikeness in movements, the patterned qualities that made series of movements look as if they were being danced for the sake of the pattern, even if those making them had neither streamlined nor embellished them with any such quality in view. There is something fortuitous in such dancelikeness. Probably the task of raising a ship's anchor by turning a capstan can only be done in a way that is so coordinated in space, time, and muscular effort that it looks like a dance. But the end to be achieved does not call for those precise movements: if the anchor could have been raised by some other, equally efficient and safe, set of concerted movements, those could have been learned instead and would have done just as well. Only if the sailors refused to change because their way was the right way, efficient or not, would we be inclined to say that they had made a ritual of their work and, in making it a ritual, had made it a dance.

Bücher wanted to make the difference between labor and dance a matter of degree. Degree of what? There are two important possibilities. One is degree of intensity of dance qualities (as defined by one's paradigms of dance). Obviously, the skills that ballet dancers and other dance specialists labor for years to acquire are dance skills, and what they do in their dancing will in consequence be so saturated in dance quality that it will be dance in a way that other dancing and dancelike behavior will not be. The other possibility is that dancelikeness is a matter of degree of separability from a functional context. A rain dance is a dance and is the very dance it is, whether or not it is danced in hope of rainfall—dancers all over the world can show you their dances, though they may not like to. A capstan chanty is a song and can be played and sung as the very song it is, miles from any capstan. But the rhythmic movement the song measures is not a dance in the same sense as the rain dance, even though a bunch of sailors may pretend to turn a capstan or really turn a pretend capstan. A choreographer could include an anchor-raising dance in a musical, but it would not be the same thing. The point of the movements, their inner direction and their outer modeling, would be transformed in a way that the rain dance would not have to be. The rain dancers would be doing their dance on stage; the sailors would not be raising their anchor on stage.[6]

A more extreme case is presented by the roustabouts driving the tent pegs in Walt Disney's *Dumbo*. Their movements are drawn and animated as dance movements; they are presented as choreographed. But they are not shown as dancing: they are raising a tent. Although they are shown as if they were dancing, and although the artists have emphasized the dance quality of the movements, what we are being shown is how dancelike the driving of a tent peg can be and has to be,[7] a real peg that will hold a big tent. To us, watching the film and in imagination watching the raising of

[6] Of course, they *could* be raising their anchor on stage. The whole shebang could be brought from their ship—the capstan screwed to the stage, the hawser run through a trapdoor to the anchor in a tank of salt water below—with their accordionist to play the tune and their officer of the watch to give the orders. But, even if they didn't spoil everything by hamming it up, would any sensible person go to see them?

[7] It is only the gross quality of the movement that the animators suggest: the actual refinements of living movement, it is beyond their skill to show or even (except by luck) to suggest. In fact, the impressiveness of the scene owes much to the graphic quality of the presentation of the animated sequence itself—we are never in danger of forgetting that this is the Disney studio at its most stylish. Adrian Stokes has remarked that because the movements are thus stylized a Disney cartoon could be completely choreographed, and in this as in other ways comes closer to ballet style than almost anything else does (Stokes 1934, 20–25).

the big top, the movement has an interest close to that of a dance. But to the roustabouts the movement is the work of driving the peg without splitting each other's heads. That is what we see them doing and think of them as thinking about, and our interest is in the dancelikeness of their intently doing just that necessary thing.

To speak in a pleasantly modulated voice is to bring to conversation some of the interest of music. To write legibly and to place one's letter neatly on the page is to give one's correspondence some of the quality of the graphic arts. And so on. If such quality were not possible in everyday actions and attractive when achieved in them, the arts would not be possible. It is a sort of quality on which we may place a very high value. But it is an occasional value. It is not to be confused with the cultivation and development of such values in art, even when, as often happens, what an artist achieves pleases us less than such casual graces. But, though we may think that the arts develop out of such incidental perfections of daily life, we have as much reason to say that if the arts were not possible and if arts were not cultivated these incidental perfections would not be possible either. People do not have to reinvent for themselves the idea of rhythm and the ideal of beauty. They live in a world where the values of art have been cultivated time out of mind; and this is something they cannot help knowing, even if they never attend to their knowledge. When people impart something dancelike to their work, it is partly because they know they might have been dancing.

7.2 Ritual

At the annual convocation of my university, my colleagues parade in colorful gowns, Latin is spoken, students kneel in turn, the Chancellor holds their hands, an audience applauds. All this has a certain symbolic efficacy: it stands for the Conferring of Degrees, the attainment of certain privileges, and the certification of a presumed level of competence. But the degree can be conferred without the ceremony (the diploma can be mailed); if the ceremony goes wrong (sometimes the President recites the wrong bit of Latin), the degree is not invalidated; and whoever invented the ceremony had only aesthetic considerations in mind—to invent something pompously reminiscent of similar academic rigmaroles, to symbolize traditional fealties. Many religious and civic ceremonies consist of regular sequences of actions, in which the immediate requirement is the repetition and the ultimate determinants are symbolic and expressive. We call them rituals.

Some rituals are dances; some dances are rituals. But rituals are not, as such, dances; and dances as such are not rituals. Why not? Well, a dance is not a ritual unless it consists of a set sequence of actions invariably performed on an occasion that is recognized as calling for it. But not all dances that comply with these conditions are rituals. Our local ballet troupe does *Nutcracker* every Christmas as part of the seasonal celebrations; the Helston Furry Dance is danced only as part of an annual festival. Why are they not rituals? *Nutcracker* is a ballet obviously fit for Christmas jollities. But it is not really a ritual. For one thing, a ritual is something done: not the dance, but the presenting of it, would be the ritual. And the rituality lies in the sequence of actions, not in the sequence of steps. If it were a ritual, there would be some sort of ceremony in which (for instance) the spirit of Yule would be invoked or that of Petipa appeased. In the Helston Furry Dance, the Mayor and the Town Clerk would do something ceremoniously official. And perhaps they do. If they do, is the Helston Furry Dance part of a ritual? We might say so. But we might not, unless there were some symbolic efficacy that the dance in its context could be thought of as having (no doubt the magical renewal of the tourist industry).

The difference between ritual and dance is conceptual. Ritual as such is not dance, not because rituals lack dance qualities, but because it is inappropriate to *demand* any sort of dance quality from a ritual.[8]

The extent of the conceptual separation may be questioned. One could argue that, although dance need not be ritual and ritual need not involve dance, one cannot understand what either is without grasping some way in which it is linked to the other. T. S. Eliot, for instance, conjoined ballet and the mass as the "highest forms" of dance. He specified as a necessary qualification for anyone who would "penetrate to the spirit of dancing"— along with "a close study of the dancing of primitive peoples" and of danc-

---

[8] But suppose a dance is performed as part of a ritual. Is it possible then to say that the ritual is not properly performed unless the dance is danced well, so that dance qualities become essential to the ritual at second hand? Certainly. Reality is untidy: various situations occur and are variously described and judged. But to say that the ritual has not been done *properly* is ambiguous. It may mean that people have been sloppy and skimpy, as people with tiresome duties often are, or that we personally have standards that are not being complied with (it isn't Christmas without real candles on a real tree—it isn't that other people are sloppy and skimpy, it's rather that they don't understand or care about *Christmas*). Or it may mean that the requirements of the ritual have not been met at all, the ritual as such has not really been performed. I would think that a cruddy performance of a dance in a ritual might well prevent it from being done properly in the first sense (cf. note 11 below) but less readily in the third. In any case, if the ritual has not been properly performed, the dance has not been performed *properly* either. The difference is that the requirements imposed by its being part of a ritual could be quite different from those imposed by its being a performance of the dance in question. For instance, the ritual might call for a part to be played by an internationally famous star or by the mayor's wife, or for the dance to be performed without certain cuts that are usual in stage performances, and so on and so forth.

ing amongst "developed peoples such as the Tibetans and the Javanese," not to mention "a first-hand knowledge of the technique of ballet from bar practice to toe work"—that "he should have studied the evolution of Christian and other liturgy. (For is not the High Mass—as performed, for instance, at the Madeleine in Paris—one of the highest developments of dancing?)" (Eliot 1925, 441). Though I have never been to the Madeleine, I should have thought the answer to that rhetorical question was "Of course not." Eliot himself neither explains nor elaborates. Perhaps he is indulging in conscious extravagance, for he goes on to say that the ideal critic "should track down the secrets of rhythm in the (still undeveloped) science of neurology" (p. 442), which even in the heyday of I. A. Richards can hardly have been meant seriously.

To be fair, we should explain that Eliot was reviewing a book in which Cecil J. Sharp proposed to replace ballet by a "native" ballet "founded on folk-dance technique." Eliot observes that "you cannot *revive* a ritual without reviving a faith," evidently supposing that sword dances and such were performed as ritual rather than as art or recreation. (Sharp himself maintained in another work that the sword dance, ubiquitous in Europe and mentioned as early as the fourteenth century by Olaus Magnus, derives from the ritual slaying of a sacred animal [Sharp 1911, 9–36]). Eliot's squib makes sense only if he thinks there are two distinct kinds of dancing: art dance and ritual dance. But the position is not developed, and I mention it chiefly because of his influence as a propounder of doctrines. (I made some remarks about ritual and artistic dance in connection with Béjart in Chapter 6, n. 22.)

Whatever may go on at the Madeleine, ritual actions can be given aesthetic quality. In a Catholic mass, the musical setting of the words may even take on the character of a free musical performance, as it conspicuously does in those of Haydn. But this is possible (despite the Council of Trent) just because all that is needed is that the words be got through somehow or other, without necessarily being attended to. Analogously, it is quite possible that there should be a ritual in which various prescribed movements could be embedded in what was otherwise a freely composed dance. Are there merely historical reasons why this is not done, if indeed it is not? Perhaps. But priests among us undergo a long and specialized training that is not that of a dancer or a singer. The choir in a Haydn mass are trained as singers. Anyone could say the words somehow, and if a priest is offering a mass while the music is sung, his words and actions are no part of the music. In a danced ritual of the sort envisaged here, our analogy would be preserved only if the priest were someone whose *priestly* functions were *confined* to making the few simple but efficacious movements, however few or however many other movements he might make as a dancer.

Rituals have to be done right; the right moves must be made in the right order. But these are actions and movements conceived in action terms ("put the right hand on the suppliant's left elbow and say 'Go in peace' "), not steps defined as elements in a formal system. In many rituals there is a qualitative requirement that the moves be made decently and in order. But such decorum is not required in every case; when it is, it is a desideratum rather than a necessary condition. And decorum is very much not a dance quality, as Adam Smith pointed out when he contrasted the values of dance with those of social intercourse. Decorum is a constraint laid equally on all actions in social space, but the qualitative requirements of dance are proper to the context of the dance and are thus essentially *anti*-social. Certainly there is no competition in quality among performers of a ritual. In our convocations some chancellors do a more gracious job than others, are more benignant, dignified, courteous, friendly, and prompt. These variations greatly affect the satisfaction one takes in the ceremony, but they are as irrelevant to the ritual as the personal morality of a priest is to the validity of the sacraments administered. The variations in style and quality are more like the variations between different social occasions than like those between different performances of a dance.

7.21 RITUAL AND CEREMONY

We have been writing of rituals and ceremonies as though these concepts were nearly identical. Really, they are not, and it is arguable that they are not even closely allied. A ceremony is a celebratory occasion, a grand affair with public significance; and whatever is done ceremoniously (whether part of a ceremony or not) is done in a way befitting the public character of such an occasion, with dignity and emphasis. Ceremonious movements draw attention to themselves and to their own importance, to advertise that they are part of a ceremony or (if they are not) that whatever affair they form part of is worthy to be a ceremony. I may open a bottle of champagne ceremoniously, make a big thing of it, to mark the fact that we are celebrating something worthy of public commemoration; I may open a bottle of beer ceremoniously to indicate that it would be champagne if I had any. A ritual, on the other hand, is a sequence of acts, repeated from occasion to occasion, in which what matters is that the things done be just these actions performed in just this sequence. Their status as ritual does not depend on there being anything ceremonious about them, severally or jointly. And why is the ritual carried out? There is a special sense of "ritual" in which a ritual is much the same as a "rite," the *dromenon* (Greek for "thing done") of a myth about the foundational realities of the world, a reenactment of what was done *in illo tempore* (Latin for "then") and is always being redone in the sustaining of social and cosmic realities. Such rites are elements in religions: rituals do not have to be rites; rites are one special sort of ritual. Rituals may give rise to the feeling that something religious is going on, but nothing of the sort need be involved. For a ritual as such, there may be any reason or no reason. There need only be a recognizable occasion, such that the pattern of action be recognizable as appropriate to it.

Not all rituals are ceremonies. It may not matter at all how the movements are carried out as long as they are recognizably performed, and there may be no public or quasi-public occasion to be marked. Nor need a ceremony be a ritual, for the occasion to be celebrated may not recur. But ceremonies do tend to be or become rituals. They are movements to mark an occasion, so the obvious thing to do is what is known to be generally done on occasions of this sort. At the most mundane level, one recites the familiar words and rehearses the trite gestures of a toast, not because they are things that have to be said and done to secure some practical or magical end, but just so that everyone will recognize that something special is going on. Even in celebrating nonrecurring occasions, like the diamond jubilee of a monarch, one tends to cobble together fragments of such analogous ceremonies as royal weddings and coronations, silver jubilees and visits of heads of state; and these, because these are the sorts of things that are always done on occasions involving potentates, will impart a ritual air to the occasion. What else could one do? Whatever one does will have to be recognizable as a celebratory ceremony; although the context will help, people will want to feel that what they are watching has the look of a ceremony. It must be the sort of thing one would expect. The planners will therefore start by asking themselves what people will expect, and they will accordingly proceed to find out what was done on similar occasions before. So a ceremony will almost certainly turn into something like a ritual if the occasion recurs often enough, especially if it works, and ceremonies at regular intervals become rituals. A good ceremony is such as to *establish* a ritual.

7.22 RITUAL, CEREMONY, DANCE

Ceremonious movement is displayed movement, as theater dance is, and is displayed as having a certain quality. Yet what is emphasized is not the quality or significance of the movement as body movement or gesture but the generalized quality of importance or portentousness. Ritual movement, on the other hand, is not necessarily flaunted, but is determined by sequence and hence, like dance, by an imposed pattern. The pattern, how-ever, consists only of the sequence being observed and does not involve taking the elements up into an overriding rhythm in a dancelike manner or, indeed, taking account of any sort of rhythmic considerations or any-thing else that would make the quality of movement in the parts add mean-ing to each other and to the whole. Both ceremony and ritual are signifi-cantly dancelike, then, but neither together nor separately is it significant to them that they have any qualities important to artistic dance (or, for that matter, to any dance). And it is never significant to any dance as dance that it have any of the qualities important to ritual or ceremony as such.

A dance can portray a ritual or a ceremony. In fact, this is often done. As with "absolute" music, the problem of providing a convincing principle of organization is very hard for the dance maker to resolve without models to go by; so the structures of rituals and ceremonies provide useful arma-tures on which dances can be built. But then the "ritual" and "ceremoni-ous" qualities in the dance are, as it were, in quotation marks, and one hopes that they will be transmuted into dance analogues as thoroughly as any other mimetic mode.[9]

A dance can portray a ritual that is also a dance, as in Stravinsky's *Rite of Spring*: whatever choreography is used, the dance performed is not the same as the dance portrayed. And a ritual can form part of a dance: those thirty-two fouettés in *Swan Lake*, no part of the original conception but regularly done, are (like the second and third encores in the old D'Oyly Carte productions of Gilbert and Sullivan) a ritual event, cherished in a special way by audiences as a separate happening within the dance—even if they can also be justified as making good dramatic and artistic sense.[10]

---

[9] In the favorite showpiece of the Bucket Dance Company of Rochester N.Y., a church service develops into an ecstatic and spontaneous celebration, following the pattern of some Protestant cults. The night I saw it, the dance did not work well: the quotation of ritual at the beginning was too literal, and the translation into ecstasy at the end did not effect the desired imaginative transfiguration. It was as if the dancers were merely impersonating wor-shippers who got out of hand. But one saw clearly what the intended effect was. (I gather that the dance usually works, in the space it was devised for; the company was using an unfamiliar and uncongenial space, the night I saw it.)

[10] These ritual supplements and inserts go three steps beyond the *scène à faire* in a play or the focal or bravura point in a role—a tenor's high C or the leap in *Spectre de la rose*—in which for artistic or technical reasons one moment stands out *within* the work. The latter are there because they are part of the work as conceived, even though they have been traditionally singled out as isolated objects of attention for audiences or even for performers. They are two steps beyond the cadenza in a virtuoso concerto, where the composer has provided for the executant to strut his or her own stuff. They go one step beyond the episode in *The Merry Widow* that provides for entertainment at a ball, in which it is expected that the *divertimenti* will be something topical and outrageous. Such episodes, like the cadenzas, are there because they are part of the work, to which they contribute as loosely connected or aleatoric parts;

A dance can sometimes simply be a ritual; a ritual sometimes just is a dance. Every five years, let us say, the whole tribe gets together and performs the sun dance. It is a dance; what else? It is a ritual; why not? It is a ceremony—of course. It can be a ceremony, as a public observance tied to a season or a *rite de passage*. It can be a ritual even in the narrowest sense as the repeated *dromenon* of a myth, a danced movement reinforcing or reenacting what was done in the exemplary time. And it can be a dance fulfilling all the conditions laid down by Judith Hanna. The difference between the three is, we said, a conceptual one. But that means that there can be no difference for those who really do not make such a conceptual distinction. It would not surprise us to learn that the people whose culture included such ritual dances used one word for both ritual and dance and had no word appropriated to dances that were not rituals or rituals that were not dances, whether or not all their rituals were such as we should call dances and all their dances such as we should call rituals. Such people would not be debarred from criticizing dance aspects and ritual aspects of what they did, but they would not consider these criticisms as pertaining to distinguishable categorizations of it.[11]

Suppose every year the men of a tribe dance in honor of the year's dead or dance in masks before the youths who are to be initiated into an age group. An individual might make his way of performing in such a dance a matter of emulation in skill, in endurance, in elegance. The dance might even be a recognized occasion for such personal displays. But it need not be a matter of emulation at all, any more than the partaking of communion is among us (some people no doubt take the paten or the chalice more clumsily than others, but to take more than fleeting note of such differences in oneself or others would be grotesque). The dancers may all be just going through the motions, getting the sequence of steps more or less right, their

---

they are not separate enclaves encysted within the work. The fouettés and the encores really have no business to be there; everyone knows that, but insists on them all the same. The fact that there is such a progression as this, however, does show that a ritual character is a matter of degree, in a way in which being a ritual in the fullest and most literal sense is not. The paradigm cases of ritual are not exceptionally ritualistic or ritual-like: they simply are rituals. And, because they really are rituals, they do not have to be ritelike at all, just as a real king does not have to be the least bit royal.

[11] In Bali, it appears, where there are many dance festivals and there are ritual dances that all must perform, but "there is no spontaneous communal dancing" (Zoete 1938, 7), and consequently there is no such thing as dancing *in general*, so that "the Balinese, deprived of his tradition, seems to have no style at all" (p. 215), dance and ritual criteria may converge: "In certain old villages the Baris has more the appearance of a ceremonial *standing* than a dance, and it is often perfunctory, even slovenly in performance, like the Mass in some Latin churches. The fact of the performance rather than its perfection seems to be the important thing" (p. 56).

bodies painted in more or less the proper way, the masks bearing reasonable approximations to the traditional iconography. Not everyone will have had time to practice, or to do a proper job with the paint. Still, it is a dance. Our uninformed anthropologists will recognize it immediately as a dance, if they happen to see it. So long as there is a sequence of steps that could be learned, a right way and a wrong way to move, there is a dance. But in the convocation at our university there is no dance. The gestural components are so interlarded with discourse, so vestigial, and in most cases so elementary that any dance quality is below the threshold of rational noticeability.

Whether a ritual or a ceremony is also a dance or not, any values of eloquence or grace, though they will be valued when they occur, are a bonus. It may be, of course, that the best dancers are chosen to perform a ritual and give it a dance quality, just as an eloquent speaker may be chosen to give a convocation address or just as the precentor in a cathedral is a priest chosen so that his voice will give the ritual of divine service a musical quality. And at Oberammergau, no doubt, the principal actors are chosen for their dramatic ability, so that the Passion Play has a theatrical quality. But nothing essential to the ritual depends on the availability of such personnel. These shows really *must* go on. The villagers of Oberammergau vowed to perform the play; they did not vow to compete in any real or imaginary drama festival.[12]

7.3 *Disciplines of Meditation*

Something has to be said about such disciplines as T'ai Ch'uan, in which something dancelike is done in a context remote from that of dance. But, rather than entangling myself in the actualities of their methods, origins, or theoretical presuppositions, of which I have no direct knowledge, I will

---

[12] According to an established literary convention, altar boys assisting at mass may like to put on airs and imagine themselves as enhancing the proceedings by their demeanor. But, according to the same convention, neither priest nor congregation is likely to pay much attention. In fact, there is a conflict of values, even a confusion of genres, at work here. Acolytes have no place in the ritual as such and do little useful work. They are, in fact, doing a sort of little dance. But if they were to do anything really dancelike it would spoil the ritual. They would distract from the main thing, which is that the ritual should be seen to be performed. If the values of the movements made are visibly appropriate to dance, the ritual value is trivialized. Ceremoniousness, on the other hand, may work both ways: it may seem to enhance the dignity and solemnity and hence the ritual character of a rite, or it may be felt to detract from it by intruding worldliness. Both attitudes are familiar among us. And it is conceivable that a dancelike quality could be felt not to trivialize but to enhance a ritual as ritual. But this last combination of values is not so easily exemplified in our society.

raise what seem to me to be the relevant issues by talking about a possible sort of practice that may or may not be exemplified.

We saw in §7.1 that a dance may perform the serious work of establishing order, by exemplification, in the microcosm and hence in the macrocosm. Confucian music and dance did this. We have also seen that rituals may reenact an original order, reestablishing the founding conditions of the world by symbolically reentering the original condition celebrated by myth. And we glanced also at ecstatic dance—Dionysian orgies and Dervish spins—in which a transformation of consciousness is brought about in the course of violent or extreme movements that are classified as dances, and the resulting transformation is thought to have some metaphysical significance, actually bringing about an important change in the kind of entity that the dancer (at least for the time being) is. In all these manifestations, the dancelikeness and the dance status of the movements performed do not seem to be affected one way or another by the significance of what they supposedly bring about.

If the foregoing sorts of behavior were paralleled by an organized set of movements designed to transform (at least temporarily) the mover by setting his or her psychic constituents in order, what would settle whether such movements were dance or not? It could not be the dominance of a dance context, because the status of the context is precisely what is in question. Nor can it be the dancelikeness of the movements, because what is merely like dance is not, as such, dance. The most probable criterion is whether the ordering principles of the movement are dance principles. But this turns out to be hard to say.

On the one hand, our imaginary analogue of T'ai Chi might be dancelike in that the motions performed are "other than ordinary" combinations of movements best described in terms of the movement system itself—its steps and gestures—based on complex and difficult rules of order, learned as one learns to dance, their inwardness mastered in the way that novice dancers, after mastering the movements, find themselves turning into dancers. And the disciplinary exercises in question would have their effect simply by being the movements they are, not through any further instrumentality. On the other hand, the people who do this are not dancers, do not necessarily think of themselves as dancing or learning to dance, may not be at all interested in dancing. If they recommend the practice to their friends, it is not as a form of dance but as a means of personal adjustment. They wish to become serene, or whatever it may be, to harmonize themselves internally or externally. They are doing therapeutic exercises. From this point of view, what they are doing is a psychophysical exercise quite distinct from dance. Or, to take a different sort of parallel, as in Eugene Herrigel's description of Zen archery (1953), a mode of behavior once utilitarian may become transformed into a set of movements abstracted from their purpose, and these in turn may become valued entirely for the way they affect and reflect the inner being. But in the end it all comes together: the inner result is the same as the unwilled coincidence of the internalized means and the repudiated end. In cultures where such practices were widespread, the concept of dance as such would have no real place.

Yoga, T'ai Chi, the "martial arts" generally are no more dance than "aerobic" exercises are: neither the context nor the end is that of dance. At no point, especially, is there any idea that the movements are to be seen or to be enjoyed by oneself or others, nor is social recreation involved. One of my friends tells me that the Chinese categorize T'ai Chi as "play," but I do not speak Chinese and I do not how the Chinese concept of play meshes with other concepts. The movements are not performed for their own sakes. But it is possible that our imaginary T'ai Chi, unlike the others, takes on the character of dance because the governing principles are those of the internal order of the embodied person, corresponding to what has been called "the expression of emotion," and accordingly perhaps responding to a refined form of whatever the original motivation of dance has traditionally been supposed to be.

We may recall here the Platonic *choreia*. In the Platonic, originally Pythagorean, theory of all art, the music (or whatever it may be) is performed and enjoyed for the sake of its "beauty," its purely musical values. It is simply held that whatever has these aesthetic values automatically reflects, symbolizes, and reinforces a desirable order within the personality. How does this differ from the sort of practice we have been considering? Because the connection alleged by Pythagoreans between the rational relationships that operate in the art and the benefits it is to achieve is merely affirmed by theorists on theoretical grounds and is extraneous to the practice of the art. The art of music was developed, and continues to be practiced, without regard to what such theorists propose. But in the discipline of meditation the dance properties and the therapeutic properties of what is done are linked only experientially. If the harmony were achieved by doing things that felt and looked ugly, that would be no reason for not doing them. That is why it is inappropriate, even rude, to watch such people at their exercises.

One last thing needs to be said. Though there is no logical or functional relationship between the dancelikeness of such practices and their meditative value, there is a relation of fittingness. Is it merely sentimental to think that the movements of any practice directed at achieving inner and outer harmony will inevitably be perceived as beautiful in a dancelike way? If not, is it sentimental to think that this coincidence is a very important fact about human beings and the way they relate to themselves, each other, and the world they live in? Or should we say that if this relationship were not normal it is unthinkable that dance practices (or any artistic practices) should have been developed? But perhaps the answer is that the very concept of inner and outer harmony already involves commitment to the values of dance and other arts, that the objectives of T'ai Chi cannot be stated in ways that are aesthetically neutral in their implications.

When I was young, before I had ever heard of T'ai Chi, I saw from a hotel window someone doing his exercises on the back lawn. Two things were evident to me: first, that he was performing a very beautiful dance; second, that he was not a dancer and was not dancing. His mind was visibly intent on something that might not have been different from the movements he was making, but was certainly different from the dance that was formed by those movements.

7.4 *Sport*

It has been a commonplace for at least fifty years—in fact, ever since the rise of organized sport as the British version of the physical culture movement in the nineteenth century—that the spectator's satisfaction in a sporting event is partly aesthetic. In ice hockey, baseball, cricket, the various forms of football, and other team sports, the rules of the game impose patterns, often quite elaborate, that are constantly repeated. These rules, when related to the exigencies imposed by whatever is defined as winning the game, give rise to further repeated and elaborated patterns of strategy, in which systematic variations to seek an advantage give rise to a third cycle of regularities. Executing these strategies makes extreme demands on the strength, agility, dexterity and specific skills of the players, whose bodies and movements thereby acquire thrilling and beautiful qualities. A sporting engagement has aesthetic appeal and approximates to dance in the same way that any controlled movement of the body does, but in a more precise way as well. The pattern of such a game is one of variation within elaborate repetition in the context of a formal unity—precisely the pattern Havelock Ellis thought most typical of a dance.

A sporting event can be described in ways that make it sound more dancelike than it is. Such games are indeed full of small graces and triumphs that could be dances in their own right (and may momentarily take on the likeness of familiar dance movements and poses, in ways that are often exploited for purposes of burlesque). But a sporting contest as a whole is not a dance, and in important ways it is very unlike one.[13] The dominant aim of the contestants is to win, within or not too noticeably outside the rules.[14] If winning can be better achieved by graceless brutality, or if the balance of movement is upset by too great a disparity in prowess between the teams, aesthetic considerations will not be allowed to interfere. In this respect, the competitive context means that the actions performed will usually be more rigidly utilitarian than what is done in the workplace, in which as we have seen there is necessarily some leeway.[15] Particular players will adopt mannerisms to amuse the spectators, and perhaps to amuse each other and themselves; they may even be kept on the team as clowns. But these are incidental and exceptional cases.[16]

It was C. J. Ducasse (coiner of the term "endotelic") who most clearly stated the main relation between spectator sports and art: both are segre-

[13] Emile Jaques-Dalcroze, speaking of the aesthetics of individual variations within group movements, takes a football game as an example, but adds: "A game of football (with a real or imaginary ball) arranged so as to obtain decorative groupings and single players crossing one another, will afford the spectators quite a different kind of emotion from that created by a real match. It will not be emotion caused by surprise, but emotion of an aesthetic order, created by the harmonies and counterpoints of movements" (Jaques-Dalcroze 1930, 42). He seems to confuse two different points here. One is the difference between the suspense engendered by partisanship, with the interest taken in each movement as contributory to success or failure, and the aesthetic interest that can be taken in the resulting patterns of movement. The other is the difference between the movements thus engendered in an actual football game and the movements that would take place in a simulated game choreographed with decorative effects in mind. I am not convinced that the latter would have a higher aesthetic value than a real game (in fact, it would risk being ridiculous); I am sure its aesthetic value would be different. Probably the aesthetic bonus that comes with a serious contest, a series of unheralded delights, cannot be simulated or planned; even a demand for something as general as more passing and less charging might well upset the effect of earnest spontaneity. Perhaps the interest in a performance of *Running Out of Breath* might lie in just this balance between task and display, which the recited commentary would enhance.

[14] It is customary at this point to mention professional all-in wrestling, in which (one is told) this is never entirely true and sometimes is not true at all. Such matches are choreographed to produce an appearance of conflict and pain, and both the winner and the time and manner of his or her victory are planned beforehand. If that is what really happens, are we to say that this is an exception among sports? Or should we say that the performers are really dancers? I think we should say neither. The participants are more like mimes, portraying the wrestlers they would be if they were in earnest. The end, one gathers, is to appear almost convincingly to suffer and inflict pain, to deceive and to be deceived. It is essential, I take it, that the spectators be able, at will, to pretend either that cruelty is taking place or that it is not, and this must call for nice judgment on the part of the athletes.

[15] I am speaking here of the exigencies of the work situation. Actual jobs often involve pointless tyrannies, as though the employers had purchased the workers' souls and not their labor power.

[16] In his last seasons with the Toronto Maple Leafs hockey team, Eddie Shack fulfilled this function. The crowd kept howling for him, but he was never allowed on the ice until the upshot of the game was clear.

gated activities set up as ends in themselves, to be enjoyed for their own sakes. But in the sporting event there is a real, though arbitrary, end (namely, to win), and everything in the game has to be understood in relation to this. In an artistic performance, it is the entire performance that is the end in itself: the form the dance takes is not determined by the requirement that it achieve anything other than to be the dance that it is. On the other hand, artistic success is really wanted; success in the game is of no value in itself outside the context of the game (Ducasse 1929, 99–110). But that is too simple. To the players of a game, the successful pursuit of the end of winning may be more important than the victory. Amateurs may have fun seeing who can win; professionals may be more interested in playing well enough to stay on the team than in actually winning. But still, the whole form of the game is that of activity organized toward the goal of victory. Again, two dancers may compete in popularity, skill, or endurance; but nothing in the fact of the competition dictates the form of the dance as dance.

The difference between dance shows and sporting events comes out in the nature of spectatorship. The spectators at a dance are an audience, a collective of individual appreciators. The spectators at a sporting event are a crowd; they take sides.

7.5 *Athletics*

Athletics in general is a matter of developing the powers of the body in movement without any ulterior end, issuing in economical displays of controlled strength. The values of athletics should accordingly be the same as those of dance, or close to them. Athletic feats, like dances, are of delimited kinds recognized and current within a society. And dancers, especially ballet dancers, are athletes, whatever else they may be; their training is athletic, ballet exercises are athletic exercises (in fact, athletes of many sorts use ballet exercises as part of their training).

Athletics should be beautiful, and the beauty of the body in motion should be a dance beauty. To develop prowess in athletics requires the utmost efficiency in movement, and it has been a commonplace for centuries that such efficiency should yield a functional beauty of a purer sort than the adventitious charms of ornament. The whole basis of Paul Souriau's *Aesthetics of Movement* (1889) was the economy of movement, as measured in the first instance by pleasures and pains generated by intramuscular energy levels, but in the last resort as evidenced in the articulate will of the mover. And the exponent of this beauty was not the dancer (the art of dance has no place in his scheme) but, at an elementary level, the natural animal in graceful motion and, at a higher level, the athlete whose achievement reflects the intelligent analysis of a task and the synthesis of appropriate motion and crowns it with the accomplished appearance of prowess.

All dance is athletics in a sense, but not all athletics seems to be dance. There is nothing notably dancelike in track events, where the sole aim is to get across the finish line first. No such patterning is imposed here as we saw imposed by the rules of sports (in team games especially, but even in such interactive duels as tennis). The same is true of long jumping. In high jumping, pole vaulting, even hurdling, the dexterity in body-management required to clear the obstacles demands some intricacy of order, and so do the material exigencies of discus-throwing (but hardly those of shot-putting and still less of caber-tossing, where matter is gross). Among athletic events other than interactive sports, the most dancelike are those in which the excellence aimed at is not simply to be highest or fastest but to fulfill elaborate specifications, as in gymnastics, where prowess is assessed by judges on graded scales. Some of these we will examine separately, but let us think first about what may be an intermediate case.

Is a swallow dive a dance in miniature? Apparently not. But why not? Is it merely a difference in context and concept? It is at least that. Divers do not think of themselves as dancing, are not so thought of by others, do not train as dancers or with dancers, have no institutional links with the dance world. But it is more than that. It is obvious that divers are not dancing. They do not look in the least as though they were. And yet the values by which diving is judged are partly aesthetic: correctness, elegance, economy of movement, perhaps including preparation and recovery. Of course, they are judged for achieving these qualities, not for displaying them: the dive must be right, not look right. But the judges know it is right only because it does look right, and we have insisted that dancers too may think about doing the dance right rather than looking right. Nor can the mere fact that the dive is submitted to judgment be what makes the difference. One can dive otherwise than in competition, and one can have dance competitions (but see §5.5127 on "ice dancing").

One of the differences between a dive and a dance is that no internal rhythm governs divers' performances. They prepare themselves, dive when they are ready, swim away. But everyone who has watched diving knows that the preparation is part of the show, a way of "entering the dance," and the closing of the waters terminates it effectively. So why should we not say that the dive is in fact just like a dance, and would be one—only it is too short to count as one?

One might compare the swallow dive with the bull-leaping dance portrayed in the frescoes of ancient Knossos. In the latter, as in the former, the bull-leaper prepares the leap (over the bull's horns, in this case), performs it, recovers from it. Why is the latter a dance, if the former is not? Why is it not just another athletic display or a competition in strength, agility, and daring? The answer is that it is by no means clear that the youths of Knossos *were* dancing. We do not know what they were doing. Neither the iconography nor any literary evidence shows what sort of performance the leap over the horns was part of. I would say that it was not a dance unless there was indeed a continuing action in which the leaps were rhythmically integrated episodes. If the young people just stood around and took turns jumping when the bull's head was rightly placed or something of that sort, then what was going on was an athletic contest, or an ordeal, or an acrobatic performance, or something else that was not a dance.

A swallow dive is not a dance but a feat. Interest is focused on the bodily development and control displayed in a tricky physical performance. It has more in common with other physical feats, like drinking a bottle of beer without taking a breath or scoring ten consecutive bull's-eyes at six hundred yards with a rifle over open sights, than it has with dancing. Jumping a Minoan bull's horns could well have been just a feat, too. The archaeologists who published the material called it a dance, and the name stuck. And why did they call it a dance? It does not really matter: they were reminded of the dance portrayed on Achilles' shield in the *Iliad*, they had romantic souls, they had been reading Jane Harrison, whatever.

When physical feats develop into arts, do they turn into dance? Apparently not, or not always. When Spanish bullfighting was turned into an art by Belmonte in about 1910, it did not become a dance. The torero's feat of courage and finesse became at once more like gymnastics as the demands on physical precision became more exacting, more like drama as the risk and the appearance of risk were enhanced by the closer work with the cape, and more like dance as the matador made the bull his partner (a passive partner) in patterned movement. But it has never been thought of as actually dance, and it is not dance. The point of the matador's part in it is to tease and kill the animal at great risk to himself, and that remains the point. A pass or series of passes with the cape may in itself take on the character of a *pas de deux* if abstracted from its context, but it belongs to its context and in separation from that context would lose all point. It is part of the matador's feat to *make a dance of it*, and we do not appreciate his feat if we take him to be merely dancing in the first place. A dance is not a feat, though dances incorporate feats, such as high leaps and long strings of pirouettes,[17] and to perform an arduous and exacting dance is a feat.

[17] When the Bolshoi Ballet came to Toronto on their first postwar American tour and performed in the local hockey arena, the locals applauded loudly every time the men propelled themselves into the air. How crass! We should have sat on our hands until the dance was over and then applauded the artistic totality. We were crass because we recognized only physical

One can break into a dance; one cannot break into a dive. One can spend an afternoon diving, but the only way to do so is by doing one dive, then another dive, then another, into and out of the pool. However fluid the sequence within one dive (and we have seen that even then there is a sort of neutral time before I have collected myself for the dive and after I have begun the bit that counts only as getting out of the pool), the relation of one dive to the next is mere sequence, of no significance. In fact, if I made the sequence of my divings meaningful, I would be making a dance out of my dives. But I can dance by starting dancing and going on till I stop, without there having to be a moment at which one dance stops and another begins. That is true even if I cannot really be said to be dancing unless I can give you some good answer to the question what it is I am dancing. Again, one of the things that makes it possible to say I am dancing in a sense quite different from any in which I could be said to be diving is that, if my dance consists of a sequence of movements ("steps"), I would still be dancing if I changed the sequence of my steps, though I might not be dancing the same dance. Nothing like that is true of diving. This and things like this are what I mean when I say that dancing is an activity: one can be dancing in a way in which it makes no sense to say that one can be diving.

Probably, the distinctions we have been groping for cannot be made in any sharp way. Ultimately, the determining factor is the overpowering contrast in context and concept. And yet, one may feel that a dance as such is never an athletic display, that dance values are never athletic values. Why does one feel that? Partly because athletic values are strictly determined by the feat to be performed, much more so than in sports. There is no room for anything except maximizing performance in the relevant respect; and even those aestheticians who have extolled functional beauty have never supposed that a literally functional aesthetic could sustain an art. In old-fashioned analyses of aesthetic values, maximizing anything never sufficed for beauty, which required balance and a choice of form. Striving for a maximum belonged not to beauty but to the sublime and necessarily involved the infinite reach of the mind. Nor does one allow that there can be art where there is no room for expressive values and symbolic meanings, which athletics as such systematically excludes. It is not that an athletic feat cannot have such a value; but it can have it only inadvertently. The athlete who goes in for that sort of thing will lose points and deserves to lose.

The training of an athletic body is not the training of a dancing person.

---

feats where we should have seen the art of ballet. Actually, we were not so crass as all that. The feats were indeed remarkable. The men were strong and well trained. Why not applaud them? There was, after all, no artistic significance in their jumping so high. And the dancing, so far as anyone could see in that monstrous shed, was nothing special.

7.51 GYMNASTS AND ACROBATS

Within the domain of athletics, some activities are more dancelike than others. Most dancelike, to the uninitiated observer, are the patterned exercises of gymnasts and acrobats, which present us with routines of complex organization, sequences of poses. I know little about these but will say some things that, right or wrong, will indicate the sort of relationships I think should be examined. Acrobatics, I take it, is the display form of the sort of movement that in gymnastics takes its physical-culture form.

Before ballet form was fully developed, tumblers, dancers, acrobats, and mimes were, at least outside the official theaters, pretty much the same people doing the same sorts of thing: putting on shows of bodily agility for amazement and amusement. Similarly, the Stearnses (1968) explain how, in American vernacular dance in the 1930s, classical tap dancing began to turn into a "flash" dancing that consisted largely of tumbling and acrobatics (partly because it was no longer possible to find musicians who would maintain the necessary subtlety in the accompanying rhythm, thus reversing the trend described by Dubos in retailing the progress of ballet style under Lully). And, as athletic achievement manifests what Souriau identified as the purest form of the aesthetics of movement, so gymnastics seems to satisfy the basic requirements of a Deweyan aesthetics more straightforwardly than dance does: it celebrates the sense of equilibrium sought, achieved, sacrificed, transcended (see Dewey 1934). This equilibrium is indeed an aspect of dance, but not the essence of it, though Edwin Denby thinks of ballet technique as developed from the problems of keeping balance in motion (Denby 1949, 12). Gymnasts who lose sight of such considerations court failure: if they seek to impart a dance quality to what they do, they violate the canons of their craft.

T. S. Eliot remarked that the difference between acrobatics and dancing is "a difference of total effect. . . . The acrobat, however bad or good, appeals to the mind rather than to the senses. We admire his skill. . . . In *dancing*, the physical skill is ancillary to another effect" (Eliot 1925, 442). Dance values are to be appreciated, acrobatic values are to be judged. The contamination of values in nudging gymnastics toward dance seems to be in bad taste, like wearing frilly underpants at Wimbledon. But, of course, people did wear frilly underpants on the Center Court, for a time; such practices become the done thing, and then the thing to do. Hybrid arts of gymnastic dance are developed and may generate the taste by which they should be enjoyed; in time, the International Olympic Committee comes to accept them. What they are, I understand, is freely combined sub-routines of manifestations of gymnastic skill. What the competitors have to learn is not how to dance as dancers dance, but how to expand their sense of form to more extended combinations than hitherto. The trainers call themselves choreographers. But the routines are, necessarily, not generated by a dance idea (or any kind of aesthetic idea: the formal sense controls but does not generate). What offends the people who still object to this sort of thing is, as I said before, that the resulting performance appears to simulate a kind of value to which it can make no authentic claim.

Even institutional differentiations have limited effect in an open society, and conceptual distinctions are driven to take refuge in the half-and-half. There is nothing to stop people doing anything they can think of: to conceive a boundary is to envisage the other side and to imagine crossing it. Intermediate and mixed practices abound, and those who develop them are not necessarily less intelligent and sensitive than those who are scandalized by them. One of the most celebrated dance groups in recent decades, Pilobolus, has avowedly made sheer athleticism the basis of its most characteristic dances, developing routines and poses like those of the eighteenth-century acrobats we mentioned earlier. Still, it is hard to cancel out the effect of centuries of divergence, and it is easy to imagine that one senses a certain tension within their practice. Arlene Croce has some thoughtful sentences on Pilobolus, identifying and accepting their chosen medium:

> "Dance" is not what I would say Pilobolus does, and it is not what I would want it to do. Its art, which is based on gymnastics, is already complete. Gymnastics present the body in complicated feats of coordination without reference to what dancers call dynamics—the play of contrasts available between extremes of pressure, speed, and direction (hard-soft, fast-slow, up-down). A gymnast wants to get from one movement to another as smoothly as possible, and his rhythm—another distinguishing factor—is adjusted to his efficiency. He can have dance timing, but he is moved more by functional logic than by dance impetus. (Croce 1978, 214)

But although what Pilobolus does is based on gymnastics and avoids dance rhythm and dance dynamics, what it does is not gymnastics. Why not? Well, what determines the movements they make? The movements they make are for display to an audience (or perhaps, in the first instance, for their own satisfaction), not to build their bodies or to satisfy judges of gymnastics displays. They have developed the possibilities of gymnastics in directions that gymnasts are not likely to take.

Gymnastics lacks metaphor. What you see is what you get. Though its movements have names, the names identify the feats and imply the relevant criteria. They do not refer to any meaning the movements may have, such that an interpretation is necessary in the way that we saw Arthur Danto said was necessary for art. Gymnastics lacks resonance. If what Pilobolus does has such resonance, it may be because of what Croce goes on to say (1978, 215): "Their stage presence is different from dancers'—it is more sexually realistic." If that is true, we should say that an art based on gymnastics is an art, not of the body as corporeal realization of a human person, but of the body as an innervated system of weights and levers. The domain of such an art is explored by Paul Souriau under the title "the expression of movement" (1889, ch. 3).

Gymnastics comprises movements of body; dance comprises movements of a person. If so, the direct sexual presence that Croce found in Pilobolus reflects not the absence of meaning but the fact that what is meant is the coupling of bodies and not the interrelation of people. Gymnastics excludes the latter; it is not so clear that dance excludes the former, if only because people may lose themselves in the ecstasies of the flesh. And we may relate to this contrast the ancient opposition (to which we have referred before and will again) between arms and legs: the true dance of gesture, the humanly meaningful movement of head and arms, versus the mere acrobatism of the agile feet with which no meaning is conveyed.[18] "But to the Girdle do the Gods inherit, beneath is all the Fiends."

7.52 SOME SPECIALTIES

Dance is partly defined by differentiating it from specific things that are not dance. But that means that the way we understand dance in general, as well as specific dances, is governed partly by the currency within our culture of particular practices that impinge more or less distinctly on our awareness of our social and cultural world. Such a practice may affect our understanding no less decisively than some outrageous piece of nonsense or novelty that belongs nowhere but in the dance world, where we have to take notice of it if only so as to avoid it. Let us remind ourselves briefly of three such practices that are distinctly other than dance.

7.521 *Fencing*

Fencing is stylized swordplay, with its rituals of salute and acknowledgment, its numbered positions and parries. It is neither dance nor dancelike:

---

[18] I have not forgotten that the converse position is sometimes taken: what the hands do is mere mime, the pure dance is what the legs and feet do. And we have already made the obvious point that the whole moving person is involved in the dance, so that the contrast is specious. But it is so obvious that the contrast is specious that we should look for a meaning important enough to motivate it, which is the one in the text. People who simply try to reverse the values have merely failed to see the point.

it may be taken up as physical exercise and, though stylized, could be a serious preparation for duelling. Why mention it, otherwise than for its formal organization, its use of something like a repertory of steps and postures? Only because men used to learn fencing and dancing together; because there used to be a genre of mock combats (still in fact a special skill of stage management) mounted by the impresarios of dance spectacles and choreographed by the same people; and because, according to some writers, but I do not know on what evidence, the erect trunk and "turned out" foot positions basic to ballet were derived from the exigencies of fencing.

7.522 *Figure Skating and Baton Twirling*

In §5.4127 we considered figure skating as a marginal case rather than an affine because we were considering the efforts of some practitioners to make it more dancelike than it is. But one thing we did not mention is that, in the skating lands where figure skating is rife, there is a traditional stereotype (discredited in some circles but still powerful in others) according to which little boys play shinny, which is much too rough for little girls; so little girls do figure skating. But little girls also learn dancing, including a sort of proto-ballet, and there may be a tendency for the two sets of movements to become assimilated. If so, the main line of influence could be that ballet affects dancing classes, which affect figure skating classes, which affect, if they do not generate, competitive figure skating among adults.

The destinies of little girls are important because of a curious relationship that has become institutionalized between daughters and mothers, a sort of prefiguring of that involved in launching a young woman on the marriage market. Behind many a young woman dancer stands an ambitious mother, commanding her daughter (as the fathers of heroes tell their sons in the *Iliad*), "Always to come first, and to be superior to the others." The decisive importance of an indomitable and emancipated mother in the careers of the pioneers of modern American dance is emphasized by Elizabeth Kendall (1979). But the phenomenon to which I primarily refer involves more indomitability than emancipation. The idea seems to be to make the girl put on a fancy costume and do something conspicuous for which one can get a trophy. Figure skating is one medium for this vicarious display. Another is baton twirling or drum-majoretting—"baton" for short.

Baton is a flourishing subculture of its own, endemic in station-wagon suburbia (though I have no data on its social and geographic distribution). Is it a form of dance? If not, it is hard to see what it is; and, if it is not, it is hard to see what would be. It is an equivalent of the Platonic *choreia* adapted to the spiritual aspirations of a consumer society. But its institutional affiliations are not directly with dance. Participants do not think of themselves as dancing or as dancers, and do not regularly engage in other forms of dance (but that is neither here nor there, for we have remarked that dancers often confine themselves to a single dance form).

As with figure skating, the forms of competition and related behavior are those associated with athletics. In itself, baton is not so much dance as *drill*. That figures: it goes with marching bands, in which the drum major on parade struts for the band and the populace. Baton is a sort of drill that has broken loose from its moorings and been developed into a rudimentary dance form.

Drilling as such is not dancing. The emphasis is on uniformity in marching and in weapons handling, in which it is presumed that the uniformity and the associated qualities of precision and "smartness" are aids to military virtue as well as evidence of it. A corps de ballet is drilled in the sense that precision and synchronization in ensemble movement are inculcated as independent values; but the process is called drilling because it is like imparting a military drill, not because what is imparted is a drill. ("Could anything be less moving than the spectacle of fifty *danseuses* obstinately bent upon inclining the head in one direction and raising the leg in the other?" asks Jaques-Dalcroze [1930, 185].)

The reason why baton is not recognized as dance may be partly institutional and partly because the aesthetic values pursued are sharply distinguished from the regnant life-form and concept of art toward which dancers are orientated. Art has connotations of openness, noncomformity, and even disreputability that are alien to the paramilitary rigors of baton. One of the major categories of baton competition is, indeed, "dance twirl," in which the competitor works out an individual routine with her instructor; but, so far as I am aware, dance values are not allowed to intrude into these performances.

People who go in for folk dancing know they are dancing. Why don't baton twirlers? Is it just the habit of speech? Perhaps. But folk dancing is something one takes up as a recreation. It is hard to imagine a group of women taking up baton twirling. The practice hardly exists without the institutional framework, supported by mothers frantically stitching costumes and urging their offspring to practice, practice, practice. Twyla Tharp's *Bix Pieces* has a wonderful episode, at once funny and pathetic, in which the baton twirler figures as harassed adolescent, succumbing in a shower of batons dropped and recovered: it is as though baton were the nightmare from which the dancer was trying to wake up.

Baton belongs to the fringes of schooling, with interschool football and marching bands and general razzmatazz—a quasi-ceremonial, quasi-cultural complex of rivalry, display, and keeping-the-kids-out-of-mischief that plays a large part in our North American folkways without ever being adequately conceptualized. To someone who never went to an American school, it seems wholly weird; the natives find it natural but have no words for it.

And what about cheerleading, another aspect of this fringe complex? Are cheerleaders dancers? Their prancing is a rudimentary dance, as their cries are rudimentary song. Both form part of our musical and physical culture. But when we speak of music and dance, we don't mean that. They belong with clowns and tumblers; but clowns and tumblers have no real place in our minds nowadays, so the cheerleaders are on their own.

Female cheerleaders at football games wear skirts too short for the weather. Why? They are not such as to incite a crowd to cheer, and the accompanying physical exertions are not such as to demand exceptional freeing of the limbs. The legs, obviously, are part of the show. Similarly, both the costumes and the movements of the baton twirlers are such as to emphasize the secondary sexual characteristics of the dancers. In fact, although the institutional links of baton are with athletics and militarism, its aesthetic is that of body display: the movements are those of show-girl strutting and other erotic flauntings. That is understandable, if the proper locale of presentation is the football game half-time and the pregame parade. But the sexual significance appears to be ignored, or at least not mentioned, by participants and promoters. At the only baton competition I expect ever to have attended, the presiding judge castigated the assembled parents because many of the contestants did not have proper costumes but wore last year's bathing suits, which they had naturally outgrown. The judge denounced the result as indecent. That the whole proceedings were indecent in just the same way did not, presumably, cross her mind.

7.6 *Parades and Spectacles*

We associated baton with marching bands, and these in turn with parades. Float parades and other musical processions are a long-established tradition among us, often associated with annual festivals—Mardi Gras, homecoming week, carnival week. As a genre of show, they have been neglected by aestheticians and, I think, not much studied by folklorists. The typical form of these parades is a procession of wagons decorated and surmounted by fantastically dressed people in tableau, interspersed with bands and accompanied by clowns and tumblers. They are, of course, in no sense dances or significantly dancelike. But dancers are likely to play a part in them, and it may become a very large part.[19] (We have to remember that autonomous dance is rare, and dancers have usually been participants in shows of wider scope: they have to catch a toehold wherever they can.) Parades, as we pointed out before, entered into the court ballets of the sixteenth century and have survived them. The structure of that strangely popular warhorse, *La Douairière de Billebahaut* (1626), was evidently that of a parade. Ménéstrier draws the analogy with Chinese ceremonial processions, and his engraving of one of the latter is again quite evidently a parade of the sort we are familiar with. Ménéstrier's book on ballet was in fact a sequel to a more general work on public spectacles (1669), one in a proposed series of studies of theatrical and other forms of representational communication. As a Jesuit, he was consciously committed to his order's perennial policy of capturing the popular imagination in good causes.

The parade tradition clearly converged for a while with the separate tradition of ceremonious public dance, but it has now diverged again. Not completely, however. Bournonville and Balanchine both from time to time mounted patriotic spectacles that appealed to the same sort of taste.

Parades are not the only popular spectacles that have formed vehicles for dance without themselves ever taking on the character of dances. Elizabeth Kendall has noted that throughout the nineteenth century, theater dance survived in the United States largely in the form of the "spectacle-extravaganza," a genre, she says, to which, rather than to ballet proper, such entertainments as *Coppélia* and *Casse-Noisette* properly belong.[20] Ruth St. Denis, Kendall says, "began the lineage of modern dance in America" with "a pantomimic shorthand of spectacle-extravaganza with religious overtones" (Kendall 1979, 4, 12). And we have drawn attention to a late survivor of the genre, Ice Capades, as affording a vehicle for the maintenance, if not for the promotion, of dancing on skates.

7.7 Theater and Drama

Drama is not, as such, a neighbor of dance in general. There is no relation between the two other than that, in both, the participants are engaged

---

[19] In a football parade, the half-time entertainers probably, and the cheerleaders almost certainly, will take part in the procession. But they will not cavort; all they will do is wave, like the eponymous hero of a Santa Claus parade (whose "Ho! Ho! Ho!" is to song as his wave is to dance) and like the Queen of Canada (whose gesture of greeting is, as someone has pointed out, that of someone unscrewing a very large bottle top). The Canadians will never admit it, but we should probably think of her as dancing, in an understated sort of way.

[20] Diaghilev, on the other hand, wrote in *Mir Iskusstva* in 1902 that "*Coppélia* is the most beautiful ballet in existence, a pearl which has no equal in the ballet repertory" (Buckle 1979, 74).

in activities that are not everyday labor. The two are connected insofar as they converge on theater. But then the connection becomes very close: dance and drama as theater arts may combine, may be institutionally allied (as opera and ballet are allied, by the similarity of the demands they make on conditions of presentation), or may be conceived as parallel.

Shall we say that theater dance and drama are akin, in some of their forms, in that both present images of human praxis, but that one uses words as the main medium of presentation and the other uses gestures? No, let's not say that. The analog of drama is not dance but pantomime, dumb-show; and the relation between dance and pantomime is a separate topic. The separation is more radical. In drama or pantomime the subject is praxis, the engagement of the character or characters in a praxis other than that of the stage action itself. When dancers interact, they do so not as participants in a social relationship but as fellow dancers, even if the dance has a joint praxis as its subject. But what is this difference?

The essential space of the dramatic action is a social space, constituted by the human interactions of the characters represented. The spatial relations of the actors on the stage function primarily as mediating these social relations, secondarily as symbolizing them. If, as sometimes happens, the director arranges the actors in tableaux or silhouettes for pictorial effect, the purpose is typically either to mark the formality of the artistic treatment (its status as artifice) or to dramatize a moment of recognition or suspense. Here the visual design of the relationship is not essential to the artistic transaction, but in a dance it would be.

The difference between dramatic space and dance space has been most emphatically stated by Paul Weiss: "The actor creates a place in a single whole prescribed by the idea of a play; the dancer creates a whole from a position prescribed by the idea of the dance. Every movement of the dancer covers the entire dancing space" (Weiss 1961, 210). The actor, he goes on, is somehow "two men in one"; but the audience, in relation to the actor, sacrifices its independence to function as a "fourth wall." In the dance, however, "the two positions are almost reversed. The dancer is in the dance. He does not assume a role; he gives himself without reserve. But the audience, though it acts as a wall or limit of the dancing space, functions at the same time as the environment for the dance" (Weiss 1961, 210).

It is interesting to compare Weiss's interpretation with Moira Shearer's way of making the same contrast: "You don't have to work on an audience, it isn't *to* them. You are creating something within the stage. . . . When you act for the straight theatre, the audience is all-important. . . . Your timing, everything, is dependent on how they react" (Newman 1982, 109; partly quoted above, §6.24). They seem to contradict each other on the relation between performer and audience. Weiss thinks of the dramatic audience as inert, Shearer as controlling the performance. Shearer thinks the dancer's audience negligible, Weiss attributes to it the function of "environment" as well as demarcation. Is the difference only that Weiss speaks from reflection, Shearer from experience? Perhaps. But we could effect a reconciliation by putting the matter as follows. Dancers generate, by their visible movements and becomings, individual fields of force that extend outward indefinitely, partly reacting against the fields of other dancers and partly combining into a wider joint field, that of the whole dance. This field of force, of course, impinges on the audience as "environment." But the dancers are not, as dancers, aware of this, since the audience generate no such force, even if they humanly emit waves of approval or disgust. Dramatic actors, in character, generate a joint practical and social space from which the audience are excluded (in terms of the action, they make up the fourth wall); but the play exists as the action from which the audience are excluded, so that it is crucial that they hold actively in abeyance the quality of the action they are excluded from. The social system of the drama can be effectively sustained only by the faith of the audience, to whose vagaries the actors must therefore incessantly respond even while purporting to take no account of them.

In making these distinctions, we must not forget that both drama and theater dance are performance arts and thus open to and dependent on audience feedback in a more constant way than artists who produce artifacts. Dance performances, like other theater performances, are open to continual modification from night to night. A writer or painter may abandon a practice that has not worked, but a stage director can change something that is not working (Royce 1984, x–xi). Yet this responsiveness is still of a different order from the immediate interaction between stage and auditorium.

We have been speaking of drama as representational theater, of the sort once called "legitimate theater" and defined by Aristotle in his *Poetics*. But not all theatrical presentations of deeds and speeches follow that model. Adrian Stokes, in a typical fit of overemphasis, said that "[i]n the theatrical sense, all plays are spectacles or pantomimes to which words are the music—that is, so far as they are plays, something played in a theater, spectacles, so far as they are drama, and not merely the dramatized vehicle of poetry, doctrines, and anything that might be read in a book" (Stokes 1934, 12). And he adds that "[b]allet is the only pure form of the theatre today with any popularity." But it is not only in the presence or absence of words or steps that the differences lie. Equally fundamental is the difference between presentation and representation, between addressing the audience and affecting to ignore them, as well as between modes that essay a form of realism and modes that are frankly symbolic or even abstract.[21] One may tell and show an audience, directly, what one wishes to relate; one can move from narration to representation to dance to dumb-show to juggling to singing in any genre. In a presentation by the Peking Opera, for instance, it seldom seems either possible or appropriate to say whether the performers are acting, dancing, doing acrobatics, miming with words, or what. Dance and representational drama can be mutually contrasted as theatrical arts, where each is separately cultivated as an art form or simply as a practice. But a given civilization may not cultivate either, preferring other theatrical modes. Once such distinctions as that between dance and drama are made, one can always apply them; but it may be overpoweringly evident that what one sees in a given performance was conceived without paying serious attention to them, and perhaps without awareness that they might be made. Of course the performers could easily see or be brought to see such distinctions, once they were pointed out; but that does not mean that they would find them practically valuable or conceptually profound.

7.71 GESTURE

Dance, we have seen, has sometimes been contrasted with gymnastics as meaningful movement. But meaningful movements—beckonings, greetings, fist-shaking threats, courtesies—are what we call gestures. And Charles Batteux distinguished dance from the other fine arts as the art of gesture. But surely that is quite wrong. People who accompany their speech with gestures are not dancing while they talk. Perhaps what we should have said is that the meaning of dance movements is always some specific dance meaning (as Lois Ellfeldt suggested). Or perhaps we could say, with Fokine, that dance movements are a spiritualized version of gesture movements, extracting the essence of the naturally eloquent gestures of humanity. If dance becomes a practice when it breaks loose from human movements that originally performed other functions, where should we look for its base? In leapings and scamperings, obviously; in the rhythms of labor, certainly; but surely also in the gestures to which people resort when and where words fail.

People who gesture while they converse are not dancing. But often the movements they make could be used for dance or already regarded as dance. In my bilingual country, Anglophone politicians usually confine the

---

[21] In speaking of modes that essay a form of realism, I am not endorsing the unfashionable position that what is realistic or naturalistic can be objectively determined—a position attacked by Gombrich (1960) and, more extravagantly, by Goodman (1968). I am distinguishing between modes for which some term like "realistic" or "lifelike" stands for an accepted aim and those for which it does not.

manual aids of their speeches to a prodding movement like that of a pecking hen—it is supposed to look decisive and emphatic. But the hands of the Francophones dance for them; and the hands of the truly bilingual pass from dumbness to eloquence as they change tongues. The repertory of "steps" in the dance of hands may be small and unimaginatively used; even so, human hands are beautiful to watch.

Why do we never count these expressive movements as dances? For one thing, the gesturer is not performing them. Neither speaker nor hearer thinks of them as a separable component in the conversation, something that calls for attention. They are *thrown away*. There are, granted, such things as gesture dances, hand dances, and hand gestures (mudras) that form components of dances. But in these the unselfconscious repertory and rhythm are given up in exchange for a special set of movements appropriate to the dance in question. An everyday gesture, however eloquent or beautiful, would be out of keeping in a formal dance. What one could do with such "natural" gestures would be to photograph them and combine the results into a film of gestures. But the dance would have to be constituted by montage and other filmic means. It might be a dance in film, but it would not be a filmed dance; and what would preserve it from being grotesque or ludicrous would be precisely that the filmmaker had made a beautiful film of naturally beautiful objects (like Leni Riefenstahl's montages of divers in her film of the Berlin Olympics).

In the preceding paragraph, the word "natural" appeared in quotation marks. Since we do not learn everyday gestures as we learn a language, we tend to think of them as being expressive iconically, by nature, and not in the conventional and rule-generated way that languages are. Dubos, for instance, makes a distinction between "natural" and "artificial" gesture. The former "gives a stronger energy to discourse, and animates at the same time the speaker and the hearer," but it can seldom be independently understood. Even when its affective meaning is plain, it is never "sufficient to render the circumstances of this affection intelligible" (Dubos 1719, 168). Artificial gestures, on the other hand, could form part of a language. We are right to think of such gestures as natural to the extent that they are not part of a formal language; but we are wrong if we think they are precultural and would be understood as we understand them by people with other cultural backgrounds. Interculturally, they function as culture; intraculturally, they function as nature. That is part of the reason why, though they are necessary ingredients in speech acts and have speech acts as their normal context, we rightly think of them as native to a different domain, a domain that might fall within the sphere of influence of dance.

The discussion so far has failed to distinguish clearly between three sorts of gestures. One is the silent eloquence of the hands that reinforces speech.

It has no set syntax or other languagelike features, but expresses as music does, if at all, by the quality of the movement: swift or slow, slight or large, vertical or horizontal, smooth or broken, and so on. It has no set meaning, but relies on the meaning of the speech it accompanies and qualifies, in much the same way that expressive music (in Hanslick's argument) relies for its precise expressive force on a text or implicit text that goes with it.

This first sort of gesture, as the speech it should enhance becomes inaudible through deafness or competing noise, shades into a second sort: visible languages of the hand that convey meanings as rudimentary or stripped-down languages. Deaf-and-dumb language is the best known and most elaborate, but there are others, such as those used by bookmakers' tick-tack men. They typically differ from spoken languages in three main ways: they are used as inferior surrogates for ordinary languages; they are relatively simple, discriminating among a narrower range of choices than regular languages offer; and they are parasitic, mediated through ordinary languages on which they rely for their concepts (and the terms of which, when necessary, they translate).

The third kind of gesture is a performative symbolism, which cannot normally be given precise verbal equivalents (and, when it can, it is the words that render the gestures and not the other way round): crossing oneself, signs to invoke and avert curses, v-for-victory and up-yours finger signs, thumbs up or down, the circle of thumb and middle finger, thumb to nose or index to temple.

None of the three kinds of gestures is dance, for reasons given. But they can be materials for dances, bases for dances, or partial analogues for kinds of dance. They have, as Doris Humphrey points out, a singularly tough identity: any suggestion of bowing carries with it the whole complex of mutual courtesy, and, on the other hand, "nothing says bow except bow" (Humphrey 1962, 116). And, as this example shows, the restriction to hand movements is misleading. A roll of the eyes, a shake of the rump, a pointing of the toe have definite meanings of the third kind, and there is much body language of the first kind.[22] Can a person really talk in a straitjacket?

Charles Batteux, we began this section by saying, identified gesture as the medium of dance—not, we now note, a rival system to dance, but its

---

[22] Sign languages of the second kind are usually confined to the hands, though the hands may be related to other parts of the body. Meaning must be controlled, and the number of variables consequently kept down. Above all, there must be a single focus for the reader's attention. As everyone knows who has ever tried to give or receive a gestural message distinct from what words simultaneously convey, the main problem is not so much to make the message clear as to make it clear that the raised eyebrow, the bruised shin, the repeated cough, is a message.

medium. This was because dance as a fine art had to be an art of imitation, so that dance movements had to be meaning-bearing movements. Non-gestural movements could form no part of the art of dance, would be mere prancing and capering. But we have now seen that gesture as gesture has its own identity which is not that of dance and cannot accordingly even be the medium of dance. Fokine got round the difficulty by making dance a transformation of gesture, spiritualized or idealized gesture. What Batteux did was identify dance as musical gesture: music and dance, though technically distinct (music is the art of tones as dance is the art of gestures), are in practice inseparable. The integration of gesture with musical principles of movement effects a transmutation analogous to that for which Fokine relies on the choreographer's imagination and the dancer's technique.

7.72 MIME

One of the neighbors of the theater art of dance is the theater art of mime; one of the neighbors of the practice of dancing is the practice of miming. By "mime" here we do not mean the mimetic aspect of dance, which will occupy us later. And we do not mean the systems of conventional gestures that pass under the name of "mime" in ballet, which serve as translations of sentences the dancers would be uttering and which (as Joan Lawson observes) are strictly analogous to the signs by which Trappist monks ask each other to pass food at table (Lawson 1957, 139–140).[23] What concerns us is a theater art distinguished from drama by its use of gestures rather than words and from dance by its concentration on praxis rather than movement. These contrasts, like others, do not amount to exclusions: of course dances incorporate mime, of course mimes can use words. But in dance as dance the structure does not depend on the mime, and in mime as mime the words are incidental and do not carry the thread of the action.

The first thing to say about our distinction between dance and mime as separate arts or practices is that most writers on mime and dance show no interest in it or even appear unaware of it. Lawson (1957) does not distinguish systematically between conventional gestures, dance mimesis, and the art form of mime; it seems not to occur to her that the scope of her discourse includes separate art forms that might have different principles. Rudolf Laban and Lisa Ullmann (1950) make a distinction between the movement principles of pure dance and of dance-mime, but not between those of dance-mime and mime that is not dance. Even in Bari Rolfe's

---

[23] The signs are analogous, but the way they are formed is not, nor is the way they are used. See Royce's development (1984, 17–19) of Lawson's discussion.

collection of texts on miming (1981), almost none of the authors take explicit note of the distinction, though it is often implicit in what they say (the exception is Etienne Decroux, one of the few who are in fact mimes by explicit profession). I was almost beginning to think I was mistaken in making this distinction, when along came Anya Royce's new book, exploring it with sensitive and erudite brilliance. But her main contrast is between ballet and Marceau's mime, not between dance and mime in general, and she is inclined to think that Decroux's mime may be further from Marceau's than it is from some modern dance (Royce 1984, ch. 4, esp. 81–83). It is not that the other authorities have denied the distinction or downplayed its importance; they have simply failed to make it systematically and, in most cases, to make any distinction among practices and art forms at all. In what follows, I have taken little account of Royce's work: to have plumbed her depths and retraced her intricacies would have obliterated the simple contours I wished to trace.

Mime theater is associated with puppet theater and, like it, has a long and complex history. Fragments of this were already assembled by Isaac D'Israeli in an essay, "The Pantomimical Characters" (1859b): mimic theater is related to the problems of making oneself heard in noisy theaters and large assemblies and, in the formative years of our theatrical institutions, to the royal monopolies in London and Paris that confined spoken drama to a few licensed houses. (D'Israeli, like many others, also associates mime theater with the copiousness and explicitness of gestures in Italy, and especially with the Neapolitan way of virtually conducting one's conversations in dumb-show.)

By "mime" in this context, one means, approximately, an action or system of action whereby the movements of the agent's body as a whole represent a different action by producing what is recognizable as a likeness of it. The body is engaged as a whole: one does not normally mime or mimic with a specific part of one's body; one simply mimes or mimics, even if in fact only part of one's body is directly involved in the mimicry. And what one mimics or mimes is an action that differs significantly from the action one is performing. One cannot mimic a man walking by being a man and walking. But the action need not be generically or specifically different. One can mime oneself walking as one walked on a specific occasion or as one walks in specific circumstances, so long as the occasion or the circumstances do not at present obtain. Or one can mime another person doing just what one is doing in mimicry, provided that the target of the mime is that person's particular way of doing it and that it is recognizably a way not one's own. Very often, the miming consists of performing the body movements of some action that involves interaction with other bodies, or tools, or material objects and using those movements to suggest the presence of the bodies, tools, or objects in question.

Miming is not impersonating. Its target is always the action or the person in action, never the person who merely happens to be acting thus and might be acting otherwise—Sartre (1940) has some eloquent pages on the very different art of the impersonator, who evokes an absent person as agent for the very actions the impersonator is performing.[24] An impersonator and a mime might for a while do the same thing and have the same target, but the point would be different insofar as what they were doing was established as miming and impersonation respectively.

Mime typically exaggerates and often caricatures. The motivation of the supposed action is absent, so its perceptible character has to be emphasized to compensate. Because of that, the typical effects of mime are comic and pathetic. In fact, if they were not, mime would be intolerably boring, as Woody Allen suggests (Rolfe 1981, 220–224) and Royce affirms (1984, 28), though her statement that such dance and mime would be "as dull and uninteresting as the reality they portray" takes too readily for granted that the commonplace cannot be transfigured. The exaggeration follows from the task of making likeness or difference emphatic. To mime effectively, one does not produce the closest possible likeness of the target. One emphasizes the way in which one's actions are typically like those of, for instance, a man carrying a ladder—a man carrying a ladder does not need to look like a man carrying a ladder; he is carrying one, no matter how he looks—or the way in which someone walking through deep snow differs from someone walking *not* through deep snow.

Mime has a tendency to take on a dancelike character, for at least five reasons. First, what is done is governed by the idea of the mimed action, not by its actuality; it depends on a movement idea, as dances do, and does not respond to the exigencies of a situation instrumentally or practically defined. Second, the mime is trained in movement, and the movements of any highly skilled and trained performer may develop an affinity with those of any other highly skilled and trained performer. Third, the exaggeration and emphasis by which mimetic meaning is conveyed are typically, and perhaps have to be, controlled by stylization in a system of enhanced movement—such clarification and magnification of gesture within a system parallel the idealization of gesture that Fokine divined in (or demanded of) dance. Fourth, in the absence of serious occasion for the mimed action to

---

[24] D'Israeli (1859b) reminds us that the "mimes" in Roman triumphs and funerals were in fact impersonators, not pantomimes. But they were not impersonators in the way that Rich Little is an impersonator: they simply figured in the procession to stand for known individuals, in the same way that an employee in a red suit stands for Santa Claus in a department store's Santa Claus parade.

impose its necessary rhythm, an independent, quasi-musical rhythm tends to take over (though we shall see that Decroux denies this). In fact, mimes often use musical accompaniments, partly to drown out irrelevant sounds and partly to sustain interest by preventing an aural vacuum, as in the silent movies. In theory, as necessarily in the movies, the musical accompaniment merely follows the action and does not control or even affect it; but since the mime can hear the music it is unlikely that these priorities will be strictly preserved. And fifth, the parallel practice of mime-dance exists and is known to exist; the conceptual confusion that Lawson exemplifies presumably reflects a practical mixture of genres. Perhaps after all I am approaching this matter from the wrong end. It is more natural to say with Royce that dance and mime are on a continuum, so far as their methods go, and that it is the recognition that we maintain two distinct genres that makes audiences uneasy when the center lines on too many of these continua are simultaneously transgressed (Royce 1984, 83).

"In a fine character ballet," says Adrian Stokes (1935,53), "the dancer lends the very facility of his art in movement to the character that he plays, whether it be the part of a toy or of an enchanted swan," but the verbal brilliance of an actor or a dramatist cannot be used in the same way in drama. Stokes may be right, though G. B. Shaw's creation of the dustman in *Pygmalion* makes me wonder a little; but one of the values of mime is achieved in the way Charlie Chaplin lent to his characterizations a personal grace that was not that of the "little fellow" represented, not something in the normal repertory of an actor, but also not that of a dancer. It was a quality of pure mime, an illumination of action from within. Buster Keaton (and other masters of the silent screen) did something analogous, but not quite the same (he converted the characters he played into fallen angels somehow capable of sustaining his own beauty through their own adventures). What Chaplin did was derived from the music-hall comedians of his youth, who shared and adapted the movement traditions of circus clowns. We have, then, a variety of movement arts, essentially taking the form of "turns," that are neither acting nor dance but belong to this alternative tradition of mime, an enhanced and poeticized presentation, neither of personality nor of body movement, but precisely of action as taking on an exemplary nature of its own.

For us, mime has above all come to be represented by an art form distinct from any of those mentioned above but manifestly belonging to the same genus: the tradition of masked mime that develops from the commedia dell'arte, a stylized theatrical form involving great precision and virtuosity in movement, persisting with its stock characters of Pierrot and Harlequin through the nineteenth century and revived in our own day in the white-face mime of Etienne Decroux and his students, Marcel Marceau and the young Jean-Louis Barrault. Why is that not a dance form?

Why is it essential that mimes in the commedia dell'arte tradition wear masks, whereas dancers in European traditions are usually maskless? Séverin, one of the last of the traditional Pierrots, said that "the naked face would introduce a discord into the symphony of white" (Rolfe 1981, 70). The aim must be to homogenize, but also to depersonalize: the mime is present neither as dancing body nor as acting person, but as element in or bearer of the abstract form of action, and a human face is inescapably the face of somebody. One thinks of the way acrobats are depicted in eighteenth-century drawings, with their faces typically shown as though themselves masks of an inexpressive beakiness. They are dehumanized. Marceau's "Bip" is disembodied, but remains human.

In contrast with the ways mimes move, consider Baryshnikov dancing Petrushka, as he appeared in a PBS video presentation. Each movement is full of expressive pathos. But each movement is unmistakably that of a dancer. The movement keeps its own time, its own form; at every transition, the pose is exquisite in itself. The movement realizes an ideal choreography. A mime's movements are also choreographed, as it were each pose calculated. But the calculation is orientated toward eloquence, a visible expressiveness. Baryshnikov's movements are continuous with his other movements in the dance and those of the other dancers: at any moment, he could move without absurdity into abstract dance. Marcel Marceau would look absurd if he began dancing; I am not so sure that he could not, without absurdity, modulate into a dramatic performance. They are extrapolating from different systems. As Royce says,

> The goal of classical ballet, with its highly stylized and patterned movements, is not to replicate ordinary movement but to present an art form that goes far beyond the ordinary. . . . Mime, by contrast, is a form of gesture and movement that has as its goal the presentation of the ordinary, and it must have the ring of authenticity. (Royce 1984, 11)

The point can be made less clearly with the help of Laban and Ullmann (1950, 17). Self-orientation in the maze of motivation, they say, gives rise to "movement-thinking," the integration and organization of movement without conceptualized purpose, according to its own internal principles. A mime's action, we said, though not motivated otherwise than by the intention of engaging in mime, makes the motivation of a targeted action its principle of organization. I would add myself that a movement generated and governed by movement-thinking can still be modified mimetically, since there is nothing to impose a rival pattern on the particular form

337

a dance movement may take; and a mimic movement can be moved toward internal order by musical accompaniment (as we said before) without for that reason becoming a product of movement-thinking. In the last resort, however, as Edwin Denby remarked, the time taken by an action in dance-mime must be determined by the shape of the contextual dance rhythm, or it will fall out of dance; but in mime proper it must take a time determined by the real time needed to accomplish it (quoted by David Michael Levin in Copeland and Cohen 1983, 135–136).

The most celebrated attempt to give a general account of the difference between what the white-face mime does and what a dancer does is an interview that Etienne Decroux gave to Eric Bentley (Copeland and Cohen 1983, 210–215). But, as we have fastened on only one sort of mime, so Decroux fastens on one sort of dance, classical ballet. (He was, as Royce points out, originally a ballet dancer in revolt against ballet, the only dance he knew; the fact that modern dance was similarly in revolt against ballet is part of what accounts for the perceived similarity between some of what Decroux did and some modern dance [Royce 1984, 82].) Dance is music-based; mime is action-based. Dance is governed by symmetry (the requirements of pattern), mime by asymmetry (the requirements of tasks). "Dance is ecstatic and vertical, Mime earthy and horizontal" (that is: dance is emotion-centered, mime is praxis-centered). "The dancer works with the leap, the mime with the walk" (that is: dances are made up of steps, movement units; mimes are made up of praxis units). "A dancer is a man taking a walk—because his energies are not used up by his work—whereas a mime is a man walking *somewhere*, to a destination." And the dancer is trained not to make the movements that show how the body does its work; whereas "your mime is trained to display, exploit, and accentuate them, to give them style." And so, "Each art has its own territory. Pantomime and dance are opposites."

The fact that Decroux contrasts mime with ballet, not modern dance or dance in general, reflects a fact alleged by R. G. Davis: Decroux "spoke in mimetic theory and performed in pantomimic form" (Rolfe 1981, 207–210). Pantomime, in Davis's usage, is what Marceau does: evoking imaginary objects in a self-generated act. Mime proper is what Chaplin does: really interacting with real props that become "symbols in a dramatic relationship." And Davis is surely right. As contrasted with Chaplin's mime, Marceau's is on the verge of dance; it is only by contrast with the most artificial of dance forms that it can be thought of as having the earthiness that Decroux assigns to it. Davis confuses the problem, however, by making a moral issue of it. Object-oriented mime in the Chaplin mode is identified with Stanislavsky's method of stage training, in which an actor's performance is to be built up from detailed imagining of a situation in all its concreteness, which Davis thinks of as a good and profound way of doing things and one supported by the deep science of psychology. Pantomime in the Marceau manner, on the other hand, is associated with the sort of actor who builds up a performance from its constituents of speech and gesture, which is a superficial and frivolous method. This seems to me to confuse the principles on which a work is constructed with the procedures by which it was put together; but it suggests, perhaps, that the relations between dance and mime are more intricate than we have suggested.

The relations between dance and mime have always been a source of confusion. We saw in Chapter 1 that the Roman pantomime was classed as dance by the commentators on whom Lucian and Athenaeus drew, and for ideological purposes it was classed with the round dances and war-dances of hallowed antiquity. But, *at the same time*, its practitioners were extolled for their supposed ability to convey, by their miming, legal and philosophical theories and arguments. What could they possibly have done that would have justified *both* the latter claim *and* the former affiliation? We do not know, and we do not know whether we should call what they did "dancing." But for a long time people tried to do something that could be described in some such way, partly in pure emulation and partly in the hope of making dance academically respectable. The result was a theoretical mess and would have been practically disastrous but for the fact that, when it comes to the crunch, one has to do something that one's imagination can envisage, one's technique encompass, and one's public tolerate. Some of Marceau's more abstract mime is confessedly difficult (Royce 1984, 104–105); but none of it is *impossible*.

7.73 HAPPENINGS AND OTHER NON-EVENTS

We have remarked before that the recurrent rediscoveries of the avant-garde in the twentieth century have given a new importance to contextually defined art. Every few years a new wave of young hopefuls discovers that there is nothing to prevent them giving the name of whatever art they practice to anything they feel like doing. Their ignorance of history and the tendency for trivial follies to pass into oblivion mean that what they feel like doing is often much the same as what a previous generation of young hopefuls felt like doing; but not always. As part of this ferment, people whose background is in the visual arts have produced, among other things, miscellaneous "pieces" involving people in motion. The people who produced "happenings" in the 1960s (typically wandering around with toilet paper, stepladders, and leotards) might be from the fringes of the theater world, from "art" schools generically, or from dance. But what they came up with did not count as dancing: it provided, rather, a magma of movement art with which dance of various sorts could be variously contrasted. At the same time, similarly adventurous people in the dance world claimed the same privilege and ventured into the same terrain (Percival 1980, 89; cf. Banes 1983).

We said before that whether something counted as dance or not might be a matter of whether it was done under the auspices of a dance organization or a music organization or whatever else might be putting it on; but we also asserted that such merely adventitious associations must be unstable. Let us tighten things up slightly, in terms of the present chapter. Can we not detect or invent such a contrast here as we found between dance and the various forms of mime? The point of a "happening" as such, we will suggest, is never a dance point, its method of organization (including randomization) would never be a distinctively dance method; whereas the adventurers from the dance world might well be exploiting dance motive and extending dance method. We cannot, of course, use the specific contrasts we used in discussing mime: we are supposing that our pioneers (or nature-ramblers) have repudiated all that. They are exploring a new set of affinities and differentiations. Only, what?

Typically, the theater people and visual artists who went in for happenings were doing concept art. They had the idea of a sort of meeting, a sort of event, a sort of shape and provided for something of that sort to happen. But there is something rather awkward in the notion of a concept dance, in that dance as the body-centered art tends to be nonconceptual; at least, such concepts as are central to it are ideas of movement types and movement schemes. The impatience that made painters abandon the plane surface, sculptors give up on chippables and moldables, musicians leave the gamut behind cannot really possess dancers. Dancers have nothing to repudiate but themselves: there is nowhere else for their intuitions to go. Practitioners of other arts can say, "Let us do this instead," and what they do may be something that does not involve the traditional tools and materials of their craft. But dancers are themselves the tools and materials of their craft. It is not that what Clayton Clevarass did is impossible, or even that it is not worth doing. It is only that such doings are not related to the internal pressures of dance in the same way that they may be to the internal pressures of painting. In the specific (and exemplary) manifestation narrated by Banes (1983), we recall, the part played by the happening-artist's directions was taken by something called a "score," which was to be followed by dancers in a way analogous to that in which musicians follow scores prepared by John Cage—not by applying conventional musical techniques of reading and interpreting, but by responding in a way effectively controlled by whatever the score might say, *in the light of their professional responsibility*. The challenge might be precisely that of responsibly expanding one's sense of responsibility.

CHAPTER 8

~ ~ ~ ~ ~ ~ ~ ~ ~ ~ ~ ~ ~ ~ ~ ~ ~ ~

What Dance Is

A CHAPTER on what is and what is not dance does not tell us directly what dance is; it only distinguishes dances from other things. Explaining the difference between cats and marmosets doesn't tell us anything about what cats are; defining a cat tells us rather little. To know what a cat is, we have to know cats. All the same, we may feel that there must be something that we could tell people who did not know cats, to let them know what they were missing. So, granted that we all know what dance is and that this knowledge cannot be encapsulated in any summary statement, we cannot quite rid ourselves of the yearning for something to say about what dance is *really*. Philosophers spend years training themselves not to ask such questions by learning why they can have no true answers. But, so long as one has thoroughly learned that lesson, there is no reason not to go back and ask and answer the same old questions.

Trying to say what dance really is is sometimes called the "ontology" of dance. We have been doing it all along: dance is a practice of the sort we have been exploring, related in such ways as we have been suggesting to the other things we are relating it to. And what we have said provides absolutely conclusive reasons for not saying in general terms what dance is. These reasons are of several sorts: the relation between life-forms and institutions, the instability and contestability of identifiable "nerves" of practices, the interchangeability of the metaphorical and the literal as between cosmic and human contexts, the different locations and relations of concepts like that of dance in the thought-worlds of different cultures. But the ontological question remains, in two forms. First, we may feel that something more *satisfying* needs to be said about how and why everything we have found it necessary to discuss holds together. And, second, nothing stops us asking the question "What *is* this?" about specific dances in specific contexts, and finding a general importance in the answers. This chapter resumes some such questions and contexts and tries to carry them further. But we must remember that nothing said here can supersede or replace what has been said already. Ontological questions satisfy a special kind of hunger. They are no more informative or illuminating than other sorts of questions.

8.1 *What Dancing Is*

The ontological question takes two forms, one for the dancer and one for the others. What am I really doing when I am dancing? What do I really see when I see a dance? (Answers: "dancing!"; "a dance!" But if those are the right answers, there is something special that I am doing and seeing; so there must be more to it than that.) I take the former question first.

What I said in §5.3 commits me to the following. In doing the things I do as a dancer, I become a different being, a dancing being. Of course I don't really: I remain and retain my social self, my corporeal identity in its biological character, my status and function as a member of the group with and for whom I dance, a person with past and future that relate to a present that is not confined to the special being of the dance. But also I do, equally really, because the being that I exist (as accessible to my practical consciousness) is predominantly taken up with dancing. "In Bali, as elsewhere in the East," says Beryl de Zoete, "the dancer is possessed by his role. He lets the dance *dance*, and functions only as a vehicle of the dance" (Zoete 1938, 20).

As we remarked before, acknowledgment of this self-transformation seems not to get us very far. In anything I do wholeheartedly, I become the being who is doing that: I am wholly myself-as-committee-man or (at this moment) myself as writer-of-this-book, occupying the vital space defined by chapters written and to come. The notion that a person consists of a sort of continuing, neutral or morally defined, core personality onto which supplementary behavioral modalities are temporarily attached, or a continuing self-contained ego persisting unchanged in its relations with other egos similarly detached, has long lost its hold on philosophers in their reflective moments. The continuity of identity implied by my hopes and fears, guilts and glories, responsibilities and strategies, as well as by my recognizability for self and others, is self-sustaining and needs no doctrinaire postulation of such a "real self" as would detract from the practical priority of myself-as-what-I-am-doing-now. An absorbing activity or context absorbs me. I am wholly the agent of that, but not exclusively that: everything else is filtered through it, a way of handling it or a distraction from it; nothing is lost, everything is transformed or, if not transformed, takes me away from being what I now am. But, if that is true of everything sufficiently engrossing, it sheds no special light on dance. It says only that when I am dancing I tend to forget everything else, just as I do now when I am stuffing sentences into an electronic store.

But no, dancing really is different. Even if the self-transformation in dancing is only an enhanced version of a condition necessary to (if not constitutive of) engagement as such, the enhancement might be expected to be such as to make it a self-transformation of a quite different order— quite sufficiently so to make this count as what dance really is. Four main factors contribute to the difference. First, there is the endotelicity of dance, the fact that (like all activities of art) the practice of dance precludes immediate consideration of any end beyond the activity itself. Second, there is the emphasis on quality: what matters overwhelmingly in dance is how one dances (according to the values and standards appropriate to what one is dancing), so that the self-transformation can be expected to be thorough and complete, self-reinforcing. These two factors are shared by dance with many other activities, especially in art and games. The other two factors are more distinctive.

The third factor is the specialness of dance (see §4.5 and especially §4.53). Dancers tend actually to transform themselves in obvious ways: to perform specifically dance movements ("other than ordinary" in Judith Hanna's significant specification), to occupy special dance places on special dance occasions, to wear special costumes and disguises (mask or make-up), to accompany themselves with music. The significance of music in this connection is that music is a wholly artificial sound system, its rhythms and scales being generated by human beings and not found in nature, so that the dancer's aural environment is a wholly special one. Even a drum serves not only to give the time, not only to excite, but also and equally importantly to drown out all other sound (hence, too, the otherwise intolerable loudness of disco music). Similarly, the caller at a square dance uses locutions, voice rhythms, and intonations far removed from those of social intercourse.

Dancing, it seems, not only shares in an emphatic form the self-transforming nature of all engrossing activities but surrounds itself with features that are themselves, first and foremost, self-transformations and self-removals from the workaday. But the most obvious and important thing about dance is that it consists of special movements of the dancer's own body as a whole. And this is the fourth and by far the most important factor that makes the self-transformation in dance something special. Dancers throw themselves into the dance. In this respect, there is an important difference between dancing and dramatic acting, in which also the actors make themselves into other people in special places and disguises. Actors use speech; and speech binds us irrevocably to the social world, for language is intrinsically a social phenomenon. The world of a dance, whatever its social significance, is immediately a nonsocial world. Even my duty to my partner, insofar as I am engaged in the dance (for we have all read novels and seen movies in which young lovers, moving together in the dance, have inwardly fallen out of the dance into a private place of their own, "waltzing just you and I in the clouds"), is a duty to my partner in the dance.

It is tempting to see in this character of dance as primarily self-transformation an explanation or an equivalent of the sacredness so often ascribed to dance. In dance we transport ourselves into a state of being, and a world, that, because it is not ours, is that of the gods. Whose else could it be? Dance is an evidently appropriate form of worship or of mediation with whatever powers are acknowledged. And, as we remarked before, Susanne Langer's equation of dance with the congruous and symbolic manifestation of vital powers fits the same pattern: the dancer is self-transmuted into a center of pure activity in a world where everything has been made into the scene and accoutrements of such activity.

It would not be a fatal objection to the present thesis if most dancers would not use such language of themselves, would repudiate it as pretentious and false to their own experience.[1] We are talking here about what dancers do, not about how they would represent it to themselves. We have already remarked that such reflection, in addition to the difficulty that results from the necessity of redirecting one's attention in unfamiliar ways, goes against the grain of dominant philosophical and social trends. Many people begin by repudiating the practice itself of considering the quality of their own experience. To do it in solitude is morbid; to do it with others shows unbecoming self-absorption or else belongs to moments of intimacy from which it should not be abstracted.

The characteristic costume, place, and props of a dance do not merely endorse the specialness of the dancer's identity. To be a conscious human being is to occupy a situation in a world, which one assumes as one's own. The accoutrements of a dance may play a more or less direct part in the construction of the world of the dance. For example, it may be impossible to dance a sword dance without a sword, even in rehearsal.[2] "You don't

---

[1] Not all dancers are so shy. "I think of dance as a constant transformation of life itself," says Merce Cunningham (1985, 84).

[2] Judy van Zile, at a colloquium at York University, spoke of her difficulties in learning the Korean knife dance *Chinju Kom Mu*. Unlike most Korean knife dances, which are danced with hinged knives, this dance is danced with ceremonial knives that are rigid—and far too valuable to use in rehearsal. So the dancer practices with the hinged knives. But, of course, their balance is quite different from that of the rigid knives, and that causes difficulties when the latter are used in actual performance. Despite these difficulties, although one could obviously practice with rigid batons weighing about the same as the knives, this is apparently not done: it is more important that one practice with knives than that one practice with an object having the right shape and weight.

become a character," says Alexander Grant, "till you put it on, sitting in the dressing room making up your face. You become the role when you actually turn into it in costume and make up" (Newman 1982, 75). Benois was speaking of a similar inner transformation when he recalled of Nijinsky's performance as Petrushka that "[t]his time also the metamorphosis took place when he put on his costume and covered his face with makeup" (Benois 1941, 338).

It is because dancing is in an important respect (perhaps, first and foremost) a special mode of being that the moments of joining the dance and leaving the dance always require special attention. Thus, in Indian dance forms, the entrance of a dancer is a very special affair. In the Chhau dance of Purulia, for instance, the dancing area, about twenty feet square, is joined by a corridor about twenty feet long and five feet wide, through which the dancers enter: "The corridor also becomes a part of the performing area and the dances are continued and started immediately with the entrance of an artiste in the corridor" (Bhattacharyya 1972, 36)—as though the dancer were being newly born.[3] In a discussion of "liminality" in her phenomenological exploration of a Cretan dance, Mary Coros writes:

On the Way to the Dance Floor
    I am not as I have just been
        and
                I am not as I am about to be

My body-being is on its way . . . to it knows not what . . .
My body-being is moving away from what is known, from what is comfortable . . . to the unknown . . .

My body-being is on its way to risk . . .

My body-being doesn't recognize itself . . .

My body-being is moving out of the mundane kinetic mode but doesn't know *what* to be-come or *how* to be-come or *when* to be-come . . .[4]

---

[3] A similar function and a similar symbolism may be found in the more familiar procedure in Kathakali, whereby the newly introduced character is slowly revealed by the lowering of a cloth. But the emphasis here is more directly on drawing the audience's attention to the new arrival, as is even more evidently the case in a South Indian provincial form, Yakshagana: "Each actor enters dancing, exchanges a few words with a musician, who now and then talks with the actors and makes comments and asks every new character who he is; and the actors thus announce themselves" (Raghavan 1979, 56–57).

[4] Coros 1982, 18. Despite the typography, this is not to be read as a poem but as an attempt to render a state of consciousness at a subverbal level (see §8.46 below).

The self-transformation in the dance, complete because all the dancer's activities, embodiment, and worldly equipment are made such as to transform the dancer into a bodily consciousness and activity sharply and unequivocally characterized, is significantly like what I take Hegel to have had in mind when he wrote, in a manuscript dating from the summer of 1803: "The noonday of our mortal life, the moment of our clearest vision, is the warrior's 'absolute life in the *Volk*', the moment when we realize what it means to say 'In God we live and move and have our being' (Harris 1983, 197). But, evidently, the contrasts are no less striking than the analogies. What Hegel has in mind is that it is the warrior's actual readiness to die with or for his comrades in battle that is the only real evidence of commitment to that membership in a human community that at once creates and clarifies personhood and thus lays the only possible foundation for individuality and freedom. In joining the dance, we may, for reasons we have now seen, have a sense of a similar clarification of our active being by transforming ourselves into something at odds with our confused and compromised animality. But, in the first place, we have only the sense of it. The transformation is phenomenologically real enough, but it has no cash value: there is nothing we are laying on the line. (Even in the legendary Bacchic frenzy, the Bacchantes were not themselves at risk: the *sparagmos*, the tearing of the prey, is not a risk for the dancers as dancers but for the victim. If the victim's mother leads the dance, as Agave did, that is an accident irrelevant to the inner meaning of the dance.) That is why dancers are not proud, think themselves nothing special and their dancing no big deal. (They may take a proper pride in their skill or their achievements; but, unlike some practitioners of other arts, dancers seldom think that being dancers is enough to make them important people.) And, in the second place, there need be no dance that is joined in any other sense than that the way of dancing is not our personal invention or discovery or property: the sort of freedom it prepares is the moral self-recollection that Schiller thought all art provided, not the real self-loss in a community of self-losers that, in Hegel's fantasy, prepares a real self-recovery.

The sorts of things we have been saying are unwelcome to philosophers because they evade the need for critical thinking. But we cannot responsibly avoid them. We have five choices: to say that something like this is going on and give the best account we can; to say that nothing like this is going on (which is already to countenance the notion that it might have been); to say that something different is going on; to say that something like this may well be going on but is only contingently connected with the concept of dance or the practice of dancing; or to ignore the matter entirely. The last option is the one that lovers of plain thinking prefer, which is one of the reasons why little of substance has been written on the aesthetics of dance. But it is not open to us, in any simple form. Once such questions have been broached, one has to have some strategy, either defensible or such as one is prepared to commit oneself to, for either dealing with them or disposing of them. The third option is not likely to provide anything easier to stomach than the first two. And the fourth option offers cold comfort if it is conceded that a practice may be what it is because its nerve is what it is.

It may be hard to keep talk of self-transformation under sober, rational control, but it has unfortunate ontological consequences only if it is combined with an ontology of persons, which itself would be likely to transgress in the same manner. If one did embrace a theory requiring some inconveniently strong criterion of "personal identity," that theory would probably require one to use some other language to label the phenomena we have called self-transformation. But there is one temptation we must guard against in any case. We said above that this aspect of dance might be one of the things that encourage people to speak of the "sacredness" of all dance, because of the specialness involved. The temptation (akin to that to which we suspected Laban of succumbing, in §5.3) is to go directly from the dancer's sense of otherness to a special sort of otherness identified as self-loss and further interpreted as a revelation of oneness with the One or the All. Dances may be used to induce special experiences interpretable in such ways—the whirlings of dervishes may be such—but they need not. There is no reason to make such a sense of oneness essential to dance and thus make all dance revelatory (as I have heard Kapilar Vatsyayan do in a brilliant oration). Our talk of "being other" does not endorse, or counter, or reduce, or explain any claims about mystical experiences of any sort; it leaves them just where they were.

Although our argument lends no support to theories that would make dance a source of special illumination or privilege, it does encourage us to assign to dance a special significance of a rather different sort. The self-transformations of dance are, on the face of it, transitory and to that extent almost illusory: one joins the dance, becomes a dancer, leaves the dance—and becomes, presumably, what one was before. But Victor Turner has drawn attention to the importance in rituals and celebrations generally of the phenomenon of "liminality," that is, the way in which participants are disengaged from their social ties and enter an indeterminate state in which "anything can happen," from which they return to a set of engagements that may be different from those that obtained before. It is for this reason transitions from one social status to another are so often marked by elaborate ceremonies and rituals (*rites de passage*) (Turner 1974). If in fact, as I have argued, the characteristic features of dance constitute a fairly thoroughgoing self-transformation of a temporary sort, dance seems to be inherently appropriate to liminal status and hence to tend to have whatever general significance liminality may be assigned in one's general anthropology. Some people go on to argue that whatever behavior has liminal significance has thereby the character of dance, but I think that is a mistake. Dance makes for liminality, but we have sufficiently seen that it is independently defined and characterized and has everywhere its own structures of institutional identity.

In a discursive article on the scope and limits of the aesthetics of music, I found myself driven to a conclusion similar to that drawn here in relation to dance:

> It is more nearly true of music than it is of anything else that it offers an alternative reality and an alternative way of being. The perennial task of the aesthetics of music is to work out unpretentiously the ways in which that is so or seems to be so, so that such affirmations can be soberly contested or supported. (Sparshott 1987)

The relation between this formula and what I have been saying about self-transformation in dance must be reserved for a more comprehensive treatment of the relations between dance and music in general—a vast topic, as I have noted before. But it should be said at once that the difference is marked. One says such things as "you are the music while the music lasts," and this self-absorption, like that in dance, is in the first instance a special case of the general tendency to become engrossed in whatever one is wholeheartedly doing. But, as special cases, they differ. Music offers an alternative way of being and an alternative reality because of the completeness of the musical universe, so that one exists as musician rather than as human. But in the dance it is rather one's humanity itself that is transformed. Insofar as in many cultures the difference between dance and music is negated or simply not thought of, of course, this contrast has no force. What the contrast amounts to when it does have force, when music and dance become mutually separable practices, is easily seen simply by exploring the two sorts of practice in their separability, as in the present book and in the article cited.

8.11 EXPRESSION

If dance is a self-transposition into one or another alternative way of being, the common saying that dance is basically, and was originally, an expression of emotion is exactly wrong.[5] People who jump for joy, fling

---

[5] Consider, for instance, the following statement on the origin of dance. "The apes, gorillas and the chimpanjis who live on trees, perhaps lived one crore years ago. These animals de-

themselves about in grief, stride up and down in anxiety, stamp with rage are not yet dancing. In fact, if the inward state is thwarted of its practical issue, the "displacement activity" that gives it motor expression is hardly made more effective by being subjected to formal control. Rather, the dancer enters into a state of being that has its inward counterpart, the associated "emotion," which may or may not be antecedently present as stimulus or as suggestion. R. G. Collingwood's famous theory, that art (including dance) is the expression of emotion in the very special sense that it is the discovery of a complex of thought and action that will uniquely clarify what is significant in a real or possible experience (Collingwood 1938), is closer to the mark but still, as many critics observe, gratuitous: what the artist or dancer may have felt or thought of in a personal capacity is surely beside the point (Sirridge and Armelagos 1977).

The dancer is transmuted into the dancer of a dance of which the precise character may, on the whole, be joyous, solemn, tetchy, or whatever. But the dance equally may have no such generic character other than that of being (say) tango-ish. A mourning dance may be congruous with what mourners conventionally are supposed to feel, and people who are actually mourning may, in performing such a dance, find their actual feelings endorsed, or normalized, or stimulated—but equally they may not. There is no reason to suppose that actual mourning or knowledge of mourning either helps or hinders in such a dance or makes it either more or less subjectively suitable. Especially, the only knowledge relevant to the composing or dancing of a work like Martha Graham's *Lamentation* is not knowledge of or about grief (in which we have no reason to suppose that Graham was adept) but knowledge of how to make and perform dances, how to conceive and realize danceable modes of being. Just so, when the Hopi Snake Dance regenerates the world, the dancers' work is not to feel anything but actually to put themselves into the condition that, by its realization, corroborates the corresponding real condition in their society and in

---

cended from the trees and learnt to stand and move with the help of hind legs. . . . With this descent from the trees there were certain changes in the physical structure of these mammals according to the use of the part of the body. Just for example the daily ascent on the trees developed the bones of wrist and further became familiar with how to catch and hold the things and after passage of time developed the toes and fingers. Now the old ape succeeded to bring the things eye-ward by holding them in hands and fingers. Then he used his thinking power to collect food and utilize the bodily organs. After the development of thinking power he represented the inner feelings in time and rhythm with the help of bodily organs. This representation of inner feelings in time and rhythm was named as dance" (Veer 1982, 9). But in his practical summary of the accepted feeling-modalities (*rasas*) of Indian dance the author gives the conventional prescriptions of movements, scenes, music, and accoutrements, without regard to any feelings the dancers may have or to the relevance of any evocation of emotion as such.

the world. Of course, it may happen that a particular dancer or a chore-ographer is unable to dance or to compose without first being in some emotional condition; but that is far from saying that, even for such people, the function of the dance is to give their inner feeling an outward form. Rather, the feeling, if any, functions as the germ of a dance or of an idea for a dance. Much less is it true that the externalization of subjective states is the function of dance in general.

8.2 *What a Dance Is*

We have been looking at things from the point of view of the dancer, who after all comes first: until there is a dancer there can be no dance for the public to see, and dancing as such needs no audience. But many dances, and many kinds of dancing and dance making, exist as for spectators: what they do is construct visible objects of cognition. What are these objects that they construct? They cannot be identical with the self-transmutations we have been talking about, which can be of interest only to those in whose lives they are episodes—and which, from a choreographer's point of view as well as from that of an audience, need not occur at all. But we should not be surprised to find that some such transformation is involved; in fact, it would be silly to suppose that it would not be.[6] How can what is essen-tial in what dancers do be unrelated to what is essential in what spectators of dance see?

We must repeat here our earlier warning, that the previous chapters did not leave undecided the question of what a dance really is. That holds for the question of what it is that the spectator really sees, as it does for the question of what it is that the dancer is really doing. We gave a variety of very solid reasons, on logically heterogeneous grounds, why no true gen-eral answers to such a question could be given; and we also gave general descriptions of some different sorts of answers that could be given in cer-tain restricted contexts of practice and inquiry. That is why we began this chapter by saying that the whole of this book so far has been nothing but an extended account of what dance is, what dancing is, what dances are; and the complex extensiveness is a good part of the answer.

It remains true, however, that there are contexts in which the question of what a dance is becomes both poignant and pointed. One such context is that of the spectator at a dance performance, such as is mounted and

[6] Many of the most durable ballets in the repertory are based on dramatic self-transforma-tions: *Sleeping Beauty, Swan Lake, Coppélia, Nutcracker*, not to mention all those in which mortals are immortalized or vice versa. So perhaps a sense that dance involves self-transfor-mation works itself out at this symbolic level.

presented for supposedly critical audiences in theaters in Europe and America.[7] Reflective spectators at such performances, which may be and are meant to be admirable and striking, may ask themselves: What is this that I am seeing? What is this dance, as a dance? And the answers they find, if they find any, may seem applicable only to the dance they are watching, or to the particular genre represented by that dance (broadly or narrowly defined, sharply or vaguely contrasted with other possible dances), or to all dance as a mode of theatrical presentation within the general understanding of public art.

To answer the sort of question now mooted cannot be to specify the essence of dance in terms of a totality of timeless realities or the place of dance in any sort of taxonomy. The task is to characterize the object of attention as an object of just the sort of appreciative scrutiny that is properly directed on it, in terms of the understandings that govern the practice of dance making, dancing, and dance going. It is to give what will be the most appropriate description in the light of a defined interest. And the task will be a possible one if alternative descriptions can be argued or felt to be less appropriate from a point of view that can be established as preemptively legitimate. Some answers may be obviously true, but open to serious objections; others may be not obviously true, but defensible in the light of reflection. It could turn out that the question (on some occasion of its asking; or wherever asked in the circumstances we are envisaging) calls for a single, complex answer. Or it could turn out that there are a lot of plausible partial answers, all of which deserve consideration but not commitment. The only sensible thing to do, I think, is to look at a few things that have been said or thought and see what they look like.

To begin with, it seems obvious that when I see a dance, what I see is a lot of people (whom I can describe and may be able to name) moving around for a given length of time in certain ways that I could specify, with equipment and in a context of presentation that I could describe. Certainly. But that is open to objection in two ways.

First, "people" is not a neutral description. What do I mean when I call them "people," exactly? People as opposed to dancers? People as members of communities of social persons? Animals of the species *homo sapiens*? Men and women? All of those things? I see them, certainly, *as* dancers and/or characters in a dance: do I see Karen Kain (who is dancing Giselle), or Giselle (who is danced by Karen Kain)? Surely whatever I see (describable

---

[7] The point of the restriction to Europe and America is not that India and China lack dance connoisseurship and dance connoisseurs but that the dance practices of North America and Europe, including European Russia, are not mutually exotic. One is socially entitled to generalize over North American and European theater dance, even if all such generalizations are based on cultural fictions.

in such terms) is not seen as superimposed on an entity identifiable in advance of any description at all or substituted for something uncontroversially describable as what I must *really* be seeing in the first instance. What I see, I see in the first instance *as* something-or-other (or someone-or-other) initially and basically describable in some way or some set of ways. But what is that way? What is supposed to be the significance of starting with the word "people"—or some other word not conceptually related to dance (or less emphatically related to dance than "dancer" would be)? It is not that I have made any mistake in choosing to start there; it is just that it turns out that I need better reasons for starting there than I have given—or, I suspect, than anyone is able to give.[8]

If one dismisses what I have just said as a typical philosophical quibble, which it is (typical philosophical quibbles typically raise fundamental problems), one is left with a second objection. Granted, what is going on is that people are moving on the stage, as described, and all of that is what the dance is—there is nothing additional that we have left out. But the fact remains that the people are not the dance. They are performing the dance, they are participating in the dance. The dance is what they are performing and participating in; so how can it also *be* them? They are not *parts* of a dance, do not collectively constitute the dance in the way that the steps performed are parts of it and are collectively identical with it. Again, that is not to say that the answer we gave is wrong, a "category mistake," only that there are objections to it, that we cannot claim for it the status of uniquely right and satisfactory answer to the question: What am I seeing when I see a dance? So there is no reason for not going further, and perhaps faring worse, by taking a quick look at some things people have said, some of them less vague than talk about "people" and some having more to do with the dance than with the dancers.

8.21 SEEING A DANCE—SOME POSSIBLE WAYS

What do I see when I see a dance? I see a dance. Gilbert Ryle used to say that the verb "see" is an "achievement verb": usually, to specify what one sees is to claim that one has grasped in what is visually present a certain character or unity that the object of the verb specifies. One is not surprised, then, to find that one is tempted to give any or many of several answers to the question of what one sees when one sees a dance, and that the answer "a dance" is by no means empty, even if it is seldom helpful and never interesting. Before we cite some particular answers, we may arm ourselves

---

[8] For a frivolous-looking romp through the difficulties connected with explaining what one sees by saying what one sees "it" as, see Sparshott 1974.

with the question of how they relate to each other. Are they (some of them) real alternatives, mutually exclusive? Do they perhaps pick out different aspects of (all or typical) dances? Or do they pick out (not so much different aspects of dances as) different emphases in dancing? Or do they represent neither aspects nor emphases, but different ways of seeing dances as wholes? (Or are those three—aspects, emphases, ways of being seen—not clearly distinguishable?) Are the proposed alternatives none of these, but rather interpretations of what is already seen under certain aspects etc.? If the last is the case, are the interpretations, or some of them, really ways of advocating special ways of dancing or, at least, ways of distinguishing different ways of dancing and emphasizing those differences?

It is indeed possible that all dances *can* be seen in all of the ways to be suggested, but some lend themselves more readily to being seen in some of these ways than others. In that case, perhaps it is being suggested that those more accessible to the modes of vision in question represent the "nerve" of the practice of dance. Or it may be that not all the suggestions are on the same level: they may relate to different levels of coding as well as to alternative codes—that is, some may refer to a basic level of structured meaning present in all dances and others to higher levels of meaning on which interest centers. (Similarly, every piece of music is structured in accordance with some sort of gamut, and the gamut itself is structured in some specific sort of way—say, in accordance with major/minor tonality—and any piece so structured is in a specific key. In hearing music, one may be hearing that in it which defines its tonality, without which it would not be music; but one will not be *listening* to that and is more likely to single out, as what one hears in the music, the specific tunes with their rhythms and harmonies.) When I watch a performance of Patsalas's *L'Île Inconnue*, it is a perceptible fact about the ballet that it is ballet and, at another level, that it is dance. My experience would be not what it is if I were not aware of both facts; but they are not what I attend to, and they are not even separable factors that *could* engage my attention. What I look at is just what the dancers are doing with what Patsalas has done.

8.211 *Dancers Dancing*

Because we could not get away with saying that a dance is people in motion, the most obvious suggestion is that what we see in a dance is what we really do see and is there to be seen: the movements (more or less skilled, structured, beautiful, etc.) of human bodies, in all their charm, vigor, prowess, and discipline, moving in real space and time, in the costumes and setting actually fabricated and lit. We will have to add something to the effect that these are movements of dancers dancing in a dance setting, and unless we are aware of this we cannot be said really to see the dance; but not too much should be made of that. It is no more than a background categorization, standing at most for the sum of the relevant experience with which our spectatorship is invested; it is vital not to let it obfuscate the nature of what it is we really see, the real movements of real humans in all their concreteness. We have already quoted Edwin Denby, for one, as emphasizing the importance in ordinary dance experience of the real charm, prowess, vigor, and dedication that we sense in the people who are dancing for us (Denby 1949, 3); Betty Redfern has urged us not to talk rubbish about "virtual space" but to respect our actual awareness that these movements are being made in real space, physical space: "Dance space is physical space attended to under a particular description" (Redfern 1983, 81).

Redfern's point, she is at pains to make clear, is not to deny that one can make sense of what such writers as Langer and Wigman say about dance space—it is, of course, true that the dance *image* is not a physical entity— but to recall us to the "philosophical point" that the basis of image and space is a physical reality. The supposedly philosophical point, however, is unclear, because the phrase "physical space" is left unexplained. Presumably she means the sort of three-dimensional framework we specify by sets of linear measurements. But the sets of coordinates we use for measuring are specifically designed to be neutral as between contexts and hence are seldom directly relevant to any contexts that are not in the first instance occasions for measurement. For real-life situations, we have to translate back into the distances and trajectories in terms of which the operations and processes we are concerned with are performed and occur. The apparent lucidity and realism of Redfern's dictum rests on a confusion, familiar to anyone who has worked in the philosophical problems of space and time, about the status and functions of mathematics and mensuration. Still, one could endorse Redfern's intent—which may have been to deny Husserl's contention that phenomenological considerations are logically and epistemically prior to postulations of scientific reality—without accepting her formulation. Similarly, one may want to insist that dance movements are real movements, their expressive and otherwise appreciable qualities depending on control of the body so precise that fine discriminations can be observed and learned. When we see a dance, we see in the first instance these real, concrete movements of actual people with the qualities they really have in the places where they really are: everything else can be referred to that as a basis.

8.2111 *The Body Affirmed*

If we follow out the implications of what we have just seen proposed, we may say that when we see a dance we are in any case seeing the movements of bodies, bodies of humans who are moving them and who are not engaged in dramatic representation as such. Even so, as we shall now see, the actuality of the body as center of our dance experience may be affirmed or denied. Besides, what "the body" should mean here is as tricky a matter as what "a person" meant before; but we postpone that issue for separate treatment (§8.3). Meanwhile we can simply think of a dance as presenting real human bodies eloquently meeting resistance, occupying space, succumbing to or overcoming constraints, and so forth. An honest dance will be one in which this is evident, and perhaps only an honest dance can be a *real* dance. Some such feeling is among the factors that have made people want to say that only with Martha Graham does dance find itself, on the ground that she was the first to construct dance movement on principles wholly consonant with the integrity of the physicality of the body.

The theme of the body's primacy was directly stated before Graham's day in a famous essay by Jacques Rivière (1913). Loie Fuller's dancing (then in vogue), he says, depends on making the body vanish; Diaghilev's Russian ballet made a point of revealing the body. But Fokine, Diaghilev's first choreographer, had still made the dancers lose themselves in the pattern of the dance. Nijinsky's choreography for *The Rite of Spring*, by contrast, emphasizes the individuality of each dancing body and makes it directly and immediately expressive: "Nothing is more moving than this physical image of the passions of the soul" (Rivière 1913, 141). In this, evidently, Rivière is only describing one kind of dance; but he goes on to claim that the very specificity of its adaptation to Stravinsky's score fits it to be a general technique. Whatever his intentions, then, we may treat his remarks as in fact representing a type of possible specification of what I see when I see a dance. I see the personal embodiment of human beings in eloquent and thereby expressive motion. I see the dancers' self-transmutations in the process of working themselves out. And because I clearly see, as they more diffusely and agonizedly feel, the corporeal substance that is transmuted and that so visibly remains what it was, the triumph and pathos of humanity is made plain to me.

8.21111 *Empathy*. This will be as good a place as any to dispose of the old theory of empathy, a theory of art that is now obsolete (it rests on a way of psychologizing that no one uses any more) but that forcibly suggests itself in the present context and pleads for resurrection. The point is this. If dancing is a matter of self-transmutation, it is so in a specific way and for specific reasons; and these are such as to be inaccessible to the spectator, who simply is not doing the appropriate things. But how can dance be for the spectator something quite different from what it is for the dancer? Obviously it can't. But two sorts of links are possible. First, it is easy to see that in changing themselves for spectators dancers also change themselves for themselves, and they may find such a change no less satisfactory (as it need certainly be no less complete) than any other. Second, what the dancer does may establish for the spectator some sympathetic link—between what the spectator knows by seeing and what the dancer knows in doing—that is less than identity. What the theory of empathy did was to seek to establish such links. Briefly, it began with the Kantian conundrum that the beauty I find in an object, which as *found* must be objectively there, is assigned to it on the basis of my own feelings, which are subjective. A typical version of the theory would go like this. Certain formal properties in an object evoke in me certain body feelings (because the only way I can perform the abstraction that enables me to observe them is by imaginatively constructing them in myself); these make me feel good in some way; I then attribute to the object a form that is actually based on the version of it I have imaginatively reconstructed in myself, and attribute to it a kind of excellence that is a sort of objectified version of the corresponding feeling.

The reason the empathy theory obtrudes itself here is that it seems to give us just the link we need. When we see a dancer in self-transmutation, in order to read the dancer's pose and movements we must ourselves realize them internally and thus effect in ourselves a comparable (though not identical) self-transmutation, which we then ascribe to (and appreciate in) the dancer. But there are two objections to this suggestion. First, as a famous psychologist once remarked, an obese and elderly person such as himself could appreciate dance, though to imagine himself doing such things was painful and ludicrous. The other objection is that the sort of self-transmutation we spoke of was not a matter of feeling, kinesthetic or other, but a matter of one's construction of the world of one's action and of oneself in it. These objections are not fatal. An empathy theorist would rightly object that, in the first place, the whole theory is carefully articulated (even in my few sentences) to preclude such literal crudities; and, in the second place, the reduction of pretentious "ontological" jargon to empirically identifiable body feelings is deliberate. So the theory of empathy remains in the wings at the theater of the mind, awaiting its cue.

8.2112 *The Body Denied*

The converse of the position just examined is that, when we see a dance as such, what we see is, as we said before, not something of which the dancers or their bodies are constituents but something they perform with their bodies. Their bodies, then, form the basis of something other than themselves—the movements abstracted from them in some way. But our glance at Rivière already furnished two ways in which this abstraction may be performed.

8.21121 *Subsumption.* Contrasting Fokine's fluid and idealizing choreography with Nijinsky's turned-in and body-centered style, Rivière says that balletic movement envelops and hides the dancer as Fuller's draperies hid her: "Something comes between him and us; it is his very movement. . . . Once the first movements have been invented by the body, it is as if, becoming conscious of themselves, they said to their author: 'Enough now! Let us take over!' " (Rivière 1913, 135).[9] At the very least, the composition takes precedence over detail. Such a dance consists of the movement patterns that the dancers generate and in which they participate, surrendering their identity to that of the dance. They are wholly transformed, not only into dancers, but into dancers of the specific dance they are dancing. And that dance is what we look at. If we allow our attention to wander into a consideration of individual personalities and styles, we may still be concentrating on the dancing, but we will have lost sight of the dance.

Such a position may be taken in three ways. First, it may be simply a description of two styles of dance making. Second, it may be taken normatively: Fokine betrays the body by losing its human eloquence in vague expressionism; Nijinsky abandons dance creation in favor of disintegrated interactions. Third, the two positions may be taken as rival claims about what it is to see any dance: either that we miss the dance if we notice the immediate involvement of the bodies, or that we lose the human force of dance practice if we allow it to degenerate into abstract pattern making or beauty mongering.

8.21122 *Pure Energy.* Rivière said that even Fokine's choreography emphasized the presence of the body, though the flowing and idealized form of the movement canceled the weight and individuality of its presence. The implied relationship is that spelled out by Sartre in *L'Idiot de la famille* and already glanced at (§6.321): the marble in a statue, the dancer in a dance, remains present as "derealizing" itself, just as the spectators "derealize" themselves, canceling out their own individuality by making themselves into spectators correlated with the spectacle, even though it is they themselves in their individuality who continue to do this (Sartre 1971, 785–

---

[9] Rivière's language, but not his thought, is echoed by Beryl de Zoete, who writes that in Balinese dancing "[p]ersonal temperament . . . has been translated into another medium. Something stands between it and the spectator, the dance body strangely modified and rarefied. This passage into a new medium, into the 'other thought,' as the Balinese call it, . . . is perhaps what we mean by 'great' " (Zoete 1938, 24). In our terms, that means that in "great" dancing the dancer's self-transformation is made directly visible to the spectator, rendering the dancer *as embodied personality* invisible. What Rivière is saying is that stylized dancing renders the dancer *as individuated body* invisible. One sees how many changes could be rung on this theme.

790). But one could argue that what such a spectator (at least in the first instance) sees is not the dance as such but the dancer in the dance, a sort of intermediary between the person who dances and the dance itself. The dance as such would be the system of energies of which the dance consists, in which the dancers lose their human identity completely. This is in fact what Paul Valéry argued (1936): what the dancer creates is a kind of time, a time of pure energy. (The language, if not the thought, reflects the nineteenth-century notion that all art is a form of play and that play is a use of "excess energy.")

Although Valéry maintains that what he says is true of all dance, and in fact of all art, one suspects that he is thinking about Loie Fuller, of whom, we recall, Rivière said much the same. Frank Kermode (1962) has reminded us of the enormous impact Fuller made on the artistic world around 1890 by her development of the "skirt dance" (so dear to young Reginald St.-Johnston) into what she claimed was a new art form.[10] The impression she made was in some ways greater than that made by Duncan, but different: Duncan showed that there could be a specific and distinctive art of dance, Fuller seemed to epitomize the formal principles of all *art nouveau* and the general aesthetic of French symbolism in which art becomes pure metaphor.[11] Fuller herself was originally an actress and not a dancer, and photographs all show her as a dumpy and undancerlike person—in fact like a won ton, a small piece of meat encased in a spreading veil of draperies.[12] Her art was an art of moving light and color. Not surprisingly, though she inspired a generation of poets and for Valéry (a belated epigone of symbolist aesthetics) epitomized what dance really was, she offered nothing for dancers as such to work on. She did not discover any new mode of self-transformation but remained undancerlike, an arranger of lights and a manipulator of veils, herself untransformed in the midst of the magic, the meat in the won ton. Or perhaps we should say that what

[10] In her autobiography Fuller writes: "I was aware that I had discovered something unique, but I was far from imagining, even in a daydream, that I had hold of a principle capable of revolutionising a branch of aesthetics. I am astounded when I see the relations that form and colour assume. The scientific admixture of chemically composed colours, heretofore unknown, fills me with admiration, and I stand before them like a miner who has discovered a vein of gold, and who completely forgets himself as he contemplates the wealth of the world before him" (Fuller 1913, 36–37). It does not sound like a dancer talking.

[11] The text is a bit unfair to Fuller. We recall that St.-Johnston's exaltation of skirt dancing went with the conviction that ballet was obsolete. In part, this was simply a matter of unfortunate timing: Diaghilev was not yet on the horizon. But partly it is that St.-Johnston thinks of skirt dancing as well as ballet dancing within the context of general theatrical dance in all its variety, a context from which old-fashioned ballet historians averted their gaze. Fuller was not a peripheral figure in that context, and contemporary reassessments of Ruth St. Denis are drawing our attention to its relevance (cf. Shelton 1981).

[12] Compare the photographs in Harris 1979. The works of art reproduced by Harris testify to the connection between Fuller's professional persona and the prevailing art of the day.

she achieved was indeed a transmutation of being by other than dance means, a simulation of dance. That would be why she was an inspiration to Yeats and other poets but never to dancers, who noticed that the body movements she relied on to produce her effects were themselves commonplace, not dance movements and hence not efficacious in achieving whatever dancers intrinsically achieve for themselves.

Valéry, for all his vagaries and vaguenesses, was a respected and sometimes a revered figure, a disturbing and disconcerting intelligence. Of course it is not the case that dancers are lost in their dances, converted into pure energy patterns for themselves or for their audiences. But that may be because, when we see a dance, it is not only the dance we see. To see a dance and only a dance might still be something of the sort Valéry indicates.

8.21123 *Virtual Powers.* The notion that a dance as such is not to be reduced to the actual movements of actual dancers is taken one stage further than Valéry by Susanne Langer in one of the best known and most thoroughly misunderstood theories about what dance is, a theory to which we have repeatedly alluded in this book without ever actually saying what it is. Whereas the energies of which Valéry speaks are presumably real energies, even if it is hard to figure out what exactly they are, Langer insists that a dance, like any other work of art, is a virtual object and not a real object. By this she means that the relationships that obtain within it as a work of art are relationships that hold among "appearances"—perceptibles as perceived, cognizables as cognized. A piece of music is made up of tones at intervals in a measure and a tempo, all terms that have meaning only within music as an auditory system and are not to be translated into specifications of the physical vibrations that produce them. Literary works are made up of words as meaningful entities that again, and even more notoriously, are not to be identified with the sounds and marks people make in producing them. Paintings are organized in two-dimensional and three-dimensional pictorial spaces that are constituted by relationships visible in the picture and are not to be identified with what can be measured on the picture surface.[13] If dance is an art like them, a dance too must be constituted by the perceptible relationships generated by the dancers in motion; and these will be purely dynamic relationships, visible exercises of force. The relations to which we attend in a dance performance are not such as

---

[13] A road leads back into the picture space, though the painting is on a flat board. In nonrepresentational paintings, colored patches generate the picture form by advancing and receding and by cohering into interrelated shapes in ways that are not to be reduced to how light is reflected by the pigments spread on the canvas. If a painter like Morris Louis contrives in his painting to affirm the flatness of the picture surface, this is a considerable achievement of spatial control, not a supine surrender to the inherent quality of paint.

could be expressed in terms of physics and optics: they are describable only in terms appropriate to dancers as related by their dancing to each other and to the dance place. In fact, much of a ballet dancer's skill goes to concealing the actual strains and stresses and inertial forces that make the labor of dancing.

If each of the arts produces a characteristic sort of appearance or virtual reality, there must in each case be some specific reason for doing so. Paintings interest us because we live in space, and the experience of this aspect of our lives is too pervasive and too elusive for us to grasp it clearly: naturally, then, we take an interest in objects in which spatiality breaks free, as it were, and does become an object for attention. Analogously, the free appearance of vital force in dance fascinates us because another elusively pervasive aspect of our affective experience is that of being exerters of force (and weakness) in a world that is itself correspondingly dynamic, experienced as yielding and resisting, crushing and reinforcing, whether or not our science and religion allow us to speak of it in such terms. So, when we see a dance, we do of course see the dancers moving themselves on the stage, but that is not the dance. It is only the "vehicle" of the dance. The dance itself is the system of virtual energies that symbolize a world of vital powers, a world familiar to us as inherent in the world as we live in it. Each dancer is no doubt, for herself or himself, a center of power, organizing a personal space in a field of force. And to the spectator, and no doubt to the dancers as well, the dance as a whole is a single field of force even while the individual powers that sustain it are individually felt and perceived.

Most criticisms of Langer are beside the point, the product of failing to attend either to the way Langer articulates her theory or to the phenomena in other arts to which she refers. Her theory is much less like Valéry's than it looks at first. Valéry describes a sort of experience that he takes to be typical of dance watching and goes on to say that the experience of all art really has the same character. Langer starts by considering the fine arts as a whole as a kind of symbol system, of which she describes the articulation and the use. She then differentiates the particular fine arts as subsystems within this system, distinguished by their means (their "primary illusions") and by their symbolic functions. Reading a work in such a symbolism is, in one essential respect, like reading a text: what one attends to is always the text as meaning-bearer. If I see someone doing something I might call dancing, but the "dance" is not meaningfully relatable to an art in a system of arts, then what I see is not a dance in this sense at all: the difference is radical.[14]

[14] Langer does not even raise the quesions of whether this possibility is fulfilled, or why it could not be if it cannot, or what she would say if it could. What is the practical basis or the practical bearing of her postulation of a set of discrete arts and genres with distinct functions? Her obliviousness to tough questions of this sort is what has prevented hard-nosed professors

What seems to be the same point was explicitly made by Charles Batteux nearly two centuries earlier, in a passage quoted above (§3.311). It is in line with a persistent tradition in Western dance theory that he distinguishes meaningless from meaningful dance movements. What is noteworthy is that he too, like Langer, says that the latter are unreal. A dance of virtuoso athleticism exceeds its proper bounds; a dance should be, like music, the artificial portrait of human passions and, as such, imaginary and unreal (Batteux 1746, 36–38). Where Langer and Batteux fundamentally differ is that the latter has a copy theory of meaning, so that meaning-bearing movements are related to gestures that would naturally or conventionally express emotions. But there is no such restriction on the sorts of movement that belong to Langer's realm of virtual powers.

8.211231 *Celebration.* If we were to take Langer's point of view and think of dance as a symbolic presentation and clarification of vital powers, it would make sense to think of the dancer's self-transmutations, in whatever form, as having a central meaning: the realization and celebration of free agency, not in the sense of lability and ability to change (which is what Schiller [1795] seems to imply), but in the sense of prowess. Dance becomes a manifestation of power in oneself and others. It is not surprising, then, that dance is often thought of as a manifestation of divine power. Whereas other arts in their solemnities may be felt as threatening, lowering, oppressive, dance should be essentially festive, representing a sense of achievement or of wonder, a celebration of life. And people do often say things like that.

Aristotle pointed out the duality we have referred to in the notion of potentiality: a power to cause change must correspond to the ability to undergo change, and in most processes, what produces a change in something else does so by changing itself. If dance is first and foremost a celebration of power, this smacks of the sort of aggressiveness that is often thought of as offensively male, needing to be tempered by female values of preservation and submission. Accordingly, we find in classical Indian dance the Tandava dance of Shiva, a masculine dance, shadowed by the quite different Lasya dance of Parvati, in which the movements are yielding and soft rather than angular and forceful. And whereas the *Natyashastra* articulates the masculine dance in terms of the movements the dancer initiates, the twelve types of Lasya dance are differentiated by the kinds of predicament a woman may find herself in (Bharata 1967, ch. 20, 132 ff.). In fact, Shiva dances to create, sustain, and destroy the world; Parvati dances to attract and maintain the love of Shiva.

---

of philosophy from taking her thesis seriously, despite the suggestive charm of her work. One need not succumb to skeptics, but one must show that one has seriously confronted their challenges.

If the association of dances of assertion and dances of passivity with the traditional power relations of the human sexes is rejected, the fact remains that a dance of power and vitality carries with it as its shadow a dance of dejection and debility and loss. With this in mind, we may look back at our rejection of the view that dance "expresses emotion" as a misrepresentation of self-tranformation and note that not all emotions are (from our point of view) equal. In the ritual exordium to her survey of Indian folk dance, extolling (as writers on dance from Lucian to Sachs and beyond have traditionally done) the antiquity and universality of the practice, Kapila Vatsyayan writes:

> Amongst the arts, dance is at once the most primitive and the most sophisticated. There is hardly a civilisation or culture where the aware-ness of human movement as a vehicle of expression of joy and of sor-row is not evident. Perhaps before man began to speak and to paint, he began to dance. . . . This urge has assumed many shapes and forms at different periods of history and in different regions of the world. On one level, whether in time or space, these forms embody man's innate universal desire to express human joys and sorrows. On an-other, they are different, clearly distinguishable on account of their particular content and the distinctive form and style through which this content is manifested. (Vatsyayan 1976, 13)

It is not every feeling that is here said to be universally expressed, but joy and sorrow. And what are these, we may ask, but the names of our engage-ment in the world as exercising and as undergoing power, as active and as passive? Joy and sorrow, the author is telling us, are a common factor in dances whose specific content is always something definite and rich, cul-turally developed and determined. And with this in mind, we may recall that conversation in *Pride and Prejudice*: dance is at once the first among polite amusements and something that every savage does (Chapter 6, note 5 above). Stripped of cultural bias, what that conversation says is that at one level dance represents something universal and basic in humanity, and at another level, by the specific way it does this, dance represents specific cultural values. And that fits the context in Austen: the young people might have been engaging in a minuet, but basically they were escaping from the polite ennui imposed by their elders and finding an outlet for their sense of vitality.

8.212 *Being Human*

All the accounts we have so far sketched of what it is that we see when we see a dance have started from the obviously primary consideration that one is looking at people moving their bodies and have varied in whether the body is emphasized or transformed or sublated in the dance. But the whole emphasis may have been subtly wrong. Granted that dances are among the things people do most essentially with their bodies, it does not follow that "the body" is to be thought of as something alien to oneself that one has to lug around, like a suitcase, or that the point of what one is using one's body to do must have something to do with its being a body as such, any more than authorship could be reduced to penmanship even in a culture where all authors wrote with pen and ink and calligraphy was practiced only by authors. Dancers are first and foremost, though not most distinctively, human beings, and they dance in and with their corporeal humanity. Perhaps what we see in a dance is people being corporeally human, or beings whose reality takes the form of embodying consciousness. Existentialist and phenomenological philosophers, if no others, have urged that this must be the starting point of all human studies and sciences.

This shift in emphasis from the body as an animated mechanism to the body as conscious corporeality or corporeal consciousness, and the equation of the latter with being human, has generated at least three ways of thinking about what a dance really is.

8.2121 *Dasein*

Maxine Sheets-Johnstone points out that Langer's account of dance can be read as equating any dance, as experienced, with "a sheer dynamic flow of force," in which dancer and spectator are absorbed and which is destroyed by reflection or by any breach in spatial or temporal continuity; such a dance is referred to the dancer not as a body or as an individual with a personal history extending beyond the dance but to the dancer as a dance being (Sheets-Johnstone 1966, 32, 4, 39, 55). The dance is not an object for the dancer, who lives the dance. In fact, what dance is for dancer and spectator alike is a modification of our way of being in the world (instrumentally, as agents) and in-the-midst-of-the-world (situatedly), temporally and spatially, in a basically human way that the reification of the body falsifies, a way that is explored by standard expositions of this or that variety of phenomenology. How, then, is dance different from the being-in-time, the *Dasein* as Heidegger has taught us to think of it, that is what we are anyway? It is different in whatever it is that makes all art distinctive (there is a good choice of formulations), a difference that in dance will manifest itself as an authentic self-choice without ulterior purpose, without discourse, without song, without other instruments than earth and heaven (a place to stand, a place to move). Or whatever. The point is that whatever one says will not speak of moving bodily but of living humanly: the body movement is the way of showing this, the only way there is.

Sheets-Johnstone actually associates the phenomenological approach with a specific set of aesthetic theories and dance values (and, in fact, with a specific choreographic method), but from our present point of view none of that is necessary. Our present point is rather that, whatever version of phenomenology one espouses as method or as doctrine, it is likely to be immediately obvious what one is to say that dance essentially is, simply from considering how one's life as an embodied consciousness would show itself.

8.2122 *People Dancing*

Another way of eliminating the tendentious emphasis on the body is to point out simply that when one sees a dance, one sees people actively and appropriately participating in dance, and dance is the practice they are engaging in. It is a thesis we have met before: dance movement has been defined as movement that actually takes place in a context socially identified as a dance context or is recognized as appropriately linked to such movement (by analogy, or however) (Best 1978, 80; cf. §5.524 above). What we see when we see a dance is something that dancers are doing: a set of actions (rather than movements) appropriately assigned to a context appropriately recognized as a dance context. Not the way they move, but what they are doing, is what counts. And what did the word "appropriately" mean in that sentence? One cannot say, because appropriateness is defined by occasion. If we do concentrate on the movements the dancers make with their bodies, or on some set of such movements, we do so only in the light of our conviction that to see how dancers are moving is the way to see what they are doing, because and only because that is what they *are* doing.

8.21221 *The Context of Art.*

For present purposes, Arthur Danto's theory of art can be treated as a version of what we have just said (see §6.31 above). To see a dance is to see something done as a dance by those who are doing it. What makes it really a dance is there being really an available way of interpreting it. It is beside the point to object here that this applies only to dances that aspire to the status of art, because to be present as a spectator at a dance performance is sufficient to establish the proper context as that of art for all relevant purposes.

It follows from the foregoing that when, at a dance performance, what I see has no meaning for me—when I can make no sense of it as a dance—then I have not seen a dance. Either there was really no dance to be seen, or I did not manage to see it. That sounds paradoxical, but in terms of Danto's theory it is not. I did not see what, if anything, they were doing, because I did not see the significant connections in what was before my eyes, connections that alone constituted the unity (or special disunified-ness) of the dance—if there was one; for there is, we recall, a sense in which one can be dancing though there is no dance one is dancing. My inability to see what is being done is analogous to my inability to hear what is being said in a foreign language: I do not even hear the words, I do not even know how to assign sounds to phonemes.

The condition of "not seeing a dance" can be exemplified from the experience of an English artist at the wedding celebrations for the eldest son of the Maharajah of Jodhpur in 1942:

> It was the fairy-tale India that one reads about but so very rarely finds. *The* most wonderful parties in the Palace, everyone a-glitter, real danc-ing-girls, each with her own musicians, one an accordion affair, one a drum and one a tooty-flute and the players get *so* worked up as they play, tho' the girl just postures nonchalantly and stamps her belled and jewelled feet occasionally. There is really very little movement in In-dian dance, but *lovely* clothes and colours. (Swayne-Thomas 1981, 16)

Presumably what the dancer did had the elaborate formal organization and subtly complex musical accompaniment that Indian dances generally have; but nothing except the stamp and jangle was recognizable to the English-woman as a dance movement or, indeed, as anything actually *done*. She was aware only of the level of vigor manifested. Her inability to see the dance seems to have had three components: lack of the necessary background knowledge (system of interpretation) to see what was being done as a dance with a specific dance character; lack of a means to articulate the dancer's movements into meaningful elements or phases; and inability to tell what to look at. It may be worth while contrasting this way of talking with that of Mary Mothersill, who, because she wants to insist that the beauty of a dance is really there to be seen, would insist that the dance is also there to be seen and that Alice Swayne-Thomas saw it (Mothersill 1984, 302–305). She saw it, but did not know what to look for, did not notice and attend to those parts and qualities of the dance on which its beauty depended. After all, she was the Maharajah's guest and was presum-ably placed so that she could see exactly what he saw.

To some degree, the difference in descriptions here is verbal, a matter of preference in rhetoric. Both parties agree that the visibilia were accessible to Alice Swayne-Thomas's eyes, which were directed vigilantly upon them; both agree that she was not aware of the dance as a significant and unified project, because she did not know how to look at Indian dancing. There are, however, two considerations that Mothersill misses. First, she speaks (in an analogous case from music) as if the inexperienced listener failed because there were *parts* that she failed to notice and *combinations* of parts

365

that she failed to make. That is, she speaks as if the articulation of the whole into parts were itself among the visually accessible data. But there is no reason to suppose that to be the case. The other thing she misses has to do with the mechanics of vision. The reason for saying that Swayne-Thomas saw the dance is that it was there before her eyes. But that is sufficient only insofar as the eye is like a camera, click open, click shut. But how far is that? One is inclined to say at first that what impinges on the painter's retinas and what is transmitted by her optic nerves are the same as they would have been for a better informed observer; but what goes on in the visual centers of the cortex may well be different—and we lack a good basis for confining what is strictly visual to precortical events. But that will not do. What goes up the optic nerve is itself affected by the redirecting and focusing of the eye, which itself depends on what the eye's owner is looking at and looking for. People confronted with the same spectacle see different things because what you see depends on what you do. Mothersill draws the line between seeing on the one hand and noticing and attending on the other hand, in a place where it cannot be drawn.—But all this, true and important as it is, and relevant as it is to the question of what is involved in seeing a dance, has taken us away from the specifics of Danto's somewhat rococo theory of art, to which we now return.

The difference between Danto's view of what makes a work of art a work of art (and, by inference and extension, what makes a dance a dance) and the view derived from David Best is that on the latter a dance may be rendered such by the context in which the dancers move, so that we can see them dance, and see the dance they are dancing, without being able to understand the dance at all. On the view derived from Danto, a dance is such only because it is understood as a dance in some quite definite way; people who see without understanding (in the way we described in the preceding sentence) have seen something, but not enough to count as actually seeing a dance.

8.2123 *Social Realism*

If what I see when I see a dance is really people doing something, then I cannot decide beforehand that what they are principally doing in their dance is performing the movements that make up the dance. That may be just their way of doing something else, which gives to their movements their most important meaning and which accordingly it is proper to identify as what they are really up to. If one description is to be given of what they do, this further meaning will provide it. I have argued against this position elsewhere (Sparshott 1982) on the grounds, pretty generally held, that what they are actually and directly doing is performing the actual dance movements they make, which can be studied and developed without regard to any further use that may be made of them or any social or political meaning that may be found in them. Someone who dances may be foreshadowing the emancipation of the slaves, and that may be the most important thing that the dancer is doing; but to say that a dance is being performed says nothing about that, and nobody seriously supposes that it does. Nobody would maintain that if I have not recognized that emancipation is foreshadowed I must have failed to see the dance, though there will be things about it that I have not understood.

The objection I have just stated can best be met by giving it the lie direct. A dance is danced by people as the human beings they are, and to be a human being is to live a life that is a variant on the common destiny of a social or economic class. Unless dancers are less than human beings, what they primarily *do* in their dancing must objectively be, whether they know it or not, to show and symbolize the social relationships into which they actually enter. Even their pure, artistically orientated or technically orientated, intentions and strivings will themselves have as their primary significance the economic and social structures in which such ambitions are defined and conceived. There is, then, no special range of dance meanings and significantly special dance contexts such as we have been postulating: there is only a familiar medium wherein dancers and audiences convey social and economic relationships by piquant exemplification. What determines the true nature of dance is not the immediate (subjective) meanings but the objective meanings of those meanings themselves.

8.213 *What Is the Body?*

We were considering ways of saying what a dance really is, all of which were based on the simple idea that in any case a dance consists entirely or principally of movements of human bodies, the question being how to specify the aspect under which those movements were viewed when they were viewed as a dance. Then we contrasted all those views with those that insisted that dancers are not primarily bodies at all—as if they were animated cadavers, or zombies—but human beings: dances are things dancers do, not merely movements they make.[15] But in all this discussion we have

[15] The abnegation of humanity, as opposed to its sublimation, is what accounts for the malaise induced in Marcia Siegel by the dancing of Erick Hawkins: "In trying to see the dancing body as a thing in itself, possessing an intrinsic beauty provided it is being faithful to its own natural rules, he comes closer than perhaps anyone to the 'objective' goals of modern art, music, and literature. But he is assuming that we can *see* the naturalness and the pure beauty as easily as someone performing in his technique can *feel* it. He asks the audience to separate the literal fact—that real persons, male and female, are doing real actions with inevitable resonances in our experience—from the aesthetic fact—that these persons can be per-

failed to notice an important ambiguity in the idea of the body itself. Where does the body end? At the skin, or at the outermost shell of clothing? One takes it for granted, I think, that the former answer is the right one—my body is what I put my clothes on. But, if that is right, the idea that dances consist mainly of body movements excludes most of the world's dance. The notion, common among us, that dance is most itself when dancers are as nearly naked as decency permits, in costumes that leave the limbs visible and untrammeled, is one that much of the world expressly repudiates. "You cannot dance our dance properly without our clothes on," said the chief's wife at Ajibame in Dahomey to Robert Thompson when he began to follow the steps of the master drum during a festival, and she rushed up to him, bringing a Yoruba robe (Thompson 1974, 253). And Ram Avtar Veer lays it on the line: "The dance in naked body undoubtedly produces a clear picture of poses of whole bodily organs used in dance. But Indian culture does not permit the nakedness of ladies in dancing" (Veer 1982, 66). It is not, obviously, that they cannot see the point; in training a dancer, one starts from the movements of the limbs. But those movements are not the substance, but the underpinning, of what the spectators are to see. And to rehearse in leotards may not, in any case, be the best way to practice for dancing in heavy robes.

The idea that a dance consists of body movements as they are without drapery associates dance with nakedness or near nakedness, and in a society (as ours has long been) in which people are expected to wear clothes except in very specific contexts, nakedness is charged with special meanings. One of these is sexuality: the naked body is, often, the sexually offered and prepared body. Insofar as that is so, naked dance may be inherently erotic—even when it is not overtly or directly so, because then the erotic suggestion is not absent but contradicted and denied. And in North America, at least, it seems that the preference for tights and body-stockings in dance has in fact coincided with the growing tendency to include nude scenes into theatrical and especially cinematic productions, scenes that seldom have any other point than sexual display.

To be human is to be a social being, unthinkable otherwise than as shaped in a community that is continually interacting and articulating that interaction in speech. It is also to be strongly individual, a single embodied consciousness subject to anxiety when the unmitigated nature of its subjective isolation is revealed. It is to be intellectual, ceaselessly analyzing and interpreting one's situation ("How are you doing?" is our common greet-

---

ceived for their form and harmony alone. . . . Some of his viewers, myself included, find in these nearly naked, hairless bodies engaging in soft, gentle play not a more human humanity but one that is somehow deficient" (Siegel 1979, 318–319).

ing and is nonchalantly answered "Good. How's yourself?"). It is to be a homeostatic organism, a self-maintaining chemical factory. And it is to be sexual, perpetually at the center of a network of attractions and repulsions that color almost all our experience. All these aspects of our humanity are inevitably involved in all that we do, though not all are equally emphasized. The dancing body, I have been suggesting, is emphatically sexual in its display and exercise of nakedness. But, at the same time, its sexuality is emphatically canceled by a diversity of factors. First, nakedness is not sexual in its implications in all contexts, but principally in situations of intimacy, real or pretended: dancers do not usually dance as to and for the audience but in essential remoteness from them. (Belly dances and other dances that mime seduction need special consideration, obviously.) Second, the nudity of dance is closer to the functional nudity of athletics: the dancers are evidently athletes working at their exercises, stripped for action. Third, if the dancers are really dancing and dancing well, their attention and ours is drawn to the dance itself, not to their and our sexual propensities and prospects. And fourth, as we have seen, the dancer tends to be subsumed in the movement of the dance. Even in Nijinsky's choreography, as Rivière thought of it, the pathos of the dancer's emphasized body is that of the world's irresistible pressure, not that of a personal vulnerability.

We see how ambiguous the idea of "the body" is when we contrast the physical body as an anatomist might conceive it, in its skin envelope more or less masked by drapery, with the social bodies of people as we meet them on the street, clothed and in their right mind. Most dances are dances of the social body, and it is in the social body that nakedness has its social meaning of *absence* of clothing. It is only in moments of confusion that a physiologist (or similar professional) thinks of the naked body as *undressed*. In terms of this contrast, the dancer's body has to be the social body rather than the physiological body: the dancer is, after all, doing something that has a distinctively social meaning. How, then, are we to account for the assumption that nudity or near nudity is the appropriate garb for a dancer? It is made to seem natural by reference to the dance as the art of body movement. But that is simply a mistake.

At least three closely related factors seem to be involved. First, there is the fact that the nineteenth-century heritage of present-day dance is that of gymnastics and body-building, a practice in which people stripped down (as they still do) for purely practical reasons. Second, there is the sentimental nineteenth-century cult of Hellenism, to which Isadora Duncan owed so much, in which the Greek ideal of physical and mental health was associated with the distinctively Hellenic practice of exercising in the nude. And third, as Elizabeth Kendall points out (1979), the first generation of modern dance in America arose in a climate of female emancipation that included protest against the tight-lacing and other stiflingly unhygienic clothing of the day. The release of the body from its clothing was symbolic; the suggestion of the presence of the unrestrained body was thematically important for Loie Fuller as well as for Duncan. Diaphanousness was not so much a tease as a promise of freedom.

8.3 *What Is Dance?*

What are we to do with all these rival accounts of what a dance is? How are they to be related to each other? Should we simply treat them as alternative characterizations, no doubt among many others, all of which fit some dances to some extent but any of which will fit some dances better than others? One thing we might say is that it depends where you sit. Can you see the sweat and hear the panting? If so, you are not likely to think that the dance denies the body weight of the dancers. Perhaps Valéry sat at the back of the gallery. On the other hand, if you are close enough to see the sweat you may be too close to see the overall pattern of the dance and will be unlikely to identify the dance (as you see it) with that. If that is how matters stand, then the question of which is the better account of what dance is reduces to the question of which is the best seat in the house—or, in more general terms, how far from the dance the audience should be and, consequently, how theaters should be built. Or again, the social relations brought to an expressive head in the dance will not be visible to the politically naive (or will be visible only to the gullible), who themselves may be blind to the formal features that for more sophisticated afficionados of dance are what the dance is actually about, so that their dismissal of such features as trivial can hardly be taken seriously—or, as they would say in their turn, they are not so indoctrinated into such frivolities as to be mystified by them.

We are bemused by the notion of a work of art, and hence by the notion that a dance is something with a determinate character. Why should it be? Choreographers, like other real-life artists, have many things in mind as they work out the complexities of their creations. It is highly unlikely that they have any single system of meanings and effects in mind. How could they? They would have to maintain not only conscious neglect of all other factors and possibilities, all alternative viewpoints, but also prevent their practice from being contaminated by all they inarticulately knew. In a dance there will be some things you can only see from real close, some things that need a panoramic view, some things that are only evident on repeated viewing, some things that only really hit you the first time, some things that depend on pure and undistracted visual impact, some things that call for technical or historical knowledge or indoctrination, some things that require you to appeciate how hard it is for the dancers to do them, some things that build on the illusion of soaring in a leap. Some aspects of the work it will be possible to appreciate simultaneously, some one will have to hold together in a sort of suspension and shifting of emphases, some may exclude each other in a given performance, some may reveal themselves differentially at different times of life or to persons of different sexual orientation. Why not? To make a dance is to make something that is to prove satisfactory as a dance under some or all of the conditions, in some or all of the ways, that we are suggesting, and under such other conditions as there may be. Dancers and dance makers please themselves, satisfy their exacting requirements, in as many ways as occur to them as they work. Why should there be any optimum way in which this inchoate totality comes together?

What bemuses us is the Aristotelian model, whereby "art imitates nature" in the sense that a natural object grows into a single, complete, mature form, the realization of which is the justification of the thing's existence—elephants grow up to be elephants just so that there shall be elephants, jointly though imperfectly manifesting the complete nature of elephantinity. Similarly, on the view that Aristotle shared with Karl Marx, the artist labors to complete a work of art, realizing the perfect and perfectly determinate form that defines the work and which is just what the artist had in mind at the moment when intentions became fully formed. Well, perhaps that does happen sometimes; but, when it does, it is very unlike what usually happens when people actually set out to do things, and I see no reason to set it up as an ideal to which they should conform.

We began this chapter by insisting that there could be no ontology of dance, that what we had already established made it impossible even to undertake the project of saying in general terms what dancing is or what a dance is. What was not ruled out, we said, was saying what a dance is from the point of view of a regular dance goer at a regular dance performance. Are we to say that that too has proved impossible? Not necessarily. Dance turns out to be the performance art whose performances sometimes or always lend themselves to such characterizations as the above (among others, no doubt), and for the reasons given. As we said in Chapter 4 that the range of meanings we went through could be presumed, in its entirety as a range of lively options, to be distinctive of the practice of dance, so we can now say that a dance is the sort of thing that sustains a structured set of alternatives of the kind presented here.

8.4 *Principles of Order*

If it is true that dances may be conceived in radically different ways, corresponding (among other things) to irreducibly different but inexpugnably legitimate ways in which we as humans can conceive and must live out our relation to the world, it follows that there can be no principles of dance order: each such conception must generate its own set of elements and its own ways of articulating them.

It is important to realize at the outset that the sort of deep ambiguity we have detected in dance, together with the multiplicity of dimensions of dance meaning, rules permanently out of order the recurrent attempts to discover a culture-free mathematical basis for aesthetic standards. At one time the canons of human proportion were thought to have the potential for emancipating sculpture and figure painting from fashion and relativity; for a longer time, the "golden section" and other proportions were asked to do the same service for architecture; and, above all, the simple principles underlying consonant intervals were expected to ground music on eternal truth. In all cases, the hope was to transcend cultural differences by eliminating as trivial all that depended on cultural understanding and interpretation. Surely the principles of true beauty must be the same everywhere. Nowadays we have mostly given up the search for a set of forms that all truly beautiful objects must share. But may we not still hope to identify, in our more sophisticated way, some system of recursive analysis, fractals or what not, that will enable us to explain how an identifiable sort of internal coherence of analyzables underlies whatever is found beautiful within the most diverse dance traditions?

It should be quite clear by now that the hope thus offered is trivial at best. It relies on an analysis that is formal from start to finish, in which the identification of relevant relationships is determined perceptually or in some a priori fashion of which no one has any inkling. It is not something unachieved, to which a more sophisticated mathematical technique might lead us; it is wrong from the start, presupposing views of human relationship and of the bases of meaningfulness for which there is nothing whatever to be said. Those who cling to the hope of a preemptively authoritative, culture-free analysis cannot have asked themselves the ontological questions from which they needed to start.

We have already remarked (§5.522) that all possible forms of patterning, such as those anatomized by Ernst Gombrich, can be expected to be exemplified in one or another dance form. And a given dance, maintained through generations with as little change as possible within a stable dance practice, may be expected to undergo subtle internal changes as its neighbor practices change, thereby promoting or preempting conceivable (and hence applicable) systems of order within which the continuing dance practice may be thought of. If one revives a dance production after ten years, keeping everything the same, differences in the ways people outside the dance world dress themselves and address each other must change many of the meanings within the dance and may add or subtract whole ranges of significance, and hence of significant patterning, within the dance as the best and most informed spectators will perceive it.

The same passage that invoked Gombrich went on to say that it was tempting to equate dance with *measured* movement. Is that temptation one that we must now more firmly resist, or can we use it to qualify our declaration that there can be no determinate principles of dance order?

8.41 BODY AND MEASURE

The very idea of time as quantifiable and measurable, as usable for dating and timing, is derived from the decision to take certain repeated units of movement as standards by which other movements may be measured. To form the basis of regularity, these standard movements must be regular in a prior sense: they must end where they begin again (as in a foot rule, if it is to be useful, one inch must end just where the next inch starts). Such movements must, Aristotle thought, be either cyclic, movement in orbit past a given mark, or reversing, like a piston or a pendulum. In his day, the natural paradigm was the apparent cyclic movement of the heavenly bodies; nowadays, these are replaced or supplemented by reversing movements—pulsing crystals, swinging pendulums, escapements rocking on wheel rims. To understand what the basis of dance pattern could be, we must note the reversing movements of the body: the pendulum swing of legs in walking, systole and diastole of the heart, intake and release of breath. These movements have, to an extent, their own rhythm, their own speed, which imposes itself. But hearts may beat faster or slower, breath may become pant or sigh; and, especially in the limbs in haste or dawdling, such natural rhythms, while their basis is unchanged, may be imperiously overridden by the decisions of the person in charge.[16]

[16] Some people might want to insert here a reference to patterns of movement in the cerebral cortex, whether of global "alpha waves" and such or of synaptic trackings down ionic pathways (as playfully hinted by T. S. Eliot, §7.2 above). No doubt there is such a counter-dance going on, but I doubt its relevance at this stage of the game. We do not know any way of making interesting correlations between any such intracortical events (which are never directly perceivable by anyone and not normally even indirectly perceivable, least of all in a dance situation) and the sort of bodily movements and motivational configurations that define the interests of dancers and dance goers alike. In any case, it is a tricky business to estab-

Dance movement is indeed likely to be measured movement. But such ways as we have indicated in which the regular and regulative movements of the body may be varied, in themselves and as against the mineral regularities we choose for our clocks, are enough to ensure that dances can be measures against measure. Movements may be fast or slow. They may be perceived by the spectator as faster or slower than the body's habit suggests, and intended or experienced by the mover as hurried or dragged against the felt impetus of the limbs. They may be accelerated or decelerated. More subtly, a movement may be imposed on the body or acquiesced in, the rhythm may be bodily or conceptual in its origin. And, as part of this patterning of impetus, movements may be large or small and in either case may be infused with little or much energy, languid or intense. Such qualities and the ways of varying them must be part of the patterning most indigenous to dance, insofar as dancing remains centered on body movement.

We have been speaking of the body kinesiologically, as a mechanical system subject to the laws of physics. Despite the misgivings expressed earlier, that seems legitimate. In our scientific world view, the laws of physics are basic, and the scientific world view with that basis defines what all things and people have in common. But we have, after all, just finished saying that it is not possible to live that way. Not science, but phenomenology, must prevail in practical thought, when we come to consider the immediate quality of the world we live in. And we have just seen that there is no one simple account of what we are as bodies, or as embodied, or as corporeal. We saw that honest, intelligent, well-informed, and sensitive people do not always want to give the same answer to the question what a dance, as such, is. And each different view of what a dance essentially is must subtend a different set of views of how it is proper to desribe the order of the dance, what its elements are and how they are related to each other and to the whole.

8.42 MUSIC AND MEASURE

The beating of the drum, the striking up of the band, is at once the invitation to the dance, the harbinger of dance, the symbol of dance, a physical incitement to dance, a metaphor of dance, the sustaining accompaniment of dance. Death leads his dance by playing a drum, a fiddle, or pipes. It is often said that dance movement is characteristically movement patterned by music—or, more precisely, since one can dance without music, movement patterned as if by music. But really, dance is in some re-

---

lish formal correlations between informational flow in control systems and mechanical changes in the gross systems they exist to control.

spects prior to abstract music. Time as the measure of movement depends on what is moved, and in music as pure form nothing is really moved. Should we not say that what singers and players of instruments do is already to dance, in that they perform the dance that will embody the form that the music identifies? No, better not; but one sees the point of saying it. We are, in any case, more used to thinking about musical form than about dance form and more adept at doing so. Music is to dance as mind is to body, conceived as the prior and regulative part even if we do not assign it any independent reality.

We cannot, however, delimit dance order by relying on the parameters of musical order. Not only do the spatial and energic determinants of actual dancing have no obvious equivalents in strictly musical terms, so that nothing is clarified by pretending to reduce the former to the latter, but musical order can share any indeterminacy we allow to dance. If anything can be dance, anything can be music; if music is restricted to specific sets of variations and variables, so can dance be, and there is no reason to suppose these two sets to be congruent. In other words, if there are reasons for thinking that dance depends on music, those reasons cannot have anything to do with formal analogies between the two realms.

When we consider the possibility of specifying principles of dance order, we must bear in mind the complexities adduced in §5.111. In a reflective society armed with such concepts as those of art and criticism, as Karl Aschenbrenner (1974) has urged, to invoke a principle is to invite its successful breach, and the language of art critics reflects this. Words of praise and dispraise tend to come in pairs, depending on whether a perceived quality in a work or performance is thought to contribute to making it better or worse. If dance can be patterned, built up from repeated elements, then it can be significantly unpatterned. If it can be metrical, danced in time to a beat, then it can be significantly unmetrical. If it can be rhythmical, with a swing we feel on our bodies, then it can be significantly unrhythmical. What is essential is never the fact that dance is any of these, but the way it is them. None the less, though to be a dance is not necessarily to have a particular one of these paired characters, it is at least to be movement to which such considerations are centrally relevant. The timing of the movement has to matter, and to matter just because it is timing. And no doubt there will often be a strong expectation, or even a demand, that dances will be of one kind rather than another.

8.43 SUBSUMPTION

We recall that Havelock Ellis identified as the leading characteristic feature of dance the way in which partial movements are caught up into wholes in a unifying rhythm (§§2.3, 7.1 and note 5 above). It may be a leading feature, but is it a distinctive feature? Susanne Langer, without reference to dance, thought it distinctive of vital processes in any living body that the built-in rhythms of pulsation of particular organs and subsystems are modified and overridden by the unifying order of the organism as a whole (Langer 1970). Every dance, then, like every organism, is a system of captured rhythms, in which a dominant patterning modifies and thus subsumes the temporal patterns of its subsystems, whether those be the predilections and capacities of individual dancers or the inertial tendencies of parts of a dancer's body. But every ordered motion of an organism or of a collaborative group must manifest a pattern of the same general sort; otherwise we would have no occasion to speak of a single organism or of collaboration. (There are, of course, other modes of group action and interaction, if not of collaboration, but we leave those on one side for now.) To assign the phenomenon specifically to dance is little more than a rhetorical gesture on Ellis's part, in a book that strikes our latter-day sensibilities as largely made up of rhetorical gestures. But not entirely so. Though the order of dance cannot be any specific sort of order but may be an ordering primarily in terms of movement type, of ritual structure, of action-sequence, or anything else, we will not think of it as dance unless the orderedness itself is evidently what dominates the situation. The order of the dance may be articulated in ways that do not depend on dance, as by narrative sequence or exposition, but we allow them to constitute dance only insofar as what dominates the experience for dancer and spectator alike is the orderedness of the ordered unity in which this is worked out. Even if a dance is arbitrarily structured or devoid of structure, as the avant-garde would say it could be, it will be a dance only insofar as dance motivation or dance context take over the whole and give it a significance that effectively restructures it. No doubt this often fails to happen; but then we may say that dance is not achieved. The avant-garde really cannot claim to be doing anything of significance if there is no way they can come to grief; like people who cheat at solitaire, they reduce their victories to the level of defeats.

8.44 PATTERNS IN SPACE

The ordering of dance that we have been talking about so far is a strictly temporal modulation, really a matter of ordering tensions and relaxations. Most of what we have said could be (and has been) said of music without regard to any physical movements of singers or instrumentalists, either as a matter of psychological anticipations and fulfillments or (less speculatively) as a system of logical implications fulfilled or negated (Meyer 1956 and 1962, respectively). But dance movement is primarily movement of the body in space and hence is patterned spatially no less than temporally.

One dances measures, we said; but one also dances *figures*. Aristotle in his *Poetics* already chooses this term (*schematia*), a term familiar in his circles as belonging to geometry, to pick out the distinctive forms of dance; and "figures" are what Hippocleides dances away his marriage with.

A person simply beating time with foot or finger might be making a dance patterned in time but not significantly patterned in space. Someone striking a pose might be making a dance (like Paul Taylor's *Duet*, §5.5216) well ordered in space but patterned in time only trivially, in that the pose must be struck and abandoned (or lit up and blacked out). And someone merely establishing presentness, like Duse as Duncan imagined her (§5.52161), would be doing something not significantly patterned at all, either in space or in time—although, as we said, the person might stand as a source of order, like Shiva as the *Natyaraj*.

The preceding paragraph led us into a trap. We spoke of a dance being patterned in space and time, as though there could be two sorts of patterns, spatial and temporal. But the concept of pattern is really not applicable to temporal series. Or at least, if we think of a pattern as an array of ordered elements laid out for our inspection, there can be no temporal pattern, because there can be no compresence of spatially distinct elements and hence no array. All we can have are repetitions and reversals, inversions and changes of scale, that present formal analogues of patterns. But the pattern is present only to reflection: what actually confronts us is always one episode of a continued series, conditioned by what precedes and follows, in what is experientially a radically different order.

We encountered the concept of pattern before, as a putatively necessary condition of dance (§5.522), and what concerned us then was the minimal conditions something must fulfill to be patterned in an appropriate sense. Our present concern is with what sorts of (spatial) patterning are indigenous to dance as dance. Many alternative ways of ordering dances in space may become prominent depending on how one is dancing and, more importantly, what one takes oneself and others to be doing in dancing. Conceptually, as geometric pattern creation, a dance may be thought of planometrically, in terms of the forms trodden out on the floor, as in the neo-Platonic ideology of the French and Italian courts. Empiricists who reduce everything to constructs from sense impressions might conceive dances as though they were silhouettes projected on a screen, in terms of line and trajectory. A scientist analyst may conceive dance three-dimensionally as solid bodies moving through Euclidean space (or, more significantly, the Cartesian space defined by coordinates on three axes).[17] A humanist may

---

[17] In a videocast called *Other Dances* (PBS, 16 August 1982), Jerome Robbins emphasized how important it is that dancers are dancing in an actual space, in definite relation to a fixed floor, wings, etc., and not in the fluctuating and indeterminate spatiality that the television camera creates for its viewers. That holds good whether or not we think of the dancers as

emphasize the order of centrifugal and centripetal movement with the body as center, without special regard to the status of the environment within which the dancer moves. And, as we have seen, if the body is the social body, one may think of the dance in terms of a topology of human relations, approaching, retreating, welcoming, rebuffing, dominating, and deferring. There are different orders because there are different spaces, with dimensions and directions differently defined according to what we think a dance really is and dancers, as such, really are.

If we were committed to some one ontological view of dance, we would thereby be committed to the corresponding analysis of dance space and the patterns it could sustain. But such a commitment would be uneasy. What would we do about alternative commitments and analyses? We cannot help noticing that there are lots of such alternatives. We could of course say that their proponents did not understand dances at all. People often do say such things, but only because they do not stop to think about the implications of what they are saying: they cannot seriously believe that their own sensitivity and intelligence are of a quite different order from those of their professional colleagues. What shall we say then? Perhaps that all humans are real virtuosos in being human, and after a lifetime we do have an indeterminate multiplicity of such alternative spatialities quite effortlessly available to our sensibilities. To find our ways in a world that is partly social, partly interpersonal, partly mechanical, and so on, we must be able, without even thinking about it, to act in terms of as many of them as are appropriate at any given moment. Why should not dances, like life, be constructed in indefinitely many spaces, in such a way that the element/ whole relationships that are relevant, and their relative importances, have to be picked up as we go along, and we may often or even usually have a choice in the weighting we may at a given moment prefer? That would be just one more aspect of the phenomenon to which Ludwig Wittgenstein drew attention in his (rather unhappy) metaphor of "language games": it is as if we had at our disposal the rules of many games of speech and practice, and slipped from one set of rules to another without notice. Only, of course, most of the time we are not playing any one determinate game— not even the Glass Bead Game of Hesse's novel.

8.45 Time, Space, Movement, Rhythm

The phrase "movement in space and time," like its twin phrase "patterns in space and time" to which we have already objected, expresses a muddle. One moves in space from one place to another; but whatever time one

---

occupying the same real space as their audience, rather than (for instance) a space made discontinuous from the place of the audience either by the edge of the dance area or by the magnetic force of the dance itself.

moves in is always now. To borrow a phrase from Lars Aagaard-Mogensen (1986, 45), "We are time dwellers (rather than travellers)." One does not move from past to future; and, if you prefer to use dates and hours as milestones, it always takes exactly six hours to get from 6 P.M. to midnight. There may be scientific contexts in which one speaks of movement in four dimensions (three spatial, one temporal) between which there can be a trade-off; but that sort of thing has no application at all to the contexts of human practice, in which we do not approximate the speed of light.

For practical purposes, it makes a lot of sense to stick with Aristotle's notion that time is the measure of movement or change. His concepts were tailor-made for the human scale, which often makes them good for practical contexts at the same time that it makes them useless for mathematical and experimental science. The movement that time measures has first to be specified, and it is typically specified in terms of a different set of measures from those we measure time with—for instance, spatial ones. We enumerate and determine the relative positions, phases, or magnitudes gone through and then use temporal measures to specify how long is taken in traversing them.

Are the spatial measures used to specify movements independent of the temporal measures used to measure the movements? To a point, yes. I can say that it takes me three breaths or twenty heartbeats to cover a distance of thirty meters, for instance, or that it it takes me ten seconds to perform twelve steps. Thus the nature of a movement and its magnitude have to be independently determined, even if we do so without stopping to think.

What about rhythm? Without committing ourselves to the strong sense of "rhythmicality" specified in Chapter 7 (note 5) above, we can at least say that rhythm has something to do with emphases and importances in transitions. There can be rhythm in space as well as in time. People tend nowadays to think of rhythm as essentially temporal, a feature internal to music, where it is almost a technical term; and it has been fashionable in aesthetics to say that its use in other contexts is metaphorical, but that is going rather far (cf. Sparshott 1963, 107). The word transliterates a Greek term that was originally used for the way a body is articulated in space— not the relative lengths of the limbs, but the angles between them and hence the dynamic poise of the body. History aside, we still can and do talk about visual rhythms in space as well as auditory rhythms in time.

But what about dance, which traditional metaphors have identified as music made visible and as pictures come to life? Does a dance have two separate rhythms, a quasi-musical rhythm and a quasi-sculptural one? One hardly thinks so. Is the rhythm of a dance then a synthesis of two partial rhythms (themselves specifiable in many different ways, according to our previous argument)? That does not sound right to me. And the reason it does not may be gathered from what we were saying about subsumption.

The dance is one: all phases of the changes in the dance are synthesized, and it is the totality that we think of as rhythmical or unrhythmical or arhythmical, or as having this rhythm or that. What is assessed for rhythm is what is happening in the dance. But that means that all units whereby the dance is, as it were, measuringly perceived must be mutually compatible or even reducible after all. And we have already seen that the neutral three-dimensional space of "Euclidean" geometry and the impersonal quartz-or-clockwork time of celestial rotations or molecular vibrations exist precisely in order to synchronize and coordinate the changes in disparate systems. Does that mean that the overall rhythm of a dance should be assessed by stopwatch and measuring tape? Presumably not, but why not? Because what calls the tune in setting up the overall rhythm is whatever in fact functions as the dominant system; and what that is, you can tell only by looking or feeling.

8.46 MOTION, MOVEMENT, ACTION

What do we see when we see a dance? There is a hierarchy in what we can see it as, the higher terms involving the lower, and it may be perceived as structured differently on these different levels. We mention four such levels; there may be others, and there may be intergradings and fusions.

At the lowest level, there are simple motions: persisting objects identified as being first in one place and then in another place and continuously occupying intervening positions, the motion consisting simply of these chartable trajectories.[18] We see what the dancers present us with as a pattern of identifiable forms in movement relative to each other and to the surrounding space and structures.

Second, there are motions perceived dynamically, as objects propelled inertially by forces along paths determined by those forces. We see the dancers as solid objects entangling with and rebounding from each other and the things on and among which they move.

Third, there are movements of the sort people make, ascribed not to forces as such but to intentions operating in, through, behind those forces—the relationship is immaterial and often indeterminate, because what counts is that the person is self-moved. The dancers move as and where they have decided to move and manage to move.

Fourth, there are actions. In making their movements, the dancers are doing things: they decide to perform the movements they do perform, but they perform them because they have decided to do something else, to

---

[18] The objects may be real or phenomenal. A succession of static images projected on a screen is what a continuously moving object in a film is based on. Since we are talking about what a dance is seen as, the difference is irrelevant here.

perform a dance or, on a smaller scale, to cross the stage or to swing their partners. An action cannot usually be specified by the movements made in performing it and does not specify in every detail what those movements are to be, though on any given occasion the action, as observed, is nothing but the movements made in performing it in a suitable situation. Full-blown action amounts to *praxis*, doing something in the world and participating in history. But the point at which an action becomes *praxis* is never quite clear, because it is not possible to get agreement on what counts as history or on how big a difference has to be before it really makes a difference.

There is nothing we know of in the irreducible data of human physiology and psychology that imposes precisely this four-level hierarchy on all observers, regardless of cultural background, though no doubt it is unavoidable that there shall be some hierarchy or other. Nor does the fact that a specific level of the hierarchy is culturally recognized mean that there is only one way in which dances can be construed at that level. On the level we have here identified as that of "action," for instance, different cultures may have very different ways of thinking about intention and will, mind and body, desire and inhibition. None of those are neutral terms; all of them are heavy with ancient doctrines structured in ways that may be inseparable from the specific cultural history of our civilization. People everywhere do things, and do some of them on purpose, but what they think is going on when people do things on purpose will be shaded or even structured differently in different cultures, and that is bound to affect how they see dances (and, probably, how they dance).[19] Similarly, at the lower level of intentional movement that does not yet amount to action, how a movement is construed will vary according to how one thinks human energies are marshaled and how one thinks the body is organized as a system. People who habitually operate with the concepts of yin and yang, for instance, are bound to construe and classify body movements accordingly; people who believe, as many Europeans believed early this century, in the vital importance of the solar plexus will draw for themselves a different internal map from any envisaged by contemporary kinesiology.

We cannot actually see how the body works as a machine or even whether it works as a machine at all. Similarly, how people seem to see

---

[19] The standard exposition of this theme used to be a paper by D. D. Lee (1950). She argued, oddly but not unpersuasively, that some Oceanic societies (which she knew only at second hand, through the writings of Malinowski) dispensed with the concept of purpose. It was not quite clear how this worked, but it was at least evident that the interaction between Trobrianders and their environment was not conceived in terms of the imposition of an imperious will on an inert world. More recent formulations of such theses (e.g., by Bateson 1972) are more tactful.

movement will depend on how they think of human bodies as information processors or whether they think of them in terms of information processing at all. Nowadays, for instance, we are told that the brain processes visual and auditory data at different speeds (a moment's thought will show that this has to be true at some level, that sound waves and light waves could not be analyzed in the same way); that must affect the way we actually see dances, and if we became systematically and self-consciously aware of it it might make much more of a difference than it does now, and a different sort of difference.

Even if we forget the possible cultural differences in how actions may be construed and classified, there is an ambiguity in the concept of action itself as applied to dance. The action we see as performed may be a dance action, such as a hay, or it may be an action mimed, such as a salutation. Often, what we see is both at once: the dancer performs a complicated lift with his partner, and the prince thereby embraces the princess in sexual ecstasy. What the characters do and what the dancers are doing are perceived with equal directness as part of the dance. And then, of course, there are the actions that the people who are dancing perform even as they dance as dancers and live as characters: they are living their working lives through the dance, and we see that with equal directness, especially if the dancers are our friends and relations. That is not part of the dance at all, in any dance; but it is there to be seen. If it were not, there could be no dance; and if we did not know that it was there to be seen, our experience of dance would lose much of its value. Angels might perform a dance on the head of a pin, but they would not be dancing on it, and what they did could not have the same interest for us that a dance has when people dance it on the bones of their own two feet (Chapter 5, note 24 above).

In the hierarchy of levels of agency, there is a logical gap between what I have called motion and movement as there is not between what I have called movement and action. Agents perform movements that involve motions of their bodies. They do not *perform* those motions as such. By performing the movements they do perform, they perform certain actions; in performing those actions, they perform the movements that make up the actions. The motions are what take place in their bodies, as situated in space, in the course of their doing what they do. Philosophers have spent much effort trying to formulate adequately precise ways of analyzing these relationships (e.g., Goldman 1970, Wolterstorff 1980), and it would be out of place to duplicate their labors here even if I could. The immediate point is to emphasize the radical importance of the break between the sorts of things one can say about dance movement that do not involve reference to its being a complex of animal and/or human self-movements but that treat the dancers merely as visual phenomena or as physical objects, and the sorts of things that involve reference to dancers as animate agents.

The hierarchy of levels of agency works itself out in many distinctions. It is the basis, for instance, of a distinction between space-founded relationships and intention-based relationships, and of one between forms as they fill a space and forms as they generate a space. The latter difference is one that dancers may find disorienting if they have rehearsed in a small space and must dance in a large one. The same dance that was shaped around themselves becomes something they have somehow to dance out to the bounds of the stage—"You have to fill the dance space *somehow*," I heard a dancer say.

The hierarchy is, then, an indeterminate one, in its structure and in the aspects of the structure that become important in different practical contexts, and also in the practical form those aspects assume as opportunities and problems for dancers and spectators. A given dance tradition may rely on a particular version of the structure in all these three ways, and those who live inside that tradition (by choice or because they know no other) may reasonably say that their version is simply what dance really is. Nothing else is dance. Other people don't dance properly, don't know how to dance, are degenerate or philistine. But we as students of philosophy are always trying to push our understanding in the direction of all the universality that we can warrant, and we will prefer to say that what dance is has to be understood in terms of all these alternatives, not just as a mass but as capable of meaningful articulation. We will not acquiesce in claims that a certain tradition is the only possible or the only legitimate one, except to the extent that there are devotions and delights that only such exclusiveness makes possible.

The four levels distinguished in our hierarchy do not exhaust the possibilities. Mary Coros, for instance, finds it necessary to write from the point of view of four distinguishable levels of conceptualization. There is the felt "language of movement" in which one's awareness of one's bodily self is immediate, "movement languaging, gesture speaking; . . . body-being speaking." There is "body-being's reflection on itself; what it 'thinks,' how it feels as it moves. . . ." There is the mediating level at which one uses common sense and whatever other resources one has to make the first two levels articulate. And there is "the epistemic conceptualization where universals arise . . ." (Coros 1982, 3). It is by no means clear what language one should use to distinguish these levels of awareness, but one instantly recognizes them and the differences between them as modes of a dancer's self-knowledge.

Whatever a dancer does will be amenable to analysis in the ways we outlined and available to the dancer's self-awareness in such ways as Coros distinguishes. But also, because the dancer is a dancing person, all the dance movements will be describable both in terms of dance analysis (as steps or whatever) and in terms of the exercise of the organism's capacities. And this distinction corresponds to the one familiar in linguistics as that between phonemic analysis and phonetic description: it is one thing to describe, in whatever terms one has available, the sounds people can be heard to make as they talk and quite another thing to identify the sounds they make in terms of the set of mutual relations whereby they are constituted as distinguishable elements capable of combining in properly formed words in a language. Such phonemes cannot be defined otherwise than by their distinguishability from other phonemes that belong to the same language.[20] Similarly, a dance movement performed as part of a dance within a formalized dance system can be identified only in relation to other movements as differentiated within that system itself.

An analysis of a dance made simply in observational terms, or in terms of movement units defined within other dance systems, will fail to show what choices the dancers are making and will not identify the respects in which the dance is performed correctly or incorrectly or in which the dancers fail to perform it at all. This point was first clearly made, so far as I am aware, by Adrienne Kaeppler in an analysis of Tongan dance. "The first task of a structural analysis of dance is to locate for a specific tradition the basic movement units [which she calls "kinemes"] and define the range of permissible variation within those units" (Kaeppler 1972, 174). Thus, in Tonga, the kinemes are defined by contours of movement, not by timing: a movement can vary in timing and still be called the same movement (p. 176). Other recognizable movements of the dancers may have no "emic" significance at all but are only stylistically relevant as helping to determine whether the dance is done well or badly, in a characteristically Tongan way or in an alien way. Hip movements, for instance, are never emic in Tonga, and the upper leg does not exist for Tongan dance terminology (pp. 177–180): "Such movements may tell us something about the dancer, but not about the dance" (p. 177).

In Kaeppler's terminology, kinemes combine into morphokines, the least movements that can be *performed*—roughly corresponding to the level

[20] The application to general anthropological contexts of this distinction between "emic" and "etic" analysis is due to Kenneth L. Pike: "Descriptions or analyses from the etic standpoint are 'alien,' with criteria external to the system. Emic descriptions provide an internal view, with criteria chosen from within the system. They represent to us the view of one familiar with this system and who knows how to function within it himself" (Pike 1954, 8). But this distinction between inside and outside is faintly misleading: the heart of the matter is rather that the emic account goes by function, having to do with the distinctions that articulate practice, whereas etic distinctions are made from the stance of an empirical observer of phenomena.

of analysis implicit in our familiar word "step." The most familiar attempt to carry through such a two-level analysis of a dance style is that of the *Natyashastra*, which lists 108 *karanas* (corresponding to kinemes), which combine, in strings of six to nine units, to form the recognized *ansaharas* (Bharata 1967, ch. 4, §§30ff.), which would correspond to the morphokines.

The *Natyashastra* does not explain the principles of its analyses and lists, and it is not really clear where the ground level of the system should be located. But then, the aptness of Kaeppler's analogy between phoneme and kineme is not clear either. If the analogy between linguistic analysis and dance analysis is to go through, the phonemic/kinemic level must distinguish between what is and is not a structural component of a dance, but the components themselves will have no meaning or value; the morphemes or morphokines will be meaning-conferring combinations of those components, but not in themselves capable of standing alone as meaningful; and morphemes will combine into sememes that have definable meanings as separable units. (In fact, what we have is a formalization and clarification of the three-level analysis of the written into letters, syllables, and words, familiar since Plato's day—and used by the Villaris [1978] to explain the articulation of disco dancing.) But this third, sememic level is not represented in Kaeppler's analysis of Tongan dance, and that means that the lower levels also cannot function as they do in the linguistic analogue.

The general question of the analogies and disanalogies between linguistic and dance systems is complex. (Paul Ziff makes a start in his contribution to Fancher and Myers 1981, 69–83.) But we can perhaps see already that the parallel can hardly go through, just because dance is inseparable from the actual flow of body movement in a way that has no linguistic analogue. Linguistic structures are equally exemplified in written and vocal discourse and hence are abstractable. That is to say, what is linguistically significant in the vocal sign can be identified as what it shares with the equivalent inscription, and vice versa. By contrast, there is no reason for dance systems to be comparably abstractable. Whatever the range of meanings they can bear, they do not perform the function of comprehensive conceptual formulation and communication that determines the kind of grammatical structure languages have to have. All human cultures have dances. But all human cultures also have languages. It is absurd to suppose that the two systems do the same job.

8.461 *Pure Dance*

Some such hierarchy as that of motion, movement, and action is inescapable once analytic attention is turned on the ways people do things. As soon as we recognize such a hierarchy, we can see that pure and autonomous dance is possible, in the sense of a practice and art that is defined in terms of body movements performed simply for their own sakes. But such arts of pure dance, dance that is nothing but dance, are not found everywhere. In fact, the very idea of an autonomous art of pure dance seems almost confined to America in the last century. None the less, it seems that people who never in fact separate dance from music or dance from drama grasp the point of that separation without even having to stop and think about it. Presumably the immediate explanation of that fact (if it is a fact; of phenomena that might lead one to think it a fact, if it is not one) is that in learning to dance one does have to learn the movements as movements; or, if one has oneself picked up the skills without thinking about them, one sees that in teaching someone else one would have to isolate and impart the movement techniques. The concept of dance is one that people who are in the least aware of cultural diversity tend to have whether they know they have it or not. Thus, though Robert F. Thompson finds that the African peoples whose culture he studies seldom have the concept of dance as such, and though he tells us many times that they conceptualize their practice in ways that do not correspond to the ones we use, we also find him reporting conversations in which he asks his informants about particular points of dance value and dance technique and they find no difficulty in giving direct and relevant answers.[21]

Thompson quotes A. M. Jones as saying, "The norm of African music is the full ensemble of the dance; all other forms of music are secondary. . . . This consists of the orchestra, the hand-clapping, the song, and the dance."[22] Thompson complains that Jones wrongly omits costume and cosmetics, coiffure and artifacts. In the same vein, we read: "May I make it clear that when I talk about music I am referring to drumming, dancing, and singing? They are all the same thing and must not be separated" (Gbeho 1952, 31; cited by Thompson 1974, 242). The point is clear and emphatic: we are dealing with a single practice. But the wording is significant. Three things are named, of which dancing is one. They are said to

---

[21] Thompson 1974. Thompson was working with an interpreter, at least some of the time. Perhaps we should ask what the interpreter was up to. Did what he reported to Thompson always faithfully represent a response to a question asked and understood in a way that Thompson would have accepted? To what extent did the interpreter's interventions represent his own education and cultural bias, and to what extent did they represent his preconceptions about the beliefs of the interlocutors? Whatever the case may be, the interpreter at least found the task one that could be straightforwardly performed.

[22] Jones 1959, I, 51; cited by Thompson 1974, 242. Note that dance is included in music here, not the other way round. This order of subordination might be thought a mere byproduct of the fact that Jones (like Gbeho, a bit further on) is writing about music in the first place. But it is quite generally true that the first place one looks for discussions of dance outside the classical dances of the great civilizations is the *Journal of Ethnomusicology*.

be the same thing, but Gbeho cannot say they are the same without naming them separately. In fact, he says not that they cannot be separated but that they *must* not be separated. Why must they not? Because we will be struck by lightning? Presumably not. The point should rather be that none of them can be understood otherwise than in a practical context that combines them, that the people would not do what they do otherwise than in such a context, and that dancing without drumming and singing would be either pointless or a relatively trivial and culturally insignificant activity. Gbeho understands the distinction perfectly well and knows that we will grasp it too; but the distinction is not one between practices separately institutionalized and endowed with autonomous principles of construction and intelligibility. The distinction is a normative one, normative in one way for the dancers and in another way for us as interpreters.

Once one realizes (or, if you think it false: once one manages to convince oneself) that the distinction between pure dance, an art centered on nonordinary body movements, and complex art practices in which such movement is combined inextricably with music, text, and spectacle, is a distinction that may be quite recognizable to people whose culture refuses to countenance it as a practical possibility, the world's languages seem to abound with conceptual slippages that can be associated with it. Some of these may represent (wholly or partly) a colonized nation's acquisition of the language of the colonizing power, misrepresenting or degrading the original institution. But this seems not to apply in all cases. A world survey, were it within my professional competence, would pertain rather to anthropological linguistics than to anything that even our liberal interpretation could count as philosophy. But we cannot leave the matter entirely alone, since the concept of practice itself was introduced as involving the terms in which practitioners define what they are doing; so I will say something about it in a separate section (§8.4611).

In general, it seems that the request "Show me how you dance" is one that is immediately grasped, even by people who would not spontaneously make the abstraction involved. But one must not therefore assume that, because the abstraction of pure dance from its context is readily understood, being already implicit in the analytic processes of learning any dance practice, and hence a practice that is dance and nothing but dance can always in principle be abstracted and cultivated, pure dance must everywhere be able to sustain itself as a socially viable practice. There are many practices that it is possible to conceive without ever being tempted to indulge in them. It is easy enough to throw a turnip at a cow, and it is easy to imagine a custom of throwing turnips at cows on Saturday afternoons. But it is not a custom that is widely followed, and if a society were to adopt it one would not be surprised to hear that the custom (if not the cows) died out. Similarly, it is easy to see what an art of pure dance might be, but that does not mean that such an art could sustain itself over a long period of time in abstraction from other, supporting institutions. It might prove, in the light of experience, to be a rather silly thing to do.

Dance in the arts has usually occurred in structured settings: oriental dance-dramas, musical comedies, operas, or such sequences of fragmentary "turns" as a vaudeville show. When it does so, it may occur as a jewel in a setting, as a divertissement or set piece; or it may be so placed and introduced as to flow out of its context. The alternatives I have in mind here are most easily illustrated by the way musical pieces are built into musical comedies. The songs may be built into the plot (which is typically a story about music making); they may emerge naturally ("Everyone suddenly burst out singing"); or they may be inserted as set pieces into a prose drama, like the arias stuck into the *recitativo secco* of an old opera. We have no difficulty in switching from one convention to another. In the movie *Top Hat* Fred Astaire plays the role of a dance entertainer, and some of his dances he performs explicitly as such within the story; but others he slips into just to dance the story along, and at least once he performs a set dance, not as the entertainer he represents but as the dancer he is. The transition is so easy from one mode to the other that one seldom notices which is being done.

A social dancer at ball, hop, disco, or other meet can dance till exhaustion sets in without getting bored. But there remains a problem for dance as a pure art form, articulated in terms of movement rather than drama and unalleviated by interludes. For how long can such pure dance sustain interest and formal satisfaction through its internal structure and its perceptible movement qualities? Is a public of sufficiently adept and devoted spectators likely to persist in any society? It seems not to have happened anywhere other than in our own turbulent times, in which so many things keep changing and happening that we do not know what we are observing, let alone what we should be predicting. But perhaps Hegel was right: perhaps the lack of an independent cognitive significance will continue to confine pure dance, for the most part, to interludes and aspects of more capacious and miscellaneous kinds of presentation.

8.4611 *No Word for It*

One of the things that has struck us about dance, as we brooded on the feasibility of a philosophical consideration of dancing, is the combination of institutional ubiquity and recognizability with a lack of conceptual focus. Everywhere we look, it seems, we find people who dance but have no single word for dance or who have only lately acquired one; quite often, it seems, two words divide the work between them.

The conceptual situation here is very unlike that with "science" and "philosophy." The latter terms stand for a single historically developed practice that has attained a sort of worldwide normativeness because it is in fact the ideology of advanced technique. Whatever the cultural cost, people want to be sure of eating; science shows the way, and philosophy provides the climate in which science is done. The situation with dance is quite different. Different people have different sets of dances, and no nation esteems another nation's practice more highly than its own. The concept of dance, with its limited and oblique representation in the world's languages, seems to stand rather for the recognition that these can all be seen as different ways of doing the same thing, but seen only from a standpoint that few people wish to adopt.

In times of cultural change and conquest, which means most of the time, dances can be uprooted in an imperial context, taken to capital or court, and displayed there with the other trophies. Pure dance, dance as such, is perhaps what can be uprooted and transported, taught to the king's dance troupe, videotaped, sent on good-will missions—dance that can accordingly be shown and recognized, observed and copied, but not shared. However that may be, the conceptual complexities of dance terminologies seem to me distinctive of the field and worthy of the attention of philosophers even if they do not know what to do about it.

One thing we have to avoid is what we found Joann Kealiinohomoku (1970) saying: "Can we really believe that only white Europeans are 'advanced' enough to speak about dance?" We observed at the time (§3.2) that she was failing to distinguish between that English word and words in other languages that covered somewhat different practices and had somewhat different connotations. What we must now insist on is that we do not mean to suggest that adoption of any particular conceptual scheme, with the associated habit of making one particular set of abstractions, is a sign of "progress" or "civilization." The material that follows is not meant to be a pathology: it merely draws attention to a range of phenomena. It may in fact be the case that the habitual use of highly general terms for cultural practices, such as "art" or "science" or "dance," is peculiar to complex imperial civilizations with highly organized literate cultures, in which a wide range of practices from widely different ethnic backgrounds is compared. It is even probable that in all such imperial meeting places the conceptual schemes used in comparison and abstraction tend to converge. But the emergence of such conceptual hierarchies is a function of the imperial situation, and the standpoint implied in their habitual use is no sign of excellence.

In one of Adrienne Kaeppler's investigations, it appears that in ancient Polynesian terminology there was no one word embracing everything that we should call dance. There was *ha'a*, a sacred dance expressing humility, and *hula*, a recreational or celebratory dance expressing joy and other up-beat emotions. The terminology attended to the nature of the context as well as to the level of formality in the dance occasion. But the conditions governing the two terms were not symmetrical: in *ha'a* the context of production was the most important thing, whereas in *hula* what mattered most was the movements performed and their meanings. But nowadays the word *hula* covers all structured movement (Kaeppler 1984). It is as if the word *hula* were all ready to take on the meaning of dance in general, as soon as the conceptual space around it was cleared.

The situation in Hawaii might be attributed to the usual cultural attrition at the hands of missionaries, traders, and other intruders. The reader may recall, however, that a similar instability infected the Hellenic terminology of dance, in which *choreia* was identified principally by its place in social life and *orchesis* by its formal properties (though the former tended to be planometric in emphasis while the latter went in for jumping), but in the instability of Greek society throughout historical times the terms tended to lose their separate identity (§2.21 above). In fact, the Romans could use the one word *saltatio* to translate both words.

The Greek dichotomy of a movement-orientated and a ceremony-orientated term, the former primarily associated with individual leaping and the other with communal circling, has a partial analogue in the Japanese situation described by Gunji. "The common words for dance," he tells us, "are *mai* and *odori*. . . . The original meaning of the word *odori* was a leaping, jumping type of dance, while *mai* denoted a rotating or circling dance." Court dances and ritual dances were *mai*; rougher and more rustic dances were *odori*. The Chinese ideograms for these words were combined into a new word, *buyo*, which "was first used by the great dance-drama scholar Tsubouchi Shoyo (1859–1935) and his associates as an abstract term for dance in general. Until the creation of this word there was no abstract term for dance in the Japanese language" (Gunji 1970, 74). But he also reports that "the word used for dance in ancient records of Japan" was *buto*, a word now "used exclusively to indicate Western-style ballroom dancing" (p. 74). Despite this, Selma Jeanne Cohen reports that careful scholar Adrienne Kaeppler as saying that the term *buyo* is in fact inseparable from the Kabuki that is Gunji's subject and coexists with *bon* (funereal dance) and *mikagura* (in Shinto ceremonial) as "simply the movement dimensions of three entirely different activities that function in three entirely distinct ways" (Cohen 1982, 21)—as, of course, ballet and disco do.

No doubt Kaeppler had her reasons for saying "movement dimensions" rather than "dance dimensions"—I wasn't there. My old Kenkyusha Japanese-English dictionary seems to be less fussy, but you never know with dictionaries. In any case, the situation is obviously too complex to be easily summarized; but it looks rather as if the term *buyo* was coined as a generic term for classical Japanese dance to distinguish it from what *buto* had become, containing within itself the older polarity of ritual versus recreation, circling versus leaping. And we note that this move took place around 1920, a great time for dance revivals—when Uday Shankar was inaugurating the recovery of Indian classical dancing, when Diaghilev was reintroducing Europe to the lost art of ballet, when it became mandatory for American popular music to be dance music (Stearns and Stearns 1968, 95).

If my conjecture about *buto* and *buyo* is right, a similar distinction is made in Russian, where one word (*pljas*) is used for native Russian-type dancing and another word (*tanc*, German *Tanz*) for European-style dancing. Friedrich Zorn, a German dancing master working in Odessa, considered himself greatly daring when he included the former as well as the latter in his *Grammar of the Art of Dancing*, though his illustrative diagrams show all the Russian-dancing legs wearing furry britches, whereas the European-dancing legs are in tights (Zorn 1887, 38 and passim). My colleague S. Whalen draws my attention to an astonishing passage in Andrei Bely's novel *Petersburg*, in which a character is described as dancing his life away, the aspects of his decline marked with a dazzling variety of prefixes and verbal forms. All but one of the word forms used are derivatives of *tanc*; once only, in the midst of these, is a form of *pljas* used, and that is to indicate the wildness with which the character dances himself out of his career (Bely 1922, ch. 4). Bely and Zorn, in their different ways, recognize that the two words designate domains of a single practice, and they are not handicapped by the conceptual and practical divergence.[23]

At least in English, in addition to a host of names for dances and dance contexts and dance varieties, we do have one single word for dance— namely, "dance." But what about European languages in general? Here, as in other cases, we have a pair of words, Germanic "dance" and Romance "ball." European languages use the two eclectically, but not, so far as I am

---

[23] Since we have more than once referred in the text to Hebrew dance terminology, a review would be in place here. But it is impracticable for a layman. Oesterley (1923, ch. 4) lists eleven roots, some related to jumping and some to twirling, but it is unclear to the reader whether or not he really knows what the words mean and how they are used; Sendrey (1974, 221–225) supplies a dozen biblical words and says there are many more in the rabbinical literature, but again he leaves it unclear what activities and occasions they properly embrace. His conclusion (p. 225) that this abundance of terms "testifies . . . to the paramount importance of dance in the life and ritual of the Jewish people" is unwarranted. One could compile an enormous list of English dance verbs if one included jumping, cavorting, waltzing, pirouetting, gamboling, skipping, and so on, all on the same level. It is quite unclear from the evidence presented by these authors how the Israelites articulated their conceptualizations of what we should call dance.

aware, in ways that embody the sort of complexities we have been looking at: usually, at least, there is one generic word for dance, depending on who was boss when the vernacular was settling down. There is no sign of a latent conceptual unity manifesting itself in diversity. The explanation is probably a simple one: the conceptual unity of dance was established for educational purposes before the vernaculars existed, by way of that Latin word *saltatio*, which the theorists of the Roman world had already established as a generic term. It is the conceptual structures of Latin and Greek, the languages reserved by the educated for their formal endeavors, that have determined what we join and what we separate in our theoretical moments, rather than the dynamics of our vernaculars.

Yet another aspect of the latency of the concept of dance is shown in what Robert Thompson (1974, 252) says he was told in 1967 by George Tabmen, a professional interpreter from Dan in Liberia: "There is not a definite word for dance in Dan. For dance, we say *ta ka*, 'feet of song', because the movement of the foot is done to the sound of singing or musical instrument." If Tabmen really did say just that, and if he was speaking truly and not accommodating himself to Thompson's prejudices, then the Dan do have a fixed expression for dance, if not a single word. Perhaps it now only means the pedal component in a mixed song-and-dance form, but Mr. Tabmen seems in no doubt that, if anyone were to do anything more straightforwardly dancelike, *ta ka* is what it would be called.

Most striking of all these latent identities is one I have often seen affirmed in treatises on classical Indian dance, including at least two by impeccable authorities. The classical Sanskrit authors, they say, recognize three kinds of dance, *natya*, *nrtta*, and *nrtya*. These can be translated roughly as dance drama, pure dance, and expressive dance. But our authorities assure us that there is no Sanskrit word for dance, or for any general practice or phenomenon of which those three words would name different varieties. What, then, are these authorities of ours telling us? And in what language are they thinking? The thought they are expressing is, it seems, one that cannot be thought in Sanskrit. But if it can be thought only in English, how can it not be a falsification of the thought-world and practice of Indian dance? Yet what it says seems to fit perfectly well the phenomena that are being described and classified, and the authorities I have in mind write from inside the world of classical Indian dance. I suspect that the situation is somewhat as follows.

The *Natyashastra*, the primary authority for Indian classical dance, lays down a codified description of *natya*, dance-drama of the kind most typically represented for us by Kathakali. In doing so, it codifies, among other aspects of the presentation (including the music and the plot requirements), both *nrtya*, the kind of dance that expresses the meaning of a poetic text to which it is danced and from which it necessarily derives its articulation, and *nrtta*, the kind of dance that is structured primarily by movement forms.[24] Now, dance is danced by dancers, who, however much music they may have to learn, are simply dance performers. What they learn to dance is one or more named varieties of dance, Kathak or Chhau or whatever; and these, as parts or wholes, may be or incorporate dance-dramas in which the dancers participate and pure or expressive dances and dance sequences that they perform. In other words, the overarching unity that links the three terms is not a generic concept of dance but the common pattern of study and performance as shared by dancers and as manifested in relation to each of the named styles and genres that do not need to be identified as instances of anything. The concept of dance as such is everywhere and nowhere; and the adept in Indian dance has no difficulty, when writing in English, in using the word "dance," although the term had no original place in the articulation of the thought-world in question.[25]

[24] Indian explanations written for Western readers tend to say that *nrtta* is pure dance and *nrtya* is expressive dance. But this is very misleading if we take "expressive" in one of the ways current in Western aesthetic theory. Ram Avtar Veer, who, despite the unorthodoxy of his English idiom, states his views with exemplary precision, puts it this way: "The movement of feet and hands in time and rhythm is called Nrata. We can also define it as a dance without acting. The expression of feelings does not play an important part in Nrata. Only the rhythmical movement of the bodily organs is essential. . . . The expression of feelings and Nrata combined together are called Nratya i.e. Nratya is the movement of bodily organs in time and rhythm representing the theme of the story, drama or some historical events" (Veer 1982, 51). The situation is really much more complex than this, because it appears that Indian theory did not develop a comprehensive concept of music in all its branches and as distinct from dance before the fourth century B.C.E. According to M. Ghose, in the introduction to the second volume of his translation of the *Natyashastra*, there were words for song, for instrumental music, and for an art form (*preksa*) comprising both forms of music and pure dance (*nrtta*)—roughly, it seems, corresponding to *natya* but thought of as music-centered rather than as drama-centered. And by the third century C.E. "[t]here came into vogue . . . the word 'Samgita' for signifying by means of a single term all the different phases of music including dance" (Bharata 1961, 5–6). What this suggests is that the Indian theorists had at their disposal a battery of different terms for different music practices and dance practices singly and in various combinations, and they never felt any need to impose artificial segregations by sorting the terms into separate categories, though it was perfectly clear that the relations among them were not homogeneous. Anyone thinking and writing in English can, without compunction and without much falsification, use the generic term "dance" to convey associations that the Indian conceptual scheme holds, as it were, in solution.

[25] My knowledge of the theory and history of Indian dance comes from English-language sources, which I am in no position to evaluate. There are problems, I know. One useful piece of information has been furnished by Mandakantra Bose, who writes from Vancouver to tell me that the word *nrtya* was not used before the fourth century C.E. If that is so, we might envisage the situation as follows. The *Natyashastra* incorporates a definition and description of *nrtta* as the dance component abstracted from the *natya* it is concerned to analyze. But *nrtta* in that context typically takes the form of what would later be called *nrtya*, though in other

8.5 *Conclusion*

This chapter has been both futile and essential. It has been futile because we knew from the start that there is no one question that can be asked with the words "What is dance?" What we mean when we say "dance" depends on context in ways that resist simplification and ordering. But the chapter was essential because the impossibility of an answer does not dispose of its necessity. There is, as it were, a pattern of positions we fall back on when we want to say what dance really is, not alternative nerves of the practice so much as places where the concept of dance plays strategic roles in our thinking. Different modes of philosophy—phenomenology, culture criticism, aesthetics, conceptual analysis—determine different strategies without articulating them; it is not even clear how many different wars are being fought. Perhaps a chapter on the ontology of dance has to do with the default value of the concept—what we mean by dance when we don't mean anything else by it; except that there seems to be no one such value, but an indefinite number answering to salient families of contexts. Since we do not have an acceptable model for structuring such discussions (I have suggested that the models whereby we structure comparable discussions of other arts are superstitious residues from more complacent ages, useless to the scrupulous and disenchanted conscience of our day), we have no compelling reason for conducting the discussion in one way rather than another, no reason even for seeking more than a formal consistency. But we had to do something, or nothing. Now, let us wind up the chapter with a reminder of two sets of alternatives within which we cannot make a definitive choice but within which the nature of the choice itself is essential to whatever dance most centrally is.

8.51 DANCE AS SIGN

What we see when we see a dance is one of three things: it is a tissue of meanings, of significances borne by the dancers in their dancing; or it is a tissue of signs, of pure meaning-bearers abstracted from the actual dancers who embody the signs; or it is a nexus of things or persons that are both realities in real relation and also signs in relations of significances. We can also see the dance simply as real people doing things, making real movements in real space. But if that is all we see it makes sense to say that we do not see the dance at all. One can argue the point, but the case is strong enough that we can concede it for now.

---

contexts it does not. So another term is called for to distinguish this special application, which differs (as my text suggests) in the very basis of its organization.

One might contend that the distinction between things and signs is illusory. Things as seen are determined by and have to be defined by cultural meanings culturally codified. If I see an apple, I already identify it as a fruit of a certain kind, and that kind has inescapable meanings. That is certainly true. But the sense in which everything I identify in what I see is accessible only by way of my culture's repertory of classifications and meanings is very different from the way in which I see certain things as entities within specific cultural systems, articulated by special codes, to which they properly belong. In the latter kind of case, a kind to which dance belongs, a specific overriding code is superimposed on the diffuse cultural codings in which all objects of cognition are alike embedded. It is important not to overlook that. But the very fact that dancers are already meaningful before they take on the meaning of dancers means that whenever we see a dance we are already enmeshed in the thing/sign complexities and ambiguities we have mentioned, which become necessary factors in our experience of dance itself. We cannot say simply what a dance is, because whatever we say it is turns out to be something it could only be by also being something else, and there is no way of stabilizing the relations between the alternatives: in positing one we posit the possibility of the other, in positing their fusion we posit the possibility of their separation, in distinguishing between them we concede their antecedent unity, and so on.

In addition to the basic ambiguities we have just recalled, there is the plethora of meaning dimensions we outlined in chapter 4, together with a lot more material of the same sort that was postponed for later consideration. Dance, we said, is in general something of which we can be more or less directly aware as bearing such meanings—any or all of them. As we become aware of such meanings in specific cases, we recognize them as dance meanings; but they do not form a totality that is ever present to our minds, far less an operational equivalent of "what we mean by dance."

8.52 BEING HUMAN

Dance is that practice that comprises arts of human movement, suitably qualified so as to exclude anything we recognize as the wrong sort of movement. If we were going to embark on an ontology of dance, we would do best to make that our starting point, qualifying and adding or subtracting later. But, if we did start there, the basis for our ontology would have to be the mutual irreducibility and inescapable validity of different views of what it is to be human. They are irreducible because they are what we arrive at when we have made all the reductions we can, absolute termini of analysis and absolute starting points of existence. They are inescapable because we have to live them. We do not have the choice of being something that excludes them, we only have the choice of not attending to them.

What are these alternative views? Just because we have made such big claims for them, we cannot say definitely what they are; such a statement would be the conclusion of a philosophical inquiry, which is a contradiction in terms. Most philosophers do not even try, but cling to their one irrefutable way of thinking their and our humanity, letting the others go hang. And it is not always clear whether two statements that seem mutually irreducible may not turn out to be mutually translatable. However that may be, every human being seems quite certainly to be each of the following: a material object locatable in place and time, describable in terms of physics and chemistry; a living animal with a lifetime and a genetic inheritance; an absurd being, unable to accept or to reject either of the foregoing self-descriptions because to know something like that of oneself is to know that it cannot be the whole truth; a being responsible for its temporal existence and for the world that existence sustains; an individual self-defined within the structured community of minds that Hegel identified as "Spirit." To repudiate such a self-description is to show that one has not understood it. Admittedly, none of them are easy to understand. Some of them are quite hard.

Even if one does not accept all the items on the little list I have given, or even if one does not accept any of them, I do not see how one can avoid recognizing that some list of that general sort must be valid, though its validity may not be exclusive.[26] Any account of what we are as human beings is going to involve listing some set of radically different alternatives covering that sort of range. But then, whatever we do we must do as all the things we so variously are. We are dancers as all of them.

That is why there can be no simple and true account of what dance is.

---

[26] I am prepared to entertain the possibility that all such lists must cover a certain range of possibilities and that lists may be judged valid or invalid for coherence, completeness, and perhaps other values, but that not all valid lists need contain all or indeed any of the same items. The list I sketched was made up of items familiar within our intellectual world, articulated and advocated within our cultural context. Given this initial background, a range of alternatives defined in the terms it makes available can tell us truly what we have to be. If we started with a different initial apparatus our savants might excogitate a different set of necessities for us. But the necessities are not invented, they are discovered.

CHAPTER 9

≈ ≈ ≈ ≈ ≈ ≈ ≈ ≈ ≈ ≈ ≈ ≈ ≈ ≈ ≈ ≈ ≈ ≈

Conclusion

I THINK what has been done in this book is the right sort of thing to have done and to do. The wrong thing to do would be to produce a tidy theory in which dance would be given a determinate place and character in the world. Hardly less wrong would be to use the skeptical dogmatism of some philosophical pundit to show that the idea of a philosophy of dance involves a category mistake or some other intellectual solecism. What I, and others, should rather do is amplify and complicate on some such lines as the ones laid down herein, refining and simplifying only to clean up a little around the edges, not to impose a simpler pattern or a clearer tendency.

The material presented here has been put forward as preliminary work for a philosophy of dance. But it is already philosophy in its way. It is by no means certain that there is any better way.

The aesthetics of dance, perhaps more than the aesthetics of any other art or practice, ought to be done in the presence of a great deal of explicit philosophizing, for reasons that emerged at the end of Chapter 8. Artistic dance has to be the art of human presence or a set of arts and practices in which the modes of human presence are at issue as they are nowhere else— except perhaps in dramatic rituals, which are constantly assimilated to dance by those who write about them. We do not always think of dancing in that sort of way—we do not always think of dance in any sort of way; but once that point of view has been grasped it cannot be got rid of. The varieties and relations of the forms actually taken by human presence and compresence are the field of anthropology and the other human sciences. But the question of what it is to be human has another dimension, the dimension of meaning, and that is what philosophers are concerned with (cf. Sparshott 1975). All philosophy, even when it looks technical, is concerned directly with the question of what it means to be human—or, more precisely, with what it means to the philosopher to be whatever he or she takes herself or himself to be. Most philosophers most of the time think about questions more sharply defined, but the scope and style of such thinking is usually more compatible with some ways of answering the existential question ("What am I?") than with others, whether one chooses to talk about it or not. We have seen that a way of answering the existential question directly affects how one thinks about dance, and how one thinks about dance shows how one would deal with the existential question, if one dealt with it.

I said in Chapter 8 that the philosophy of humanity cannot be simplified beyond a certain point. There are a number of ways of answering the existential question that, once their point has really been grasped, can neither be denied nor reduced to each other. Nor can they be effectively handled by saying things like "we are always in question to ourselves," which prove to be in their turn positions that, once grasped, can neither be denied nor reduced to other positions equally incontestable. And that, as we said, is one reason why the philosophy of dance cannot be simplified without bare-faced lying.

We began this book by asking why the philosophy of dance had been neglected or, when not neglected, treated in a discouraging way. We can now supplement what we said there. If the aesthetics of dance is inseparable from intractably self-referential questions about the status of the would-be aesthetician, it is not surprising that the subject has been dealt with in a way that strikes clear-headed thinkers as dirty, corrupt, contaminated, or at best mushy. Workers in the humanities are regarded by all other academics as mushy; all other humanists detect mushiness in the alleged discipline of philosophy; all other philosophers despise aesthetics for its hopeless mushiness; and the aestheticians of dance are so mushy that even the other aestheticians notice. This is because, as we now see, their topic systematically resists the establishing of a stable starting point, in a way that the aesthetics of other arts does not.[1] This is felt, but not seen; so workers in the aesthetics of dance either commit themselves to blatantly inadequate premises or else succumb to evasive rhetoric. The proper solution is not to abstain from discussion in the interests of respectability, for nothing is more pathetically ridiculous than a philosopher determined to be respectable. The solution is never to forget just how messy one is being, so that one can be reasonably sure that one is being messy in a fully justifiable way.

9.1 *Dance Philosophy and World System*

We are now better able to see why it was hard to fit artistic dance into the canon of the fine arts. It was not, as we suggested before, merely be-

---

[1] The aesthetics of theater and drama is contaminated with the same trouble, for the same reason, but not to the same extent. The way drama establishes a connection between the stage and the social world (§7.7) has a sobering effect, and the authority of Aristotle's *Poetics* provides a stable point of reference.

cause of its triviality from the point of view of intellectual development, but because of its elusiveness as an object of thought. One can form a clear and straightforward notion of what dance is only if one can form a correspondingly sharp notion of what a human being is and hence of what one is oneself; and it is preposterous to suppose that, in making oneself an object for one's own cognitive operations, one could *reduce* oneself to such an object. Things are made much worse by the fact that, while one can think of music and poetry as a connoisseur rather than as a practitioner, dancing has almost always been something one approaches as a participant (at least potentially) before one is an observer. In whatever mode of dance, I have suggested, however quotidian or even vestigial, to stand forth as a dancer or to enter the dance is to undertake what amounts to a marked change in one's way of being; and to be aware of others dancing, in however refined a way, is to be aware of them as entering upon a transformation such as one might oneself undertake. One may be excluded from many dances, but there is this one important way in which one cannot be excluded from dancing.

Now that we see what the problem is, can we reintegrate dance into the fine arts on a special footing, as an art that necessarily involves self-reference and to which the philosophical aesthetician must accordingly devote special handling? Presumably not. We did say that the time has passed when systems of fine arts could be set up without absurdity, because we no longer have an intellectual world to map. Everything is too complicated and is changing too fast.

One can be much more specific than we were about the conditions in which the systems of fine arts (and of their predecessors, the imitative arts) could flourish. They depended on a philosophical world view that still tantalizes us; that is, it is desperately attractive but systematically eludes us. It has been called *philosophia perennis*, the perennial philosophy, but has been somewhat misidentified and misdescribed. This world view has appeared in Western thought, quite self-consciously, in two phases, that of Aristotle and that of Hegel. Aristotle knew he was summing up the work of his predecessors; Hegel knew he was correcting Aristotle's summation in the light of what had happened since. Briefly, the view is that the world in its entirety is revealed by objective inquiry to be a single whole that is fully real.

To explain and establish the view we have just rather puzzlingly named, the only starting point we need is the recognition that science exists. That is, the world has a certain structure, and we can find out what it is; or, at least, our attempts to do so can keep getting better and better. But if science exists, so do scientists; they are part of the world. The world as a whole is thus a self-knowing (or at least a self-discovering) system. In Aristotle's old version, the world thus self-known is a finite structure in eternal equilibrium. Humans are the parts of it through which it knows itself. This being so, human culture has as definite a structure as any other aspect or part of the world. That applies to the arts too. It must, accordingly, apply to the practice or practices of dance. Scientists will be able to anatomize dance, to distinguish its developed from its undeveloped forms, to separate what is accidental and unknowable (and creative) from what is part of the knowable system—Aristotle's analysis of tragedy shows just what sort of work has to be done. Dance would turn out to have—or, as in Hegel's system, definitely not to have—a determinate place or places in the system of human practice as it worked itself out in cycles of cultural regeneration and catastrophe. So there would be a definite philosophy of dance, which would be a definite part of philosophy as a whole, and philosophy as a whole would be the same as science as a complete or completable system.

It is essential to realize the force of the underlying contention here. Knowledge is possible, science is real; a world with scientists in it is a self-knowing totality. The alternative view, associated with the name of Karl Popper, that science advances by guesses that can be shown to be wrong but never shown to be true, looks like a real alternative only if we think of the guesswork as relating to isolated phenomena. But science is an immense mass of interrelated knowledge. As that mass builds up, the places where fundamental error could remain, and the kinds of error that are still possible, become more and more limited. It is not that Popper is wrong; it is only that the consequences of his views are far less skeptical than they can be made to sound when presented in the abstract. There are always indefinitely many theories that will accommodate the data as well as the theories we have; but those are not theories that anyone is going to take seriously.

Aristotle was wrong about almost everything. So was Hegel. What Hegel did was recast the self-knowing world of science to take account of world history. Instead of permanent structures of culture, we have the development of self-knowledge and the world. The culminating phase is the development, within a fully articulated political system, of a world scientific community, through which is diffused not only knowledge of the world system as discovered by scientific investigation but also a deeper understanding of what is involved in the possibility and process of that discovery itself. In the course of working all this out, the fine arts will find their place as articulating a specific phase in the self-knowledge of the world. Again, the philosophy of the arts will be a definite part of philosophy as a whole, and the philosophy of dance will consist of articulating the part or parts played by dancing in the development of human culture, which of course is the locus of the world's self-knowledge.

Talk about the world's self-knowledge (or about "the Absolute") sounds grandiose, as though the World Mind were some mysteriously unfamiliar entity, like a very large but spectral Napoleon. But no more grandiosity is involved than is implicit in the very attempt to consider the overall context of scientific progress. Is there such a thing as scientific progress, or isn't there? Are scientists real, or aren't they? Is science carried on by a single worldwide scientific community, or isn't it? To answer no to these questions requires a certain hardihood. But to answer yes is to say that the world is a self-knowing system. And to say that the world is a self-knowing system is no more than that.

Hegel was wrong about one important thing. He was wrong about many things, partly because he was exceptionally well informed about the latest developments in the science of his day and partly because he shared Aristotle's prejudice in favor of hierarchical structures. But what cuts us off from the really important thing, his conviction that the world can be viewed practically as well as theoretically as a single self-knowing system, is his belief that the solar system is unique. If it is, human scientists and their successors are the only scientific community that will ever develop, so that the actual shapes of human culture are the definitive form that the world's self-knowledge takes. If we are going to evaluate the tantalizing ideal of a philosophy of dance that will be radically different in its ambitions from what this book presents, what we have to do is differentiate between what is inescapably valid and what is definitely unacceptable in the vision that Hegel and Aristotle shared, in which humanity is the unique locus of the world's self-knowledge and the forms of human culture as we know them have exemplary standing.

It is easy to show what has changed. Science and scientists are as real as they ever were. In fact, the scale and security of scientific achievement are of a quite different order from what they were even a century ago. From now on, any paradigm shifts that occur—any radical changes in the organization of scientific method and the world views that go with that method—will have to leave an enormous amount in place. And one of the things that is new in our science is that cosmology and cosmogony begin to be built solidly into the texture of positive science. (What our science radically lacks is a way of integrating our own conscious operations into the physical world; but that is another story.)

The important change, from the point of view of our present inquiry, is that the status of human culture as the sole or privileged locus of the world's self-knowledge has gone. The world to which we know ourselves to belong is one in which there may be many scientific communities, of the cultural organization of which we know nothing.

The story of the universe starts with a "big bang" some billions of years ago. Or so it seems.[2] Our science converges on this, and we presume that it will continue to converge on this (or, if we are mistaken, on some other cosmic origin; but the alternatives become ever fewer and less believable) to the point where no other origin will be seriously thinkable. In any case, our science begins to converge on some definite cosmology (and cosmogony) or other; and it is to be expected that in due course this will be built solidly into the corpus of mutually supporting and supported mainstream science. But that holds equally for any community of scientists anywhere in any galaxy. All galaxies belong to the world that shares that real origin, so that the discoveries of any kind of being or beings that comes to know the world will come to incorporate that origination in their understanding. It is not that science everywhere must be the same in its structures, its development, or its concerns; probably it won't. It is rather that any cognizing community within the world that our science establishes as real must establish as real what is compatible with what we establish—including, of course, our own possibility. It is merely preposterous to suppose that a radically different cosmology, equally solidly established and methodically developed, could come to be in place anywhere else. The discoverables, and hence the discoveries, must be mutually translatable. The world, then, remains a self-knowing system, but not at all in the way that Aristotle or Hegel could envisage. It no longer requires—indeed, it no longer tolerates—a unified scientific culture.

It has been conjectured that any beings capable of developing knowledge of the physical world would have to be rather like human beings. Since they would need to be information processors capable of processing information of the same sort that we have to deal with, their logical structure as processors would have to be analogous and probably their physical structure would have to be too. But we do not really know that. We do not know anything solid about the conditions that beings must fulfill if they are actually to *do* science. Especially, we do not know anything about the social, political, or cultural setting necessary for world-knowing. (We must bear in mind that the very words "social," "political," and "cultural" take their concrete meaning from terrestrial goings on.)

It follows that, although we are still bound to the recognition of the world as a self-knowing system, the system we recognize is not one in which human science and (much less) human culture form a distinctive part. They provide only one locus among indefinitely many loci of self-knowledge between the "big bang" (or whatever it turns out to be) and

---

[2] The text assumes that the scenario of Weinberg's *First Three Minutes* (1977) has not been and will not be replaced by a totally different scenario and, more importantly, that it cannot now be simply abandoned but only displaced by a more solidly established scenario. Once cosmology gets built into normal science, it is very hard to get rid of it.

whatever terminus of diffusion or return may constitute the completion or noncompletability of the world. So the notion of a philosophy of art, in which the philosophy of dance would be definitely located and which would occupy a definite place in a general philosophy that would establish the shape of the world as real and knowable, vanishes. We are left with dance and its theory as a local actuality and a permanent possibility, in the sort of way we considered when we were discussing the identifiability of practices and their imputed "nerves" in §3.21.

So long as the world view of progressive science could include within itself the scientific community as an integrated and locatable center of knowledge, it necessarily preempted other world views and defined for philosophy the unique task of a self-critical interpretation of all real and possible knowledge. Without that focus for self-reference, science cannot encompass a world view at all; it is enough for the sciences to go their ways, separately or together, as they do today. We are therefore left where we found ourselves in Chapter 8, with a number of alternative views of humanity and consciousness, and consequently of the worlds with which they are correlated. Even the pragmatist theory of truth—that truth could be defined as that on which all disinterested inquiry would ultimately converge—really loses its force without the conviction that there is a single intellectual framework within which convergence is possible. It becomes hard to resist arguments that reduce philosophy to conversation, a mutually enlightening exchange of views in which the very ideas of truth and progress lose all pretense to systematic force.

We launched ourselves on this discourse about world views and their conditions by way of the thought that, now that we understood why dance was such a tricky business, we could perhaps reinstate dance within a well-formed theory of the fine arts. But we cannot. Not only must we remind ourselves that dance was in fact excluded from the more carefully constructed systems; we can now add that neither in the Aristotelian world nor in its Hegelian revision could dance really play its part in the supposed self-knowledge of the world. Dance could not articulate permanent or evolving structure, could not help to articulate the scientific and cultural world. Dance is irremediably transient, and its transience cannot sum through any dialectic. This deficiency (as in the light of those world views it must seem) could not be remedied by any discovery that dance is more deeply and puzzlingly related to self-knowledge than the other arts.

Aristotle and Hegel belong to a quaintly archaic past, and the systems of the fine arts survive only by the inertia of practical and administrative tradition. What makes dance hard to fit in to views now obsolete might make it exceptionally consonant with whatever it is that made them obsolete.

Dance, more than other arts, has to do with self-knowledge as in process and in question. If all art is art by being subject to an interpretation, it is typical of dance that it necessarily goes beyond its interpretations. In a world in which we do not know what we are, there is one thing we can thereby ever more certainly know. We can know that we are dancing.'

REFERENCE LIST

〜 〜 〜 〜 〜 〜 〜 〜 〜 〜 〜 〜 〜 〜 〜 〜 〜 〜 〜

IF THE DATE by which a work is keyed here and in the text differs from the edition for which bibliographic data are given, it is the date of the first edition in the original language unless otherwise specified. The edition for which data are provided is in each case that consulted in the preparation of this book.

Aagaard-Mogensen, Lars. 1986. "Do You Have Time to Go?" In Cécile Cloutier and Paul Perron, eds., *New Perspectives in Aesthetics*, 44–51. Toronto: University of Toronto Department of French.

Akenside, Mark. 1744. "Imagination." In his *Poetical Works*. Edited by Alexander Dyce. Boston: Little, Brown and Co., 1854.

Alain [Chartrier, Émile]. 1920. *Système des beaux arts*. 4th ed. Paris: Gallimard, 1926.

Aldrich, Virgil. 1963. *Philosophy of Art*. Englewood Cliffs: Prentice-Hall.

Arbeau, Thoineau. 1588. *Orchésographie*. Translated by Cyril Beaumont. New York: Dance Horizons, 1968.

Arendt, Hannah. 1958. *The Human Condition*. New York: Doubleday, 1959.

Aschenbrenner, Karl. 1974. *The Concepts of Criticism*. Dordrecht: Reidel.

Astaire, Fred. 1959. *Steps in Time*. New York: Harper.

Austen, Jane. 1813. *Pride and Prejudice*. In *The Novels of Jane Austen*. Edited by R. W. Chapman, 3d ed. Vol. 2. London: Oxford University Press, 1932.

Balanchine, George. 1984. *Portrait of Mr. B: Photographs of George Balanchine*. With an essay by Lincoln Kirstein. New York: Viking Press/Ballet Society.

Banes, Sally. 1983. *Democracy's Body: Judson Dance Theater 1962–1964*. Ann Arbor: UMI Research Press.

Bateson, Gregory. 1972. *Steps to an Ecology of Mind*. San Francisco: Chandler.

Batteaux, Charles. 1746. *Les Beaux arts reduits à un même principe*. Paris: Saillart et Nyon, et veuve Desaire, 1773.

Bazin, Germain. 1967. *The Museum Age*. New York: Universe Books.

Beardsley, Monroe C. 1958. *Aesthetics*. New York: Harcourt, Brace.

Beardsley, Monroe C. 1977. "The Philosophy of Literature." In George Dickie and Richard Sclafani, eds., *Aesthetics: A Critical Anthology*, 317–333. New York: St. Martin's Press.

Bely, Andrei. 1922. *Petersburg*. Translated by Robert A. Maguire and John E. Malmstad. Bloomington: Indiana University Press, 1978.

Benois, Alexandre. 1941. *Reminiscences of the Russian Ballet*. Translated by Mary Britnieva. London: Putnam.

Benois, Alexandre. 1964. *Memoirs*. Translated by Moura Budberg. London: Chatto.

Bernheimer, Richard. 1961. *The Nature of Representation: A Phenomenological Inquiry*. New York: New York University Press.

Best, David. 1978. *Philosophy and Human Movement*. London: Unwin.

Bharata. 1961. *The Natyasastra: A Treatise on Hindu Dramaturgy and Histrionics Ascribed to Bharata-Muni*. Edited and translated by Manomohan Ghosh. Vol. 2. Calcutta: The Asian Society.

Bharata. 1967. *The Natyashastra Attributed to Bharata-Muni*. Edited and translated by Manomohan Ghosh. Vol. 1. Calcutta: Manisha Granthalaya Private Ltd. (Cited by chapter and section.)

Bhattacharyya, Asutosh. 1972. *Chhau Dance of Purulia*. Calcutta: Rabindra Bharati University.

Booth, Mark W. 1981. *The Experience of Song*. New Haven: Yale University Press.

Boswell, James. 1791. *The Life of Samuel Johnson, Ll.D*. Vol. 2. London: J. M. Dent, 1949. (Everyman's Library.)

Bournonville, August. 1848. *Mit Theaterliv*. Translated by Patricia N. McAndrews as Part 1 of *My Theatre Life*. Middletown: Wesleyan University Press, 1979.

Bournonville, August. 1865. *Mit Theaterliv*. Vol. 2. Translated by Patricia N. McAndrews as Part 2 of *My Theatre Life*. Middletown: Wesleyan University Press, 1979.

Bournonville, August. 1878. *Mit Theaterliv*. Vol. 3. Translated by Patricia N. McAndrews as Part 3 of *My Theatre Life*. Middletown: Wesleyan University Press, 1979.

Brahms, Caryl. 1936. *Footnotes to the Ballet*. London: Peter Davies.

Bücher, Karl. 1902. *Arbeit und Rhythmus*. 3d ed. Leipzig: B. G. Teubner.

Buckle, Richard. 1979. *Diaghilev*. London: Hamish Hamilton, 1984.

Burne-Jones, Georgina ["G B-J"]. 1904. *Memorials of Edward Burne-Jones*. Vol. 2. New York: Macmillan.

Cahusac, Louis de. 1754. *La Danse ancienne et moderne, ou Traité historique de la danse*. Geneva: Slatkin Reprints, 1971.

Carroll, Noël. 1981. "Post-Modern Dance and Expression." In Fancher and Myers 1981, 95–104.

Cavell, Stanley. 1971. *The World Viewed: Reflections on the Ontology of Film*. New York: Viking Press.

Cavell, Stanley. 1976. *Must We Mean What We Say?* Cambridge: Cambridge University Press.

Chernoff, John Miller. 1979. *African Rhythm and African Sensibility*. Berkeley and Los Angeles: University of California Press.

Christout, M. F. 1967. *Le Ballet de cour de Louis XIV*. Paris: Picard.

Clark, Kenneth. 1949. *Landscape into Art*. London: John Murray.

Cohen, Selma Jeanne, ed. 1966. *The Modern Dance*. Middletown: Wesleyan University Press.

Cohen, Selma Jeanne. 1982. *Next Week, Swan Lake: Reflections on Dance and Dances*. Middletown: Wesleyan University Press.

Colletet, G. 1632. *Grand Ballet des Effects de la Nature*. Paris: J. Martin.

Collingwood, R. G. 1938. *Principles of Art*. Oxford: Clarendon Press.

Condillac, Etienne Bonnot de. 1746. *Essai sur l'origine des connoissances humaines*. Paris: Galilée, 1973.

Copeland, Roger. 1979. "Merce Cunningham and the Politics of Perception." In Copeland and Cohen 1983, 307–324.

Copeland, Roger, and Marshall Cohen, eds., 1983. *What Is Dance?* New York: Oxford University Press.

Coros, Mary. 1982. *Sousta*. Privately distributed.

Crabb, Michael, ed. 1978. *Visions*. Toronto: Simon and Pierre.

Croce, Arlene. 1978. *Afterimages*. New York: Knopf.

Crompton, Robert Morris, ed. 1892. *Dancing: A Journal Devoted to the Terpsichorean Arts, Physical Culture, and Fashionable Entertainments*, 1891–1893. Facsimile reprint. Toronto: Press of Terpsichore, 1984.

Cunningham, Merce, in conversation with Jacqueline Lesschaeva. 1985. *The Dancer and the Dance*. New York and London: Marion Boyars.

D'Alembert, Jean le Rond. 1751. *Preliminary Discourse to the Encyclopedia of Diderot*. Translated by Richard Schwab and Walter Rex. New York: Liberal Arts Press, 1963.

Danto, Arthur C. 1981. *The Transfiguration of the Commonplace: A Philosophy of Art*. Cambridge, Mass.: Harvard University Press.

[Davies, John]. 1596. *Orchestra or a Poeme on Dauncing*. In his *Complete Poems*. Edited by Alexander B. Grosart. London: Chatto and Windus, 1876.

Denby, Edwin. 1949. *Looking at the Dance*. New York: Pellegrini and Cudahy.

Dewey, John. 1934. *Art as Experience*. New York: Minton, Balch.

Dickie, George. 1974. *Art and the Aesthetic: An Institutional Analysis*. Ithaca: Cornell University Press.

D'Israeli, Isaac. 1859a. "Fire, and the Origin of Fireworks." In his *Curiosities of Literature*, vol. 2, 15–19. London: Routledge, Warner, and Routledge.

D'Israeli, Isaac. 1859b. "The Pantomimical Characters." In his *Curiosities of Literature*, vol. 2, 116–130. London: Routledge, Warner, and Routledge.

Dubos [Du Bos], J. B. 1719. *Critical Reflections on Poetry, Painting and Music*. Translated from the fifth edition by Thomas Nugent. Vol. 3. London: John Nourse, 1748.

Ducasse, C. J. 1929. *The Philosophy of Art*. New York: Dial Press.

Dufrenne, Mikel. 1953. *The Phenomenology of Aesthetic Experience*. Translated by Edward S. Casey and Albert A. Anderson. Evanston: Northwestern University Press, 1973.

Duncan, Isadora. 1928. *The Art of the Dance*. New York: Theatre Arts.

Eliot, T. S. 1925. "The Ballet." *The Criterion* 3 (April 1925), 441–443.

Ellfeldt, Lois. 1976. *Dance from Magic to Art*. Dubuque: William C. Brown.

Ellis, Havelock. 1923. *The Dance of Life*. New York: Houghton Mifflin.

Elyot, Thomas. 1531. *The Boke Named The Gouernour*. London: Thomas Berthelet.

Erlanger, Philippe. 1970. *Louis XIV*. New York: Praeger.

Fancher, Gordon, and Gerald Myers, eds. 1981. *Philosophical Essays on Dance*. Brooklyn: Dance Horizons.

Feinman, Jana. 198?. "The Creative Personality as It Relates to Women." *Graduate Dance Review* 1 (n.d.), 40–48.

Fetherston, Christopher. 1582. *A Dialogue Agaynst light, lewde, and lasciuious dauncing*. London: Thomas Dawson.

Feyerabend, Paul. 1978. *Against Method*. New York: Schocken.

Fokine, Michel. 1961. *Fokine: Memoirs of a Ballet Master*. London: Constable.

Foster, John. 1977. *The Influence of Rudolph Laban*. London: Lupus Books.

Foster, Susan Leigh. 1983. "On Dancing and the Dance." In Sixth Annual Conference of Dance History Scholars, *Proceedings*, 133–141. Riverside, Calif.: Society of Dance History Scholars.

Foucault, Michel. 1966. *Les Mots et les choses*. Translated as *The Order of Things*. London: Tavistock, 1970.

Frankl, Paul. 1968. *Principles of Architectural History*. Cambridge, Mass.: MIT Press.

Fried, Michael. 1977. "Art and Objecthood." In George Dickie and R. F. Sclafani, eds., *Aesthetics: A Critical Anthology*, 438–460. New York: St. Martin's Press.

Frisch, Karl von. 1950. *Bees: Their Vision, Chemical Senses, and Language*. Ithaca: Cornell University Press.

Frye, Northrop. 1963. "Introduction" to his *Romanticism Reconsidered*. New York: Columbia University Press.

Fuller, Loie. 1913. *Fifteen Years of a Dancer's Life*. Reprinted. New York: Dance Horizons, n.d.

Gadamer, Hans-Georg. 1960. *Truth and Method*. Translated. London: Sheed and Ward, 1975.

Gallini, Giovanni-Andrea. 1762. *A Treatise on the Art of Dancing*. London: printed for the author.

Gbeho, Philip. 1952. "The Indigenous Gold Coast Music." *Journal of the African Music Society* 1 (1952). Cited from Thompson 1974.

Goldman, Alvin I. 1970. *A Theory of Human Action*. Englewood Cliff: Prentice-Hall.

Gombrich, E. H. 1960. *Art and Illusion*. New York: Pantheon.

Gombrich, Ernst. 1979. *The Sense of Order*. Ithaca: Cornell University Press.

Goodman, Nelson. 1968. *Languages of Art*. Indianapolis: Bobbs-Merrill.

Goodman, Nelson. 1972. *Problems and Projects*. Indianapolis: Bobbs-Merrill.

Goodman, Paul. 1960. *Growing Up Absurd*. New York: Vintage Books.

Gordon, Suzanne. 1983. *Off Balance: The Real World of Ballet*. New York: McGraw-Hill.

Gore, Catherine G. F. ["Lorgnon"]. 1844. "A Word or Two of the Opera-tive Classes." *Blackwood's* 55 (1844), 292–298.

Graves, Robert. 1969. "The Decline in Bullfighting." In his *The Crane Bag*, 153–158. London: Cassell.

Greenberg, Clement. 1971. *Art and Culture*. Boston: Beacon Press.

Griaule, Marcel. 1948. *Conversations with Ogotemmöli.* Translated. London: Oxford University Press, 1965.

Guest, Ivor. 1966. *Romantic Ballet in Paris.* Middletown: Wesleyan University Press.

Guest, Ivor. 1984. *Jules Perrot: Master of the Romantic Ballet.* London: Dance Books.

Gunji, Masakatsu. 1970. *Buyo: The Classical Dance.* Translated by Don Kenny. New York: Walker/Weatherhill.

Hacking, Ian. 1983. *Representing and Intervening: Introductory Topics in the Philosophy of Natural Science.* Cambridge: Cambridge University Press.

Hall, Edward T. 1966. *The Hidden Dimension.* Garden City: Doubleday.

Hanna, Judith Lynne. 1979. *To Dance Is Human: A Theory of Non-Verbal Communication.* Austin: University of Texas Press.

Hanna, Judith Lynne. 1983. *The Performer-Audience Connection: Emotion to Metaphor in Dance and Society.* Austin: University of Texas Press.

Harris, H. S. 1983. *Night Thoughts.* Vol. 2 of *Hegel's Development.* Oxford: Clarendon Press.

Harris, Margaret Haile. 1979. *Loie Fuller: Magician of Light.* Richmond: The Virginia Museum.

Haskell, Arnold L. 1948. *Ballet Panorama.* 3d ed. London: B. T. Batsford.

H'Doubler, Margaret. 1940. *Dance: A Creative Art Experience.* New York: F. S. Crofts.

Hegel, G.W.F. 1835. *Aesthetik.* Edited by F. Bassenge from H. G. Hotho's second edition (1842). Frankfurt: Europäisch Verlagsanstalt GmbH, 1955.

Hegel, G.W.F. 1968. Gesammelte Werke. Hamburg: F. Meiner, 1968–.

Hegel, G.W.F. 1975. *Aesthetics.* Translated from Hegel 1835 by T. M. Knox. Oxford: Clarendon Press.

Heppenstall, Rayner. 1936. *Apology for Dancing.* London: Faber and Faber.

Herrigel, Eugene. 1953. *Zen in the Art of Archery.* New York: Pantheon Books.

Hood, Hugh. 1984. *The Scenic Art.* Toronto: Stoddart.

Horst, Louis. 1940. *Pre-Classic Dance Forms.* New York: The Dance Observer.

Howard, V. A. 1982. *Artistry: The Work of Artists.* Indianapolis: Hackett.

Huizinga, Johan. 1955. *Homo Ludens: A Study of the Play Element in Culture.* Translated by R.C.F. Hull. Boston: Beacon Hill.

Humphrey, Doris. 1962. *The Art of Making Dances.* New York: Grove Press.

Huxley, Julian S. 1914. "The Courtship-Habits of the Great Crested Grebe." Zoological Society of London, *Proceedings* (1914), 491–562.

Jaques-Dalcroze, Emile. 1930. *Eurhythmics Art and Education.* Translated by Frederick Rothwell. Edited by Cynthia Cox. New York: A. S. Barnes.

Jenkyns, Richard. 1980. *The Victorians and Ancient Greece.* Cambridge, Mass.: Harvard University Press.

Johnson, Tom. 1976. "Running Out of Breath." In Copeland and Cohen 1983, 332–335.

Jones, A. M. 1959. *Studies in African Music.* London: Oxford University Press.

Jowitt, Deborah. 1974. "Rebel Turned Classicist." *New York Times*, 10 March, 1974. Cited from Van Camp 1981.

Jowitt, Deborah. 1977. *Dance Beat: Selected Views and Readings 1967–76*. New York: Marcel Dekker.

Jowitt, Deborah. 1985. *The Dance in Mind*. Boston: Godine.

Kaeppler, Adrienne L. 1972. "Method and Theory in Analyzing Dance Structure, With an Analysis of Tongan Dance." *Ethnomusicology* 16 (1972), 173–215.

Kaeppler, Adrienne L. 1984. "The Use of Historical Sources in the Study of Hawaiian Hula." Paper presented to the annual conference of the Society of Dance History Scholars, 18 February 1984.

Kant, Immanuel. 1790. *Kritik der Urtheilskraft*. Translated as *The Critique of Judgement* by J. C. Meredith. Oxford: Clarendon Press, 1952.

Kaprelian, Mary H. 1976. *Aesthetics for Dancers*. Washington: AAHPER.

Katz, Ruth. 1973. "The Egalitarian Waltz." In Copeland and Cohen 1983, 521–532.

Kealiinohomoku, Joann. 1970. "An Anthropologist Looks at Ballet as a Form of Ethnic Dance." In Copeland and Cohen 1983, 533–549.

Keller, Evelyn Fox. 1983. *A Feeling for the Organism*. New York and San Francisco: W. H. Freeman.

Kendall, Elizabeth. 1979. *Where She Danced*. New York: Knopf.

Kermode, Frank. 1962. "Poet and Dancer Before Diaghilev." In his *Puzzles and Epiphanies*, 1–28. London: Routledge and Kegan Paul.

Kipling, Rudyard. 1894. *The Jungle Book*. London: Macmillan.

Kirstein, Lincoln. 1935. *Dance: A Short History of Classic Theatrical Dancing*. Brooklyn: Dance Horizons, 1969.

Kirstein, Lincoln. 1970. *Movement and Metaphor: Four Centuries of Ballet*. New York: Praeger.

Kirstein, Lincoln. 1987. "The Monstrous Itch." *New York Review of Books*, 34, no. 10, 11 June 1987, 30–32.

Kraus, Richard. 1969. *History of the Dance in Art and Education*. Englewood Cliffs: Prentice-Hall.

Kristeller, Paul Oskar. 1951. "The Modern System of the Arts." In Morris Weitz, ed., *Problems in Aesthetics*, 108–163. 2d ed. New York: Macmillan, 1970.

Laban, Rudolf. 1974. *The Language of Movement*. Boston: PLAYS, Inc.

Laban, Rudolf, and Lisa Ullman. 1950. *The Mastery of Movement*. By Rudolf Laban, third edition enlarged by Lisa Ullmann. New York: PLAYS Inc., 1971.

Lambranzi, Gregorio, 1716. *New and Curious School of Theatrical Dancing*. Translated by Derra de Moroda. Brooklyn: Dance Horizons, 1966.

Langer, Susanne K. 1953. *Feeling and Form*. New York: Scribners.

Langer, Susanne K. 1970. *Mind: An Essay on Human Feeling*. Vol. 1, Baltimore: Johns Hopkins University Press.

Lawson, Joan. 1957. *Mime: The Theory and Practice of Expressive Gesture*. Reprinted. New York: Dance Horizons, n.d.

Lee, Dorothy Demetriakopoulos. 1950. "Linear and Non-Linear Codifications of Reality." *Psychosomatic Medicine* 12 (1950), 89–97.

Legge, James, trans. 1885. *Yo Ki or the Record of Music*. In Max Mueller, ed., *Sacred Books of the East*, vol. 28. London: Oxford University Press.

Leonardo da Vinci. 1939. *Paragone*. Edited and translated by Irma A. Richter. London: Oxford University Press, 1949.

Levin, David Michael. 1977. "Philosophers and the Dance." *Ballet Review* 6 (1977–1978), 71–78.

Levinson, André. 1927. "The Idea of the Dance: From Aristotle to Mallarmé." In Copeland and Cohen 1983, 47–55.

Locke, John. 1693. "Some Thoughts Concerning Education." In his *Works*, vol. 3, 1–95. London: Awnsham Churchill, 1723.

Louis, Murray. 1980. *Inside Dance*. New York: St. Martin's Press.

Lukács, Georg. 1963. *Die Eigenart des Ästhetischen*. Darmstadt: Luchterhand.

McDonagh, Don. 1973. *Martha Graham: A Biography*. New York: Praeger.

McGowan, Margaret M. 1963. *L'Art du ballet de cour en France 1581–1643*. Paris: C.N.R.S.

McGuinness-Scott, Julia. 1983. *Movement Study and Benesh Movement Notation*. London: Oxford University Press.

MacIntyre, Alasdair. 1981. *After Virtue*. London: Duckworth.

Maritain, Jacques. 1922. *Art and Scholasticism*. Translated by J. F. Scanlan. London: Sheed and Ward, 1930.

Mas i Solench, Josep M. 1981. *Diccionari breu de la Sardana*. Santa Coloma de Farners: Estudis Colomencs.

Mason, W. A. 1970. "Chimpanzee Social Behavior." In G. H. Bourne, ed., *The Chimpanzee*, vol. 2, 265–288. Basel: S. Karger.

Ménéstrier, Claude-François. 1669. *Traité des tournois, joustes, carrousels et autres spectacles publics*. Lyons: Jacques Muguet.

Ménéstrier, Claude-François. 1682. *Des Ballets anciens et modernes selon les règles du théâtre*. Paris: René Guignard.

Mersenne, Marin. 1636. *Harmonie Universelle*. Paris: S. Cramoisy.

Meyer, Leonard B. 1956. *Emotion and Meaning in Music*. Chicago: University of Chicago Press.

Meyer, Leonard B. 1962. *Music, the Arts, and Ideas*. Chicago: University of Chicago Press.

Mill, John Stuart. 1833. "Thoughts on Poetry and Its Varieties." In his *Autobiographical and Literary Essays, Collected Works*, vol. 1. Toronto: University of Toronto Press, 1981. (Quoted from 1859 version.)

Miller, James Lester. 1979. "Choreia: Visions of the Cosmic Dance in Western Literature from Plato to Jean de Meun." Ph.D. diss., University of Toronto.

Miller, James. 1986. *Measures of Wisdom: The Cosmic Dance in Classical and Christian Antiquity*. Toronto: University of Toronto Press.

Mothersill, Mary. 1984. *Beauty Restored*. Oxford: Clarendon Press.

Murray, Jan. 1979. *Dance Now*. Harmondsworth: Penguin Books.

Nadel, M. H., and G. C. Nadel, eds. 1970. *The Dance Experience*. New York: Praeger.

Newman, Barbara. 1982. *Striking a Balance: Dancers Talk About Dancing*. Boston: Houghton Mifflin.

Noverre, Jean Georges. 1760. *Letters on Dancing and Ballets*. Translated by Cyril W. Beaumont. London: Beaumont, 1951.

Oesterley, W.E.O. 1923. *The Sacred Dance: A Study in Comparative Folklore*. New York: Macmillan.

Payzant, Geoffrey. 1978. *Glenn Gould: Music and Mind*. Toronto: Van Nostrand Reinhold.

Percival, John. 1971. *Experimental Dance*. London: Studio Vista.

Percival, John. 1980. *Modern Ballet*. Rev. ed. London: The Herbert Press.

Pike, Kenneth L. 1954. *Language in Relation to a Unified Theory of the Structure of Human Behavior*. Glendale: Summer Institute of Linguistics.

Pike, Bob, and Dave Martin. 1973. *The Genius of Busby Berkeley*. Reseda, Calif.: cfs books.

Pirsig, Robert M. 1974. *Zen and the Art of Motorcycle Maintenance*. New York: Bantam Books, 1975.

Prunières, Henry. 1914. *Le Ballet de cour en France avant Benserade et Lully*. Paris: Henry Laurens.

Pure, Michel de. 1668. *Idée des spectacles anciens et nouveaux*. Paris: M. Brunet.

Raghavan, V. 1979. "Yakshagana." In Gowri Kuppuswamy and M. Hariharan, eds., *Readings on Music and Dance*, 51–63. Delhi: B. R. Publishing Corporation.

Rainer, Yvonne. 1966. "A Quasi Survey of Some 'Minimalist' Tendencies in the Quantitatively Minimal Dance Activity Midst the Plethora, or an Analysis of Trio A." In Copeland and Cohen 1983, 325–332.

Ralph, Richard. 1985. *The Life and Works of John Weaver*. London: Dance Books.

Redfern, Betty. 1983. *Dance, Art and Aesthetics*. London: Dance Books.

Rio, Janice A. 1981. "Contemporary Aesthetic Theory Applied to Dance as a Performing Art." Ph.D. diss., University of Nebraska.

Rivière, Jacques. 1913. "Le Sacre du printemps." In his *The Ideal Reader*, 125–147. New York: Meridian, 1960.

Rolfe, Bari, ed. 1981. *Mimes on Miming*. London: Millington Books.

Rousseau, Jean Jacques. 1972. *Correspondance complète*. Vol. 15. Edited by R. A. Leigh. Banbury: Voltaire Foundation.

Royce, Anya Peterson. 1984. *Movement and Meaning: Creativity and Interpretation in Ballet and Mime*. Bloomington: Indiana University Press.

Ruskin, John. 1849. *Seven Lamps of Architecture*. London: Swan, Elder and Company.

Sachs, Curt. 1937. *World History of the Dance*. New York: Norton.

Saint-Hubert, M. de. 1641. *La Manière de composer et faire réussir les ballets*. Paris: F. Targa.

St.-Johnston, Reginald. 1906. *A History of Dancing*. London: Simpkin, Marshall, Hamilton, Kent, and Company.

Sartre, Jean-Paul. 1940. *L'Imaginaire*. Translated by Bernard Frechtman as *The Psychology of Imagination*. New York: Washington Square Press, 1965.

Sartre, Jean-Paul. 1943. *L'Être et le Néant*. Translated by Hazel Barnes as *Being and Nothingness*. New York: Philosophical Library, 1956.

Sartre, Jean-Paul. 1971. *L'Idiot de la famille*. Vol. 1. Paris: Gallimard.

Sathyanarayana, R. 1969. *Bharatanatya: A Critical Study*. Mysore: Sri Varalakshmi Academia of Fine Arts.

Schiller, J.C.F. 1795. *On the Aesthetic Education of Man*. Translated by Elizabeth M. Wilkinson and L. A. Willoughby. Oxford: Clarendon Press, 1967.

Scruton, Roger. 1977. *The Aesthetics of Architecture*. Princeton: Princeton University Press.

Sendrey, Alfred. 1974. *Music in the Social and Religious Life of Antiquity*. Rutherford: Fairleigh Dickinson University Press.

Sharp, Cecil J. 1911. *The Sword Dance of Northern England*. Three parts, 1911–1913. Reprinted. East Ardsley: EP Publishing, 1977.

Sheets-Johnstone, Maxine. 1966. *The Phenomenology of Dance*. Madison and Milwaukee: University of Wisconsin Press.

Sheets-Johnstone, Maxine. 1978. "An Account of Recent Changes in Dance in the U.S.A." *Leonardo* 11 (1978), 197–201.

Sheets-Johnstone, Maxine, ed. 1984. *Illuminating Dance*. Lewisburg: Bucknell University Press.

Shelton, Suzanne. 1981. *Divine Dancer: A Biography of Ruth St. Denis*. Garden City: Doubleday.

Shelton, Suzanne. 1983. "Jungian Roots of Martha Graham's Dance Imagery." Sixth Annual Conference of Dance History Scholars, *Proceedings*, 119–132. Riverside, Calif.: Society of Dance History Scholars.

Siegel, Marcia B. 1977. *Watching the Dance Go By*. Boston: Houghton Mifflin.

Siegel, Marcia B. 1979. *The Shapes of Change: Images of American Dance*. Berkeley: University of California Press, 1985.

Sirridge, Mary, and Adina Armelagos. 1977. "The In's and Out's of Dance: Expression as an Aspect of Style." *Journal of Aesthetics and Art Criticism* 36 (1977), 15–24.

Smith, Adam. 1795. "Of the Nature of that Imitation Which Takes Place In What Are Called the Imitative Arts." In Karl Aschenbrenner and Arnold Isenberg, eds., *Aesthetic Theories*, 227–252. Englewood Cliffs: Prentice-Hall, 1965.

Soanes, Sidney V., ed. 1976. *Ice Dancing*. 2d ed. Toronto: Queen City Publishing.

Sorell, Walter. 1971. *The Dancer's Image: Points and Counterpoints*. New York: Columbia University Press.

Souriau, Paul. 1889. *The Aesthetics of Movement*. Translated by Manon Souriau. Amherst: University of Massachusetts Press, 1983.

Sparshott, F. E. 1963. *The Structure of Aesthetics*. Toronto: University of Toronto Press.

Sparshott, Francis. 1970a. "First Steps in the Theory of Practice." Howard E. Kiefer and Milton J. Munitz, eds., *Ethics and Social Justice*, 21–44. Albany: State University of New York Press.

Sparshott, Francis. 1970b. "Play." In Ralph A. Smith, ed., *Aesthetic Concepts and Education*, 107–134. Urbana: University of Illinois Press.

Sparshott, Francis. 1972. *Looking for Philosophy*. Montreal: McQill-Queen's University Press.

Sparshott, Francis. 1973. "Work—The Concept: Past, Present, and Future." *Journal of Aesthetic Education* 7 (1973), 23–38.

Sparshott, Francis. 1974. "As: Or, the Limits of Metaphor." *New Literary History* 6 (1974), 75–94.

Sparshott, Francis. 1975. "On Saying What Philosophy Is." *Philosophy in Context* 4 (1975), 17–27.

Sparshott, Francis. 1976. "How To Build Without Really Trying." *Journal of Aesthetic Education* 10 (1976), 93–108.

Sparshott, Francis. 1982. *The Theory of the Arts*. Princeton: Princeton University Press.

Sparshott, Francis. 1984. "The Dancing Body." In Sheets-Johnstone 1984, 188–202.

Sparshott, Francis. 1985a. "Text and Process in Poetry and Philosophy," *Philosophy and Literature* 9 (1985), 1–20.

Sparshott, Francis. 1985b. "Aristotle on Women." *Philosophical Inquiry* 7 (1985), 177–200.

Sparshott, Francis. 1987. "Aesthetics of Music—Limits and Grounds." In Philip Alperson, ed., *What Is Music?* New York: Haven Publications, forthcoming.

Stearns, Marshall, and Jean Stearns. 1968. *Jazz Dance: The Story of American Vernacular Dance*. New York: Schirmer Books.

Stodelle, Ernestine. 1984. *Deep Song: The Dance Story of Martha Graham*. New York: Schirmer Books.

Stokes, Adrian. 1934. *To-Night the Ballet*. 2d ed. London: Faber and Faber, 1935.

Stokes, Adrian. 1935. *Russian Ballets*. London: Faber and Faber.

Suits, Bernard. 1978. *The Grasshopper*. Toronto: University of Toronto Press.

Swayne-Thomas, April. 1981. *Indian Summer*. London: New English Library.

Taper, Bernard. 1984. *Balanchine: A Biography*. 3d ed. New York: Times Books.

Thompson, Robert Farris. 1974. *African Art in Motion: Icon and Act*. Los Angeles: University of California Press.

Tilghman, B. R. 1984. *But Is It Art? The Value of Art and the Temptation of Theory*. Oxford: Basil Blackwell.

Tuccaro, Archange. 1959. *Trois dialogues de l'exercice de sauter et voltiger en l'air*. Paris: Claude de Monstr'oeil.

Turner, Victor. 1974. *Dramas, Fields, and Metaphors: Symbolic Action in Human Society*. Ithaca: Cornell University Press.

Valéry, Paul. 1936. "Philosophy of the Dance." In his *Collected Works*, Bollingen Series 45, vol. 13, *Aesthetics*, 197–211. Translated by Ralph Mannheim. Princeton: Princeton University Press, 1964.

Van Camp, Julie Charlotte. 1981. "Philosophical Problems of Dance Criticism." Ph.D. diss., Temple University.

Vatsyayan, Kapila. 1976. *Traditions of Indian Folk Dance*. New Delhi: Indian Book Company.

Veer, Ram Avtar [Sangeetacharya]. 1982. *Natraj: Indian Dances Through the Ages*. New Delhi: Pankaj Publications.

Véron, Eugène. 1878. *L'Esthétique*. 2d ed. Paris: Reinwald. 1883.

Villari, Jack, and Kathleen Sims Villari. 1978. *The Official Guide to Disco Dance Steps*. Northbrook, Ill.: Quality Books.

Voltaire. 1973. *Oeuvres complètes*. Vol. 111. Banbury: Voltaire Foundation.

Walter, L. Edna, ed. 1919. *Mother Goose's Nursery Rhymes*. London: A. and C. Black.

Weaver, John. 1706. *Orchesography; or, the Art of Dancing, by Characters and Demonstrative Figures . . . Being an Exact and Just Translation from the French of Monsieur Feuillet*. In Ralph 1985, 175–285.

Weaver, John. 1712. *An Essay Towards an History of Dancing*. In Ralph 1985, 391–672.

Weaver, John. 1728. *History of the Mimes and Pantomimes*. In Ralph 1985, 677–732.

Weinberg, Steven. 1977. *The First Three Minutes: A Modern View of the Origin of the Universe*. New York: Basic Books.

Weiss, Paul. 1961. *Nine Basic Arts*. Carbondale: Southern Illinois University Press.

Wigman, Mary. 1963. *The Language of Dance*. Translated by Walter Sorell. Middletown: Wesleyan University Press, 1974.

Wigman, Mary. 1975. *The Mary Wigman Book*. Edited and translated by Walter Sorell. Middletown: Wesleyan University Press.

Willis, Paul. 1974. "Youth Groups in Birmingham and Their Specific Relation to Pop Music." In Irmgard Bontinck, ed., *New Patterns of Musical Behaviour*, 108–113. Vienna: Universal Edition.

Winter, Marian Hannah. 1974. *The Pre-Romantic Ballet*. New York: Pitman.

Wolterstorff, Nicholas. 1980. *Works and Worlds of Art*. Oxford: Clarendon Press.

Wright, Wilmer Cave, ed. and trans. 1913. *The Works of the Emperor Julian*. Vol. 1. New York: Macmillan. (Loeb Classical Library.)

Yates, Frances A. 1969. *Theatre of the World*. Chicago: University of Chicago Press.

Zoete, Beryl de, and Walter Spier. 1938. *Dance and Drama in Bali*. New York: Thomas Yoseloff, 1958.

Zorn, Friedrich A. 1887. *Grammar of the Art of Dancing*. Translated by Alfonso Josephs Sheafe. Reprinted. New York: Dance Horizons, n.d.

INDEX

INDEX

D'Alembert, Jean le Rond, 30–33, 44, 45–
46, 53, 148–149, 201
Damascius, 92
Dan, 392
dance: Aristotelian definition of, 240; as an
art, ch. 6; as art, 267; artistic, 22; autonomy of, 57, 149, 386–388; awareness in,
170; as basic, 3–5, 77, 98, 101–102,
105; character, 78, 170–171; as classical
art, 38–40; cognitive significance of,
158–160, 182–183; context, 78–80,
253–254, 256–257, 364–367; default
values of term, 394; definition of, ch. 5;
domain of, 151; and drama, 343; existence of, 169–170; as fine art, 23–63, 66–
67, 81–82, 109–113, 141–164, 191,
359–360, 399; going, 178–179; inacces-
sibility of, 10–11; indeterminacy of,
370–371; learnability of, 270–271; of
life, 101–106, 229–230; marginal cases
of, 213–230; meaning of, ch. 4, 213; as
mimetic, 145–149; motivation, 264–
265; movement, 206; as movement type,
102, 231–234; neglected by philosophy,
ch. 1; neighbors of, ch. 7; ontology of,
ch. 8; and physical education, 14, 75n,
134; as practice, 113–130; presence in,
207–208; as primitive, 37, 37–38n, 44,
68, 88, 362; problematic status of, xvii,
81; pure, 231, 285–288; quality, 256–
257, 304, 306; recognizability of, 208–
210; and ritual, 209; as romantic art, 36,
42–43, 53, 59–63, 135n; as sacred, 17,
260, 268, 295–296, 344, 347; and setting, 388; as symbolic art, 37–38, 83; as
typical art, 142–143; ubiquity of, xvii, 3,
4–5, 37, 169, 211, 264, 276n, 362; and
utility, 209n, 299–305; as visual, 184–
185; world, 111, 254
Dance in America, 11
dancelikeness, 266, 268, 299, 302–305,
314
dancers: and choreographers, 95, 133,
222–223, 231, 255, 278; and dances,
352; lack of esteem for, 20–21; as people, 382; reality of, 353–362; in relation,
180–182
dances: and dancers, 352; and dancing,
264, 320; entering and leaving, 172–
173, 176–179, 279, 318, 345–346, 347;

identification of, 184, 233; meanings in,
183–186; ontology of, 350–370; proprietorship in, 181–182; repeatability of,
233
dancing a dance, 257–260, 261; ontology
of, 342–350
dancing masters, 51n, 64–65, 178–179,
277n
danse noble, 51
Dante Alighieri, 214n, 237
Danto, Arthur C., 77, 108, 289–290, 322–
323, 364–366
Dark Elegies, 70
Darwinism, 5, 125, 139n
Dasein, 363–364
Dauberval, Jean, 34
David, king of Israel, 22, 29, 87n, 93n,
259–260
Davidson, T., 264
Davies, John, 49, 50, 95–100, 101, 106,
212, 250
Davis, R. G., 338–339
Decroix, Etienne, 334, 336–338
definitions, 188–192; and investigation,
262; persuasive, 201; stipulative, 201–
202
Delphic oracle, 4
Delsarte, François, 76
demi-caractère, 51
Demosthenes, 20
Denby, Edwin, 131, 338, 354
Denishawn, 76, 139n, 282, 286
derealization, 291–292, 357–358
Descartes, René, 88, 89n, 98
Desrosiers, Robert, 132
Dewey, John, 321
Diaghilev, Sergei, 3, 66, 67, 69, 71–72,
327n, 355, 358n, 391
Dickie, George, 79, 254, 290
dictionaries, 144n, 192, 201, 215n, 220,
222, 264, 390
Diderot, Denis, 54, 110
digital and analog, 232–234
Dilthey, Wilhelm, 89
Dionysia, 89
Dionysius the Areopagite, 93, 94
Dionysus, 27n, 68, 85, 176, 212, 277, 313,
346
disco dancing, 139, 258, 260, 273, 284–
285, 343, 385